Study Guide and Solutions Manual

for

Fundamentals of General, Organic, and Biological Chemistry

Susan McMurry

Cornell University

Production Editor: *Lynn Barret*
Acquisitions Editor: *Diana Farrel*
Supplements Acquisitions Editor: *Susan Black*
Prepress Buyer: *Paula Massenaro*
Manufacturing Buyer: *Lori Bulwin*

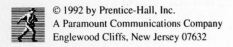

© 1992 by Prentice-Hall, Inc.
A Paramount Communications Company
Englewood Cliffs, New Jersey 07632

Printed in the United States of America

10 9 8 7 6

ISBN 0-13-351891-4

Prentice-Hall International (UK) Limited, *London*
Prentice-Hall of Australia Pty. Limited, *Sydney*
Prentice-Hall Canada Inc., *Toronto*
Prentice-Hall Hispanoamericana, S.A., *Mexico*
Prentice-Hall of India Private Limited, *New Delhi*
Prentice-Hall of Japan, Inc., *Tokyo*
Simon & Schuster Asia Pte. Ltd., *Singapore*
Editora Prentice-Hall do Brasil, Ltda., *Rio de Janeiro*

Contents

Preface

How is food digested? What is a polymer? How do anesthetics work?

For all of these questions, chemistry provides an answer. Chemistry, the study of matter, is essential to an understanding of the scientific events in the world, from acid rain to DNA to the ozone layer. Chemical laboratory tests are a routine part of medical care. The functioning of our bodies is a result of thousands of biochemical reactions. To study life, you must first study chemistry.

Both the textbook and this Study Guide and Solutions Manual have tried to be as helpful as possible to you in your chemistry course. The textbook contains numerous solved problems that show you techniques for solving specific types of chemistry problems. In addition, the text includes applications of chemistry to present-day scientific affairs. This Study Guide consists of several types of study aids: detailed solutions to all textbook problems, brief summaries of the chapters, and self-tests.

The following suggestions may help you:

(1) Attend all classes. Although it's possible to learn chemistry just by reading the textbook and study guide, a lecturer makes difficult topics much easier to understand and ties together seemingly unrelated topics.

(2) Read the textbook. The best way to study is to skim the chapter to be covered before class, and then to read it more thoroughly after the teacher has discussed the material. Use the textbook to help you understand subjects you find especially difficult.

(3) Work the problems. Start by reading carefully the Solved Problems in the textbook. Next, try to work the Practice Problems, using the steps outlined in the Solved Problems. Finally, attempt the Additional Problems at the end of the chapter. Although this Study Guide and Solutions Manual has detailed solutions to all text problems, it's better to use the solutions in this book as a last resort. You will learn more if you first struggle a bit with a problem before checking its answer, than if you look up the answer right away.

(4) Use the supplementary material in this Study Guide to help you review each chapter. Each "Chapter in Brief" states in the fewest sentences possible the major topics of each chapter. Go over the "Checklist of Terms" in each chapter and make sure that you know the meaning of each important term. Test yourself with the self-tests, which include sentence completions, matching, and true/false questions.

Acknowledgments

This Study Guide and Solutions Manual is a genuine home-grown product. My husband John proofread and edited this book, and my son David produced it on a Macintosh II using the programs WordPerfect (text), Expressionist (equations), and ChemConnection (chemical structures.) I am grateful to them both.

Chapter 1 – Matter, Energy, and Life

1.1 *Physical changes*: (a) grinding a metal surface; (c) bubbles rising in a bottle of soda
Chemical changes: (b) fruit ripening; (d) an explosion of TNT

1.2 All of the listed items are made of chemicals.

1.3 Formaldehyde is a gas at room temperature (75°F).

1.4 At 32 °F, acetic acid is a solid.

1.5 *Mixtures*: (a) concrete; (d) wood
Pure substances: (b) helium; (c) a lead weight

1.6 *Physical changes*: (a) separation by filtration; (c) mixing alcohol and water
Chemical changes: (b) production of carbon dioxide by heating limestone

1.7 (a) U = uranium; (b) Ti = titanium; (c) W = tungsten

1.8 (a) Na = sodium; (b) Ca = calcium; (c) Pd = palladium; (d) K = potassium
(e) Sr = strontium; (f) Sn = tin

1.9 *Potential energy* (a) a book on the edge of a desk; (c) sandwich;
(d) flashlight battery
Kinetic energy: (b) a just-pitched baseball

1.10 All of the listed items are made of chemicals.

1.11 Physical properties include weight, volume, color, temperature, melting point, boiling point.

1.12 Physical properties: (a), (c), (e)

1.13 Physical properties: (a), (b), (e)

1.14 Physical properties: (a), (b), (c); chemical property: (d)

1.15 Baking soda:

White powder	Physical property
Odorless	Physical property
Dissolves in water	Physical property
Decomposes at 270°C	Chemical property
Does not burn	Chemical property

1.16 A *gas* is a fluid that has no definite shape or volume.
A *liquid* is a fluid that has no definite shape but has a definite volume.
A *solid* has a definite volume and a definite shape.

1.17 Melting, boiling and freezing, all changes of state, occur when a substance is converted from one state to another. All changes of state are physical changes.

1.18 Sulfur dioxide is a gas at 25°C.

1.19 Hexyl alcohol is a liquid at 75°F.

1.20 (a) solid; (b) liquid

1.21 Mixtures: (a), (b), (d), (f);   Pure substances: (c), (e)

1.22 Mixtures: (a), (c), (d);   Pure substances: (b), (e), (f)

1.23 An *element* is a substance that can't be broken down into simpler substances.
A *compound* has a definite composition and properties and can be broken down into simpler substances (elements) only by chemical reactions.
A *mixture* has components in varying proportions, which can be separated by physical methods.

1.24 Elements: (a);   Compounds: (b), (c);   Mixtures: (d), (e), (f)

1.25 (a) motor oil - liquid; mixture
(b) copper - solid; chemical element
(c) carbon dioxide - gas; chemical compound
(d) nitrogen - gas; chemical element
(e) sodium bicarbonate - solid; chemical compound

1.26   *Reactant*   *Products*

Hydrogen peroxide ⟶ water + oxygen
chemical compound   *chemical compound*   *element*

1.27   *Reactants*   *Products*

Sodium + water ⟶ hydrogen + sodium hydroxide
element   chemical compound   *element   chemical compound*

1.28 *Metals* are lustrous malleable elements that are good conductors of heat and electricity. *Nonmetals* are elements that are poor conductors.

1.29 (a) Zn; (b) Hg; (c) Ba; (d) Au; (e) Si; (f) C; (g) Na; (h) Pb

1.30 (a) nitrogen; (b) potassium; (c) chlorine; (d) calcium; (e) phosphorus;
(f) magnesium;   (g) manganese

1.31 The first letter of a chemical symbol is always capitalized; the second letter, if any, is never capitalized. Thus, Co stands for cobalt, and CO stands for carbon monoxide, a compound composed of carbon (C) and oxygen (O).

1.32 (a) The symbol for bromine is Br.
   (b) The symbol for manganese is Mn.
   (c) The symbol for carbon is C.
   (d) The symbol for potassium is K.

1.33 Oxygen is the most abundant element in the earth's crust and in the human body.

1.34 (a) Fe; (b) Cu; (c) Co; (d) Mo; (e) Cr; (f) F; (g) S

1.35 (a) Water has the formula H_2O.
   (b) Water is composed of hydrogen and oxygen.

1.36 (a) $MgSO_4$: magnesium, sulfur, oxygen
   (b) $FeBr_2$: iron, bromine
   (c) CoP: cobalt, phosphorus
   (d) AsH_3: arsenic, hydrogen
   (e) $CaCr_2O_7$: calcium, chromium, oxygen

1.37 (a) Osmium is a metal.
   (b) Xenon is a nonmetal.

1.38 Carbon, hydrogen, nitrogen and oxygen are present in glycine. The formula represents ten atoms.

1.39 The formula of ribose ($C_5H_{10}O_5$) represents 20 atoms.

1.40 Penicillin V: $C_{16}H_{18}N_2O_5S$.

1.41 *Kinetic energy* is the energy of an object in motion. *Potential energy* is stored energy.

1.42 All of the examples have mainly potential energy.

1.43 Kinetic energy: (b); Potential energy: (a), (c)

1.44 Food is the principal source of energy for human beings.

1.45 (a) False. Plants store energy from the sun as potential energy.
   (b) False. Chemical changes in your body produce the energy you need to run up a flight of stairs.

1.50 (a) See Problem 1.41.
   (b) *Melting point* is the temperature at which a change of state from solid to liquid occurs; *boiling point* is the temperature at which a change of state from liquid to gas occurs.
   (c) A *reactant* is a substance that undergoes change in a chemical reaction; a *product* is a substance formed as a result of a chemical reaction.
   (d) A *metal* is a lustrous malleable element that is a good conductor of heat and electricity; a *nonmetal* is an element that is a poor conductor.

1.51   (a) True; (b) False; melting is a physical change.

1.52   (a) False; it also has potential energy due to gravity.
(b) False; the correct formula is PbO.
(c) False; the resulting product is a mixture, not a compound.

1.53   Chemical compounds: (a) H_2O_2; (d) NO; (e) $NaHCO_3$
Elements: (b) Mo; (c) C

1.54   The white solid is a chemical compound; the brown gas and the molten metal are elements.

1.55   The liquid was a mixture.

1.56   Remove the iron filings with a magnet. Add water to the remaining mixture and filter out the sand. Evaporate the water to recover the salt.

The Chapter in Brief

Matter and its Properties (Sections 1.1, 1.2) Chemistry is the study of matter, which is defined as anything that has mass and volume. Matter has physical properties and chemical properties, and undergoes physical changes and chemical changes. The states of matter are solid, liquid, and gas.

Classification of Matter (Sections 1.3–1.5) Matter can exist either as a pure substance or as a mixture of substances. Compounds and elements are the two types of pure substances. There are over one hundred elements, each of which is represented by a one- or two-letter symbol. A chemical formula lists the elements in a compound.

Energy (Section 1.6) Energy is the capacity to do work. Potential energy is stored energy, and kinetic energy is the energy of motion. Energy in the human body is produced by chemical reactions.

Self-Test for Chapter 1

Complete the following sentences:

1.   A swinging pendulum has _____ energy.

2.   Color is a _____ property.

3.   _____ is the symbol for the element bismuth.

4.   When a substance _____, it changes from gas to liquid.

5.   Matter is anything that has _____ and _____.

6.   A _____ has definite volume but indefinite shape.

7.   A _____ _____ doesn't vary in its properties or composition.

8.   Energy stored in chemical compounds is _____ energy.

Tell whether each of the following statements is true or false:

1.   The forms of energy are interchangeable.

2.   Rust formation is a chemical change.

3.   A chemical compound is a pure substance.

4.   The components of a solution are separable by chemical methods.

5.   The formula C_2H_4O represents three atoms.

6.   Spontaneous changes lead to lower potential energy.

7.   The chemical symbol for silver is Si.

8.   In the chemical reaction carbon + oxygen —> carbon dioxide, the reactants are elements.

Chapter 2 – Measurements in Chemistry

2.1   cL = centiliter

2.2   (a) mL = milliliter   (b) kg = kilogram
          (c) cm = centimeter   (d) km = kilometer
          (e) μg = microgram

2.3   (a) liter = L   (b) microliter = μL
          (c) nanometer = nm   (d) megameter = Mm

2.4   (a) 1 nm = 10^{-9} m   (b) 1 dg = 10^{-1} g
          (c) 1 km = 10^3 m   (d) 1 mL = 10^{-3} L
          (e) 1 ng = 10^{-9} g

2.5   In scientific notation, a number is written as the product of a number between one and ten times ten raised to a power. In (a), 58 g = 5.8 x 10 g.

Value	Scientific Notation
(a) 58 g	5.8 x 10 g
(b) 46,792 m	4.6792 x 10^4 m
(c) 0.000 672 0 cm	6.720 x 10^{-4} cm
(d) 345.3 kg	3.453 x 10^2 kg

2.6

Value in Scientific Notation	Value In Normal Notation
(a) 4.885 x 10^4 mg	48,850 mg
(b) 8.3 x 10^{-6} m	0.0000083 m
(c) 4.00 x 10^{-2} mL	0.0400 mL

2.7   0.000 000 000 278 = 2.78 x 10^{-10} m (The decimal point must be moved ten places to the right.)

$$2.78 \times 10^{-10} \text{ m} \times \frac{1 \text{ pm}}{10^{-12} \text{ m}} = 2.78 \times 10^2 \text{ pm}$$

2.8

Number	Significant Figures	Reason
(a) 3.45 m	3	
(b) 0.1400 kg	4	Rule 4
(c) 10.003 L	5	Rule 1
(d) 35 cents	Exact	

2.9   (a) 6.0 x 10^5 (b) 1300 or 1.300 x 10^3 (c) 7.942 x 10^{11}

2.10 (a) 2.30 g   (b) 188.38 mL   (c) 0.009 L   (d) 1.000 kg

2.11   Remember:

(1) The sum or difference of two numbers can't have more digits to the right of the decimal point than either of the two numbers.

(2) The product or quotient of two numbers can't have more significant figures than either of the two numbers.

(a) 4.87 mL + 46.0 mL = 50.87 mL = 50.9 mL

(b) 3.4 x 0.023 g = 0.0782 g = 0.078 g

(c) 19.333 m - 7.4 m = 11.933 m = 11.9 m

(d) 55 mg - 4.671 mg + 0.894 mg = 51.223 mg = 51 mg

(e) 62,911 ÷ 611 = 102.96399 = 103

2.12   (a) 10^3 mL/L   (b) 28.35 g/oz   (c) 1.057 quarts/L

2.13

(a) 16.0 oz x $\dfrac{28.35 \text{ g}}{1 \text{ oz}}$ = 454 g   (b) 2500 mL x $\dfrac{1 \text{ L}}{1000 \text{ mL}}$ = 2.5 L

(c) 99.0 L x $\dfrac{1 \text{ quart}}{0.9464 \text{ L}}$ = 105 quarts

2.14

0.840 quart x $\dfrac{1 \text{ L}}{1.057 \text{ quart}}$ x $\dfrac{1000 \text{ mL}}{1 \text{ L}}$ = 795 mL

2.15

(a) 7.5 lb x $\dfrac{1 \text{ kg}}{2.205 \text{ lb}}$ = 3.4 kg

(b) 4.0 oz x $\dfrac{29.57 \text{ mL}}{1 \text{ oz}}$ = 120 mL

Remember: The answers must have the correct number of significant figures.

2.16

2 x 0.324 g x $\dfrac{1000 \text{ mg}}{1 \text{ g}}$ x $\dfrac{1}{135 \text{ lb}}$ x $\dfrac{2.205 \text{ lb}}{1 \text{ kg}}$ = 10.6 $\dfrac{\text{mg}}{\text{kg}}$

2 x 0.324 g x $\dfrac{1000 \text{ mg}}{1 \text{ g}}$ x $\dfrac{1}{40 \text{ lb}}$ x $\dfrac{2.205 \text{ lb}}{1 \text{ kg}}$ = 36 $\dfrac{\text{mg}}{\text{kg}}$

2.17

°C = $\dfrac{(°F - 32)}{1.8}$; In this case, °F = 103°

= $\dfrac{(103° - 32°)}{1.8}$ = $\dfrac{71.0°}{1.8}$ = 39.4 °C

2.18   °F = (1.8 x °C) + 32° ; In this case, °C = -38.9°

= (1.8 x -38.9°) + 32° = -38.0°F

2.19

$$\text{Specific heat} = \frac{\text{calories}}{\text{gram} \times {}^\circ C}$$

$$\text{Calories} = \text{Specific heat} \times g \times {}^\circ C$$

$$= \frac{1.0 \text{ cal}}{g \, {}^\circ C} \times 350 \text{ g} \times 22{}^\circ C$$

$$= 7700 \text{ cal}$$

2.20

$$\text{Specific heat} = \frac{161 \text{ cal}}{75 \text{ g} \times 10{}^\circ C} = 0.21 \frac{\text{cal}}{g \, {}^\circ C}$$

2.21   Solids with densities greater than water will sink; solids with densities less than water will float.
Solids that float: ice, human fat, cork, balsa wood
Solids that sink: gold, table sugar, earth

2.22

$$\frac{12.37 \text{ g}}{1.474 \frac{g}{mL}} = 8.392 \text{ mL}$$

2.23

$$\text{Density} = \frac{\text{Mass}}{\text{Volume}} = \frac{16.8 \text{ g}}{7.6 \text{ cm}^3} = 2.2 \text{ g} / \text{cm}^3$$

2.24   A *physical quantity* is a physical property that can be measured, and consists of a number plus a unit.

2.25 - 2.26

Quantity	Metric Unit	SI Unit
Mass	gram (g)	kilogram (kg)
Volume	liter (L)	cubic meter (m^3)
Length	meter (m)	meter (m)

2.27   (a) centiliter   (b) decimeter   (c) millimeter   (d) nanoliter
(e) milligram   (f) cubic meter   (g) cubic centimeter

2.28   (a) pg   (b) cm   (c) dL   (d) μL   (e) mL

2.29

$$\frac{10^{-3} \frac{g}{mg}}{10^{-12} \frac{g}{pg}} = 10^9 \frac{pg}{mg} ; \quad 35 \text{ ng} \times \frac{10^{-9} \frac{g}{ng}}{10^{-12} \frac{g}{pg}} = 35 \times 10^3 \text{ pg} = 3.5 \times 10^4 \text{ pg}$$

2.30

$$1\,L \times \frac{10^6\,\mu L}{L} = 10^6\,\mu L\,; \quad 20\,mL \times \frac{10^3\,\mu L}{mL} = 2 \times 10^4\,\mu L$$

2.31 A quart is about 5% smaller than a liter: 1 quart = 0.9464 L

2.32 (a) 9.457×10^3 (b) 7×10^{-5} (c) 2×10^{10}
(d) 1.2345×10^{-2} (e) 6.5238×10^2

2.33 (a) 4870 (b) 5,501,000
(c) 0.002 540 (d) 36,800

2.34 (a) six (b) three (c) three (d) four
(e) can't tell (f) three

2.35 (a) 2.4×10^5 (b) 3.0×10^{-1} (c) 3.0
(d) 2.4×10^2 (e) 5.0×10^4 (f) 6.6×10^2

2.36 (a) five (b) three (c) four
(d) one (e) three

2.37 (a) 7,926 miles; 7,900 miles; 7,926.38 miles
(b) 7.926381×10^3 miles

2.38 (a) 12.1 g (b) 96.19 cm (c) 263 mL (d) 20.9 mg

2.39 (a) $43.0\,m^2$ (b) $22\,mi^2$ (c) 184.7 mi/hr (d) $1360\,cm^3$

2.40 (a) 0.3614 cg (b) 0.0120 ML (c) 0.0144 mm (d) 6.03×10^1 ng

2.41

(a) $56.4\,mi \times \dfrac{1.609\,km}{1\,mi} = 90.1\,km$

$56.4\,mi \times \dfrac{1.609\,km}{1\,mi} \times \dfrac{1\,Mm}{10^3\,km} = 9.01 \times 10^{-2}\,Mm$

(b) $2.0\,L \times \dfrac{1.057\,quarts}{1\,L} = 2.1\,quarts$

$2.0\,L \times \dfrac{10^3\,mL}{1\,L} \times \dfrac{1\,fl\,oz}{29.57\,mL} = 68\,fl\,oz$

(c) $86.0\,in \times \dfrac{1\,cm}{0.3937\,in} = 218\,cm; \quad 218\,cm \times \dfrac{1\,m}{100\,cm} = 2.18\,m$

(d) $1.35\,lb \times \dfrac{1\,kg}{2.205\,lb} = 0.612\,kg; \quad 0.612\,kg \times \dfrac{10^4\,dg}{1\,kg} = 6.12 \times 10^3\,dg$

2.42   (a) 97.8 kg   (b) 0.133 mL   (c) 0.46 ng

2.43 3.9×10^{-2} g/dL iron, 8.3×10^{-3} g/dL calcium, 2.24×10^{-1} g/dL cholesterol

2.44

$$\frac{100 \text{ km}}{1 \text{ hr}} \times \frac{0.6214 \text{ mi}}{1 \text{ km}} = 62.1 \text{ mi/hr}$$

$$\frac{62.1 \text{ mi}}{1 \text{ hr}} \times \frac{5280 \text{ ft}}{1 \text{ mi}} \times \frac{1 \text{ hr}}{60 \text{ min}} \times \frac{1 \text{ min}}{60 \text{ s}} = 91.1 \text{ ft/s}$$

2.45

$$\frac{55 \text{ mi}}{1 \text{ hr}} \times \frac{1 \text{ km}}{0.6214 \text{ mi}} = 89 \text{ km/hr}$$

$$\frac{89 \text{ km}}{1 \text{ hr}} \times \frac{10^3 \text{ m}}{1 \text{ km}} \times \frac{1 \text{ hr}}{60 \text{ min}} \times \frac{1 \text{ min}}{60 \text{ s}} = 25 \text{ m/s}$$

2.46

$$6 \times 12 \text{ oz} \times \frac{29.57 \text{ mL}}{1 \text{ oz}} \times \frac{1 \text{ L}}{10^3 \text{ mL}} = 2.1 \text{ L}; \quad \frac{\$2.59}{2.1 \text{ L}} = \$1.20/\text{L}$$

$$\$1.59 / 2.0 \text{ L} = \$0.80/\text{L}$$

2.47

$$\frac{1 \text{ cell}}{6 \times 10^{-6} \text{ m}} \times \frac{1 \text{ m}}{39.37 \text{ in}} = 4 \times 10^3 \text{ cells / inch}$$

2.48 $1 \text{ ft}^2 = (0.3048 \text{ m})^2 = 0.0929 \text{ m}^2$

$$\frac{406,000 \text{ m}^2}{0.0929 \frac{\text{m}^2}{\text{ft}^2}} = 4,370,000 \text{ ft}^2$$

2.49

$$13.0 \text{ in} \times \frac{25.4 \text{ mm}}{1 \text{ in}} = 330 \text{ mm}$$

2.50

$$\frac{200 \text{ mL}}{1 \text{ dL}} \times \frac{10 \text{ dL}}{1 \text{ L}} \times 5 \text{ L} = 10^4 \text{ mg} = 10 \text{ g}$$

2.51

$$\frac{1.2 \times 10^4 \text{ cells}}{1 \text{ mm}^3} \times \frac{10^6 \text{ mm}^3}{1 \text{ L}} \times 5 \text{ L} = 6 \times 10^{10} \text{ cells}$$

2.52

$$1200 \text{ mg} \times \frac{1.0 \text{ cup}}{290 \text{ mg}} = 4.1 \text{ cups}$$

2.53

$$°C = \frac{(°F - 32°)}{1.8} = \frac{(98.6° - 32°)}{1.8} = \frac{66.6°}{1.8} = 37.0 \ °C, \ or \ 310 \ K$$

2.54 $°F = (1.8 \times °C) + 32° = (1.8 \times 39.3°) + 32° = 102.7°F$

2.55 $78 \ K; \ °F = (1.8 \times °C) + 32° = 1.8 \times (-195.8°C) + 32° = -320.4°F$

2.56 calories = specific heat $\times$ g $\times$ °C

$$= \frac{0.895 \ cal}{g \ °C} \times 30.0 \ g \times 20°C = 537 \ calories$$

$$= 0.537 \ kcal$$

2.57

$$Specific \ heat = \frac{cal}{g \ °C} = \frac{23 \ cal}{5.0 \ g \times 50°C} = 0.092 \ \frac{cal}{g \ °C}$$

2.58

$$0.175 \ \frac{cal}{g \ °C} = \frac{50 \ cal}{15 \ g \times X°C} ; \ X = 19°$$

Since X is the difference between the initial and final temperature, and since 20°C is the initial temperature, the final temperature is 20°C + 19°C = 39°C.

2.59 See problem 2.58 for help in solving this problem.

$$For \ mercury: \ 0.033 \ cal/g \ °C = \frac{250. \ cal}{150. \ g \times X° \ C}; \ X = 51° \ C; \ 25° \ C + 51° \ C = 76° \ C$$

$$For \ iron: \ 0.106 \ cal / g \ °C = \frac{250. \ cal}{150. \ g \times X°C}; \ X = 15.9 \ °C; \ 25.0 \ °C + 15.9 \ °C = 40.9 \ °C$$

2.60

$$\frac{0.25 \ g}{1.40 \ \frac{g}{cm^3}} = 0.178 \ cm^3$$

2.61

$$\frac{3.928 \ g}{5.000 \ mL} = 0.7856 \ \frac{g}{mL}; \ specific \ gravity = 0.7856$$

2.62 Specific gravity = 1.1088; density = 1.1088 g/mL

$$1000 \ g \times \frac{1 \ mL}{1.1088 \ g} = 901.0 \ mL; \ 2 \ lb \times \frac{453 \ g}{lb} \times \frac{1 \ mL}{1.1088 \ g} = 817.1 \ mL$$

2.63 A urinometer will float higher in chloroform than in ethanol.

2.64

(a) $\dfrac{1 \text{ grain}}{64.8 \text{ mg}} = \dfrac{0.0154 \text{ grain}}{1 \text{ mg}}$ (b) $\dfrac{1 \text{ fluid oz}}{8 \text{ fluidram}} = \dfrac{0.13 \text{ fluid oz}}{1 \text{ fluidram}}$

(c) $\dfrac{1 \text{ fluidram}}{3.70 \text{ mL}} = \dfrac{0.270 \text{ fluidram}}{1 \text{ mL}}$ (d) $\dfrac{1 \text{ minim}}{0.062 \text{ mL}} = \dfrac{16.1 \text{ minim}}{1 \text{ mL}}$

(e) $\dfrac{1 \text{ fluid oz}}{480. \text{ minim}} = \dfrac{2.08 \times 10^{-3} \text{ fluid oz}}{1 \text{ minim}}$

2.65

(a) $5 \text{ grains} \times \dfrac{64.8 \text{ mg}}{1 \text{ grain}} = 324 \text{ mg}$ (b) $1.5 \text{ oz} \times \dfrac{8 \text{ dram}}{1 \text{ oz}} = 12 \text{ drams}$

2.66   Body fat acts as a shock absorber, a thermal insulator and as an energy storehouse.

2.67

Body volume = (land weight - underwater weight) kg x $\dfrac{1 \text{ L}}{\text{kg}}$ = 79.4 kg x $\dfrac{1 \text{ L}}{\text{kg}}$ = 79.4 L

Body density = $\dfrac{\text{body weight}}{\text{body volume}} = \dfrac{85.0 \text{ kg}}{79.4 \text{ L}} = 1.07 \text{ kg/L}$

2.68

$5.0 \text{ lb} \times \dfrac{454 \text{ g}}{1 \text{ lb}} \times \dfrac{1 \text{ mL}}{0.94 \text{ g}} = 2.4 \times 10^3 \text{ mL or } 2.4 \text{ L}$

2.69   One carat = 200 mg = 0.200 g

$0.200 \dfrac{\text{g}}{\text{carat}} \times 44.4 \text{ carat} = 8.88 \text{ g}$

$8.88 \text{ g} \times \dfrac{1 \text{ oz}}{28.35 \text{ g}} = 0.313 \text{ oz}$ (three significant figures)

2.70

$°C = \dfrac{(°F - 32°)}{1.8} = \dfrac{(350° - 32°)}{1.8} = \dfrac{318°}{1.8} = 177°C$

2.71

$\dfrac{293{,}000 \text{ people}}{6.2 \text{ mi}^2} = 4.7 \times 10^4 \dfrac{\text{people}}{\text{mi}^2}$

2.72

$\dfrac{2 \times 0.25 \text{ g}}{130 \text{ lb} \times 0.454 \dfrac{\text{kg}}{\text{lb}}} = \dfrac{0.50 \text{ g}}{59 \text{ kg}} = 8.5 \times 10^{-3} \dfrac{\text{g}}{\text{kg}}$ for the woman

$8.5 \times 10^{-3} \dfrac{\text{g}}{\text{kg}} \times 40 \text{ lb} \times 0.454 \dfrac{\text{kg}}{\text{lb}} = 0.154 \text{ g}$

A 40-lb child would need 0.154 g, or 154 mg, of penicillin to receive the same dose as a 130-lb woman. The child would thus need about 1.2 of the 125 mg penicillin tablets.

2.73

$$1.3 \frac{g}{L} \times 4.0\,m \times 3.0\,m \times 2.5\,m \times 1000 \frac{L}{m^3} = 3.9 \times 10^4\,g$$

$$\frac{3.9 \times 10^4\,g}{453 \frac{g}{lb}} = 86\,lb$$

2.74

$$75 \frac{mL}{beat} \times 72 \frac{beat}{min} \times 60 \frac{min}{hr} \times 24 \frac{hr}{day} = 7.8 \times 10^6 \frac{mL}{day}$$

2.75

$$15\,g \times \frac{1000\,mL}{50\,g} = 30\,mL$$

2.76   (a) 13.6   (b) An iron ball would float.

(c) $2.00\,L \times \dfrac{10^3\,mL}{L} \times \dfrac{13.6\,g}{mL} \times \dfrac{1\,lb}{454\,g} = 60.0\,lb$

2.77

$$\frac{85\,mg}{mL} \times \frac{10^3\,mL}{1\,L} \times \frac{0.9464\,L}{qt} \times \frac{1\,qt}{2\,pt} \times 11\,pt = 440 \times 10^3\,mg = 440\,g$$

$$440\,g \times \frac{1\,lb}{454\,g} = 0.97\,lb$$

2.78

$$\frac{3000\,mL}{1\,day} \times \frac{5\,g}{100\,mL} \times \frac{4\,kcal}{1\,g} = 600\,kcal\,/\,day$$

2.79

$$\left(\frac{100\,mL}{1\,kg} \times 10\,kg\right) + \left(\frac{50\,mL}{1\,kg} \times 10\,kg\right) + \left(\frac{20\,mL}{1\,kg} \times 35\,kg\right) = 2200\,mL$$

2.80

$$7.5\,grains \times \frac{1\,fluidram}{10\,grains} \times \frac{3.70\,mL}{1\,fluidram} = 2.8\,mL$$

2.81   calories needed $=$ specific heat of H_2O $\times$ g $\times$ °C

for water: specific heat $= 1.00\,cal\,/\,g\,°C$; $g = 3.0\,L \times \dfrac{10^3\,mL}{1\,L} \times \dfrac{1.00\,g}{1\,mL}$; °C $= 72°$

calories needed $= \dfrac{1.00\,cal}{g\,°C} \times 3 \times 10^3\,g \times 72°C = 2.2 \times 10^5\,cal = 220\,kcal$

$$220\,kcal \times \frac{1\,tbsp}{100\,kcal} = 2.2\,tbsp\ butter$$

The Chapter in Brief

Physical Quantities (Sections 2.1 - 2.2) Physical quantities are any physical properties that can be measured; they consist of a number plus a unit. Commonly used units are based on the SI and metric systems. These units can be modified by prefixes for smaller or larger quantities.

Measurements of Matter (Sections 2.3–2.5, 2.10) Mass, volume, length, and temperature are four commonly measured physical properties. For each of these properties, unit conversion tables are given in the text.

Measurement and Accuracy (Sections 2.6–2.7) The accuracy of a measurement is indicated by the number of significant figures. Section 2.6 gives rules for determining significant figures. Very large and very small numbers are often represented in scientific notation as the product of a number between one and ten times 10 raised to a power. Numbers with more digits than are significant should be rounded off.

Conversion of Units, and Problem Solving (Sections 2.8–2.9) The factor-label method is used to convert from one scientific unit to another, as shown in dosage calculation problems.

Specific Heat, Density, and Specific Gravity (Sections 2.11–2.13) These physical quantities can be calculated using the techniques developed in this chapter.

Self-Test for Chapter 2

1. Write the full name of these units:
    (a) µm   (b) dL   (c) Mg   (d) L   (e) ng

2. Write the abbreviation for each of the following units:
    (a) kiloliter   (b) picogram   (c) centimeter   (d) hectoliter

3.   *Quantity   Significant Figures?*

    (a) 1.0037 g
    (b) 0.0080 L
    (c) 0.008 L
    (d) 2 aspirin
    (e) 273,000 mi

4. Express the following in scientific notation:
    (a) 0.000 070 3 g   (b) 137,100 m   (c) 0.011 L   (d) 18,371,008 mm
    How many significant figures do each of the above quantities have?

5. Round the following to three significant figures:
    (a) 807.3 L   (b) 4,773,112 people   (c) 0.00127 g   (d) 10370 µm
    Express each of the above quantities in scientific notation.

6. Convert the following quantities:
    (a) 256 g = _____ lbs   (b) 417 mm = _____ m
    (c) 2.0 gallons = _____ L   (d) 2.17 m = _____ inches
    (e) 35°C = _____ °F   (f) 298 K = _____ °C
    (g) 175 mL = _____ oz   (h) 175 mg = _____ oz

7. If the specific heat of gold is 0.031 cal/g °C, how many calories does it take to heat 10 g of gold from 0°C to 100°C?

8. If the density of ethanol is 0.7893 g/mL, how many grams does 275 mL weigh?

Complete the following sentences:

1. The fundamental SI units are _____, _____, _____, and _____.

2. Physical quantities are described by a _____ and a _____.

3. The amount of heat necessary to raise the temperature of one gram of a substance by one degree is the substance's _____ _____.

4. The prefix _____ indicates 10^{-9}.

5. The number 0.00306 has _____ significant figures.

6. To convert from grams to pounds, use the conversion factor _____.

7. Two units for measuring energy are _____ and _____.

8. The method used for converting units is called the _____ _____ method.

9. _____ _____ is the density of a substance divided by the density of water at the same temperature.

10. The size of a degree is the same in both _____ and _____ units.

Tell whether the following statements are true or false:

1. The units of specific gravity are g/mL.

2. The number 0.07350 has four significant figures.

3. The sum of 57.35 and 1.3 has four significant figures.

4. The conversion factor 1.057 quarts/liter is used to convert quarts into liters.

5. Some SI units are the same as metric units.

6. The temperature in °C is always a larger number than the temperature in K.

7. Raising the temperature of 10 g of water by 10°C takes less heat than raising the temperature of 10 g of gold by 10°C.

8. Mass measures the amount of matter in an object.

9. Ice is more dense than water.

10. A nanogram is larger than a picogram.

Match each entry on the left with its partner on the right:

1.	5003	(a) Converts pounds to kilograms
2.	1 centimeter	(b) 0.1 grams
3.	$\dfrac{2.205\ \text{lb}}{1\ \text{kg}}$	(c) Larger than one inch
4.	263 K	(d) -17.8°C
5.	1 dekagram	(e) Four significant figures
6.	0.0486	(f) SI unit of volume measure
7.	1 m³	(g) Converts kilograms to pounds
8.	1 liter	(h) 10 grams
9.	1 decimeter	(i) -10°C
10.	$\dfrac{1\ \text{kg}}{2.205\ \text{lb}}$	(j) Smaller than one inch
11.	0°F	(k) Metric unit of volume measure
12.	1 decigram	(l) Three significant figures

Chapter 3 – Atoms and the Periodic Table

3.1

$$2.33 \times 10^{-23} \text{ g} \times \frac{1 \text{ amu}}{1.6606 \times 10^{-24} \text{ g}} = 14.0 \text{ amu}$$

3.2

$$10^5 \text{ atoms} \times \frac{197 \text{ amu}}{1 \text{ atom}} \times \frac{1.6606 \times 10^{-24} \text{ g}}{1 \text{ amu}} = 3.27 \times 10^{-17} \text{ g}$$

3.3

(a) $1.0 \text{ g} \times \dfrac{1 \text{ amu}}{1.6606 \times 10^{-24} \text{ g}} \times \dfrac{1 \text{ atom}}{1.0 \text{ amu}} = 6.0 \times 10^{23}$ atoms

(b) $12.0 \text{ g} \times \dfrac{1 \text{ amu}}{1.6606 \times 10^{-24} \text{ g}} \times \dfrac{1 \text{ atom}}{12.0 \text{ amu}} = 6.02 \times 10^{23}$ atoms

(c) $230 \text{ g} \times \dfrac{1 \text{ amu}}{1.6606 \times 10^{-24} \text{ g}} \times \dfrac{1 \text{ atom}}{230 \text{ amu}} = 6.02 \times 10^{23}$ atoms

3.4 In each of the above examples, the mass in grams equals the mass in amu, and the number of atoms in all three samples is identical.

3.5 (a) Re (b) Li (c) Te

3.6 Recall that the *atomic number* shows how many protons an atom contains. Uranium, with an atomic number of 92 thus contains 92 protons.
The *mass number* shows the number of protons plus the number of neutrons. To find the number of neutrons in an atom, subtract the atomic number from the mass number.
For uranium: Mass number - atomic number = 235 - 92 = 143
The uranium atom therefore has 143 neutrons.

3.7 Both chlorine isotopes have 17 protons. The chlorine isotope with mass number 35 has 18 neutrons, and the isotope with mass number 37 has 20 neutrons.

3.8 Atomic number is written at the lower left of the element symbol, and mass number is written at the upper left.

$$^{35}_{17}\text{Cl} \quad \text{and} \quad ^{37}_{17}\text{Cl}$$

3.9

(a) $^{11}_{5}\text{B}$ (b) $^{56}_{26}\text{Fe}$

3.10 (a) 6 (b) 2 (c) 6

3.11 Ten electrons are present in this atom, which is neon.

3.12 Twelve electrons are present in this atom, which is magnesium.

3.13   To find the electron configuration of an atom, first find its atomic number. For C (carbon), the atomic number is 6; thus carbon has 6 protons and 6 electrons. Then, assign electrons to the proper orbitals, two to each orbital. For carbon, the electron configuration is $1s^2$ $2s^2$ $2p^4$.

Element	Atomic Number	Electron Configuration
(a) C (carbon)	6	$1s^2 \, 2s^2 \, 2p^2$
(b) Na (sodium)	11	$1s^2 \, 2s^2 \, 2p^6 \, 3s^1$
(c) Cl (chlorine)	17	$1s^2 \, 2s^2 \, 2p^6 \, 3s^2 \, 3p^5$
(d) Ca (calcium)	20	$1s^2 \, 2s^2 \, 2p^6 \, 3s^2 \, 3p^6 \, 4s^2$

3.14   Element 11 (Na): $1s^2 \, 2s^2 \, 2p^6 \, 3s^1$
Element 36 (Kr): $1s^2 \, 2s^2 \, 2p^6 \, 3s^2 \, 3p^6 \, 4s^2 \, 3d^{10} \, 4p^6$

3.15   Element 33 (As): $1s^2 \, 2s^2 \, 2p^6 \, 3s^2 \, 3p^6 \, 4s^2 \, 3d^{10} \, 4p^3$. The $4p$ shell is incompletely filled. Notice that only one electron occupies each orbital of the $4p$ subshell.

$\uparrow \; \uparrow \; \uparrow$ $4p^3$

3.16   Aluminum is in Group 3A and period 3.

3.17   (a) krypton - noble gas   (b) strontium - metal
(c) nitrogen - non-metal   (d) cobalt - transition metal
(a), (b) and (c) are main group elements.

3.18   Arsenic: $1s^2 \, 2s^2 \, 2p^6 \, 3s^2 \, 3p^6 \, 4s^2 \, 3d^{10} \, 4p^3$

3.19   In Group 2A, all elements have the outer-shell configuration ns^2.

3.20   Chlorine, in Group 7A, has seventeen electrons. Its electron configuration is $1s^2 \, 2s^2 \, 2p^6$ $3s^2 \, 3p^5$. Two electrons are in shell 1, ten electrons are in shell 2 and nine electrons are in shell 3. The outer shell configuration is $3s^2 \, 3p^5$.

3.21   Atoms of different elements differ in the number of protons and electrons they have.

3.22

(a) Bi: $208.9804 \text{ amu} \times \dfrac{1.6606 \times 10^{-24} \text{ g}}{1 \text{ amu}} = 3.4703 \times 10^{-22} \text{ g}$

(b) Xe: $131.29 \text{ amu} \times \dfrac{1.6606 \times 10^{-24} \text{ g}}{1 \text{ amu}} = 2.1802 \times 10^{-22} \text{ g}$

(c) He: $4.0026 \text{ amu} \times \dfrac{1.6606 \times 10^{-24} \text{ g}}{1 \text{ amu}} = 6.6467 \times 10^{-24} \text{ g}$

3.23

(a) $5.00 \times 10^6 \text{ atoms} \times \dfrac{1.99 \times 10^{-23} \text{ g}}{\text{atom}} \times \dfrac{1 \text{ amu}}{1.6606 \times 10^{-24} \text{ g}} = 5.99 \times 10^7 \text{ amu}$

(b) $\dfrac{2.66 \times 10^{-23} \text{ g}}{1 \text{ atom O}} \times \dfrac{1 \text{ amu}}{1.6606 \times 10^{-24} \text{ g}} = 16.0 \text{ amu}$

(c) $\dfrac{1.31 \times 10^{-22} \text{ g}}{1 \text{ atom Br}} \times \dfrac{1 \text{ amu}}{1.6606 \times 10^{-24} \text{ g}} = 78.9 \text{ amu}$

3.24

$6.022 \times 10^{23} \text{ atoms} \times \dfrac{1.6606 \times 10^{-24} \text{ g}}{1 \text{ amu}} \times 14.01 \text{ amu} = 14.01 \text{ g}$

3.25

Particle	Mass in amu	Charge
Proton	1.007	+1
Neutron	1.009	0
Electron	5.486×10^{-4}	−1

3.26 Protons and neutrons are found in a dense central region called the nucleus. Electrons orbit the nucleus.

3.27 (a) fluorine   (b) tin   (c) zinc

3.28

Isotope	Argon-36	Argon-38	Argon-40
Number of neutrons	18	20	22

3.29

Isotope	(a) $^{27}_{13}\text{Al}$	(b) $^{28}_{14}\text{Si}$	(c) $^{11}_{5}\text{B}$	(d) $^{224}_{88}\text{Ra}$
# of protons	13	14	5	88
# of neutrons	14	14	6	136
# of electrons	13	14	5	88

3.30 (a) and (c) are isotopes because they have the same atomic number, but different mass numbers.

3.31 (a) fluorine-19   (b) neon-19   (c) fluorine-21   (d) magnesium-21

3.32

(a) $^{14}_{6}\text{C}$ (b) $^{39}_{19}\text{K}$ (c) $^{20}_{10}\text{Ne}$

3.33

(a) $^{206}_{84}\text{Po}$ (b) $^{224}_{88}\text{Ra}$ (c) $^{197}_{79}\text{Au}$ (d) $^{84}_{36}\text{Kr}$

3.34 (a) 122   (b) 136   (c) 118   (d) 48

3.35

$^{12}_{6}C$ - six neutrons $^{13}_{6}C$ - seven neutrons

3.36

$^{131}_{53}I$

3.37   Each element occurs in nature as a mixture of isotopes. The atomic weight represents the average mass of the naturally-occurring isotope mixture and is determined by calculating the percent of atoms contributed by each isotope.

3.38   Contribution from ^{63}Cu: 69.09% of 62.93 amu = 43.48 amu
Contribution from ^{65}Cu: 30.91% of 64.93 amu = 20.07 amu
Atomic weight = 63.55 amu

3.39   A maximum of two electrons can go into an orbital.

3.40   First shell - 2 electrons
Second shell - 8 electrons
Third shell - 18 electrons

3.41   An s orbital is spherical and centered on the nucleus. A p orbital is dumbbell-shaped, and the three p orbitals extend out from the nucleus at 90° angles to each other.

3.42   Ten electrons are present; the element is neon.

3.43   Fourteen electrons are present; the element is silicon.

3.44   (a) sulfur   (b) bromine   (c) silicon

⇅ ↑ ↑   ⇅ ⇅ ↑   ↑ ↑ _

$3p^4$ $4p^5$ $3p^2$

3.45   *Element*   *Electron configuration*

(a) Mg	$1s^2 2s^2 2p^6 3s^2$
(b) S	$1s^2 2s^2 2p^6 3s^2 3p^4$
(c) Ne	$1s^2 2s^2 2p^6$
(d) Cd	$1s^2 2s^2 2p^6 3s^2 3p^6 4s^2 3d^{10} 4p^6 5s^2 4d^{10}$

3.46   The element with atomic number 20 (Ca) has two electrons in its outer shell.

3.47   The third period in the periodic table contains eight elements because eight electrons are needed to fill the s and p subshells of the third shell.

3.48   The fourth period contains 18 elements because 18 electrons are needed to fill the s and p subshells of the fourth shell, plus the d subshell of the third shell.

3.49 Americium-241 (Am; atomic number 95) has 95 protons and 241 - 95 = 146 neutrons and is a metal.

3.50 (a) They are metals.
(b) They are transition metals.
(c) The $3d$ subshell is being filled.

3.51 The number of valence electrons for elements in a group is the same as the group number. Thus, Group 4A elements have four valence electrons.

3.52 (a) calcium: (i) (iv) (vii) (b) palladium: (i) (iii)
(c) carbon: (ii) (iv)   (d) radon: (ii) (iv) (v)

3.53 beryllium: $2s$ arsenic: $4p$

3.54 Group 6A

3.55 The elements immediately above and below sulfur in the periodic table - oxygen and selenium - are chemically most similar to sulfur.

3.56

Element	(a) Kr	(b) C	(c) Ca	(d) K	(e) B	(f) Cl
# of valence-shell electrons	8	4	2	1	3	7

3.57 The alkali metal family is composed of lithium, sodium, potassium, rubidium, cesium and francium.

3.58 Fluorine, chlorine, bromine, iodine, and astatine make up the halogen family.

3.59 Helium, neon, argon, krypton, xenon, and radon make up the noble-gas family.

3.60 The chemical behavior of elements is determined by the number of electrons in their outer shell; elements with different number of outer-shell electrons differ in reactivity. In this problem, xenon, with eight outer-shell electrons, is unreactive, but cesium, with one outer-shell electron, is very reactive.

3.61 Group 7A: $ns^2\,np^5$ Group 1A: ns^1

3.62 Because cesium resembles potassium in its electronic structure and chemical behavior, radioactive cesium in the food chain can become incorporated into organisms, where its harmful radiation can cause damage.

3.63 (a) Usually, strontium has no electron in a shell higher than the fifth shell. When radiant energy interacts with strontium, an electron may be raised to the sixth shell. This state is of higher energy than the usual ground state, and is said to be *excited*.
(b) To return to the ground state, the excited electron must release energy.

3.64 Higher energy: (a) cosmic rays   (b) gamma rays   (c) cosmic rays

3.65 Ultraviolet radiation is more damaging because it is of higher energy.

3.66 This radiation is ultraviolet radiation.

3.67 Hydrogen is placed in Group 1A because it has one electron in its outermost (only) electron shell. Hydrogen is placed in Group 7A because only one electron is needed to fill its outermost (only) electron shell.

3.68 A normal light microscope can't reach the degree of precision of a scanning tunneling microscope.

3.69 Pb: $1s^2\ 2s^2\ 2p^6\ 3s^2\ 3p^6\ 4s^2\ 3d^{10}\ 4p^6\ 5s^2\ 4d^{10}\ 5p^6\ 6s^2\ 4f^{18}\ 5d^{10}\ 6p^2$
Shell 1: 2 electrons   Shell 2:   8 electrons   Shell 3: 18 electrons
Shell 4: 32 electrons   Shell 5: 18 electrons   Shell 6:   4 electrons

3.70 Highest occupied subshell: (a) Ar - $3p$ (b) Mg - $3s$ (c) Tc - $4d$ (d) Fe - $3d$

3.71 Contribution from ^{79}Br: 50.54% of 78.92 amu = 39.89 amu
Contribution from ^{81}Br: 49.46% of 80.91 amu = 40.02 amu
Atomic weight = 79.91 amu

3.72 Contribution from ^{24}Mg: 78.70% of 23.99 amu = 18.88 amu
Contribution from ^{25}Mg: 10.13% of 24.99 amu =   2.53 amu
Contribution from ^{26}Mg: 11.17% of 25.98 amu =   2.90 amu
Atomic weight = 24.31 amu

3.73 One atom of carbon weighs more than one atom of hydrogen because the mass of carbon (12 amu) is greater than the mass of hydrogen (1 amu).

3.74 10^{23} atoms of carbon weigh 12 x 10^{23} amu, and 10^{23} atoms of hydrogen weigh 1 x 10^{23} amu. Thus the weight of carbon is 12 times greater than that of hydrogen.

3.75 If 10^{23} hydrogen atoms weigh 1 gram, then 10^{23} carbon atoms will weigh 12 grams.

3.76 Using the above reasoning, we predict that 10^{23} sodium atoms will weigh 23 grams.

3.77 Strontium occurs directly below calcium in Group 2A and thus has similar chemical behavior. Strontium is a metal, has 38 protons, and is in the fifth period.

3.78 The outer-shell electrons of titanium are in the $4s$ orbital.

3.79 Zirconium, a metal, has an electron configuration by shell of 2 8 18 10 2.

3.80

$$8.6 \text{ mg } \times \frac{1 \text{ g}}{10^3 \text{ mg}} \times \frac{1 \text{ amu}}{1.6606 \times 10^{-24} \text{ g}} \times \frac{1 \text{ atom}}{40.08 \text{ amu}} = 1.3 \times 10^{20} \text{ atoms}$$

3.81 (a) Electrons must fill the 4s subshell before entering the 3d subshell. The correct configuration:

$$1s^2 \, 2s^2 \, 2p^6 \, 3s^2 \, 3p^6 \, 4s^2 \, 3d^4$$

(b) Electrons must fill the 2s subshell before entering the 2p subshell. The correct configuration:

$$1s^2 \, 2s^2 \, 2p^3$$

(c) Silicon has fourteen electrons. The correct configuration:

$$1s^2 \, 2s^2 \, 2p^6 \, 3s^2 \, \uparrow \, \uparrow \, \_$$
$$3p$$

(d) The 3s electrons must have opposite spins. The correct configuration:

$$1s^2 \, 2s^2 \, 2p^6 \, \uparrow\downarrow$$
$$3s$$

3.82 Count the electrons in each example to arrive at the atomic number. Then look up the answer in the periodic table.
(a) Cu   (b) Mo

The Chapter in Brief

Atoms (Sections 3.1–3.6) An atom is the smallest amount of an element that still retains the element's chemical properties. Atoms are composed of protons, neutrons, and electrons, with protons and neutrons comprising the nucleus. The atomic number of an element indicates the number of protons (and the number of electrons) the element has. The mass number indicates the number of protons plus neutrons. Atoms with identical atomic numbers but different mass numbers are called isotopes.

Electrons (Sections 3.7–3.8) Electrons occupy specific regions, or "shells," around the nucleus. Within each shell are subshells, and within each subshell the electrons are grouped by pairs into orbitals. The distribution of electrons throughout an atom's shells is called the atom's electron configuration.

The Periodic Table (Sections 3.9–3.10) The periodic table organizes the elements according to their atomic numbers. Elements in the same group (or column) of the table have similar chemical properties and similar electron configurations.

Self-Test for Chapter 3

Complete the following statements:

1. A _____ orbital is dumbbell-shaped.

2. An atomic mass unit is also known as a _____.

3.   The nucleus of an atom is made up of _____ and _____.

4.   The _____ _____ indicates the number of protons in an atom.

5.   The electrons in an atom are grouped by energy into _____.

6.   Elements belonging to the same _____ have similar chemical properties.

7.   The atomic number of aluminum is _____.

8.   Protons, neutrons, and electrons are known as _____ _____.

9.   Atoms having the same number of protons but different numbers of neutrons are called _____.

10.   The third shell contains _____ electrons.

Tell whether the following statements are true or false:

1.   Bismuth is a metal.

2.   The mass of an electron is approximately 1 amu.

3.   A $4s$ electron is higher in energy than a $3d$ electron.

4.   Isotopes have the same number of protons but different numbers of neutrons.

5.   An atom's atomic number indicates the number of protons and neutrons the atom has.

6.   Elements in Group 2A are more reactive than elements in Group 1A.

7.   Elements in the same period have similar chemical properties.

8.   More elements are metals than are nonmetals.

9.   All compounds obey the law of definite proportions.

10.   A subshell contains only two electrons.

Match the items on the left with those on the right.

1. $1s^2\ 2s^2$ (a) Mendeleev

2.   Group   (b) Number of protons in an element

3.   Atomic mass unit   (c) Reactive metals

4.   Formulated the periodic   (d Average mass of a large number of an
       table   element's atoms

5.   Neutron   (e) Column in the periodic table

6. $^{28}_{14}\text{Si}$

(f) Row in the periodic table

7. Group 1A

(g) Element with atomic mass of 14 amu

8. Atomic number

(h) Electron configuration of beryllium

9. $^{29}_{14}\text{Si}$

(i) Element having 15 neutrons

10. Atomic weight

(j) Subatomic particle with zero charge

11. $^{14}_{7}\text{N}$

(k) Dalton

12. Period

(l) Element with atomic number 14

Chapter 4 – Nuclear Chemistry

4.1 For alpha emission, subtract 2 from the atomic number of radon and 4 from the mass number:

$$^{222}_{86} Rn \rightarrow \, ^4_2 He + \, ^{218}_{84} ?$$

Then, look in the periodic table for the element with atomic number 84:

$$^{222}_{86} Rn \rightarrow \, ^4_2 He + \, ^{218}_{84} Po$$

4.2 Add 4 to the mass number of radon-222 to calculate the isotope of radium:

$$^{226}_{88} Ra \rightarrow \, ^4_2 He + \, ^{222}_{86} Rn$$

4.3

$$^{14}_6 C \rightarrow \, ^0_{-1} e + ?$$

The mass number of the product element stays the same, but the atomic number increases by 1, to 7. Looking in the periodic table, we find that ^{14}N is the element formed:

$$^{14}_6 C \rightarrow \, ^0_{-1} e + \, ^{14}_7 N$$

4.4

(a) $^3_1 H \rightarrow \, ^0_{-1} e + \, ^3_2 He$ (b) $^{210}_{82} Pb \rightarrow \, ^0_{-1} e + \, ^{210}_{83} Bi$

4.5 $17,000 \div 5730 = 2.97$, or approximately 3 half-lives.

The final percentage of $^{14}_6 C$ is 100% x (1/2) x (1/2) x (1/2)
= 100 /8 = 12.5%.

4.6

$$\frac{I_1}{I_2} = \frac{d_2^2}{d_1^2}; \; I_1 = 250 \text{ units}; \; d_1 = 4.0 \text{ m}; \; I_2 = 25 \text{ units}; \; d_2 = ? \text{ m}^2$$

$$\frac{250 \text{ units}}{25 \text{ units}} = \frac{d_2^2}{16 \text{ m}^2}; \; 10 \, x \, 16 \text{ m}^2 = d_2^2; \; 160 \text{ m}^2 = d_2^2; \; d_2 = 13 \text{ m}$$

4.7

$$\frac{5 \text{ mrem}}{120 \text{ mrem}} \, x \, 100\% = 4.2\%$$

Thus, the annual dose of radiation for most people will increase by approximately 4%.

$^3_1 H \rightarrow \, ^0_{-1} \beta + \, ^3_2 He$ $^{210}_{82} \rightarrow \, ^0_{-1} \beta + \, ^{210}_{83} Bi$

4.8

$$175 \, \mu Ci \times \frac{1 \, mL}{44 \, \mu Ci} = 4.0 \, mL$$

4.9

$$^{241}_{95}Am \rightarrow \, ^{4}_{2}He + \, ^{237}_{93}Np$$

4.10

$$^{241}_{95}Am + \, ^{4}_{2}He \rightarrow 2 \, ^{1}_{0}n + \, ^{243}_{97}Bk$$

4.11

$$^{40}_{18}Ar + \, ^{1}_{1}H \rightarrow \, ^{1}_{0}n + \, ^{40}_{19}K$$

4.12

$$^{235}_{92}U + \, ^{1}_{0}n \rightarrow 2 \, ^{1}_{0}n + \, ^{137}_{52}Te + \, ^{97}_{40}Zr$$

4.13   A substance is said to be radioactive if it emits radiation by decay of an unstable nucleus.

4.14   Transmutation is the change of one element into another brought about by nuclear decay.

4.15

Radiation	Particle Produced	Atomic Number	Mass Number	Penetrating Power
α emission	$^{4}_{2}He$	decreases by 2	decreases by 4	low
β emission	$^{0}_{-1}e$	increases by 1	unchanged	medium
γ emission	none	unchanged	unchanged	high

4.16   The symbol for an alpha particle is $^{4}_{2}He$.

4.17   The symbol for a beta particle is $^{0}_{-1}e$.

4.18   Gamma radiation has the highest penetrating power, and alpha radiation has the lowest penetrating power.

4.19   When ionizing radiation strikes a molecule, a high-energy reactive ion is produced.

4.20   Ionizing radiation causes cell damage by breaking bonds in DNA. The resulting damage may lead to mutation, cancer, or cell death.

4.21   Background radiation may arise from naturally occurring radioactive isotopes or from cosmic rays.

4.22   A neutron in the nucleus decomposes to a proton and an electron, which is emitted as a beta particle.

4.23   An alpha particle is a helium nucleus, $^{4}_{2}He$; a helium atom is a helium nucleus plus two electrons.

4.24   If strontium-90 has a half-life of 28.8 years, half of a given quantity of strontium-90 will have decayed after 28.8 years.

4.25   100% x 1/2 x 1/2 = 25%
Thus, 25% of the original radioactivity remains in a sample after 2 half-lives.

4.26   The inside walls of a Geiger counter tube are negatively charged, and a wire in the center is positively charged. Radiation ionizes argon gas inside the tube, which creates a conducting path for current between the wall and the wire. The current is detected, and the Geiger counter makes a clicking sound.

4.27   A film badge is protected from light exposure, but exposure to other radiation causes the film to get cloudy. Photographic development of the film and comparison with a standard allows the amount of exposure to be calculated.

4.28   Rems indicate the amount of tissue damage from any type of radiation, and allow comparisons between different types of radiation to be made.

4.29   According to Table 20.5, any amount of radiation above 25 rems produces detectable effects in humans.

4.30   (1) c ;   (2) b ;   (3) d ;   (4) a

4.31   A nuclear equation is balanced if the sum of the atomic numbers is the same on both sides and if the sum of the mass numbers is the same on both sides.

4.32   For an atom emitting an alpha particle, the atomic number decreases by two, and the mass number decreases by four.
For an atom emitting a beta particle, the atomic number increases by one, and the mass number is unchanged.
For an atom emitting a gamma ray, both atomic number and mass number are unchanged.

4.33   A transuranium element is an element with an atomic number greater than 92; it is produced by bombardment of a lighter element with high-energy particles.

4.34   In nuclear fission, bombardment of a nucleus causes fragmentation in many different ways to yield a large number of smaller fragments. Normal radioactive decay of a nucleus produces an atom with a similar mass and yields a predictable product.

4.35   Bombardment of a $^{235}_{92}U$ nucleus with one neutron produces three neutrons, which, on collision with three $^{235}_{92}U$ nuclei, yield nine neutrons, and so on. Because the reaction is self-sustaining, it is known as a chain reaction.

4.36

$$^{75}_{34}Se \rightarrow {}^{0}_{-1}e + {}^{75}_{35}Br$$

4.37 $365 \div 120 = 3.04$, or approximately 3 half-lives.

$$0.050 \text{ g } \times \frac{1}{2} \times \frac{1}{2} \times \frac{1}{2} = 0.0062 \text{ g}$$

Approximately 0.006 grams of $^{75}_{34}\text{Se}$ will remain after a year.

4.38   After seven half-lives, 99% of any sample will have decayed. Since the half-life of $^{75}_{34}\text{Se}$ is approximately 1/3 year, 99% of the sample will have disintegrated in $7 \times 1/3 = 2\ 1/3$ years.

4.39

(a) $^{35}_{16}\text{S} \rightarrow\ ^{0}_{-1}\text{e} +\ ^{35}_{17}\text{Cl}$ (b) $^{24}_{10}\text{Ne} \rightarrow\ ^{0}_{-1}\text{e} +\ ^{24}_{11}\text{Na}$

(c) $^{90}_{38}\text{Sr} \rightarrow\ ^{0}_{-1}\text{e} +\ ^{90}_{39}\text{Y}$

4.40

(a) $^{140}_{55}\text{Cs} \rightarrow\ ^{0}_{-1}\text{e} +\ ^{140}_{56}\text{Ba}$ (b) $^{246}_{96}\text{Cm} \rightarrow\ ^{4}_{2}\text{He} +\ ^{242}_{94}\text{Pu}$

4.41

(a) $^{190}_{78}\text{Pt} \rightarrow\ ^{4}_{2}\text{He} +\ ^{186}_{76}\text{Os}$ (b) $^{208}_{87}\text{Fr} \rightarrow\ ^{4}_{2}\text{He} +\ ^{204}_{85}\text{At}$

(c) $^{245}_{96}\text{Cm} \rightarrow\ ^{4}_{2}\text{He} +\ ^{241}_{94}\text{Pu}$

4.42

(a) $^{109}_{47}\text{Ag} +\ ^{4}_{2}\text{He} \rightarrow\ ^{113}_{49}\text{In}$ (b) $^{10}_{5}\text{B} +\ ^{4}_{2}\text{He} \rightarrow\ ^{13}_{7}\text{N} +\ ^{1}_{0}n$

4.43

(a) $^{235}_{92}\text{U} +\ ^{1}_{0}n \rightarrow\ ^{160}_{62}\text{Sm} +\ ^{72}_{30}\text{Zn} + 4\ ^{1}_{0}n$

(b) $^{235}_{92}\text{U} +\ ^{1}_{0}n \rightarrow\ ^{87}_{35}\text{Br} +\ ^{146}_{57}\text{La} + 3\ ^{1}_{0}n$

4.44

$$^{198}_{80}\text{Hg} +\ ^{1}_{0}n \rightarrow\ ^{198}_{79}\text{Au} +\ ^{1}_{1}\text{H}$$

A proton is produced in addition to gold-198.

4.45

$^{209}_{83}\text{Bi} +\ ^{58}_{26}\text{Fe} \rightarrow\ ^{266}_{109}\text{Une} +\ ^{1}_{0}n$ A neutron is also produced.

4.46   6 days = 144 hrs = approx 2 half-lives
27 days = 648 hrs = approx 10 half-lives
5.0 ng x 1/2 x 1/2 = approx 1 ng of mercury-197 remains after 6 days.
5.0 ng x $(1/2)^{10}$ = approx 5 x 10^{-3} ng of mercury-197 remains after 27 days.

4.47

$$\frac{I_1}{I_2} = \frac{d_2^2}{d_1^2}; \frac{300 \text{ rems}}{25 \text{ rems}} = \frac{d_2^2}{4.0 \text{ m}^2}; \frac{1200 \text{ m}^2}{25} = d_2^2; \ d_2 = 6.9 \text{ m}$$

4.48

$$\frac{650 \text{ rems}}{I_2} = \frac{(50.0 \text{ m})^2}{(1.0 \text{ m})^2}; \ I_2 = 0.26 \text{ rems}$$

4.49

(a) $^{198}_{79}\text{Au} \longrightarrow \ ^{0}_{-1}\text{e} + \ ^{198}_{80}\text{Hg}$

(b) $\dfrac{30.0 \text{ mCi}}{3.75 \text{ mCi}}$ = 8 half lives; 8 x 2.7 days = 21.6 days

(c) $\dfrac{1.0 \text{ mCi}}{1 \text{ kg}}$ x 70 kg = 70 mCi

4.50

68 kg x $\dfrac{180 \ \mu\text{Ci}}{1 \text{ kg}}$ x $\dfrac{1 \text{ mCi}}{10^3 \ \mu\text{Ci}}$ x $\dfrac{1 \text{ mL}}{5.0 \text{ mCi}}$ = 2.4 mL

4.51   An antigen is a substance that stimulates antibody production.

4.52   Large doses of radiation may disturb cell biochemistry, cause tissue damage and lead to mutations.

4.53   The body-imaging techniques, CT and PET, are noninvasive and yield a large array of images that can be processed by computer to produce a three-dimensional image of an organ.

4.54   It takes three half-lives for radiation to decay to one eighth of its original value.
3 x 5730 years = 17,200 years old

4.55   Only living organisms can incorporate atmospheric $^{14}\text{CO}_2$.

4.56   The age of the leather sample is so much smaller than the half-life of $^{14}\text{CO}_2$ that the ratio of ^{14}C to ^{12}C is almost the same as the atmospheric ratio.

4.57   Since radiation occurs spontaneously, no substance can neutralize radioactive emission.

4.58   Dosimeters and film badges are more useful for measuring radiation exposure over a period of time; scintillation counters and geiger counters are more useful for measuring a current source of radiation.

4.59   An internally administered radioisotope must have a short half-life to minimize prolonged exposure to ionizing radiation.

4.60

(a) $^{99}_{42}\text{Mo} \rightarrow ^{0}_{-1}\text{e} + ^{99}_{43}\text{Tc}$. ^{99}Mo decays to Tc-99m by beta-emission.

.(b) $^{98}_{42}\text{Mo} + ^{1}_{0}n \rightarrow ^{99}_{42}\text{Mo}$

4.61 24 hours = approx 4 half-lives. 15 Ci x $(1/2)^4$ = 0.94 Ci

4.62

(a) $^{238}_{94}\text{Pu} \rightarrow ^{4}_{2}\text{He} + ^{234}_{92}\text{U}$

(b) The metal case serves as a shield to protect the wearer from alpha radiation.

4.63 The apron protects parts of the body that are not being X-rayed from radiation.

4.64 Embryos and fetuses are particularly susceptible to the effects of radiation because their cells divide frequently.

4.65 Nuclear fusion produces few radioactive by-products, and the deuterium fuel used is abundant and inexpensive.

The Chapter In Brief

Introduction to Radioactivity (Sections 4.1–4.6) A radioactive substance produces radiation. The three types of radiation are alpha (α), beta (β), and gamma (γ). These types differ in particle size, charge, and penetrating power. Every element has both natural and artificial isotopes. A radioisotope of one element can change into another element by transmutation. The amount of time required for one-half of a radioactive sample to decay is called its half-life ($t_{1/2}$).

Detection and Measurement of Radiation (Sections 4.7–4.10) All high-energy radiation is known as ionizing radiation. Radiation can be detected by film badges and by Geiger counters. Units for measuring radiation are the curie, the roentgen, the rad, and the rem. Among important medical uses of radiation are imaging, in vivo and in vitro procedures, and tumor therapy.

Artificial Transmutation and Nuclear Fission (Sections 4.11–4.12) Atoms of one element can be bombarded with small particles to yield different elements. When bombardment produces many small fragments, it is called nuclear fission. Some fission reactions, including that of uranium-238 can be chain reactions.

Self-Test For Chapter 4

Complete the following sentences:

1. The change of one element to another is called _____.

2. _____ _____ cause the most tissue damage.

3. A uranium-containing mineral is _____.

4. All people are exposed to _____ radiation.

5. _____ is an *in vitro* technique used in nuclear medicine.

6. The age of a sample can be determined by measuring the amount of _____ it contains.

7. The _____ is a unit for measuring the number of radioactive disintegrations per second.

8. In _____ _____, an atom is split apart by neutron bombardment to give small fragments.

9. People who work around radiation sources wear _____ _____ for detection of radiation.

10. PET and CT are techniques for _____ _____.

Match the entries on the left with their partners on the right:

1. Rutherford   (a) Alpha particle

2. $^{245}_{96}Cm$ (b) Used in cancer therapy

3. $t_{1/2}$ (c) Discovered radioactivity

4. $^{0}_{-1}e$ (d) Neutron

5. Becquerel   (e) Used for archeological dating

6. $^{90}_{38}Sr$ (f) Discovered α, β particles

7. $^{1}_{0}n$ (g) Natural radioactive element that undergoes fission

8. P. and M. Curie   (h) Discovered radium

9. $^{60}_{27}Co$ (i) Transuranium element

10. $^{4}_{2}He$ (j) Component of radioactive waste

11. $^{11}_{6}C$ (k) Beta particle

12. $^{235}_{92}U$ (l) Half-life

Tell whether the following statements are true or false:

1. If a sample has a half-life of 12 days, it will have decayed completely in 24 days.

2. X-rays are considered to be ionizing radiation.

3. The ratio of carbon-14 to carbon-12 in the atmosphere is constant.

4.   Pierre and Marie Curie discovered radioactivity.

5.   A β particle travels at nearly the speed of light.

6.   An α particle travels at nearly the speed of light.

7.   The product of β emission has an atomic number one amu smaller than the starting material.

8.   A nuclear power plant can undergo a nuclear explosion in an accident.

9.   The rad is the unit most commonly used in medicine to measure radiation dosage.

10. Radiation causes injury by ionizing molecules.

11. Most of the known radioisotopes are naturally occurring.

12. Many isotopes undergo nuclear fission.

Chapter 5 – Ionic Compounds

5.1

$\cdot \overset{\displaystyle \cdot}{\underset{}{X}} \cdot$

5.2

$:\!\overset{\displaystyle \cdot\cdot}{\underset{\displaystyle \cdot\cdot}{Rn}}\!:$ $\qquad$ $\cdot\overset{\displaystyle \cdot}{\underset{\displaystyle \cdot}{Pb}}\cdot$ $\qquad$ $:\!\overset{\displaystyle \cdot\cdot}{\underset{\displaystyle \cdot\cdot}{Br}}\cdot$ $\qquad$ $\cdot Ra\cdot$

5.3

$K\cdot \longrightarrow K^+ + e^-$

$:\!\overset{\displaystyle \cdot\cdot}{\underset{\displaystyle \cdot\cdot}{Cl}}\cdot \ + \ e^- \longrightarrow :\!\overset{\displaystyle \cdot\cdot}{\underset{\displaystyle \cdot\cdot}{Cl}}\!:^{-}$

5.4

(a) $:\!\overset{\displaystyle \cdot}{\underset{\displaystyle \cdot\cdot}{Se}}\cdot \ + \ 2\,e^- \longrightarrow :\!\overset{\displaystyle \cdot\cdot}{\underset{\displaystyle \cdot\cdot}{Se}}\!:^{2-};$ $\qquad$ $Se + 2\,e^- \longrightarrow Se^{2-}$

(b) $\cdot Ba\cdot \longrightarrow Ba^{2+} + 2\,e^-;$ $\qquad$ $Ba \longrightarrow Ba^{2+} + 2\,e^-$

(c) $:\!\overset{\displaystyle \cdot\cdot}{\underset{}{Br}}\cdot \ + \ e^- \longrightarrow :\!\overset{\displaystyle \cdot\cdot}{\underset{\displaystyle \cdot\cdot}{Br}}\!:^{-};$ $\qquad$ $Br + e^- \longrightarrow Br^-$

5.5 Potassium (atomic number 19): $1s^2\,2s^2\,2p^6\,3s^2\,3p^6\,4s^1$
Argon (atomic number 18): $1s^2\,2s^2\,2p^6\,3s^2\,3p^6$
Potassium can attain the noble-gas configuration of argon by losing an electron from its $4s$ orbital.

5.6 Magnesium (atomic number 12): $1s^2\,2s^2\,2p^6\,3s^2$
Neon (atomic number 10): $1s^2\,2s^2\,2p^6$
Magnesium can attain the noble-gas configuration of neon by losing two electrons from its $3s$ orbital

5.7 Oxygen atom (atomic number 8): $1s^2\,2s^2\,2p^4$
Neon atom (atomic number 10): $1s^2\,2s^2\,2p^6$
Oxygen can attain the noble-gas configuration of neon by gaining two electrons in its $2p$ orbital. The electron configuration of the oxygen ion and the neon atom are the same.

5.8 Molybdenum, a transition metal, is more likely to form a cation than an anion.

5.9 Strontium loses two electrons to form the Sr^{2+} cation; bromine gains an electron to form the Br^- anion. Only chromium can form more than one cation.

5.10 Cu, Mg, and Cl are present in the human body as ions.

5.11 Cu^{2+} – copper (II) ion $\qquad$ F^- – fluoride ion
Mg^{2+} – magnesium ion $\qquad$ S^{2-} – sulfide ion

5.12 Ag^+, Fe^{2+}, Cu^+, Te^{2-}

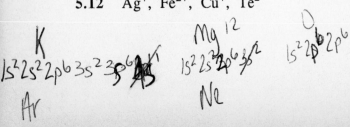

5.13 Na+ – sodium ion K^+ – potassium ion
       Ca^{2+} – calcium ion Cl^- – chloride ion

5.14 NO_3^- – nitrate ion CN^- – cyanide ion
       OH^- – hydroxide ion HPO_4^{2-} – hydrogen phosphate ion

5.15 HCO_3^- – bicarbonate ion OH^- – hydroxide ion
       NO_2^- – nitrite ion MnO_4^- – permanganate ion

5.16 (a) AgI   (b) Ag_2O (c) Ag_3PO_4

5.17 (a) Na_2SO_4 (b) $FeSO_4$ (c) $Cr_2(SO_4)_3$

5.18 $(NH_4)_2CO_3$

5.19 $Al_2(SO_4)_3$, $Al(CH_3CO_2)_3$

5.20 $BaSO_4$. One barium ion is present for each sulfate ion.

5.21 Ag_2S – silver(I) sulfide. The charge on silver is +1.

5.22 (a) CuO – copper(II) oxide   (b) $Ca(CN)_2$ – calcium cyanide
       (c) $NaNO_3$ – sodium nitrate   (d) Cu_2SO_4 – copper(I) sulfate
       (e) Li_3PO_4 – lithium phosphate   (f) NH_4Cl – ammonium chloride

5.23 (a) $Ba(OH)_2$ (b) $CuCO_3$ (c) $Mg(HCO_3)_2$ (d) CuF   (e) $Fe_2(SO_4)_3$
       (f) $Fe(NO_3)_2$

5.24 (a) Ca_3N_2 (b) $CaHPO_4$
       3 Ca = 3 x 40.1 amu = 120.3 amu   1 Ca   = 40.1 amu
       2 N = 2 x 14.0 amu = 28.0 amu   1 H   = 1.0 amu
                             _____   1 P   = 31.0 amu
                             = 148.3 amu   4 O = 4 x 16.0 amu   = 64.0 amu
                                                                             _____
                                                                             = 136.1 amu

       (c) $Ca(OH)_2$ (b) $Ca(MnO_4)_2$
       1 Ca   = 40.1 amu   1 Ca   = 40.1 amu
       2 O = 2 x 16.0 amu = 32.0 amu   2 Mn = 2 x 54.9 amu = 109.8 amu
       2 H = 2 x 1.0 amu   = 2.0 amu   8 O = 8 x 16.0 amu   = 128.0 amu
                             _____   _____
                             = 74.1 amu   = 277.9 amu

5.25 (a) CuO   – two ions   (b) $Ca(CN)_2$ – three ions
       (c) $NaNO_3$ – two ions   (d) Cu_2SO_4 – three ions
       (e) Li_3PO_4 – four ions   (f) NH_4Cl – two ions

$40 \times 3 = 120.0$ 40
19×2 28.0   1
                            31   74
$\overline{Ca_3 N_2} = \overline{148.0}$ 16×4   64
                                   $\overline{118}$

5.26 (a) MgO

		(b) CuO		(c) MnSO$_4$	
1 Mg	= 24.3 amu	1 Cu	= 63.5 amu	1 Mn	= 54.9 amu
1 O	= 16.0 amu	1 O	= 16.0 amu	1 S	= 32.1 amu
				4 O = 4 x 16.0 amu	= 64.0 amu
	= 40.3 amu		= 79.5 amu		= 151.0 amu

5.27 (a) An *ion* is an electrically charged atom or group of atoms.
(b) An *anion* is a negatively charged ion.
(c) A *cation* is a positively charged ion.
(d) An *ionic bond* is a bond formed when a positively charged ion and a negatively charged ion interact.
(e) An *ionic compound* is a chemical compound in which cations and anions are attracted to each other by ionic bonds.

5.28 (a) H ·   (b) He :(c) Li ·

5.29

(a) $:\!\overset{.}{\underset{.}{P}}\cdot$ (b) $:\!\overset{.}{\underset{..}{S}}\cdot$ (c) $:\!\overset{..}{\underset{..}{Cl}}\cdot$ (d) $\cdot Ba \cdot$ (e) $\cdot \overset{.}{Al}\cdot$

5.30

(a) $\cdot Ca \cdot \longrightarrow Ca^{2+} + 2\,e^-$ (b) $Au \longrightarrow Au^+ + e^-$

(c) $:\!\overset{..}{\underset{..}{F}}\cdot\, + e^- \longrightarrow F^-$ (d) $Cr \longrightarrow Cr^{3+} + 3\,e^-$

5.31 (a) $N + 3\,e^- \rightarrow N^{3-}$ (b) $Li \rightarrow Li^+ + e^-$
(c) $Ti \rightarrow Ti^{2+} + 2\,e^-$ (d) $Au \rightarrow Au^{3+} + 3\,e^-$

5.32 Statement (c) is true. (a) Ions have a regular arrangement in ionic solids. (b) Ions vary in size. (d) Ionic solids have high melting points.

5.33 The *octet rule* states that atoms undergo reactions in order to obtain a noble-gas electronic configuration with eight outer-shell electrons.

5.34 An ion with 34 protons and 36 electrons has a 2– charge.

5.35 An ion with 11 protons and 10 electrons has a +1 charge.

5.36 Strontium, a Group 2A element, must lose two electrons in order to achieve a noble-gas configuration.

3.37 Strontium (atomic number 38) has 38 protons and 38 electrons. The strontium ion Sr^{2+} has 38 protons and 36 electrons.

5.38 (a) Rb^+ $1s^2\,2s^2\,2p^6\,3s^2\,3p^6\,4s^2\,3d^{10}\,4p^6$
(b) Br^- $1s^2\,2s^2\,2p^6\,3s^2\,3p^6\,4s^2\,3d^{10}\,4p^6$
(c) S^{2-} $1s^2\,2s^2\,2p^6\,3s^2\,3p^6$
(d) Ba^{2+} $1s^2\,2s^2\,2p^6\,3s^2\,3p^6\,4s^2\,3d^{10}\,4p^6\,5s^2\,4d^{10}\,5p^6$
(e) Al^{3+} $1s^2\,2s^2\,2p^6$

5.39 (a) Ar (b) He (c) Ne (d) Ne (e) Ne

5.40 (a) *Atomic radius* is the distance between the nucleus and the outermost electrons in an atom.
(b) The *ionization energy* is the energy required to remove one electron from a single atom in the gaseous state.

5.41 (a) O (b) Li (c) Zn (d) N

5.42 All alkali metals have relatively low ionization energies.

5.43 (a) Al^{3+} (b) Fe^{2+} and Fe^{3+} (c) Cl^-

5.44 (a) Elements in Groups 1A, 2A, and 3A all commonly form cations.
(b) Elements in Groups 6A and 7A all commonly form anions.

5.45 None of the ions are stable because all lack eight outer-shell electrons.

5.46 (a) Magnesium forms only the Mg^{2+} cation.
(b) Silicon does not form cations.
(c) Manganese, a transition metal, can form several different cations.

5.47 Cr^{2+} $1s^2\, 2s^2\, 2p^6\, 3s^2\, 3p^6\, 3d^4$
Cr^{3+} $1s^2\, 2s^2\, 2p^6\, 3s^2\, 3p^6\, 3d^3$

5.48 The ionization energy of Li^+ is much greater than that of Li. Li loses an electron to form an ion with eight outer-shell electrons, but Li^+ would need to lose one electron from a stable octet to form the Li^{2+} cation.

5.49 S^{2-} has a larger ionic radius than S because S^{2-} has two additional electrons that are not as tightly held by the positively charged nucleus as are the electrons of the S atom.

5.50 (a) S^{2-} – sulfide ion (b) Sn^{2+} – tin(II) ion (c) Sr^{2+} – strontium ion
(d) Mg^{2+} – magnesium ion (e) Au^+ – gold(I) ion

5.51 (a) Cu^+ cuprous ion copper(I) ion
(b) Fe^{3+} ferric ion iron(III) ion
(c) Hg^{2+} mercuric ion mercury(II) ion

5.52 (a) Se^{2-} (b) O^{2-} (c) Ag^+ (d) Co^{2+}

5.53 (a) OH^- (b) SO_4^{2-} (c) $CH_3CO_2^-$ (d) MnO_4^- (e) OCl^- (f) NO_3^-
(g) HCO_3^-

5.54 (a) NH_4^+ ammonium ion (b) CN^- cyanide ion
(c) CO_3^{2-} carbonate ion (d) SO_3^{2-} sulfite ion

5.55 (a) $Al(NO_3)_3$ (b) $AgNO_3$ (c) $Zn(NO_3)_2$ (d) $Ba(NO_3)_2$

5.56 $Mg(OH)_2$, $Al(OH)_3$

5.57 (a) $NaHCO_3$ (b) KNO_3 (c) $CaCO_3$

5.58   (a) $Ca(OCl)_2$ (b) $CuSO_4$ (c) Na_3PO_4

5.59

	S^{2-}	Cl^-	PO_4^{3-}	CO_3^{2-}
copper(II)	CuS	$CuCl_2$	$Cu_3(PO_4)_2$	$CuCO_3$
Ca^{2+}	CaS	$CaCl_2$	$Ca_3(PO_4)_2$	$CaCO_3$
NH_4^+	$(NH_4)_2S$	NH_4Cl	$(NH_4)_3PO_4$	$(NH_4)_2CO_3$
iron(III)	Fe_2S_3	$FeCl_3$	$FePO_4$	$Fe_2(CO_3)_3$

5.60   (a) $MgCO_3$ magnesium carbonate   (b) $Ca(CH_3CO_2)_2$ calcium acetate
(c) $AgCN$ silver cyanide   (d) $Na_2Cr_2O_7$ sodium dichromate

5.61 $Ca_3(PO_4)_2$ is the correct formula because the six positive charges from the three Ca^{2+} ions are balanced by the six negative charges of the two PO_4^{3-} ions.

5.62

Compound	One formula unit contains
(a) $AgCl$	1 Ag^+ ion, 1 Cl^- ion
(b) CaF_2	1 Ca^{2+} ion, 2 F^- ions
(c) Ag_2SO_4	2 Ag^+ ions, 1 SO_4^{2-} ion

5.63   (a) ZnO 65.4 amu + 16.0 amu = 81.4 amu
(b) TiO_2 47.9 amu + (2 x 16.0 amu) = 79.9 amu
(c) $PbCrO_4$ 207.2 amu + 52.0 amu + (4 x 16.0 amu) = 323.2 amu
(d) $CdSe$ 112.4 amu + 79.0 amu = 191.4 amu

5.64   (a) $(NH_4)_2Cr_2O_7$ (2 x 14.0 amu) + (8 x 1.0 amu) + (2 x 52.0 amu) + (7 x 16.0 amu)
= 252.0 amu
(b) $Cr(NO_3)_3$ 52.0 amu + (3 x 14.0 amu) + 9 x 16.0 amu) = 238.0 amu
(c) $LiHSO_4$ 6.9 amu + 1.0 amu + 32.1 amu + (4 x 16.0 amu) = 104.0 amu

5.65   Homeostasis is the maintenance of a constant internal environment in the body.

5.66

$$\frac{60\ \mu g}{1\ dL} \times \frac{1\ g}{10^6\ \mu g} \times \frac{10\ dL}{1\ L} = 6 \times 10^{-4}\ g/L$$

5.67   Most of the calcium present in the body is found in bones and teeth.

6.68   Sodium protects against fluid loss and is necessary for muscle contraction and transmission of nerve impulses.

5.69   Too little iron in the blood leads to anemia, which becomes more severe if blood is removed.

5.70   "hyper" – too high; above normal
"hypo" – too low; below normal

5.71   To a geologist, a mineral is a naturally occurring crystalline compounds. To a nutritionist, a mineral is a metal ion essential for human health.

5.72

Ion	Name	Charge	Total charge
Ca^{2+}	calcium ion	2+	5 x (2+) = 10+
PO_4^{3-}	phosphate ion	3–	3 x (3–) = 9–
OH^-	hydroxide ion	1–	1–

The formula correctly represents a neutral compound because the number of positive charges equals the number of negative charges.

5.73 $Ca_5(PO_4)_3OH$

5 Ca	= 5.40.1 amu	= 200.5 amu
3 P	= 3 x 31.0 amu	= 93.0 amu
13 O	= 13 x 16.0 amu	= 208.0 amu
1 H	= 1 x 1.0 amu	= 1.0 amu

$$492.5 \text{ amu}$$

5.74   The hydride ion has the same electron configuration as the noble gas neon.

5.75   (a) CrO_3 (b) VCl_5 (c) MnO_2 (d) MoS_2

5.76 $Pb_3(AsO_4)_2$

3 Pb	= 3 x 207.2 amu	= 621.6 amu
2 As	= 2 x 74.9 amu	= 149.8 amu
8 O	= 8 x 16.0 amu	= 128.0 amu

$$899.4 \text{ amu}$$

5.77   (a) A gluconate ion has one negative charge.
(b) Three gluconate ions are in one formula unit of iron(III) gluconate.

5.78   (a) Cu_3PO_4 copper(I) phosphate   (b) Na_2SO_3 sodium sulfite
(c) MnO_2 manganese(IV) oxide   (d) $AuCl_3$ gold(III) chloride
(e) $Pb(CO_3)_2$ lead(IV) carbonate   (f) Ni_2S_3 nickel(III) sulfide

5.79   (a) $Co(CN)_2$ (b) UO_3 (c) $SnSO_4$ (d) K_3PO_4 (e) Ca_3P_2

5.80

Ion	Protons	Electrons	Neutrons
(a) $^{16}O^{2-}$	8	10	8
(b) $^{89}Y^{3+}$	39	36	50
(c) $^{133}Cs^+$	55	54	78
(d) $^{81}Br^-$	35	36	46

The Chapter in Brief

Ions and Ionic Bonds (Sections 5.1–5.3) Ions form when atoms either gain or lose electrons. Ionic bonds can form between positive ions and negative ions. Atoms and ions can be represented by electron-dot structures. Ionic compounds are high-melting crystalline solids that are often water soluble.

The Octet Rule and Periodic Properties (Sections 5.4– 5.5) Main-group atoms tend to combine in chemical compounds to attain eight outer-shell electrons (the octet rule). Periodic properties such as atomic radii and ionization energy are related to the octet rule.

Ions and Ionic Compounds (Sections 5.6–5.10) Metals form cations, and group 6A and 7A elements form anions. Polyatomic ions are also common. When cations and anions form compounds, the total charge must be zero.

Formula Weights (Section 5.11) The formulas of ionic compounds are simplest formulas, and the formula weight of an ionic compound is the sum of the atomic weights of the individual atoms in the compound.

Self-Test for Chapter 5

Complete the following sentences:

1.   _____ _____ measures the ease with which an atom gives up an electron.

2.   The name of K_3PO_4 is _____ _____.

3.   Radium (atomic number 88) loses _____ electrons to achieve a noble-gas configuration.

4. NO_3^- is an example of a _____ ion.

5.   The formulas of ionic compounds are _____ formulas.

6.   Atoms of main-group elements tend to combine in chemical compounds so that they attain _____ outer-shell electrons.

7.   The formula weight of $Fe_3(PO_4)_2$ is _____.

8.   _____ is the maintenance of a constant internal environment in the body.

9.   Ionic compounds are usually _____ solids.

10.   The first three elements in group ____ form neither cations nor anions.

Tell whether the following statements are true or false:

1.   Zinc can form ions with different charges.

2. Na^+ and F^- have the same electron configuration.

3. Na^+ has a larger atomic radius than F^-.

4. $Co(CO_3)_2$ is a possible compound.

5.   Hyponatremia means too much sodium in blood serum.

6.   Ionic crystals conduct electricity.

7.   Cuprous ion is the same as copper(II) ion.

8.   Many ionic compounds are not water-soluble.

9.   Group 5A consists of metals and nonmetals.

10.   Elements in group 7A have the largest ionization energies.

11.   The octet rule is limited to main-group elements.

Match each item on the left with its partner on the right:

1. $FeBr_2$ (a) sulfite anion

2. S^{2-} (b) electron-dot symbol

3. NH_4^+ (c) alkali metal

4. SO_3^{2-} (d) has the same electron configuration as Na^+

5.   Ca   (e) iron(II) bromide

6. $FeBr_3$ (f) transition metal

7.   Ar   (g) sulfate anion

8.   ·Be·   (h) alkaline earth metal

9.   CO   (i) has the same electron configuration as Cl^-

10. SO_4^{2-} (j) iron(III) bromide

11.   Ne   (k) polyatomic cation

12.   K   (l) polyatomic anion

Chapter 6 – Molecular Compounds

6.1   The two hydrogen atoms achieve the electron configuration of helium: $1s^2$

6.2

shared electron pair

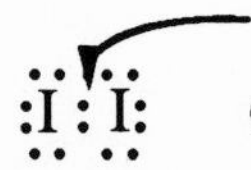

$$:\ddot{I}:\ddot{I}: \quad \text{or} \quad I\text{–}I \quad \text{or} \quad I_2$$

Each iodine achieves the noble gas configuration of xenon.

6.3   (a) PH_3 hydrogen – one covalent bond; phosphorus – three covalent bonds
(b) H_2Se hydrogen – one covalent bond; selenium – two covalent bonds
(c) HCl hydrogen – one covalent bond; chlorine – one covalent bond
(d) SiF_4 fluorine – one covalent bond; silicon – four covalent bonds

6.4   Lead is a member of Group 4A and should form four covalent bonds as do carbon and silicon. $PbCl_4$ is thus a more likely formula for a compound containing lead and chlorine than is $PbCl_5$.

6.5   Form ionic and covalent bonds: N, O, S, F, Cl, Br, I
Form only covalent bonds: B, C, Si, P

The latter four elements form only covalent compounds because it is too difficult to add or remove electrons to form an ion with a complete octet.

6.6   In acetic acid, all hydrogen atoms have two outer-shell electrons and all carbon and oxygen atoms have eight outer-shell electrons.

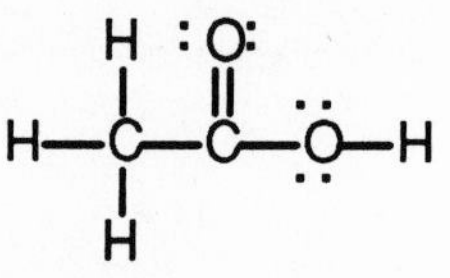

Acetic acid

6.7   (a) H_2O_2
(b) $(2 \times 1.0 \text{ amu}) + (2 \times 16.0 \text{ amu}) = 34.0 \text{ amu}$
(c) By removing two protons (H^+ ions), the peroxide ion O_2^{2-} has only 16 protons but still has its 18 electrons (14 outer-shell plus 4 inner-shell). Since there are two more electrons that protons, the charge of the peroxide ion is –2.

$$:\ddot{O}:\ddot{O}:^{2-} \quad \text{peroxide ion}$$

6.8 $C_2Cl_3H_3O_2$ $(2 \times 12.0 \text{ amu}) + (3 \times 35.5 \text{ amu}) + (3 \times 1.0 \text{ amu}) + (2 \times 16.0 \text{ amu})$
$= 165.5 \text{ amu}$

6.9   (a) for phosgene, $COCl_2$

Step 1: Total valence electrons –
$4 e^-$ (from C) + $6 e^-$ (from O) + $2 \times 7 e^-$ (from Cl) = $24 e^-$

Step 2: Six electrons are involved in the covalent bonds.

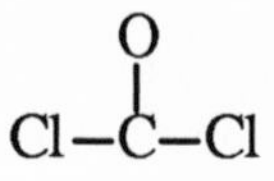

$$Cl-\overset{\overset{\displaystyle O}{|}}{C}-Cl$$

Step 3: The other 18 electrons are placed in nine lone pairs.

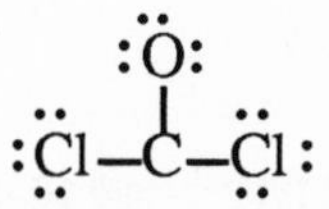

$$:\ddot{C}l-\overset{\overset{\displaystyle :\ddot{O}:}{|}}{C}-\ddot{C}l:$$

Step 4: All electrons are used up in the above structure, but carbon doesn't have an electron octet, so an electron pair must be moved from oxygen to form a carbon-oxygen double bond.

Step 5: The 24 electrons have been used up, and all atoms have a complete octet.

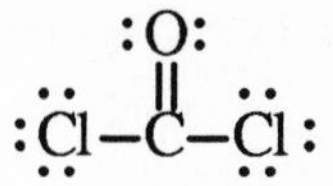

$$:\ddot{C}l-\overset{\overset{\displaystyle :O:}{||}}{C}-\ddot{C}l:$$

(b) for OCl^-

Step 1: Total valence electrons –
$6 e^-$ (from O) + $7 e^-$ (from Cl) + $1 e^-$ (negative charge) = $14 e^-$

Step 2: Two electrons used.   O—Cl

Step 3: Twelve additional electrons used.

$$:\ddot{O}-\ddot{C}l:^{-}$$

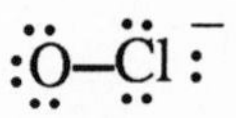

Step 4: The above structure uses fourteen valence electrons, and all atoms have complete octets.

6.10   (a) for CO

Step 1: $4 e^- + 6 e^- = 10$ electrons

Step 2:   Two electrons used.   C—O

Steps 3-4: Eight additional electrons used.

$$:\ddot{C}-\ddot{O}:$$

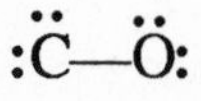

Step 5: Since neither carbon nor oxygen has a complete octet, electron pairs must be moved. The structure :C≡O: now has complete octets for both atoms.

(b) SCl_2 : 20 electrons

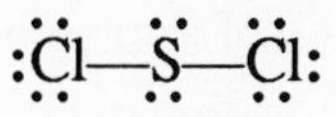

$$:\ddot{C}l-\ddot{S}-\ddot{C}l:$$

6.11

HNO_3 :   24 electrons

$$:\ddot{O}-\overset{\overset{\displaystyle :O:}{||}}{N}-\ddot{O}-H$$

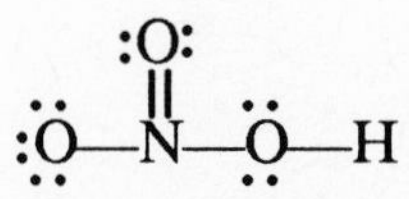

6.12

CH_5N :   14 electrons

$$H-\overset{\overset{\displaystyle H}{|}}{\underset{\underset{\displaystyle H}{|}}{C}}-\overset{\cdot\cdot}{\underset{\underset{\displaystyle H}{|}}{N}}-H$$

6.13

C_3H_8 :   20 electrons

$$H-\overset{\overset{\displaystyle H}{|}}{\underset{\underset{\displaystyle H}{|}}{C}}-\overset{\overset{\displaystyle H}{|}}{\underset{\underset{\displaystyle H}{|}}{C}}-\overset{\overset{\displaystyle H}{|}}{\underset{\underset{\displaystyle H}{|}}{C}}-H$$

6.14

CH_2O :   12 electrons

$$H-\underset{\underset{\displaystyle H}{|}}{C}=\overset{\cdot\cdot}{\underset{\cdot\cdot}{O}}$$

6.15

(a)
$$H-\overset{\overset{\displaystyle H}{|}}{\underset{\underset{\displaystyle H}{|}}{C}}-\overset{\cdot\cdot}{\underset{\cdot\cdot}{O}}-H$$

(b)
$$:N\equiv C-\overset{\overset{\displaystyle H}{|}}{\underset{\underset{\displaystyle H}{|}}{C}}-H$$

(c)
$$:\overset{\cdot\cdot}{\underset{\cdot\cdot}{Cl}}-\overset{\cdot\cdot}{\underset{\underset{\displaystyle :\overset{\cdot\cdot}{Cl}:}{|}}{N}}-\overset{\cdot\cdot}{\underset{\cdot\cdot}{Cl}}:$$

6.16   (a) Carbon, the central atom, is surrounded by four bonds. Referring to Table 6.2, we see that chloroform has tetrahedral geometry.

$$\underset{\underset{\displaystyle Cl}{\diagdown}}{Cl}\cdots\overset{\overset{\displaystyle Cl}{|}}{C}-H \qquad \text{Chloroform}$$

(b) Dichloroethylene is planar, with 120° bond angles.

$$\underset{Cl}{\overset{Cl}{\diagup}}C=C\underset{H}{\overset{H}{\diagdown}} \qquad \text{Dichloroethylene}$$

6.17`   Ammonium ion is tetrahedral.

$$H\cdots\overset{\overset{\displaystyle H}{|}+}{\underset{\underset{\displaystyle H}{\diagup}}{N}}-H \qquad \text{Ammonium ion}$$

6.18   Both molecules are bent and have bond angles of approximately 105°.

6.19 Use Figure 6.10 to predict electronegativity:

Least electronegative ⎯⎯⎯⎯⎯⎯⎯⎯⎯> Most electronegative

   H (2.1), P (2.1) < S (2.6) < N (3.0) < O (3.5)

6.20

Electronegativity	Difference	Type of Bond
(a) I (2.5) , Cl (3.0)	0.5	polar covalent
(b) Li (1.0) , O (3.5)	2.5	ionic
(c) Br (2.8) , Br (2.8)	0	covalent
(d) P (2.1) , Br (2.8)	0.7	polar covalent

6.21

Electronegativity	Bond polarity
(a) F (4.0) , S (2.5)	$\overset{\delta^-}{F}-\overset{\delta^+}{S}$
(b) P (2.1) , O (3.5)	$\overset{\delta^+}{P}-\overset{\delta^-}{O}$
(c) As (2.0) , Cl (3.0)	$\overset{\delta^+}{As}-\overset{\delta^-}{Cl}$

6.22

(a) 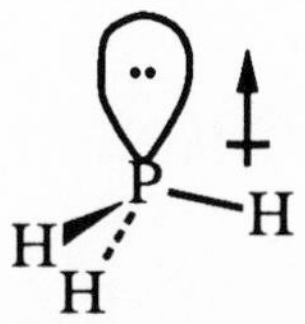   (b) 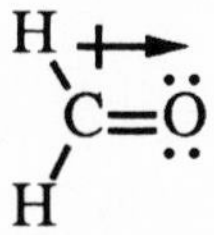   (c)

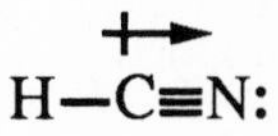

The bonds of PH_3 are covalent, but the molecule is polar because of the lone electron pair on phosphorus.

6.23 (a) S_2Cl_2 disulfur dichloride   (b) ICl iodine chloride
   (c) ICl_3 iodine trichloride

6.24 (a) SeF_4 (b) P_2O_5 (c) BrF_3

6.25 A covalent bond is a chemical bond in which electrons are shared between two atoms. When two atoms are far apart, neither feels the effect of the other. As the atoms move closer together, they are attracted to each other. Potential energy is at a minimum at a distance that is the bond length between the two atoms. If the atoms move closer to each other than the bond length, they repel each other, and potential energy increases.

6.26 (a) oxygen (i) (iv)   (b) potassium (iii)   (c) phosphorus (ii)
   (d) iodine (i) (iv)   (e) hydrogen (i) (iv)   (f) cesium (iii)

6.27 Form covalent bonds: (b) carbon and fluorine, (d) silicon and fluorine

6.28 Tellurium, a Group 6A element, forms two covalent bonds, as do oxygen, sulfur, and other members of Group 6A.

6.29 Germanium, a Group 4A element, forms four covalent bonds.

6.30   *Hydrogen* has only one valence electron to share in one covalent bond.
Boron has only three valence electrons to share in three covalent bonds.
Phosphorus and *sulfur* can expand the number of bonds to five and six, respectively.

6.31   (a) N – three covalent bonds;   Cl – one covalent bond
(b) H – one covalent bond;   I – one covalent bond
(c) C – four covalent bonds;   H – one covalent bond;   Cl – one covalent bond
(d) P – five covalent bonds;   Br – one covalent bond

6.32   Coordinate covalent bonds: (b) $Cu(NH_3)_4{}^{2+}$ (c) $NH_4{}^+$ (f) H_3O^+

6.33   Since tin is a member of Group 4A, it forms four covalent bonds. $SnCl_4$ is the most likely formula for a molecular compound of tin and chlorine.

6.34   (a) A *molecular formula* shows the numbers and kinds of atoms in a molecule; a *structural formula* shows how the atoms in a molecule are bonded to each other.
(b) A *structural formula* shows the bonds between atoms; a *condensed structure* shows central atoms and the bonds between them as groups.
(c) A *lone pair* of valence electrons is a pair that is not shared; a *shared pair* of electrons is shared between two atoms.

6.35   (a) N_2 – 10 valence electrons   (b) CO – 10 valence electrons
(c) CH_3CH_2CHO – 24 valence electrons   (d) OF_2 – 20 valence electrons

6.36

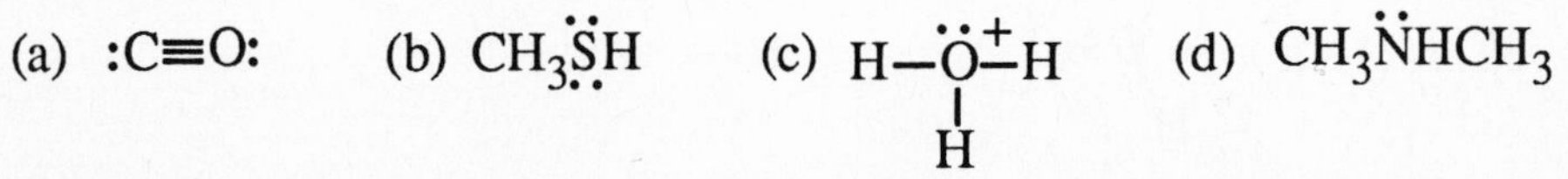

(a) $:C{\equiv}O:$ (b) $CH_3\ddot{\underset{..}{S}}H$ (c) $H-\overset{+}{\underset{\underset{H}{|}}{\ddot{O}}}-H$ (d) $CH_3\dot{\ddot{N}}HCH_3$

6.37   A compound with the formula C_2H_8 cannot exist because any structure drawn would violate the rules of valence.

6.38   Structure (a) is correct. Structure (b) has two carbons with incomplete octets. Structure (c) has one carbon with an incomplete octet and an oxygen bonded to three groups.

6.39

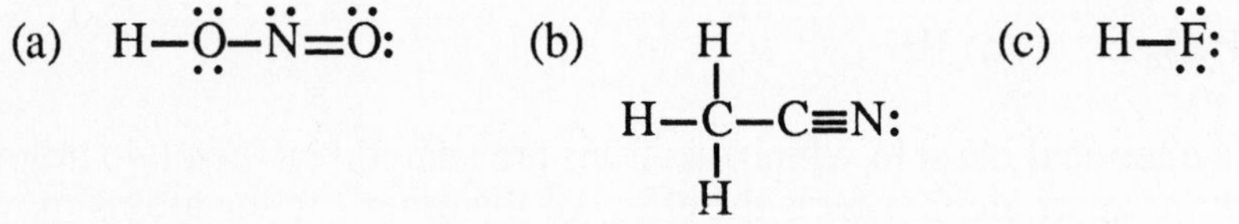

(a) $H-\underset{..}{\ddot{O}}-\ddot{N}{=}\ddot{O}:$ (b) $H-\underset{\underset{H}{|}}{\overset{\overset{H}{|}}{C}}-C{\equiv}N:$ (c) $H-\ddot{\underset{..}{F}}:$

6.40   (a) $CH_3CH_2CH_3$ (b) $H_2C{=}CHCH_3$ (c) CH_3CH_2Cl

6.41

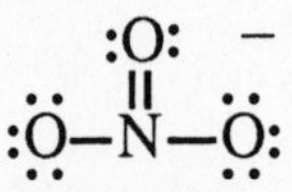

$:\underset{..}{\ddot{O}}-\underset{\underset{\ddot{O}:}{\|}}{\overset{\overset{:O:}{\|}}{N}}-\underset{..}{\ddot{O}}:{}^{-}$

Each oxygen atom has eight protons, and nitrogen has seven, for a total of 31 protons. The structure shown for nitrate has 24 outer-shell electrons which, when added to the 8 inner-shell electrons, add up to 32 electrons. Since there is one more electron than proton, nitrate ion has a –1 charge.

6.42

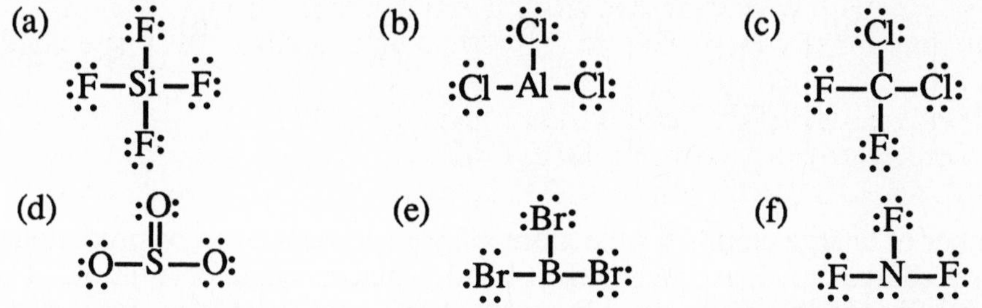

(a)

$$:\!\ddot{F}\!:$$
$$:\!\ddot{F}\!-\!Si\!-\!\ddot{F}\!:$$
$$:\!\ddot{F}\!:$$

(b)

$$:\!\ddot{Cl}\!:$$
$$:\!\ddot{Cl}\!-\!Al\!-\!\ddot{Cl}\!:$$

(c)

$$:\!\ddot{Cl}\!:$$
$$:\!\ddot{F}\!-\!C\!-\!\ddot{Cl}\!:$$
$$:\!\ddot{F}\!:$$

(d)

$$:\!\ddot{O}\!:$$
$$:\!\ddot{O}\!-\!S\!-\!\ddot{O}\!:$$

(e)

$$:\!\ddot{Br}\!:$$
$$:\!\ddot{Br}\!-\!B\!-\!\ddot{Br}\!:$$

(f)

$$:\!\ddot{F}\!:$$
$$:\!\ddot{F}\!-\!N\!-\!\ddot{F}\!:$$

6.43

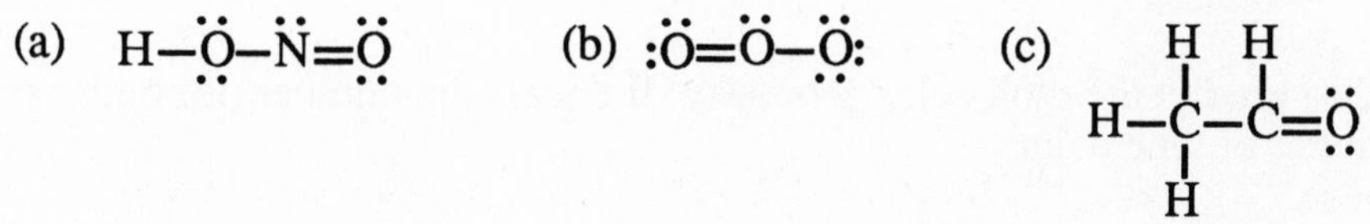

(a) $H\!-\!\ddot{O}\!-\!\ddot{N}\!=\!\ddot{O}$

(b) $:\!\ddot{O}\!=\!\ddot{O}\!-\!\ddot{O}\!:$

(c)

$$\begin{array}{cc} H & H \\ | & | \\ H\!-\!C\!-\!C\!=\!\ddot{O} \\ | \\ H \end{array}$$

6.44

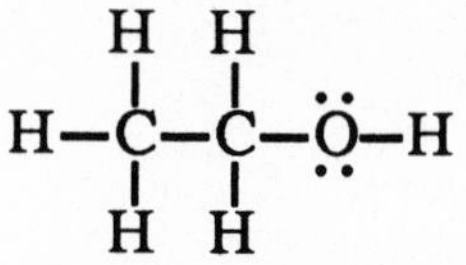

$$\begin{array}{cc} H & H \\ | & | \\ H\!-\!C\!-\!C\!-\!\ddot{O}\!-\!H \\ | & | \\ H & H \end{array}$$ Ethanol

6.45

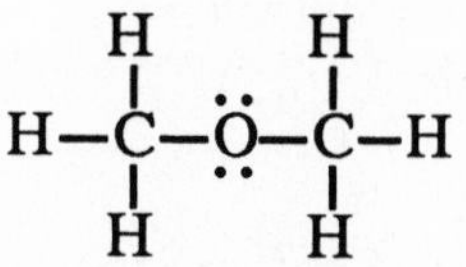

$$\begin{array}{cc} H & H \\ | & | \\ H\!-\!C\!-\!\ddot{O}\!-\!C\!-\!H \\ | & | \\ H & H \end{array}$$ Dimethyl ether

6.46

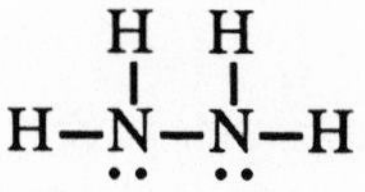

$$\begin{array}{cc} H & H \\ | & | \\ H\!-\!\ddot{N}\!-\!\ddot{N}\!-\!H \end{array}$$ Hydrazine

6.47

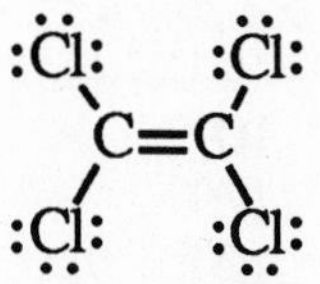

$$\begin{array}{cc} :\!\ddot{Cl}\!: & :\!\ddot{Cl}\!: \\ \diagdown & \diagup \\ C\!=\!C \\ \diagup & \diagdown \\ :\!\ddot{Cl}\!: & :\!\ddot{Cl}\!: \end{array}$$ Tetrachloroethylene contains a double bond

6.48

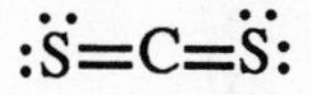

$:\!\ddot{S}\!=\!C\!=\!\ddot{S}\!:$ Carbon disulfide contains two carbon–sulfur double bonds.

6.49   (a) It was thought that noble gases couldn't form bonds because they already had eight valence electrons.

(b)

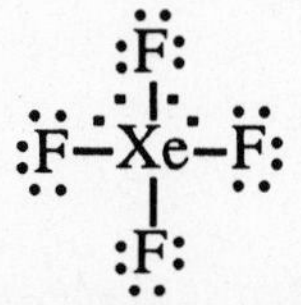

$$:\!\ddot{F}\!:$$
$$:\!\ddot{F}\!-\!Xe\!-\!\ddot{F}\!:$$
$$:\!\ddot{F}\!:$$ Xenon tetrafluoride

6.50

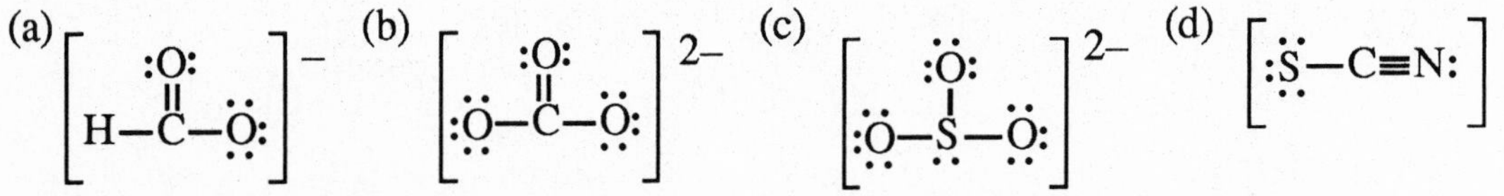

(a) $\left[\begin{array}{c} \ddot{O} \\ \parallel \\ H-C-\ddot{O}: \end{array} \right]^{-}$ (b) $\left[:\ddot{O}-\overset{\displaystyle \ddot{O}}{\underset{\displaystyle \parallel}{C}}-\ddot{O}: \right]^{2-}$ (c) $\left[:\ddot{O}-\overset{\displaystyle \ddot{O}}{\underset{\displaystyle }{S}}-\ddot{O}: \right]^{2-}$ (d) $\left[:\ddot{S}-C\equiv N: \right]^{-}$

6.51   Count the number of charge clouds for the atom whose geometry is to be predicted. An electron pair is a charge cloud, as is a covalent bond, whether single or multiple. Then consult Table 6.2 for possible geometries for atoms having the calculated number of charge clouds.

6.52   Use Table 6.2 to predict the molecular geometry. **B** equals the number of bonds, and **E** equals the number of lone pairs:

Molecule	# of bonds	# of lone pairs	Shape	Bond angle
(a) AB_4	4	0	tetrahedral	109°
(b) AB_3E	3	1	pyramidal	109°
(c) AB_2E	2	1	angular	120°

6.53

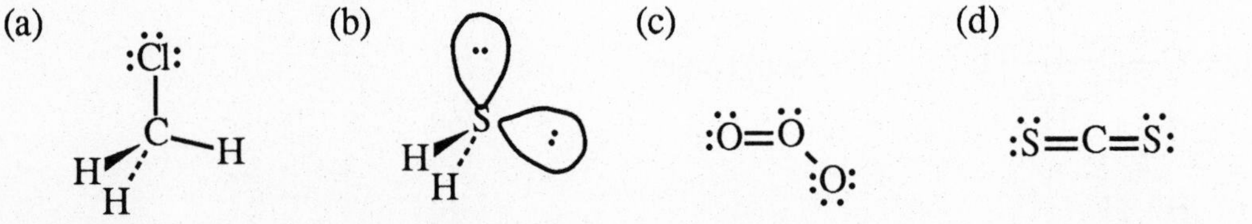

(a)   (b)   (c)   (d)

bond angle – 109°   bond angle – 105°   bond angle – 120°   bond angle – 180°

6.54

Molecule	# of bonding pairs	# of lone pairs	Shape	Bond angle
(a) SiF_4	4	12	tetrahedral	109°
(b) $AlCl_3$	3	9	planar	120°
(c) CF_2Cl_2	4	12	tetrahedral	120°
(d) SO_3	4	8	planar	120°
(e) BBr_3	3	9	planar	120°
(f) NF_3	3	10	pyramidal	107°

6.55

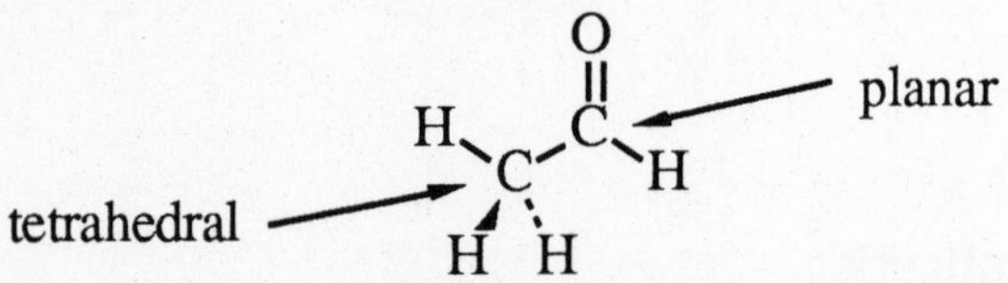

planar

tetrahedral

6.56   Bonds that are 100% covalent occur only between atoms with identical electronegativities. Bonds that are ionic occur only between atoms with a difference in electronegativity greater than 2.0. Most bonds fall into neither category and are neither 100% covalent nor ionic.

6.57

$$\overset{\delta^+\ \ \delta^-}{\text{(a) I—Br}} \quad \overset{\delta^-\ \ \delta^+}{\text{(b) O—H}} \quad \overset{\delta^+\ \ \delta^-}{\text{(c) C—F}} \quad \overset{\delta^-\ \ \delta^+}{\text{(d) N—C}} \quad \text{(e) nonpolar}$$

6.58

Electronegativity		*Difference*	*Type of bond*
(a) Na (0.9) ,	F (4.0)	3.1	ionic
(b) C (2.5) ,	Cl (3.0)	0.5	polar covalent
(c) N (3.0) ,	H (2.1)	0.9	polar covalent
(d) Be (1.5) ,	Br (2.8)	1.3	polar covalent

6.59 Use Figure 6.10 to determine bond polarities

Least polar bonds ———> Most polar bonds

$$PH_3 \ < \ HCl \ < \ H_2O \ < \ CF_4$$

6.60 The individual bonds in BCl_3 are polar, but BCl_3 is nonpolar overall because all bond polarities cancel.

6.61

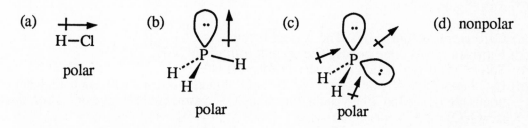

6.62 (a) PI_3 phosphorus triiodide   (b) $AsCl_3$ arsenic trichloride
       (c) P_4S_3 tetraphosphorus trisulfide   (d) Al_2F_6 dialuminum hexafluoride
       (e) NI_3 nitrogen triiodide   (f) IF_7 iodine heptafluoride

6.63 (a) NO_2 (b) SF_6 (c) BrI_5 (d) P_4O_{10} (e) N_2O_4 (f) $AsCl_5$

6.64

	Ionic compounds	*Molecular compounds*
(a) smallest particles:	individual ions	individual molecules
(b) melting point:	high	low
(c) existence as gas, liquid, or solid:	solid	low-melting solid, liquid, or gas

6.65 A coordinate covalent bond is one in which both bonding electrons are donated by the same atom.

6.66 In biological molecules, magnesium, iron, cobalt, copper, and zinc are associated with coordinate covalent bond formation.

6.67 A polymer is formed of many repeating units contained in a long chain.

6.68 Diamonds and graphite are both formed of large numbers of carbon atoms. In diamonds, each carbon is covalently bonded to four neighboring carbons with tetrahedral geometry. In graphite, each carbon is bonded to three other carbons in two-dimensional sheets that are stacked on top of each other. Diamond has a rigid three-dimensional structure that is responsible for its strength and hardness. Graphite is formed of two-dimensional sheets that slip past each other.

6.69 Diamonds are used for cutting and as abrasives. Graphite is used in pencil lead and as a lubricant.

6.70

(a)
$$
\begin{array}{ccc}
 & \text{H} & \text{O} & \text{H} \\
 & | & || & | \\
\text{H}-\text{C}-&\text{C}-&\text{C}-\text{H} \\
 & | & & | \\
 & \text{H} & & \text{H}
\end{array}
\qquad
\begin{array}{ccc}
 & \text{H} & \text{H} & \text{O} \\
 & | & | & || \\
\text{H}-\text{C}-&\text{C}-&\text{C}-\text{H} \\
 & | & | & \\
 & \text{H} & \text{H} &
\end{array}
$$

(b) The C=O carbon atoms have planar geometry; the other carbons have tetrahedral geometry.
(c) The C=O bonds are polar.
(d) Formula weight of acetone: 58.0 amu

6.71 Consult Figure 6.3 for help.

(a) Carbon forms four bonds. The correct formula is CCl_4.
(b) Nitrogen forms three bonds. The correct formula is N_2H_4.
(c) Sulfur forms two bonds. The correct formula is H_2S.
(d) C_2OS *could* actually be correct (S=C=C=O), but compounds with such adjacent double bonds are rare. More likely is the formula COS, a structural relative of carbon dioxide (S=C=O).

6.72 Cyanide ion has 4 inner-shell electrons plus the 10 electrons pictured for a total of 14. Together, carbon and nitrogen have 13 protons. Since there is one more electron than proton, cyanide ion has a charge of –1.

6.73 (a) $CaCl_2$ (i)   (b) $Mg(NO_3)_2$ (i), (ii)   (c) BF_4^- (ii), (iii)   (d) CBr_4 (ii)

6.74

(a)
$$
\left[
\begin{array}{c}
\text{H} \\
| \\
\text{H}-\text{P}-\text{H} \\
| \\
\text{H}
\end{array}
\right]^+
$$

(b) Phosphonium ion is tetrahedral

(c) An H^+ ion forms a coordinate covalent bond with phosphorus
(d) # of electrons: 15 (from P) + 3 (from 3 H) = 18
   # of protons: 15 (from P) + 4 (from 4 H) = 19
   PH_4^+ is positive because the number of protons exceed the number of electrons by one.

6.75-6.76

Compound	Name	Formula weight
(a) $CaCl_2$	calcium chloride	110.0 amu
(b) $TeCl_2$	tellurium dichloride	198.5 amu
(c) BF_3	boron trifluoride	67.8 amu
(d) $MgSO_4$	magnesium sulfate	120.4 amu
(e) K_2O	potassium oxide	94.2 amu
(f) FeF_3	iron(III) fluoride	112.8 amu
(g) PF_3	phosphorus trifluoride	88.0 amu

6.77 (a) H_3PO_4 phosphoric acid (b) H_2CO_3 carbonic acid
     (c) HNO_3 nitric acid (d) H_2SO_4 sulfuric acid

6.78

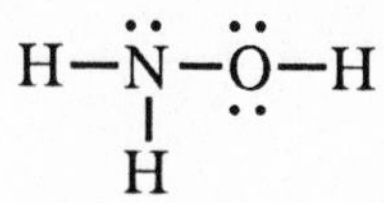

$$H-\overset{..}{\underset{|}{N}}-\overset{..}{\underset{..}{O}}-H$$
$$\overset{|}{H}$$

Hydroxylamine is polar because it contains polar O–H, N–H, and N–O bonds.

The Chapter in Brief

Covalent Bonds (Sections 3.1–3.3, 3.5) Covalent bonds are formed when two atoms share electrons; in most cases, atoms that form covalent bonds achieve a noble-gas configuration. Multiple bonds and coordinate bonds are other types of covalent bonds.

Lewis Structures and Molecular Shapes (Sections 3.4, 3.6, 3.7) Structural formulas show how atoms in a molecule are connected to each other. In Lewis structures, a covalent bond is indicated by a line, and lone electron paris are shown as pairs of dots. The VSEPR model shows how to predict the shapes of molecules.

Bond Polarity (Sections 3.8, 3.9) The difference in electronegativities of atoms can be used to predict if bonds are polar or nonpolar. Molecules containing polar bonds may or may not be polar.

Molecular Compounds (Sections 3.10–3.12) The weak intermolecular forces between molecules in molecular compounds cause the properties of these compounds to differ from those of ionic compounds. Acids are molecular compounds that dissolve in water to give H^+ and an anion.

Self-Test for Chapter 6

Complete the following sentences:

1. An _____ element strongly attracts electrons.

2. A molecular compound that occurs in living organisms is called a _____ _____.

3. In Lewis structures, a line represents a _____ bond.

4. A _____ adds a hydrogen ion.

5. The formula X_2 represents a _____ molecule.

6. A molecule whose central atom forms three bonds and has no lone pairs has a _____ shape.

7. _____ orbitals in sulfur and phosphorus can be used for covalent bonds.

8. N_2 contains a _____ bond.

9. _____ molecular compounds are formed from only two elements.

10. Many molecular compounds are soluble in _____ liquids.

Tell whether the following statements are true or false:

1. Br_2 is a molecular compound.

2. Six electrons are used to form a triple bond.

3. Coordinate covalent bonds occur only in cations or anions, not in neutral compounds.

4. The first step in drawing a Lewis structure is to find the total number of electrons in the combined atoms.

5. $AlCl_3$ is a pyramidal molecule.

6. The shape of ionic compounds can be predicted by the VSEPR model.

7. Electronegativity decreases in going down the periodic table.

8. CI_4 contains polar covalent bonds.

9. Both planar and bent molecules have bond angles of 120°.

10. Group 7A elements can form more than one covalent bond.

Match each item on the left with its partner on the right:

1. BCl_3 (a) contains a pure covalent bond

2. planar molecule   (b) SO_2

3. bent molecule   (c) acid

4. Cl_2 (d) NH_3

5. BCl_4^- (e) contains a triple bond

6. NaI   (f) H_2O

7. C≡O   (g) contains a double bond

8. HNO_3 (h) central atom doesn't have an electron octet

9. angular molecule   (i) contains an ionic bond

10. O=C=O   (j) $AlCl_3$

11. pyramidal molecule   (k) contains a coordinate covalent bond

12. CH_3Cl (l) contains a polar covalent bond

Chapter 7 – Chemical Reactions: Classification and Mass Relationships

7.1 An equation is balanced if the number and types of atoms on the left side equals the number and types of atoms on the right side.
(a) On the left: 2 H + Cl + K + O
  On the right: 2 H + Cl + K + O The equation is balanced.
(b) On the left: 1 C + 4 H + 2 Cl
  On the right: 1 C + 3 H + 3 Cl The equation is not balanced.
(c) Balanced
(d) Not balanced in H, O.

7.2 (a) Solid cobalt (II) chloride plus gaseous hydrogen fluoride yields solid cobalt (II) fluoride plus gaseous hydrogen chloride.
(b) Aqueous lead (II) nitrate plus aqueous potassium iodide yields solid lead (II) iodide plus aqueous potassium nitrate.

7.3 *Step 1.* Write the unbalanced equation

$$Na + Cl_2 \longrightarrow NaCl$$

Step 2. Balance the atoms of each type, one by one. Here, the equation is balanced for sodium. To balance for chlorine:

$$Na + Cl_2 \longrightarrow 2\,NaCl$$

Unfortunately, the equation is no longer balanced for sodium. To balance for sodium:

$$2\,Na + Cl_2 \longrightarrow 2\,NaCl$$

The equation is now balanced.

7.4 *Step 1:* $O_2 \longrightarrow O_3$

Step 2: $3\,O_2 \longrightarrow 2\,O_3$ The equation is balanced.

7.5 (a) $Ca(OH)_2 + 2\,HCl \longrightarrow CaCl_2 + 2\,H_2O$
(b) $4\,Al + 3\,O_2 \longrightarrow 2\,Al_2O_3$
(c) $2\,CH_3CH_3 + 7\,O_2 \longrightarrow 4\,CO_2 + 6\,H_2O$
(d) $2\,AgNO_3 + MgCl_2 \longrightarrow 2\,AgCl + Mg(NO_3)_2$

7.6 Molar mass of C_2H_6O = 46.0 g

$$10.0\ g\ \times\ \frac{1\ mol}{46.0\ g}\ =\ 0.217\ mol\ in\ a\ 10.0\ g\ sample$$

$$0.10\ mol\ \times\ \frac{46.0\ g}{1\ mol}\ =\ 4.6\ g\ in\ a\ 0.10\ mol\ sample$$

7.7

Carbon: 0.025 mol aspirin x $\dfrac{6.02 \times 10^{23} \text{ molecules aspirin}}{1 \text{ mol aspirin}}$

x $\dfrac{9 \text{ C atoms}}{1 \text{ molecule aspirin}}$ = 1.4 x 10^{23} C atoms

Hydrogen: 0.025 mol aspirin x $\dfrac{6.02 \times 10^{23} \text{ molecules aspirin}}{1 \text{ mol aspirin}}$

x $\dfrac{8 \text{ H atoms}}{1 \text{ molecule aspirin}}$ = 1.2 x 10^{23} H atoms

Oxygen: 0.025 mol aspirin x $\dfrac{6.02 \times 10^{23} \text{ molecules aspirin}}{1 \text{ mol aspirin}}$

x $\dfrac{4 \text{ O atoms}}{1 \text{ molecule aspirin}}$ = 6.0 x 10^{22} O atoms

7.8   Molar mass of NaOH = 40.0 g

1.0 L x $\dfrac{1.5 \text{ mol}}{1 \text{ L}}$ x $\dfrac{40.0 \text{ g}}{1 \text{ mol}}$ = 60. g NaOH

7.9   (a) Ni (*s*) + 2 HCl (*aq*) $\longrightarrow$ $NiCl_2$ (*aq*) + H_2 (*g*)

9.81 mol HCl x $\dfrac{1 \text{ mol Ni}}{2 \text{ mol HCl}}$ = 4.90 mol Ni

(b) 6.0 mol Ni x $\dfrac{1 \text{ mol } NiCl_2}{1 \text{ mol Ni}}$ = 6.0 mol $NiCl_2$ from 6.0 mol Ni

6.0 mol HCl x $\dfrac{1 \text{ mol } NiCl_2}{2 \text{ mol HCl}}$ = 3.0 mol $NiCl_2$ from 6.0 mol HCl

3.0 mol $NiCl_2$ is the maximum number of moles that can be formed because HCl is the limiting reagent.

7.10   6 CO_2 + 6 H_2O $\longrightarrow$ $C_6H_{12}O_6$ + 6 O_2

15.0 mol glucose x $\dfrac{6 \text{ mol } CO_2}{1 \text{ mol glucose}}$ = 90.0 mol CO_2

7.11   (a) This is a mole-to-mole problem.

9.90 mol SiO_2 x $\dfrac{4 \text{ mol HF}}{1 \text{ mol } SiO_2}$ = 39.6 mol HF

(b) This is a mass-to-mass problem.

$$23 \text{ g SiO}_2 \text{ x } \frac{1 \text{ mol SiO}_2}{60.1 \text{ g SiO}_2} \text{ x } \frac{2 \text{ mol H}_2\text{O}}{1 \text{ mol SiO}_2} \text{ x } \frac{18.0 \text{ g H}_2\text{O}}{1 \text{ mol H}_2\text{O}} = 14 \text{ g H}_2\text{O}$$

7.12 $NH_3 + HCl \longrightarrow NH_4Cl$

$$15.0 \text{ g HCl x } \frac{1 \text{ mol HCl}}{36.5 \text{ g HCl}} \text{ x } \frac{1 \text{ mol NH}_4\text{Cl}}{1 \text{ mol HCl}} \text{ x } \frac{53.5 \text{ g NH}_4\text{Cl}}{1 \text{ mol NH}_4\text{Cl}} = 22.0 \text{ g}$$

$$\frac{19.4 \text{ g}}{22.0 \text{ g}} \text{ x } 100 = 88.2\%$$

7.13   (a) $CaO (s) + H_2O (l) \longrightarrow Ca(OH)_2 (aq)$

This reaction is a combination reaction, since two compounds combine to form a third compound.

(b) $Fe (s) + H_2SO_4 (aq) \longrightarrow FeSO_4 (aq) + H_2 (g)$ displacement reaction

(c) $Fe (s) + Cl_2 (g) \longrightarrow FeCl_2 (s)$ combination reaction

7.14 $Mg (s) + ZnCl_2 (aq) \longrightarrow Zn (s) + MgCl_2 (aq)$

7.15 $CuCO_3 (s) \longrightarrow CuO (s) + CO_2 (g)$

7.16 $2 HgO (s) \longrightarrow 2 Hg (l) + O_2 (g)$

7.17   (a) $2 Al(NO_3)_3 (aq) + 3 Na_2S (aq) \longrightarrow Al_2S_3 (s) + 6 NaNO_3 (aq)$

(b) $CaCO_3 (s) + 2 HCl (aq) \longrightarrow CaCl_2 (aq) + H_2O (l) + CO_2 (g)$

7.18   (a) displacement (b) exchange (c) decomposition

7.19 $NH_4NO_3 (s) \longrightarrow N_2O (g) + 2 H_2O (l)$

This is a decomposition reaction.

7.20   (a) Write the equation, including all ions.

$$2 K (s) + Pb^{2+} + 2 NO_3^- \longrightarrow 2 K^+ + 2 NO_3^- + Pb (s)$$

The nitrate ions on each side cancel.

$$2 K (s) + Pb^{2+} \longrightarrow 2 K^+ + Pb (s)$$

(b) $2 OH^- + 2 H^+ \longrightarrow 2 H_2O \ (l)$

K^+ and SO_4^{2-} cancel, and coefficients are reduced.

(c) $CuS \ (s) + 2 H^+ \ (aq) \longrightarrow Cu^{2+} \ (aq) + H_2S \ (g)$

7.21

	Oxidizing agent	Reducing agent
(a)	Cu^{2+}	Fe
(b)	Cl_2	Mg
(c)	Cr_2O_3	Al

The oxidizing agent gains electrons, and the reducing agent loses electrons.

7.22 $\underset{\textit{Reducing agent}}{2 K \ (s)} + \underset{\textit{Oxidizing agent}}{Br_2 \ (l)} \longrightarrow 2 KBr \ (s)$

7.23

	Compound	Oxidation number of metal	Name
(a)	VCl_3	+3	vanadium (III) chloride
(b)	MgO	+2	magnesium (II) oxide
(c)	$SnCl_4$	+4	tin (IV) chloride
(d)	CrO_3	+6	chromium (VI) oxide
(e)	$Cu(NO_3)_2$	+2	copper (II) nitrate
(f)	$NiSO_4$	+2	nickel (II) sulfate

7.24   Oxidation numbers are written above the atoms.

(a) $\overset{+1 \ -2}{Na_2S} (aq) + \overset{+2 \ -1}{NiCl_2} (aq) \longrightarrow 2 \overset{+1 \ -1}{NaCl} (aq) + \overset{+2 \ -2}{NiS} (s)$

This reaction is an exchange reaction and is not a redox reaction, since no atoms change oxidation numbers.

(b) $2 \overset{0}{Na} (s) + 2 \overset{+1 \ -2}{H_2O} (l) \longrightarrow 2 \overset{+1 \ -2 +1}{NaOH} (aq) + \overset{0}{H_2} (g)$

Sodium is oxidized and hydrogen is reduced in this displacement reaction.

7.25

$2 \overset{+2 \ -2}{PbS} (s) + 3 \overset{0}{O_2} (g) \longrightarrow 2 \overset{+2 \ -2}{PbO} (s) + 2 \overset{+4 \ -2}{SO_2} (g)$

Sulfide is oxidized and O_2 is reduced in the above reaction.

7.26   (a) Carbon is oxidized and oxygen is reduced in this redox reaction.
(b) This is not a redox reaction because no atoms change oxidation number.
(c) $CH_3CH=CH_2$ is reduced because H_2 is added (H_2 is oxidized).
(d) In this reaction, Mn is reduced [from Mn (VII) to Mn (II)] and S is oxidized [from S (IV) to S (VI)].

7.27   A balanced equation is an equation in which the number of atoms of each kind is the same on both sides of the reaction arrow.

7.28   (a) $2\,C_2H_6 \;+\; 7\,O_2 \longrightarrow 4\,CO_2 \;+\; 6\,H_2O$

      (b) balanced

      (c) $2\,Mg \;+\; O_2 \longrightarrow 2\,MgO$

      (d) $(NH_4)_3P \;+\; 3\,NaOH \longrightarrow Na_3P \;+\; 3\,NH_3 \;+\; 3\,H_2O$

      (e) $2\,K \;+\; 2\,H_2O \longrightarrow 2\,KOH \;+\; H_2$

7.29   (a) $SO_2\,(g) \;+\; H_2O\,(g) \longrightarrow H_2SO_3\,(l)$

      (b) $2\,K\,(s) \;+\; Br_2\,(l) \longrightarrow 2\,KBr\,(s)$

      (c) $C_3H_8\,(g) \;+\; 5\,O_2\,(g) \longrightarrow 3\,CO_2\,(g) \;+\; 4\,H_2O\,(l)$

7.30   (a) $Hg(NO_3)_2 \;+\; 2\,LiI \longrightarrow 2\,LiNO_3 \;+\; HgI_2$

      (b) $I_2 \;+\; 5\,Cl_2 \longrightarrow 2\,ICl_5$

      (c) $4\,Al \;+\; 3\,O_2 \longrightarrow 2\,Al_2O_3$

      (d) $CuSO_4 \;+\; 2\,AgNO_3 \longrightarrow Ag_2SO_4 \;+\; Cu(NO_3)_2$

      (e) $2\,Mn(NO_3)_3 \;+\; 3\,Na_2S \longrightarrow Mn_2S_3 \;+\; 6\,NaNO_3$

      (f) $4\,NO_2 \;+\; O_2 \longrightarrow 2\,N_2O_5$

      (g) $P_4O_{10} \;+\; 6\,H_2O \longrightarrow 4\,H_3PO_4$

7.31 $2\,NaHCO_3 \;+\; H_2SO_4 \longrightarrow 2\,CO_2 \;+\; Na_2SO_4 \;+\; 2\,H_2O$

7.32 $C_2H_6O \;+\; O_2 \longrightarrow C_2H_4O_2 \;+\; H_2O$

7.33 $6\,CO_2 \;+\; 6\,H_2O \longrightarrow C_6H_{12}O_6 \;+\; 6\,O_2$

7.34   (a) $2\,C_4H_{10} \;+\; 13\,O_2 \longrightarrow 8\,CO_2 \;+\; 10\,H_2O$

      (b) $C_2H_6O \;+\; 3\,O_2 \longrightarrow 2\,CO_2 \;+\; 3\,H_2O$

      (c) $2\,C_8H_{18} \;+\; 25\,O_2 \longrightarrow 16\,CO_2 \;+\; 18\,H_2O$

7.35   One mole of a substance is equal to its formula weight in grams. One mole of a molecular compound contains 6.02×10^{23} molecules.

7.36

$$16.2 \text{ g Ca} \;\times\; \frac{1 \text{ mol}}{40.1 \text{ g Ca}} \;\times\; \frac{6.02 \times 10^{23} \text{ atoms}}{1 \text{ mol}} = 2.43 \times 10^{23} \text{ atoms}$$

7.37

$$2.68 \times 10^{22} \text{ atoms} \;\times\; \frac{1 \text{ mol}}{6.02 \times 10^{23} \text{ atoms}} \;\times\; \frac{238.0 \text{ g}}{1 \text{ mol}} = 10.6 \text{ g uranium}$$

7.38   molar mass of caffeine = 194 g

$$125 \text{ mg } \times \frac{1 \text{ g}}{10^3 \text{ mg}} \times \frac{1 \text{ mol}}{194 \text{ g}} = 6.44 \times 10^{-4} \text{ mol caffeine}$$

7.39   molar mass of aspirin = 180 g

$$500 \text{ mg } \times \frac{1 \text{ g}}{10^3 \text{ mg}} \times \frac{1 \text{ mol}}{180 \text{ g}} = 2.78 \times 10^{-3} \text{ mol aspirin}$$

7.40 $(16 \times 12.0 \text{ g}) + (13 \times 1.0 \text{ g}) + (35.5 \text{ g}) + (2 \times 14.0 \text{ g}) + 16.0 \text{ g} = 284.5$ g/mol: molar mass of $C_{16}H_{13}ClN_2O$.

7.41 - 7.43

Compound	Molar Mass	Number of Moles in 5.00 g	Number of Grams in 0.050 mol
(a) C_6H_6	78.0 g	0.0641 mol	3.90 g
(b) $NaHCO_3$	84.0 g	0.0595 mol	4.20 g
(c) $CHCl_3$	119.5 g	0.0418 mol	5.98 g
(d) $C_{16}H_{18}N_2O_5S$	350 g	0.0143 mol	17.5 g

7.44   molar mass of $FeSO_4$ = 151.8 g

$$300 \text{ mg } \times \frac{1 \text{ g}}{10^3 \text{ mg}} \times \frac{1 \text{ mol}}{151.8 \text{ g}} = 1.98 \times 10^{-3} \text{ mol}$$

7.45   A limiting reagent is the reagent that limits the maximum amount of product that can be formed.

7.46   (a) $N_2 + O_2 \longrightarrow 2 \text{ NO}$

(b) 7.50 mol of N_2 are needed to react with 7.50 mol of O_2.

(c) $3.81 \text{ mol } N_2 \times \dfrac{2 \text{ mol NO}}{1 \text{ mol } N_2} = 7.62 \text{ mol NO}$

(d) $0.250 \text{ mol NO } \times \dfrac{1 \text{ mol } O_2}{2 \text{ mol NO}} = 0.125 \text{ mol } O_2$

(e) $12 \text{ mol } O_2 \times \dfrac{2 \text{ mol NO}}{1 \text{ mol } O_2} = 24 \text{ mol NO}$

$16 \text{ mol } N_2 \times \dfrac{2 \text{ mol NO}}{1 \text{ mol } N_2} = 32 \text{ mol NO}$

In this reaction, O_2 is the limiting reagent, and 24 mol NO is the maximum number of moles that can form.

7.47 (a) $C_4H_8O_2 + 2\ H_2 \longrightarrow 2\ C_2H_6O$

(b) 3.0 mol of ethyl alcohol are produced from 1.5 mol of ethyl acetate.

(c) $1.5\ \text{mol}\ C_4H_8O_2 \times \dfrac{2\ \text{mol}\ C_2H_6O}{1\ \text{mol}\ C_4H_8O_2} \times \dfrac{46.0\ \text{g}\ C_2H_6O}{1\ \text{mol}\ C_2H_6O} = 138\ \text{g}\ C_2H_6O$

(d) $12.0\ \text{g}\ C_4H_8O_2 \times \dfrac{1\ \text{mol}\ C_4H_8O_2}{88.0\ \text{g}\ C_4H_8O_2} \times \dfrac{2\ \text{mol}\ C_2H_6O}{1\ \text{mol}\ C_4H_8O_2}$

$$\times \dfrac{46.0\ \text{g}\ C_2H_6O}{1\ \text{mol}\ C_2H_6O} = 12.5\ \text{g}\ C_2H_6O$$

(e) $12.0\ \text{g}\ C_4H_8O_2 \times \dfrac{1\ \text{mol}\ C_4H_8O_2}{88.0\ \text{g}\ C_4H_8O_2} \times \dfrac{2\ \text{mol}\ H_2}{1\ \text{mol}\ C_4H_8O_2} \times \dfrac{2.0\ \text{g}\ H_2}{1\ \text{mol}\ H_2} = 0.55\ \text{g}\ H_2$

7.48 (a) $N_2 + 3\ H_2 \longrightarrow 2\ NH_3$

(b) $16.0\ \text{g}\ NH_3 \times \dfrac{1\ \text{mol}\ NH_3}{17.0\ \text{g}\ NH_3} \times \dfrac{1\ \text{mol}\ N_2}{2\ \text{mol}\ NH_3} = 0.471\ \text{mol}\ N_2$

(c) $75.0\ \text{g}\ N_2 \times \dfrac{1\ \text{mol}\ N_2}{28.0\ \text{g}\ N_2} \times \dfrac{3\ \text{mol}\ H_2}{1\ \text{mol}\ N_2} \times \dfrac{2.0\ \text{g}\ H_2}{1\ \text{mol}\ H_2} = 16.1\ \text{g}\ H_2$

(d) $0.62\ \text{mol}\ N_2 \times \dfrac{2\ \text{mol}\ NH_3}{1\ \text{mol}\ N_2} \times \dfrac{17.0\ \text{g}\ NH_3}{1\ \text{mol}\ NH_3} = 21.1\ \text{g}\ NH_3$

$1.33\ \text{mol}\ H_2 \times \dfrac{2\ \text{mol}\ NH_3}{3\ \text{mol}\ H_2} \times \dfrac{17.0\ \text{g}\ NH_3}{1\ \text{mol}\ NH_3} = 15.1\ \text{g}\ NH_3$

Hydrogen is the limiting reagent, and 15.1 g NH_3 can be formed from 1.33 mol H_2.

7.49

(a) $10.0\ \text{g}\ CO \times \dfrac{1\ \text{mol}\ CO}{28.0\ \text{g}\ CO} \times \dfrac{1\ \text{mol}\ CH_3OH}{1\ \text{mol}\ CO} \times \dfrac{32.0\ \text{g}\ CH_3OH}{1\ \text{mol}\ CH_3OH} = 11.4\ \text{g}\ CH_3OH$

(b) $\dfrac{9.55\ \text{g}}{11.4\ \text{g}} \times 100 = 83.8\%$ yield

7.50

(a) $75 \times 10^3\ \text{g}\ Fe_2O_3 \times \dfrac{1\ \text{mol}\ Fe_2O_3}{159.6\ \text{g}\ Fe_2O_3} \times \dfrac{4\ \text{mol}\ Fe}{2\ \text{mol}\ Fe_2O_3} \times \dfrac{55.8\ \text{g}\ Fe}{1\ \text{mol}\ Fe} = 52.4 \times 10^3\ \text{g}\ Fe$

$= 52.4\ \text{kg}\ Fe$

(b) $\dfrac{51.3\ \text{kg}}{52.4\ \text{kg}} \times 100 = 97.9\%$ yield of Fe

7.51 (a) $CH_4 + 2\,Cl_2 \longrightarrow CH_2Cl_2 + 2\,HCl$

(b) $50.0 \text{ g } CH_4 \times \dfrac{1 \text{ mol } CH_4}{16.0 \text{ g } CH_4} \times \dfrac{2 \text{ mol } Cl_2}{1 \text{ mol } CH_4} \times \dfrac{71.0 \text{ g } Cl_2}{1 \text{ mol } Cl_2} = 444 \text{ g } Cl_2$

(c) From part (b), we see that 50.0 g CH_4 reacts with 444 g Cl_2. However, if we have only 50.0 g Cl_2, it will react with much less than 50.0 g CH_4, and thus Cl_2 is the limiting reagent. To calculate the amount of CH_2Cl_2 formed:

$$50.0 \text{ g } Cl_2 \times \dfrac{1 \text{ mol } Cl_2}{71.0 \text{ g } Cl_2} \times \dfrac{1 \text{ mol } CH_2Cl_2}{2 \text{ mol } Cl_2} \times \dfrac{85.0 \text{ g } CH_2Cl_2}{1 \text{ mol } CH_2Cl_2} = 29.9 \text{ g } CH_2Cl_2 \text{ formed}$$

7.52 (a) $FeCl_2\,(aq) + 2\,Ag\,(s) \longrightarrow 2\,AgCl\,(s) + Fe\,(s)$

(b) $Ba\,(s) + 2\,H_2O\,(l) \longrightarrow Ba(OH)_2\,(aq) + H_2\,(g)$

(c) $CuSO_4\,(aq) + Zn\,(s) \longrightarrow ZnSO_4\,(aq) + Cu\,(s)$

(d) $Mg(NO_3)_2\,(aq) + Pb\,(s) \longrightarrow Pb(NO_3)_2\,(aq) + Mg\,(s))$

7.53 If products consist of soluble ions, then no reaction will occur.

(a) $2\,NaBr\,(aq) + Hg_2(NO_3)_2\,(aq) \longrightarrow Hg_2Br_2\,(s) + 2\,NaNO_3\,(aq)$

(b) $SrCl_2\,(aq) + K_2SO_4\,(aq) \longrightarrow SrSO_4\,(s) + 2\,KCl\,(aq)$
(c) no reaction

(d) $(NH_4)_2CO_3\,(aq) + CaCl_2\,(aq) \longrightarrow CaCO_3\,(s) + 2\,NH_4Cl\,(aq)$

(e) $2\,KOH\,(aq) + MnBr_2\,(aq) \longrightarrow Mn(OH)_2\,(s) + 2\,KBr\,(aq)$

(f) $3\,Na_2S\,(aq) + 2\,Al(NO_3)_3\,(aq) \longrightarrow Al_2S_3\,(s) + 6\,NaNO_3\,(aq)$

7.54 In net ionic reactions, no spectator ions appear. Otherwise, the equations are balanced for number of atoms and charge, and equations are reduced to their lowest common denominators.

(a) $Mg\,(s) + Cu^{2+}\,(aq) \longrightarrow Mg^{2+}\,(aq) + Cu\,(s)$

(b) $2\,Cl^-\,(aq) + Pb^{2+}\,(aq) \longrightarrow PbCl_2\,(s)$

(c) $2\,Cr^{3+}\,(aq) + 3\,S^-\,(aq) \longrightarrow Cr_2S_3\,(s)$

(d) $2\,Au^{3+}\,(aq) + 3\,Sn\,(s) \longrightarrow 3\,Sn^{2+}\,(aq) + 2\,Au\,(s)$

(e) $2\,I^-\,(aq) + Br_2\,(l) \longrightarrow 2\,Br^-\,(aq) + I_2\,(s)$

7.55 The element reduced gains electrons and is the oxidizing agent; the element oxidized loses electrons and is the reducing agent.

	(a)	(b)	(c)	(d)	(e)
Reduced / oxidizing agent	O_2	Cl_2	Cu^{2+}	F_2	Cl_2
Oxidized / reducing agent	S^{4+}	Na	Zn	Cl^-	Bi^{3+}

7.56 (a) Co^{3+} (b) Fe^{2+} (c) U^{6+} (d) Cu^{2+} (e) Ti^{4+} (f) Sn^{2+}

7.57   Qualitative: (a), (c), (d)
      Quantitative: (b), (e)

7.58   In organic redox reactions, *oxidation* is the addition of oxygen or the removal of hydrogen, and *reduction* is the addition of hydrogen or the removal of oxygen.

7.59   (a) reduction   (b) reduction   (c) neither oxidation nor reduction   (d) oxidation

7.60   Electrochemical cells are used for direct production of electricity from redox reactions.

7.61   Corrosion is the deterioration of materials resulting from exposure to the environment. Symptoms of corrosion include rust, which can cause complete deterioration, and surface oxidation, which forms a white layer on many metals.

7.62

(a) $15.0 \text{ g Zn} \times \dfrac{1 \text{ mol Zn}}{65.4 \text{ g Zn}} \times \dfrac{1 \text{ mol H}_2}{1 \text{ mol Zn}} \times \dfrac{2.0 \text{ g H}_2}{1 \text{ mol H}_2} = 0.459 \text{ g H}_2$

(b) This is a displacement reaction.
(c) In this redox reaction H^+ is reduced (oxidizing agent) and Zn is oxidized (reducing agent).

7.63

$80.0 \times 10^3 \text{ g H}_2\text{O} \times \dfrac{1 \text{ mol H}_2\text{O}}{18.0 \text{ g H}_2\text{O}} \times \dfrac{1 \text{ mol Li}_2\text{O}}{1 \text{ mol H}_2\text{O}} \times \dfrac{29.8 \text{ g Li}_2\text{O}}{1 \text{ mol Li}_2\text{O}}$

$= 132 \times 10^3 \text{ g Li}_2\text{O} = 132 \text{ kg Li}_2\text{O}$

This combination reaction is not a redox reaction since the oxidation numbers of reagent and product atoms remain the same.

7.64   molar mass of batrachotoxin $(C_{31}H_{42}N_2O_6) = 538 \text{ g}$

$0.05 \text{ μg} \times \dfrac{1 \text{ g}}{10^6 \text{ μg}} \times \dfrac{1 \text{ mol}}{538 \text{ g}} \times \left[6.02 \times 10^{23} \dfrac{\text{molecules}}{\text{mol}} \right] = 5.6 \times 10^{13} \text{ molecules}$

7.65   (a) $3 \text{ CuCl}_2 \text{ (}aq\text{)} + 2 \text{ Na}_3\text{PO}_4 \text{ (}aq\text{)} \longrightarrow \text{Cu}_3(\text{PO}_4)_2 \text{ (}s\text{)} + 6 \text{ NaCl (}aq\text{)}$
         A precipitate of $\text{Cu}_3(\text{PO}_4)_2$ forms

(b) $3 \text{ Cu}^{2+} \text{ (}aq\text{)} + 2 \text{ PO}_4{}^{3-} \text{ (}aq\text{)} \longrightarrow \text{Cu}_3(\text{PO}_4)_2 \text{ (}s\text{)}$

7.66   (a) $\text{C}_{12}\text{H}_{22}\text{O}_{11} \text{ (}s\text{)} \longrightarrow 12 \text{ C (}s\text{)} + 11 \text{ H}_2\text{O (}l\text{)}$

(b) $60.0 \text{ g sucrose} \times \dfrac{1 \text{ mol sucrose}}{342 \text{ g sucrose}} \times \dfrac{12 \text{ mol C}}{1 \text{ mol sucrose}} \times \dfrac{12.0 \text{ g C}}{1 \text{ mol C}} = 25.2 \text{ g carbon}$

(c) $6.50 \text{ g C} \times \dfrac{1 \text{ mol C}}{12.0 \text{ g C}} \times \dfrac{11 \text{ mol H}_2\text{O}}{12 \text{ mol C}} \times \dfrac{18.0 \text{ g H}_2\text{O}}{1 \text{ mol H}_2\text{O}} = 8.94 \text{ g H}_2\text{O}$

7.67   (a) $Cu\ (s) + 4\ H^+\ (aq) + 2\ NO_3^-\ (aq) \longrightarrow Cu^{2+}\ (aq) + 2\ NO_2\ (g) + 2\ H_2O\ (l)$

(b) $35.0\ g\ HNO_3 \times \dfrac{1\ mol\ HNO_3}{63.0\ g\ HNO_3} \times \dfrac{1\ mol\ Cu}{4\ mol\ HNO_3} \times \dfrac{63.5\ g\ Cu}{1\ mol\ Cu} = 8.82\ g\ Cu$

$35.0\ g\ HNO_3$ is more than enough to dissolve $5.00\ g\ Cu$.

7.68   (a) Ethanol is oxidized because hydrogen is removed from it.

(b) $1.50\ g\ C_2H_6O \times \dfrac{1\ mol\ C_2H_6O}{46.0\ g\ C_2H_6O} \times \dfrac{2\ mol\ K_2Cr_2O_7}{3\ mol\ C_2H_6O} \times \dfrac{294.2\ g\ K_2Cr_2O_7}{1\ mol\ K_2Cr_2O_7}$

$= 6.40\ g\ K_2Cr_2O_7$

(c) $80.0\ g\ C_2H_6O \times \dfrac{1\ mol\ C_2H_6O}{46.0\ g\ C_2H_6O} \times \dfrac{3\ mol\ C_2H_4O_2}{3\ mol\ C_2H_6O} \times \dfrac{60.0\ g\ C_2H_4O_2}{1\ mol\ C_2H_4O_2}$
$= 104\ g\ C_2H_4O_2$

7.69

$100.0\ lb\ C_6H_{12}O_6 \times \dfrac{454\ g}{1\ lb} \times \dfrac{1\ mol\ C_6H_{12}O_6}{180.0\ g\ C_6H_{12}O_6} \times \dfrac{2\ mol\ C_2H_6O}{1\ mol\ C_6H_{12}O_6}$

$\times \dfrac{46.0\ g\ C_2H_6O}{1\ mol\ C_2H_6O} = 2.32 \times 10^4\ g\ C_2H_6O$

$2.32 \times 10^4\ g\ C_2H_6O \times \dfrac{1\ mL}{0.789\ g} \times \dfrac{1\ qt}{946.4\ mL} = 31.1\ qts\ ethanol$

7.70   (a) exchange (b) combination   (c) combination (d) exchange (e) exchange (f) combination   (g) combination

7.71   (a) $Al(OH)_3 + 3\ HNO_3 \longrightarrow Al(NO_3)_3 + 3\ H_2O$

(b) $3\ AgNO_3 + FeCl_3 \longrightarrow 3\ AgCl + Fe(NO_3)_3$

(c) $(NH_4)_2Cr_2O_7 \longrightarrow Cr_2O_3 + 4\ H_2O + N_2$

(d) $Mn_2(CO_3)_3 \longrightarrow Mn_2O_3 + 3\ CO_2$

7.72   (a) exchange   (b) exchange   (c) decomposition   (d) decomposition

The Chapter in Brief

Chemical Equations (Sections 7.1, 7.2) Chemical equations are shorthand representations of chemical reactions. Chemical equations must be balanced — that is, they must have the same number and kinds of atoms on both sides of the reaction arrow.

The Mole (Sections 7.3–7.7) A mole of a substance is its formula weight in grams (molar mass) and contains Avogadro's number of particles. Grams and moles can be interconverted by using the molar mass as a conversion factor. A chemical equation shows the mole ratios of products and reactants in a chemical reaction. Both molar mass and mole ratios can be used as conversion factors in mass-to-mass calculations.

Types of Chemical Reactions (Sections 7.8–7.14) Chemical reactions can be classified as combination, decomposition, displacement, or exchange reactions. In some reactions, elements gain or lose electrons; these are known as redox reactions. Oxidation numbers are used to show electron ownership in redox reactions.

Self-Test for Chapter 7

Complete the following sentences:

1. The numbers placed in front of formulas to balance equations are called _____.

2. A _____ is a solid that forms during a reaction.

3. Ions that appear on both sides of the reaction arrow are _____ ions.

4. The substances in a reaction can be solids, liquids, or gases, or they can be in _____ solution.

5. Grams and moles can be converted by using _____ _____ as a conversion factor.

6. When one reagent in a chemical reaction is not fully consumed, the other reagent is known as a _____ _____.

7. In a chemical equation, _____ are shown on the left of the reaction arrow.

8. The oxidation state of gold in $AuCl_3$ is _____.

9. In the reaction $2 Mg + O_2 \longrightarrow 2 MgO$, Mg is the _____ agent.

10. A reaction in which an element reacts with a compound to yield a different element and compound is called a _____ reaction.

11. A reaction between an acid and a base is a _____ reaction.

Tell whether the following statements are true or false:

1. A mole of oxygen atoms has the same mass as a mole of nitrogen atoms.

2. The coefficients in chemical reactions show the relative numbers of moles of reactants and products.

3. A combination reaction is an example of a redox reaction.

4. In a redox equation, the oxidizing agent is oxidized and the reducing agent is reduced.

5.   If all coefficients in a chemical equation are even numbers, the equation is not completely balanced.

6.   Mole ratios are used to convert between moles and grams of a compound.

7.   In the reaction between K and Cl_2, K is the oxidizing agent.

8.   In the reaction $4\,Al + 3\,O_2 \longrightarrow 2\,Al_2O_3$, the mole ratio of product to Al is 2.

9.   Most sodium salts are soluble.

10.   The same compound can be both oxidized and reduced in a reaction.

Match each item on the left with its partner on the right:

1.	$20\text{ g C} + 60\text{ g O}_2 \longrightarrow CO_2$	(a) converts moles Na to grams Na
2.	$C_3H_8O + O_2 \longrightarrow C_3H_6O + H_2O$	(b) molar mass of NaF
3.	42.0 amu	(c) exchange reaction
4.	23.0 g sodium / 1 mol	(d) decomposition reaction
5.	$H^+(aq) + OH^-(aq) \longrightarrow H_2O(l)$	(e) carbon is the limiting reagent
6.	$S + O_2 \longrightarrow SO_2$	(f) unbalanced equation
7.	$HCl + NaOH \longrightarrow NaCl + H_2O$	(g) converts grams Na to moles Na
8.	42.0 g	(h) oxygen is the limiting reagent
9.	1 mol / 23.0 g sodium	(i) combination reaction
10.	$CaCO_3 \longrightarrow CaO + CO_2$	(j) displacement reaction
11.	$20\text{ g C} + 20\text{ g O}_2 \longrightarrow CO_2$	(k) formula weight of NaF
12.	$Mg + 2\,HCl \longrightarrow MgCl_2 + H_2$	(l) net ionic equation

Chapter 8 – Chemical Reactions: Energy, Rates, and Equilibrium

8.1   (a) Since heat appears on the left side of the equation, the reaction is endothermic.
(b) $\Delta H = +678$ kcal

(c) $C_6H_{12}O_6 (s) + 6\,O_2 (g) \longrightarrow 6\,CO_2\,g) + 6\,H_2O\,(l) + 678$ kcal

8.2   (a) The reaction is endothermic because ΔH is positive.
(b) $\dfrac{801\ \text{kcal}}{4\ \text{mol Al}} = \dfrac{200\ \text{kcal}}{1\ \text{mol Al}}$; 200 kcal are required

(c) $10\ \text{g Al}\ \times\ \dfrac{1\ \text{mol Al}}{27.0\ \text{g}}\ \times\ \dfrac{200\ \text{kcal}}{1\ \text{mol Al}} = 74$ kcal

8.3

$$145\ \text{g NO}\ \times\ \frac{1\ \text{mol}}{30.0\ \text{g NO}}\ \times\ \frac{43\ \text{kcal}}{2\ \text{mol NO}} = 104\ \text{kcal}$$

8.4   (a) Entropy decreases.
(b) Entropy increases because disorder increases when fuel vaporizes.
(c) Entropy decreases because one mole of product is formed for each two moles of reactant.

8.5   (a) Sodium iodide dissolves spontaneously because ΔG is negative.
(b) Entropy increases because two moles of ions are formed from one mole of solid.

8.6

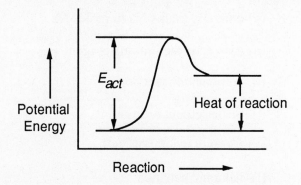

In this reaction E_{act} is large because the reaction is slow, and heat of reaction is large and positive because the reaction is endothermic.

8.7

$$K = \frac{[\text{products}]}{[\text{reactants}]}$$

(a) $K = \dfrac{[NO_2]^2}{[N_2O_4]}$ (b) $K = \dfrac{[CH_3Cl][HCl]}{[CH_4][Cl_2]}$ (c) $K = \dfrac{[Br_2][F_2]^5}{[BrF_5]^2}$

8.8   If K is greater than 1, the reaction favors products. If K is less than 1, the reaction favors reactants.
(a) Products are strongly favored.
(b) Reactants are strongly favored.
(c) Products are somewhat favored.

8.9   Since increasing pressure shifts equilibrium in the direction that decreases the number of molecules in the system, high pressure favors the production of SO_3.

8.10   (a) Increasing the temperature shifts the equilibrium to the left.
(b) Increasing the pressure shifts the equilibrium to the right.
(b) Removing CH_4 from the reaction vessel causes more CH_4 to be formed and shifts the equilibrium toward the right.

8.11   In an endothermic reaction, the total bond energies of the reactants are less than the bond energies of the products.

8.12   The Law of Conservation of Energy: Energy can neither be created nor destroyed in any chemical or physical process.

8.13   In a chemical reaction, the difference in bond energies between reactants and products is known as the *heat of reaction* (enthalpy).

8.14   (a) ΔH is positive.

(b) $6.5 \text{ mol } Br_2 \times \dfrac{7.4 \text{ kcal}}{1 \text{ mol } Br_2} = 48 \text{ kcal}$

(c) $75 \text{ g } Br_2 \times \dfrac{1 \text{ mol } Br_2}{159.8 \text{ g } Br_2} \times \dfrac{7.4 \text{ kcal}}{1 \text{ mol } Br_2} = 3.5 \text{ kcal}$

8.15   (a) $C_6H_{12}O_6 + 6\,O_2 \longrightarrow 6\,CO_2 + 6\,H_2O$

(b) $\dfrac{4.1 \text{ kcal}}{1 \text{ g glucose}} \times \dfrac{180 \text{ g glucose}}{1 \text{ mol glucose}} \times 1.50 \text{ mol glucose} = 1100 \text{ kcal}$

(c) The production of glucose from CO_2 and H_2O is an endothermic process.

$\dfrac{4.1 \text{ kcal}}{1 \text{ g glucose}} \times 15.0 \text{ g glucose} = 62 \text{ kcal needed to produce 15 g glucose}$

8.16   (a) $C_2H_5OH + 3\,O_2 \longrightarrow 2\,CO_2 + 3\,H_2O + 35.5 \text{ kcal}$

(b) ΔH is negative because energy is released.

(c) $\dfrac{35.5 \text{ kcal}}{5.00 \text{ g } C_2H_5OH} \times \dfrac{46.0 \text{ g } C_2H_5OH}{1 \text{ mol } C_2H_5OH} = \dfrac{327 \text{ kcal}}{1 \text{ mol } C_2H_5OH} \text{ released}$

(d) 450. kcal $\times$ $\dfrac{1 \text{ mol } C_2H_5OH}{327 \text{ kcal}}$ = 1.38 mol C_2H_5OH

1.38 mol $\times$ $\dfrac{46.0 \text{ g}}{1 \text{ mol}}$ = 63.5 g C_2H_5OH

(e) 10.0 g C_2H_5OH $\times$ $\dfrac{35.5 \text{ kcal}}{5.00 \text{ g } C_2H_5OH}$ = 71.0 kcal

(f) calories needed = specific heat of H_2O $\times$ g $\times$ °C

Specific heat of water = 1.00 cal /°C $\times$ g; mass of 500 mL H_2O = 500 g; °C = 80.0

$= \dfrac{1.00 \text{ cal}}{1°C \times 1 \text{ g}}$ $\times$ 500.0 g $\times$ 80.0°C = 4×10^4 cal = 40.0 kcal

40.0 kcal $\times$ $\dfrac{5.00 \text{ g } C_2H_5OH}{35.5 \text{ kcal}}$ = 5.63 g C_2H_5OH

8.17   Entropy is a measure of the disorder of a system.

8.18   Increased disorder: (a)
Increased order: (b) (c) (d) (e)

8.19   A spontaneous process proceeds without any external influence.

8.20   A reaction with a negative free energy is spontaneous.

8.21   The free energy change (ΔG) of a chemical reaction shows whether or not a reaction is spontaneous. If the sign of ΔG is negative, the reaction is spontaneous. Of the two factors that contribute to ΔG (ΔH and ΔS), ΔH is usually larger at low temperatures. Thus if a reaction is spontaneous (negative ΔG) it is usually exothermic (negative ΔH).

8.22   (a) Dissolution of NaCl is endothermic since ΔH is positive.
(b Entropy increases because disorder increases.
(c) Since the dissolution of NaCl is spontaneous, ΔG for the reaction must be negative. Because we already know that ΔH is positive, it must be true that $T\Delta S$ is the major contributor to the size of ΔG.
(d) NaCl is even more soluble in hot water than in cold water because $T\Delta S$ (and also ΔG) becomes even larger at higher temperatures.

8.23   (a) This reaction is spontaneous because ΔG is negative.
(b) Entropy decreases because two atoms of liquid and one molecule of gas react to yield two molecules of solid.

8.24   (a) $H_2(g) + Br_2(l) \longrightarrow 2 HBr(g)$
(b) Entropy increases because the number of product molecules is greater than the number of reactant molecules.
(c) The process is spontaneous at all temperatures because ΔH is negative and ΔS is positive.

8.25 The *activation energy* of a reaction is the amount of energy needed for reactants to surmount the energy barrier to reaction.

8.26 A reaction with E_{act} = 5 kcal/mol is faster because less energy is needed to surmount the energy barrier.

8.27

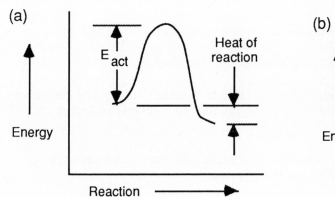

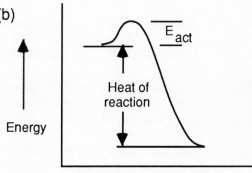

8.28

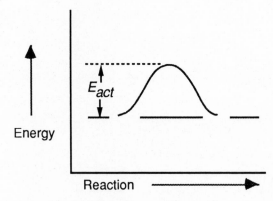

The heat of reaction is zero.

8.29, 8.33

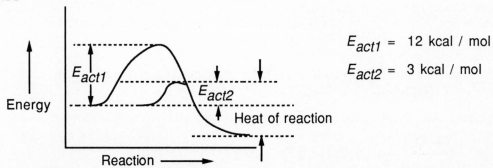

E_{act1} = 12 kcal / mol

E_{act2} = 3 kcal / mol

8.30 Increasing temperature increases reaction rate for two reasons:
1. Particles move faster and are more likely to collide.
2. A larger fraction of particles move faster at high temperatures, causing more collisions.

8.31 Increasing concentrations increases reaction rate because the increased crowding of reactants causes more collisions.

8.32 A catalyst is a substance that increases reaction rate by lowering the activation energy barrier, yet remains unchanged when the reaction is completed.

8.33 See Problem 8.29

8.34 (a) The value of ΔG indicates that diamonds spontaneously turn into graphite.
(b) Because this behavior is not observed, the activation energy of the above reaction must be extremely high or the reaction rate must be extremely slow.

8.35 In a reversible reaction, chemical equilibrium is a state in which the rates of the forward reaction and the reverse reaction are equal. The amounts of reactants and products are rarely equal at equilibrium.

8.36 As the forward reaction proceeds, products accumulate and react to reform starting material, slowing down the rate of formation of products.

8.37 Catalysts lower the height of the activation energy barrier for both forward and reverse reactions but don't change the equilibrium constant.

8.38

(a) $K = \dfrac{[CO_2]^2}{[CO]^2[O_2]}$ (b) $K = \dfrac{[C_2H_4Cl_2][HCl]^2}{[C_2H_6][Cl_2]^2}$

(c) $K = \dfrac{[CaO][CO_2]}{[CaCO_3]}$ (d) $K = \dfrac{[H_3O^+][F^-]}{[HF][H_2O]}$ (e) $K = \dfrac{[O_3]^2}{[O_2]^3}$

8.39 A reaction with K greater than 1 favors products.
A reaction with K less than 1 favors reactants.
Favors reactants: (a) (d)
Favors products: (b) (c) (e)

8.40

(a) $K = \dfrac{[N_2O_4]}{[NO_2]^2} = \dfrac{[0.0869 \text{ mol/L}]}{[0.025 \text{ mol/L}]^2} = 140$

(b) $139 = \dfrac{0.40 \text{ mol/L}}{[NO_2]^2}$; $[NO_2]^2 = \dfrac{0.40 \text{ mol/L}}{139}$; $[NO_2] = 0.054 \text{ mol/L}$

8.41

$139 = \dfrac{[N_2O_4]}{[0.12 \text{ mol/L}]^2}$; $[N_2O_4] = 139 \times [0.12]^2 = 2.0 \text{ mol/L}$

8.42 If the pressure is raised, more products than reactants are found at equilibrium, because high pressure favors the reaction that produces fewer molecules.

8.43

$$K = \frac{[OF_2]^2}{[F_2]^2[O_2]} = \frac{[0.0633 \text{ mol/L}]^2}{[0.0100 \text{ mol/L}]^2[0.200 \text{ mol/L}]} = 200$$

8.44 (a) The reaction is endothermic.
(b) Reactants are favored at equilibrium.
(c) (i) Increasing pressure favors formation of ozone, since increased pressure shifts the equilibrium in the direction of the reaction than produces fewer molecules.
(ii) Increasing $[O_2]$ (g) increases the amount of O_3 formed.
(iii) Increasing the concentration of O_3 shifts the equilibrium to the left.
(iv) A catalyst has no effect on the equilibrium.
(v) Increasing the temperature shifts the equilibrium to the right.

8.45 (a) This reaction is exothermic.
(b) Products are favored at equilibrium.
(c) (i) Increasing pressure has no effect on the equilibrium.
(ii) Increasing $[HCl]$ (g) increases the amount of H_2 (g) and Cl_2 (g) formed.
(iii) Increasing $[Cl_2]$ (g) increases the amount of HCl (g) formed.
(iv) Decreasing $[H_2]$ (g) decreases the amount of HCl (g) formed.
(v) A catalyst has no effect on the equilibrium.

8.46 Nitrogen fixation is the conversion of N_2 into chemically usable nitrogen compounds.

8.47 (a) The production of ammonia from its elements is an exothermic process.

(b) $\dfrac{22 \text{ kcal}}{2 \text{ mol NH}_3} \times 0.500 \text{ mol NH}_3 = 5.5 \text{ kcal}$

8.48 Body temperature is regulated by the thyroid gland and by the hypothalamus region of the brain.

8.49 Dilation of the blood vessels cools the body by allowing more blood to flow close to the surface of the body.

8.50 The hormone epinephrine stimulates the metabolic rate.

8.51 Hemoglobin is responsible for oxygen transport in the body.

8.52 Training at high altitude stimulates the production of more hemoglobin molecules to allow for transport of additional oxygen.

8.53 (a) Fe_3O_4 (s) + 4 H_2 (g) $\longrightarrow$ 3 Fe (s) + 4 H_2O (g)

(b) $75 \text{ g Fe} \times \dfrac{1 \text{ mol Fe}}{55.8 \text{ g Fe}} \times \dfrac{36 \text{ kcal}}{3 \text{ mol Fe}} = 16 \text{ kcal}$

(c) $75 \text{ g Fe} \times \dfrac{1 \text{ mol Fe}}{55.8 \text{ g Fe}} \times \dfrac{4 \text{ mol H}_2}{3 \text{ mol Fe}} \times \dfrac{2.0 \text{ g H}_2}{1 \text{ mol H}_2} = 3.6 \text{ g H}_2$

(d) Reactants are favored in this reaction.

8.54 (a) Since the reaction of CO with Hb is more favored than the reaction of O_2 with Hb, CO removes Hb from the bloodstream. Less Hb is available to react with O_2, and less HbO_2 is available to the tissues.

(b) Administering high doses of O_2 to a victim of CO poisoning shifts the equilibrium in the following reaction to the right.

$$Hb(CO)\ (aq) + O_2\ (aq) \longrightarrow Hb(O_2)\ (aq) + CO\ (aq)$$

This shift results in displacement of CO from Hb(CO) and in formation of $Hb(O_2)$ to replenish body tissues with O_2.

8.55

$$1700\ \text{kcal}\ \times\ \frac{1\ \text{gram}}{4.1\ \text{kcal}}\ =\ 420\ \text{grams glucose}$$

8.56

(a) $10.0\ \text{g}\ H_2O\ \times\ \dfrac{1\ \text{mol}\ H_2O}{18.0\ \text{g}\ H_2O}\ \times\ \dfrac{9.72\ \text{kcal}}{1\ \text{mol}\ H_2O}\ =\ 5.40\ \text{kcal}$

(b) 5.40 kcal

8.57 (a) $4\ NH_3\ (g) + 5\ O_2\ (g) \longrightarrow 4\ NO\ (g) + 6\ H_2O\ (g) + \text{heat}$

(b) $K = \dfrac{[NO]^4\,[H_2O]^6}{[NH_3]^4\,[O_2]^5}$

(c) (i)   Raising the pressure shifts the equilibrium to the left.
(ii) Adding NO (g) shifts the equilibrium to the left.
(iii) Decreasing $[NH_3]$ shifts the equilibrium to the left.
(iv) Lowering the temperature shifts the equilibrium to the left.

8.58 (a) $2\ CH_3OH + 3\ O_2 \longrightarrow 2\ CO_2 + 4\ H_2O$

(b) $50.0\ \text{g}\ CH_3OH\ \times\ \dfrac{1\ \text{mol}\ CH_3OH}{32.0\ \text{g}\ CH_3OH}\ \times\ \dfrac{174\ \text{kcal}}{1\ \text{mol}\ CH_3OH}\ =\ 272\ \text{kcal}$

8.59

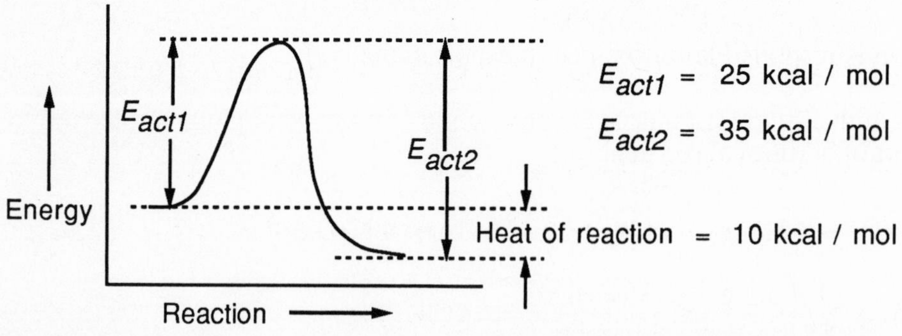

$E_{act1} = 25\ \text{kcal / mol}$

$E_{act2} = 35\ \text{kcal / mol}$

Heat of reaction $= 10\ \text{kcal / mol}$

The forward process is exothermic.

8.60 A catalyst can't increase the amount of product formed from a given amount of reactants because a catalyst affects only reaction rate, not equilibrium.

The Chapter in Brief

Reaction Energy (Sections 8.1–8.5) Chemical reactions occur when there is a difference in energy between products and reactants. The heat of reaction measures this difference. Reactions that absorb heat are endothermic, and reactions that release heat are exothermic. Food produces the energy for biochemical processes to occur. The free energy of a reaction (ΔG) measures the spontaneity of the chemical reaction and is determined by the heat of reaction (ΔH) and the entropy change (ΔS).

Reaction Rates (Sections 8.6, 8.7) The rate of a reaction is determined by the number of collisions of reacting molecules. Energy of activation is the amount of energy needed for a reaction to surmount the barrier to reaction. Temperature, concentration, and catalysts all affect the reaction rate.

Equilibrium (Sections 8.8–8.10) Reactions that can proceed in either direction are reversible. At equilibrium, the rates of the forward and reverse reactions are equal. An equilibrium constant relates the concentration of reactants and products at equilibrium. Le Chatelier's principle states that an equilibrium subjected to stress shifts to relieve that stress.

Self-Test for Chapter 8

Complete the following sentences:

1.   Grams and moles can be converted by using _____ _____ as a conversion factor.

2.   _____ occurs when the human body is unable to generate enough body heat.

3.   In a chemical equation, _____ are shown on the left.

4.   Catalysts in the human body are called _____.

5.   A reaction that absorbs heat from the surroundings is an _____ reaction.

6.   The number placed before each substance in a balanced equation is called a _____.

7.   A mole of any substance contains _____ _____.

8.   When one reagent in a chemical reaction is not fully consumed, the other reagent is known as a _____ _____.

9.   Three methods of speeding up a reaction are _____, _____, and _____.

10.   If products and reactants are of similar stability, the reaction is considered a _____ _____.

Match the entries on the left with their partners on the right:

1.   Enzyme   (a) Shows energy relationships in a reaction

2. $20 \text{ g C} + 60 \text{ g O}_2 \longrightarrow CO_2$ (b) A reaction that gives off heat

3. $H_2O + CO_2 \longrightarrow H_2CO_3$ (c) Converts starch to sugar in saliva

4.   Heat of reaction   (d) Energy needed for a reaction to occur

5.   Reaction energy diagram   (e) Converts grams of Na to moles

6.   23.0 g sodium / 1 mol   (f) Carbon is the limiting reagent

7.   Exothermic reaction   (g) Reaction that can go in either direction

8.   20 g C + 20 g O_2 ——> CO_2 (h) Reaction that absorbs heat

9. E_{act} (i) Difference in energy of products and reactants

10.   1 mol / 23.0 g sodium   (j) Oxygen is the limiting reagent

11.   Reversible reaction   (k) Converts moles Na to grams

12.   Endothermic reaction   (l) Balanced equation

Tell whether the following statements are true or false:

1.   The caloric value of food tells how much energy is used when food is burned in oxygen.

2.   In a chemical equilibrium, both product and reactant concentrations remain constant.

3.   If all coefficients in a chemical equation are even numbers, the equation is not completely balanced.

4.   The term "mole" refers only to chemical quantities.

5.   A reaction with a large E_{act} will probably have a large heat of reaction.

6.   Raising the temperature of a reaction always increases the rate of reaction.

7.   You must always use the coefficients in a chemical equation to convert between grams of one reactant and grams of another reactant.

8.   Catalysts increase the rate of a reaction by increasing the number of collisions between reactants.

9.   At chemical equilibrium, all chemical reaction stops.

10.   Humans can't digest cellulose because the E_{act} for the reaction is too high.

Chapter 9 – Gases, Liquids, and Solids

9.1 Use the appropriate conversion factor from Section 9.3

$$220 \text{ mm Hg} \times \frac{1 \text{ atm}}{760 \text{ mm Hg}} = 0.289 \text{ atm}$$

$$0.289 \text{ atm} \times 14.7 \frac{\text{psi}}{\text{atm}} = 4.25 \text{ psi}$$

$$0.289 \text{ atm} \times 101,325 \frac{\text{Pa}}{\text{atm}} = 29,300 \text{ Pa}$$

9.2 $0.98 \times 9.5 \text{ atm} = 9.3 \text{ atm He}$
$0.020 \times 9.5 \text{ atm} = 0.19 \text{ atm } O_2$

9.3 The partial pressure of oxygen in diving gas (0.19 atm) is approximately equal to the partial pressure of oxygen in air (0.21 atm).

9.4

$$\frac{573 \text{ mm Hg}}{760 \text{ mm Hg}} \times 100 = 75.4\% \text{ N}_2; \quad \frac{100 \text{ mm Hg}}{760 \text{ mm Hg}} \times 100 = 13.2\% \text{ O}_2$$

$$\frac{40 \text{ mm Hg}}{760 \text{ mm Hg}} \times 100 = 5.3\% \text{ CO}_2; \quad \frac{47 \text{ mm Hg}}{760 \text{ mm Hg}} \times 100 = 6.2\% \text{ H}_2\text{O}$$

9.5 $685 \text{ mm} \times 0.132 \text{ O}_2 = 90.4 \text{ mm Hg}$ is the pressure of O_2

9.6 *Ballpark Solution:* Since the pressure is reduced by almost 100 times, the volume must increase by almost 100 times, from 5 L to 500 L.

Exact Solution: $P_1 \times V_1 = P_2 \times V_2$

$$V_2 = \frac{P_1 \times V_1}{P_2} = \frac{(90 \text{ atm}) \times (5.0 \text{ L})}{(1.0 \text{ atm})} = 450 \text{ L}$$

The ball park solution and the exact solution agree.

9.7 *Ballpark Solution:* Since the volume increases by four times, the pressure must decrease by four times, from 5.0 atm to 1.25 atm.

Exact Solution: $P_1 \times V_1 = P_2 \times V_2$

$$P_2 = \frac{P_1 \times V_1}{V_2} = \frac{(5.0 \text{ atm}) \times (2.5 \text{ L})}{(10.0 \text{ L})} = 1.2 \text{ atm}$$

The ballpark solution and the exact solution agree.

$$P_2 = \frac{P_1 \times V_1}{V_2} = \frac{(5.0 \text{ atm}) \times (2.5 \text{ L})}{(0.20 \text{ L})} = 62 \text{ atm}$$

9.8 *Ballpark Solution:* Since the temperature increases by about 25%, the volume must also increase by about 25%, from 0.30 L to around 0.38 L.

Exact Solution:

$$\frac{V_1}{T_1} = \frac{V_2}{T_2}$$

$$V_2 = \frac{V_1 \times T_2}{T_1} = \frac{(0.30 \text{ L}) \times (350 \text{ K})}{273 \text{ K}} = 0.38 \text{ L}$$

The ballpark solution and exact solution agree.

At 500°C (773 K): $V_2 = \dfrac{V_1 \times T_2}{T_1} = \dfrac{(0.30 \text{ L}) \times (773 \text{ K})}{273 \text{ K}} = 0.85 \text{ L}$

9.9 *Ballpark Solution:* Since the pressure increases by 50%, the temperature must also increase by 50%, from 273 K to around 400 K.

Exact Solution:

$$\frac{P_1}{T_1} = \frac{P_2}{T_2}$$

$$T_2 = P_2 \times \frac{T_1}{P_1} = 45 \text{ psi} \times \frac{273 \text{ K}}{30 \text{ psi}} = 410 \text{ K} \quad (137°C)$$

The ballpark solution and the exact solution agree.

9.10 In this problem, P, V, and T vary.

$$\frac{P_1V_1}{T_1} = \frac{P_2V_2}{T_2}; \quad P_1 = 745 \text{ mm Hg}; \quad V_1 = 250. \text{ L}; \quad T_1 = 295 \text{ K}$$

$$P_2 = 570 \text{ mm Hg}; \quad V_2 = 232 \text{ L}; \quad T_2 = ?$$

$$T_2 = \frac{P_2V_2T_1}{P_1V_1} = \frac{570 \text{ mm Hg} \times 232 \text{ L} \times 295 \text{ K}}{745 \text{ mm Hg} \times 250 \text{ L}} = 209 \text{ K, or -64° C}$$

9.11

$$\frac{P_1V_1}{T_1} = \frac{P_2V_2}{T_2}; \quad P_1 = 775 \text{ mm Hg}; \quad V_1 = 0.590 \text{ L}; \quad T_1 = 352 \text{ K}$$

$$P_2 = 760 \text{ mm Hg}; \quad V_2 = ?; \quad T_2 = 273 \text{ K}$$

$$V_2 = \frac{P_1V_1T_2}{P_2T_1} = \frac{775 \text{ mm Hg} \times 0.590 \text{ L} \times 273 \text{ K}}{760 \text{ mm Hg} \times 352 \text{ K}} = 0.467 \text{ L} = 467 \text{ mL}$$

9.12 *Ballpark Solution:* Since one mole of a gas occupies 22.4 L, a 100,000 L container holds 100,000/22.4 moles, or about 4500 moles.

Exact Solution:

$$\frac{V_1}{n_1} = \frac{V_2}{n_2}$$

$$n_2 = V_2 \; x \; \frac{n_1}{V_1} = 100,000 \text{ L CH}_4 \; x \; \frac{1.0 \text{ mol}}{22.4 \text{ L}} = 4460 \text{ mol CH}_4$$

The same container could also hold 4460 mol CO_2. Thus, the ballpark solution and the exact solution agree.

$$4460 \text{ mol CH}_4 \; x \; 16.0 \frac{\text{g CH}_4}{\text{mol CH}_4} = 71,400 \text{ g CH}_4 = 7.14 \text{ x } 10^4 \text{ g CH}_4$$

$$4460 \text{ mol CO}_2 \; x \; 44.0 \frac{\text{g CO}_2}{\text{mol CO}_2} = 19,600 \text{ g CO}_2 = 1.96 \text{ x } 10^5 \text{ g CO}_2$$

9.13 $PV = n\,RT$; $P = nRT/V$

$$n = 3.2 \text{ g } x \; \frac{1 \text{ mol}}{44.0 \text{ g}} = 0.073 \text{ mol}; \quad R = 0.0821 \frac{\text{L atm}}{\text{mol K}}$$

$$T = 20°C = 293 \text{ K}; \quad V = 350 \text{ mL} = 0.35 \text{ L}$$

$$P = \frac{0.073 \text{ mol } x \; \dfrac{0.0821 \text{ L atm}}{\text{mol K}} \; x \; 293 \text{ K}}{0.35 \text{ L}} = 5.0 \text{ atm}$$

9.14 $PV = nRT$; $n = PV/RT$

$P = 150$ atm; $V = 180$ L He; $R = 0.0821 \dfrac{\text{L atm}}{\text{mol K}}$; $T = 25°C = 298$ K

$$n = \frac{150 \text{ atm } x \; 180 \text{ L He}}{0.0821 \dfrac{\text{L atm}}{\text{mol K}} \; x \; 298 \text{ K}} = 1.10 \text{ x } 10^3 \text{ mol He}$$

$$1.10 \text{ x } 10^3 \text{ mol He } x \; 4.0 \frac{\text{g}}{1 \text{ mol He}} = 4.40 \text{ x } 10^3 \text{ g He}$$

9.15 Remember that boiling points increase with increasing molecular (or atomic) weight.
(a) Kr, Ar, Ne. This series is arranged in order of decreasing boiling point.
(b) CH_3CH_3, $CH_3CH_2CH_3$, $CH_3CH_2CH_2CH_3$. This series is arranged in order of increasing boiling point.

9.16 Methyl alcohol (a) and methylamine (c) are capable of hydrogen bonding because each contains a hydrogen atom bonded to an electronegative atom. Ethylene does not hydrogen-bond.

9.17 (a) *London forces* are the only intermolecular forces between ethane molecules, and thus ethane has a low boiling point.

(b) The major intermolecular force between ethyl alcohol molecules is *hydrogen bonding*, which causes ethyl alcohol to be high boiling. Other molecular forces are also present but are much weaker than hydrogen bonding.

(c) *Dipole-dipole* interactions are the principal forces between ethyl chloride molecules and cause the boiling point of ethyl chloride to be higher than that of ethane.

9.18 One atmosphere is the amount of pressure needed to hold a column of mercury 760 mm high.

9.19 Partial pressure is the pressure contribution of one component of a mixture of gases to the total pressure.

9.20 Dalton's law of partial pressure says that the total pressure exerted by a gas mixture is the sum of the individual pressures of the components in the mixture.

9.21 (1) A gas consists of many tiny particles moving about at random with no attractive forces between particles.

(2) Gas particles move in a straight line with an energy proportional to temperature.

(3) The amount of space occupied by gas molecules is much smaller than the amount of space between molecules.

(4) When molecules collide, they spring apart elastically without reacting, and their total energy is conserved.

9.22 According to the kinetic theory of gases, gas pressure is due to collisions with the walls of the container. The more collisions, the higher the pressure.

9.23

(a) $1 \text{ atm } \times 760 \dfrac{\text{mm Hg}}{\text{atm}} = 760 \text{ mm Hg}$

(b) $0.25 \text{ atm } \times 760 \dfrac{\text{mm Hg}}{\text{atm}} = 190 \text{ mm Hg}$

(c) $7.5 \text{ atm } \times 760 \dfrac{\text{mm Hg}}{\text{atm}} = 5.7 \times 10^3 \text{ mm Hg}$

(d) $28.0 \text{ in. Hg } \times 25.4 \dfrac{\text{mm}}{\text{in.}} = 711 \text{ mm Hg}$

(e) $41.8 \text{ Pa } \times \dfrac{760 \text{ mm Hg}}{101{,}325 \text{ Pa}} = 0.314 \text{ mm Hg}$

9.24

(a) $440 \text{ mm Hg } \times \dfrac{1 \text{ atm}}{760 \text{ mm Hg}} = 0.579 \text{ atm}$

(b) $440 \text{ mm Hg } \times \dfrac{1 \text{ in. Hg}}{25.4 \text{ mm Hg}} = 17.3 \text{ in. Hg}$

9.25

$0.579 \text{ atm } \times 160 \dfrac{\text{mm Hg}}{\text{atm}} = 92.6 \text{ mm Hg}$

9.26 Boyle's law: $P_1V_1 = P_2V_2$ at constant temperature and number of moles.

9.27 $P_1V_1 = P_2V_2$; $P_1 = 65.0$ mm Hg; $P_2 = 385$ mm Hg; $V_1 = 600.$ mL $= 0.600$ L; $V_2 = ?$

$$\frac{P_1V_1}{P_2} = V_2 = \frac{65.0 \text{ mm Hg} \times 0.600 \text{ L}}{385 \text{ mm Hg}} = 0.101 \text{ L} = 101 \text{ mL}$$

9.28 $P_1V_1 = P_2V_2$; $P_1 = 1.00$ atm; $P_2 = ?$; $V_1 = 3.50$ L; $V_2 = 2.00$ L

$$\frac{P_1V_1}{V_2} = P_2 = \frac{1.00 \text{ atm} \times 3.50 \text{ L}}{2.00 \text{ L}} = 1.75 \text{ atm}$$

9.29 $P_1V_1 = P_2V_2$; $P_1 = 150$ atm; $P_2 = 1.00$ atm; $V_1 = 50.0$ L; $V_2 = ?$

$$\frac{P_1V_1}{P_2} = V_2 = \frac{150 \text{ atm} \times 50.0 \text{ L}}{1.00 \text{ atm}} = 7500 \text{ L}$$

9.30 $P_1V_1 = P_2V_2$; $P_1 = 14.7$ psi; $P_2 = ?$; $V_1 = 10.0$ cc; $V_2 = 2.00$ cc

$$\frac{P_1V_1}{V_2} = P_2 = \frac{14.7 \text{ psi} \times 10.0 \text{ cc}}{2.00 \text{ cc}} = 73.5 \text{ psi}$$

9.31 (a) For N_2: $P_1V_1 = P_2V_2$; $P_1 = 35.0$ atm; $P_2 = ?$; $V_1 = 25.0$ L; $V_2 = 15.0$ L

$$\frac{P_1V_1}{V_2} = P_2 = \frac{35.0 \text{ atm} \times 25.0 \text{ L}}{15.0 \text{ L}} = 58.3 \text{ atm}$$

For O_2: $P_1 = 15.0$ atm; $P_2 = ?$; $V_1 = 10.0$ L; $V_2 = 15.0$ L

$$\frac{P_1V_1}{V_2} = P_2 = \frac{15.0 \text{ atm} \times 10.0 \text{ L}}{15.0 \text{ L}} = 10.0 \text{ atm}$$

(b) Total pressure $= 58.3$ atm $+ 10.0$ atm $= 68.3$ atm.

9.32 Charles' law: $V_1/T_1 = V_2/T_2$ at constant pressure and number of moles.

9.33

$$\frac{V_1}{T_1} = \frac{V_2}{T_2}; V_1 = 960 \text{ L}; V_2 = 1200 \text{ L}; T_1 = 18°\text{ C} = 291 \text{ K}; T_2 = ?$$

$$T_2 = \frac{V_2T_1}{V_1} = \frac{1200 \text{ L} \times 291 \text{ K}}{960 \text{ L}} = 364 \text{ K} = 91°\text{ C}$$

9.34

$$\frac{V_1}{T_1} = \frac{V_2}{T_2}; V_1 = 125 \text{ mL}; V_2 = ?; T_1 = 25°\text{ C} = 298 \text{ K}; T_2 = 37°\text{ C} = 310 \text{ K}$$

$$V_2 = \frac{V_1T_2}{T_1} = \frac{125 \text{ mL} \times 310 \text{ K}}{298 \text{ K}} = 130. \text{ mL}$$

9.35

$$\frac{V_1}{T_1} = \frac{V_2}{T_2}; \quad V_1 = 43.0 \text{ L}; \quad V_2 = ?; \quad T_1 = 20°\text{ C} = 293 \text{ K}; \quad T_2 = -5°\text{ C} = 268 \text{ K}$$

$$V_2 = \frac{V_1 T_2}{T_1} = \frac{43.0 \text{ L} \times 268 \text{ K}}{293 \text{ K}} = 39.3 \text{ L}$$

9.36   In order to use the combined gas law, the quantity of gas must remain constant.

9.37   The conditions of STP are 760 mm Hg pressure and 273 K temperature.

9.38

$$\frac{P_1 V_1}{T_1} = \frac{P_2 V_2}{T_2}; \quad P_1 = 760 \text{ mm Hg}; \quad V_1 = 2.84. \text{ L}; \quad T_1 = 273 \text{ K}$$
$$P_2 = 520 \text{ mm Hg}; \quad V_2 = 7.50 \text{ L}; \quad T_2 = ?$$

$$T_2 = \frac{P_2 V_2 T_1}{P_1 V_1} = \frac{520 \text{ mm Hg} \times 7.50 \text{ L} \times 273 \text{ K}}{760 \text{ mm Hg} \times 2.84 \text{ L}} = 493 \text{ K} = -220°\text{ C}$$

9.39

$$\frac{P_1 V_1}{T_1} = \frac{P_2 V_2}{T_2}; \quad P_1 = 1.14 \text{ atm}; \quad V_1 = 3.50. \text{ L}; \quad T_1 = 22.0°\text{ C} = 295 \text{ K}$$

$$P_2 = 1.20 \text{ atm}; \quad V_2 = ?; \quad T_2 = 30.0°\text{C} = 303 \text{ K}$$

$$V_2 = \frac{P_1 V_1 T_2}{T_1 P_2} = \frac{1.14 \text{ atm} \times 3.50 \text{ L} \times 303 \text{ K}}{295 \text{ K} \times 1.20 \text{ atm}} = 3.42 \text{ L}$$

9.40

$$\frac{P_1 V_1}{T_1} = \frac{P_2 V_2}{T_2}; \quad P_1 = 749 \text{ mm Hg}; \quad V_1 = 55.0 \text{ mL}; \quad T_1 = 26°\text{ C} = 299 \text{ K}$$

$$P_2 = 760 \text{ mm Hg}; \quad V_2 = ?; \quad T_2 = 0°\text{C} = 273 \text{ K}$$

$$V_2 = \frac{P_1 V_1 T_2}{T_1 P_2} = \frac{749 \text{ mm Hg} \times 55.0 \text{ mL} \times 273 \text{ K}}{299 \text{ K} \times 760 \text{ mm Hg}} = 49.5 \text{ mL}$$

9.41

$$\frac{P_1 V_1}{T_1} = \frac{P_2 V_2}{T_2}; \quad P_1 = 140 \text{ atm}; \quad V_1 = 8.0 \text{ L}; \quad T_1 = 20°\text{ C} = 293 \text{ K}$$

$$P_2 = 1.0 \text{ atm}; \quad V_2 = ?; \quad T_2 = 273 \text{ K}$$

$$V_2 = \frac{P_1 V_1 T_2}{T_1 P_2} = \frac{140 \text{ atm} \times 8.0 \text{ L} \times 273 \text{ K}}{293 \text{ K} \times 1.0 \text{ atm}} = 1040 \text{ L}$$

9.42 $0.21 \times 140 \text{ atm} = 29 \text{ atm } O_2$

9.43 (a) For one mole of gas, the universal gas law says that P is proportional to T/V, or $P \propto T/V$. Thus, if the temperature doubles, and the volume is halved, the new pressure is four times greater than the original pressure:

$$P \propto \frac{T}{V} = \frac{2}{0.5} = 4$$

(b) If the temperature is halved and the volume is doubled, the new pressure is one fourth of the original pressure:

$$P \propto \frac{T}{V} = \frac{0.5}{2} = 0.25$$

9.44 Avogadro's Law states that equal volumes of gases at the same temperature and pressure contain equal numbers of molecules. Since the volume of space taken up by gas molecules is so much smaller than the amount of space between molecules, Avogadro's Law is true regardless of the chemical identity of the gas.

9.45 A mole of gas at STP occupies 22.4 L.

9.46 The samples contain equal numbers of molecules.

9.47 1.0 L of O_2 weighs more that 1.0 L of H_2 because the formula weight of O_2 is greater than the formula weight of H_2, and equal numbers of moles of both are present.

9.48

$$0.20 \text{ g Cl}_2 \ \times \ \frac{1 \text{ mol Cl}_2}{71 \text{ g}} \ \times \ \frac{22.4 \text{ L}}{1 \text{ mol Cl}_2} = 0.063 \text{ L} = 63 \text{ mL}$$

9.49

(a) $V = 4.0 \text{ m} \times 5.0 \text{ m} \times 2.5 \text{ m} = 50 \text{ m}^3$; $50 \text{ m}^3 \times \dfrac{1000 \text{ L}}{1 \text{ m}^3} = 5.0 \times 10^4 \text{ L}$

$$\frac{1 \text{ mol}}{22.4 \text{ L}} \ \times \ = 5.0 \times 10^4 \text{ L} = 2230 \text{ mol gas}$$

$0.21 \times 2230 = 470 \text{ mol O}_2$; $470 \text{ mol O}_2 \times \dfrac{32.0 \text{ g O}_2}{1 \text{ mol O}_2} = 15000\text{g O}_2 = 15 \text{ kg O}_2$

(b) $0.79 \times 2230 = 1760 \text{ mol N}_2$; $1760 \text{ mol N}_2 \times \dfrac{28.0 \text{ g N}_2}{1 \text{ mol N}_2} = 49000\text{g N}_2 = 49 \text{ kg N}_2$

(c) $15 \text{ kg} + 49 \text{ kg} = 64 \text{ kg air}$

9.50 The universal gas law : $PV = nRT$

9.51 $PV = nRT$; $n = PV/RT$;

For Cl_2: $P = 1.0 \text{ atm}$; $V = 2.0 \text{ L}$; $R = 0.082 \dfrac{\text{L atm}}{\text{mol K}}$; $T = 273 \text{ K}$

$$n = \frac{1.0 \text{ atm} \times 2.0 \text{ L}}{0.082 \dfrac{\text{L atm}}{\text{mol K}} \times 273 \text{ K}} = 0.089 \text{ mol Cl}_2$$

$$0.089 \text{ mol Cl}_2 \ \times \ \frac{71 \text{ g}}{1 \text{ mol Cl}_2} = 6.3 \text{ g Cl}_2$$

For CH$_4$:   P = 1.5 atm;   V = 3.0 L;   R = 0.082 $\dfrac{L\,atm}{mol\,K}$;   T = 300 K

$$n = \dfrac{1.5\,atm \times 3.0\,L}{0.082\,\dfrac{L\,atm}{mol\,K} \times 300\,K} = 0.18\,mol\,CH_4$$

$$0.18\,mol\,CH_4 \times \dfrac{16.0\,g}{1\,mol\,CH_4} = 2.9\,g\,CH_4$$

There are more molecules in the CH$_4$ sample than in the Cl$_2$ sample. The Cl$_2$ sample, however, weighs more.

9.52   As in the preceding problem, use the relationship $n = PV/RT$

For CO$_2$: $n = \dfrac{500\,mm\,Hg \times 2.0\,L\,CO_2}{62.3\,\dfrac{mm\,Hg\,L}{mol\,K} \times 300\,K} = 0.054\,mol\,CO_2$

$$0.054\,mol\,CO_2 \times \left[6.02 \times 10^{23}\,\dfrac{molecules}{mol}\right] = 3.2 \times 10^{22}\,molecules\,CO_2$$

For N$_2$: $n = \dfrac{760\,mm\,Hg \times 1.5\,L\,N_2}{62.3\,\dfrac{mm\,Hg\,L}{mol\,K} \times 330\,K} = 0.055\,mol\,N_2$

$$0.055\,mol\,N_2 \times \left[6.02 \times 10^{23}\,\dfrac{molecules}{mol}\right] = 3.3 \times 10^{22}\,molecules\,N_2$$

The CO$_2$ sample has slightly fewer molecules. Since the formula weight of CO$_2$ is much greater than the formula weight of N$_2$, however, the CO$_2$ sample weighs more (2.4 g) than the N$_2$ sample (1.5 g).

9.53

$$n = 15.0\,g\,CO_2 \times \dfrac{1\,mol}{44\,g} = 0.34\,mol\,CO_2\,;   T = 300\,K;   V = 0.30\,L$$

$$P = \dfrac{nRT}{V} = \dfrac{0.34\,mol\,CO_2 \times 62.3\,\dfrac{mm\,Hg\,L}{mol\,K} \times 300\,K}{0.30\,L} = 2.1 \times 10^4\,mm\,Hg$$

9.54

$$PV = nRT;   n = 20.0\,g\,N_2 \times \dfrac{1\,mol}{28.0\,g} = 0.71\,mol\,N_2;   V = 0.40\,L;   P = 6.0\,atm$$

$$T = \dfrac{PV}{nR} = \dfrac{6.0\,atm \times 0.40\,L}{0.71\,mol \times 0.082\,\dfrac{L\,atm}{mol\,K}} = 41\,K$$

9.55

$$n = 18.0 \text{ g } O_2 \text{ x } \frac{1 \text{ mol}}{32.0 \text{ g}} = 0.56 \text{ mol } O_2 \text{ ;} \quad T = 350 \text{ K ;} \quad P = 550 \text{ mm Hg}$$

$$V = \frac{nRT}{P} = \frac{0.56 \text{ mol } O_2 \text{ x } 62.3 \frac{\text{mm Hg L}}{\text{mol K}} \text{ x } 350 \text{ K}}{550 \text{ mm Hg}} = 22 \text{ L } O_2$$

9.56

$$n = \frac{PV}{RT}; \quad P = 2.5 \text{ atm}; \quad V = 0.55 \text{ L}; \quad T = 347 \text{ K}$$

$$= \frac{2.5 \text{ atm x } 0.55 \text{ L}}{0.082 \frac{\text{L atm}}{\text{mol K}} \text{ x } 347 \text{ K}} = 0.048 \text{ moles}$$

9.57 The vapor pressure of a liquid is the partial pressure of the vapor above the liquid.

9.58 At a liquid's boiling point, its vapor pressure equals atmospheric pressure.

9.59 Increased pressure raises a liquid's boiling point; decreased pressure lowers a liquid's boiling point.

9.60 A liquid's heat of vaporization is the amount of heat needed to vaporize one gram of the liquid at its boiling point.

9.61 (a) At 400 mm Hg, water boils at approximately 83°C.
(b) Diethyl ether is a gas at 20°C and 400 mm Hg.
(c) At 40°C, ethanol boils at approximately 140 mm Hg.

9.62 (a) All molecules exhibit *London forces*, but they are significant only for non-polar molecules and for noble gases. London forces increase in strength with increasing molecular weight.
(b) *Dipole-dipole interactions* are important for molecules that have polar covalent bonds.
(c) *Hydrogen bonding* occurs between a molecule that contains an electronegative atom and a molecule that has a hydrogen bonded to an electronegative atom.

9.63 London forces are the attractive forces between these non-polar molecules. Since London forces are stronger with increasing molecular weight, the melting point of the halogens increase with increasing molecular weight.

Halogen:	F_2	Cl_2	Br_2	I_2
Melting point:	-220°C	-101°C	-7°C	113.5°C

9.64 Dipole-dipole interactions are most important in compounds that do not exhibit ionic bonding or hydrogen bonding and have polar covalent bonds. Thus, dipole-dipole interactions are most important only for HCN (b) and CH_3Cl (e).

9.65 Ethanol is higher-boiling because of hydrogen bonding. Since molecules of ethanol are strongly attracted to each other, the boiling point of ethanol is higher than that of dimethyl ether, whose molecules are held together by weaker dipole-dipole interactions.

9.66

(a) $9.72 \frac{kcal}{1\ mol} \times 3.00\ mol = 29.2\ kcal$

(b) $9.72 \frac{kcal}{1\ mol} \times \frac{1\ mol}{18.0\ g} \times 255\ g = 138\ kcal$ of heat is released

9.67   The atoms in a crystalline solid are arranged in a regular, orderly network. The atoms in an amorphous solid have no regular arrangement.

9.68   Use Table 9.2 if you need help.
Ionic attractions: KBr (a), $MgCO_3$ (e)
Intermolecular attractions: CO_2 (b), Ne (d), NH_3 (f)
Metallic bonding: Ca (c)

9.69   In diamond, a network covalent solid, each atom is covalently bonded to several other atoms in a huge, three-dimensional array.

9.70   In a solid, molecules are held in a rigid position; in a liquid, molecules can move past each other but are still attracted to each other; in a gas, practically no attractive forces exist between molecules. Since is takes more energy for molecules to break away from one another than to loosen the attractive forces between molecules, heats of vaporization are larger than heats of fusion.

9.71   A systolic pressure reading measures the maximum pressure developed in the artery just after contraction. A diastolic pressure reading measures the minimum pressure at the end of the heart cycle.

9.72   A blood pressure reading of 180 / 110 indicates high blood pressure. The systolic reading is 180, and the diastolic reading is 110.

9.73   Ether was used as the first general anesthetic.

9.74   Bioglass and bone chemically bond to each other, thus eliminating the junction between them.

9.75   A large body of water stores heat and releases it when the temperature drops. When a body of water freezes, the heat released keeps the temperature of neighboring regions from falling.

9.76   Ice has a lower density then liquid water because crystalline water has more space between molecules than liquid water has.

9.77   The water sprayed on plants releases heat on cooling that keeps the crops from freezing.

9.78   As the temperature is increased, the kinetic energy of gas molecules increases, and the force per unit area which they exert against the walls of a container increases, thus increasing pressure.

9.79   Two moles of hydrogen react with one mole of oxygen according to the balanced equation. Since equal volumes of gases have equal numbers of moles at STP, 5.0 L of H_2 reacts with 2.5 L of O_2.

9.80 3.0 L of H_2 and 1.5 L of O_2 react completely. At STP, one mole of H_2 occupies 22.4 L. Thus, 3.0 L of hydrogen = 3.0/22.4 or 0.13 mol. This is also the number of moles of H_2O formed.

$$n = 0.13 \text{ mol } H_2O \; ; \quad T = 373 \text{ K} \; ; \quad P = 1.0 \text{ atm}$$

$$V = \frac{nRT}{P} = \frac{0.13 \text{ mol } H_2O \; \times \; 0.0821 \frac{L \text{ atm}}{\text{mol K}} \; \times \; 373 \text{ K}}{1.0 \text{ atm}} = 4.0 \text{ L } H_2O$$

9.81 $PV = nRT$; $P = 1.0$ atm; $V = 0.24$ L; $T = 310$ K

$$n = \frac{PV}{RT} = \frac{1.0 \text{ atm} \times 0.24 \text{ L}}{0.0821 \frac{L \text{ atm}}{\text{mol K}} \times 310 \text{ K}} = 0.0094 \text{ mol} = 9.4 \text{ mmol } CO_2$$

9.82

$$0.0094 \text{ mol } CO_2 \times 44.0 \frac{g}{\text{mol}} = 0.42 \text{ g } CO_2$$

$$0.42 \frac{g \, CO_2}{\text{min}} \times 60 \frac{\text{min}}{\text{hr}} \times 24 \frac{\text{hr}}{\text{day}} = 600 \frac{g \, CO_2}{\text{day}}$$

9.83 At STP, equal volumes of gases have an equal number of moles. However, O_2 has a greater formula weight than H_2, and the vessel containing O_2 will therefore be heavier.

9.84

Gas	Formula Weight	Density (g/L) at STP
(a) CH_4	16.0 amu	0.714
(b) CO_2	44.0 amu	1.96
(c) O_2	32.0 amu	1.42
(d) UF_6	352 amu	15.7

9.85 $n = 1$ mol ; $T = 1$ K ; $P = 1 \times 10^{-14}$ mm Hg

$$V = \frac{nRT}{P} = \frac{1 \text{ mol} \times 62.3 \frac{\text{mm Hg L}}{\text{mol K}} \times 1 \text{ K}}{1 \times 10^{-14} \text{ mm Hg}} = 6 \times 10^{15} \text{ L}$$

$$\text{Density} = \frac{6.02 \times 10^{23} \text{ atoms}}{6 \times 10^{15} \text{ L}} = 10^8 \frac{\text{atoms}}{\text{L}}$$

9.86 $PV = nRT$; $V = 300.$ mL; $T = 150°C = 423$ K

(a) For CH_3OH: $n = 2.50 \text{ g} \times \dfrac{1 \text{ mol}}{32.0 \text{ g}} = 0.0781$ mol

$$P = \frac{0.0781 \text{ mol} \times 0.0821 \frac{L \text{ atm}}{\text{mol K}} \times 423 \text{ K}}{0.300 \text{ L}} = 9.04 \text{ atm}$$

For H_2O: $n = 1.50$ g x $\dfrac{1 \text{ mol}}{18.0 \text{ g}}$ $= 0.0833$ mol

$$P = \dfrac{0.0833 \text{ mol} \times 0.0821 \dfrac{L \text{ atm}}{\text{mol K}} \times 423 \text{ K}}{0.300 \text{ L}} = 9.64 \text{ atm}$$

(b) Total pressure is equal to the sum of partial pressures.
$P_{Total} = 9.04$ atm $+ 9.64$ atm $= 18.68$ atm

(c) A container such as a pressure cooker must be vented because the large pressure buildup inside can lead to an explosion or to the sudden release of hot gases if the container is opened without venting.

9.87

(a)

```
      H  H  H
  ..  |  |  |  ..
 :O - C - C - O:
  ..  |  |  |  ..
      H  H  H
```
Ethylene glycol

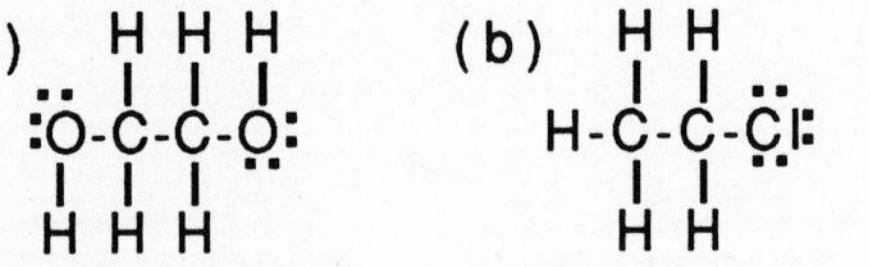

(b)

```
     H  H
     |  |   ..
 H - C - C - Cl:
     |  |   ..
     H  H
```
Chloroethane

(c) Ethylene glycol is higher melting and higher boiling than chloroethane because it forms hydrogen bonds.

The Chapter in Brief

Gas Laws (Sections 9.5–9.9) Gas laws can be used to predict the influence on gases of changing pressure (P), volume (V), temperature (T), and number of moles (n). Boyle's law states that $P_1V_1 = P_2V_2$; Charles' law states that $V_1/T_1 = V_2/T_2$; and Avogadro's law states that $V_1/n_1 = V_2/n_2$. The combined gas law states that $P_1V_1/T_1 = P_2V_2/T_2$. These laws can be combined into the universal gas law: $PV = nRT$.

Liquids (Sections 9.10–9.12) Intermolecular forces are the forces of attraction or repulsion between molecules. In liquids, dipole-dipole interactions, London forces, and hydrogen bonding are the three types of attractive intermolecular forces.

Self-Test for Chapter 9

Complete the following sentences:

1.   In Boyle's law, the _____ of a gas is inversely proportional to its _____.

2.   A liquid has _____ volume and _____ shape.

3.   _____ law states that the total pressure of a gas mixture is the sum of the individual pressure of the components in the mixture.

4.   A pressure of 760 mm Hg and a temperature of 273 K are known as _____.

5.   _____ law says that equal volumes of gases at the same temperature contain equal numbers of molecules.

6.   In a closed container, liquid and vapor are at _____.

7.   Units for measuring pressure include _____, _____, _____, and _____.

8.   The _____ _____ _____ is the heat necessary to melt one gram of a solid at its melting point.

9.   In Charles' law, _____ and _____ are kept constant.

10. Gas particles move in straight lines, with energy proportional to _____.

11. The transformation of a substance from one state to another is known as a _____ _____ _____.

Tell whether the following statements are true or false:

1.   Molecules of ethyl alcohol exhibit hydrogen bonding.

2.   All gases are similar in their physical behavior.

3.   Molecules of CH_3Cl experience both dipole-dipole interactions and London forces.

4.   Doubling the pressure of a gas at constant temperature doubles the volume.

5.   R = 0.082 L atm / mol K is a value for the gas constant.

6.   Atoms in solids have an orderly arrangement.

7.   Standard temperature and pressure are 760 mm Hg and 273 °C.

8.   All substances become solids if the temperature is low enough.

9.   The atmospheric pressure in Death Valley (282 ft below sea level) is lower than the atmospheric pressure at sea level.

10. The more liquid there is in a closed container, the higher the vapor pressure.

Match the entries on the left with their partners on the right

1. $P_1V_1 = P_2V_2$ (a) Avogadro's law

2. Dipole-dipole attraction   (b) Gas constant

3. $P_{total} = P_{gas\ 1} + P_{gas\ 2} + ...$ (c) Force per unit area

4. 760 mm Hg at 273 K   (d) Charles' law

5. Hydrogen bonding   (e) Occurs between molecules of CH_3Br

6. $V_1/n_1 = V_2/n_2$ (f) STP

7. 0.007500 mm Hg   (g) Boyle's law

8. London forces   (h) Gay-Lussac's law

9. 62.3 mm Hg L / mol K   (i) Universal gas law

10. $V_1/T_1 = V_2/T_2$ (j) Pascal

11. Pressure   (k) Dalton's law of partial pressure

12. $PV = nRT$ (l) Occurs between molecules of N_2

Chapter 10 – Solutions

10.1 Apple juice and gasoline are true solutions because they are nonfilterable and transparent to light. Milk and hand lotion are colloids.

10.2 Remember the rule "like dissolves like".
(a) CCl_4 and H_2O do not form solutions because CCl_4 is non-polar and H_2O is polar.
(b) Gasoline and $MgSO_4$ do not form solutions because $MgSO_4$ is polar and gasoline is nonpolar.
(c)(d) These two pairs of substances form solutions because they are chemically similar.

10.3 Glauber's salt: $Na_2SO_4 \cdot 10 \ H_2O$

10.4 Molar mass of Glauber's salt: 322 g / mol. 322 g of Glauber's salt provides 1.00 mol of sodium sulfate.

10.5

$$\frac{C_1}{P_1} = \frac{C_2}{P_2}; \ P_1 = 760 \text{ mm Hg}; \ C_1 = 0.169 \text{ g} / 100 \text{ mL}; \ P_2 = 2.5 \times 10^4 \text{ mm Hg}; \ C_2 = ?$$

$$\frac{C_1 P_2}{P_1} = C_2 = \frac{0.169 \text{ g} \ \times \ 2.5 \times 10^4 \text{ mm Hg}}{760 \text{ mm Hg}} = 5.56 \text{ g } CO_2 / 100 \text{ mL}$$

10.6 1 dL = 100 mL

$$\frac{8.6 \text{ mg}}{100 \text{ mL}} \ \times \ \frac{1 \text{ g}}{1000 \text{ mg}} \ \times \ 100\% = 0.0086\% \ (w/v) \ Ca^{2+}$$

10.7

$$\frac{23 \text{ g KI}}{350 \text{ mL}} \ \times \ 100\% = 6.6\% \ (w/v) \ KI$$

10.8 Depending on the solubility of the solute in the solvent, a saturated solution may be either dilute or concentrated. If a solute is only slightly soluble in a solvent, a saturated solution will be dilute. If the solute is very soluble in the solvent, a saturated solution will be concentrated.

10.9 (a) A 12% solution contains 12 g of solute per 100 mL of solution. Thus, 12 g of glucose are needed.

(b) A 2% solution contains 2 g of solute per 100 mL of solution.

$$75 \text{ mL} \ \times \ \frac{2.0 \text{ g KCl}}{100 \text{ mL}} = 1.5 \text{ g KCl}$$

10.10 A 7.5% (*v/v*) solution contains 7.5 mL of solute per 100 mL of solution.

$$500 \text{ mL solution } \times \frac{7.5 \text{ mL acetic acid}}{100 \text{ mL solution}} = 38 \text{ mL acetic acid}$$

To prepare the desired solution, you would measure 38 mL of acetic acid into a 500 mL volumetric flask and add water to the 500 mL mark.

10.11 (a) 22 mL of ethyl alcohol are needed.
   (b)

$$150 \text{ mL solution } \times \frac{12 \text{ mL acetic acid}}{100 \text{ mL solution}} = 18 \text{ mL acetic acid}$$

10.12 A 0.9% (*w/w*) solution contains 0.9 g solute per 100 g solution. Thus:

$$\frac{0.9 \text{ g}}{100 \text{ g}} \times 10^6 = 9000 \text{ ppm NaCl}$$

10.13

$$\frac{32 \text{ mg NaF}}{20 \text{ kg}} \times \frac{1 \text{ kg}}{10^6 \text{ mg}} \times 10^6 = 1.6 \text{ ppm}$$

10.14

$$50 \text{ g } \times \frac{1 \text{ mol}}{337 \text{ g}} = 0.15 \text{ mol}; \quad \frac{0.15 \text{ mol}}{.160 \text{ L}} = 0.93 \text{ M}$$

10.15 (a) First, determine the number of moles of NaOH needed:

$$500 \text{ mL } \times \frac{1.25 \text{ mol NaOH}}{1000 \text{ mL}} = 0.62 \text{ mol NaOH}$$

Then determine the molar mass of NaOH:

$$23.0 \text{ g (Na)} + 16.0 \text{ g (O)} + 1.0 \text{ g (H)} = 40.0 \text{ g}$$

Finally, convert moles to grams by using the molar mass as a conversion factor:

$$0.62 \text{ mol NaOH } \times 40.0 \frac{\text{g}}{\text{mol}} = 25 \text{ g NaOH}$$

   (b)

$$1.5 \text{ L } \times \frac{0.25 \text{ mol glucose}}{1 \text{ L}} = 0.38 \text{ mol glucose}$$

M.M. of glucose = 180 g

$$0.38 \text{ mol glucose } \times 180.0 \frac{\text{g}}{\text{mol}} = 68 \text{ g glucose}$$

10.16 (a)

$$125 \text{ mL } \times \frac{0.20 \text{ mol NaHCO}_3}{1000 \text{ mL}} = 0.025 \text{ mol NaHCO}_3$$

(b)

$$650 \text{ mL } \times \frac{2.5 \text{ mol } H_2SO_4}{1000 \text{ mL}} = 1.6 \text{ mol } H_2SO_4$$

10.17 Using the molar mass of glucose (180.0 g) as a conversion factor, find the number of moles in 25.0 g glucose:

$$25.0 \text{ g glucose } \times \frac{1 \text{ mol}}{180.0 \text{ g}} = 0.139 \text{ mol glucose}$$

Now find the number of mL of 0.200 M glucose solution that contain 0.139 mol.:

$$0.139 \text{ mol glucose } \times \frac{1 \text{ L}}{0.200 \text{ mol glucose}} \times 1000 \frac{\text{mL}}{\text{L}} = 695 \text{ mL}$$

10.18 First, find the number of moles of cholesterol in 750 mL of blood:

$$750 \text{ mL } \times \frac{0.0050 \text{ mol cholesterol}}{1000 \text{ mL}} = 0.0040 \text{ mol cholesterol}$$

Next, find the molar mass of cholesterol:

$$27 \times 12.0 \text{ g (C)} + 46 \times 1.0 \text{ g (H)} + 16.0 \text{ g (O)} = 386 \text{ g}$$

Now, convert moles into grams:

$$0.0040 \text{ mol cholesterol } \times 386 \frac{\text{g}}{\text{mol}} = 1.5 \text{ g cholesterol}$$

10.19 Molar mass of $CaCO_3$ = 100. g

$$0.075 \text{ L } \times \frac{0.1 \text{ mol HCl}}{1 \text{ L}} \times \frac{1 \text{ mol } CaCO_3}{2 \text{ mol HCl}} \times \frac{100. \text{ g } CaCO_3}{1 \text{ mol } CaCO_3} = 0.38 \text{ g } CaCO_3$$

10.20 M_{orig} = 12.0 M ; V_{orig} = 100 mL ;   and V_{final} = 500 mL

$$M_{final} = M_{orig} \times \frac{V_{orig}}{V_{final}} = 12.0 \text{ M } \times \frac{100 \text{ mL}}{500 \text{ mL}} = 2.4 \text{ M}$$

10.21 V_{final} = 500 mL ; M_{final} = 1.25 M ; M_{orig} = 16.0 M

$$V_{orig} = V_{final} = \times \frac{M_{final}}{M_{orig}} = 500 \text{ mL } \times \frac{1.25 \text{ M}}{16.0 \text{ M}} = 39.1 \text{ mL}$$

10.22 - 10.23

Ion	Molar Mass	Charge	Equivalent Weight	Milliequivalent Weight
(a) K^+	39.1 g	+1	39.1 g	39.1 mg
(b) Br^-	79.9 g	-1	79.9 g	79.9 mg
(c) Mg^{2+}	24.3 g	+2	12.2 g	12.2 mg
(d) SO_4^{2-}	96.0 g	-2	48.0 g	48.0 mg

10.24 One equivalent of Mg^{2+} = 12.2 g (Problem 10.22 (c))

$$\frac{g\ Mg^{2+}}{L} = \frac{12\ g\ Mg^{2+}}{1\ Eq} \times \frac{1\ Eq}{1000\ mEq} \times 3.0\ \frac{mEq}{L} = 0.036\ \frac{g\ Mg^{2+}}{L}$$

$$0.036\ \frac{g\ Mg^{2+}}{L} \times 1000\ \frac{mg}{g} \times \frac{1\ L}{1000\ mL} \times 250\ mL = 9\ mg\ Mg^{2+}$$

10.25 (a) A mole of $CaCl_2$ produces three moles of solute particles, lowering the freezing point of H_2O by 5.58°C. A mole of NaCl produces two moles of solute particles, lowering the freezing point of water by 3.72°C. Thus, on a molar basis, $CaCl_2$ is more effective than NaCl at lowering the freezing point of water.

(b) From part (a), we can see than 1.5 mol NaCl produces the same number of solute particles as 1.0 mol $CaCl_2$. Comparing the amount of the two compounds:

$$1.0\ mol\ CaCl_2 \times \frac{111\ g}{1\ mol\ CaCl_2} = 111\ g\ CaCl_2\ needed$$

$$1.5\ mol\ NaCl \times \frac{58.5\ g}{1\ mol\ NaCl} = 88\ g\ NaCl\ needed$$

Thus, 88 g NaCl is as effective as 111 g $CaCl_2$ in melting ice.

10.26 (a) Glucose is not an electrolyte. Thus 1.0 mol glucose lowers the freezing point of 1 kg H_2O by 1.86°C.
(b) 1.0 mol of NaCl yields 2.0 mol solute particles, which raise the boiling point of H_2O by 2 x 0.51°C = 1.02°C.

10.27 Osmolarity = molarity x number of particles
(a) For 0.35 M KBr, Osmolarity = 0.35 M x 2 = 0.70 Osmol, since KBr yields two particles (K^+ and Br^-) in solution.
(b) For 0.15 M glucose, Osmolarity = 0.15 M x 1 = 0.15 Osmol, since glucose yields only one particle in solution.

10.28 A homogeneous mixture (such as Coca Cola) is uniform throughout, but a heterogeneous mixture (such as beef stew) is nonuniform.

10.29 A solution is transparent to light; a colloid is opaque. The components of a colloid remain suspended; the components of a suspension settle out.

10.30 The polarity of water enables it to dissolve many ionic solids.

10.31 Because the surface area of powdered salt is greater than that of a salt block, powdered salt dissolves more rapidly.

10.32 Add water to the mixture. The insoluble aspirin settles out and can be removed by filtration, and the salt can be recovered by evaporation of the water. Alternatively, add chloroform to the mixture and filter off the insoluble salt. The aspirin can then be recovered by evaporating the chloroform.

10.33 Rubbing alcohol (b) and black coffee (d) are true solutions.

10.34 The liquids in (a) are miscible, as are the liquids in (b), (c) and (d).

10.35

$$C_2 = \frac{C_1 P_2}{P_1}; \quad C_1 = 51.8 \text{ g} / 100 \text{ mL}; \quad P_1 = 760 \text{ mm Hg}; \quad P_2 = 250 \text{ mm Hg}$$

$$= \frac{51.8 \text{ g} / 100 \text{ mL} \times 250 \text{ mm Hg}}{760 \text{ mm Hg}} = 17.0 \text{ g} / 100 \text{ mL}$$

10.36

$$C_2 = \frac{C_1 P_2}{P_1}; \quad C_1 = 0.44 \text{ g} / 100 \text{ mL}; \quad P_1 = 159 \text{ mm Hg}; \quad P_2 = 760 \text{ mm Hg}$$

$$= \frac{0.44 \text{ g} / 100 \text{ mL} \times 760 \text{ mm Hg}}{159 \text{ mm Hg}} = 2.1 \text{ g} / 100 \text{ mL} \ O_2$$

10.37 Weight/volume percent (*w/v* %) is defined as the number of grams of solute per 100 mL of solution.

10.38 Molarity (M) is defined as the number of moles of solute per liter of solution.

10.39 Volume/volume percent concentration (*v/vi%*) is defined as the volume of solute in 100 mL of solution.

10.40

$$20\% \ (v/v) \ \text{means} : \quad \frac{20 \text{ mL concentrate}}{100 \text{ mL juice}}$$

$$\text{Thus,} \quad 100 \text{ mL concentrate} \times \frac{100 \text{ mL juice}}{20 \text{ mL concentrate}} = 500 \text{ mL juice}$$

Since the final volume of the diluted juice is 500 mL, you would have to add 400 mL water to the original 100 mL of concentrate.

10.41

$$\frac{5.0 \text{ mL ethyl alcohol}}{100 \text{ mL solution}} \times 500 \text{ mL solution} = 25 \text{ mL ethyl alcohol}$$

Add water to 25 mL of ethyl alcohol to make a final volume of 500 mL.

10.42

$$500 \text{ mL solution} \times \frac{0.50 \text{ g B(OH)}_3}{100 \text{ mL solution}} = 2.5 \text{ g B(OH)}_3$$

Dissolve 2.5 g B(OH)$_3$ in water to a final volume of 500 mL.

10.43

$$1.5 \text{ mg} \times \frac{1 \text{ g}}{1000 \text{ mg}} \times \frac{100 \text{ mL}}{0.40 \text{ g}} = 0.38 \text{ mL}$$

10.44

$$250 \text{ mL solution } \times \frac{0.10 \text{ mol NaCl}}{1000 \text{ mL solution}} = 0.025 \text{ mol NaCl}$$

$$0.025 \text{ mol NaCl } \times 58.5 \frac{g}{mol} = 1.5 \text{ g NaCl}$$

Dissolve 1.5 g NaCl in water to a final volume of 250 mL.

10.45

$$1000 \text{ mL solution } \times \frac{7.5 \text{ g KBr}}{100 \text{ mL solution}} = 75 \text{ g KBr}$$

Dissolve 75 g KBr in water and dilute to 1.0 L.

10.46 (a)

For 0.50 M KCl : $0.50 \frac{\text{mol KCl}}{L} \times 74.6 \frac{g}{mol} = 37.3 \frac{\text{g KCl}}{L} = 3.73 \frac{\text{g KCl}}{100 \text{ mL}}$

For 5% (w/v) KCl : $5.0 \frac{\text{g KCl}}{100 \text{ mL}}$

The 5% (*w/v*) solution is more concentrated.

(b)

$$2.5\% \text{ (w/v) NaHSO}_4 = 2.5 \frac{\text{g NaHSO}_4}{100 \text{ mL solution}}$$

$$0.025 \frac{\text{mol NaHSO}_4}{L} \times 120 \frac{g}{mol} = 3.0 \frac{\text{g NaHSO}_4}{L} = 0.30 \frac{\text{g NaHSO}_4}{100 \text{ mL}}$$

The 2.5% (*w/v*) solution is more concentrated.

10.47

(a) $5.0 \frac{\text{g KCl}}{75 \text{ mL}} \times 100 \text{ mL} = 6.7 \text{ g KCl} ;$ 6.7% (w/v) KCl

(b) $\frac{15 \text{ g sucrose}}{350 \text{ mL}} \times 100 \text{ mL} = 4.3 \text{ g sucrose} ;$ 4.3% (w/v) sucrose

10.48

(a) $50.0 \text{ mL } \times 8.0 \frac{\text{g KCl}}{100 \text{ mL}} = 4.0 \text{ g KCl}$

(b) $200. \text{ mL } \times 7.5 \frac{\text{g acetic acid}}{100 \text{ mL}} = 15 \text{ g acetic acid}$

10.49

$$23 \text{ g KOH} \times \frac{100 \text{ mL}}{10 \text{ g KOH}} = 230 \text{ mL of a 10\% (w/v) solution}$$

$$23 \text{ g KOH} \times \frac{1 \text{ mol}}{56.1 \text{ g KOH}} = 0.41 \text{ mol KOH}$$

$$0.41 \text{ mol KOH} \times \frac{1000 \text{ mL}}{0.25 \text{ mol KOH}} = 1640 \text{ mL of 0.25 M solution}$$

10.50

$$\frac{90 \text{ mg glucose}}{100 \text{ mL}} \times \frac{1 \text{ g}}{1000 \text{ mg}} = \frac{0.090 \text{ g glucose}}{100 \text{ mL}} ; \quad 0.090\% \text{ (w/v) glucose}$$

10.51

$$\frac{90 \text{ mg glucose}}{100 \text{ mL}} \times 1000 \frac{\text{mL}}{\text{L}} \times 5 \text{ L} = 4500 \text{ mg glucose} = 4.5 \text{ g glucose}$$

10.52

$$1 \text{ kg} = 10^6 \text{ mg}; \quad \frac{10 \text{ mg}}{10^6 \text{ mg}} \times 10^6 = 10. \text{ ppm}$$

10.53

$$\frac{0.050 \text{ mg}}{10^6 \text{ mg}} \times 10^6 = 0.050 \text{ ppm}; \quad \frac{0.050 \text{ mg}}{10^6 \text{ mg}} \times 10^9 = 50 \text{ ppb}$$

10.54

(a) $12.5 \text{ g NaHCO}_3 \times \dfrac{1 \text{ mol}}{84.0 \text{ g}} = 0.149 \text{ mol NaHCO}_3 ; \dfrac{0.149 \text{ mol}}{0.350 \text{ L}} = 0.425 \text{ M}$

(b) $45.0 \text{ g H}_2\text{SO}_4 \times \dfrac{1 \text{ mol}}{98.0 \text{ g}} = 0.459 \text{ mol H}_2\text{SO}_4 ; \dfrac{0.459 \text{ mol}}{0.300 \text{ L}} = 1.53 \text{ M}$

(c) $30.0 \text{ g NaCl} \times \dfrac{1 \text{ mol}}{58.5 \text{ g}} = 0.512 \text{ mol NaCl}; \dfrac{0.512 \text{ mol}}{0.500 \text{ L}} = 1.02 \text{ M}$

10.55

(a) $0.200 \text{ L} \times \dfrac{0.30 \text{ mol acetic acid}}{\text{L}} = 0.060 \text{ mol acetic acid}$

(b) $1.50 \text{ L} \times \dfrac{0.25 \text{ mol NaOH}}{\text{L}} = 0.38 \text{ mol NaOH}$

(c) $0.750 \text{ L} \times \dfrac{2.5 \text{ mol nitric acid}}{\text{L}} = 1.88 \text{ mol nitric acid}$

10.56

(a) 0.060 mol acetic acid $\times$ $60 \frac{g}{mol}$ $=$ 3.6 g acetic acid

(b) 0.38 mol NaOH $\times$ $40 \frac{g}{mol}$ $=$ 15 g NaOH

(c) 1.88 mol nitric acid $\times$ $63 \frac{g}{mol}$ $=$ 118 g nitric acid

10.57

0.0040 mol HCl $\times$ $\frac{1000 \text{ mL}}{0.75 \text{ mol}}$ $=$ 5.3 mL HCl

10.58 First, calculate the number of moles of H_2SO_4 spilled:

0.450 L $\times$ $0.50 \frac{\text{mol } H_2SO_4}{L}$ $=$ 0.22 mol H_2SO_4

According to the equation given in the problem, each mole of H_2SO_4 reacts with two moles of $NaHCO_3$. Thus, the 0.22 mol of H_2SO_4 spilled needs to be neutralized with 0.44 mol of $NaHCO_3$.

0.44 mol $NaHCO_3$ $\times$ $84 \frac{g}{mol}$ $=$ 37 g $NaHCO_3$

10.59

0.450 g AgBr $\times$ $\frac{1 \text{ mol AgBr}}{187.8 \text{ g}}$ $=$ 0.00240 mol AgBr

According to the equation given, one mole of AgBr reacts with 2 moles of $Na_2S_2O_3$. Thus, 0.00240 mol AgBr reacts with 0.00480 mol $Na_2S_2O_3$. To calculate how many mL of 0.0200 M $Na_2S_2O_3$:

0.00480 mol $\times$ $\frac{1000 \text{ mL}}{0.0200 \text{ mol}}$ $=$ $240.$ mL of 0.0200 M $Na_2S_2O_3$

10.60

(a) 13.0 mL $\times$ $\frac{0.0100 \text{ mol}}{1000 \text{ mL}}$ $=$ 0.130×10^{-3} mol I_2

According to the equation, one mole of I_2 reacts with one mole of $C_6H_8O_6$. Thus, the 25.0 mL sample contains 0.130×10^{-3} mol $C_6H_8O_6$.

$\frac{0.130 \times 10^{-3} \text{ mol}}{25 \text{ mL}}$ $\times$ $\frac{1000 \text{ mL}}{1 \text{ L}}$ $=$ 0.00520 M

(b) Molar mass of $C_6H_8O_6$ = 186 g.

$$\frac{186 \text{ g}}{1 \text{ mol}} \times \frac{0.00520 \text{ mol}}{1 \text{ L}} = \frac{0.967 \text{ g ascorbic acid}}{1 \text{ L}} = \frac{967 \text{ mg ascorbic acid}}{1 \text{ L}}$$

$$60 \text{ mg} \times \frac{1 \text{ L}}{967 \text{ mg ascorbic acid}} = 0.062 \text{ L} = 62 \text{ mL juice}$$

10.61

$$V_{final} = V_{orig} \times \frac{M_{orig}}{M_{final}}; \quad V_{orig} = 25.0 \text{ mL}; \quad M_{orig} = 12.0 \text{ M}; \quad M_{final} = 0.500 \text{ M}$$

$$= 25.0 \text{ mL} \times \frac{12.0 \text{ M}}{0.500 \text{ M}} = 600. \text{ mL of } 0.500 \text{ M HCl solution}$$

10.62

$$V_{orig} = V_{final} \times \frac{M_{final}}{M_{orig}}; \quad V_{final} = 750. \text{ mL}; \quad M_{orig} = 0.100 \text{ M}; \quad M_{final} = 0.0500 \text{ M}$$

$$= 750 \text{ mL} \times \frac{0.0500 \text{ M}}{0.100 \text{ M}} = 375 \text{ mL of } 0.100 \text{ M NaHCO}_3$$

10.63 An electrolyte is a substance that conducts electricity when dissolved in water. Sodium chloride is an example.

10.64 If the concentration of Ca^{2+} is 3.0 mEq/L, there are 3.0 mmol of charges due to calcium per liter of blood. Since calcium has a charge of +2, there are 1.5 mmol of calcium per liter of blood.

10.65

$$10\% \text{ (w/v)} = \frac{10 \text{ g KCl}}{100 \text{ mL}} \; ; \quad 30 \text{ mL} \times \frac{10 \text{ g KCl}}{100 \text{ mL}} = 3.0 \text{ g KCl}$$

The molar mass of KCl is 74.6 g/mol. Thus:

$$3.0 \text{ g KCl} \times \frac{1 \text{ mol}}{74.6 \text{ g}} = 0.040 \text{ mol KCl}$$

Since one equivalent equals one mole when an ion has only one charge, there are 0.040 Eq, or 40 mEq, of K^+ in a 30 mL dose.

10.66 Use the value 100 mEq/L for the concentration of Cl^- in blood:
For Cl^- ion, 100 mEq = 100 mmol = 0.100 mol

$$\frac{0.100 \text{ mol Cl}^-}{L} \times 0.100 \text{ L} = 0.0100 \text{ mol Cl}^- \text{ in 100 mL blood}$$

$$0.0100 \text{ mol Cl}^- \times 35.5 \frac{\text{g}}{\text{mol}} = 0.355 \text{ g Cl}^- \text{ in 100 mL blood}$$

10.67 Because SO_4^{2-} has a charge of 2, each mole of SO_4^{2-} contains two equivalents. Thus a concentration of 0.025 M SO_4^{2-} equals 0.050 Eq/L or 50 mEq/L.

10.68 Syrup is composed of water molecules, which evaporate, and sugar molecules, which are nonvolatile. These non-volatile molecules lower the vapor pressure of water and make the syrup solution evaporate more slowly.

10.69 Methanol has a molar mass of 30.0 g and provides one mole of solute particles per mole of methanol.

$$10.0° \text{ C } \times \frac{1 \text{ mol}}{1.86° \text{ C} \times 1 \text{ kg}} \times 5 \text{ kg} = 26.9 \text{ mol methanol}$$

$$26.9 \text{ mol } \times \frac{30.0 \text{ g}}{1 \text{ mol}} = 807 \text{ g of methanol needed}$$

10.70

$$\frac{26.9 \text{ mol CH}_3\text{OH}}{5 \text{ kg}} \times \frac{0.51° \text{ C} \times 1 \text{ kg}}{1 \text{ mol}} = 2.74° \text{ C; The boiling point is elevated by } 2.74° \text{ C.}$$

10.71 0.2 mol NaOH contains 0.4 mol solute particles, and 0.2 mol $Ba(OH)_2$ contains 0.6 mol solute particles. Since $Ba(OH)_2$ produces more solute particles, it produces greater freezing point lowering of 2 kg of water.

10.72 The inside of a red blood cell contains dissolved substances and therefore has a higher osmolarity than pure water. Water thus passes through the cell membrane to dilute the inside until pressure builds up and the cell eventually bursts.

10.73 If a 0.15 M NaCl solution is isotonic with blood, then the NaCl solution has the same osmolarity as blood. If distilled water is hypotonic with blood, then the water has a lower osmolarity than blood.

10.74 Distilled water separated from a 1.0 M NaCl solution by an osmotic membrane would pass through the membrane to dilute the NaCl until the maximum osmotic pressure of the solution was reached.

10.75

Solution	Molarity	# of Particles	Osmolarity
(a) 0.25 M KBr	0.25 M	2	0.50 Osmol
0.40 M Na_2SO_4	0.40 M	3	1.2 Osmol (greater)
(b) 0.30 M NaOH	0.30 M	2	0.60 Osmol
3% (w/v) NaOH	0.75 M	2	1.5 Osmol (greater)

10.76 Since a 0.40 M NaCl solution has a higher osmolarity than a 0.40 M glucose solution, water would pass through the osmotic membrane from the glucose solution to the NaCl solution until the two were of equal osmolarity.

10.77 Molar mass of uric acid ($C_5H_4N_4O_3$) = 168 g.

$$(a) \text{ } (w/v)\%: \frac{0.067 \text{ g}}{1 \text{ L}} = \frac{0.0067 \text{ g}}{100 \text{ mL}}; \frac{0.0067 \text{ g}}{100 \text{ mL}} \times 100\% = 0.0067\% \text{ } (w/v)$$

(b) ppm: One L of water weighs 1 kg. Thus:

$$\frac{0.067 \text{ g}}{1 \text{ L}} = \frac{0.067 \text{ g}}{1 \text{ kg}} \times \frac{1 \text{ kg}}{1000 \text{ g}}; \quad \frac{0.067 \text{ g}}{1000 \text{ g}} \times 10^6 = 67 \text{ ppm}$$

(c) $\dfrac{0.067 \text{ g}}{1 \text{ L}} \times \dfrac{1 \text{ mol}}{168 \text{ g}} = 0.00040 \text{ M} = 0.40 \text{ mM}$

10.78 When uncooked meat or vegetables are salted before cooking, water is drawn out by osmosis to dilute the salt.

10.79 A dialysis membrane has larger pores than an osmotic membrane so that ions and small covalent molecules can pass through a dialysis membrane, whereas only water or other small solvent molecules can pass through an osmotic membrane.

10.80 In hemodialysis, the dialysis fluid concentration can be controlled to correct electrolyte imbalances and thus to maintain homeostasis.

10.81

$$5.0\% \text{ (w/v)} = \frac{5.0 \text{ g } CaCl_2}{100 \text{ mL}}; \quad \frac{5.0 \text{ g } CaCl_2}{100 \text{ mL}} \times 5.0 \text{ mL} = 0.25 \text{ g } CaCl_2$$

$$0.25 \text{ g } CaCl_2 \times \frac{1 \text{ mol}}{111 \text{ g}} = 0.0023 \text{ mol } CaCl_2 = 0.0023 \text{ mol } Ca^{2+}$$

$$0.0023 \text{ mol } Ca^{2+} \times 2 \frac{Eq}{mol} = 0.0046 \text{ Eq } Ca^{2+} = 4.6 \text{ mEq } Ca^{2+}$$

10.82 $M_{orig} = 16 \text{ M}, \quad M_{final} = 0.20 \text{ M}, \quad V_{final} = 750 \text{ mL}$

$$V_{orig} = V_{final} \times \frac{M_{final}}{M_{orig}} = 750 \text{ mL} \times \frac{0.20 \text{ M}}{16 \text{ M}} = 9.4 \text{ mL}$$

10.83

$$5.50 \text{ g KOH} \times \frac{1 \text{ mol}}{56.1 \text{ g}} = 0.0980 \text{ mol KOH}$$

According to the balanced equation, one mole of KOH reacts with one mole of HNO_3. Thus, 0.0980 mol of KOH reacts with 0.0980 mol of HNO_3.

$$0.0980 \text{ mol } HNO_3 \times \frac{1 \text{ L}}{16 \text{ mol}} = 0.0061 \text{ L } HNO_3 = 6.1 \text{ mL } HNO_3$$

10.84 $M_{orig} = 12.0 \text{ M}, \quad V_{orig} = 25 \text{ mL}, \quad V_{final} = 525 \text{ mL}$

$$M_{final} = M_{orig} \times \frac{V_{orig}}{V_{final}} = 12.0 \text{ M} \times \frac{25 \text{ mL}}{525 \text{ mL}} = 0.57 \text{ M}$$

10.85 - 10.86

Component	Weight	Molar Mass	Molarity	Osmolarity
(a) NaCl	8.6 g	58.5	0.147 M	0.294 Osmol
(b) KCl	0.30 g	74.6	0.0040 M	0.0080 Osmol
(c) $CaCl_2$	0.33 g	111	0.0030 M	0.0090 Osmol

10.87

$$0.10\% \ (v/v) = \frac{0.10 \ mL}{100 \ mL} = 1.0 \ \frac{mL}{L}$$

$$1.0 \ \frac{mL}{L} \times 5 \ L = 5 \ mL \ alcohol$$

10.88

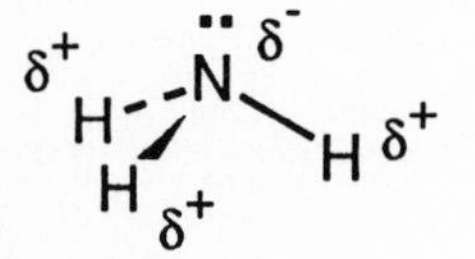

10.89

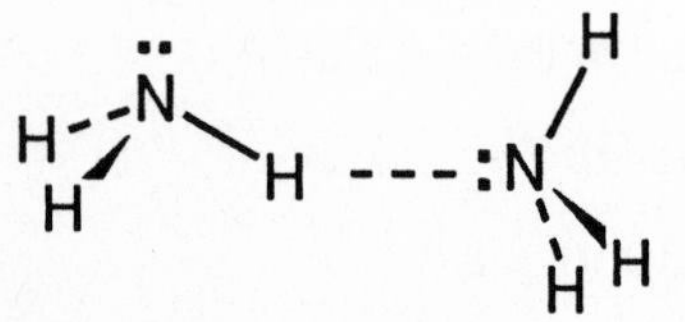

10.90 (a)

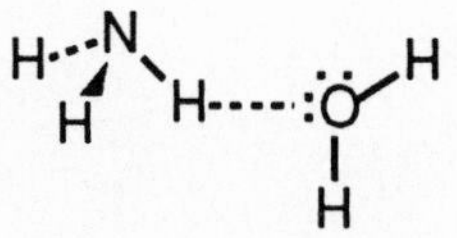

(b) $\dfrac{51.8 \ g}{1 \ L} \times \dfrac{1 \ mol}{17.0 \ g} = 3.05 \ mol / L$

10.91 (a) $CoCl_2 + 6 \ H_2O \ \rightleftharpoons \ CoCl_2 \cdot 6 \ H_2O$

(b) Molar mass of $CoCl_2 \cdot 6 \ H_2O = 238 \ g$

$$2.50 \ g \ CoCl_2 \times \frac{1 \ mol \ CoCl_2 \cdot 6 \ H_2O}{238 \ g} \times \frac{6 \ mol \ H_2O}{1 \ mol \ CoCl_2 \cdot 6 \ H_2O} \times \frac{18.0 \ g \ H_2O}{1 \ mol \ H_2O} = 1.13 \ g \ H_2O$$

The Chapter in Brief

Mixtures and Solutions (Sections 10.1–10.7, 10.15) A mixture is a combination of two or more substances that retain their chemical identities. A mixture may be either homogeneous or heterogeneous, and may be either a solution, a colloid, or a suspension. In a solution, the dissolved substance is called the solute and the liquid is called the solvent. Water, with its polar covalent bonds, can dissolve many polar covalent compounds and ionic salts. The solubility of a substance is the maximum amount that will dissolve in a given solvent and is dependent on temperature and pressure (Henry's law). Two liquids that are soluble in all proportions are miscible.

Concentration (Sections 10.8–10.10)   The amount of solute dissolved in a solvent is the solution's concentration. Three common ways to describe concentration are weight/volume percent (*w/v%*), volume/volume percent (*v/v%*), and mole/volume concentration (molarity, M). To calculate the dilution of a solution, the expression $M_{orig} \times V_{orig} = M_{final} \times V_{final}$ is used.

Electrolytes and Osmosis (Sections 10.11–10.14)   An electrolyte is a solution of ions that conducts electricity. An equivalent of an ion is the amount of the ion in grams that contains Avogadro's number of charges. Osmosis is the passage of solvent or small solute molecules through a semipermeable membrane, and is determined by the concentration of particles on each side of the membrane. Osmolarity is defined as the molarity times the number of particles in the solute. Dissolved particles can lower the freezing point or raise the boiling point of a solution.

Self-Test for Chapter 10

Complete the following sentences:

1.   Two liquids soluble in each other are said to be _____.

2.   An _____ is the amount of an ion in grams that contains Avogadro's number of charges.

3.   A weight/volume solution can be made up in a piece of glassware called a _____ _____.

4.   According to Henry's law, the _____ of a gas varies with its _____.

5.   In the _____ _____, the particles in a colloid scatter light.

6.   Compounds that attract water from the atmosphere are called _____.

7.   The formula used for calculating dilutions is _____.

8.   Milk is an example of a _____.

9.   _____ and _____ can pass through a dialysis membrane.

10.   A solution that has reached its solubility limit is said to be _____.

11.   An example of a nonelectrolyte is _____.

12.   A solution that is hypotonic with respect to blood has a _____ osmolarity than blood plasma.

Tell whether the following statements are true or false:

1.   A solute is the liquid used to dissolve a substance.

2.   It is possible to have a solution of a solid in a solid.

3.   In making a volume/volume percent solution, one liquid is added to 100 mL of the other liquid.

4.   All ionic compounds are soluble in water.

5.   A solution of 0.10 M Na_3PO_4 has a greater osmolarity than a solution of 0.15 M NaCl.

6.   Weight/weight percent is a particularly useful way to express concentration.

7.   In carrying out a dilution, the number of moles of solute remains constant.

8.   The solubility of most substances increases with temperature.

9.   A colloid differs from a solution in its ability to transmit light.

10.   A blood cell undergoes crenation when placed in distilled water.

11.   Particles dissolved in water lower the boiling point of water.

12.   The amount of gas dissolved in a liquid increases with increasing pressure.

Match the entries on the left with their partners on the right.

1.   Osmotic membrane   (a) Muddy water

2. V_{orig} / V_{final} (b) Molarity x number of particles

3.   Solution   (c) Conducts electricity in water

4.   Equivalent   (d) Vinegar

5.   Suspension   (e) Crystalline compound that holds water

6.   Dialysis membrane   (f) Dilution factor

7.   Osmolarity   (g) Butter

8.   Hypotonic   (h) Permeable only to water

9.   Colloid   (i) A solution of lower osmolarity than another

10.   Crenation   (j) Formula weight / number of charges

11.   Hydrate   (k) Permeable to water and small molecules

12.   Electrolyte   (l) Happens to cell in hypertonic solution

11.1 Look in Table 11.2 to find strong acids. Acids not in the table are weak acids.
Strong acids: HBr (*aq*), HNO_3 (*aq*)
Weak acids: HCN (*aq*), HF (*aq*), HNO_2 (*aq*)

11.2 $HCOOH$ (a) and H_2S (b) are Brønsted-Lowry acids because they have protons to donate.

11.3 SO_3^{2-} (a) and F^- (c) are Brønsted-Lowry bases because they can be proton acceptors.

11.4 Water acts as an acid when it reacts to form OH^-; water acts as a base when it reacts to form H_3O^+.

Water as an acid: (b) F^- (*aq*) + H_2O (*l*) $\rightleftharpoons$ HF (*aq*) + OH^- (*aq*)

Water as a base: (a) H_3PO_4 (*aq*) + H_2O (*l*) $\rightleftharpoons$ H_2PO^-(*aq*) + H_3O^+ (*aq*)

(c) NH_4^+ (*aq*) + H_2O (*l*) $\rightleftharpoons$ H_3O^+ (*aq*) + NH_3 (*aq*)

11.5 (a) HNO_3 (*aq*) + KOH (*aq*) $\longrightarrow$ H_2O (*l*) + KNO_3 (*aq*) potassium nitrate

(b) H_2SO_4 (*aq*) + 2 $LiOH$ (*aq*) $\longrightarrow$ 2 H_2O (*l*) + Li_2SO_4 (*aq*) lithium sulfate

(c) 2 HCl (*aq*) + $Mg(OH)_2$ (*aq*) $\longrightarrow$ 2 H_2O (*l*) + $MgCl_2$ (*aq*) magnesium chloride

11.6 3 HCl (*aq*) + $Al(OH)_3$ (*aq*) $\longrightarrow$ 3 H_2O (*l*) + $AlCl_3$ (*aq*)

11.7 (a) $KHCO_3$ (*aq*) + HNO_3 (*aq*) $\longrightarrow$ H_2O (*l*) + CO_2 (*g*) + KNO_3 (*aq*)

(b) $MgCO_3$ (*aq*) + H_2SO_4 (*aq*) $\longrightarrow$ H_2O (*l*) + CO_2 (*g*) + $MgSO_4$ (*aq*)

(c) HI (*aq*) + $LiHCO_3$ (*aq*) $\longrightarrow$ H_2O (*l*) + CO_2 (*g*) + LiI (*aq*)

11.8 H_2SO_4 (*aq*) + 2 NH_3 (*aq*) $\longrightarrow$ $(NH_4)_2SO_4$ (*aq*)

11.9

11.10 (a) The conjugate acid of HS^- is H_2S.
(b) The conjugate acid of PO_4^{3-} is HPO_4^{2-}.
(c) The conjugate base of H_2CO_3 is HCO_3^-.
(d) The conjugate base of NH_4^+ is NH_3.

11.11 Use Table 11.3 for help. The stronger acid is listed *higher* in the table than the weaker acid.
Stronger acids: (a) NH_4^+ (b) H_2SO_4 (c) H_2CO_3

11.12 In Table 11.3, the stronger base is listed *lower* in the table than the weaker base.
Stronger bases: (a) F^- (b) OH^-

11.13 HPO_4^{2-} + OH^- $\rightleftharpoons$ PO_4^3 + H_2O
acid   base   conjugate base   conjugate acid

From Table 11.3, we see that OH^- is a stronger base than PO_4^{3-} and that HPO_4^{2-} is a stronger acid than H_2O. Thus, the forward direction of the equilibrium is favored.

HPO_4^{2-} + OH^- $\rightleftharpoons$ PO_4^3 + H_2O
stronger acid   stronger base   weaker base   weaker acid

11.14 (a) Beer is slightly acidic. Since $10^{-14} = [H_3O^+][OH^-]$,

$$[OH^-] = \frac{K_w}{[H_3O^+]} = \frac{10^{-14}}{3.2 \times 10^{-5}} = 3.1 \times 10^{-10} \text{ mol/L}$$

(b) Ammonia is alkaline.

$$[OH^-] = \frac{K_w}{[H_3O^+]} = \frac{10^{-14}}{3.1 \times 10^{-12}} = 3.2 \times 10^{-3} \text{ mol/L}$$

11.15 (a) If $[H_3O^+] = 1 \times 10^{-5}$ mol/L, then pH = 5.

(b) If $[OH^-] = 1 \times 10^{-9}$ mol/L, then $[H_3O^+] = \dfrac{1 \times 10^{-14}}{1 \times 10^{-9}} = 1 \times 10^{-5}$; pH = 5.

11.16 (a) For pH = 13, $[H_3O^+] = 1 \times 10^{-13}$ mol/L.
(b) For pH = 3, $[H_3O^+] = 1 \times 10^{-3}$ mol/L.
(c) For pH = 8, $[H_3O^+] = 1 \times 10^{-8}$ mol/L.
The solution of pH = 3 is most acidic, and the solution of pH = 13 is most basic.

11.17 - 11.18

Solution	pH	Acidic/Basic	$[H_3O^+]$
(a) Saliva	6.5	acidic	3×10^{-7} M
(b) Pancreatic juice	7.9	basic	1×10^{-8} M
(c) Orange juice	3.7	acidic	2×10^{-4} M
(d) Wine	3.5	acidic	3×10^{-4} M

Pancreatic juice   Saliva   Orange juice   Wine

Least
acidic   Most
                                                             acidic

11.19 Use your calculator or use the log table to determine pH.
(a) $[H_3O^+] = 5.3 \times 10^{-9}$ mol/L: pH = 8.28
(b) $[H_3O^+] = 8.9 \times 10^{-6}$ mol/L: pH = 5.05

11.20 If a small amount of extra base is added to a mixture of HCl and NaCl, the base is neutralized to form H_2O, and the pH of the solution changes slightly. If extra acid is added, however, it can't be neutralized because Cl^- is too weak a base. Thus, the HCl - NaCl system is a poor buffer.

11.21

$$pH = pK_a + \log \frac{\left[HPO_4{}^{2-}\right]}{\left[H_2PO_4{}^-\right]}; K_a = 6.6 \times 10^{-8}$$

If $[HPO_4{}^{2-}] = [H_2PO_4{}^-]$ then $\log \frac{\left[HPO_4{}^{2-}\right]}{\left[H_2PO_4{}^-\right]} = 0$ and $pH = pK_a$; $pH = -\log [6.6 \times 10^{-8}] = 7.18$.

reaction with H^+: $HPO_4{}^{2-}$ *(aq)* + H_3O^+ *(aq)* $\longrightarrow$ $H_2PO_4{}^-$ *(aq)* + H_2O *(l)*

reaction with OH^-: $H_2PO_4{}^-$ *(aq)* + OH^- *(aq)* $\longrightarrow$ $HPO_4{}^{2-}$ *(aq)* + H_2O *(l)*

11.22 - 11.23

Sample	Weight	Molar Mass	# of Ions	Equivalent Weight	# of Equivs	Normality
(a) HNO_3	5.0 g	63.0 g	1	63.0 g	0.079	0.26 N
(b) $Ca(OH)_2$	12.5 g	74.1 g	2	37.0 g	0.338	1.13 N
(c) H_3PO_4	4.5 g	98.0 g	3	32.7 g	0.14	0.47 N

11.24 (a) 0.037 L HCl x $\dfrac{0.50 \text{ mol}}{1 \text{ L HCl}}$ = 0.019 mol HCl. Since HCl produces only one H^+ ion,

there are also 0.019 eq (or 19 meq) of HCl in 37 mL of 0.50 N solution.

(b) One eq of OH^- ion neutralizes one eq of H^+, and thus 19 meq of NaOH will neutralize the 19 meq of HCl from part (a).

11.25 First, write the balanced equation for the neutralization reaction:

HCl *(aq)* + NaOH *(aq)* $\longrightarrow$ H_2O *(l)* + NaCl *(aq)*

We see from this equation that one mole of base is needed to neutralize each mole of acid.

Ballpark Solution: Since the volume of base is about three times larger than the volume of acid, the acid must be three times more concentrated than the base - perhaps about 0.7 M HCl.

Exact Solution:

Moles NaOH = 58.4 mL x $\dfrac{0.250 \text{ mol NaOH}}{1 \text{ L}}$ x $\dfrac{1 \text{ L}}{1000 \text{ mL}}$

= 0.146 moles NaOH

Since we know from the equation that moles NaOH = moles HCl, we can find the concentration of HCl:

$$\frac{0.0146 \text{ mol HCl}}{20.0 \text{ mL}} \times \frac{1000 \text{ mL}}{1 \text{ L}} = 0.730 \text{ M HCl}$$

The ballpark solution and the exact solution agree.

11.26 $2 \text{ NaOH } (aq) + H_2SO_4 (aq) \longrightarrow 2 H_2O (l) + Na_2SO_4 (aq)$
Notice that two moles of base are needed to neutralize one mole of acid.

$$\text{Moles } H_2SO_4 = 50.0 \text{ mL} \times 0.200 \frac{\text{mol } H_2SO_4}{L} \times \frac{1 \text{ L}}{1000 \text{ mL}}$$

$$= 0.0100 \text{ mol } H_2SO_4$$

$$\text{Moles NaOH} = 2 \times \text{moles } H_2SO_4 = 0.0200 \text{ moles NaOH}$$

$$0.0200 \text{ mol NaOH} \times \frac{1 \text{ L}}{0.150 \text{ mol}} = 0.133 \text{ L NaOH} = 133 \text{ mL NaOH}$$

11.27 $2 \text{ KOH } (aq) + H_2SO_4 (aq) \longrightarrow 2 H_2O (l) + Na_2SO_4 (aq)$

$$0.0161 \text{ L} \times \frac{0.15 \text{ mol}}{1 \text{ L}} \times \frac{2 \text{ eq } H_2SO_4}{1 \text{ mol}} = 0.00483 \text{ eq } H_2SO_4$$

0.00483 eq of H_2SO_4 neutralizes 0.00483 eq (and 0.00483 mol) of KOH

$$\frac{0.00483 \text{ mol}}{0.0215 \text{ L}} = 0.22 \text{ M KOH}$$

11.28 The salt of a weak acid and a strong base produces an alkaline solution; the salt of a strong acid and a weak base produces an acidic solution. Of the salts listed, only MgF_2 (c) produces an alkaline solution.

11.29 Only NH_4Cl produces an acidic solution.

11.30 (a) H_2SO_4 (b) HNO_3 (c) $Mg(OH)_2$ (d) $Al(OH)_3$ (e) HF (f) KOH

11.31 In water, HBr dissociates almost completely. Water acts as a base to accept the proton, and a solution of H_3O^+ and Br^- results.

11.32 In water, 0.1 M CH_3COOH dissociates only to the extent of about 1%. Water acts as a base, yielding a solution of CH_3COOH, along with smaller amounts of H_3O^+ and CH_3COO^-.

11.33 In water, KOH dissociates completely to yield K^+ and OH^- ions.

11.34 A monoprotic acid such as HCl has only one proton to give up, whereas a diprotic acid such as H_2SO_4 has two protons to give up.

11.35 Strong acids: (a) $HClO_4$ (e) HI

11.36 Weak bases: (a) NH_3 (c) HPO_4^{2-} (e) CN^-

11.37 $H_3PO_4\ (aq) + H_2O\ (l) \rightleftharpoons H_2PO_4^-\ (aq) + H_3O^+\ (aq)$

$H_2PO_4^-\ (aq) + H_2O\ (l) \rightleftharpoons HPO_4^{2-}\ (aq) + H_3O^+\ (aq)$

$HPO_4^{2-}\ (aq) + H_2O\ (l) \rightleftharpoons PO_4^{3-}\ (aq) + H_3O^+\ (aq)$

11.38 Brønsted-Lowry acids: (a) HCN (d) H_2CO_3 (f) $CH_3NH_3^+$
Brønsted-Lowry bases: (b) $C_2H_3O_2^-$
Neither: (c) $AlCl_3$ (e) Mg^{2+}

11.39 Base and conjugate acid are pairs, as are acid and conjugate base.

(a) $CO_3^{2-}\ (aq) + HCl\ (aq) \rightleftharpoons HCO_3^-\ (aq) + Cl^-\ (aq)$
    base   acid   conjugate acid   conjugate base

(b) $H_3PO_4\ (aq) + NH_3\ (aq) \rightleftharpoons H_2PO_4^-\ (aq) + NH_4^+\ (aq)$
    acid   base   conjugate base   conjugate acid

(c) $NH_4^+\ (aq) + CN^-\ (aq) \rightleftharpoons NH_3\ (aq) + HCN\ (aq)$
    acid   base   conjugate base   conjugate acid

(d) $HBr\ (aq) + OH^-\ (aq) \rightleftharpoons H_2O\ (l) + Br^-\ (aq)$
    acid   base   conjugate acid   conjugate base

(e) $H_2PO_4^-\ (aq) + N_2H_4\ (aq) \rightleftharpoons HPO_4^{2-}\ (aq) + N_2H_5^+\ (aq)$
    acid   base   conjugate base   conjugate acid

11.40 Base   (a) CH_2ClCOO^- (b) C_5H_5N (c) SeO_4^{2-} (d) $(CH_3)_3N$
Conjugate $CH_2ClCOOH$ $C_5H_5NH^+$ $HSeO_4^-$ $(CH_3)_3NH^+$
acid

11.41 Acid   (a) HCN   (b) $(CH_3)_2NH_2^+$ (c) H_3PO_4 (d) $HSeO_3^-$
Conjugate CN^- $(CH_3)_2NH$ $H_2PO_4^-$ SeO_3^{2-}
base

11.42 (a) $HCO_3^-\ (aq) + HCl\ (aq) \longrightarrow H_2O\ (l) + CO_2\ (g) + Cl^-\ (aq)$

$HCO_3^-\ (aq) + NaOH\ (aq) \longrightarrow H_2O\ (l) + Na^+\ (aq) + CO_3^{2-}\ (aq)$

(b) $H_2PO_4^-\ (aq) + HCl\ (aq) \longrightarrow H_3PO_4\ (aq) + Cl^-\ (aq)$

$H_2PO_4^-\ (aq) + NaOH\ (aq) \longrightarrow HPO_4^{2-}\ (aq) + H_2O\ (l) + Na^+\ (aq)$

11.43 The stronger base appears lower in the "Base" column of Table 11.3.
(a) OH^- (b) NO_2^- (c) CH_3O^- (d) CN^- (e) HPO_4^{2-}

11.44 The stronger acid and weaker base are conjugate pairs, as are the stronger base and weaker acid. The reaction to form weaker base and weaker acid is favored.

(a) HCl (*aq*)   + PO_4^{3-} (*aq*) $\rightleftharpoons$ HPO_4^{2-} (*aq*) + Cl^- (*aq*)
stronger acid   stronger base   weaker acid   weaker base

(b) CN^- (*aq*) + HSO_4^- (*aq*) $\rightleftharpoons$ HCN (*aq*) + SO_4^{2-} (*aq*)
stronger base   stronger acid   weaker acid   weaker base

(c) $HClO_4$ (*aq*) + NO_2^- (*aq*) $\rightleftharpoons$ ClO_4^- (*aq*) + HNO_2 (*aq*)
stronger acid   stronger base   weaker base   weaker acid

(d) CH_3O^- (*aq*) + HF (*aq*) $\rightleftharpoons$ CH_3OH (*l*) + F^- (*aq*)
stronger base   stronger acid   weaker acid   weaker base

11.45 2 HCl (*aq*) + $CaCO_3$ (*s*) $\longrightarrow$ H_2O (*l*) + CO_2 (*g*) + $CaCl_2$ (*aq*)

11.46 Citric acid reacts with sodium bicarbonate to release CO_2 bubbles.

$C_6H_5O_7H_3$ (*aq*) + 3 $NaHCO_3$ (*aq*) $\longrightarrow$ $C_6H_5O_7Na_3$ (*aq*) + 3 H_2O (*l*) + 3 CO_2 (*g*)

11.47 (a) LiOH (*aq*) + HNO_3 (*aq*) $\longrightarrow$ H_2O (*l*) + $LiNO_3$ (*aq*)

(b) $BaCO_3$ (*aq*) + 2 HI (*aq*) $\longrightarrow$ H_2O (*l*) + CO_2 (*g*) + BaI_2 (*aq*)

(c) H_3PO_4 (*aq*) + 3 KOH (*aq*) $\longrightarrow$ 3 H_2O (*l*) + K_3PO_4 (*aq*)

(d) $Ca(HCO_3)_2$ (*aq*) + 2 HCl (*aq*) $\longrightarrow$ 2 H_2O (*l*) + 2 CO_2 (*g*) + $CaCl_2$ (*aq*)

(e) $Ba(OH)_2$ (*aq*) + H_2SO_4 (*aq*) $\longrightarrow$ 2 H_2O (*l*) + $BaSO_4$ (*s*)

11.48 (a) HF is slightly stronger   (b) HSO_4^- is a stronger acid
(c) $H_2PO_4^-$ is a stronger acid   (d) CH_3COOH is slightly stronger

11.49 K_w is the product of the concentrations of H_3O^+ and OH^- in any aqueous solution and is numerically equal to 10^{-14} at 25°C.

11.50 When H_3O^+ concentration is expressed as a power of 10, pH is defined as the negative of the exponent of the 10. For example, if $[H_3O^+] = 10^{-3}$ M, then pH = 3 (the negative of -3). In mathematical terms, pH is the negative logarithm of H_3O^+ concentration.

11.51

pH	*Phenolphthalein*
(a) 4.5	colorless
(b) 11.2	red
(c) 7.1	pink

11.52 Urine (pH = 7.9) is weakly basic, since a solution with a pH greater than 7.0 is basic.

11.53 The concentration of HCl in gastric juice is 10^{-2} M.

11.54 $[H_3O^+] = 10^{-pH}$. Since in this problem, $[H_3O^+] = 0.10$ M $= 10^{-1}$ M, the pH = 1.00.

11.55 Since the pH of a 0.10 N HCN solution is lower than 7.0, the solution is acidic. If HCN were a strong acid, the pH of the 0.10 N solution would be 1 (Problem 7.34). Thus, HCN is a weak acid.

11.56 (a) $[H_3O^+] = 1 \times 10^{-4}$ M   (b) $[H_3O^+] = 1 \times 10^{-11}$ M
(c) $[H_3O^+] = 1$ M   (d) $[H_3O^+] = 4.2 \times 10^{-2}$ M
(e) $[H_3O^+] = 1.1 \times 10^{-8}$ M

11.57 (a) $[OH^-] = 1 \times 10^{-10}$ M   (b) $[OH^-] = 1 \times 10^{-3}$ M
(c) $[OH^-] = 1 \times 10^{-14}$ M   (d) $[OH^-] = 2.4 \times 10^{-13}$ M
(e) $[OH^-] = 9.1 \times 10^{-7}$ M

11.58 $[H_3O^+] = 4 \times 10^{-8}$ M

11.59 - 11.60

	$[H_3O^+]$	pH	$[OH^-]$
(a) egg white	2.5×10^{-8} M	7.60	4×10^{-7}
(b) apple cider	5.0×10^{-4} M	3.30	2.0×10^{-11}
(c) ammonia	2.3×10^{-12} M	11.63	4.3×10^{-3}

Ammonia is least acidic and apple cider is most acidic.

11.61 A buffer is composed of a weak acid and its anion. Any added H_3O^+ can react with the anion and be neutralized, and any added OH^- can react with the acid. In either case, the pH of a buffered solution remains nearly constant.

11.62 $CH_3COOH + CH_3COO^- Na^+$ is a better buffer than $HNO_3 + NaNO_3$ because acetic acid is a weak acid and acetate ion is the salt of its anion. Nitric acid, however, is a strong acid, and nitrate ion is nonbasic. Thus, the nitric acid / sodium nitrate mixture can't be an effective buffer and cannot control pH.

11.63 $CH_3COO^- Na^+ (aq) + HNO_3 (aq) \longrightarrow CH_3COOH (aq) + NaNO_3 (aq)$.
The added acid is neutralized by sodium acetate.

$CH_3COOH (aq) + OH^- (aq) \longrightarrow CH_3COO^- (aq) + H_2O (l)$
The added base is neutralized by acetic acid.

11.64 *Acidosis*, which results when blood pH drops below pH 7.35, may be caused by breathing difficulties and by fasting.
Alkalosis, which results when blood pH rises above pH 7.45, may be caused by hyperventilation and by repeated vomiting.

11.65 An equivalent of an acid or base is its formula weight in grams divided by the number of H_3O^+ or OH^- ions it produces.

11.66 The normality of an acid or base solution is a measure of concentration expressed in number of equivalents per liter of solution.

11.67 The number of equivalents is equal to the number of moles divided by the number of H^+ or OH^- ions produced. In this problem, we first find the number of moles of each acid and then divide by the number of H^+ ions available.

$$\text{For } HNO_3 : \quad 0.500 \text{ L} \times \frac{0.50 \text{ mol } H^+}{1 \text{ L}} \times 1\frac{eq}{mol} = 0.25 \text{ eq } H^+$$

$$\text{For } H_3PO_4 : \quad 0.500 \text{ L} \times \frac{0.50 \text{ mol } H^+}{1 \text{ L}} \times 3\frac{eq}{mol} = 0.75 \text{ eq } H^+$$

11.68 Since one equivalent of any base neutralizes one equivalent of any acid, 0.035 equivalents of NaOH neutralize 0.035 equivalents of H_3PO_4.

11.69 Since a 0.005 N solution of any acid has 0.005 equivalents per liter, 25 mL of a 0.005 N KOH solution is needed to neutralize 25 mL of either 0.005 N H_2SO_4 or 0.005 N HCl.

11.70 For HCl, molarity equals normality. Thus, we can use the dilution formula from Chapter 6:

$$M_{orig} \times V_{orig} = M_{final} \times V_{final}$$

$$V_{orig} = \frac{M_{final}}{M_{orig}} \times V_{final} = \frac{0.10 \text{ M}}{12.0 \text{ M}} \times 250 \text{ mL} = 2.1 \text{ mL}$$

Thus, you would have to dilute 2.1 mL of 12.0 M HCl to a final volume of 250 mL in order to make a 0.10 N solution.

11.71 The molarity of an acid solution is equal to normality divided by the number of H^+ ions produced. Thus:

$$\frac{0.10 \text{ N } H_3PO_4}{3} = 0.033 \text{ M } H_3PO_4$$

11.72

$$PV = nRT \text{ or } V = \frac{nRT}{P}; \quad T = 273 \text{ K}; \quad P = 1 \text{ atm}; \quad R = \frac{0.0821 \text{ L atm}}{mol \text{ K}}$$

For HCN, molarity equals normality. Thus:

$$n = 0.250 \text{ L} \times \frac{0.10 \text{ mol}}{1 \text{ L}} = 0.025 \text{ mol HCN}$$

$$V = \frac{0.025 \text{ mol} \times 0.0821 \text{ L atm / mol K} \times 273 \text{ K}}{1 \text{ atm}} = 0.56 \text{ L HCN}$$

11.73 (a) $0.25 \text{ mol } Mg(OH)_2 \times 2 \text{ equiv/mol} = 0.50 \text{ equiv } Mg(OH)_2$

(b) F.W. of $Mg(OH)_2 = 58.3$ amu ;   1 equiv $Mg(OH)_2 = 29.6$ g

$$2.5 \text{ g } Mg(OH)_2 \times \frac{1 \text{ eq}}{29.6 \text{ g}} = 0.084 \text{ eq } Mg(OH)_2$$

(c) F.W. of CH_3COOH = 60.0 amu ;   1 equiv CH_3COOH = 60.0 g

$$15 \text{ g } CH_3COOH \times \frac{1 \text{ eq}}{60 \text{ g}} = 0.25 \text{ eq } CH_3COOH$$

11.74 Normality is equal to molarity times the number of H^+ or OH^- ions produced.
(a) 0.75 M H_2SO_4 x 2 = 1.5 N H_2SO_4
(b) 0.13 M $Ba(OH)_2$ x 2 = 0.26 N $Ba(OH)_2$
(c) 1.4 M HF x 1 = 1.4 N HF

11.75 Molar mass of $Ca(OH)_2$ = 74.1 g; 1 eq $Ca(OH)_2$ = 37.0 g

$$\frac{5.0 \text{ g}}{0.400 \text{ L}} \times \frac{1 \text{ mol}}{74.1 \text{ g}} = 0.17 \text{ M}; \quad 0.17 \frac{\text{mol}}{\text{L}} \times \frac{2 \text{ eq}}{\text{mol}} = 0.34 \frac{\text{eq}}{\text{L}} = 0.34 \text{ N}$$

11.76 Molar mass of $C_6H_5O_7H_3$ = 192 g; 1 eq $C_6H_5O_7H_3$ = 64.0 g

$$\frac{25 \text{ g}}{.750 \text{ L}} \times \frac{1 \text{ mol}}{192 \text{ g}} = 0.17 \text{ M}; \quad 0.17 \frac{\text{mol}}{\text{L}} \times \frac{3 \text{ eq}}{\text{mol}} = 0.51 \frac{\text{eq}}{\text{L}} = 0.51 \text{ N}$$

11.77 Recall that one equivalent of an acid neutralizes one equivalent of base.

Thus, $V_1N_1 = V_2N_2$; V_1 = 25 mL; N_1 = 0.34 N; N_2 = 0.51 N

$$V_2 = \frac{V_1N_1}{N_2} = \frac{25 \text{ mL} \times 0.34 \text{ N}}{0.51 \text{ N}} = 17 \text{ mL of } 0.51 \text{ N citric acid}$$

11.78 $2 \text{ KOH } (aq) + H_2SO_4 (aq) \longrightarrow 2 H_2O (l) + K_2SO_4 (aq)$

$[H_2SO_4]$ = 0.0250 M = 0.0500 N

$V_1N_1 = V_2N_2$; V_1 = 15.0 mL; N_1 = 0.0500 N; V_2 = 10.0 mL

$$\frac{V_1N_1}{V_2} = N_2; \quad \frac{15.0 \text{ mL} \times 0.0500 \text{ N}}{10.0 \text{ mL}} = 0.075 \text{ N} = 0.075 \text{ M KOH}$$

11.79 $V_1N_1 = V_2N_2$; V_1 = 35 mL; N_1 = 0.10 N; V_2 = 21.5 mL

$$\frac{V_1N_1}{V_2} = N_2; \quad \frac{35 \text{ mL} \times 0.10 \text{ N}}{21.5 \text{ mL}} = 0.16 \text{ N}$$

11.80 (a) $NaAl(OH)_2CO_3 (aq) + 4 HCl (aq) \longrightarrow$
$CO_2 (aq) + 3 H_2O (l) + NaCl (aq) + AlCl_3 (aq)$

(b) Molar mass of $NaAl(OH)_2CO_3 (aq)$ = 144 g

$$\frac{0.0955 \text{ mol HCl}}{1 \text{ L}} \times 0.0150 \text{ L} = 0.00143 \text{ mol HCl}$$

$$0.00143 \text{ mol HCl} \times \frac{1 \text{ mol antacid}}{4 \text{ mol HCl}} \times \frac{144 \text{ g}}{1 \text{ mol antacid}} = 0.0515 \text{ g} = 51.5 \text{ mg}$$

11.81   pH of acid rain = 5.6; $[H_3O^+] = 2 \times 10^{-6}$

11.82   (a) $[H_3O^+] = .03$ M

(b) $25 \text{ L} \times \dfrac{.03 \text{ mol}}{1 \text{ L}} \times \dfrac{63 \text{ g}}{1 \text{ mol}} = 47$ g, or approximately 50 g HNO_3

11.83   Gastric juice is the most acidic body fluid, and pancreatic fluid is the least acidic.

11.84 $2 \text{ NaOH } (aq) + H_2SO_4 \, (aq) \longrightarrow 2 \text{ H}_2O \, (l) + Na_2SO_4 \, (aq)$

$V_1N_1 = V_2N_2$; $V_1 = 40.0$ mL; $N_1 = 2 \times 0.10$ M $H_2SO_4 = 0.20$ N; $N_2 = 0.50$ N

$V_2 = \dfrac{N_1V_1}{N_2} = \dfrac{0.20 \text{ N} \times 40.0 \text{ mL}}{0.50 \text{ N}} = 16$ mL

11.85

(a) $0.020 \text{ L} \times \dfrac{0.015 \text{ eq } HNO_3}{1 \text{ L}} = 0.00030 \text{ eq} = 0.30 \text{ meq } HNO_3$

(b) $0.170 \text{ L} \times \dfrac{0.025 \text{ eq } H_2SO_4}{1 \text{ L}} = 0.0042 \text{ eq} = 4.2 \text{ meq } H_2SO_4$

11.86 $2 \text{ HCl } (aq) + Ca(OH)_2 \, (aq) \longrightarrow 2 \text{ H}_2O \, (l) + CaCl_2 \, (aq)$

One equivalent of HCl reacts with one equivalent of $Ca(OH)_2$.

$\text{Equiv HCl} = \dfrac{0.15 \text{ eq HCl}}{1 \text{ L}} \times 140 \text{ mL} \times \dfrac{1 \text{ L}}{1000 \text{ mL}} = 0.021 \text{ eq HCl}$

$= 0.021 \text{ eq } Ca(OH)_2$

$\dfrac{0.021 \text{ eq } Ca(OH)_2}{0.030 \text{ L}} = 0.70 \text{ N } Ca(OH)_2 = 0.35 \text{ M } Ca(OH)_2$

11.87   The concentration of H_3O^+ and OH^- ions is too low for pure water to conduct electricity.

11.88   Both 50 mL of a 0.20 N HCl solution and 50 mL of a 0.20 acetic acid solution contain the same number of moles of acid - 0.010 moles. Since HCl is a strong acid, it is almost completely dissociated in water, and the H_3O^+ concentration approaches 0.20 N. Acetic acid, however, is a weak acid that is only slightly dissociated, and the H_3O^+ concentration is much lower - around 0.002 N. Since the HCl solution has a higher H_3O^+ concentration, it has a lower pH.

11.89   If aspirin were a strong acid, the H_3O^+ concentration of a 0.010 N solution would be nearly 0.010 N, or 10^{-2} N, and the pH of the solution would be around 2. Since the observed pH is 3.3, aspirin must be a weak acid.

11.90 Both (a), NaF and HF, and (c), NH_4Cl and NH_3 are buffer systems. The NaF / HF system is a solution of a weak acid and the salt of its anion. The NH_4Cl / NH_3 system is a solution of a weak base and the salt of its cation. Neither (b) nor (d) are buffer systems since $HClO_4$ and HBr are both strong acids.

11.91 (a) $NH_4^+ (aq) + OH^- (aq) \longrightarrow NH_3 (g) + H_2O (l)$
acid   base   conjugate base   conjugate acid

(b) $PV = nRT$; $P = 755$ mm Hg; $V = 2.86$ L; $T = 333$ K; $R = \dfrac{62.3 \text{ mm Hg L}}{\text{mol K}}$

$$\frac{PV}{RT} = n = \frac{755 \text{ mm} \times 2.86 \text{ L}}{62.3 \text{ mm Hg L / mol K} \times 333 \text{ K}} = 0.104 \text{ mol } NH_3$$

$$.0104 \text{ mol} \times \frac{53.5 \text{ g}}{1 \text{ mol}} = 5.56 \text{ g } NH_4Cl$$

11.92 $M_{orig}V_{orig} = M_{final}V_{final}$; $V_{orig} = 0.025$ L; $M_{orig} = 0.40$ M; $V_{final} = 2.00$ L

$$M_{final} = \frac{M_{orig}V_{orig}}{V_{final}} = \frac{0.40 \text{ M} \times 0.025 \text{ L}}{2.00 \text{ L}} = 0.005 \text{ M} = 5 \times 10^{-3} \text{ M } OH^-$$

$$[H_3O^+] = \frac{10^{-14}}{[OH^-]} = \frac{10^{-14}}{5 \times 10^{-3}} = 2 \times 10^{-12}; \text{ pH} = 11.70$$

The Chapter in Brief

Acids and Bases (Sections 11.1–11.3) An acid is a substance that can donate a proton, and a base is a substance that can accept a proton. When an acid is dissolved in water, a water molecule accepts a proton to form a hydronium ion, H_3O^+. The reaction of an acid with a base yields water and a salt, and is called a neutralization reaction. When an acid reacts with carbonate or bicarbonate ion, carbon dioxide is also formed.

Acidity (Sections 11.7–11.13) Some acids are completely dissociated in water and are called strong acids. Others are only slightly dissociated and are called weak acids. The anion of a strong acid is a weak base, and the anion of a weak acid is a strong base. These pairs are known as conjugate acid-base pairs; acid-base reactions favor the formation of the weaker acid and the weaker base. The degree of dissociation of a weak acid is measured by K_a, the acid dissociation constant. Water dissociates to a slight degee into H_3O^+ and OH^- ions; the product of $[H_3O^+]$ and $[OH^-]$ is k_w, whose value is 10^{-14}. The pH of a solution is a measure of the solution's acidity and can be measured either by a pH meter or by use of an indicator dye.

Buffers, Equivalents, Normality (Sections 11.14–11.17) A buffer is a solution of a weak acid and the anion of that acid, and serves to stabilize a solution's pH. The bicarbonate and phosphate systems are two important buffer systems in the body. An equivalent of an acid or base is equal to the formula weight in grams divided by the number of H^+ or OH^- ions produced. Normality is the number of acid or base equivalents per liter of solution. Titration is a technique for measuring the acid (or base) concentration of a solution by reacting a known amount of the solution with a known quantity of base (or acid) until an endpoint is reached.

Self-Test for Chapter 11

Complete the following sentences:

1. One _____ of an acid reacts with one _____ of a base.

2. Phenolphthalein turns _____ in basic solution.

3. H_2CO_3 is a _____ acid.

4. The anion of a weak acid is a _____ base.

5. _____ is the splitting apart of an acid into a proton and an anion.

6. An Arrhenius base yields _____ when dissolved in water.

7. _____ is the reaction of an acid with a base.

8. _____ is the measure of a solution's acidity.

9. To completely neutralize 10 mL of 1 M H_3PO_4, you need _____ mL of 1 M NaOH.

10. CH_3COOH and CH_3COO^- are known as a _____ acid-base pair.

11. The buffer system of blood is the _____ / _____ system.

12. Substances that can act as either acids or bases are _____.

Tell whether the following statements are true or false:

1. 30 mL of 0.10 M H_2SO_4 is neutralized by 30 mL of 0.10 M NaOH.

2. A change of one pH unit is a tenfold change in $[H_3O^+]$.

3. H_2SO_4 and HSO_4^- is a good buffer system.

4. All bases are negatively charged.

5. Bicarbonate ion neutralizes more acid than carbonate ion.

6. If the pH of a solution is 7.0, $[OH^-]$ is 10^{-7}.

7. Water can act as both an acid and a base.

8. According to the Brønsted definition, an acid is a substance that dissolves in water to give H_3O^+ ions.

9. Ammonia reacts with an acid to yield ammonium hydroxide.

10. Whether an acid or a base is strong or weak depends on its percent dissociation in water.

11. The reaction $H_2O + H_2PO_4^- \longrightarrow H_3O^+ + HPO_4^{2-}$ proceeds in the direction written.

12. One equivalent of $Ca(OH)_2$ equals 37 g.

Match the entries on the left with their partners on the right:

1. Strong acid   (a) $[H_3O^+]\,[OH^-]$

2. 1 M HCl   (b) Cl^-

3. $[H_3O^+] = 10^{-8}$ (c) pH = 6

4. Alkalosis   (d) HCl

5. K_w (e) 1 N acid

6. Weak base   (f) CH_3COOH

7. Strong base   (g) $[OH^-] = 10^{-6}$

8. Salt   (h) Blood pH lower than 7.35

9. $[H_3O^+] = 10^{-6}$ (i) CH_3COO^-

10. Weak acid   (j) Na_2SO_4

11. 1 M H_3PO_4 (k) 3 N acid

12. Acidosis   (l) Blood pH higher than 7.35

Chapter 12 – Introduction to Organic Chemistry: Alkanes

12.1

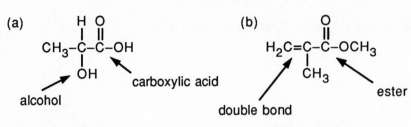

(a)

$CH_3-\overset{\overset{\displaystyle H}{|}}{C}-\overset{\overset{\displaystyle O}{\|}}{C}-OH$

$\overset{|}{OH}$ ← carboxylic acid

↗ alcohol

Lactic acid

(b)

$H_2C=\overset{}{C}-\overset{\overset{\displaystyle O}{\|}}{C}-OCH_3$

$\overset{|}{CH_3}$

double bond ↗   ↖ ester

Methyl methacrylate

12.2

(a)

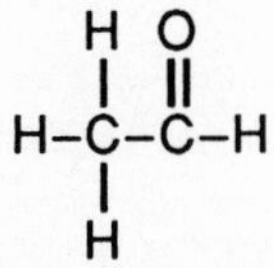

$H-\overset{\overset{\displaystyle H}{|}}{\underset{\underset{\displaystyle H}{|}}{C}}-\overset{\overset{\displaystyle O}{\|}}{C}-H$

An aldehyde

(b)

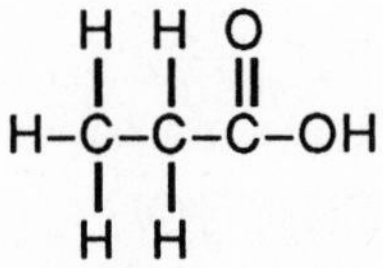

$H-\overset{\overset{\displaystyle H}{|}}{\underset{\underset{\displaystyle H}{|}}{C}}-\overset{\overset{\displaystyle H}{|}}{\underset{\underset{\displaystyle H}{|}}{C}}-\overset{\overset{\displaystyle O}{\|}}{C}-OH$

A carboxylic acid

12.3

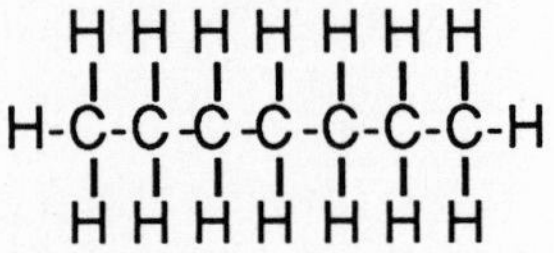

$H-\overset{\overset{\displaystyle H}{|}}{\underset{\underset{\displaystyle H}{|}}{C}}-\overset{\overset{\displaystyle H}{|}}{\underset{\underset{\displaystyle H}{|}}{C}}-\overset{\overset{\displaystyle H}{|}}{\underset{\underset{\displaystyle H}{|}}{C}}-\overset{\overset{\displaystyle H}{|}}{\underset{\underset{\displaystyle H}{|}}{C}}-\overset{\overset{\displaystyle H}{|}}{\underset{\underset{\displaystyle H}{|}}{C}}-\overset{\overset{\displaystyle H}{|}}{\underset{\underset{\displaystyle H}{|}}{C}}-\overset{\overset{\displaystyle H}{|}}{\underset{\underset{\displaystyle H}{|}}{C}}-H$ C_7H_{16} - Heptane

12.4   There are eight branched-chain heptanes:

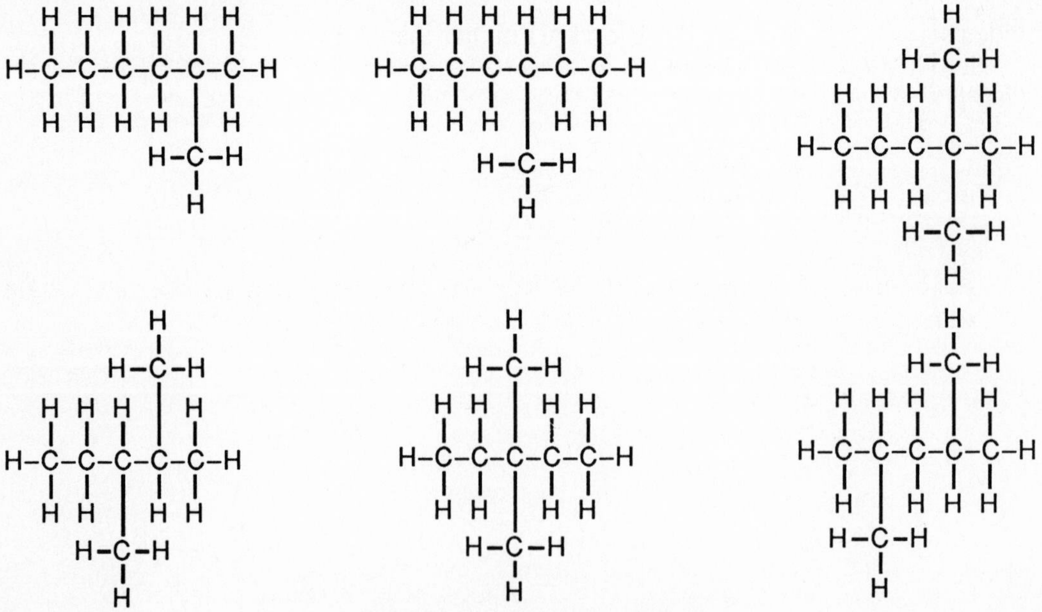

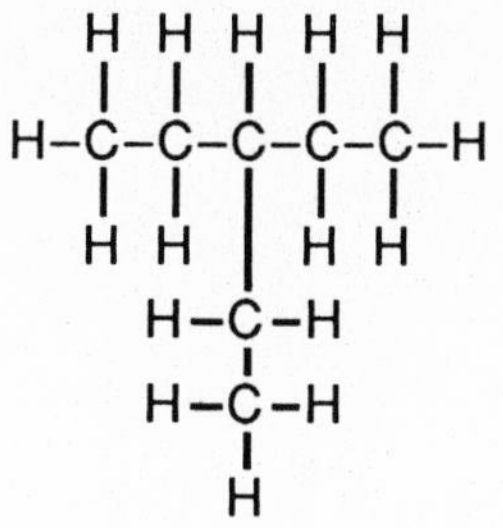

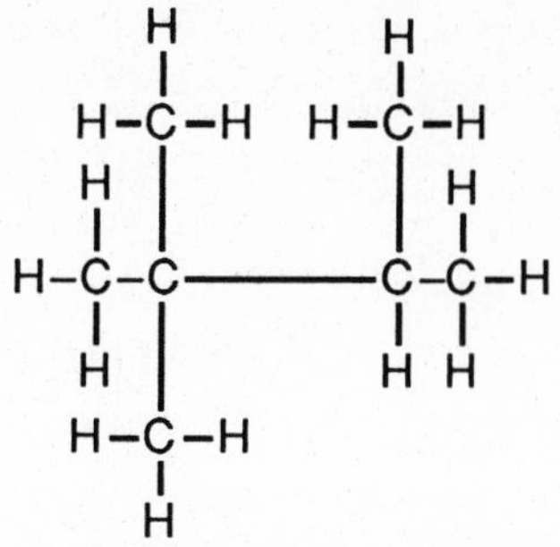

$$H-\overset{\overset{\displaystyle H}{|}}{C}-\overset{\overset{\displaystyle H}{|}}{\underset{\underset{\displaystyle H}{|}}{C}}-\overset{\overset{\displaystyle H}{|}}{\underset{\underset{\displaystyle H-\overset{\overset{\displaystyle H}{|}}{\underset{\underset{\displaystyle H-\overset{\overset{\displaystyle H}{|}}{\underset{\underset{\displaystyle H}{|}}{C}}}{|}}{C}}}{|}}{C}}-\overset{\overset{\displaystyle H}{|}}{\underset{\underset{\displaystyle H}{|}}{C}}-\overset{\overset{\displaystyle H}{|}}{\underset{\underset{\displaystyle H}{|}}{C}}-H$$

12.5

(a)   (b)   (c)

$CH_3CH_2CH_2CH_2CH_3$ $CH_3\overset{\overset{\displaystyle CH_3}{|}}{C}HCH_2CH_3$ $CH_3-\overset{\overset{\displaystyle CH_3}{|}}{\underset{\underset{\displaystyle CH_3}{|}}{C}}-CH_3$

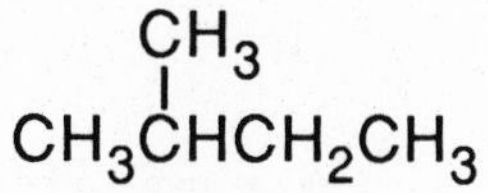

Pentane   2-Methylbutane

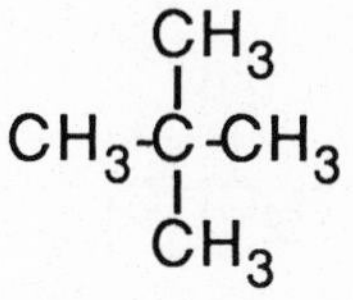

2,2-Dimethylpropane

12.6   All three structures have the same molecular formula (C_7H_{16}). Structures (a) and (c) are identical.

12.7   To solve this problem in a systematic way, use the following method:

(a) Draw the isomer of C_6H_{14} having no branches:

$CH_3CH_2CH_2CH_2CH_2CH_3$

(b) Draw the C_5H_{12} isomer having no branches, and replace one of the -CH_2- hydrogens with a -CH_3. There are two different isomers:

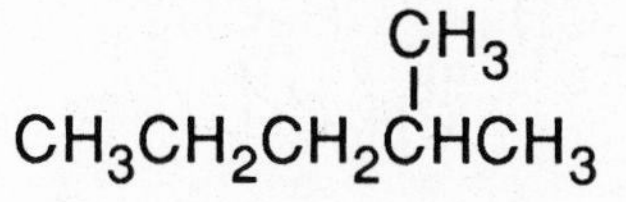

$CH_3CH_2CH_2\overset{\overset{\displaystyle CH_3}{|}}{C}HCH_3$ and $CH_3CH_2\overset{\overset{\displaystyle CH_3}{|}}{C}HCH_2CH_3$

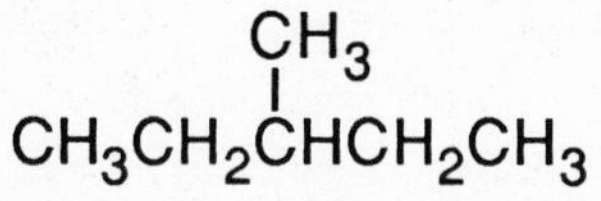

(c) Draw the C_4H_{10} isomer having no branches, and replace two of the -CH_2- hydrogens with -CH_3 groups. There are two different isomers:

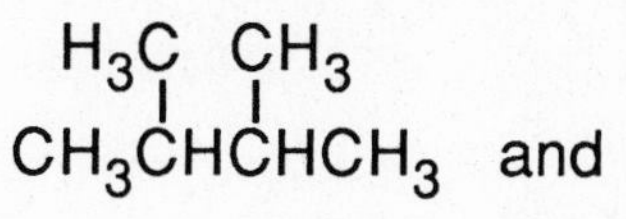

$CH_3\overset{\overset{\displaystyle H_3C}{|}}{C}H\overset{\overset{\displaystyle CH_3}{|}}{C}HCH_3$ and $CH_3CH_2-\overset{\overset{\displaystyle CH_3}{|}}{\underset{\underset{\displaystyle CH_3}{|}}{C}}-CH_3$

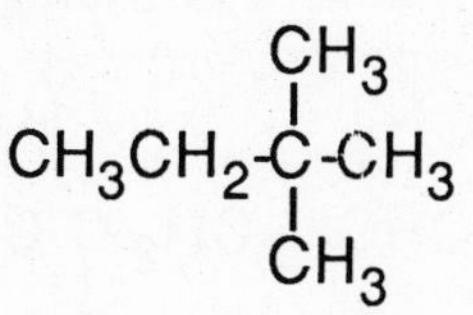

12.9

(a)

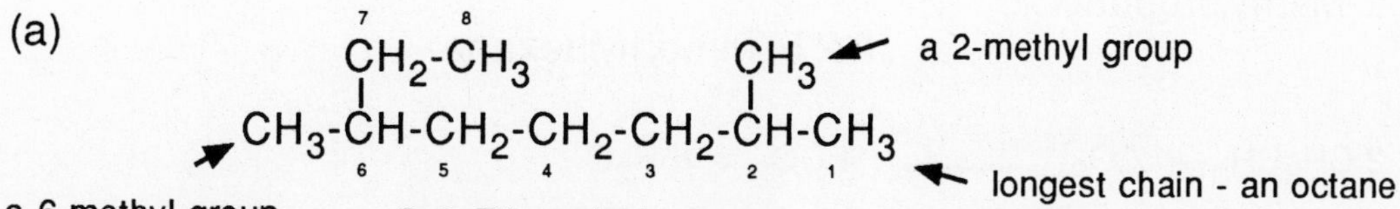

$\overset{7}{C}H_2-\overset{8}{C}H_3$ CH_3 ← a 2-methyl group

↗$CH_3-\overset{|}{C}H-CH_2-CH_2-CH_2-\overset{|}{C}H-CH_3$

        6   5   4   3   2   1   ← longest chain - an octane

a 6-methyl group   2,6-Dimethyloctane

(b)

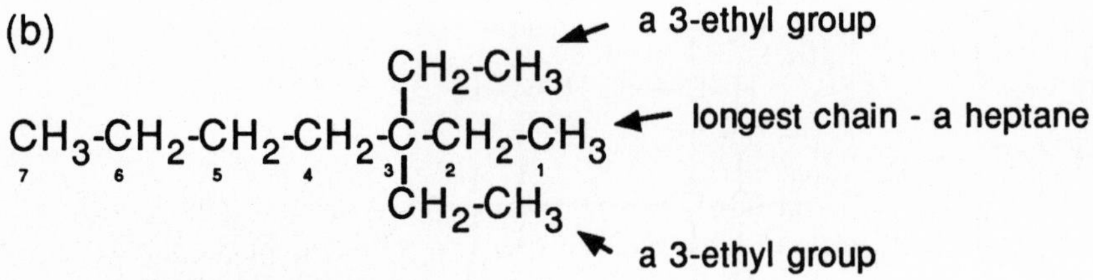

a 3-ethyl group

$$CH_2\text{-}CH_3$$

$$CH_3\text{-}CH_2\text{-}CH_2\text{-}CH_2\text{-}\underset{3}{C}\text{-}\underset{2}{CH_2}\text{-}\underset{1}{CH_3}$$
$$\quad\;\; 7 \quad\;\; 6 \quad\;\; 5 \quad\;\; 4$$

longest chain - a heptane

$$CH_2\text{-}CH_3$$

a 3-ethyl group

3,3-Diethylheptane

12.10 To answer this problem, draw the straight-chain hydrocarbon corresponding to the parent name, and replace -H's with the groups indicated.

(a)

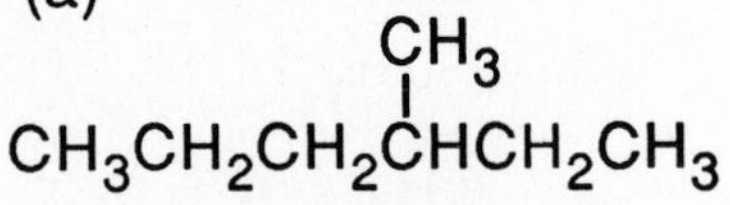

$$CH_3$$
$$CH_3CH_2CH_2CHCH_2CH_3$$

3-Methylhexane

(b)

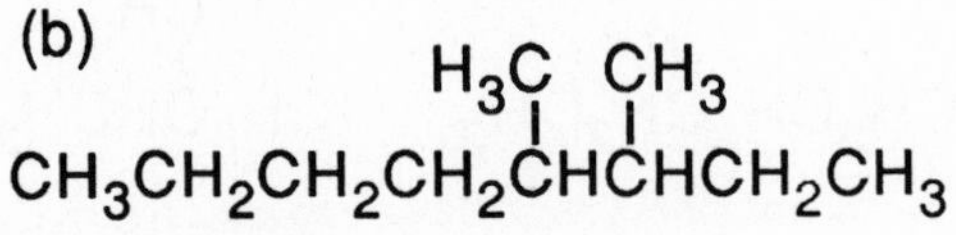

$$H_3C \quad CH_3$$
$$CH_3CH_2CH_2CH_2CHCHCH_2CH_3$$

3,4-Dimethyloctane

(c)

$$CH_3 \qquad CH_3$$
$$CH_3CHCH_2\text{-}C\text{-}CH_3$$
$$CH_3$$

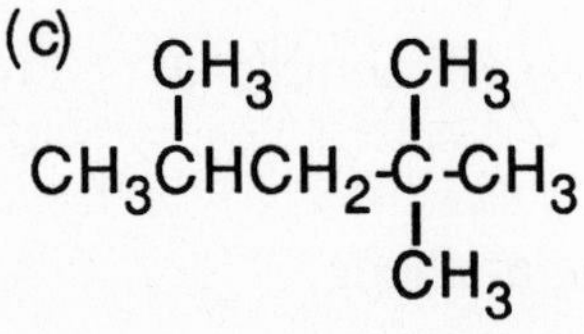

2,2,4-Trimethylpentane

12.11

(a)

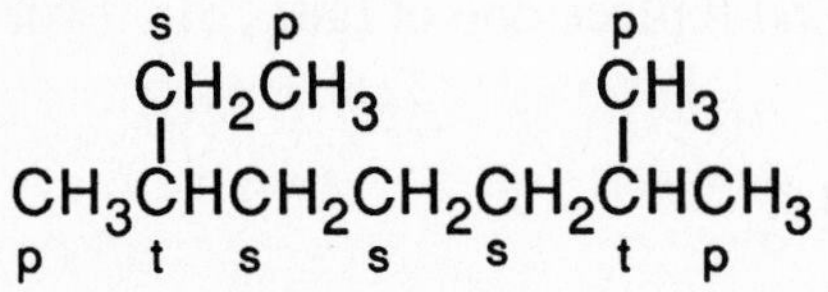

$$\underset{s}{CH_2}\underset{p}{CH_3} \qquad\qquad \underset{p}{CH_3}$$
$$CH_3CHCH_2CH_2CH_2CHCH_3$$
$$\;\; p \quad t \quad s \quad\; s \quad\; s \quad t \quad p$$

(b)

$$\underset{s}{CH_2}\underset{p}{CH_3}$$
$$CH_3CH_2CH_2CH_2\text{-}C\text{-}CH_2CH_3$$
$$\;\; p \quad\; s \quad\; s \quad\; s \quad\underset{q}{|}\;\underset{s}{}\;\;\underset{p}{}$$
$$CH_2CH_3$$
$$\;\; s \quad\; p$$

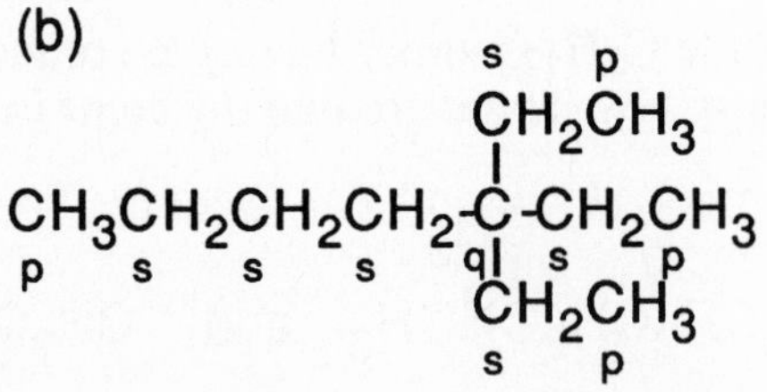

Where p = primary,   s = secondary,   t = tertiary,   q = quaternary

12.12 There are many answers to this question.   For example:

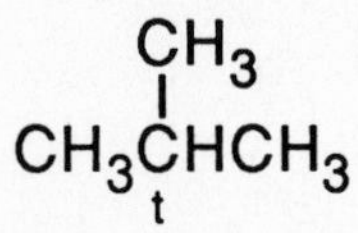

$$CH_3$$
$$CH_3\underset{t}{C}HCH_3$$

2-Methylpropane

$$CH_3 \qquad\qquad CH_3$$
$$CH_3\underset{t}{C}HCH_2CH_2\text{-}\underset{q}{C}\text{-}CH_3$$
$$CH_3$$

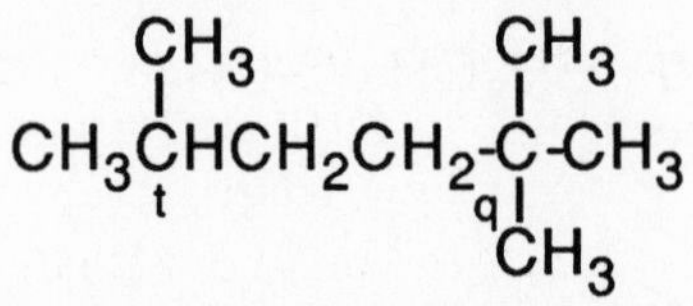

2,2,5-Trimethylhexane

12.13

$$2\,CH_3CH_3 + 7\,O_2 \longrightarrow 4\,CO_2 + 6\,H_2O$$

12.14

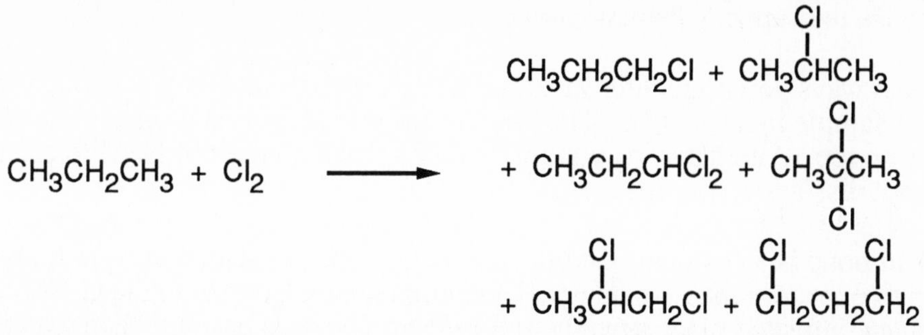

$$CH_3CH_2CH_3 + Cl_2 \longrightarrow$$

$$CH_3CH_2CH_2Cl + CH_3\overset{\underset{|}{Cl}}{C}HCH_3$$

$$+ CH_3CH_2CHCl_2 + CH_3\overset{\underset{|}{Cl}}{\underset{|}{C}}CH_3$$

$$+ CH_3\overset{\underset{|}{Cl}}{C}HCH_2Cl + \overset{\underset{|}{Cl}}{C}H_2CH_2\overset{\underset{|}{Cl}}{C}H_2$$

Six different mono- and di-substitution products can be formed from the reaction of propane with chlorine.

12.15

(a)

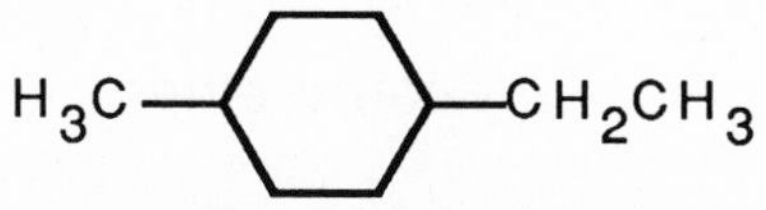

$$H_3C-\langle\ ring\ \rangle-CH_2CH_3$$

1-Ethyl-4-methylcyclohexane

The parent ring is cyclohexane The two substituents are an ethyl group and a methyl group. The ethyl group receives the smaller number because it has alphabetical priority.

(b)

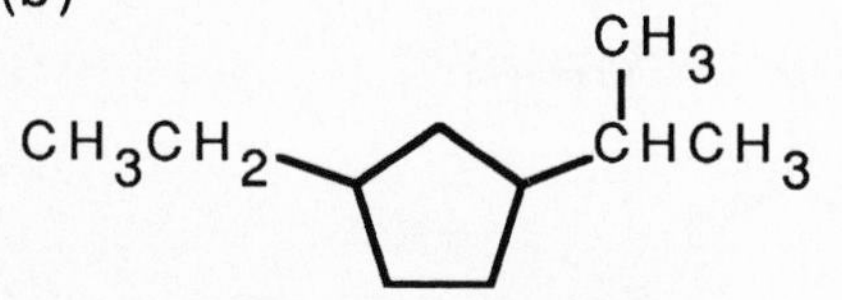

$$CH_3CH_2-\langle\ ring\ \rangle-\overset{CH_3}{\underset{|}{C}}HCH_3$$

1-Ethyl-3-isopropylcyclopentane

The parent ring is cyclopentane. The two substituents are an ethyl group and an isopropyl group. The ethyl group receives the smaller number because it has alphabetical priority.

12.16

(a)

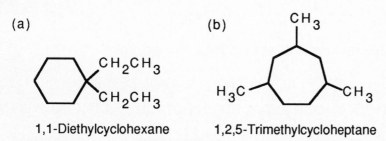

$$CH_2CH_3$$
$$CH_2CH_3$$

1,1-Diethylcyclohexane

(b)

$$CH_3$$
$$H_3C \quad CH_3$$

1,2,5-Trimethylcycloheptane

12.17 Carbon is unique in that it can form four strong bonds to other elements and to other carbon atoms, making possible a great many different compounds.

12.18 Functional groups are groups of atoms that have a characteristic chemical behavior. They are important because most of the chemistry of organic compounds is determined by functional groups. The reactivity of a functional group is similar in all compounds in which it occurs.

12.19 Organic compounds are nonpolar and do not dissolve in water. They do not conduct electricity because they are covalent, not ionic.

12.20 There are several ways you might tell water and hexane apart. One way is to put a small amount of each sample in a test tube. The two liquids do not mix, and the less dense hexane will lie on top. Alternatively, you might add a small amount of NaCl to each liquid. The salt does not dissolve in hexane.

12.21 A polar covalent bond is a covalent bond in which electrons are shared unequally, being more attracted to one atom than the other. For example, the electrons in the C-Br bond of bromomethane are attracted more strongly to the electronegative bromine than to carbon.

12.22 There are many possible answers to this question. For example:

(a)   (b)   (c)   (d)

CH_3CH_2OH CH_3NH_2 $CH_3-\overset{\overset{\displaystyle O}{\|}}{C}-OH$ $CH_3CH_2-O-CH_2CH_3$

Ethanol   Methylamine   Acetic acid   Diethyl ether

12.23

(a)   alcohol

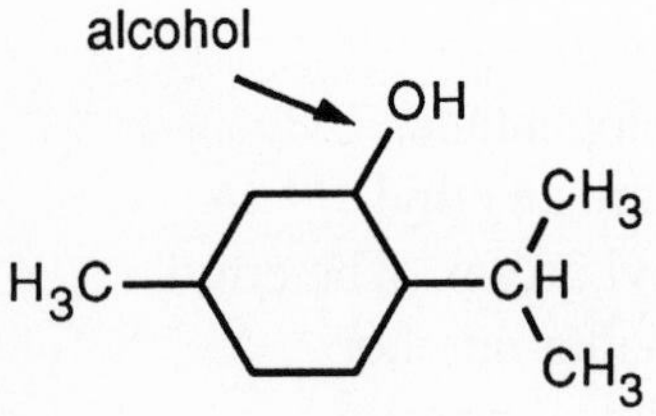

Menthol

(b)

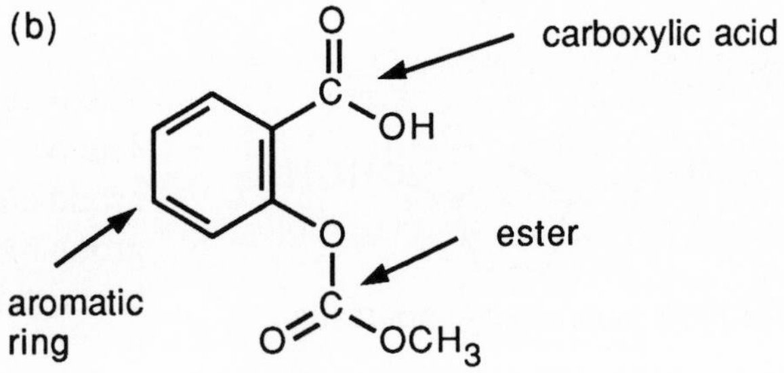

Aspirin

12.24 There are several possible answers to these questions. For example:

(a) $CH_3CH_2CH_2\overset{\overset{\displaystyle O}{\|}}{C}CH_3$ (b) $CH_3CH_2CH_2\overset{\overset{\displaystyle O}{\|}}{C}-OCH_2CH_3$ (c) $H_2NCH_2\overset{\overset{\displaystyle O}{\|}}{C}-OH$ (d) $CH_3CH_2CH_2\overset{\overset{\displaystyle O}{\|}}{C}-NH_2$

A ketone   An ester   An amine-acid   An amide

12.25

(a)

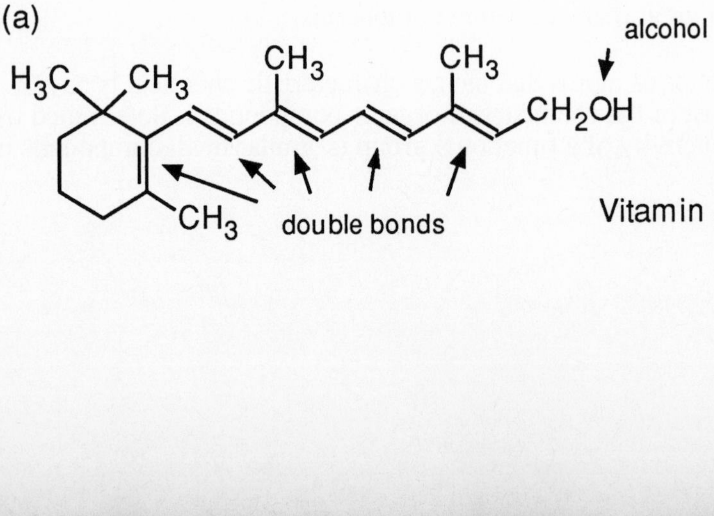

Vitamin A

(b)

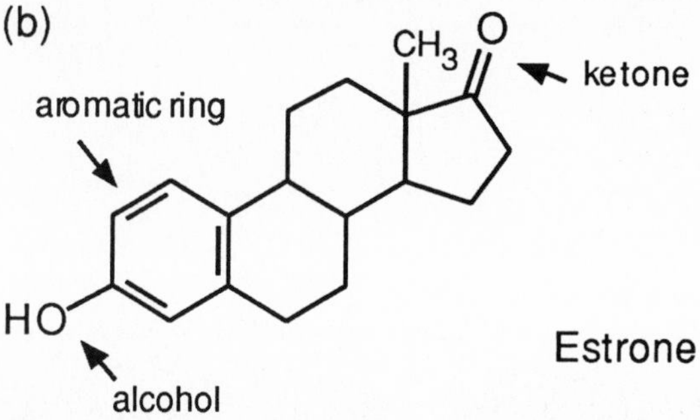

Estrone

12.26 In a straight-chain alkane, all carbons are connected in a row and it is possible to draw a path connecting them without retracing or lifting your pen from the paper. A branched-chain alkane has one or more carbon branches, and it is not possible to draw a path connecting all carbons without either retracing your path or lifting your pen from the paper.

12.27 In order for two compounds to be isomers, they must have the same molecular formula but different structures.

12.28 Compounds with the formulas C_5H_{10} and C_4H_{10} are not isomers because they do not have the same molecular formulas.

12.29 A primary carbon is bonded to one other carbon; a secondary carbon is bonded to two other carbons; a tertiary carbon is bonded to three other carbons; and a quaternary carbon is bonded to four other carbons.

12.30 A compound can't have a quintary carbon because carbon forms only four bonds, not five.

12.31 There are many possible answers to this question. For example:

(a)

$$\begin{array}{cc} H_3C & CH_3 \\ | & | \\ CH_3CHCHCH_3 \end{array}$$

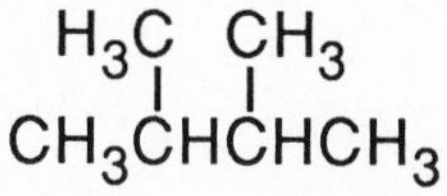

2,3-Dimethylbutane

(b)

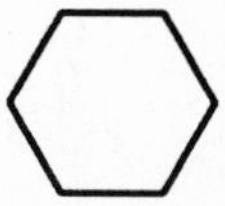

Cyclohexane

12.32

$$CH_3CH_2CH_2OH \qquad \overset{OH}{\underset{|}{CH_3CHCH_3}} \qquad CH_3CH_2\text{-}O\text{-}CH_3$$

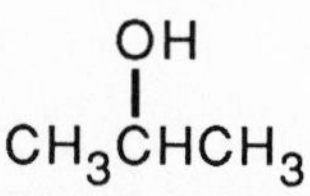

12.33 There are several possible answers to this question. For example:

(a) $CH_3CH_2NH_2$

(b) □ or $CH_3CH=CHCH_3$

(c) $CH_3\overset{\overset{\displaystyle O}{\|}}{C}\text{-}H$

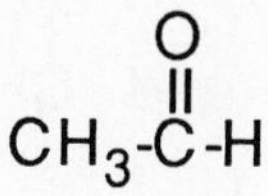

(d) $H\text{-}\overset{\overset{\displaystyle O}{\|}}{C}\text{-}OH$

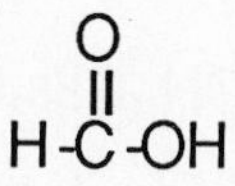

12.34 Since carbon forms only four bonds, the largest number of hydrogens that can be bonded to three carbons is eight - C_3H_8.

$$\begin{array}{ccc} H & H & H \\ | & | & | \\ H-C-C-C-H \\ | & | & | \\ H & H & H \end{array} \qquad C_3H_8$$

12.35

(a)

$CH_3CH_2CH_2CH_2OH$ $CH_3CH_2\overset{\displaystyle OH}{\overset{|}{C}}HCH_3$ $CH_3\overset{\displaystyle CH_3}{\overset{|}{C}}HCH_2OH$ $CH_3\overset{\displaystyle CH_3}{\underset{\displaystyle CH_3}{\overset{|}{\underset{|}{C}}}}-OH$

(b)

$CH_3CH_2CH_2NH_2$ $CH_3\overset{\displaystyle NH_2}{\overset{|}{C}}HCH_3$ $CH_3CH_2-\overset{\displaystyle H}{\overset{|}{N}}-CH_3$ $CH_3-\overset{\displaystyle CH_3}{\overset{|}{N}}-CH_3$

(c)

$CH_3CH_2CH_2\overset{\displaystyle O}{\overset{\|}{C}}CH_3$ $CH_3CH_2\overset{\displaystyle O}{\overset{\|}{C}}CH_2CH_2$ $CH_3\overset{\displaystyle O}{\overset{\|}{\underset{\displaystyle CH_3}{\underset{|}{C}H}}}CCH_3$

(d)

$CH_3CH_2CH_2CH_2\overset{\displaystyle O}{\overset{\|}{C}}-H$ $CH_3CH_2\overset{\displaystyle O}{\underset{\displaystyle CH_3}{\overset{\|}{\underset{|}{C}H}}}C-H$ $CH_3\overset{\displaystyle CH_3}{\overset{|}{C}}HCH_2\overset{\displaystyle O}{\overset{\|}{C}}-H$ $CH_3-\overset{\displaystyle H_3C}{\underset{\displaystyle H_3C}{\overset{|}{\underset{|}{C}}}}\overset{\displaystyle O}{\overset{\|}{C}}-H$

(e)

$CH_3CH_2\overset{\displaystyle O}{\overset{\|}{C}}OCH_3$ $CH_3\overset{\displaystyle O}{\overset{\|}{C}}OCH_2CH_3$ $H\overset{\displaystyle O}{\overset{\|}{C}}OCH_2CH_2CH_3$ $H\overset{\displaystyle O}{\overset{\|}{C}}O\overset{\displaystyle CH_3}{\overset{|}{C}}HCH_3$

(f)

$CH_3CH_2CH_2\overset{\displaystyle O}{\overset{\|}{C}}OH$ $CH_3\overset{\displaystyle CH_3}{\overset{|}{C}}H-\overset{\displaystyle O}{\overset{\|}{C}}OH$

In parts (c) and (d), remember that the C=O group of an aldehyde occurs only at the end of a chain, and the C=O group of a ketone must occur in the middle.

12.36

(a)

$CH_3CH_2CH_3$ and $\overset{\displaystyle CH_3}{\overset{|}{C}}H_2CH_3$ are identical

(b)

$CH_3-\overset{\displaystyle H}{\overset{|}{N}}-CH_3$ and $CH_3CH_2-\overset{\displaystyle H}{\overset{|}{N}}-H$ are isomers

(c)

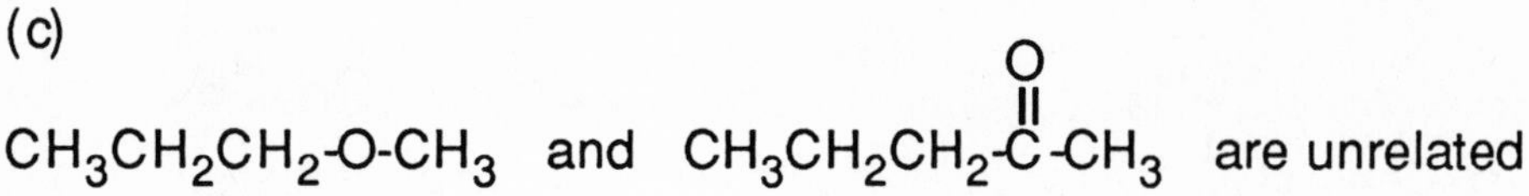

CH$_3$CH$_2$CH$_2$-O-CH$_3$ and CH$_3$CH$_2$CH$_2$-$\overset{\overset{\displaystyle O}{\|}}{C}$-CH$_3$ are unrelated

(d)

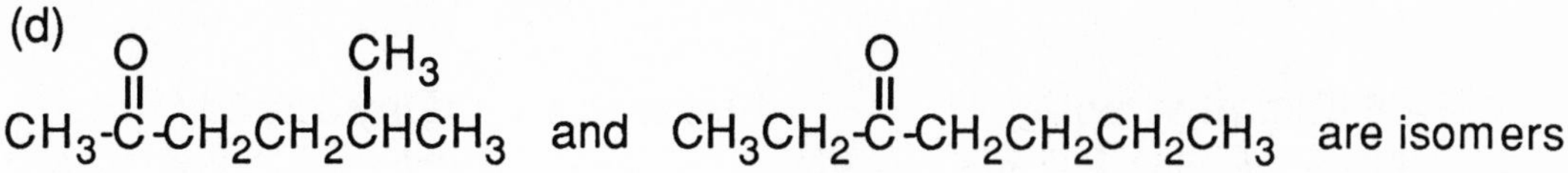

CH$_3$-$\overset{\overset{\displaystyle O}{\|}}{C}$-CH$_2CH_2$$\overset{\overset{\displaystyle CH_3}{|}}{C}HCH_3$ and CH$_3$CH$_2$-$\overset{\overset{\displaystyle O}{\|}}{C}$-CH$_2CH_2CH_2CH_3$ are isomers

(e)

CH$_3$CH=CHCH$_2$CH$_2$-OH and CH$_3$CH$_2$$\overset{\overset{\displaystyle H_3C}{|}}{C}$H-$\overset{\overset{\displaystyle O}{\|}}{C}$-H are isomers

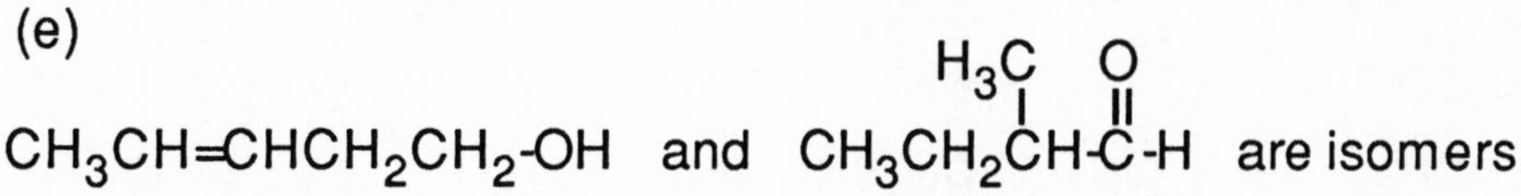

12.37 All three structures have a carbon atom with five bonds - not allowed!

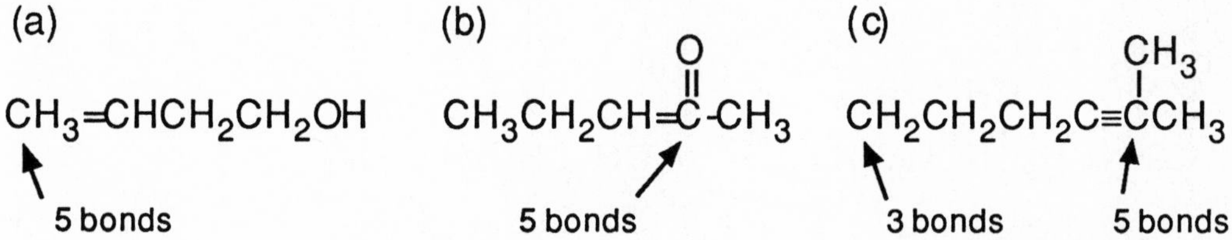

(a)

CH$_3$=CHCH$_2$CH$_2$OH

5 bonds

(b)

CH$_3$CH$_2$CH=$\overset{\overset{\displaystyle O}{\|}}{C}$-CH$_3$

5 bonds

(c)

CH$_2$CH$_2$CH$_2$C≡$\overset{\overset{\displaystyle CH_3}{|}}{C}CH_3$

3 bonds   5 bonds

12.38

(a)

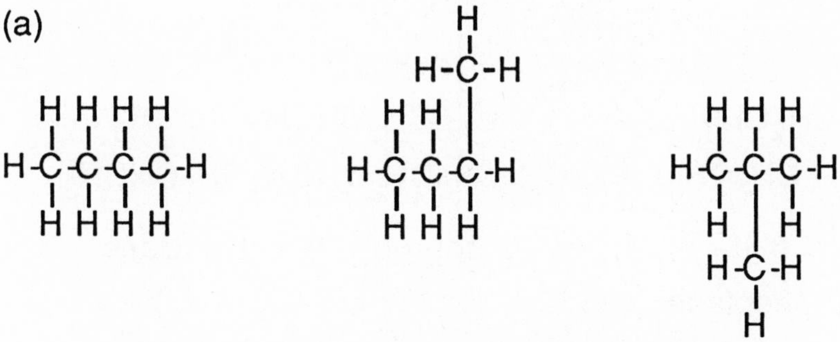

The first two are identical; the third is an isomer.

(b)

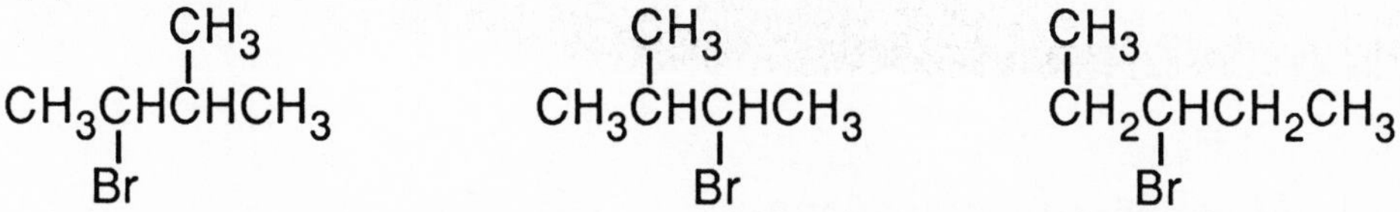

$\overset{\overset{\displaystyle CH_3}{|}}{CH_3CHCHCH_3}$
  $|$
  Br

$\overset{\overset{\displaystyle CH_3}{|}}{CH_3CHCHCH_3}$
    $|$
    Br

$\overset{\overset{\displaystyle CH_3}{|}}{CH_2CHCH_2CH_3}$
  $|$
  Br

The first two are identical; the third is an isomer.

12.39

(a)

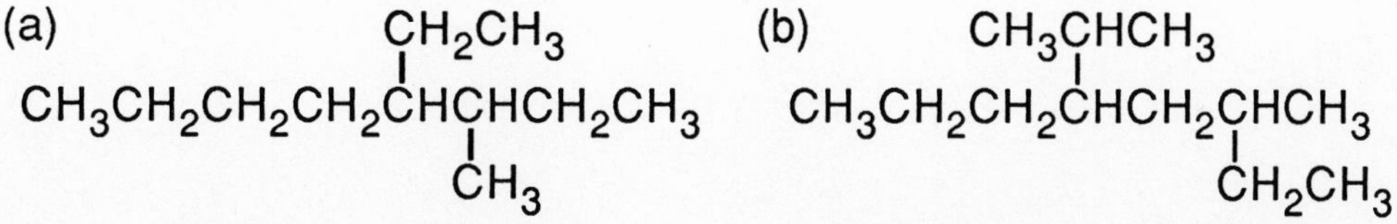

$\overset{\overset{\displaystyle CH_2CH_3}{|}}{CH_3CH_2CH_2CH_2CHCHCH_2CH_3}$
              $|$
             CH$_3$

4-Ethyl-3-methyloctane

(b)

$\overset{\overset{\displaystyle CH_3CHCH_3}{|}}{CH_3CH_2CH_2CHCH_2CHCH_3}$
                    $|$
                   CH$_2$CH$_3$

5-Isopropyl-3-methyloctane

(c)

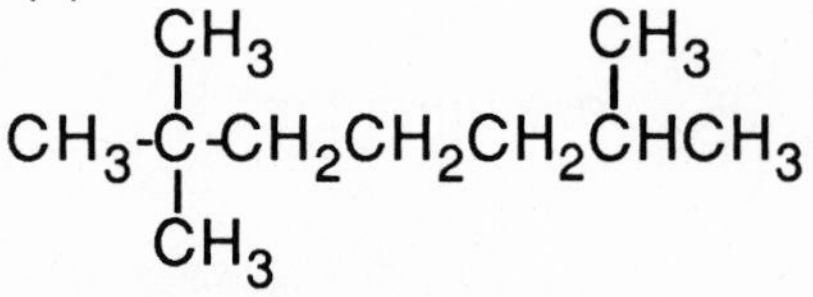

$$CH_3\text{-}\underset{\underset{CH_3}{|}}{\overset{\overset{CH_3}{|}}{C}}\text{-}CH_2CH_2CH_2\underset{}{\overset{\overset{CH_3}{|}}{CH}}CH_3$$

2,2,6-Trimethylheptane

(d)

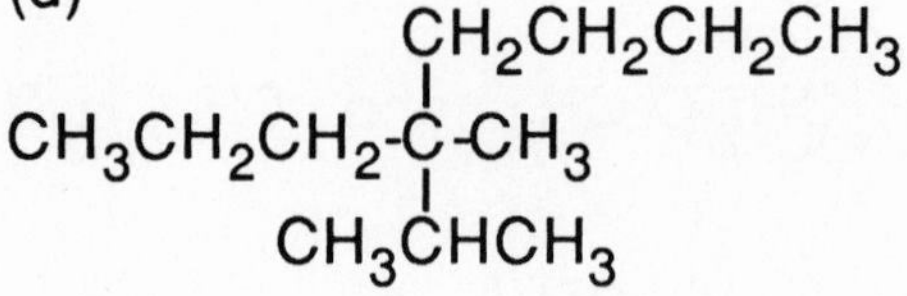

$$CH_3CH_2CH_2\text{-}\underset{\underset{CH_3CHCH_3}{|}}{\overset{\overset{CH_2CH_2CH_2CH_3}{|}}{C}}\text{-}CH_3$$

4-Isopropyl-4-methyloctane

(e)

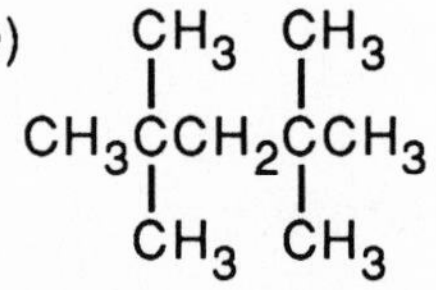

$$CH_3\underset{\underset{CH_3}{|}}{\overset{\overset{CH_3}{|}}{C}}CH_2\underset{\underset{CH_3}{|}}{\overset{\overset{CH_3}{|}}{C}}CH_3$$

2,2,4,4-Tetramethylpentane

(f)

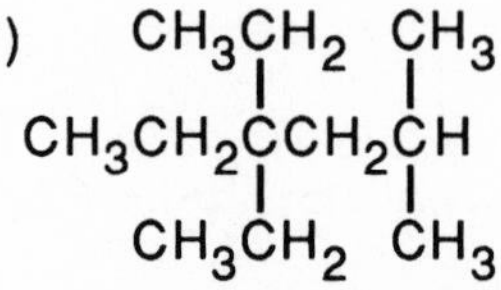

$$CH_3CH_2\underset{\underset{CH_3CH_2}{|}}{\overset{\overset{CH_3CH_2}{|}}{C}}CH_2\underset{}{\overset{\overset{CH_3}{|}}{CH}}$$

4,4-Diethyl-2-methylhexane

(g)

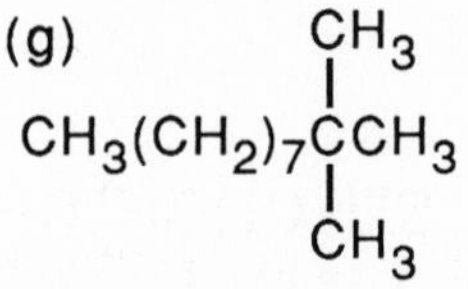

$$CH_3(CH_2)_7\underset{\underset{CH_3}{|}}{\overset{\overset{CH_3}{|}}{C}}CH_3$$

2,2-Dimethyldecane

12.40

(a)

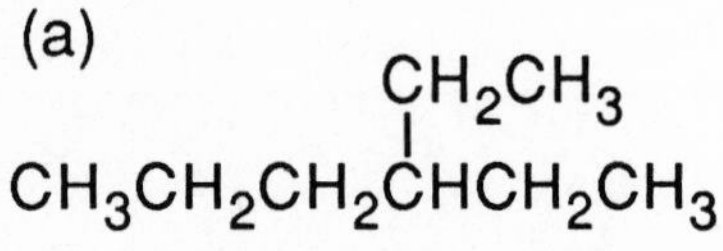

$$CH_3CH_2CH_2\underset{}{\overset{\overset{CH_2CH_3}{|}}{CH}}CH_2CH_3$$

3-Ethylhexane

(b)

$$CH_3CH_2\underset{}{\overset{\overset{H_3C}{|}}{CH}}\text{-}\underset{\underset{CH_3}{|}}{\overset{\overset{CH_3}{|}}{C}}\text{-}CH_3$$

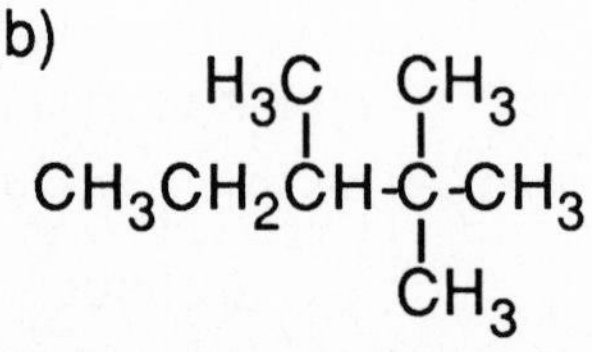

2,2,3-Trimethylpentane

(c)

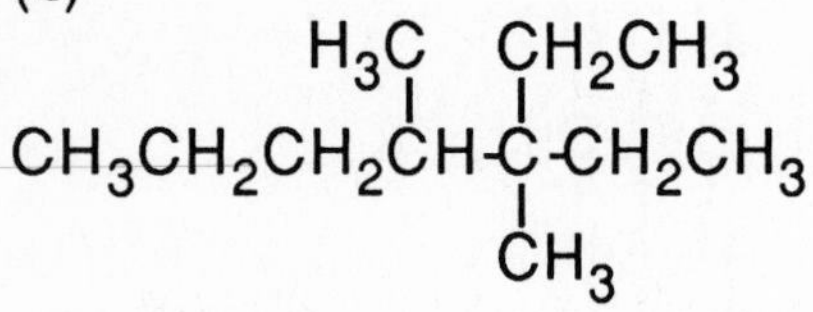

$$CH_3CH_2CH_2\underset{}{\overset{\overset{H_3C}{|}}{CH}}\text{-}\underset{\underset{CH_3}{|}}{\overset{\overset{CH_2CH_3}{|}}{C}}\text{-}CH_2CH_3$$

3-Ethyl-3,4-dimethylheptane

(d)

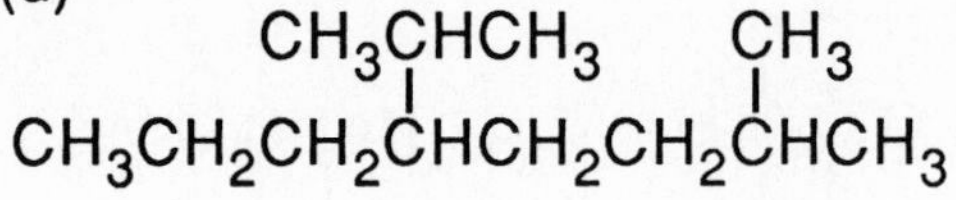

$$CH_3CH_2CH_2\underset{}{\overset{\overset{CH_3CHCH_3}{|}}{CH}}CH_2CH_2\underset{}{\overset{\overset{CH_3}{|}}{CH}}CH_3$$

5-isopropyl-2-methyloctane

(e)

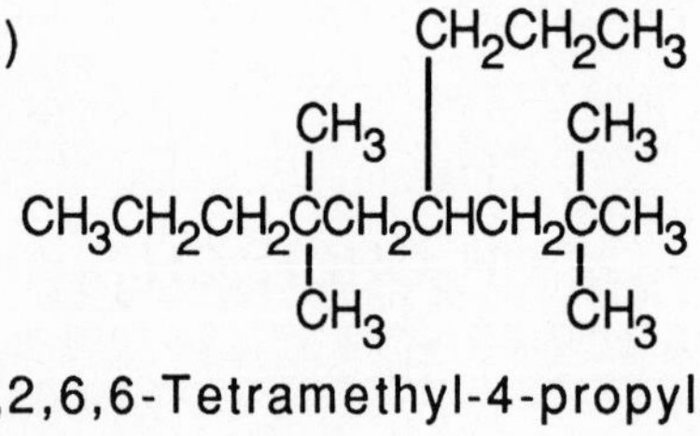

$$CH_3CH_2CH_2\underset{\underset{CH_3}{|}}{\overset{\overset{CH_3}{|}}{C}}CH_2\underset{}{\overset{\overset{CH_2CH_2CH_3}{|}}{CH}}CH_2\underset{\underset{CH_3}{|}}{\overset{\overset{CH_3}{|}}{C}}CH_3$$

2,2,6,6-Tetramethyl-4-propylnonane

12.41

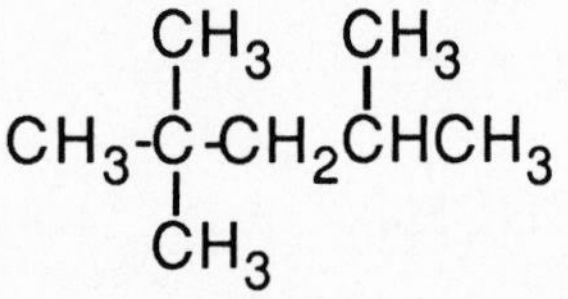

$$CH_3\text{-}\underset{\underset{CH_3}{|}}{\overset{\overset{CH_3}{|}}{C}}\text{-}CH_2\underset{}{\overset{\overset{CH_3}{|}}{CH}}CH_3 \quad \text{2,2,4-Trimethylpentane (isooctane)}$$

12.42

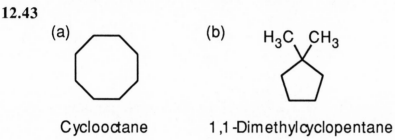

$CH_3CH_2CH_2CH_2CH_2CH_3$

Hexane

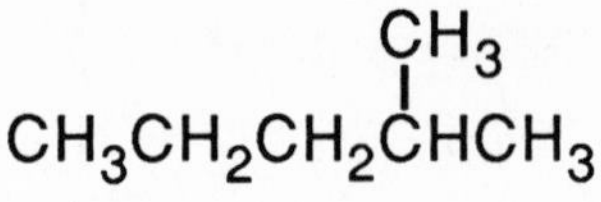

CH_3
|
$CH_3CH_2CH_2CHCH_3$

2-Methylpentane

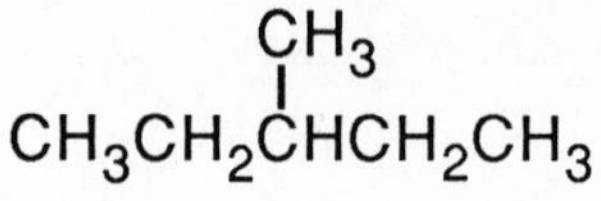

CH_3
|
$CH_3CH_2CHCH_2CH_3$

3-Methylpentane

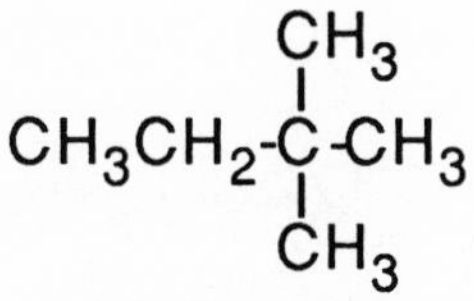

CH_3
|
$CH_3CH_2-C-CH_3$
|
CH_3

2,2-Dimethylbutane

H_3C CH_3
| |
$CH_3CHCHCH_3$

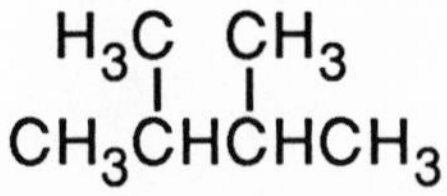

2,3-Dimethylbutane

12.43

(a)

Cyclooctane

(b) H_3C CH_3

1,1-Dimethylcyclopentane

(c) H_3C CH_3

     H_3C CH_3

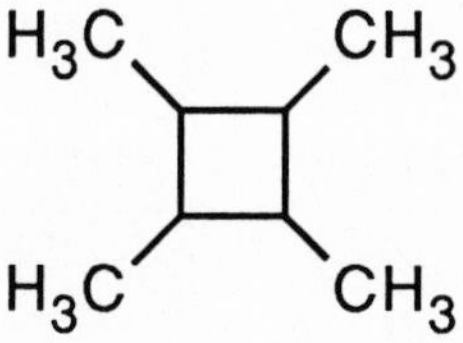

1,2,3,4-Tetramethylcyclobutane

(d)

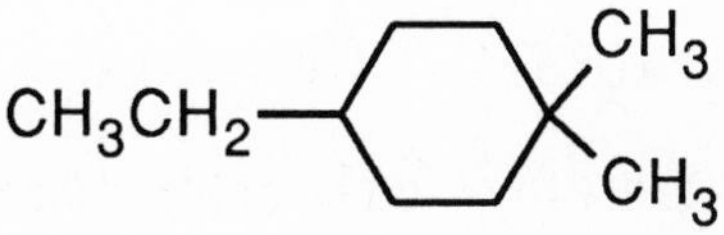

CH_3CH_2- CH_3

              CH_3

4-Ethyl-1,1-dimethylcyclohexane

(e) $-CH_2CH_3$

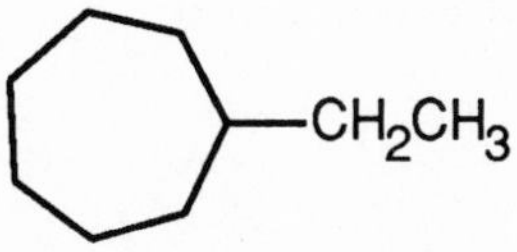

Ethylcycloheptane

(f) CH_3CH_2 CH_2CH_3

            CH_2CH_3

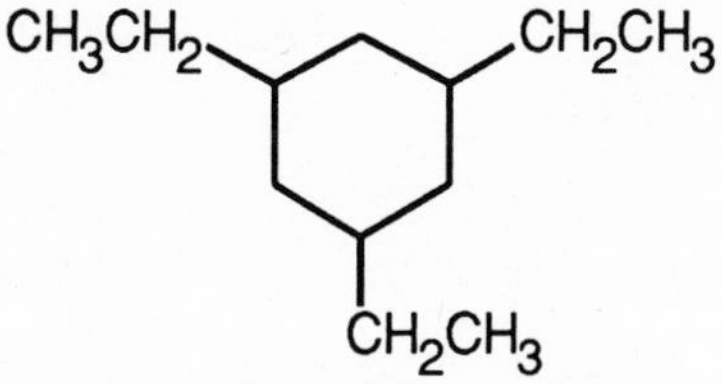

1,3,5-Triethylcyclohexane

(g) CH_3
              |
$CH_3CH_2CH_2$ $CHCH_3$

              $-CH_3$

          CH_3

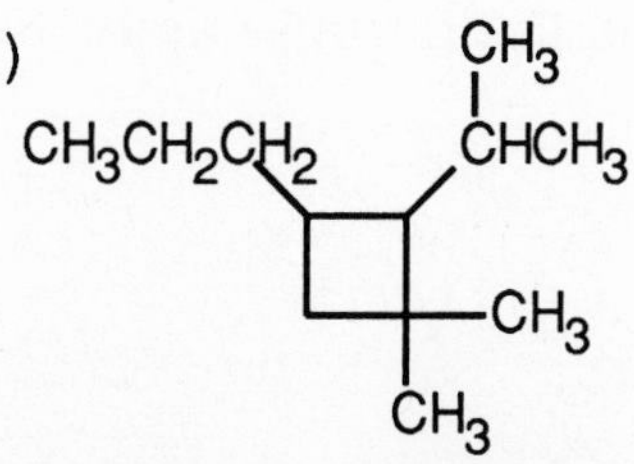

2-Isopropyl-1,1-dimethyl-3-propylcyclobutane

(h) CH_3

H_3C CH_3

              CH_3

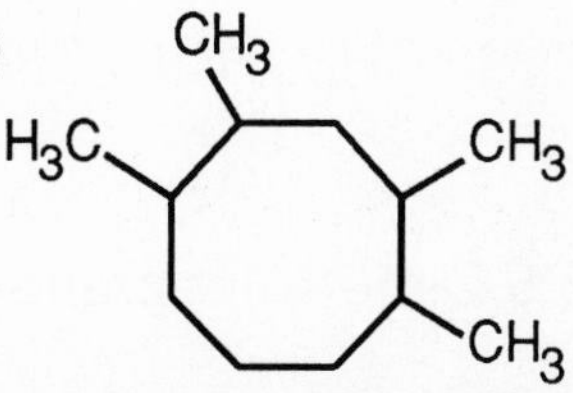

1,2,4,5-Tetramethylcyclooctane

12.44

(a)

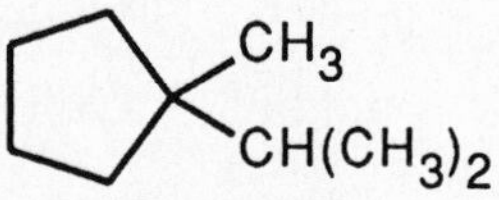
CH3
CH(CH3)2

1-Isopropyl-1-methylcyclopentane

(b)

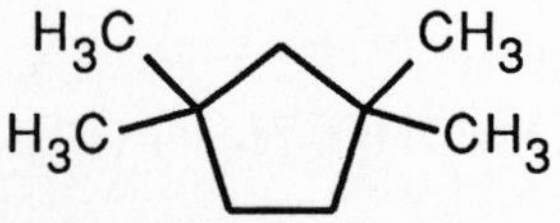
H3C
CH3
H3C
CH3

1,1,3,3-Tetramethylcyclopentane

(c)

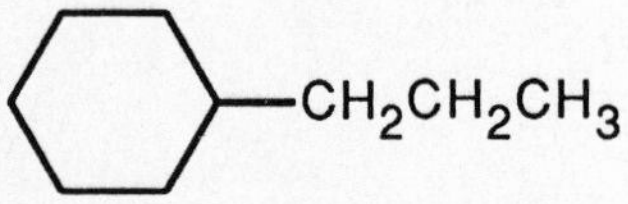
CH2CH2CH3

Propylcyclohexane

(d)

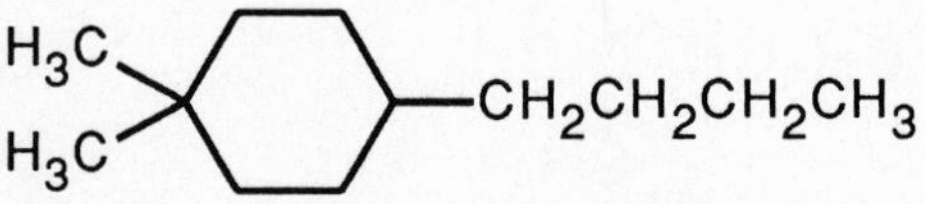
H3C
H3C
CH2CH2CH2CH3

4-Butyl-1,1-dimethylcyclohexane

(e)

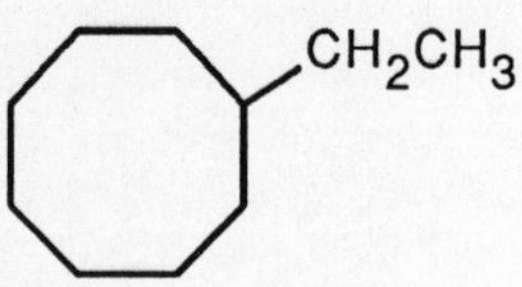
CH2CH3

Ethylcyclooctane

(f)

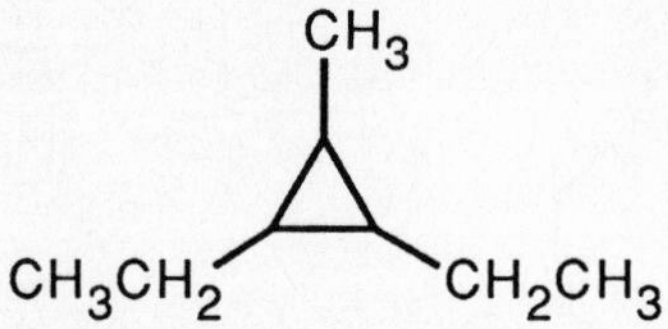
CH3
CH3CH2
CH2CH3

1,2-Diethyl-3-methylcyclopropane

(g)

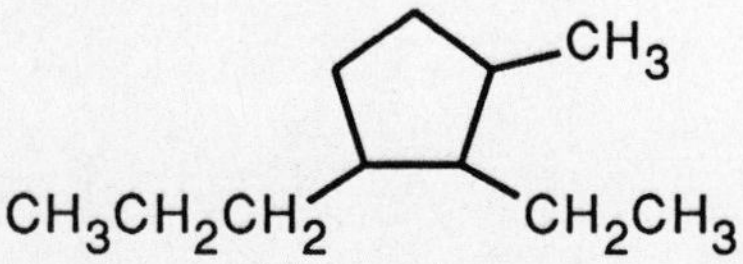
CH3
CH3CH2CH2
CH2CH3

2-Ethyl-1-methyl-3-propylcyclopentane

12.45

(a)

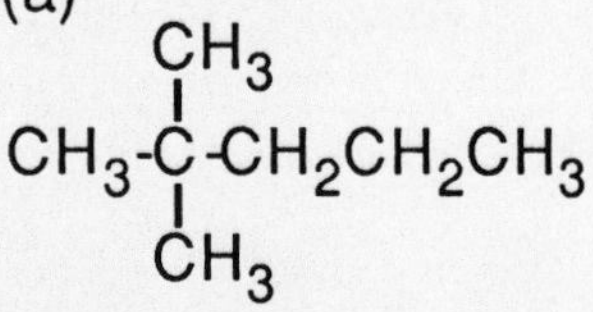
CH3
CH3-C-CH2CH2CH3
CH3

2,2-Dimethylpentane

The prefix "di" must appear when two substituents are the same.

(b)

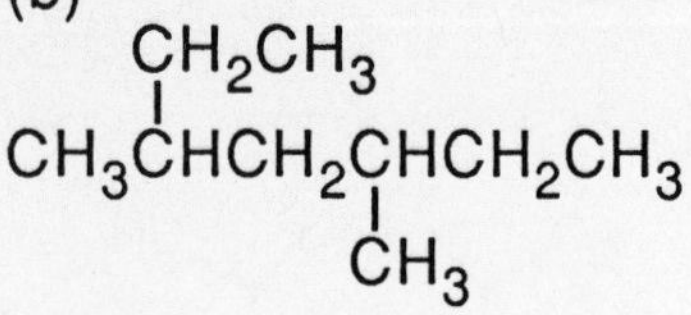
CH2CH3
CH3CHCH2CHCH2CH3
CH3

3,5-Dimethylheptane

You must choose the longest carbon chain as the parent name.

(c)

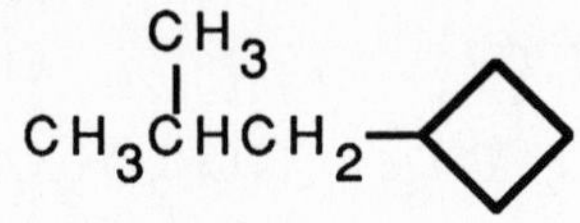

$$CH_3CHCH_2-\square$$
with CH_3 above

sec-Butylcyclobutane

This compound is an alkyl-substituted cycloalkane.

12.46

$$CH_3CH_2CH_2CH_2CH_2CH_2CH_3$$

Heptane

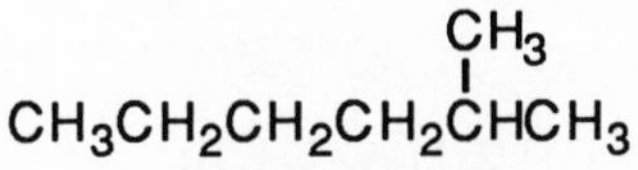

$$CH_3CH_2CH_2CH_2CHCH_3$$
with CH_3 above

2-Methylhexane

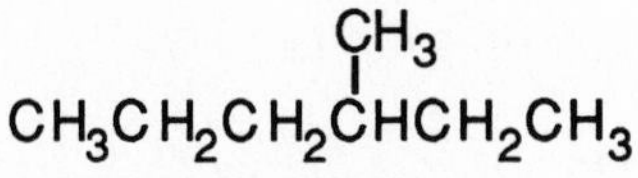

$$CH_3CH_2CH_2CHCH_2CH_3$$
with CH_3 above

3-Methylhexane

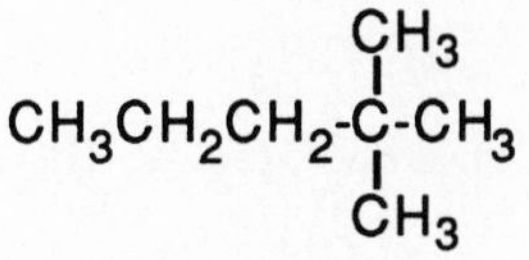

$$CH_3CH_2CH_2-C-CH_3$$
with CH_3 above and CH_3 below

2,2-Dimethylpentane

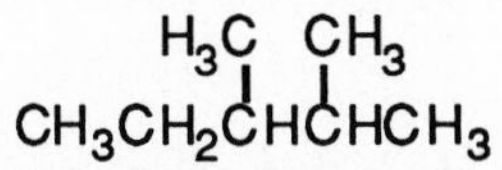

$$CH_3CH_2CHCHCH_3$$
with H_3C and CH_3 above

2,3-Dimethylpentane

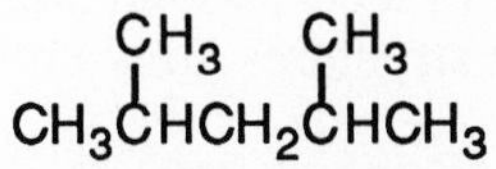

$$CH_3CHCH_2CHCH_3$$
with CH_3 and CH_3 above

2,4-Dimethylpentane

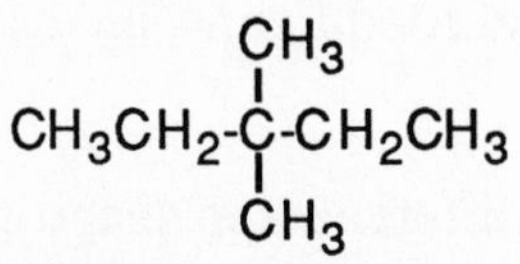

$$CH_3CH_2-C-CH_2CH_3$$
with CH_3 above and CH_3 below

3,3-Dimethylpentane

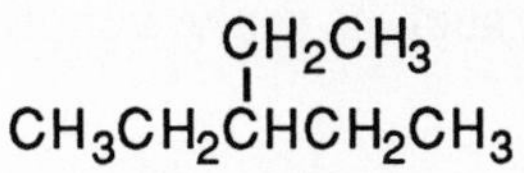

$$CH_3CH_2CHCH_2CH_3$$
with CH_2CH_3 above

3-Ethylpentane

$$CH_3CH-C-CH_3$$
with H_3C, CH_3 above and CH_3 below

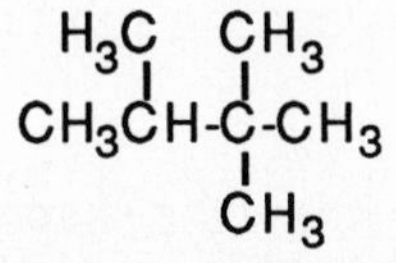

2,2,3-Trimethylbutane

12.47 $CH_3CH_2CH_3 + 5 O_2 \longrightarrow 3 CO_2 + 4 H_2O$

12.48 $2 C_8H_{18} + 25 O_2 \longrightarrow 16 CO_2 + 18 H_2O$

12.49 $C_{25}H_{52} + 38 O_2 \longrightarrow 25 O_2 + 26 H_2O$

12.50 A halogen atom replaces a hydrogen atom in a substitution reaction.

12.51

$$CH_3CH_2\overset{\underset{\displaystyle CH_3}{|}}{\underset{\underset{\displaystyle CH_3}{|}}{C}}CH_3 + Cl_2 \xrightarrow[\text{light}]{\text{heat or}} CH_3CH_2\overset{\underset{\displaystyle CH_3}{|}}{\underset{\underset{\displaystyle CH_3}{|}}{C}}CH_2Cl + CH_3\overset{\underset{\displaystyle CH_3}{|}}{\underset{\underset{\displaystyle CH_3}{|}}{CH}}\overset{Cl}{\underset{}{C}}CH_3 + ClCH_2CH_2\overset{\underset{\displaystyle CH_3}{|}}{\underset{\underset{\displaystyle CH_3}{|}}{C}}CH_3$$

12.52

$$CH_3CH_2\overset{\underset{\displaystyle CH_3}{|}}{\underset{\underset{\displaystyle CH_3}{|}}{C}}CHBr_2 + CH_3CH_2\overset{\underset{\displaystyle CH_2Br}{|}}{\underset{\underset{\displaystyle CH_3}{|}}{C}}CH_2Br + CH_3\overset{Br}{\underset{}{CH}}\overset{\underset{\displaystyle CH_3}{|}}{\underset{\underset{\displaystyle CH_3}{|}}{C}}CH_2Br + BrCH_2CH_2\overset{\underset{\displaystyle CH_3}{|}}{\underset{\underset{\displaystyle CH_3}{|}}{C}}CH_2Br$$

$$+ CH_3\overset{\underset{\displaystyle Br}{|}}{\underset{\underset{\displaystyle Br}{|}}{C}}-\overset{\underset{\displaystyle CH_3}{|}}{\underset{\underset{\displaystyle CH_3}{|}}{C}}CH_3 + BrCH_2\overset{Br}{\underset{}{CH}}\overset{\underset{\displaystyle CH_3}{|}}{\underset{\underset{\displaystyle CH_3}{|}}{C}}CH_3 + Br_2CHCH_2\overset{\underset{\displaystyle CH_3}{|}}{\underset{\underset{\displaystyle CH_3}{|}}{C}}CH_3$$

12.53 A synthetically produced version of a compound and a "natural" compound have the same properties because their chemical structures are identical.

12.54 A semisynthetic penicillin is produced by adding the appropriate chemicals to the medium in which the penicillin mold grows.

12.55 Many naturally occurring substances, such as snake venoms and food toxins, are extremely hazardous.

12.56 It is important to know the shape of a molecule because minor differences in shape can cause differences in chemical behavior and physiological activity.

12.57 Natural gas consists of C_1 - C_4 hydrocarbons and is a gas at room temperature. Petroleum consists of other alkanes, some of which are very high boiling.

12.58 Branched chain hydrocarbons burn more efficiently in an internal combustion engine.

12.59 Since alkanes differ in boiling point, a mixture can be separated by distillation, in which the lower-boiling components are boiled off and the vapor is recondensed.. The higher-boiling alkanes are distilled under reduced pressure.

12.60 The boiling points of the higher molecular weight alkanes are higher than those of CH_4 and C_2H_6 because London forces, which increase with increased formula weight, are greater for $C_{16}H_{34}$ and $C_{17}H_{36}$. The difference between the boiling points of CH_4 and C_2H_6 is greater than that between the boiling points of $C_{16}H_{34}$ and $C_{17}H_{36}$ because the percent difference in formula weight between CH_4 and C_2H_6 is greater than that between $C_{16}H_{34}$ and $C_{17}H_{36}$.

12.61 - 12.62

(a)

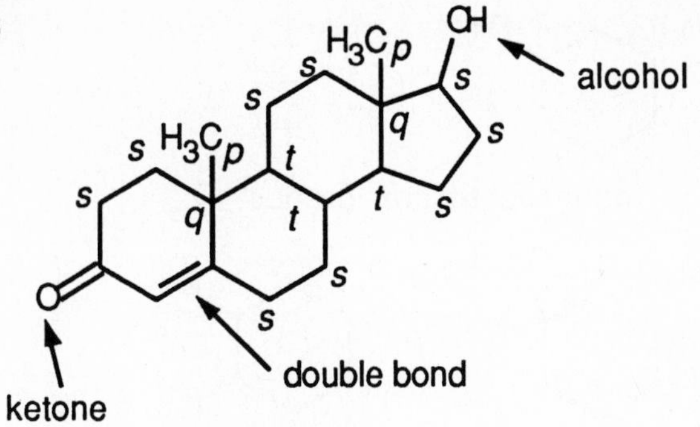

Testosterone

(b)

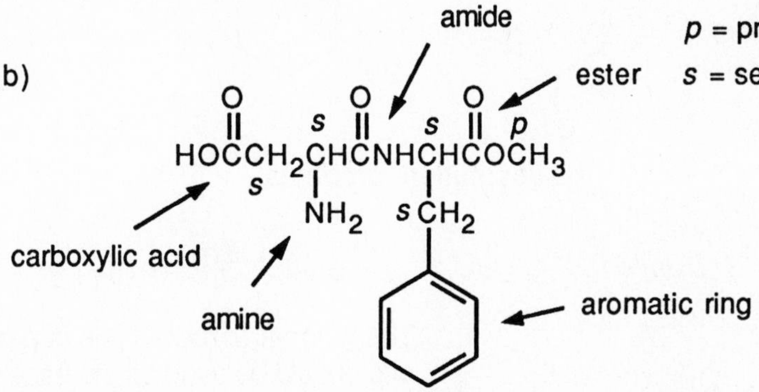

p = primary t = tertiary
s = secondary q = quaternary

Aspartame

12.63 The two compounds are isomers, which have the same molecular formula but differ in structure and properties. The less branched isomer boils at a higher temperature.

12.64 Since "like dissolves like," lipstick, which is composed primarily of hydrocarbons, is more soluble in the hydrocarbon petroleum jelly than in water.

12.65

$$2\ C_{12}H_{26} + 37\ O_2 \longrightarrow 24\ CO_2 + 26\ H_2O$$

12.66

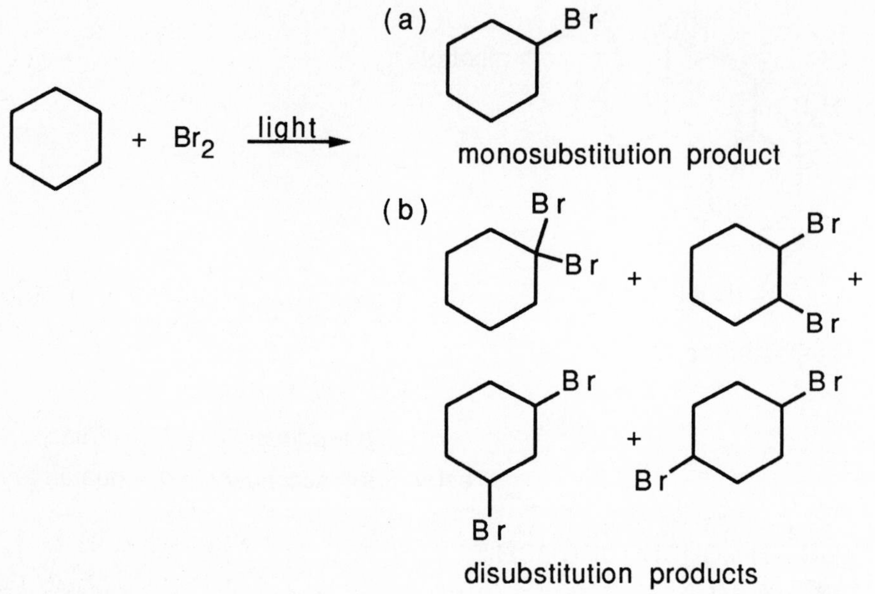

(a) monosubstitution product

(b) disubstitution products

12.67   *Structure*   *Error*

(a)

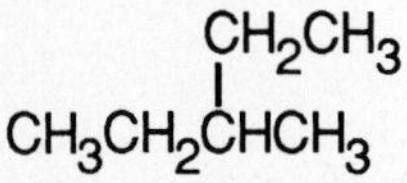

$$CH_3CH_2CHCH_3$$
with CH_2CH_3 substituent

3-Methylpentane

The longest carbon chain is a pentane and should be used as the base name.

(b)

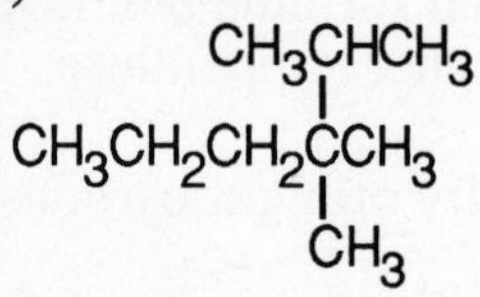

$$CH_3CH_2CH_2CCH_3$$
with CH_3CHCH_3 and CH_3 substituents

2,3,3-Trimethylhexane

The longest carbon chain is a haxane and should be used as the base name.

(c)

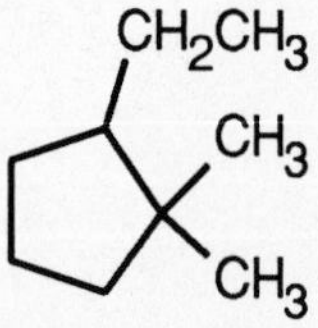

2-Ethyl-1,1-dimethylcyclopentane

The substituents should be given the lowest possible numbers.

(d)

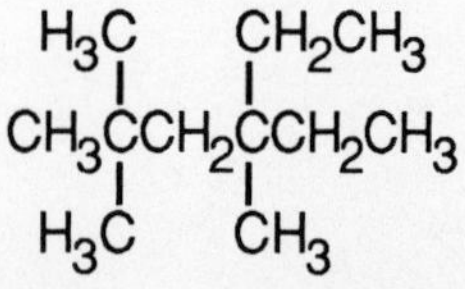

$$CH_3CCH_2CCH_2CH_3$$
with H_3C, CH_2CH_3, H_3C, CH_3 substituents

4-Ethyl-2,2,4-trimethylhexane

Numbering must start from the end nearest the first substituent.

(e)

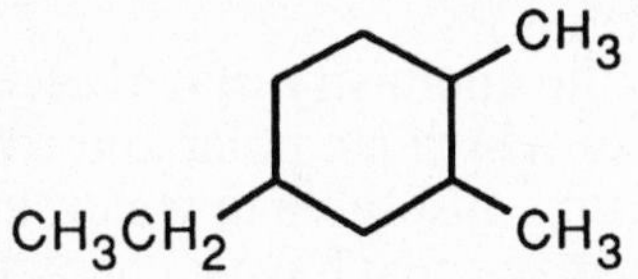

4-Ethyl-1,2-dimethylcyclohexane

Substituents must be cited in alphabetical order (prefixes are not used for alphabetizing).

(f)

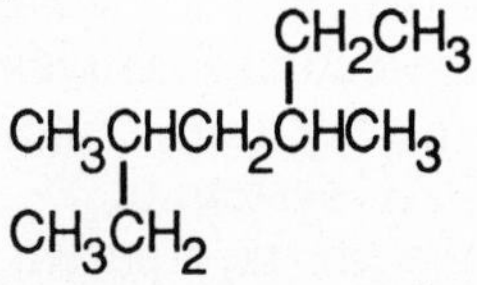

$$CH_3CHCH_2CHCH_3$$

with CH_2CH_3 and CH_3CH_2 substituents

3,5-Dimethylheptane

The longest chain is a heptane and should be used as the base name.

(g)

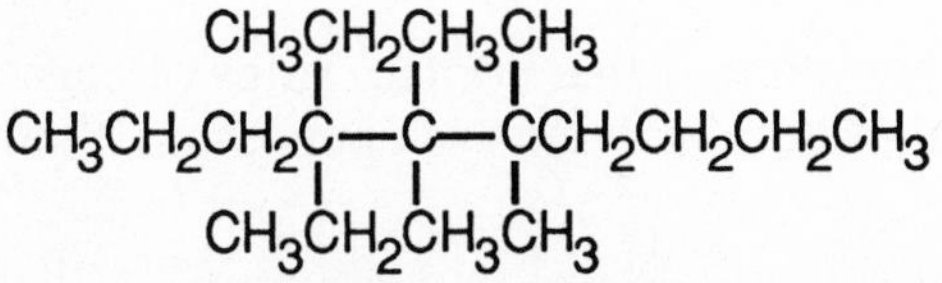

$$CH_3CH_2CH_2C-C-CCH_2CH_2CH_2CH_3$$

4,4-Diethyl-5,5,6,6-tetramethyldecane

The prefixes "tetra" and "di" must be included in the name. Substituents must be cited in alphabetical order. Numbering must start from the other end.

12.68

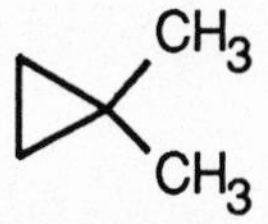

1,1-Dimethylcyclopropane

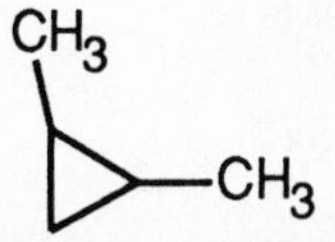

1,2-Dimethylcyclopropane

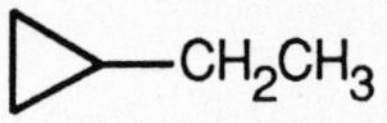

Ethylcyclopropane

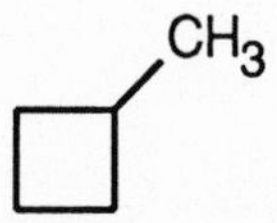

Methylcyclobutane

Cyclopentane

12.69 Pentane has a higher boiling point than neopentane because London forces, which must be overcome in boiling, are greater for linear than for more spherical or nonlinear compounds of the same formula weight.

The Chapter In Brief

Organic Molecules (Sections 12.1, 12.2) Organic chemistry is the chemistry of carbon compounds. Organic molecules contain covalent bonds, some of which are polar and some of which are multiple. Organic compounds are generally low-melting, insoluble in water, and are poor conductors of electricity. Functional groups are groups of atoms that have a characteristic reactivity.

Alkanes (Sections 12.3–12.8) Alkanes are organic compounds that contain only carbon and hydrogen and that have only single bonds. Some alkanes are straight-chain, and some are branched-chain. Condensed formulas are a simplified way of writing molecular formulas. Isomers are compounds having the same molecular formula but different structures. An alkane is capable of existing in many three-dimensional conformations. The IUPAC system of nomenclature is used to name compounds; an IUPAC name consists of a prefix, a parent, and a suffix. Carbons can be designated as primary, secondary, tertiary, or quaternary depending on how many other carbons they are bonded to. Alkanes are chemically quite unreactive; their main reactions are combustion and thermal cracking.

Cycloalkanes (Sections 12.9, 12.10) Cycloalkanes are alkanes that contain rings of carbon atoms. They are named by the IUPAC system and undergo the same reactions as open-chain alkanes.

Self-Test for Chapter 12

Complete the following sentences:

1. C_{20} to C_{36} alkanes are known as _____.

2.   Alkynes are compounds that contain _____ bonds.

3.   Alcohols and ether are functional groups that contain _____.

4.   Mixtures of hydrocarbons can be separated by _____.

5.   A _____ _____ is a shorthand way of drawing a chemical structure.

6.   A _____carbon is bonded to four other carbons.

7.   Organic compounds generally have _____ melting points that inorganic compounds.

8.   Cycloalkanes are compounds that contain carbon atoms joined together in a _____.

9.   Organic molecules are named by the _____ system.

10.   Compounds with the same formula but different structures are called _____.

Tell whether the following statements are true or false:

1.   Cyclohexane and hexane are isomers.

2.   A molecule with the formula C_5H_{12} can have the parent name pentane, butane, or propane.

3. The preferred conformation of a straight-chain alkane is twisted.

4. The correct name of the following alkane is 1,3-dimethylpentane.

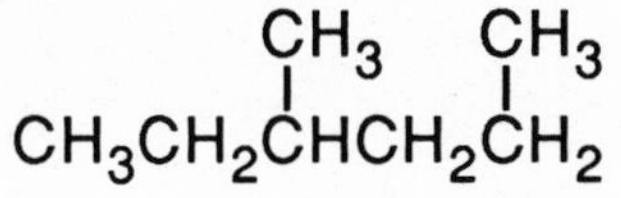

$$CH_3CH_2CHCH_2CH_2$$

with CH_3 and CH_3 substituents

5. The compound 2,3-dimethylbutane has only primary and tertiary carbons.

6. Acyclic alkanes and cycloalkanes have the same chemical reactivity.

7. The C-Cl bond in CH_3Cl is ionic.

8. The compound 1,4-dimethylcyclohexane is correctly named.

9. Alkanes with one to four carbons exist as gases at room temperature.

10. Compounds with many functional groups are more reactive than compounds with few functional groups.

11. 2-Methylpentane and 3-methylpentane probably have nearly identical boiling points.

Match the entries on the left with their partners on the right:

1. $RCH=O$	(a) contains polar covalent bonds
2. C_5H_{12}	(b) Butyl group
3. $CH_3CH(CH_3)_2$	(c) Ketone
4. $CH_3CH_2CH_2CH_3$	(d) Natural gas
5. $CH_3CH_2CH_2-$	(e) Formula of methylcyclobutane
6. $R_2C=O$	(f) Branched-chain alkane
7. CH_2Cl_2	(g) An alkene
8. $C_{30}H_{62}$	(h) Propyl group
9. C_5H_{10}	(i) Aldehyde
10. $CH_3CH_2CH_2CH_2-$	(j) Formula of 2-methylbutane
11. $CH_3CH=CH_2$	(k) A solid
12. CH_4	(l) Straight-chain alkane

13.1

(a)

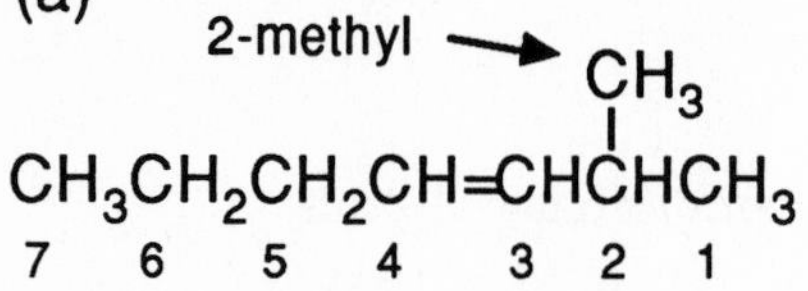

2-methyl → CH$_3$

CH$_3$CH$_2$CH$_2$CH=CHCHCH$_3$
  7   6   5   4   3   2   1

2-Methyl-3-heptene

(b)

  6   5   4   3   2   1

H$_2$C=CHCH$_2$CH$_2$C=CH$_2$
                  CH$_3$ ← 2-methyl

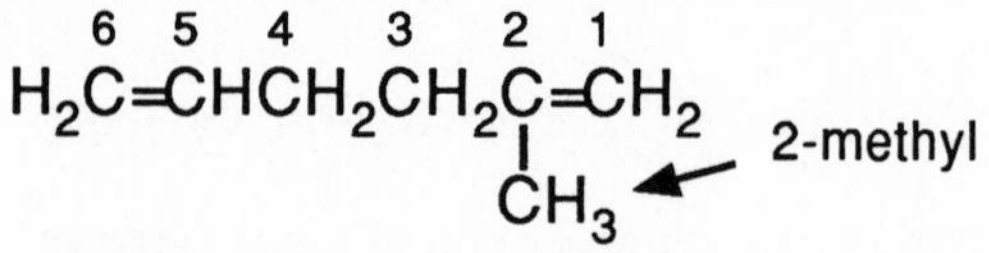

2-Methyl-1,5-hexadiene

13.2

(a)

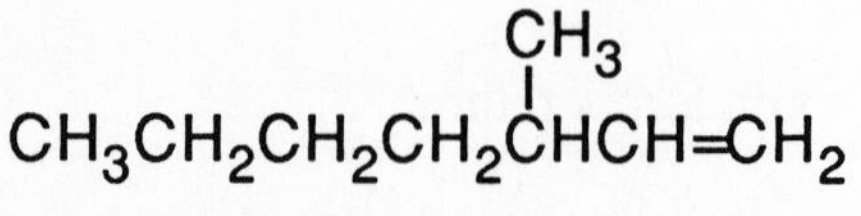

              CH$_3$

CH$_3$CH$_2$CH$_2$CH$_2$CHCH=CH$_2$

3-Methyl-1-heptene

(b)

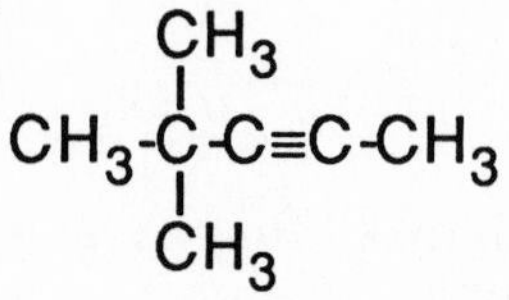

       CH$_3$

CH$_3$-C-C≡C-CH$_3$
       CH$_3$

4,4-Dimethyl-2-pentyne

(c)

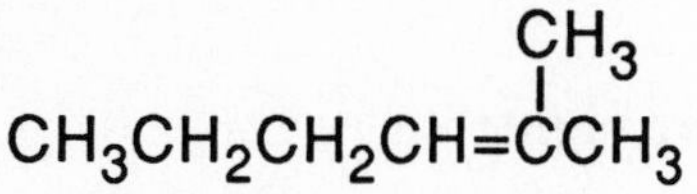

             CH$_3$

CH$_3$CH$_2$CH$_2$CH=CCH$_3$

2-Methyl-2-hexene

(d)

        CH$_3$CH$_2$ CH$_3$

CH$_3$CH$_2$CH=C—C-CH$_3$
                 CH$_3$

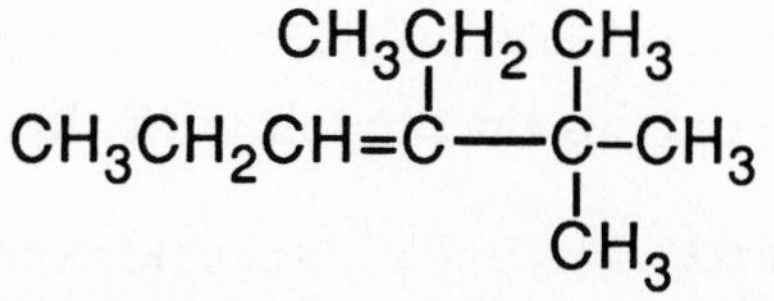

3-Ethyl-2,2-dimethyl-3-hexene

13.3 (a) Attached to C3: -H, -CH$_2$CH$_3$
           Attached to C4: -H, -CH$_2$CH$_2$CH$_3$

Since each of the double-bond carbons has two different groups attached to it, 3-heptene can exist as cis-trans isomers:

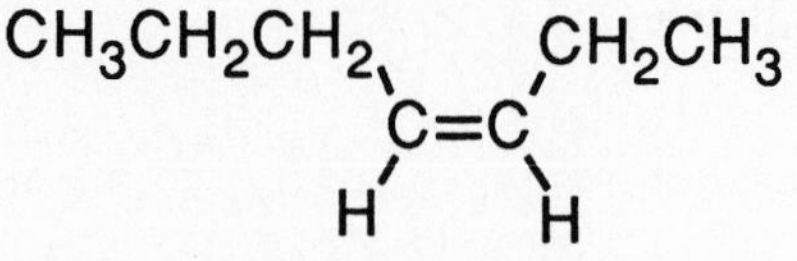

CH$_3$CH$_2$CH$_2$ CH$_2$CH$_3$
       C=C
    H   H

cis-3-Heptene

CH$_3$CH$_2$CH$_2$ H
       C=C
    H   CH$_2$CH$_3$

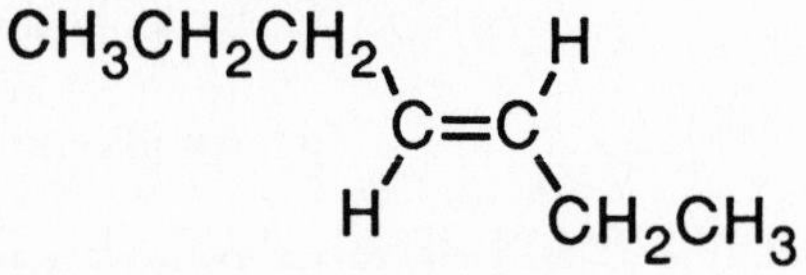

trans-3-Heptene

(b) Attached to C2: -CH$_3$, -CH$_3$
    Attached to C3: -H, -CH$_2$CH$_2$CH$_3$

Since the two groups attached to C2 are identical, 2-methyl-2-hexene does not exist as cis-trans isomers:

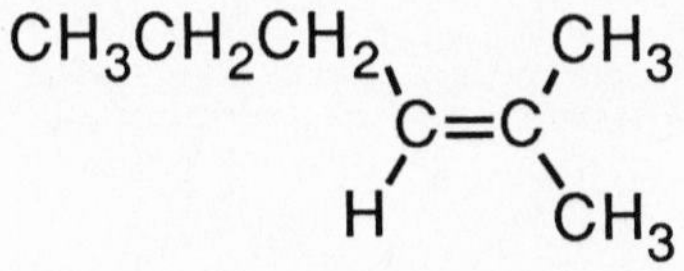

$$CH_3CH_2CH_2 \atop H \diagdown C=C \diagup CH_3 \atop CH_3$$

2-Methyl-2-hexene

(c) Attached to C2: $-H$, $-CH_3$
Attached to C3: $-H$, $-CH_2CH(CH_3)_2$

Since each carbon has two different groups attached to it, 5-methyl-2-hexene can exist as cis-trans isomers:

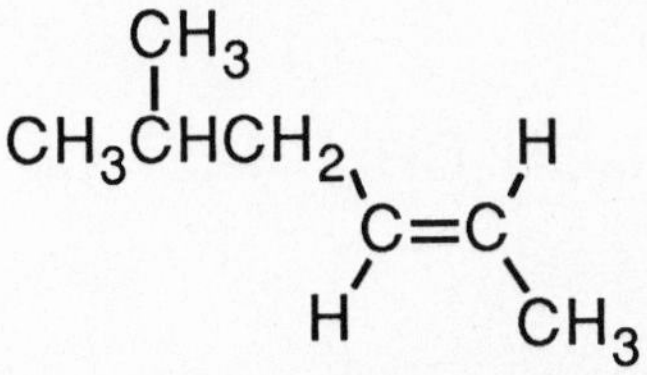

$$CH_3 \atop | \atop CH_3CHCH_2 \diagdown C=C \diagup H \atop H \qquad CH_3$$

$$CH_3 \atop | \atop CH_3CHCH_2 \diagdown C=C \diagup CH_3 \atop H \qquad H$$

trans-5-Methyl-2-hexene 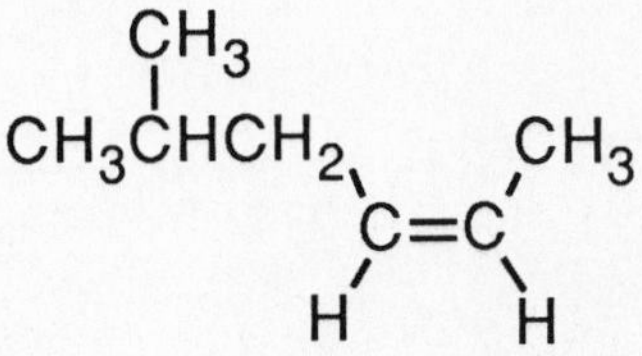   *cis*-5-Methyl-2-hexene

(Corresponds to Solved Problem 9.2 in the text)

13.4

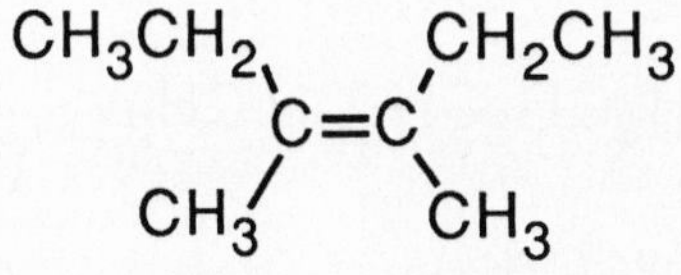

$$CH_3CH_2 \atop CH_3 \diagdown C=C \diagup CH_2CH_3 \atop CH_3$$

$$CH_3CH_2 \atop CH_3 \diagdown C=C \diagup CH_3 \atop CH_2CH_3$$

cis-3,4-Dimethyl-3-hexene 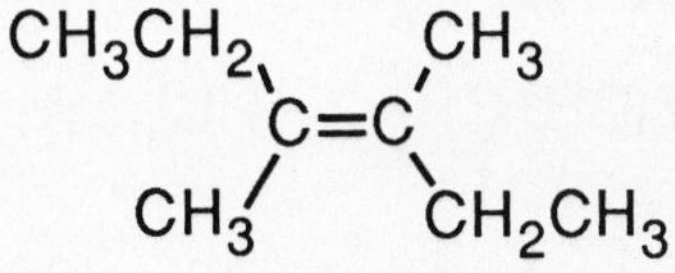   *trans*-3,4-Dimethyl-3-hexene

13.5

(a)

$$CH_3CH_2CH=CH_2 + H_2 \xrightarrow{Pd} CH_3CH_2CH_2CH_3$$

(b)

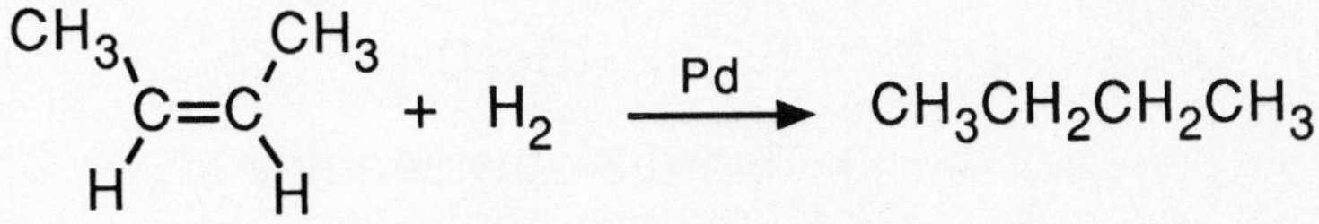

$$CH_3 \atop H \diagdown C=C \diagup CH_3 \atop H + H_2 \xrightarrow{Pd} CH_3CH_2CH_2CH_3$$

(c)

$$CH_3 \atop H \diagdown C=C \diagup H \atop CH_3 + H_2 \xrightarrow{Pd} CH_3CH_2CH_2CH_3$$

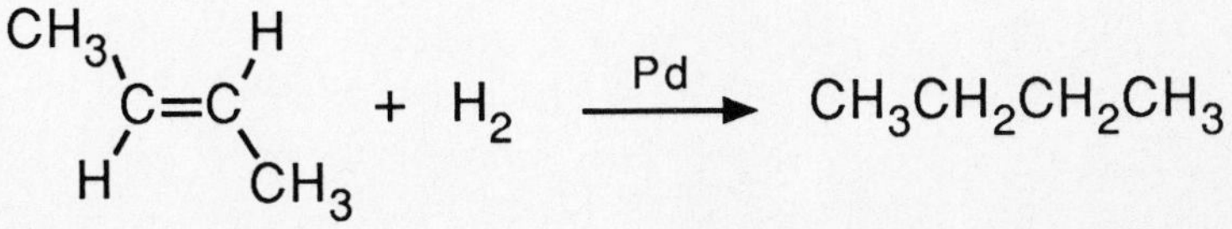

(d)

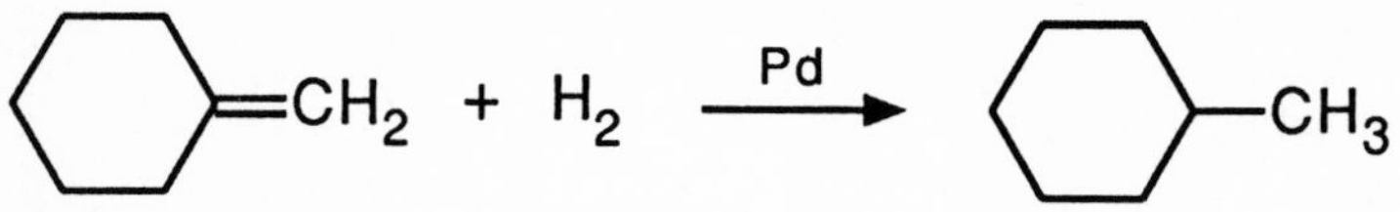
=CH2 + H2
Pd
-CH3

13.6

(a)

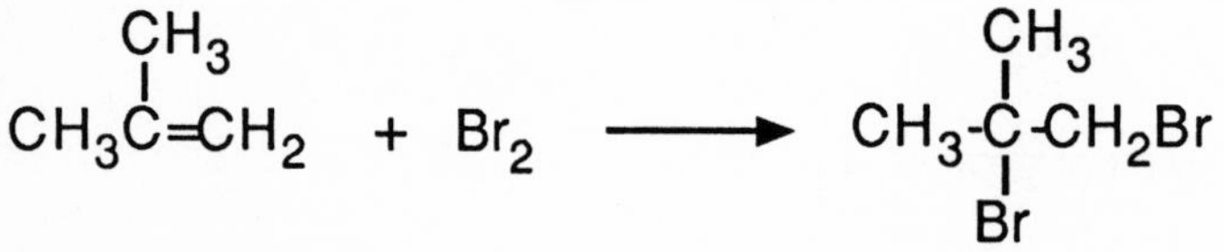
CH3
CH3C=CH2 + Br2
CH3
CH3-C-CH2Br
Br

(b)

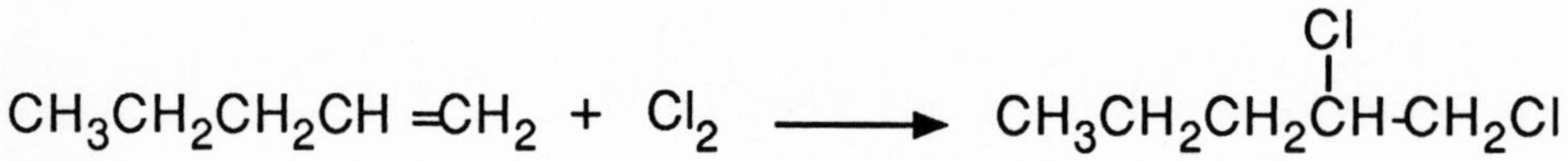
CH3CH2CH2CH =CH2 + Cl2
Cl
CH3CH2CH2CH-CH2Cl

13.7

(a)

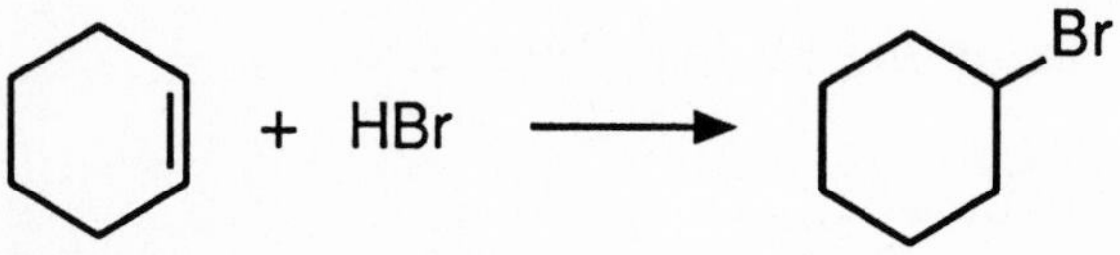
+ HBr
Br

(b)

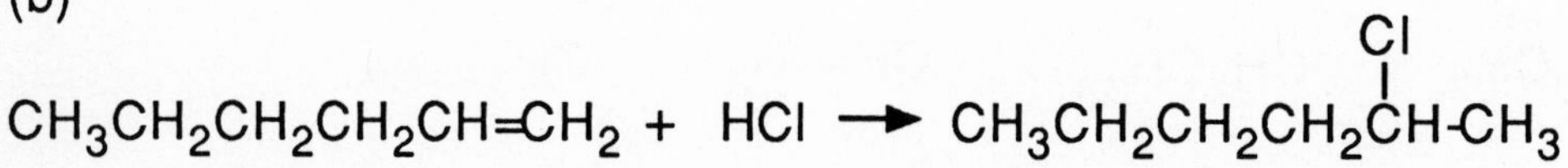
CH3CH2CH2CH2CH=CH2 + HCl
Cl
CH3CH2CH2CH2CH-CH3

Chlorine attaches to the carbon that has fewer hydrogens.

(c)

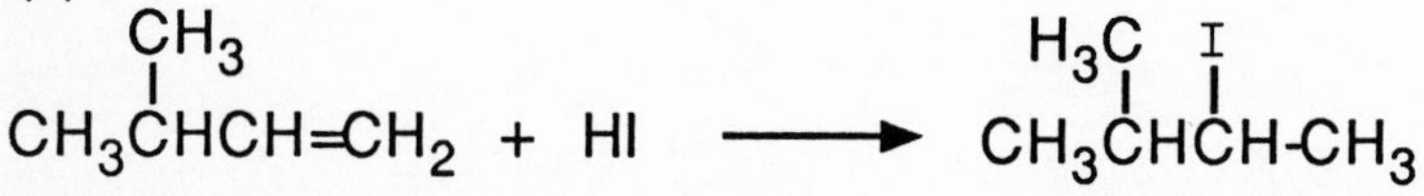
CH3
CH3CHCH=CH2 + HI
H3C I
CH3CHCH-CH3

13.8

(a)

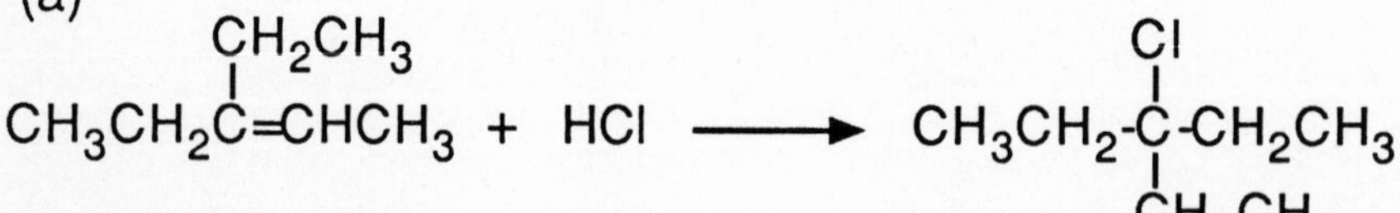
CH2CH3
CH3CH2C=CHCH3 + HCl
Cl
CH3CH2-C-CH2CH3
CH2CH3

3-Ethyl-2-pentene

3-Chloro-3-ethylpentane

(b)

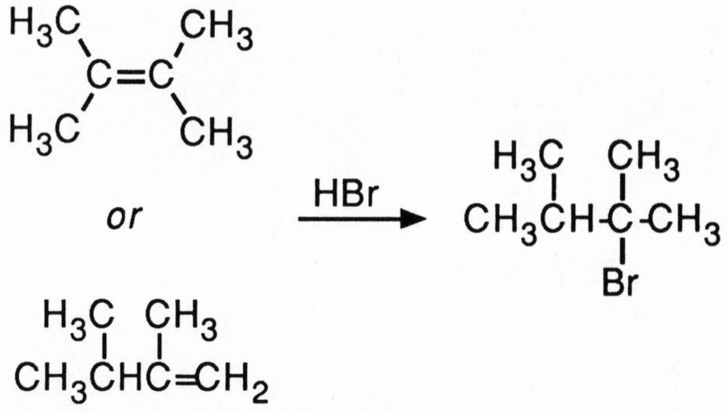

$$H_3C\text{-}C(CH_3)=C(CH_3)\text{-}CH_3$$

$$\text{or} \xrightarrow{\text{HBr}} CH_3CH\text{-}C\text{-}CH_3$$

$$CH_3CHCHC=CH_2$$

13.9

(a)

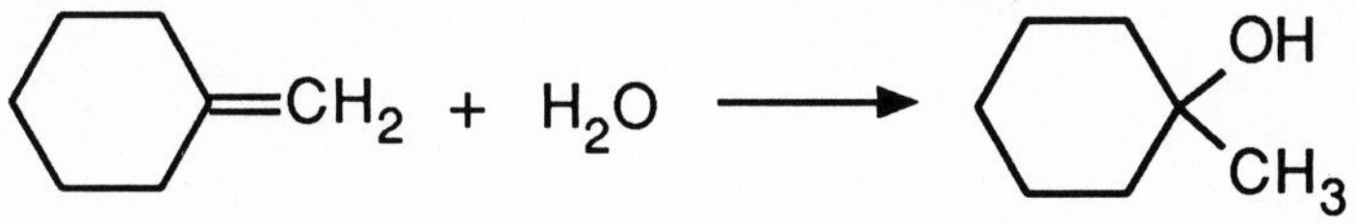

$$\text{(cyclohexylidene)}=CH_2 + H_2O \longrightarrow \text{(cyclohexyl-OH, CH}_3\text{)}$$

(b)

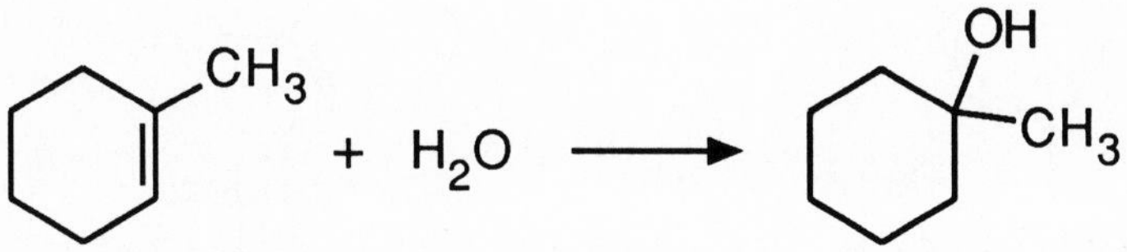

$$\text{(1-methylcyclohexene)} + H_2O \longrightarrow \text{(1-methylcyclohexanol)}$$

13.10

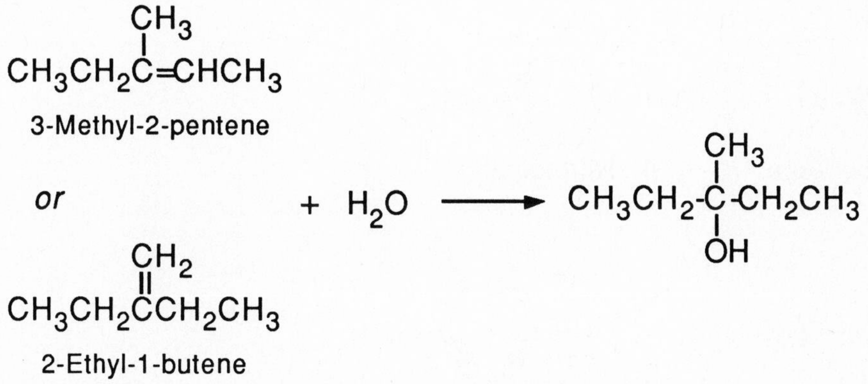

$$CH_3CH_2\overset{CH_3}{\underset{}{C}}=CHCH_3$$

3-Methyl-2-pentene

$$\text{or} \qquad + H_2O \longrightarrow CH_3CH_2\overset{CH_3}{\underset{OH}{C}}CH_2CH_3$$

$$CH_3CH_2\overset{CH_2}{\underset{}{C}}CH_2CH_3$$

2-Ethyl-1-butene

13.11

$$CH_3\overset{CH_3}{\underset{}{CH}}=CH_2 + HCl \longrightarrow \left[CH_3\text{-}\overset{CH_3}{\underset{+}{C}}\text{-}CH_3 \right] \longrightarrow CH_3\overset{CH_3}{\underset{Cl}{C}}CH_3$$

2-Methylpropene

Carbocation intermediate

2-Chloro-2-methylpropane

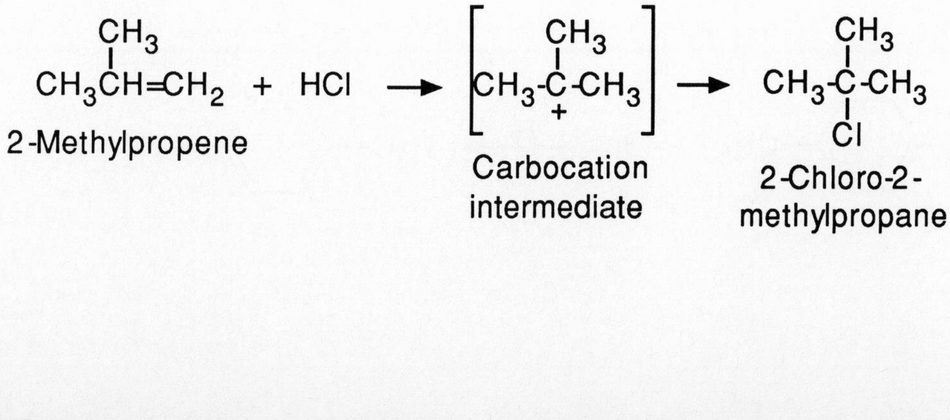

13.12   *Monomer*   *Polymer*

(a)

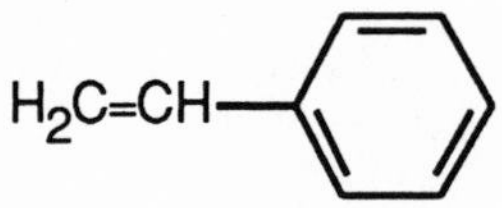

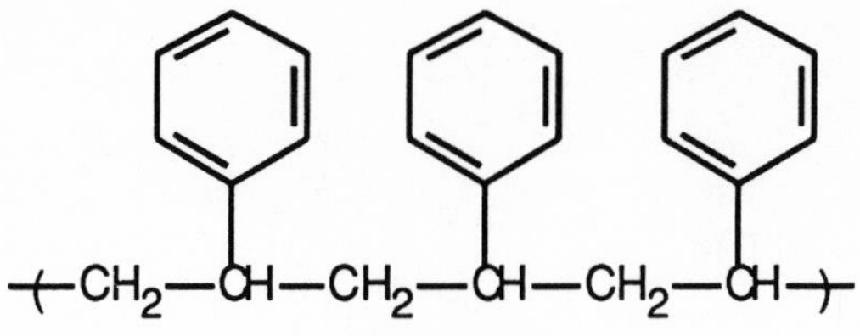

$H_2C=CH-$⬡

Styrene   Polystyrene

$+CH_2-CH-CH_2-CH-CH_2-CH+$

(b)

$H_2C=CH-C\equiv N$

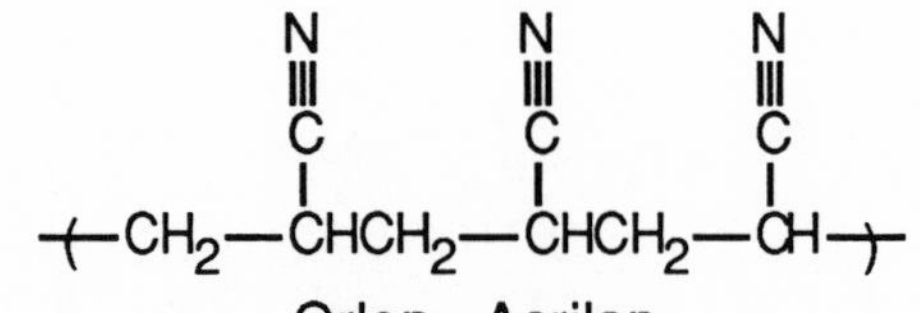

Acrylonitrile   Orlon, Acrilan

$+CH_2-CHCH_2-CHCH_2-CH+$
with $C\equiv N$ groups

13.13

(a)   *o*-Bromochlorobenzene

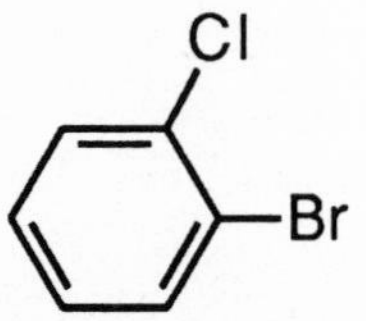

(b)   Butylbenzene $CH_2CH_2CH_2CH_3$

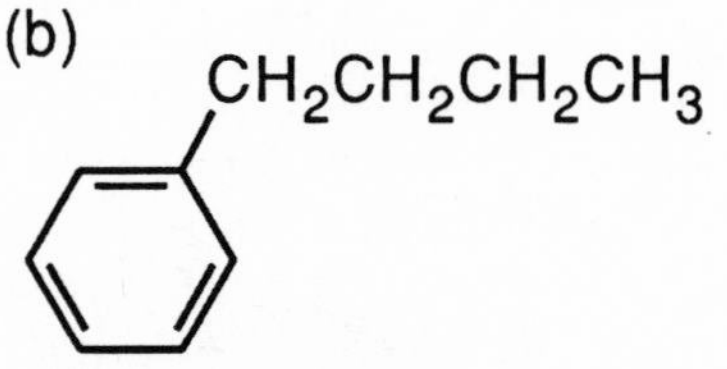

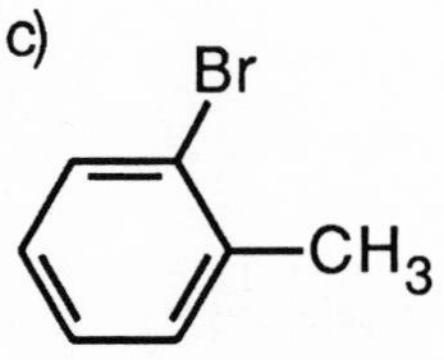

(c)   *o*-Bromotoluene

13.14

(a)   *o* -Dibromobenzene

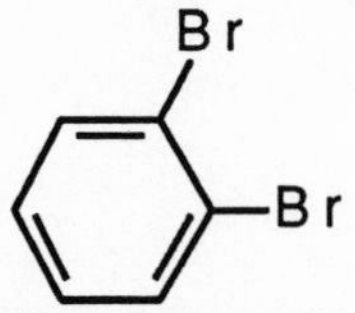

(b) O_2N-⬡$-CH_3$ *p* -Nitrotoluene

(c) CH_2CH_3 CH_2CH_3 *m* -Diethylbenzene

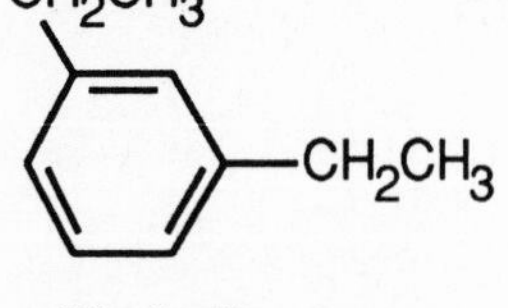

(d)   2-Chloro-4-isopropylphenol

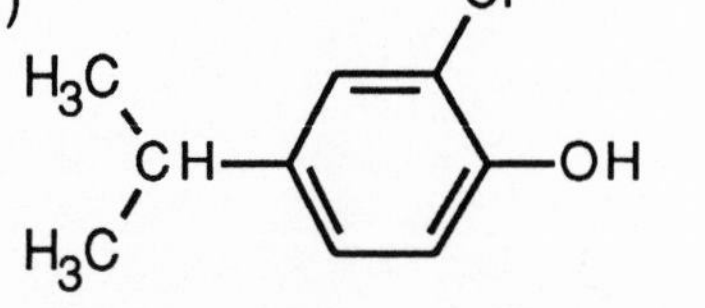

13.15

(a)

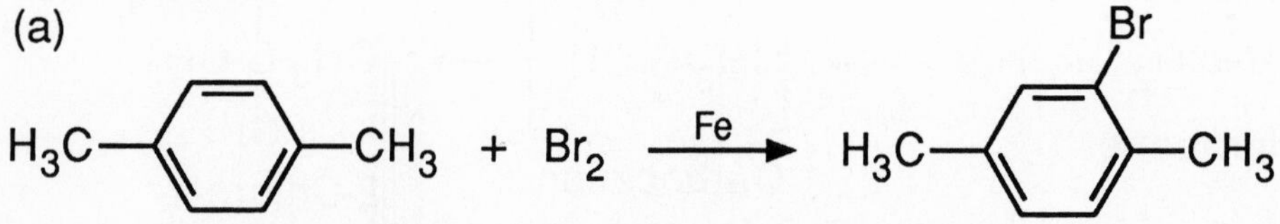

H_3C-⬡$-CH_3$ + Br_2 $\xrightarrow{Fe}$ H_3C-⬡$(Br)-CH_3$

(b)

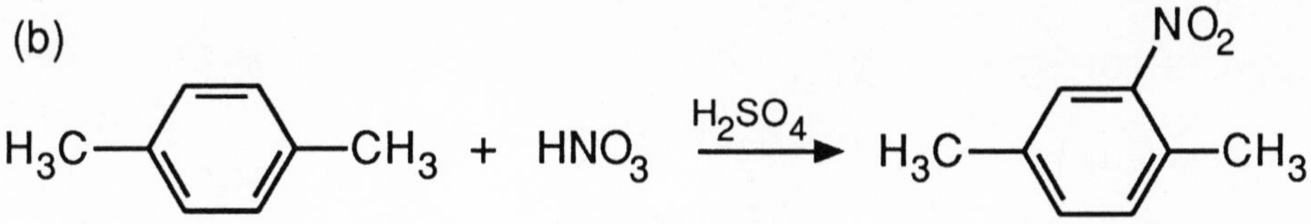

$$H_3C-\bigcirc-CH_3 + HNO_3 \xrightarrow{H_2SO_4} H_3C-\bigcirc\overset{NO_2}{-}CH_3$$

(c)

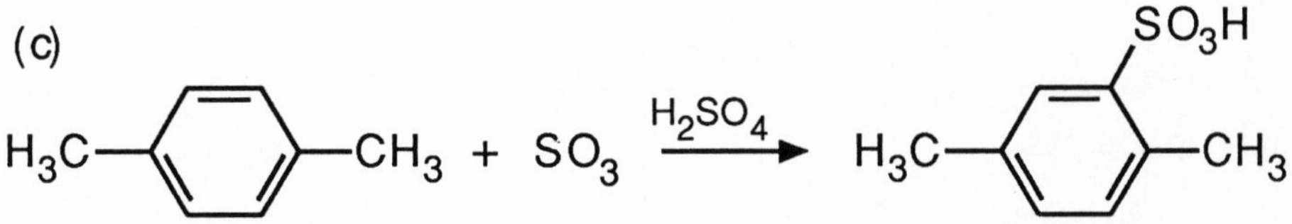

$$H_3C-\bigcirc-CH_3 + SO_3 \xrightarrow{H_2SO_4} H_3C-\bigcirc\overset{SO_3H}{-}CH_3$$

13.16

$$\bigcirc\overset{CH_3}{} + Br_2 \xrightarrow{Fe} \bigcirc\overset{CH_3}{-}Br + \bigcirc\overset{CH_3}{-}Br + \bigcirc\overset{CH_3}{-}Br$$

ortho   *meta*   *para*

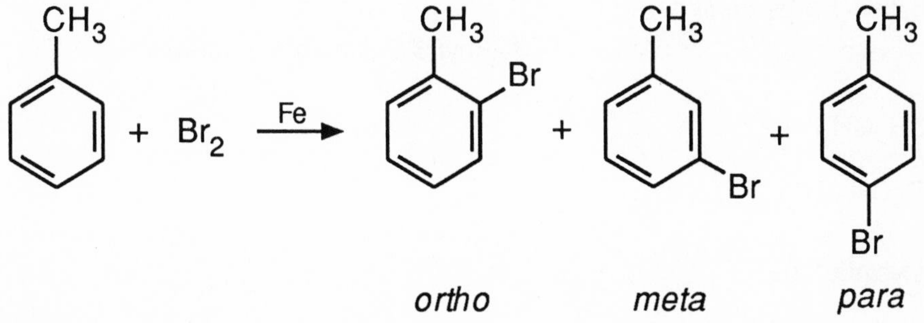

13.17 Alkenes, alkynes, and aromatic compounds are said to be unsaturated because they have fewer hydrogens per carbon than alkanes.

13.18 The term "aromatic" in chemistry refers to compounds that have a six-membered ring containing three double bonds. The association with aroma is of historical origin but no longer has any meaning.

13.19

(a)

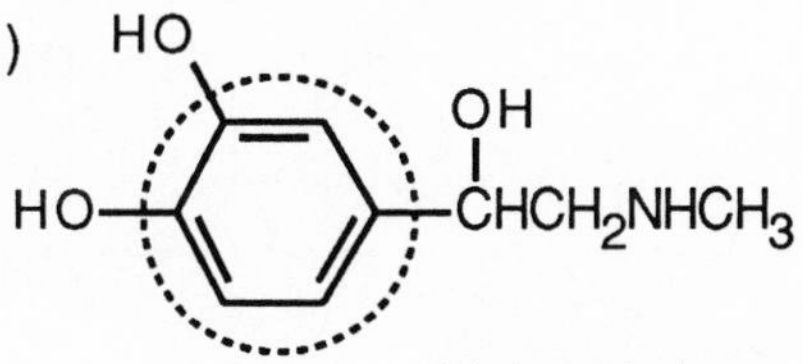

$$HO-\bigcirc-\overset{OH}{C}HCH_2NHCH_3$$
$$HO$$

Epinephrine

(b)

$$\bigcirc-OCH_2\overset{O}{C}-NH$$ ... Penicillin V

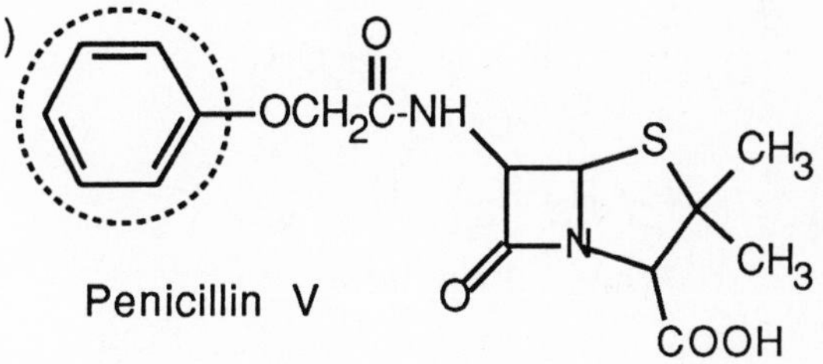

Penicillin V

13.20

Family:	Alkene	Alkyne	Aromatic Compound
Name Ending:	-ene	-yne	-benzene

13.21 There are many possible answers to this question. For example:

(a)

$$CH_3CH_2CH_2CH=CH_2$$

1-Pentene

(b)

$$CH_3CH_2C\equiv C\text{-}H$$

1-Butyne

(c)

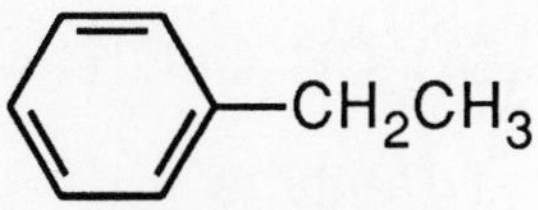

$$\bigcirc-CH_2CH_3$$

Ethylbenzene

13.22

(a) $CH_3CH_2CH_2CH=CH_2$

1-Pentene

(b)
$$\underset{\displaystyle CH_3}{CH_3CHCH_2C\equiv CCH_3}$$

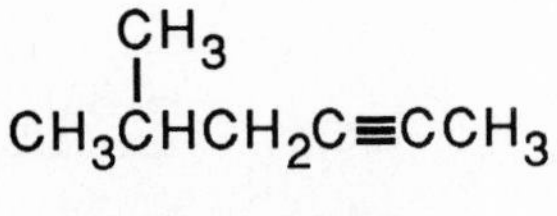

5-Methyl-2-hexyne

(c)

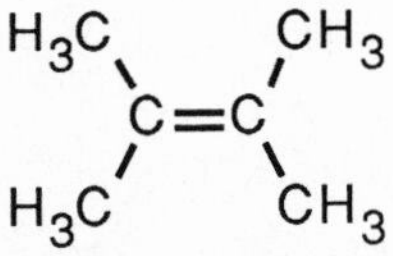

2,3-Dimethyl-2-butene

(d)
$$CH_3CH=\underset{\displaystyle \underset{CH_2CH_3}{|}}{\overset{\displaystyle \overset{CH_3}{|}}{C}}-C=CH_2$$

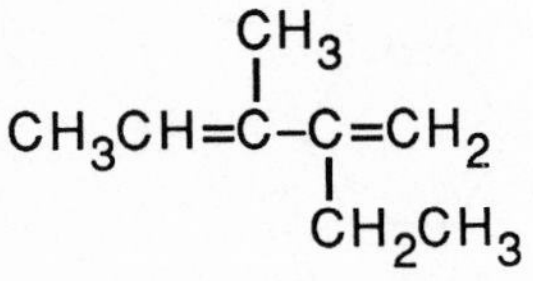

2-Ethyl-3-methyl-1,3-pentadiene

(e)

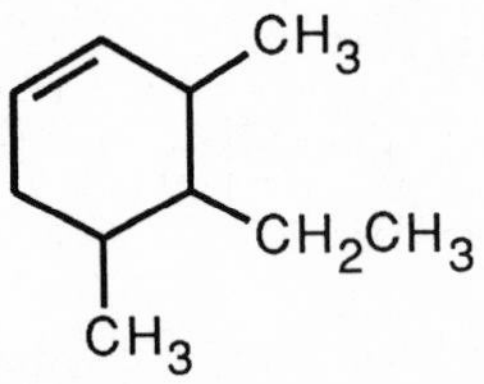

4-Ethyl-3,5-dimethylcyclohexene

(f)

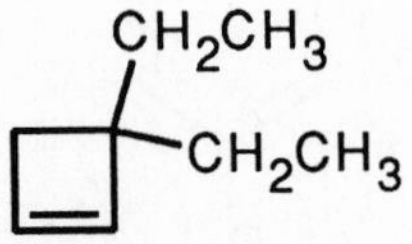

3,3-Diethylcyclobutene

13.23

(a)

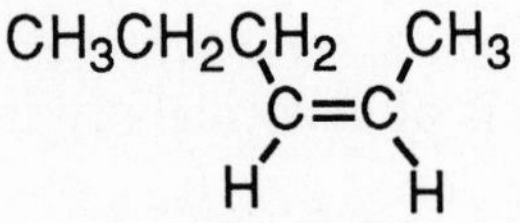

cis-2-Hexene

(b)
$$\underset{\displaystyle CH_3}{CH_3CH_2CH=CHCHCH_3}$$

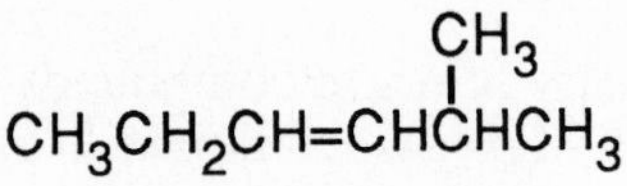

2-Methyl-3-hexene

(c)
$$\underset{\displaystyle CH_3}{CH_2=CH-C=CH_2}$$

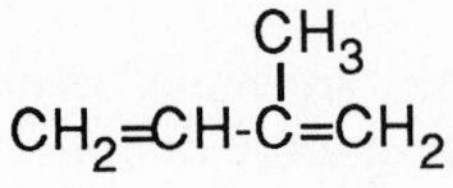

2-Methyl-1,3-butadiene

(d)

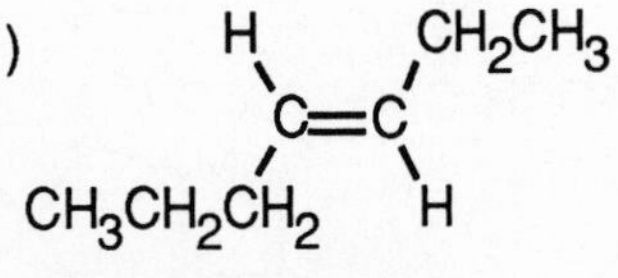

Trans-3-heptene

(e)
$$\underset{\displaystyle \underset{CH_2CH_3}{|}}{\overset{\displaystyle \overset{CH_3\quad CH_2CH_3}{|\qquad |}}{CH_3CH_2CH_2CHCH=CHCCH_2CH_3}}$$

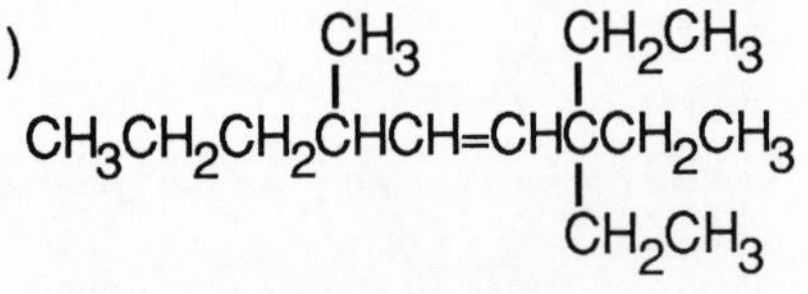

3,3-Diethyl-6-methyl-4-nonene

(f)
$$\underset{\displaystyle \underset{H_3C\ \ CH_3}{|\ \ \ |}}{\overset{\displaystyle \overset{CH_3CHCH_3}{|}}{CH_3CH=C-CCH=CH_2}}$$

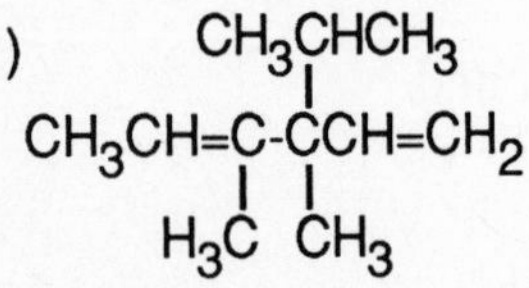

3-Isopropyl-3,4-dimethyl-1,4-hexadiene

13.24

$CH_3CH_2CH_2C\equiv CH$

1-Pentyne

$CH_3CH_2C\equiv CCH_3$

2-Pentyne

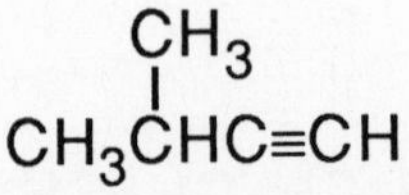

$$\underset{\displaystyle CH_3CHC\equiv CH}{\overset{\displaystyle \overset{CH_3}{|}}{}}$$

3-Methyl-1-butyne

13.25

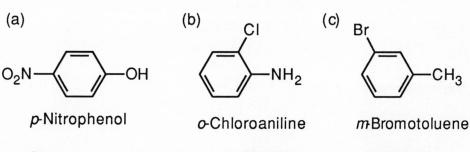

(a)

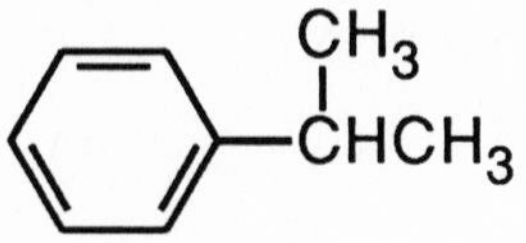

Isopropylbenzene

(b)

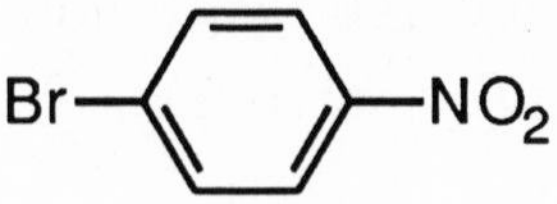

p-Bromonitrobenzene

(c)

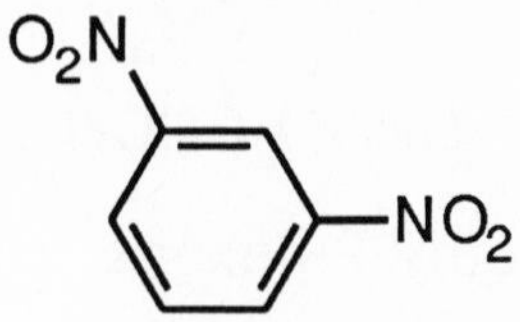

m-Dinitrobenzene

13.26

(a)

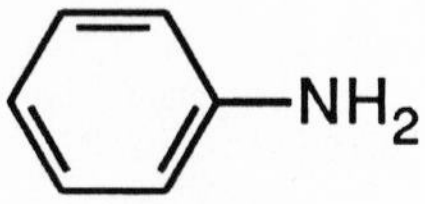

Aniline

(b)

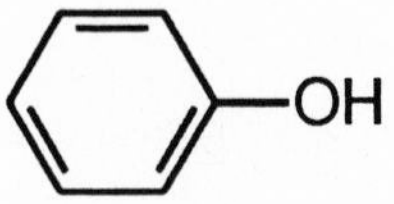

Phenol

(c)

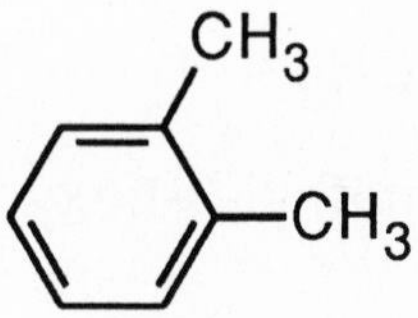

o-Xylene

(d)

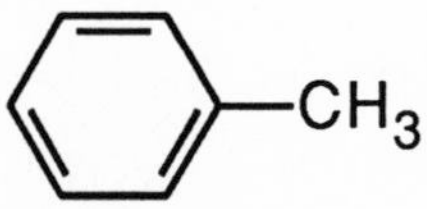

Toluene

(e)

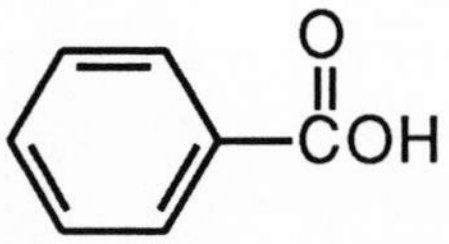

Benzoic acid

13.27

(a)

p-Nitrophenol

(b)

o-Chloroaniline

(c)

m-Bromotoluene

(d)

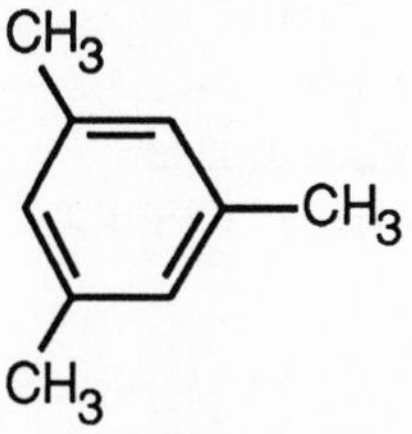

1,3,5-Trimethylbenzene

(e)

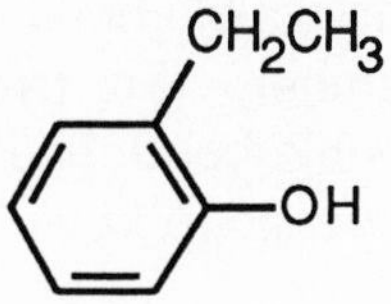

o-Ethylphenol

(f)

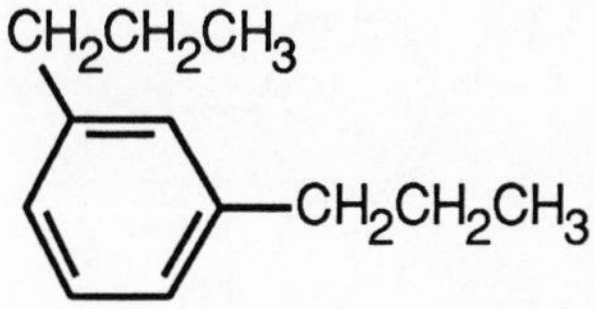

m-Dipropylbenzene

13.28

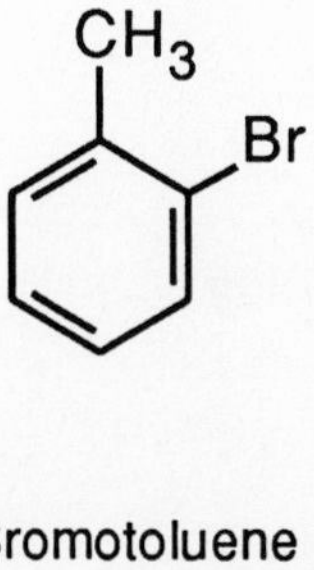

o–Bromotoluene

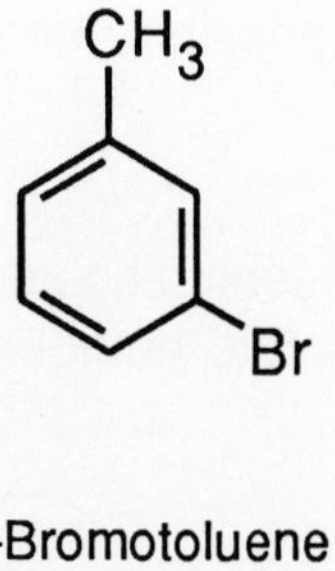

m–Bromotoluene

p–Bromotoluene

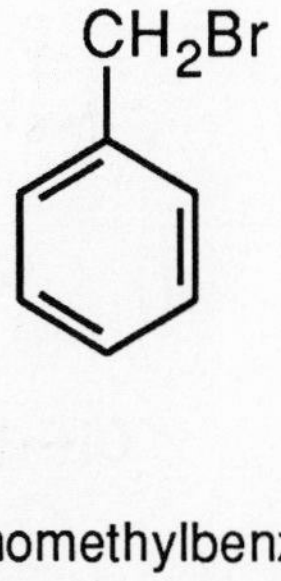

Bromomethylbenzene

13.29

(a)

$$CH_3CH=CHCH_2\overset{\overset{\displaystyle CH_3}{|}}{C}HCH_3$$

5-Methyl-2-hexene

Numbering should start from the end nearer the double bond.

(b)

$$CH_3-\overset{\overset{\displaystyle CH_3}{|}}{\underset{\underset{\displaystyle CH_3}{|}}{C}}-C\equiv CCH_2CH_3$$

2,2-Dimethyl-3-hexyne

Numbering should start from the end nearer the first substituent.

(c)

$$CH_3CH_2CH_2CH_2-\overset{\overset{\displaystyle CH_3}{|}}{C}=CH_2$$

2-Methyl-1-hexene

The longest chain should be used as a base name.

(d)

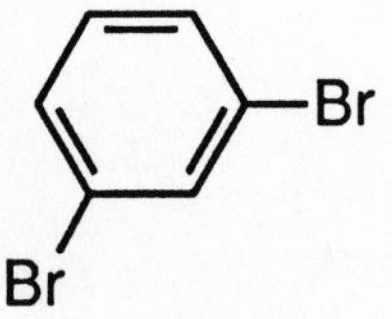

1,3-Dibromobenzene *or*

m-Dibromobenzene

Substituents should be given lowest possible numbers.

(e)

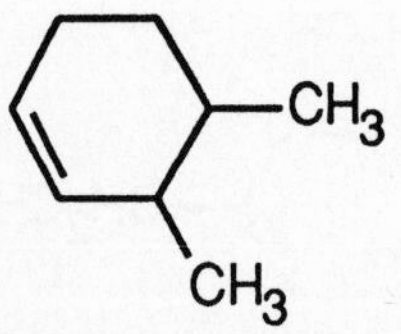

3,4-Dimethylcyclohexene

The double bond receives the lowest number. (For cyclic alkenes the double bond receives no number but is understood to be between carbons 1 and 2.)

(f)

$$CH_2=CH\overset{\overset{\displaystyle CH_3}{|}}{C}=CHCH_3$$

3-Methyl-1,3-pentadiene

The double bonds should receive the lowest possible numbers.

(g)

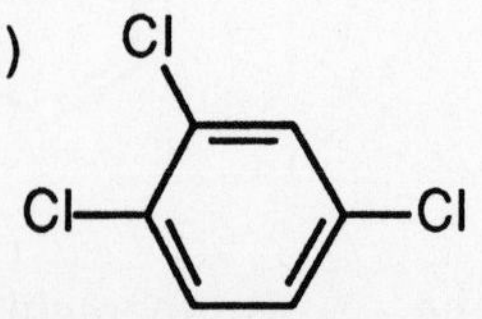

1,2,4-Trichlorobenzene

The substituents should be given the lowest possible numbers.

13.30

$CH_3CH_2CH=C=CH_2$ $CH_3CH=CHCH=CH_2$ $CH_2=CHCH_2CH=CH_2$

   1,2-Pentadiene   1,3-Pentadiene   1,4-Pentadiene

$$CH_2=CH\overset{\overset{\textstyle CH_3}{|}}{C}=CH_2 \qquad CH_3\overset{\overset{\textstyle CH_3}{|}}{C}=C=CH_2 \qquad CH_3CH=C=CHCH_3$$

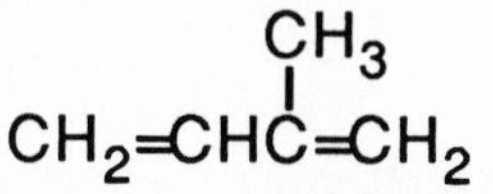

2-Methyl-1,3-butadiene 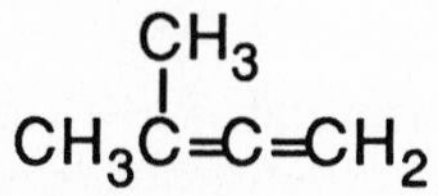   3-Methyl-1,2-butadiene   2,3-Pentadiene

13.31 For cis-trans isomers to exist, each carbon of the double bond must be bonded to two different groups.

13.32 Alkynes don't show cis-trans isomerism because only one group is bonded to each alkyne carbon.

13.33

$CH_3CH_2CH_2CH=CH_2$ $CH_3CH_2CH=CHCH_3$ $CH_3CH_2\overset{\overset{\textstyle CH_3}{|}}{C}=CH_2$

    1-Pentene   2-Pentene   2-Methyl-1-butene

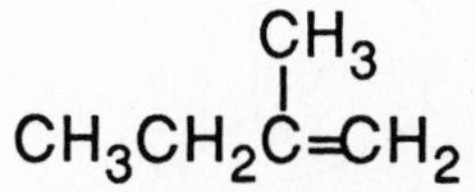

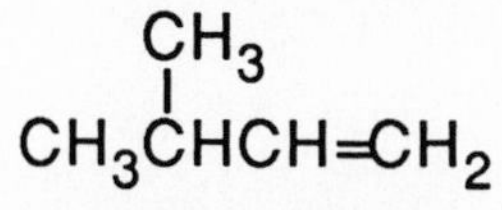

$CH_3\overset{\overset{\textstyle CH_3}{|}}{C}HCH=CH_2$ $CH_3CH=\overset{\overset{\textstyle CH_3}{|}}{C}CH_3$

3-Methyl-1-butene 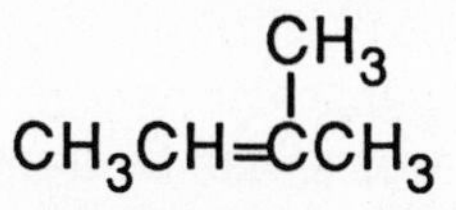   2-Methyl-2-butene

13.34 Only 2-pentene can exist as cis-trans isomers:

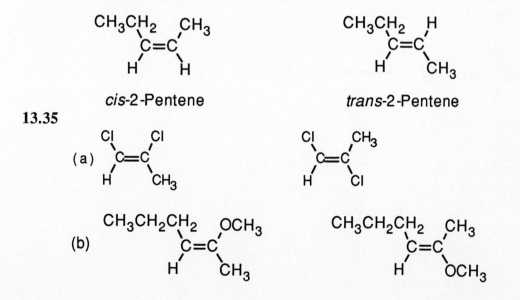

   cis-2-Pentene   *trans*-2-Pentene

13.35

13.36 (a) These compounds are identical:

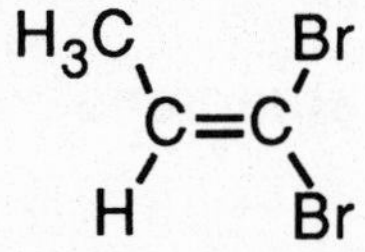

and

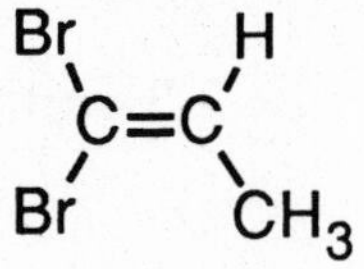

(b) These compounds are also identical:

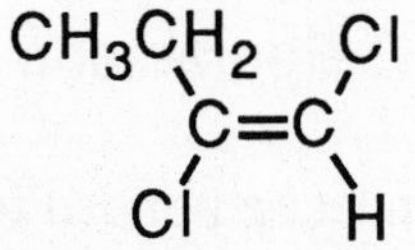

and

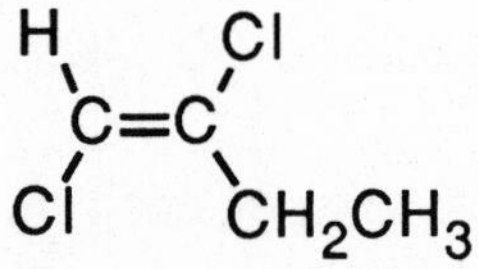

13.37 A trans double bond is too strained to exist in a small ring like cyclohexene, but a large ring is more flexible and can include a trans double bond:

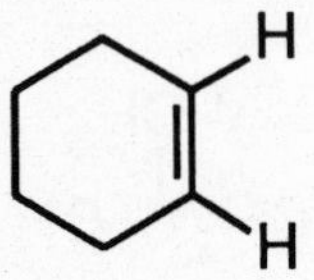

double bond must be cis in this six-membered ring

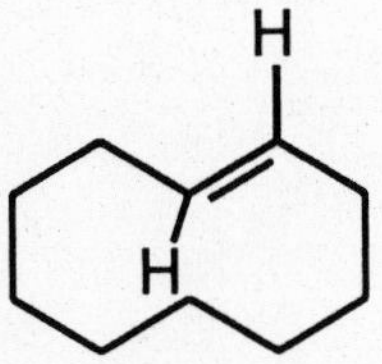

double bond can be trans in this ten-membered ring

13.38 An addition reaction is a reaction in which a reagent X-Y adds to a double (or triple) bond to yield a product having only single bonds.

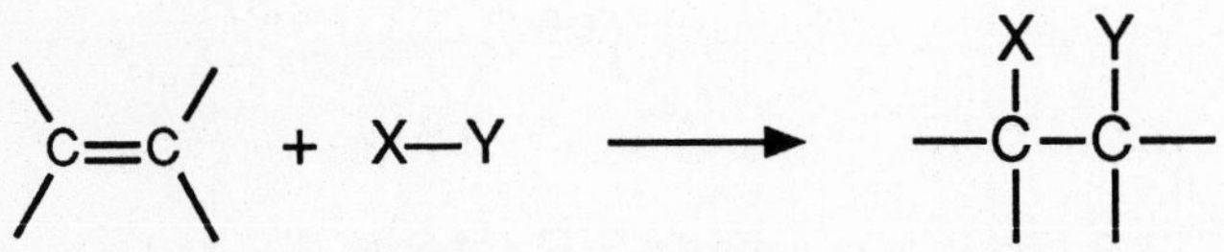

13.39

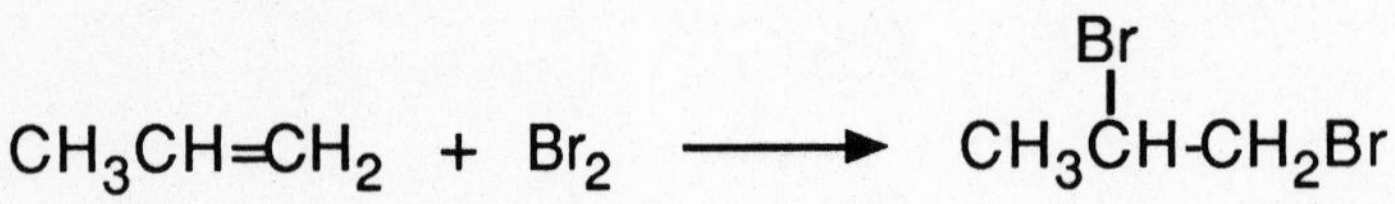

$$CH_3CH=CH_2 + Br_2 \longrightarrow CH_3\overset{\overset{\displaystyle Br}{|}}{C}H\text{-}CH_2Br$$

13.40

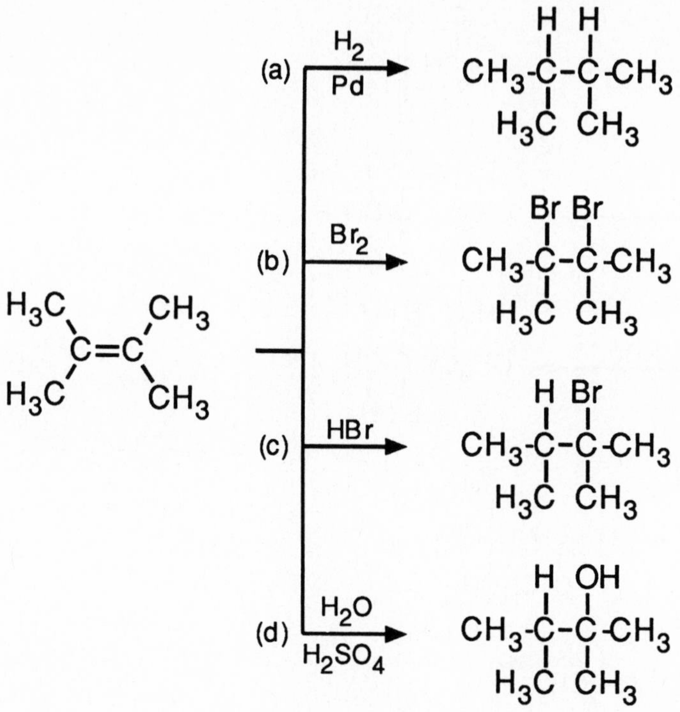

(a) $\dfrac{H_2}{Pd}$

$$\underset{\underset{\displaystyle H_3C \quad CH_3}{|}}{CH_3-\overset{\displaystyle \overset{H}{|}}{C}-\overset{\displaystyle \overset{H}{|}}{C}-CH_3}$$

(b) Br_2

$$\underset{\underset{\displaystyle H_3C \quad CH_3}{|}}{CH_3-\overset{\displaystyle \overset{Br}{|}}{C}-\overset{\displaystyle \overset{Br}{|}}{C}-CH_3}$$

$$\underset{H_3C}{\overset{H_3C}{>}}C=C\underset{CH_3}{\overset{CH_3}{<}}$$

(c) HBr

$$\underset{\underset{\displaystyle H_3C \quad CH_3}{|}}{CH_3-\overset{\displaystyle \overset{H}{|}}{C}-\overset{\displaystyle \overset{Br}{|}}{C}-CH_3}$$

(d) $\dfrac{H_2O}{H_2SO_4}$

$$\underset{\underset{\displaystyle H_3C \quad CH_3}{|}}{CH_3-\overset{\displaystyle \overset{H}{|}}{C}-\overset{\displaystyle \overset{OH}{|}}{C}-CH_3}$$

13.41

(a) $\dfrac{H_2}{Pd}$

$$\underset{\underset{\displaystyle H \quad CH_3}{|}}{CH_3-\overset{\displaystyle \overset{H}{|}}{C}-\overset{\displaystyle \overset{H}{|}}{C}-CH_3}$$

(b) Br_2

$$\underset{\underset{\displaystyle H \quad CH_3}{|}}{CH_3-\overset{\displaystyle \overset{Br}{|}}{C}-\overset{\displaystyle \overset{Br}{|}}{C}-CH_3}$$

$$\underset{H}{\overset{H_3C}{>}}C=C\underset{CH_3}{\overset{CH_3}{<}}$$

(c) HBr

$$\underset{\underset{\displaystyle H \quad CH_3}{|}}{CH_3-\overset{\displaystyle \overset{H}{|}}{C}-\overset{\displaystyle \overset{Br}{|}}{C}-CH_3}$$

(d) $\dfrac{H_2O}{H_2SO_4}$

$$\underset{\underset{\displaystyle H \quad CH_3}{|}}{CH_3-\overset{\displaystyle \overset{H}{|}}{C}-\overset{\displaystyle \overset{OH}{|}}{C}-CH_3}$$

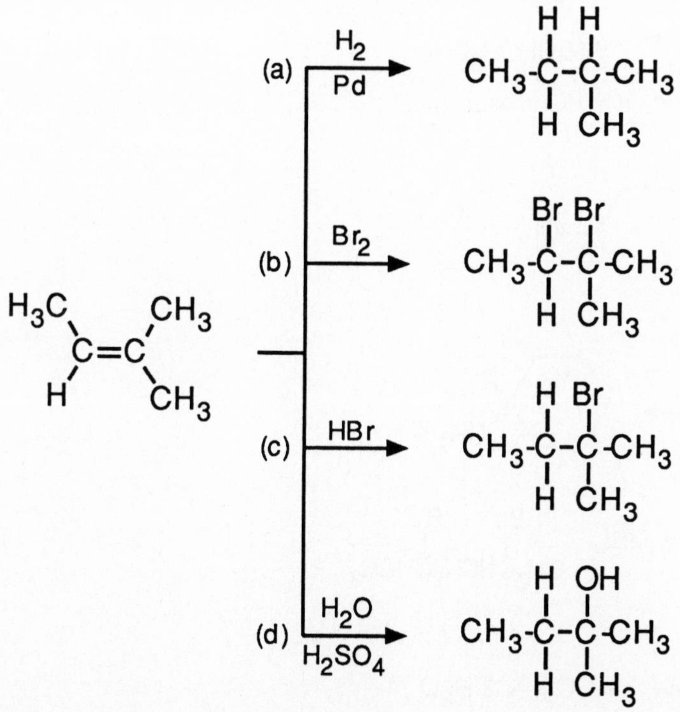

13.42

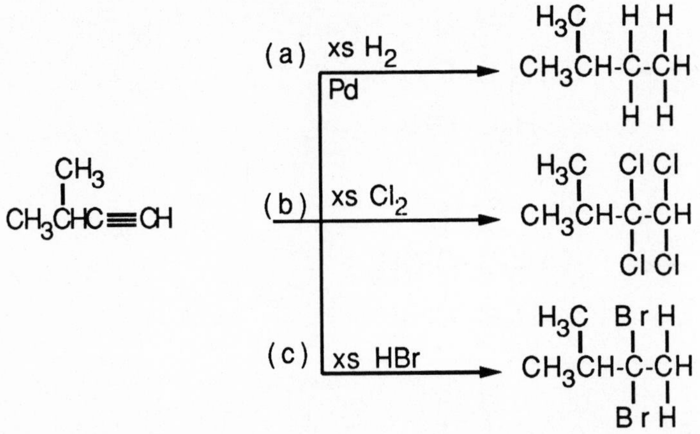

CH₃CHC≡CH (with CH₃ branch)

(a) xs H₂ / Pd →

$$H_3C \quad H \quad H$$
$$CH_3CH-C-CH$$
$$H \quad H$$

(b) xs Cl₂ →

$$H_3C \quad Cl \quad Cl$$
$$CH_3CH-C-CH$$
$$Cl \quad Cl$$

(c) xs HBr →

$$H_3C \quad Br \quad H$$
$$CH_3CH-C-CH$$
$$Br \quad H$$

13.43 (a)

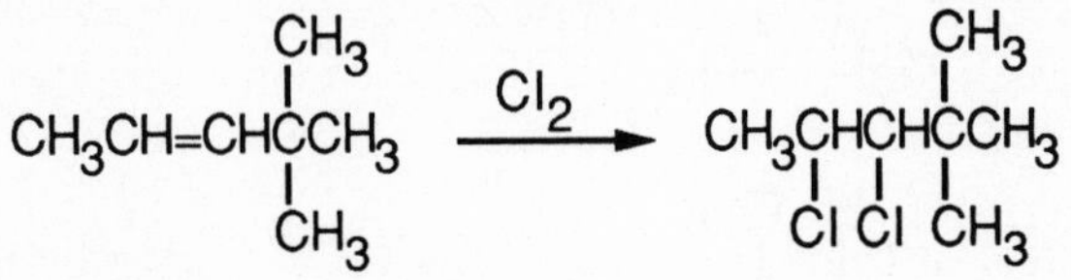

$$CH_3CH=CHCCH_3 \quad \xrightarrow{Cl_2} \quad CH_3CHCHCCH_3$$

with CH₃ groups; products: Cl Cl CH₃

(b)

$$CH_3CH=CH_2 \quad \xrightarrow{H_2/Pd} \quad CH_3CH_2CH_3$$

(c)

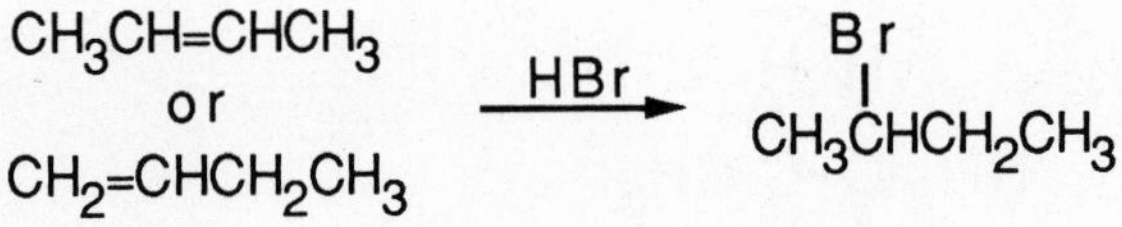

$$\begin{array}{c} CH_3CH=CHCH_3 \\ or \\ CH_2=CHCH_2CH_3 \end{array} \quad \xrightarrow{HBr} \quad \begin{array}{c} Br \\ CH_3CHCH_2CH_3 \end{array}$$

(d)

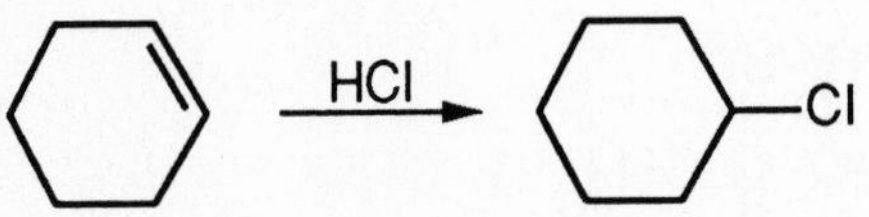

cyclohexene $\xrightarrow{HCl}$ chlorocyclohexane —Cl

(e)

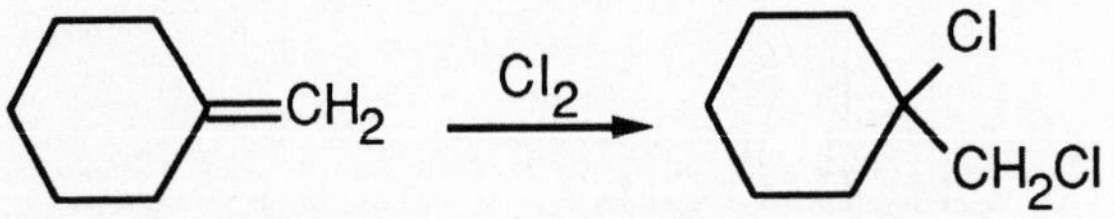

cyclohexane=CH₂ $\xrightarrow{Cl_2}$ ring with Cl and CH₂Cl

(f)

$$CH_2=CHCH_2CH=CH_2 \quad \xrightarrow{xs\ HBr} \quad \begin{array}{cc} Br & Br \\ CH_3CHCH_2CHCH_3 \end{array}$$

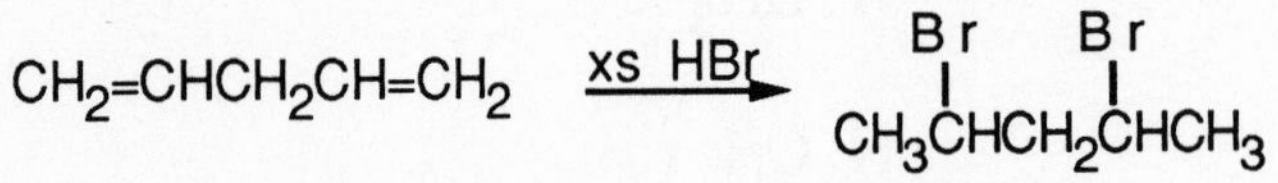

13.44

$$2\ HC\equiv CH + 5\ O_2 \longrightarrow 4\ CO_2 + 2\ H_2O$$

13.45

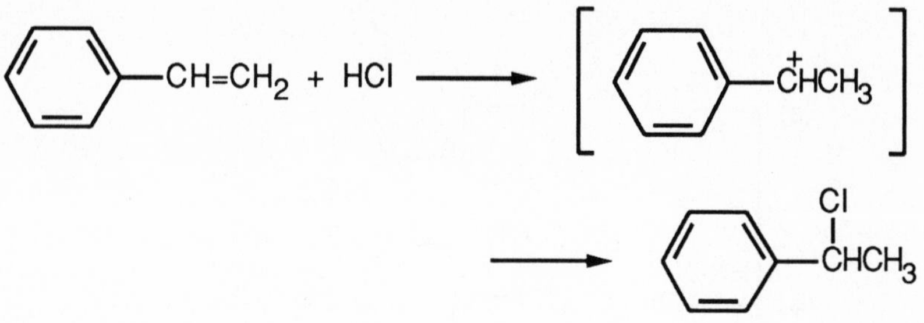

13.46

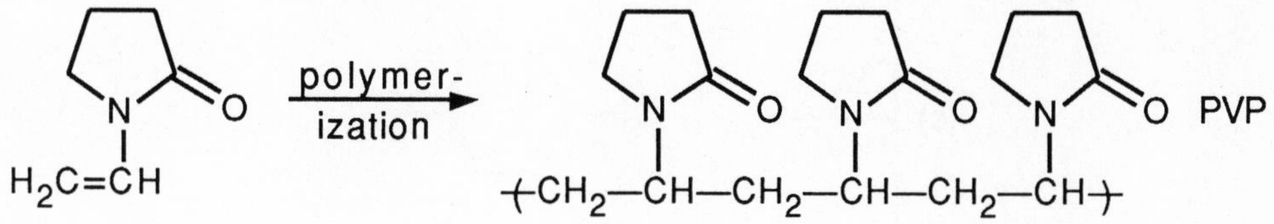

13.47

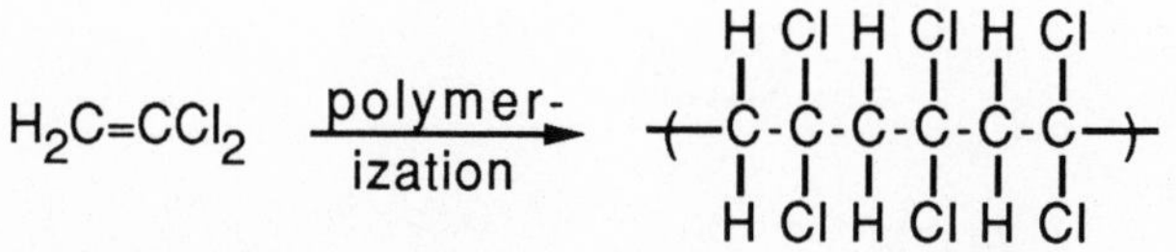

13.48 A substitution reaction is a reaction in which one atom or group of atoms replaces (substitutes for) another atom or group of atoms. For example:

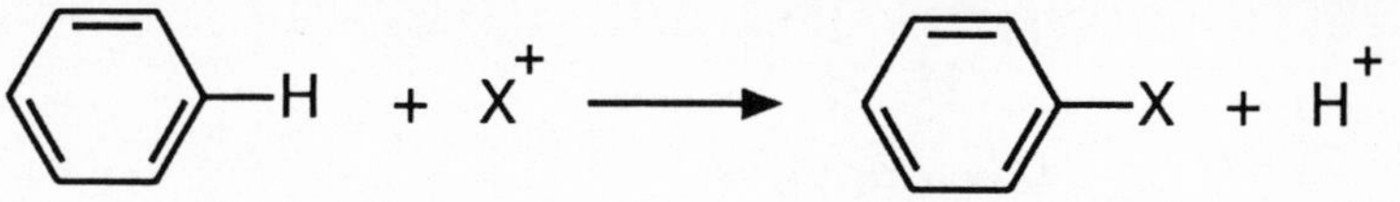

13.49

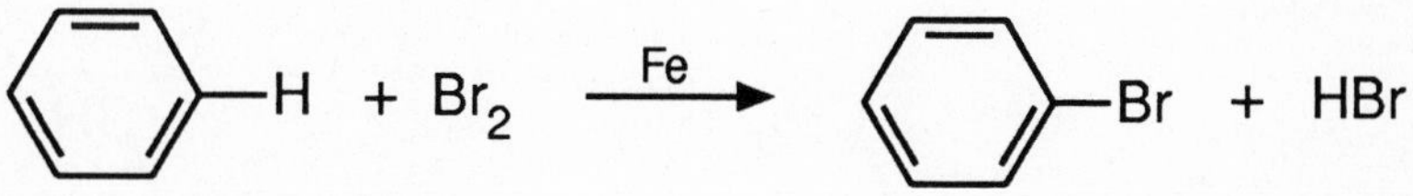

13.50 Under conditions where an alkene would react with all four reagents, benzene reacts only with Br_2 (b) to give the product shown in the previous problem.

13.51

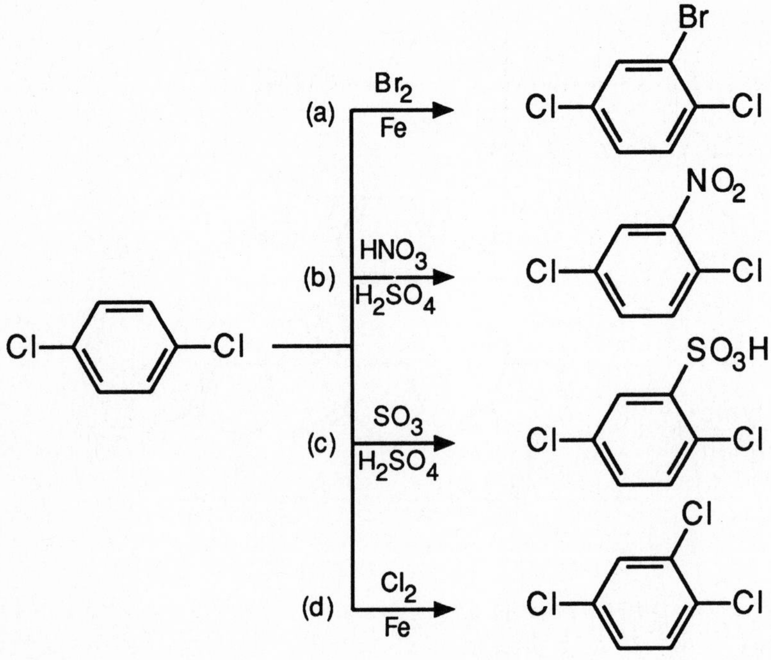

13.52

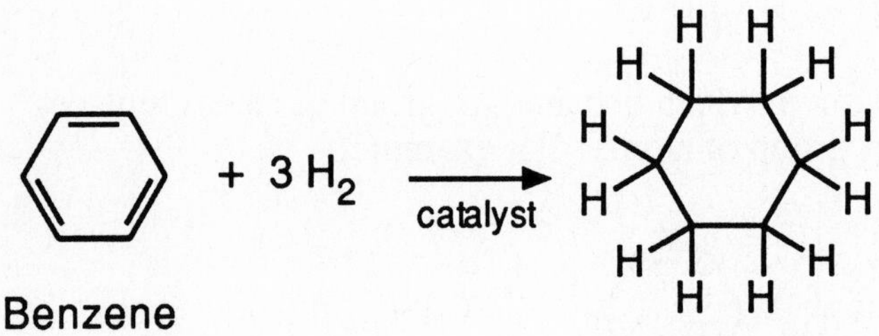

Benzene   Cyclohexane

13.53 There is only one kind of site on the benzene ring, but there are two different sites on the *o*-xylene ring for Br_2 to react.

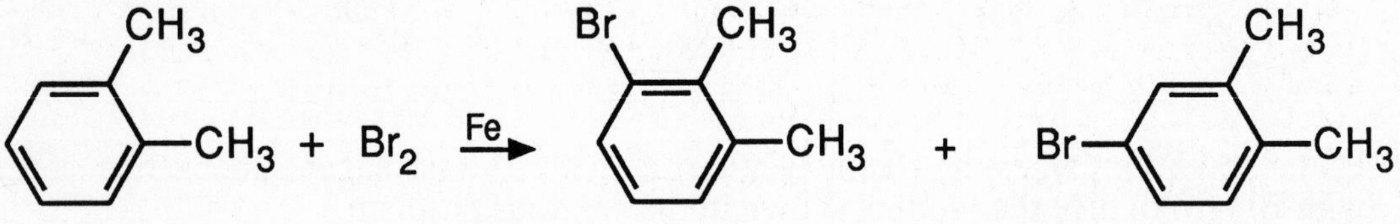

o-Xylene   3-Bromo-1,2-Dimethylbenzene   4-Bromo-1,2-Dimethylbenzene

13.54

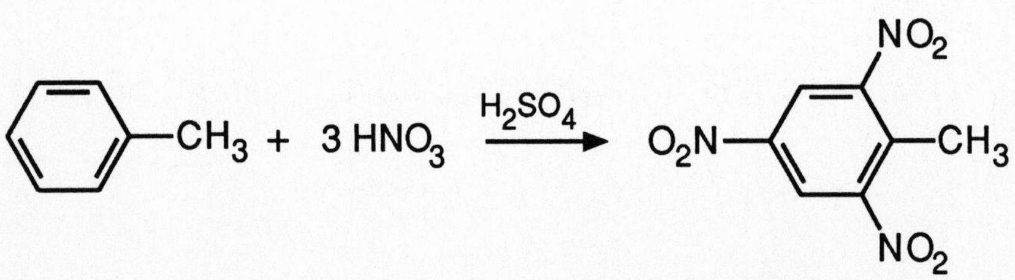

TNT

13.55 The rod cells are responsible for vision in dim light, and the cone cells are responsible for color vision.

13.56 When light strikes rhodopsin, the cis double bond between C11 and C12 is isomerized to a trans double bond. The resulting isomerization causes a change in molecular geometry that causes a nerve impulse to be sent to the brain.

13.57

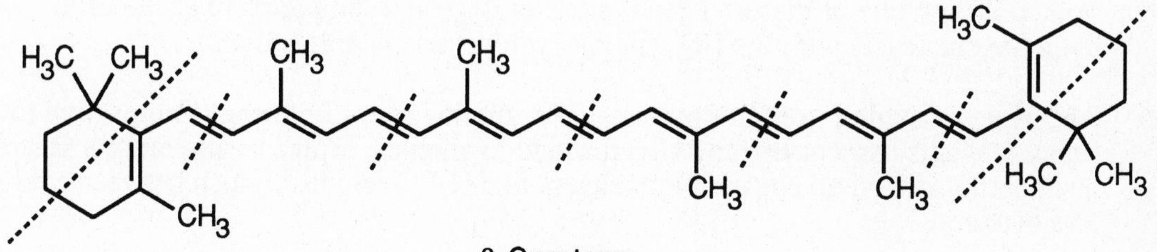

β-Carotene

13.58

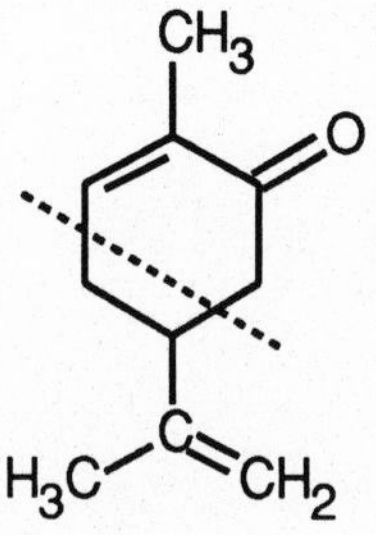

Carvone

13.59

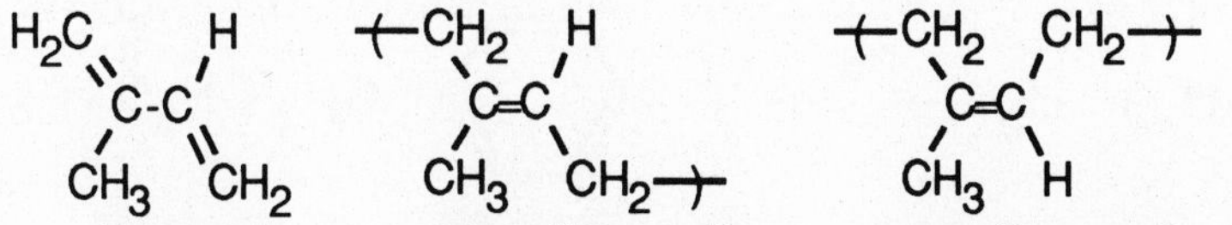

Isoprene   repeating unit   repeating unit
          (trans double bond) (cis double bond)

Isoprene doesn't show cis-trans isomerism because one end of each double bond is bonded to two hydrogens. In polymeric isoprene, however, each end of the double bond is bonded to two different substituents, giving rise to cis-trans isomerism.

13.60 Since naphthalene is white, it must absorb color in the ultraviolet range.

13.61 Tetrabromofluorescein is colored because it contains many alternating single and double bonds. Since tetrabromofluorescein is purple, it must absorb yellow light. (Yellow is the complement of purple.)

13.62 Alkanes have no double bonds and thus can't undergo the addition reactions that result in polymerization.

13.63

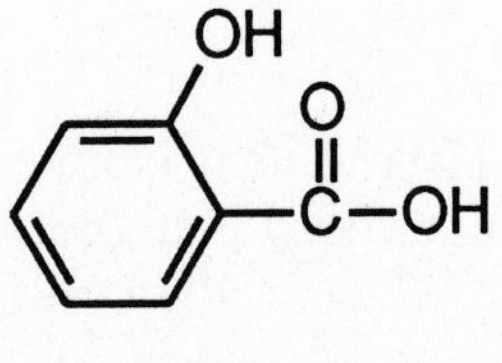

Salicylic acid

13.64 None of the reagents that add to alkenes react with alkanes such as cyclohexane. Thus, you could use one of these reagents, such as Br_2, on a sample from each bottle. The cyclohexene reacts with the Br_2, but the cyclohexane is unreactive.

13.65 The same reasoning used in Problem 13.64 applies here. Benzene is unreactive toward many reagents (except Br_2 and Cl_2) that add to alkenes. Thus, treatment of a sample from each bottle with an alkene addition reagent like H_3O^+ can distinguish between cyclohexene and benzene.

13.66

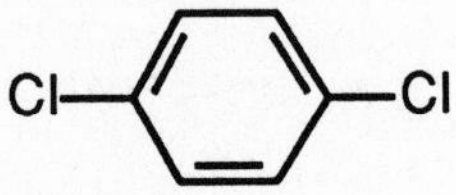

p-Dichlorobenzene

13.67

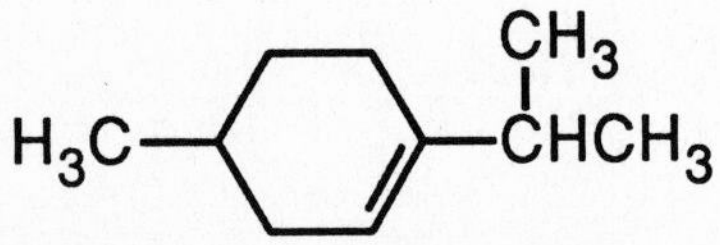

Menthene

13.68

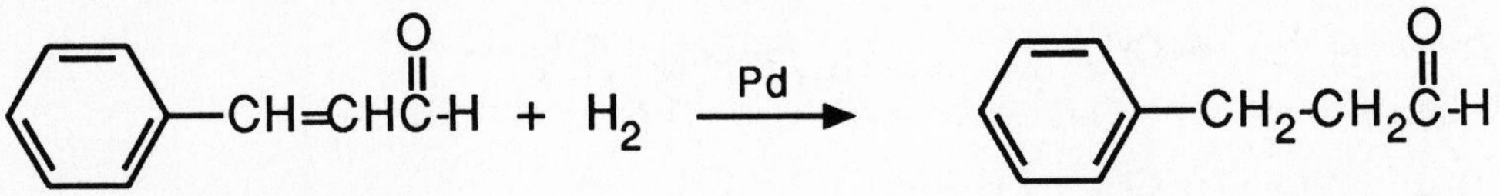

Cinnamaldehyde   3-Phenylpropanal

13.69

(a)

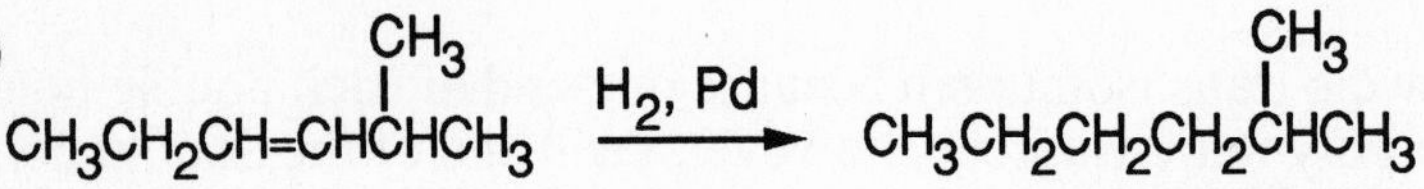

(b)

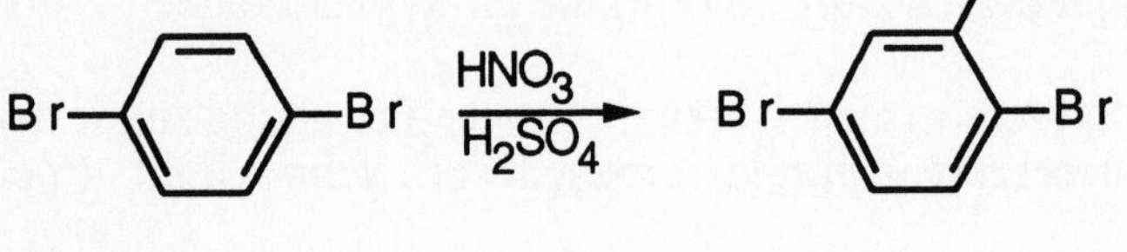

(c)

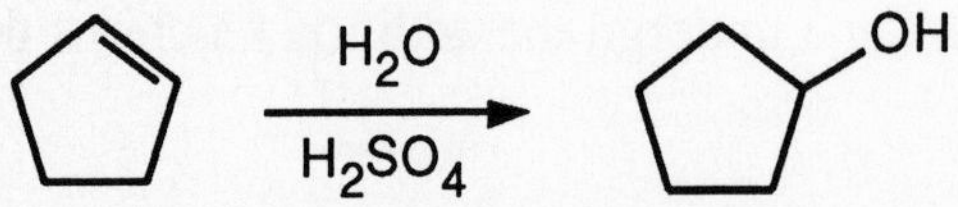

(d)

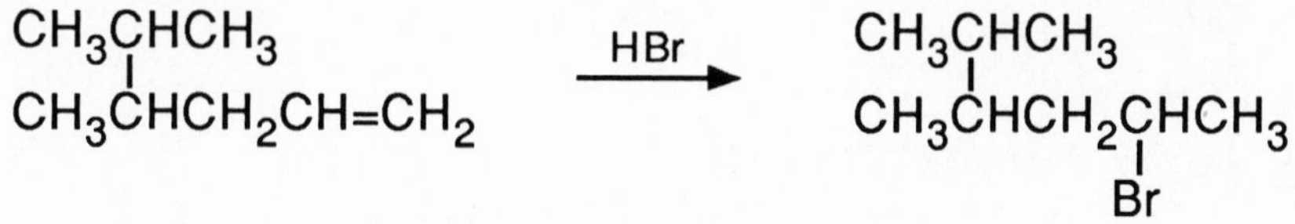

$$CH_3CHCH_3$$
$$CH_3CHCH_2CH=CH_2 \xrightarrow{HBr} $$

$$CH_3CHCH_3$$
$$CH_3CHCH_2CHCH_3$$
$$\overset{|}{Br}$$

(e)

$$CH_3C\equiv CCH_2CH_3 \xrightarrow{H_2, Pd} CH_3CH_2CH_2CH_2CH_3$$

(f)

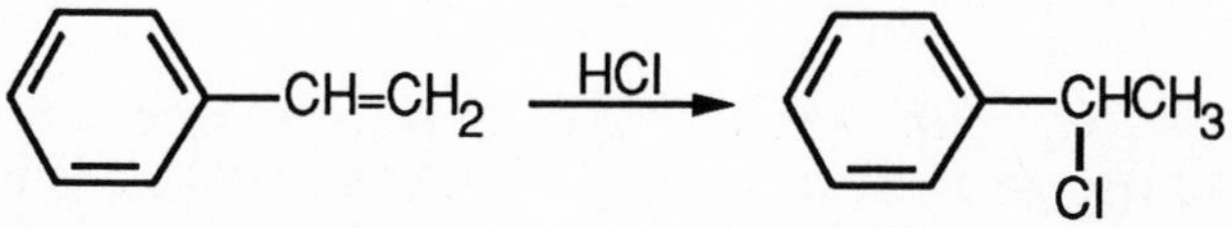

⬡—CH=CH$_2$ $\xrightarrow{HCl}$ ⬡—CHCH$_3$
                                                  |
                                                  Cl

13.70

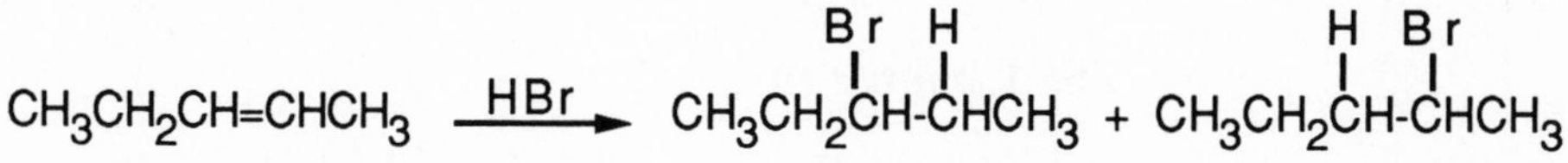

$$CH_3CH_2CH=CHCH_3 \xrightarrow{HBr}$$
$$\overset{Br\ \ H}{\underset{}{CH_3CH_2CH-CHCH_3}} + \overset{H\ \ Br}{\underset{}{CH_3CH_2CH-CHCH_3}}$$

The products are formed in equal amounts because each end of the double bond has the same number of hydrogens.

13.71 In contrast to benzene, naphthalene is a solid at room temperature because it has a greater formula weight and thus is subject to stronger London forces.

13.72

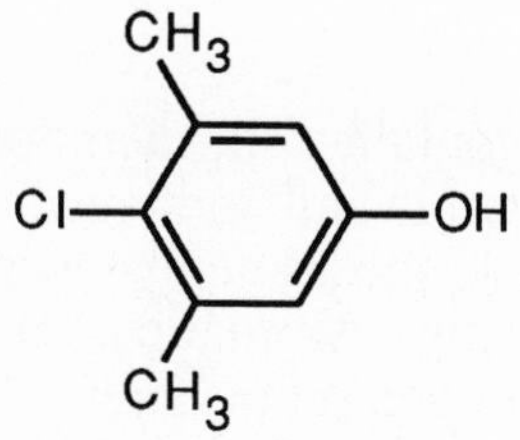

CH$_3$
|
Cl—⬡—OH   4-Chloro-3,5-dimethylphenol
|
CH$_3$

13.73 (a)(b)

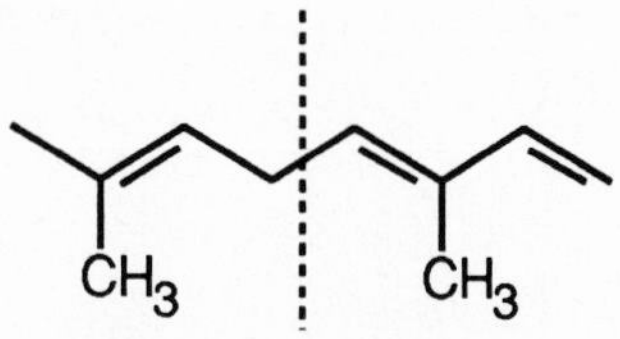

Ocimene (3,7-Dimethyl-1,3,6-octatriene)

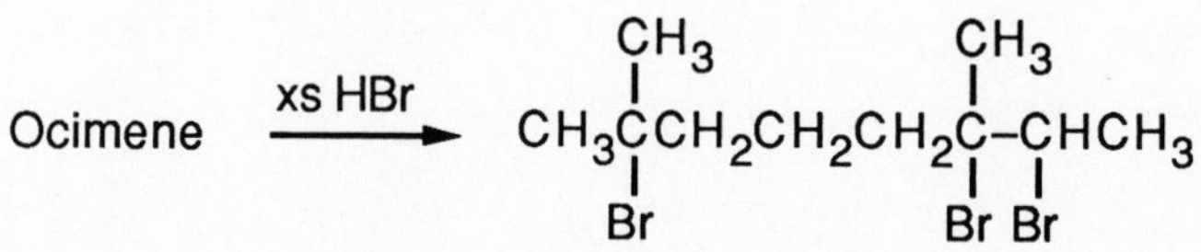

$$Ocimene \xrightarrow{xs\ HBr}$$
$$\overset{CH_3}{\underset{Br}{CH_3CCH_2CH_2CH_2}}\overset{CH_3}{\underset{Br\ Br}{C-CHCH_3}}$$

13.74

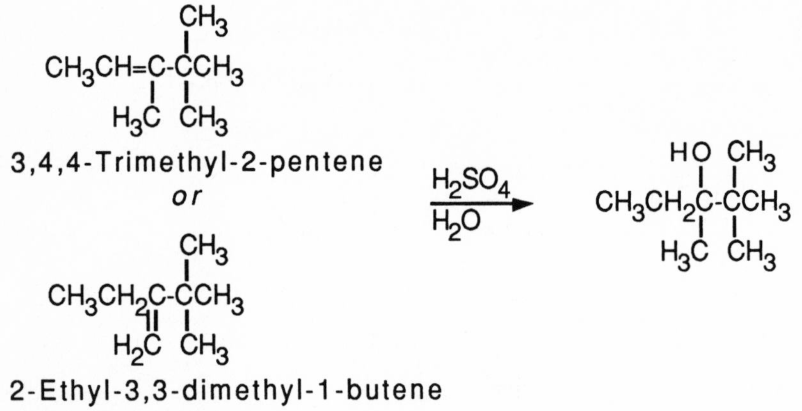

$$CH_3CH=C-CCH_3$$

with CH_3 above and H_3C CH_3 below

3,4,4-Trimethyl-2-pentene

or

$$CH_3CH_2C-CCH_3$$

with CH_3 above and H_2C CH_3 below

2-Ethyl-3,3-dimethyl-1-butene

$$\xrightarrow[\text{H}_2\text{O}]{\text{H}_2\text{SO}_4}$$

$$CH_3CH_2C-CCH_3$$

with HO CH_3 above and H_3C CH_3 below

The Chapter in Brief

Alkenes and Alkynes (Sections 13.1–13.9) An alkene is a hydrocarbon that contains one or more double bonds; an alkyne is a hydrocarbon that contains one or more triple bonds. Alkenes and alkynes are named by IUPAC rules that are similar to the rules for naming alkanes, with the name-endings -*ene* and -*yne* used to indicate a double bond or a triple bond. Alkene double bonds can show cis-trans isomerism if each carbon in the bond has two different groups attached to it. Alkenes and alkynes undergo addition reactions, in which a reagent X-Y adds to the multiple bond to give a product that has only single bonds. H_2, H_2O, Cl_2, Br_2, HCl, and HBr all add to multiple bonds. Many addition reactions take place through carbocation intermediates. Alkenes can undergo polymerization reactions to yield huge molecules.

Aromatic Compounds (Sections 13.10–13.13) Aromatic compounds contain a six-membered ring of carbons with three double bonds. These compounds are unusually stable and don't react readily with the reagents that add to alkenes. Aromatic compounds are named as substituted benzenes, using the prefixes *ortho*-, *meta*-, or *para*- to locate substituents on the ring. Aromatic compounds undergo substitution reactions in which a group Y substitutes for a hydrogen on the ring. Nitration, halogenation, and sulfonation are examples of substitution reactions. Polycyclic aromatic compounds contain two or more benzene rings sharing a common bond.

Self-Test for Chapter 13

Complete the following sentences:

1. The name of $CH_3CH_2CH_2CH_2C{\equiv}CCH_3$ is _____.

2. Addition of hydrogen to an alkene or alkyne is known as _____.

3. A benzene ring with substituents at the 1 and 4 positions is said to be _____ disubstituted.

4. In the addition of HX to an alkene, the H becomes attached to the carbon that already has ____ H's, and the X becomes attached to the carbon that has _____ H's.

5. Ethanol can be produced by the _____ of ethylene.

6. In the nitration of benzene, H_2SO_4 is used as a _____.

7. The intermediate formed during the addition of HBr to an alkene is called a _____.

8. Compounds with double or triple bonds are said to be _____.

9. _____ is another name for methylbenzene.

10. The reaction of Br_2 with benzene is an example of a _____ reaction.

11. Polymers containing more than one kind of monomer are called _____.

12. Simple alkenes are made by _____ _____ of natural gas and petroleum.

Tell whether the following statements are true or false:

1. Cis-trans isomers have identical physical properties.

2. Addition of one equivalent of H_2 to an alkyne yields an alkene.

3. Aromatic compounds are less reactive than alkenes.

4. The product of addition of HBr to 1-butene is 1-bromobutane.

5. The reaction of HBr with an alkene is known as halogenation.

6. A compound with the formula C_4H_6 can be either an alkyne or an alkene.

7. 1-Methylcyclohexene can exhibit cis-trans isomerism.

8. Mixing an alkene with water causes the hydration of the double bond.

9. Addition of HBr to an alkene is a two-step reaction.

10. Benzene and 1-butene react with Br_2 under the same reaction conditions.

11. Only aromatic compounds with more than one ring are carcinogenic.

12. Natural rubber is a polymer of isoprene.

Match the entries on the left with their partners on the right:

1. HNO_3, H_2SO_4 (a) Does not have cis-trans isomers

2. H_2O, H_2SO_4 (b) Used to hydrogenate an alkene

3. $CH_3C{\equiv}CH$ (c) Polycyclic aromatic hydrocarbon

4. Hydroxybenzene   (d) Addition reaction

5. H_2, Pd   (e) Used to nitrate aromatic compounds

6. $(CH_3)_2CH^+$ (f) Substitution reaction

7. Propene + Br_2 (g) Exhibits cis-trans isomerism

8. Naphthalene   (h) Teflon monomer

9. 2-Methylpropene   (i) Alkyne

10. Benzene + Br_2 (j) Phenol

11. 2-Butene   (k) Used to hydrate an alkene

12. $CF_2{=}CF_2$ (l) Carbocation

Chapter 14 – Some Compounds with Oxygen, Sulfur, or Halogens

14.1

(a)

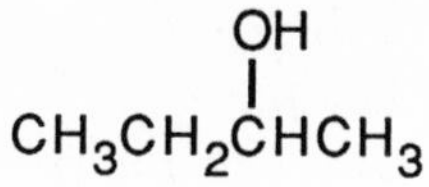

$$CH_3CH_2\overset{\overset{\displaystyle OH}{|}}{C}HCH_3$$

an alcohol

(b)

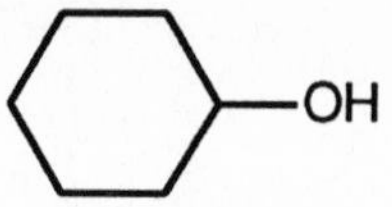

[cyclohexane ring]—OH

an alcohol

(c)

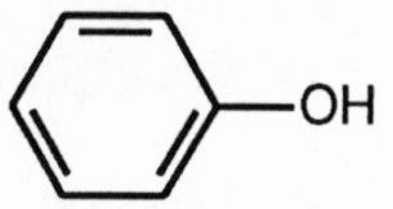

[benzene ring]—OH

a phenol

(d)

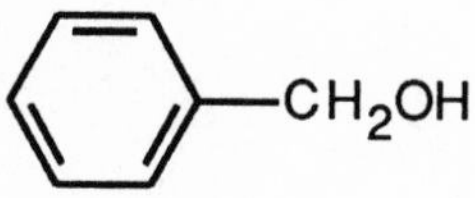

[benzene ring]—CH$_2$OH

an alcohol

(e)

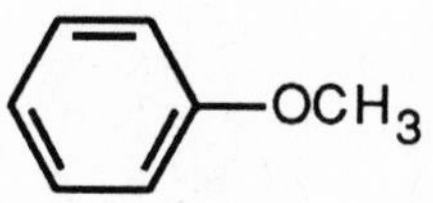

[benzene ring]—OCH$_3$

an ether

(f)

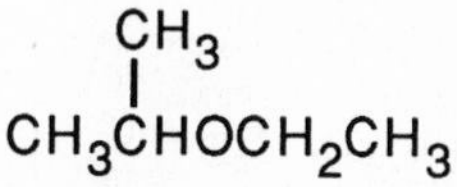

$$\overset{\overset{\displaystyle CH_3}{|}}{CH_3CHOCH_2CH_3}$$

an ether

14.2

$$^-:\ddot{O}\text{-H} \qquad\qquad (R\text{-}\!\!)\ddot{O}\text{-H}$$

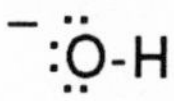

hydroxide ion 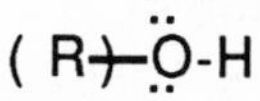   hydroxyl group

A hydroxide ion has three lone electron pairs and a negative charge. A hydroxyl group is part of an organic molecule.

14.3

(a)

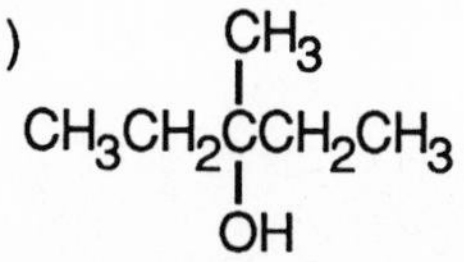

$$CH_3CH_2\overset{\overset{\displaystyle CH_3}{|}}{\underset{\underset{\displaystyle OH}{|}}{C}}CH_2CH_3$$

3-Methyl-3-pentanol
tertiary alcohol

(b)

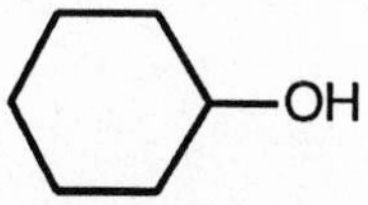

[cyclohexane ring]—OH

Cyclohexanol
secondary alcohol

(c)

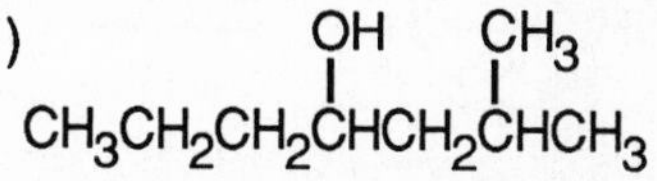

$$CH_3CH_2CH_2\overset{\overset{\displaystyle OH}{|}}{C}HCH_2\overset{\overset{\displaystyle CH_3}{|}}{C}HCH_3$$

2-Methyl-4-heptanol
secondary alcohol

(d)

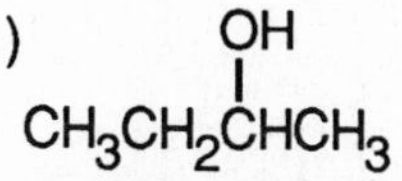

$$CH_3CH_2\overset{\overset{\displaystyle OH}{|}}{C}HCH_3$$

2-Butanol
secondary alcohol

(e)

$$ClCH_2CH_2CH_2OH$$

3-Chloro-1-propanol
primary alcohol

14.4

(a)

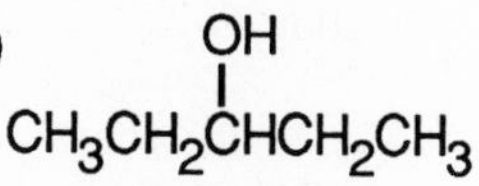

$$CH_3CH_2\overset{\overset{\displaystyle OH}{|}}{C}HCH_2CH_3$$

3-Pentanol
secondary alcohol

(b)

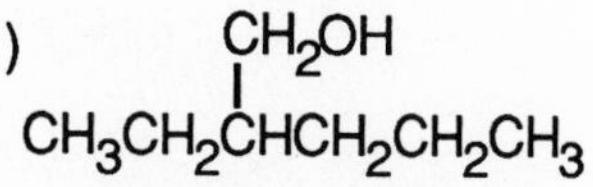

$$CH_3CH_2\overset{\overset{\displaystyle CH_2OH}{|}}{C}HCH_2CH_2CH_3$$

2-Ethyl-1-pentanol
primary alcohol

(c)

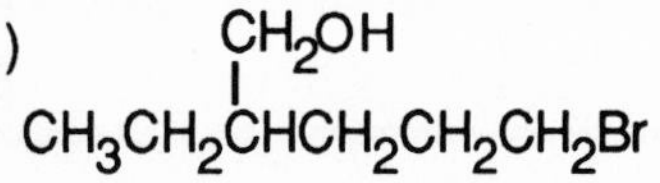

$$CH_3CH_2\overset{\overset{\displaystyle CH_2OH}{|}}{CH}CH_2CH_2CH_2Br$$

5-Bromo-2-ethyl-1-pentanol
primary alcohol

(d)

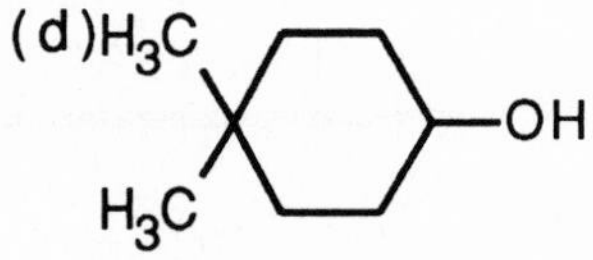

4,4-Dimethylcyclohexanol
secondary alcohol

14.5 See Problems 14.3 and 14.4.

14.6 $CH_3CH_2CH_2OH$ has the highest boiling point because it's the only compound listed that can form hydrogen bonds.

14.7

(a)

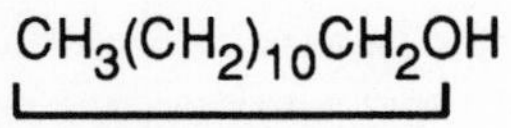

$$CH_3(CH_2)_{10}CH_2OH$$

This alkane-like part makes this alcohol water-insoluble.

(b)

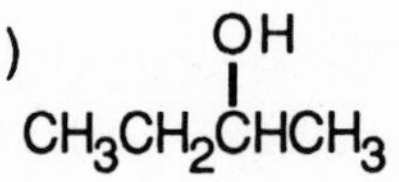

$$CH_3CH_2\overset{\overset{\displaystyle OH}{|}}{CH}CH_3$$

Very water-soluble.

(c)

$$CH_3CH_2OCH_3$$

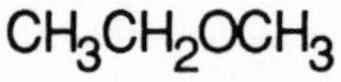

An ether - slightly water-soluble.

14.8

(a)

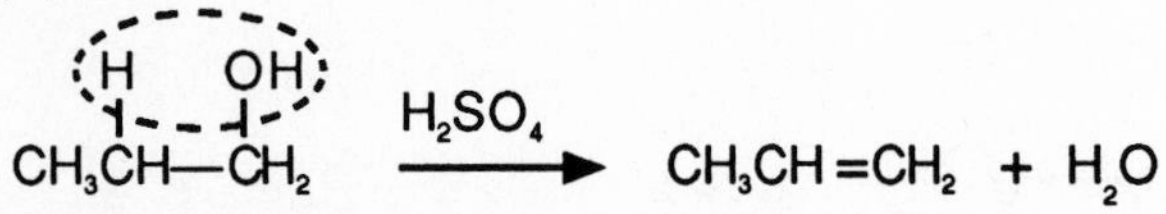

$$CH_3CH-CH_2 \xrightarrow{H_2SO_4} CH_3CH=CH_2 + H_2O$$

(b)

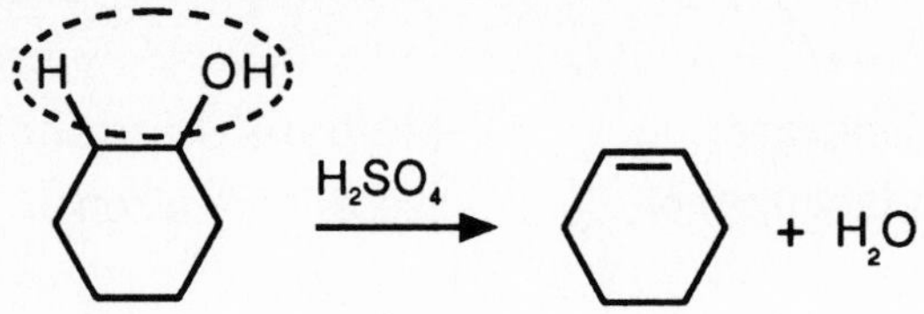

$$\xrightarrow{H_2SO_4} + H_2O$$

(c)

$$CH_2-CH-CHCHCH_3 \xrightarrow{H_2SO_4} H_2C=CHCH_2CHCH_3 + CH_3CH=CHCHCH_3 + H_2O$$

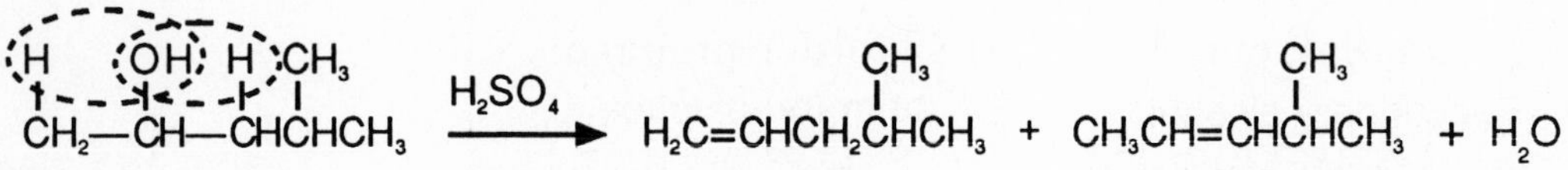

minor   major

14.9

(a)

$$CH_3\overset{\overset{\displaystyle H}{|}}{\underset{\underset{\displaystyle H_3C}{|}}{C}}-\overset{\overset{\displaystyle OH}{|}}{\underset{\underset{\displaystyle CH_3}{|}}{C}}CH_3 \xrightarrow{H_2SO_4} \overset{H_3C}{\underset{H_3C}{>}}C=C\overset{CH_3}{\underset{CH_3}{<}} + H_2O$$

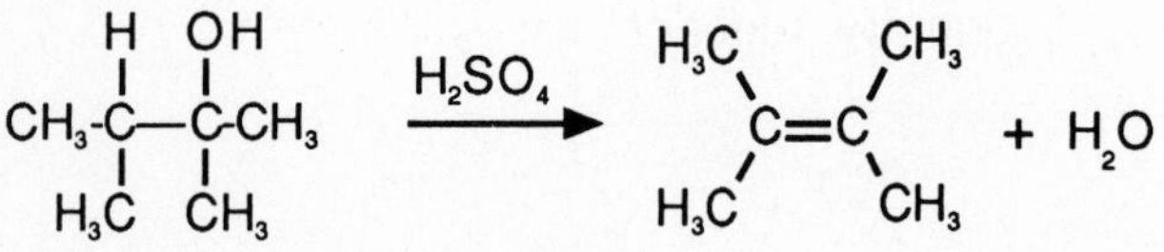

(b)

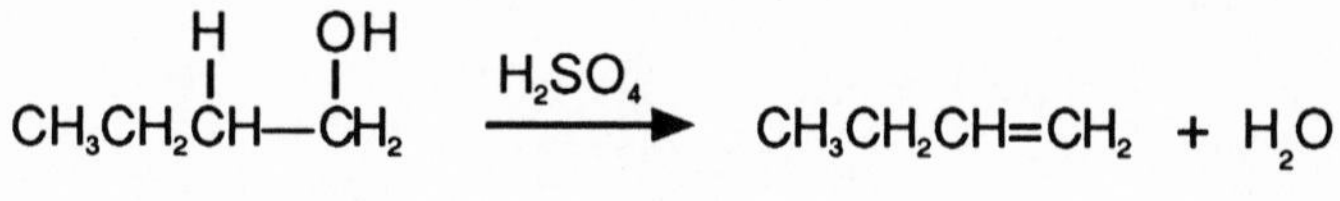

$$\underset{\underset{CH_3CH_2CH}{|}}{\overset{\overset{H \quad OH}{|\quad\ |}}{}}\!\!-CH_2 \xrightarrow{H_2SO_4} CH_3CH_2CH{=}CH_2 + H_2O$$

or

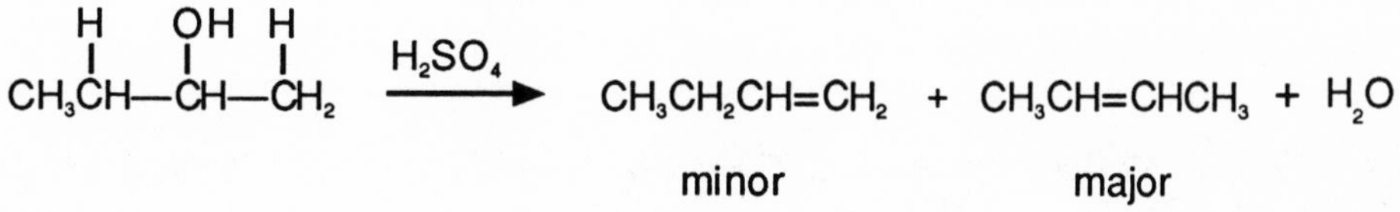

$$CH_3\overset{\overset{H}{|}}{CH}-\overset{\overset{OH}{|}}{CH}-\overset{\overset{H}{|}}{CH_2} \xrightarrow{H_2SO_4} CH_3CH_2CH{=}CH_2 + CH_3CH{=}CHCH_3 + H_2O$$

minor   major

14.10 (a)

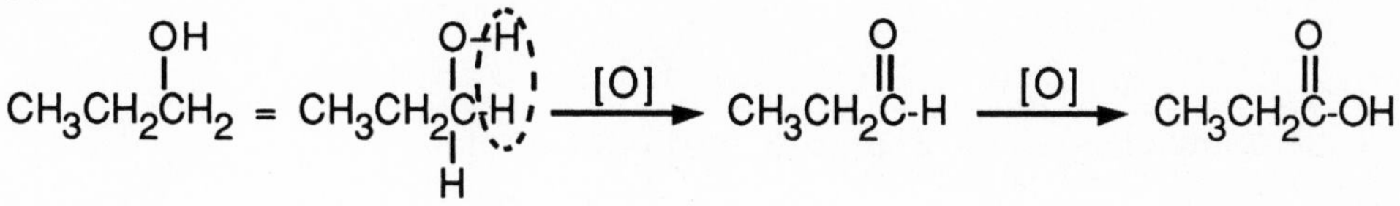

$$CH_3CH_2CH_2 = CH_3CH_2\overset{\overset{O-H}{|}}{\underset{\underset{H}{|}}{C}}{}H \xrightarrow{[O]} CH_3CH_2\overset{\overset{O}{\|}}{C}{-}H \xrightarrow{[O]} CH_3CH_2\overset{\overset{O}{\|}}{C}{-}OH$$

(b)

$$CH_3\overset{\overset{OH}{|}}{C}HCH_2CH_2CH_3 = CH_3\overset{\overset{O-H}{|}}{\underset{\underset{CH_2CH_2CH_3}{|}}{C}}{-}H \xrightarrow{[O]} CH_3\overset{\overset{O}{\|}}{C}CH_2CH_2CH_3$$

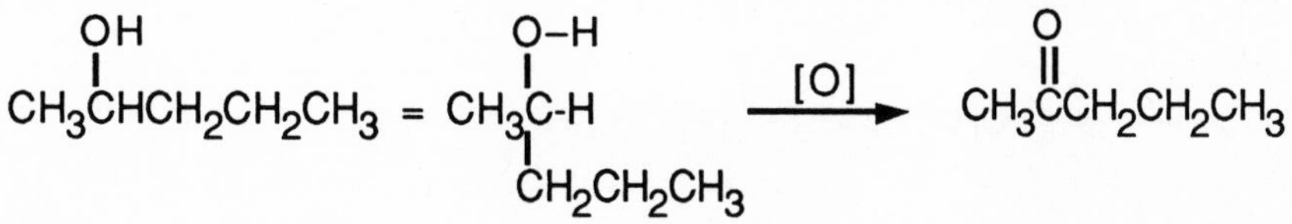

(c)

$$\text{(cyclopentyl)}-\overset{\overset{OH}{|}}{C}HCH_3 = \text{(cyclopentyl)}-\overset{\overset{O-H}{|}}{\underset{\underset{CH_3}{|}}{C}}{-}H \xrightarrow{[O]} \text{(cyclopentyl)}-\overset{\overset{O}{\|}}{C}CH_3$$

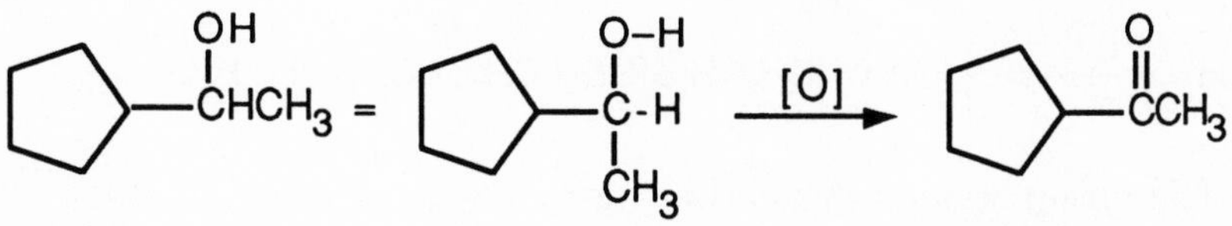

14.11

(a)

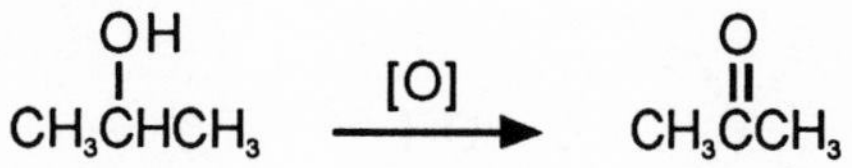

$$CH_3\overset{\overset{OH}{|}}{C}HCH_3 \xrightarrow{[O]} CH_3\overset{\overset{O}{\|}}{C}CH_3$$

(b)

$$\text{(cycloheptyl)}{-}OH \xrightarrow{[O]} \text{(cycloheptanone)}$$

(c)

$$CH_3\overset{\overset{CH_3}{|}}{C}HCH_2CH_2OH \xrightarrow{[O]} CH_3\overset{\overset{CH_3}{|}}{C}HCH_2\overset{\overset{O}{\|}}{C}{-}H \xrightarrow{[O]} CH_3\overset{\overset{CH_3}{|}}{C}HCH_2\overset{\overset{O}{\|}}{C}{-}OH$$

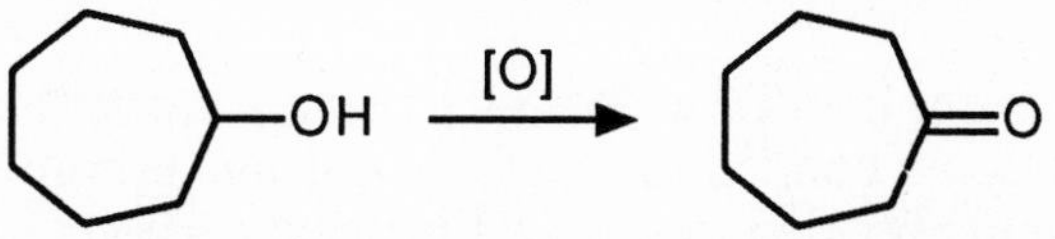

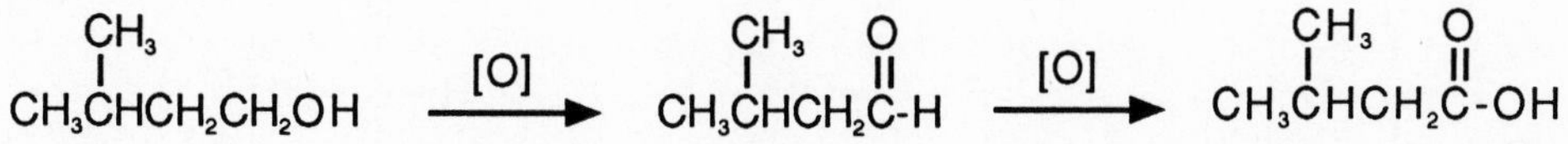

14.12

(a)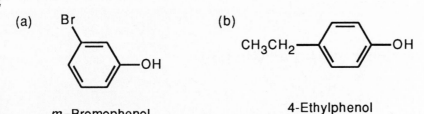

m−Bromophenol

(b)

4-Ethylphenol

14.13

(a)

p-Chlorophenol

(b)

4-Bromo-3-methylphenol

14.14

(a)

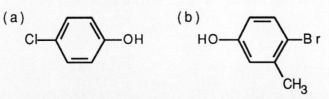

$$2 \ CH_3CH_2CH_2SH \xrightarrow{\text{[O]}} CH_3CH_2CH_2S\text{-}SCH_2CH_2CH_3 \ + \ H_2O$$

(b)

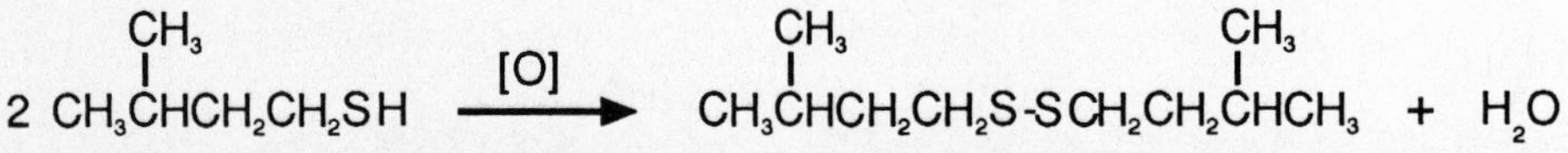

$$2 \ CH_3CHCH_2CH_2SH \xrightarrow{\text{[O]}} CH_3CHCH_2CH_2S\text{-}SCH_2CH_2CHCH_3 \ + \ H_2O$$

14.15 *Alcohols* have an -OH group bonded to a carbon atom.
Ethers have an oxygen atom bonded to two carbon substituents.
Phenols have an -OH group bonded to an aromatic ring.

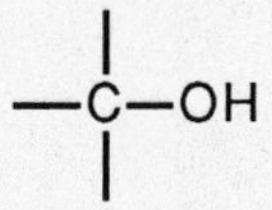

An alcohol 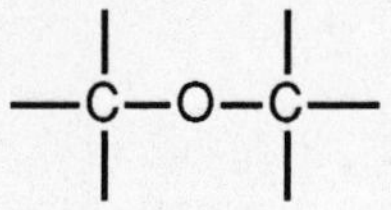   An ether 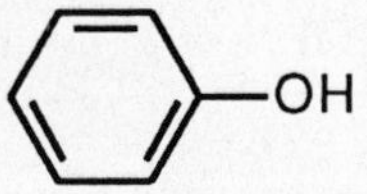   A phenol

14.16 A primary alcohol has one carbon substituent bonded to the -OH-bearing carbon; a secondary alcohol has two carbon substituents bonded to the -OH-bearing carbon; and a tertiary alcohol has three carbon substituents bonded to the -OH-bearing carbon.

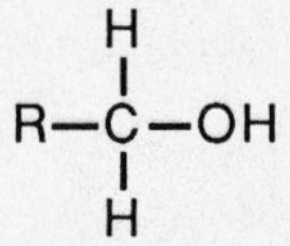

A primary alcohol 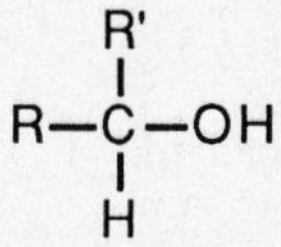   A secondary alcohol 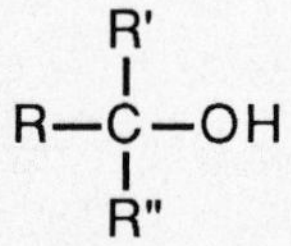   A tertiary alcohol

14.17 Alcohols contain -OH groups, which can form hydrogen-bonds to each other. Since extra energy (heat) must be supplied to break these hydrogen bonds, alcohol are higher boiling than ethers, which can't hydrogen bond.

14.18 Phenol is a stronger acid than ethanol.

14.19

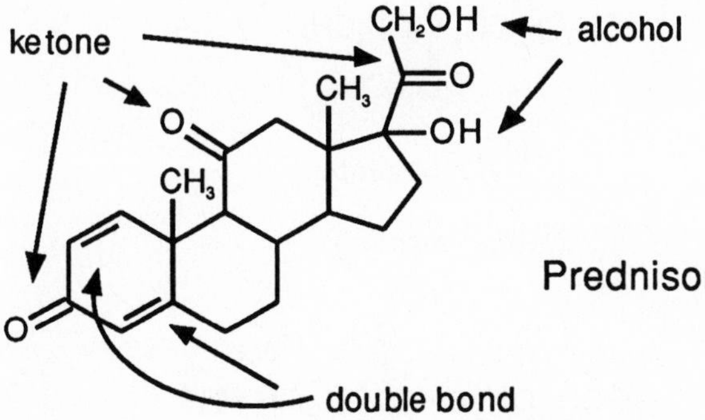

ketone
CH₂OH
alcohol
CH₃
O
OH
CH₃
O
double bond

Prednisone

14.20

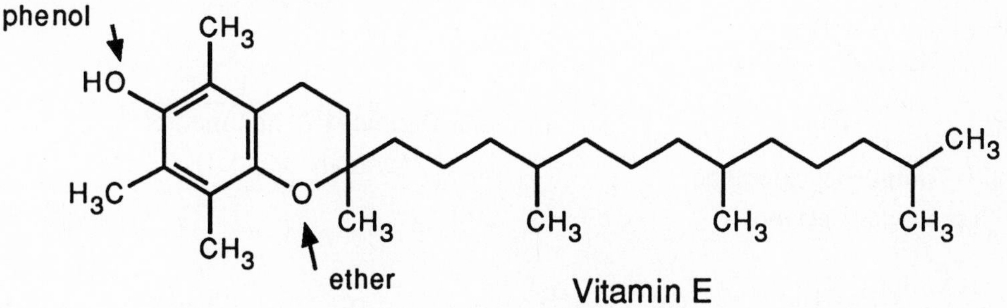

phenol
CH₃
HO
H₃C
O
CH₃
CH₃
CH₃
CH₃
CH₃
CH₃
ether

Vitamin E

14.21

(a)

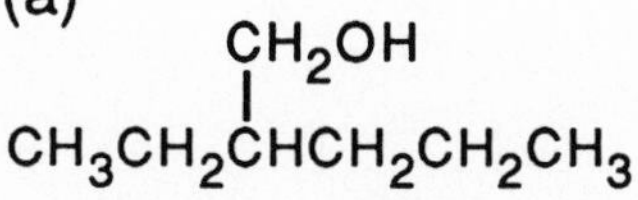

CH₂OH
CH₃CH₂CHCH₂CH₂CH₃

2-Ethyl-1-pentanol

(b)

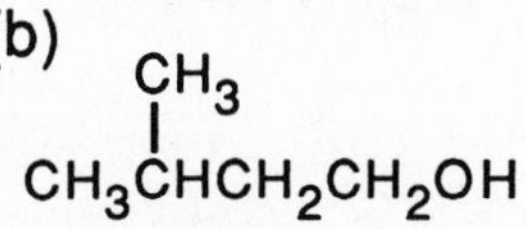

CH₃
CH₃CHCH₂CH₂OH

3-Methyl-1-butanol

(c)

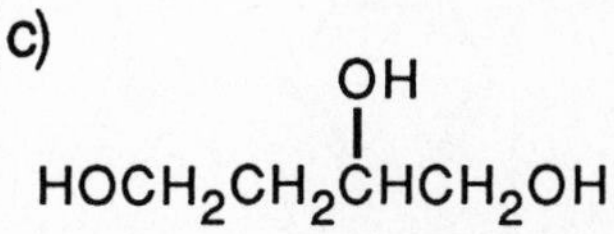

OH
HOCH₂CH₂CHCH₂OH

1,2,4-Butanetriol

(d)

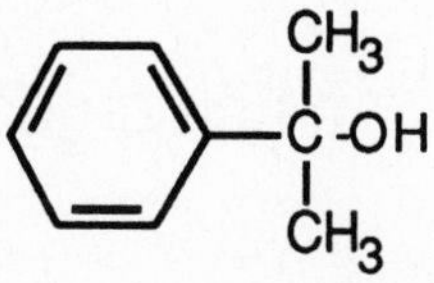

CH₃
C -OH
CH₃

2-Phenyl-2-propanol

(e)

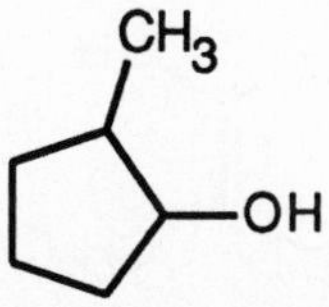

CH₃
OH

2-Methylcylopentanol

(f)

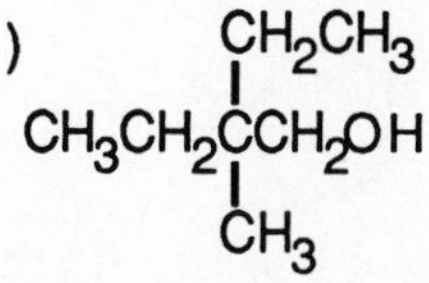

CH₂CH₃
CH₃CH₂CCH₂OH
CH₃

2-Ethyl-2-methyl-1-butanol

14.22 - 14.23

(a)

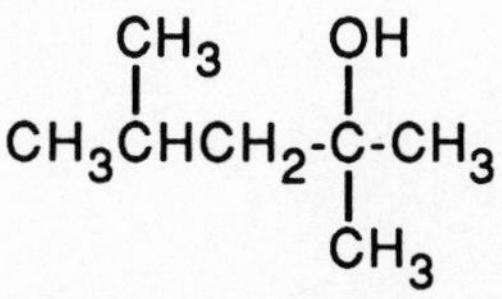

CH₃
OH
CH₃CHCH₂-C-CH₃
CH₃

2,4-Dimethyl-2-pentanol

(tertiary alcohol)

(b)

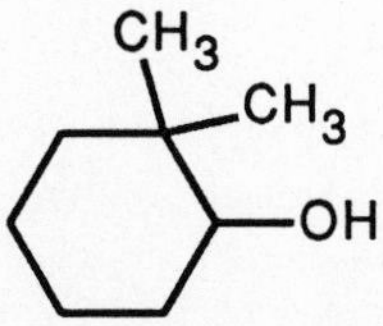

CH₃
CH₃
OH

2,2-Dimethylcyclohexanol

(secondary alcohol)

(c)

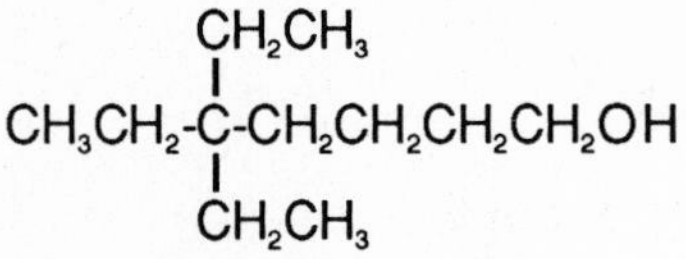

$$CH_3CH_2-\underset{\underset{CH_2CH_3}{|}}{\overset{\overset{CH_2CH_3}{|}}{C}}-CH_2CH_2CH_2CH_2OH$$

5,5-Diethyl-1-heptanol

(*primary alcohol*)

(d)

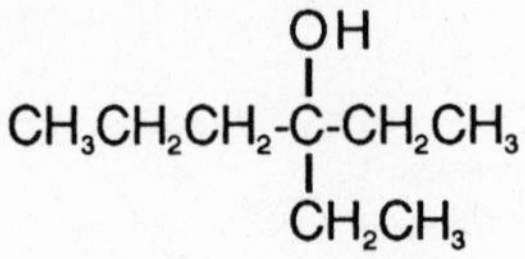

$$CH_3CH_2CH_2-\underset{\underset{CH_2CH_3}{|}}{\overset{\overset{OH}{|}}{C}}-CH_2CH_3$$

3-Ethyl-3-hexanol

(*tertiary alcohol*)

(e)

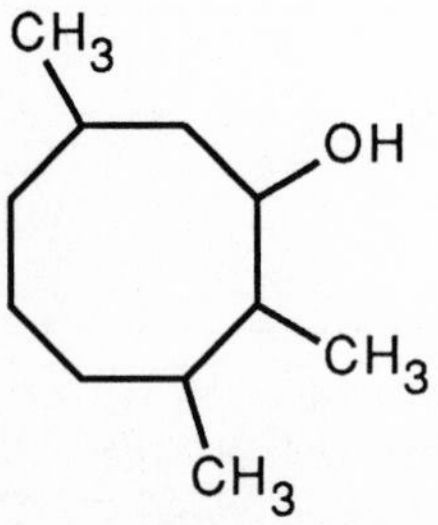

2,3,7–Trimethylcyclooctanol

(*secondary alcohol*)

(f)

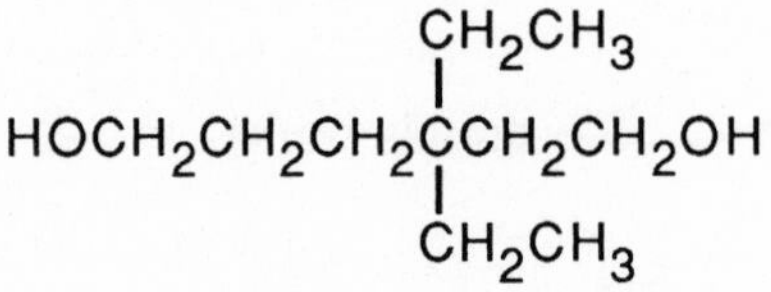

$$HOCH_2CH_2CH_2\underset{\underset{CH_2CH_3}{|}}{\overset{\overset{CH_2CH_3}{|}}{C}}CH_2CH_2OH$$

3,3–Diethyl–1,6–hexanediol

(*primary alcohol*)

14.24

(a)

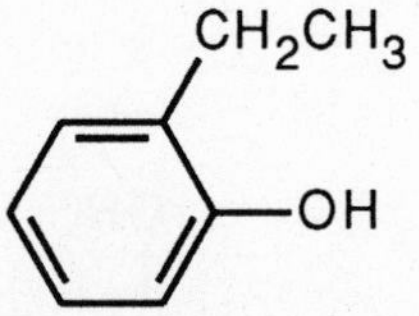

o–Ethylphenol

(b)

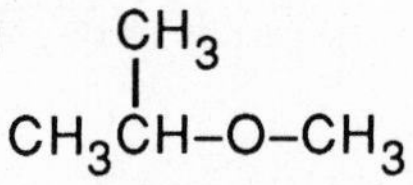

$$CH_3\underset{\underset{CH_3}{|}}{CH}-O-CH_3$$

Isopropyl methyl ether

(c)

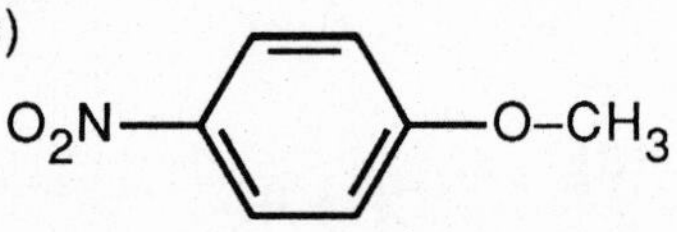

Methyl *p*–nitrophenyl ether

(d)

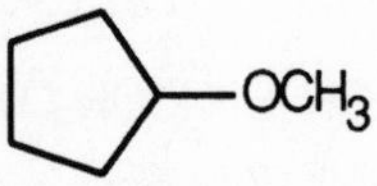

Cyclopentyl methyl ether
or
Methoxycyclopentane

(e)

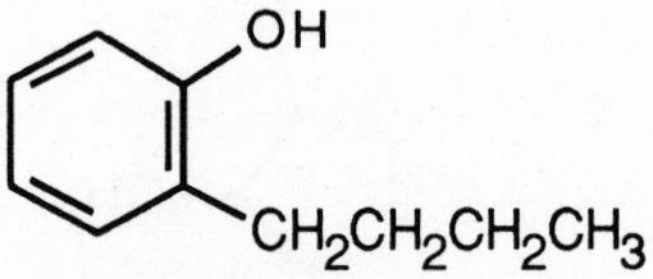

o-Butylphenol

(f)

$$CH_3CH_2CH_2OCH_2CH_2CH_3$$

Dipropyl ether

14.25

(a)

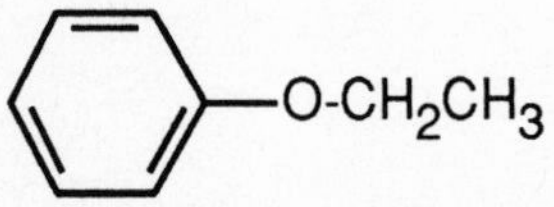

Ethyl phenyl ether

(b)

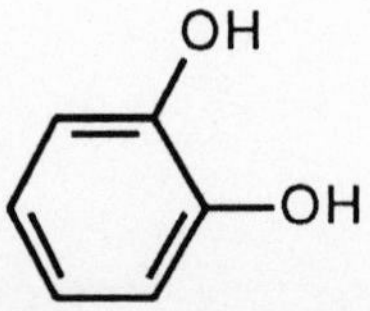

o-Dihydroxybenzene

(c)

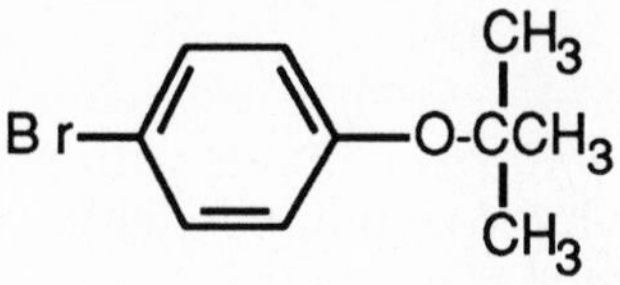

$$Br-\!\!\!\!\bigcirc\!\!\!\!-O-\underset{\underset{CH_3}{|}}{\overset{\overset{CH_3}{|}}{C}}CH_3$$

tert -Butyl-*p* -bromophenyl ether

(d)

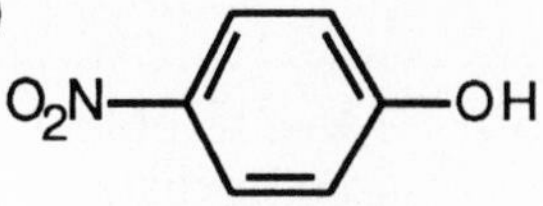

$$O_2N-\!\!\!\!\bigcirc\!\!\!\!-OH$$

p -Nitrophenol

(e)

$$\underset{\underset{CH_3}{|}}{CH_3CH}\overset{CH_3CH_2O \qquad OCH_2CH_3}{\underset{}{CHCHCH_3}}$$

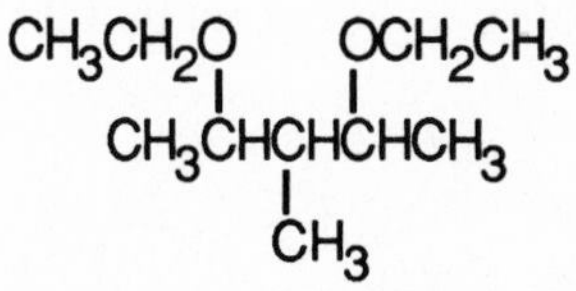

2,4-Diethoxy-3-methylpentane

(f)

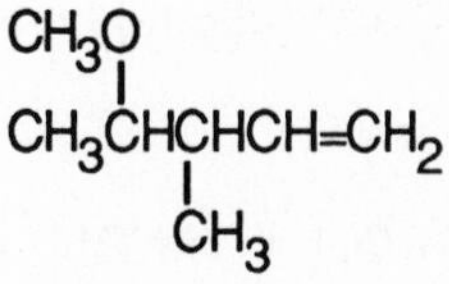

$$\overset{CH_3O}{\underset{\underset{CH_3}{|}}{CH_3CHCHCH=CH_2}}$$

4-Methoxy-3-methyl-1-pentene

14.26

Compound	Boiling Point	Reason
Hexanol	Highest	Forms hydrogen bonds
Dipropyl ether	Middle	Polar, but no hydrogen bonds
Hexane	Lowest	Nonpolar

14.27

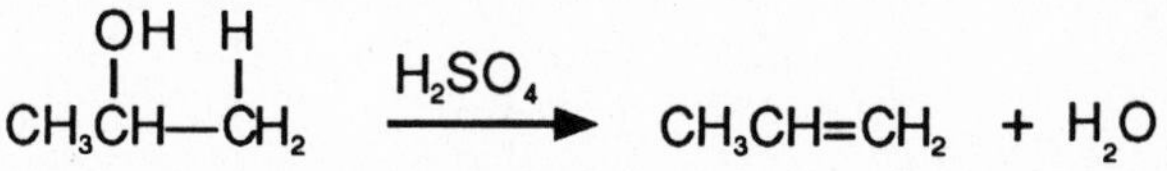

$$\underset{CH_3CH-CH_2}{\overset{OH \quad H}{\overset{|}{}\quad\overset{|}{}}} \xrightarrow{H_2SO_4} CH_3CH=CH_2 + H_2O$$

14.28 A ketone is formed on oxidation of a secondary alcohol:

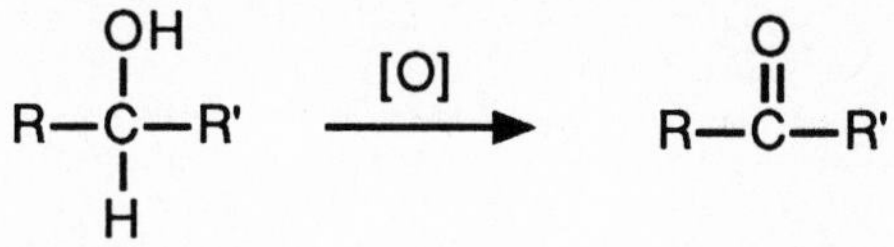

$$\underset{H}{\overset{OH}{R-\underset{|}{\overset{|}{C}}-R'}} \xrightarrow{[O]} \overset{O}{\overset{\|}{R-C-R'}}$$

A secondary alcohol   A ketone

14.29 Tertiary alcohols are not oxidized because they have no -H bonded to the -OH bearing carbon:

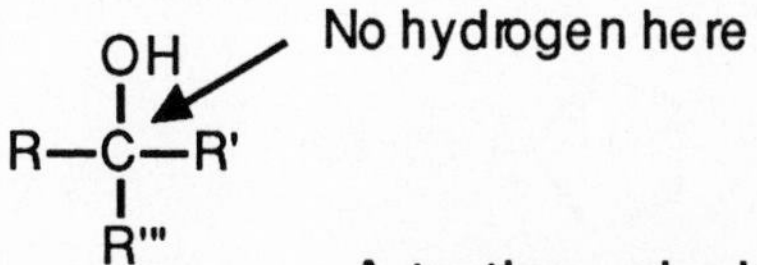

$$\underset{R'''}{\overset{OH}{R-\underset{|}{\overset{|}{C}}-R'}} \qquad \text{No hydrogen here}$$

A tertiary alcohol

14.30 Either an aldehyde or a carboxylic acid can be formed by oxidation of a primary alcohol:

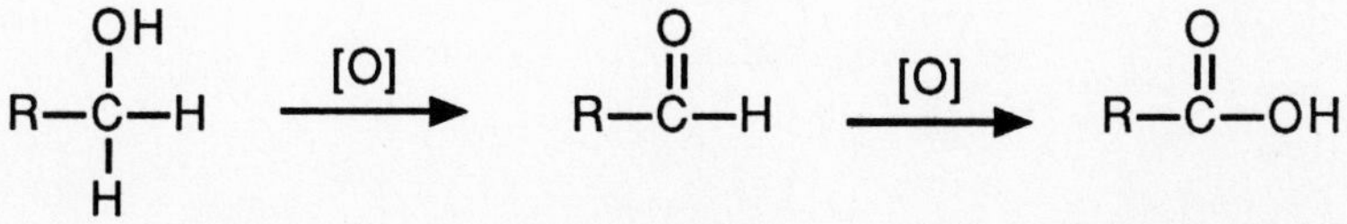

$$\underset{H}{\overset{OH}{R-\underset{|}{\overset{|}{C}}-H}} \xrightarrow{[O]} \overset{O}{\overset{\|}{R-C-H}} \xrightarrow{[O]} \overset{O}{\overset{\|}{R-C-OH}}$$

A primary alcohol   An aldehyde   A carboxylic acid

14.31

Compound	Solubility	Reason
1,2,3-Propanetriol	Most soluble	Forms most hydrogen bonds with water
1-Pentanol	Intermediate	Forms some hydrogen bonds with water
Ethane	Least soluble	Forms no hydrogen bonds

14.32 Phenols are more acidic than alcohols and are converted into their sodium salts on reaction with NaOH. Thus, only phenols and not alcohols dissolve in aqueous NaOH .

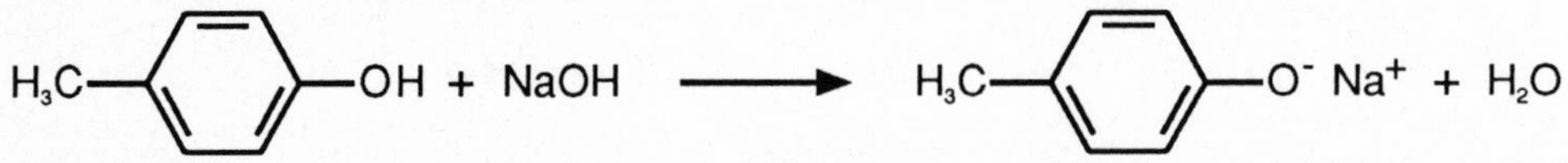

14.33 The simplest way to distinguish the two alcohols is to try to oxidize them. The tertiary alcohol is unreactive toward oxidizing agents, but the secondary alcohol would be converted to a ketone.

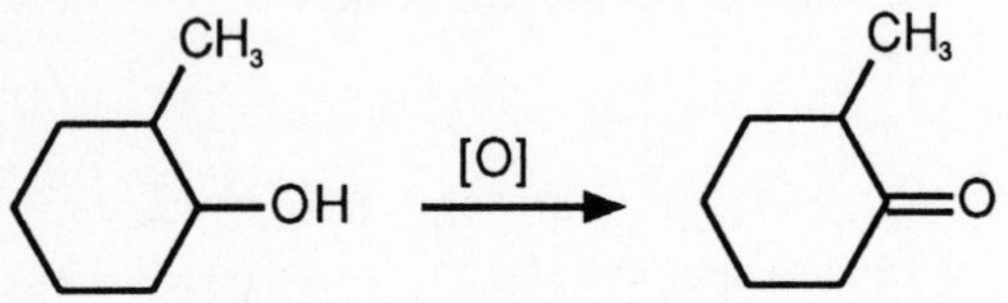

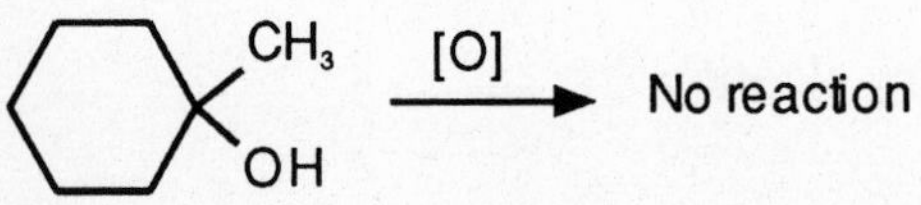

14.34

(a)

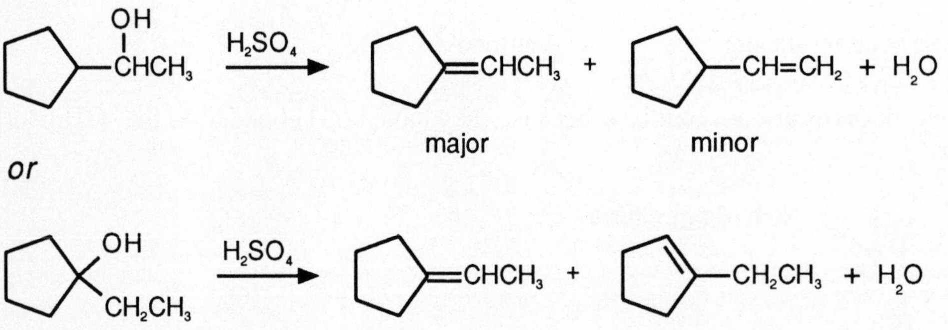

or

(b)

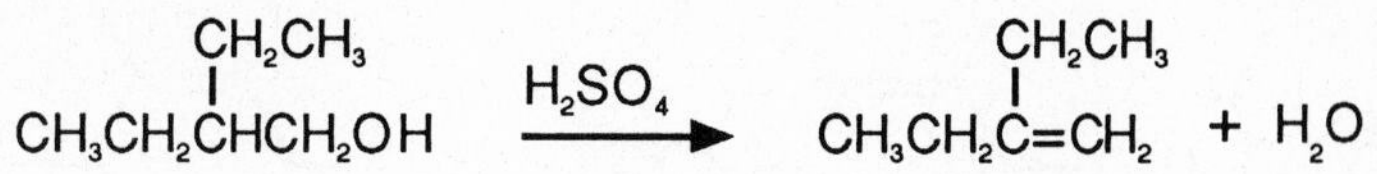

$$CH_3CH_2\overset{\overset{\displaystyle CH_2CH_3}{|}}{CH}CH_2OH \xrightarrow{H_2SO_4} CH_3CH_2\overset{\overset{\displaystyle CH_2CH_3}{|}}{C}{=}CH_2 \ + \ H_2O$$

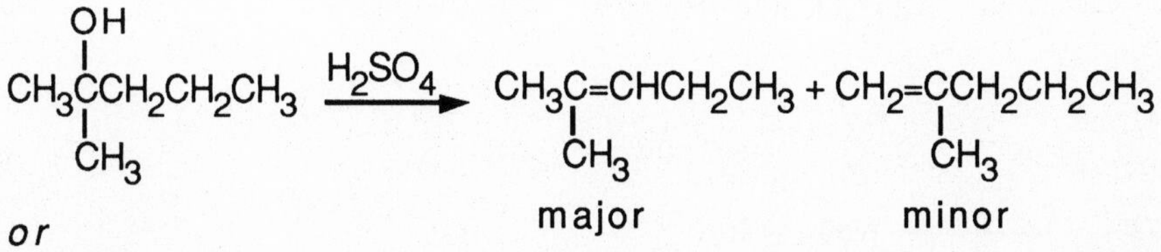

or

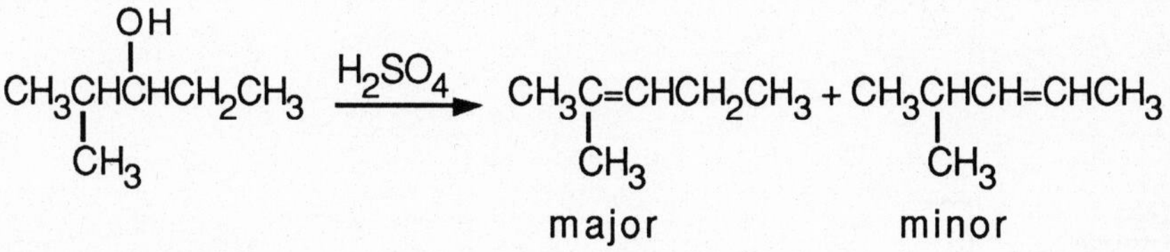

$$CH_3CH_2\overset{\overset{\displaystyle OH}{|}}{\underset{\underset{\displaystyle CH_3}{|}}{C}}{-}CH_2CH_3 \xrightarrow{H_2SO_4} CH_3CH_2\overset{\overset{\displaystyle CH_2CH_3}{|}}{C}{=}CH_2 \ + \ CH_3CH_2\overset{\overset{\displaystyle CH_3}{|}}{C}{=}CHCH_3 \ + \ H_2O$$

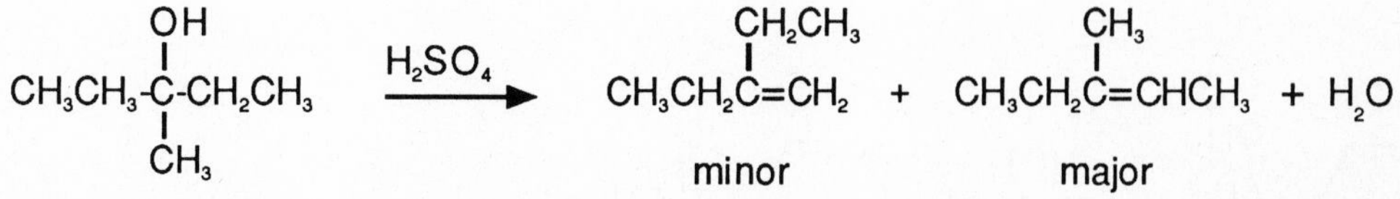

$$\quad\qquad\qquad\qquad\qquad\qquad\qquad\text{minor} \qquad\qquad\qquad \text{major}$$

(c)

$$CH_3CH_2CH_2\overset{\overset{\displaystyle OH}{|}}{CH}CH_2CH_3 \xrightarrow{H_2SO_4} CH_3CH_2CH{=}CHCH_2CH_3 \ + \ CH_3CH_2CH_2CH{=}CHCH_3$$

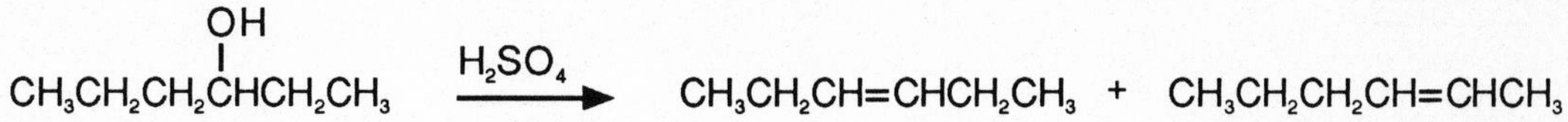

(d)

$$CH_3\overset{\overset{\displaystyle OH}{|}}{\underset{\underset{\displaystyle CH_3}{|}}{C}}CH_2CH_2CH_3 \xrightarrow{H_2SO_4} CH_3\overset{\overset{}{}}{\underset{\underset{\displaystyle CH_3}{|}}{C}}{=}CHCH_2CH_3 + CH_2{=}\overset{}{\underset{\underset{\displaystyle CH_3}{|}}{C}}CH_2CH_2CH_3$$

$$\qquad\qquad\qquad\qquad\qquad\qquad\qquad \text{major} \qquad\qquad\qquad \text{minor}$$

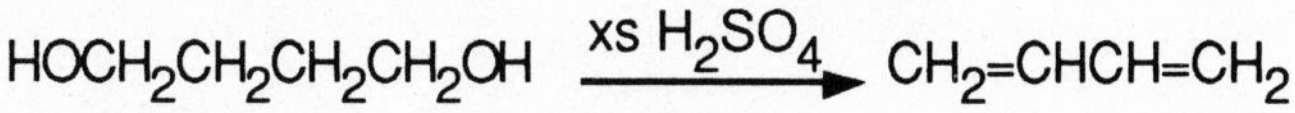

or

$$CH_3\overset{\overset{\displaystyle OH}{|}}{CH}\overset{}{\underset{\underset{\displaystyle CH_3}{|}}{CH}}CH_2CH_3 \xrightarrow{H_2SO_4} CH_3\overset{}{\underset{\underset{\displaystyle CH_3}{|}}{C}}{=}CHCH_2CH_3 + CH_3\overset{}{\underset{\underset{\displaystyle CH_3}{|}}{CH}}CH{=}CHCH_3$$

$$\qquad\qquad\qquad\qquad\qquad\qquad\qquad \text{major} \qquad\qquad\qquad \text{minor}$$

(e)

$$HOCH_2CH_2CH_2CH_2OH \xrightarrow{\text{xs } H_2SO_4} CH_2{=}CHCH{=}CH_2$$

or

$$CH_3\overset{\overset{\displaystyle OH}{|}}{CH}CH_2CH_2OH \xrightarrow{\text{xs } H_2SO_4} CH_2{=}CHCH{=}CH_2$$

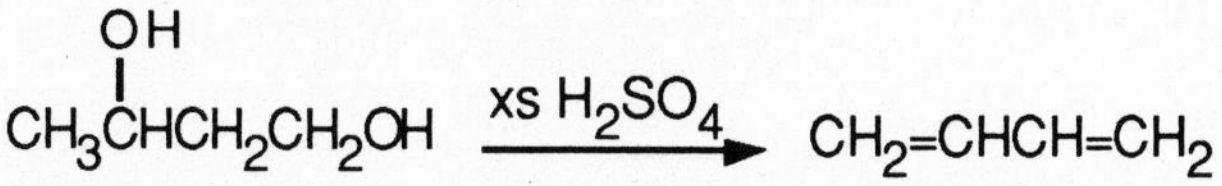

(f)

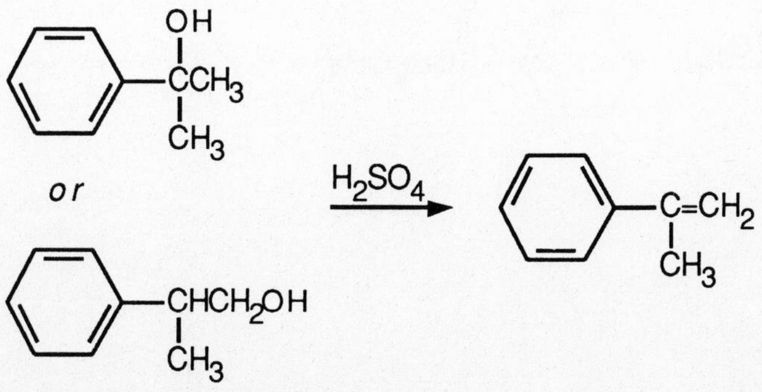

14.35

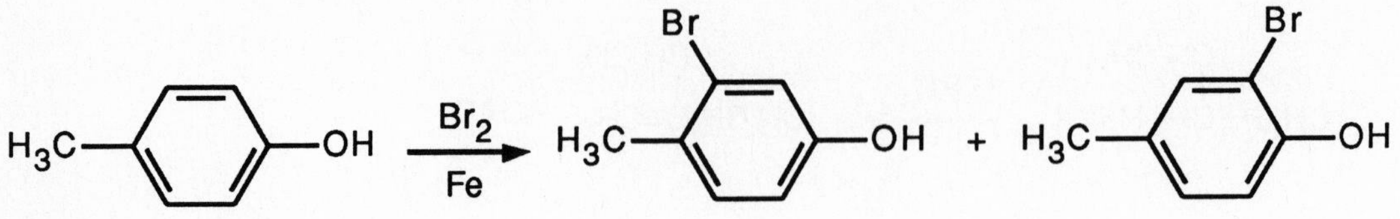

14.36

(a)

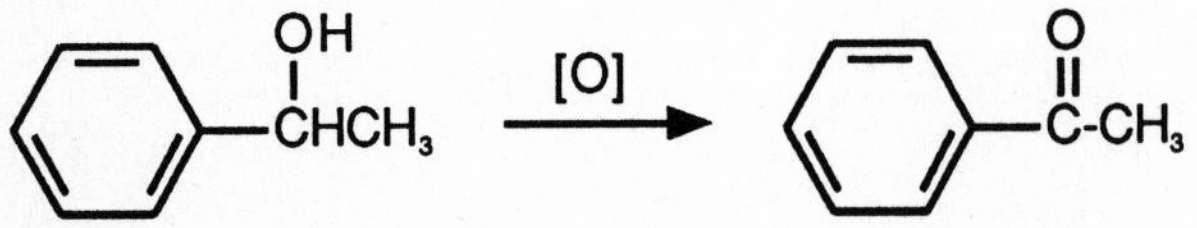

(b)

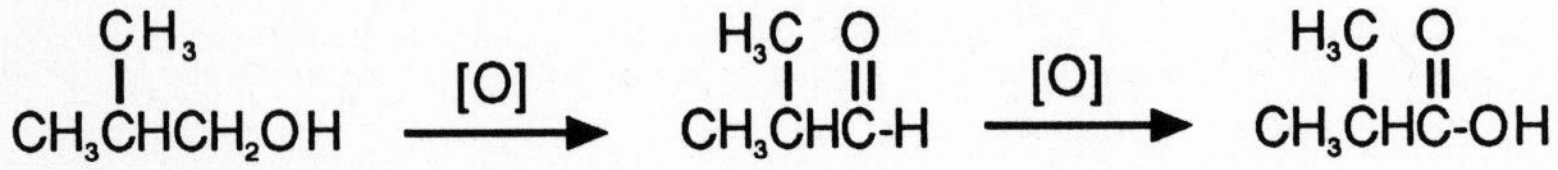

(c)

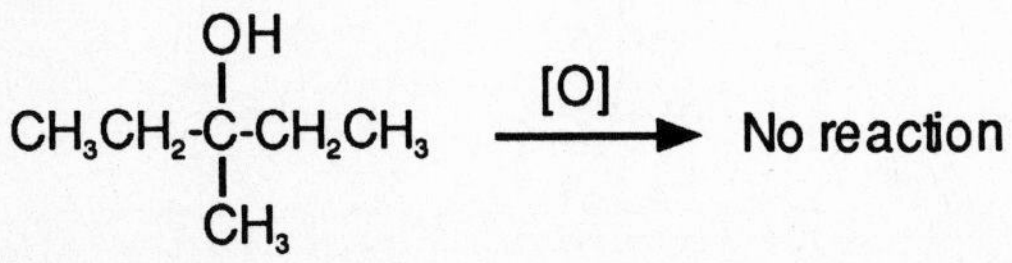

(d)

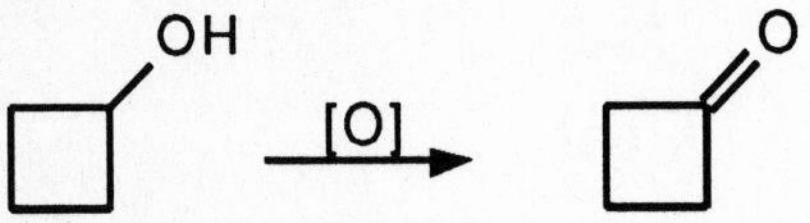

(e)

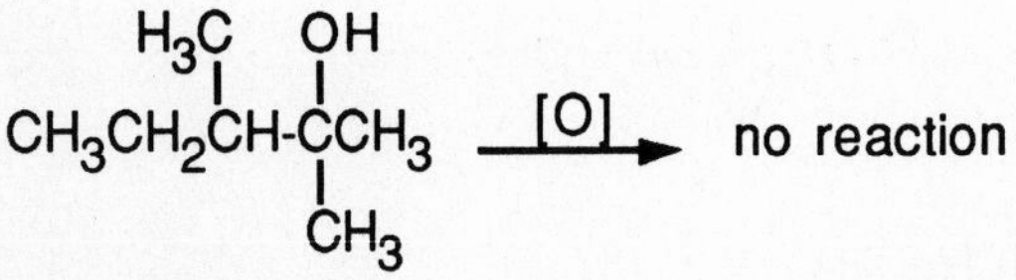

(f)

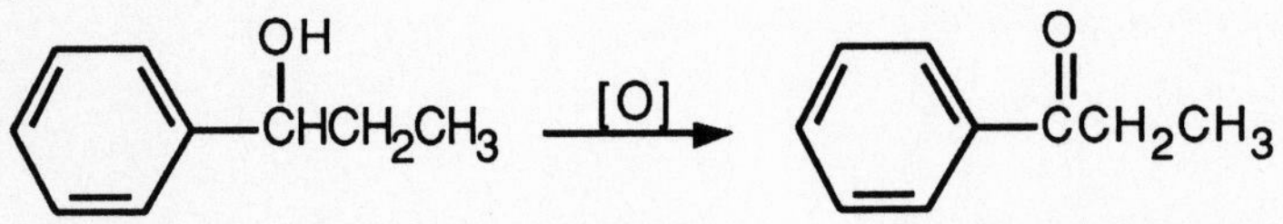

14.37

(a)

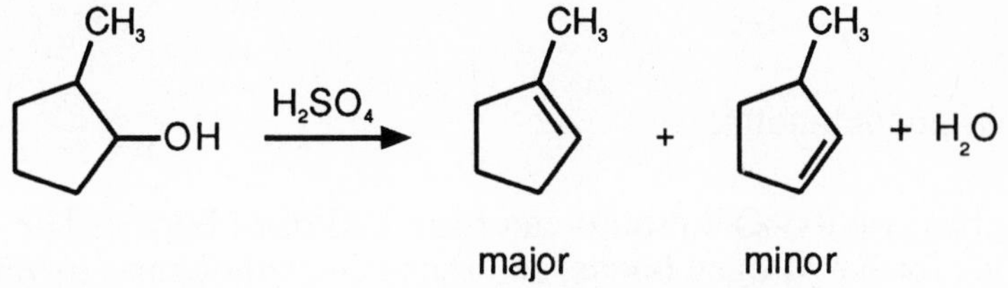

major   minor

(b)

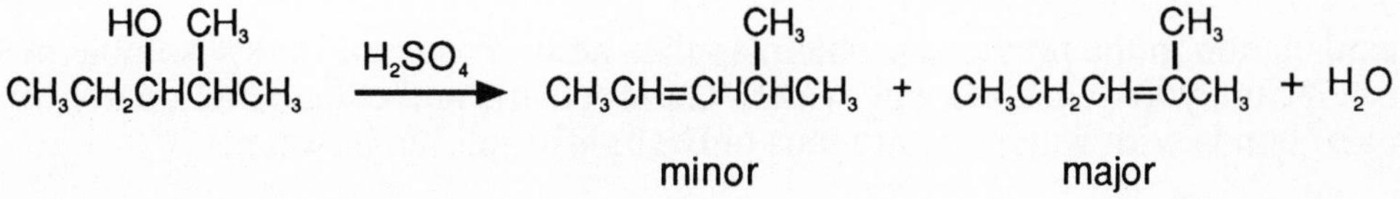

minor   major

(c)

major   minor

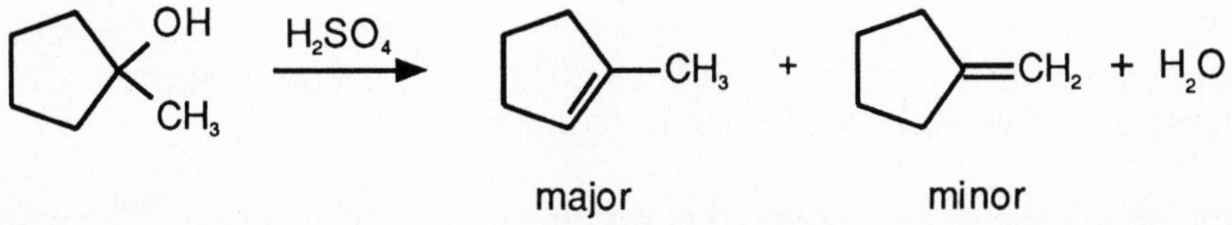

(d)

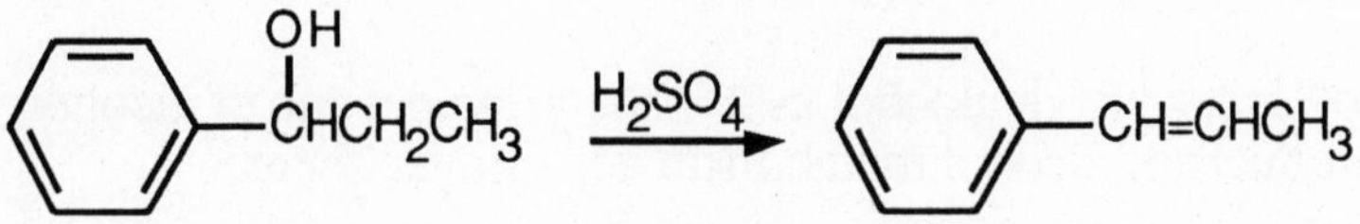

(e)

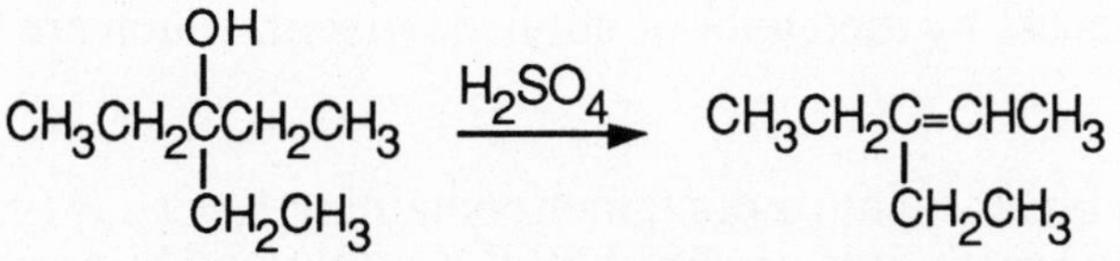

14.38 The most noticeable characteristic of thiols is their vile stench.

14.39 A thiol is the sulfur analog of an alcohol.

R–S–H   R–O–H

A thiol   An alcohol

14.40

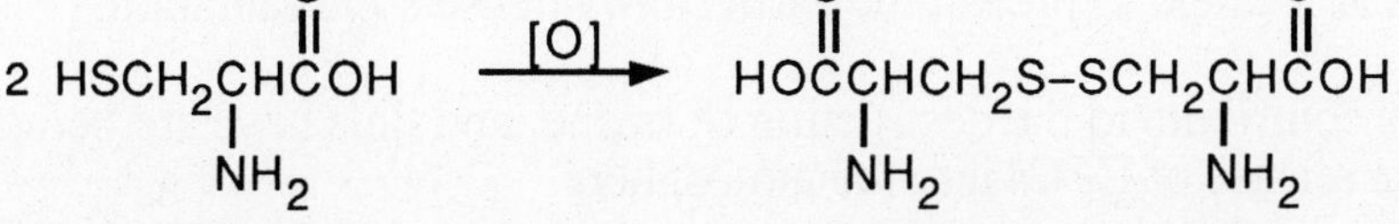

Cysteine   Cysteine disulfide

14.41

(a) CH_3CHCH_3
         |
         SH

2-Propanethiol

(b) [cyclopentane ring]—SH

Cyclopentanethiol

14.42 Propanol is high-boiling because its –OH groups can form hydrogen bonds. The –SH groups of ethanethiol don't form hydrogen bonds, and thus ethanethiol has a lower boiling point.

14.43 The explanation in the previous problem applies here. Propanol is very soluble in water because it can hydrogen-bond with water. Chloroethane and ethanethiol do not form hydrogen bonds with water and are thus only slightly soluble in water.

14.44 Ethanol is a depressant because its effects on the central nervous system are like those of anesthetics and other central nervous system depressants.

14.45 At a blood alcohol concentration of 100 - 300 mg/dL speech becomes slurred. At a blood alcohol concentration above 600 mg/dL, death may result.

14.46 Alcohol inhibits the release of an enzyme that regulates urine production. The result is increased urine output, which causes dehydration.

14.47 The liver is vulnerable to damage from alcohol as it is the principal site of alcohol metabolism, and toxic products of alcohol metabolism accumulate there.

14.48 Alcohol dehydrogenase is the enzyme responsible for alcohol metabolism. In case of methanol or ethylene glycol poisoning, ethanol is administered because it binds with alcohol dehydrogenase, blocking access by methanol or ethylene glycol, which are then eliminated from the body.

14.49 In the "breathalyzer test," a person breathes into a container containing $K_2Cr_2O_7$ (yellow-orange). If alcohol is present in the breath, it is oxidized by $K_2Cr_2O_7$, which is reduced to a Cr (III) compound (blue-green). The color change can be measured accurately enough to predict blood alcohol concentration.

14.50 Alcohol was consumed because of its anesthetic properties.

14.51 A free radical is a reactive intermediate that contains an unpaired electron.

14.52 Vitamin E is an antioxidant.

14.53 The ozone layer acts as a shield to protect the earth from intense solar radiation.

14.54 Chlorofluorocarbons contribute to the destruction of ozone, and thus laws are being enacted to restrict the release of CFCs into the atmosphere.

14.64 (a)

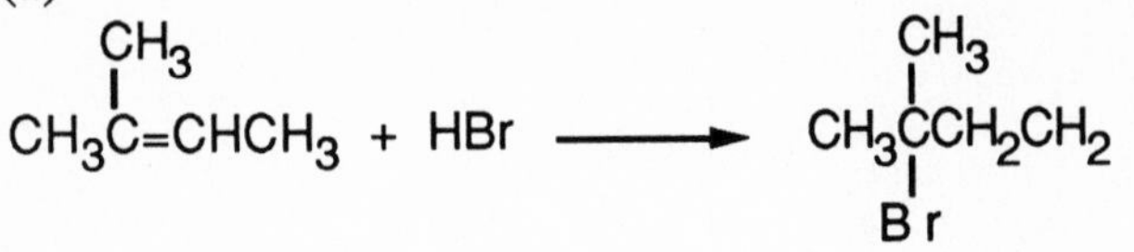

$$CH_3C{=}CHCH_3 + HBr \longrightarrow CH_3\underset{Br}{\overset{CH_3}{C}}CH_2CH_2$$

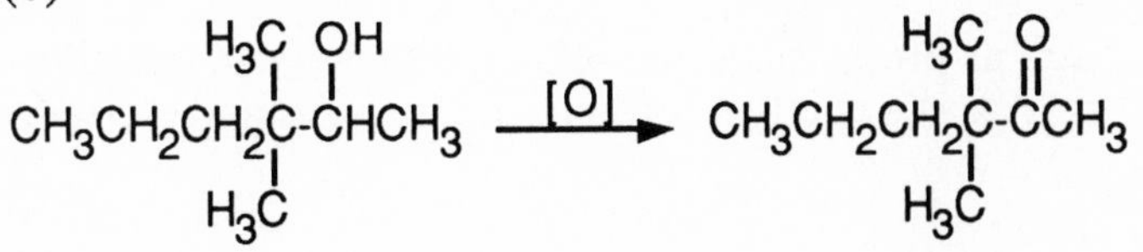

(b)

$$CH_3CH_2CH_2\underset{H_3C}{\overset{H_3C\ OH}{C}}{-}CHCH_3 \xrightarrow{[O]} CH_3CH_2CH_2\underset{H_3C}{\overset{H_3C\ O}{C}}{-}CCH_3$$

(c)

$$CH_3CH_2CH_2\underset{H_3C}{\overset{H_3C\ OH}{C}}{-}CHCH_3 \xrightarrow{H_2SO_4} CH_3CH_2CH_2\underset{H_3C}{\overset{H_3C}{C}}{-}CH{=}CH_2$$

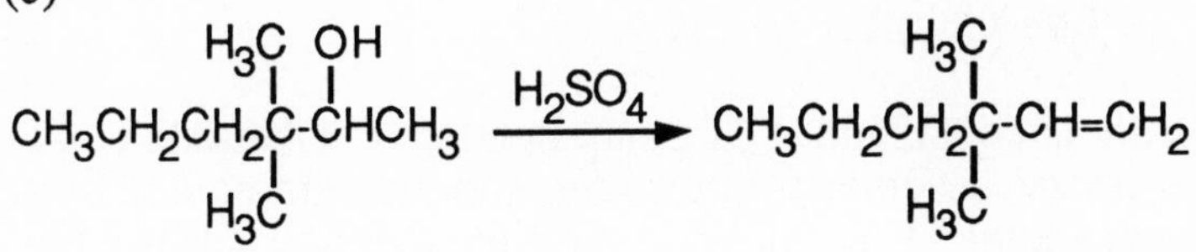

(d)

$$(CH_3)_2\underset{CH_3}{\overset{HO}{C}}C{=}C(CH_3)_2 + Br_2 \longrightarrow (CH_3)_2\overset{HO}{C}{-}\underset{CH_3}{\overset{Br}{C}}{-}\overset{Br}{C}(CH_3)_2$$

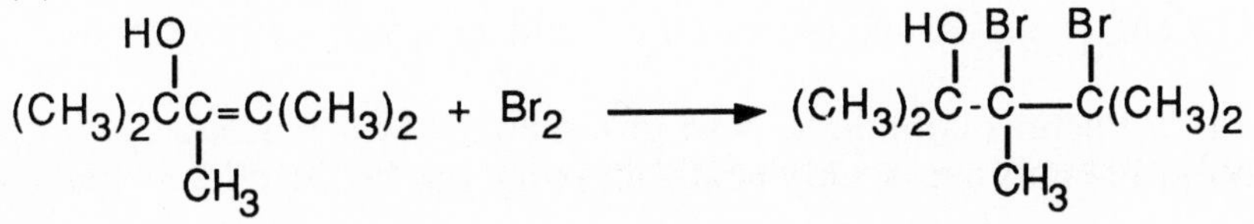

(e)

$$2\,(CH_3)_3CSH \xrightarrow{[O]} (CH_3)_3CS{-}SC(CH_3)_3$$

(f)

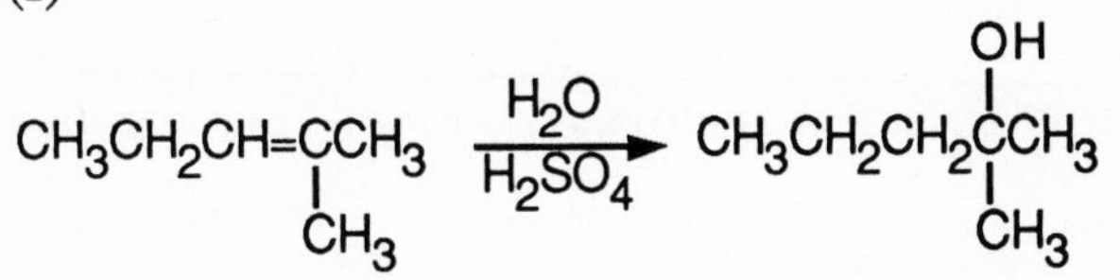

$$CH_3CH_2CH{=}\underset{CH_3}{C}CH_3 \xrightarrow[H_2SO_4]{H_2O} CH_3CH_2CH_2\underset{CH_3}{\overset{OH}{C}}CH_3$$

(g)

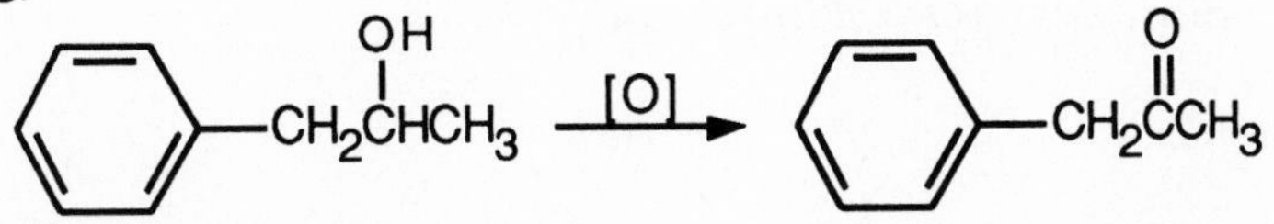

14.65

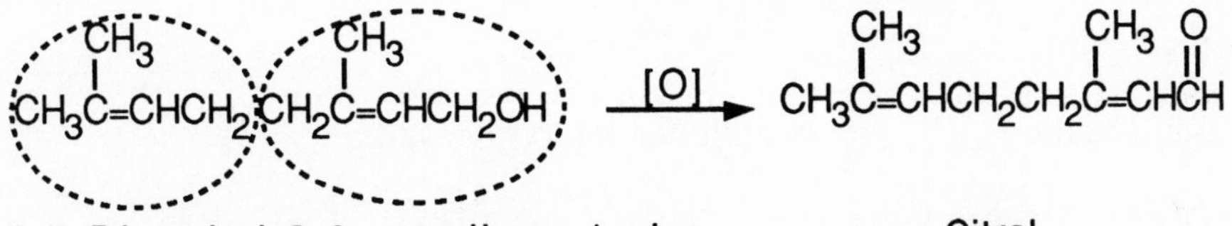

3,7-Dimethyl-2,6-octadiene-1-ol   Citral

14.66

$$CH_3CH_2OH \xrightarrow{[O]} CH_3\overset{O}{\overset{\|}{C}}OH \ \ (Acetic\ acid)$$

14.67

$$CH_3CH_2OH + 3\,O_2 \longrightarrow 2\,CO_2 + 3\,H_2O$$

14.68 Fructose is very water-soluble because it contains five hydroxyl groups, which hydrogen-bond with water.

14.69

$$CH_3CH_2CH_2OH \underset{}{\overset{H_2SO_4}{\rightleftharpoons}} CH_3CH=CH_2 + H_2O$$

The conversion of an alcohol, such as propanol, to the related alkene is an equilibrium reaction in which sulfuric acid serves as a catalyst for both the forward and the reverse reaction.

The Chapter in Brief

Alcohols (Sections 14.1–14.5) Alcohols contain an -OH group bonded to a saturated, alkane-like carbon. They can be classified as primary, secondary, or tertiary, and they are named by adding the suffix *-ol* to the name of the parent alkane. Low-molecular-weight alcohols are soluble in water and are relatively high-boiling. Alcohols are also weakly acidic. Two important reactions of alcohols are dehydration to yield an alkene and oxidation to yield an aldehyde or ketone.

Phenols (Sections 14.6, 14.7) Phenols contain an -OH group bonded to an aromatic ring and are named as substituted phenols. Phenols are weakly acidic and undergo the reactions typical of other aromatic compounds.

Ethers (Sections 14.8, 14.9) Ethers contain an oxygen bonded to two organic groups and are named by citing the two organic groups and adding the word "ether". Ethers do not form hydrogen bonds, are not acidic, and are relatively unreactive.

Thiols and Disulfides (Sections 14.10) Thiols are sulfur analogs of alcohols, and can be oxidized to yield disulfides.

Self-Test for Chapter 14

Complete the following statements:

1.   The common name for methanol is _____.

2.   Dialcohols are often called _____.

3.   Aromatic compounds called _____ react with NaOH to give salts.

4.   The dehydration of an alcohol yields an _____.

5.   Compounds called _____ are noted for their foul odors.

6.   _____ can be used to oxidize an alcohol.

7.   Ethers are _____ boiling than alcohols of similar molecular weight.

8.   _____ is a phenol used as a food additive.

9.   The major product of alcohol dehydration has the _____ number of alkyl groups attached to the double bond carbons.

10. A _____ _____ is a reactive intermediate containing an unpaired electron.

11. On prolonged contact with air, an ether forms a _____.

Match the entries on the left with their partners on the right:

1. CCl_3F (a) Peroxide

2. $(CH_3)_2CHS\text{-}SCH(CH_3)_2$ (b) Thiol

3. $CH_3CH(OH)CH_2CH_2CH_3$ (c) Phenol

4. $CH_3CH_2OCH_3$ (d) Alcohol that is not water soluble

5. CH_3OH (e) Tertiary alcohol

6. CH_3SH (f) Forms two alkenes on dehydration

7. $(CH_3)_3C\text{-}OH$ (g) Disulfide

8. $CH_3CH_2OOCH_3$ (h) Ether

9. $(CH_3)_3CCOCH_3$ (i) Glycol

10. $CH_3(CH_2)_{10}CH_2OH$ (j) Chlorofluorocarbon

11. $CH_3CH(OH)CH_2OH$ (k) Oxidation product of 3,3-dimethyl-2-butanol

12. C_6H_5OH (l) Formed from CO and H_2

Tell whether the following statements are true or false:

1.   Phenols can form hydrogen bonds.

2.   An aldehyde can be formed by oxidation of a secondary alcohol.

3.   Two different alkenes result from dehydration of 2-pentanol.

4.   Another name for phenol is carbonic acid.

5.   Phenols are more acidic than alcohols.

6.   Another name for a thiol is a mercaptan.

7.   Phenol, isopropyl alcohol, and chloroethane are all antiseptics.

8.   Oxidation is the removal of two hydrogen ions.

9.   Several halogenated alkanes are used as anesthetics.

10. Under careful reaction conditions, a primary alcohol is oxidized to an aldehyde.

Chapter 15 – Amines

15.1

(a)

$CH_3CH_2CH_2NH_2$

primary amine

(b)

$CH_3CH_2NHCH_2CH_3$

secondary amine

(c)

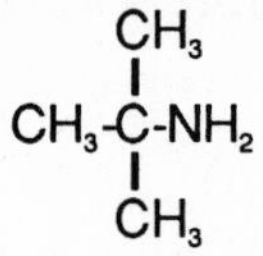

$CH_3-\underset{\underset{CH_3}{|}}{\overset{\overset{CH_3}{|}}{C}}-NH_2$

primary amine

(d)

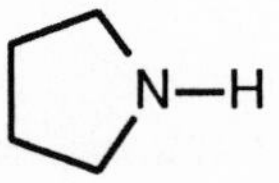

secondary amine

(e)

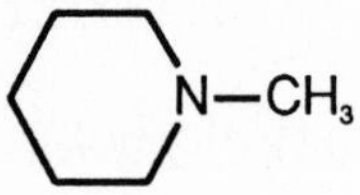

tertiary amine

15.2

(a)

$CH_3CH_2CH_2NH_2$

Propylamine

(b)

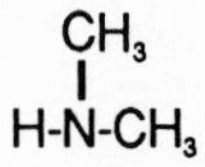

$H-\underset{}{\overset{\overset{CH_3}{|}}{N}}-CH_3$

Dimethylamine

(c)

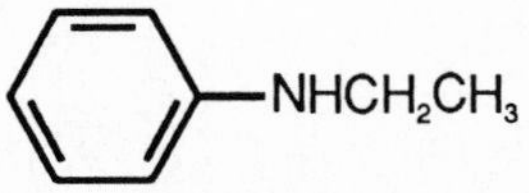

N-Ethylaniline

15.3

(a) $CH_3CH_2CH_2CH_2NH_2$

Butylamine

(b) $CH_3-\overset{\overset{H}{|}}{N}-CH_2CH_3$

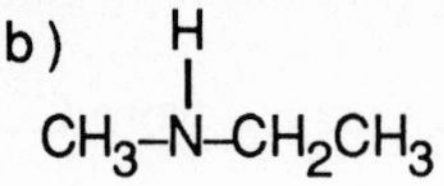

N -Methylethylamine

(c)

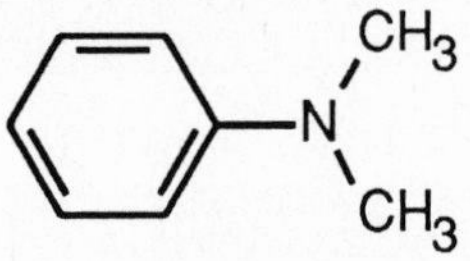

N,N -Dimethylaniline

(d)

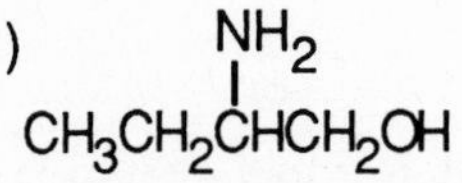

$CH_3CH_2\underset{\underset{NH_2}{|}}{C}HCH_2OH$

2-Aminobutanol

15.4

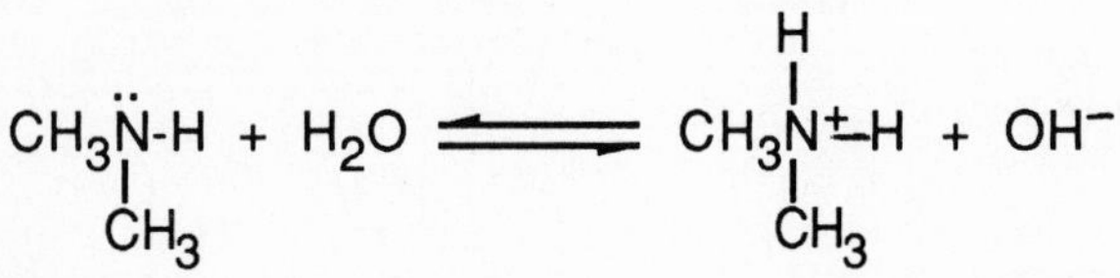

$CH_3\ddot{N}\text{-}H + H_2O \rightleftharpoons CH_3\overset{+}{N}\text{-}H + OH^-$

with CH_3 below each nitrogen

15.5 - 15.6

(a)

$CH_3CH_2\underset{\underset{CH_3}{|}}{C}HNH_2 + HBr(aq) \longrightarrow CH_3CH_2\underset{\underset{CH_3}{|}}{C}HNH_3^+ \ Br^-$

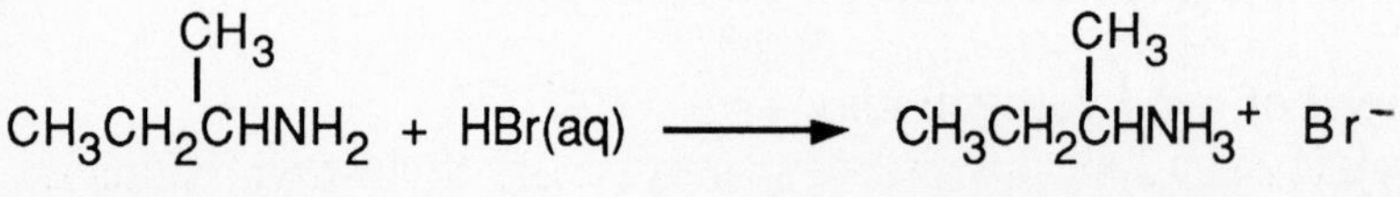

sec -Butylamine   *sec* -Butylammonium bromide

(b)

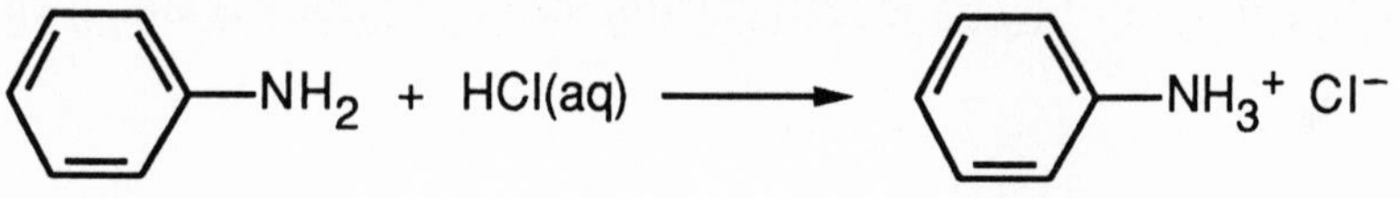

Aniline → Anilinium chloride

$$\text{Aniline} + HCl(aq) \longrightarrow \text{Anilinium chloride}$$

(c)

$$CH_3CH_2NH_2 + CH_3COOH(aq) \longrightarrow CH_3CH_2NH_3^+CH_3COO^-$$

Ethylamine → Ethylammonium acetate

(d)

$$CH_3NH_3^+Cl^- + NaOH(aq) \rightleftharpoons CH_3NH_2 + H_2O(l) + NaCl(aq)$$

Methylammonium chloride → Methylamine

15.7 Use Table 15.3 to choose the stronger base. A larger value of K_b indicates a stronger base.

(a) Ethylamine ($K_b = 4.4 \times 10^{-4}$) is a stronger base than ammonia ($K_b = 1.7 \times 10^{-5}$).

(b) Triethylamine ($K_b = 5.7 \times 10^{-4}$) is a stronger base than pyridine ($K_b = 1.8 \times 10^{-9}$).

15.8 - 15.9

(a)

$$CH_3CH_2CH_2CH_2CH_2CH_2\overset{\overset{\displaystyle CH_3}{|}}{\underset{\underset{\displaystyle CH_3}{|}}{N}}^+\!H\ \ Cl^-$$

Hexyldimethylammonium chloride
salt of a tertiary amine

(b)

$$CH_3CH_2NH_3^+\ Br^-$$

Ethylammonium bromide
salt of a primary amine

15.10

N-Ethyl-*N,N*-dimethylcyclohexylammonium chloride

15.11

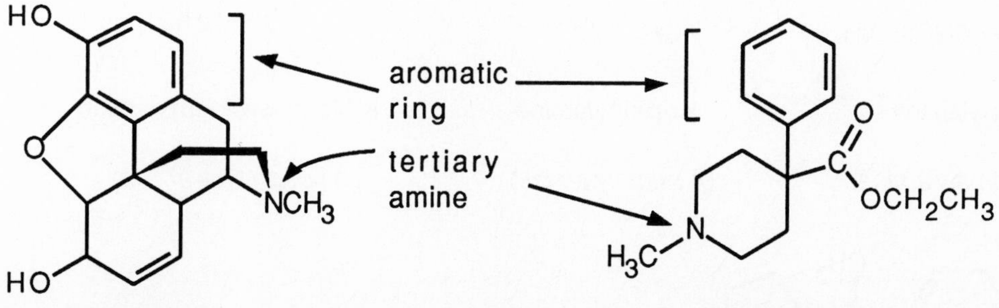

Codeine   Demerol

Codeine, Demerol, and methadone all contain aromatic rings and tertiary amines.

15.12 The family-name ending for amines is *-amine*.

15.13 Primary amines have one organic group bonded to nitrogen; secondary amines have two organic groups bonded to nitrogen; and tertiary amines have three organic groups bonded to nitrogen:

$$R-\underset{\underset{\textstyle H}{|}}{\overset{\overset{\textstyle H}{|}}{N}}-H \qquad R-\underset{\underset{\textstyle H}{|}}{\overset{\overset{\textstyle H}{|}}{N}}-R' \qquad R-\underset{\underset{\textstyle R'}{|}}{\overset{\overset{\textstyle R''}{|}}{N}}-R'$$

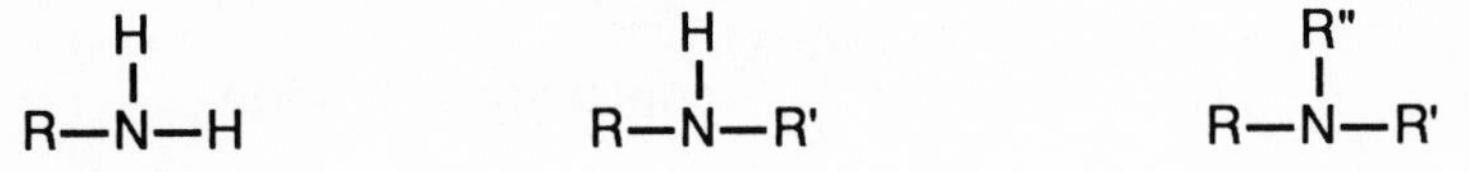

A primary amine   A secondary amine   A tertiary amine

15.14, 15.16

(a) $CH_3CH_2CH_2NH_2$

Propylamine

(*A primary amine*)

(b) $CH_3CH_2-\underset{\underset{\textstyle H}{|}}{\overset{\overset{\textstyle H}{|}}{N}}-CH_2CH_3$

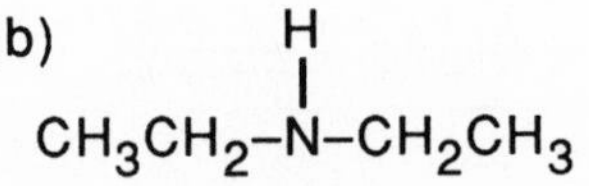

Diethylamine

(*A secondary amine*)

(c) $CH_3CH_2CH_2-\underset{\underset{\textstyle H}{|}}{\overset{\overset{\textstyle H}{|}}{N}}-CH_3$

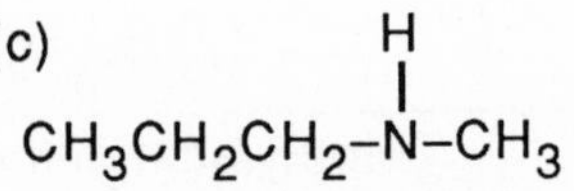

N–Methylpropylamine

(*A secondary amine*)

(d) $CH_3CH_2CH_2CH_2CH_2CH_2\underset{\underset{\textstyle |}{|}}{N}CH_3$ with $CH_3CH_2CH_2CH_2$ group

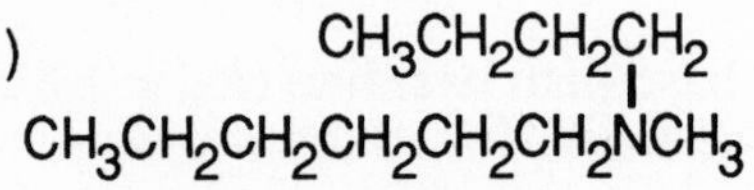

N–Butyl–N–Methylhexylamine

(*A tertiary amine*)

(e)   cyclopentyl–$\underset{\underset{\textstyle H}{|}}{N}$–$CH_2CH_3$

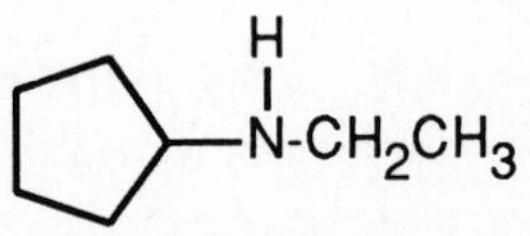

N–Ethylcyclopentylamine

(*A secondary amine*)

(f) $CH_3CH_2CH_2O$ CH_3 on benzene ring with $-NH_2$

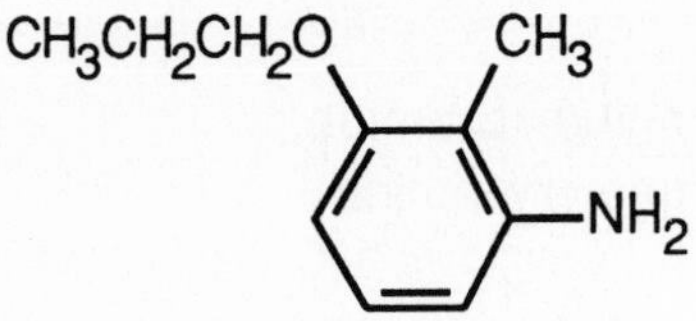

2-Methyl-3-propoxyaniline

(*A primary amine*)

15.15, 15.16

(a) $CH_3CH_2CH_2CH_2NH_2$

Butylamine

(*A primary amine*)

(b) $CH_3\underset{\underset{\textstyle NH_2}{|}}{CH}CH_3$

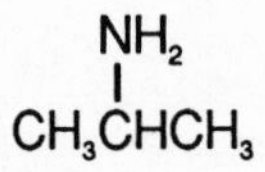

Isopropylamine

(*A primary amine*)

(c)   cyclobutyl–$NHCH_3$

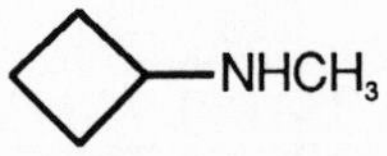

N-Methylcyclobutylamine

(*A secondary amine*)

(d)   phenyl–$\underset{\underset{\textstyle |}{|}}{\overset{\overset{\textstyle CH_3}{|}}{N}}$–cyclopentyl

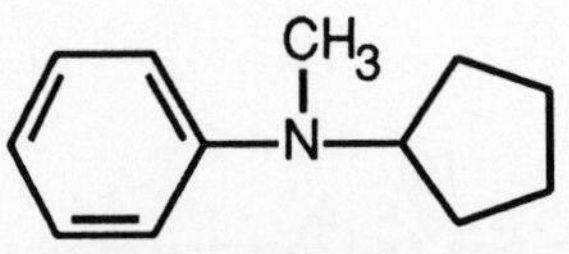

N–Cyclopentyl–N–methylaniline

(*A tertiary amine*)

15.17 There are many possible answers to this question. Here are some:

(a)   (b)

CH$_3$CH$_2$CH$_2$NHCH$_2$CH$_3$ ⬡N—CH$_3$

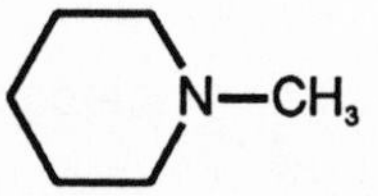

15.18 Pyridine ($K_b = 1.8 \times 10^{-9}$) is a weaker base than ammonia ($K_b = 1.7 \times 10^{-5}$).

15.19 A solution of 0.20 M methylamine has a higher pH than a solution of 0.20 M pyridine because the K_b of methylamine is larger than the K_b of pyridine. When K_b is larger, [OH$^-$] is larger, and the solution has a higher pH.

15.20

(a) $\boxed{CH_3CH_2NH_2}$ + H$_2$O $\rightleftharpoons$ CH$_3$CH$_2$NH$_3^+$ + OH$^-$

Ethylamine is the predominant species. In water, the ethylammonium ion is present to an extent of only 2%.

(b) At pH = 5.0, CH$_3$CH$_2$NH$_3^+$ is the predominant species.

15.21, 15.23

(a) CH$_3$NH$_3^+$ Cl$^-$

(b) ⬡—NH$_2^+$ Br$^-$
        |
        CH$_3$

Methylammonium chloride   *N* -Methylanilinium bromide
(*Salt of a primary amine*)   (*Salt of a secondary amine*)

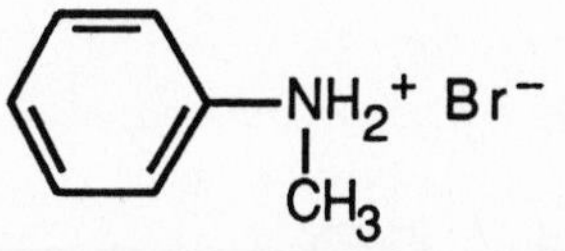

(c)   ⬠—NH$_2^+$ NO$_3^-$
              |
              CH$_3$

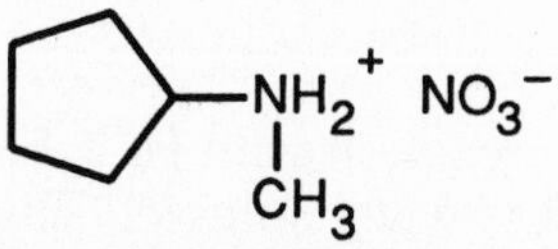

N -Methylcyclopentylammonium nitrate
      (*Salt of a secondary amine*)

15.22, 15.23

(a) ⬡—NH$_3^+$ Cl$^-$

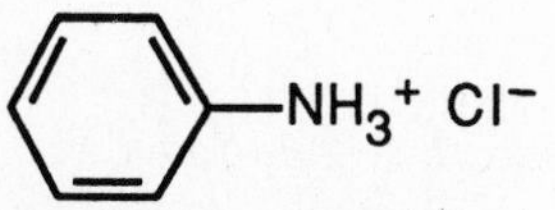

(b)   CH$_3$CH$_2$CH$_2$
              |
     CH$_3$CH$_2$CH$_2$CH$_2$NH$_2^+$ Br$^-$

Anilinium chloride   *N* -Propylbutylammonium bromide
(*Salt of a primary amine*)   (*Salt of a secondary amine*)

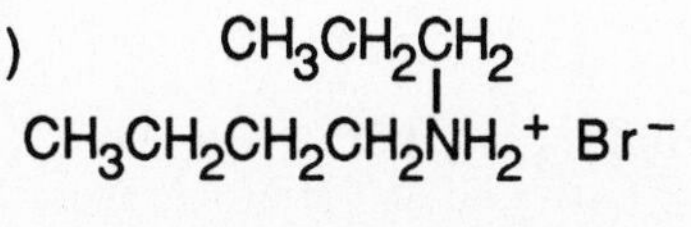

(c)   CH$_3$CH$_2$
                        |
   CH$_3$CH$_2$CH$_2$CH$_2$CH$_2$CH$_2$NH$^+$ Cl$^-$
                        |
                 CH$_2$CHCH$_3$

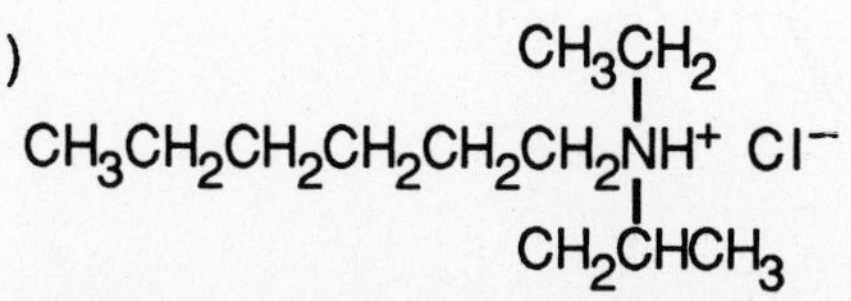

N –Ethyl–*N*–isopropylhexylammonium chloride
      (*Salt of a tertiary amine*)

15.24 Diethylamine is a stronger base than diethyl ether because amines are more basic than ethers.

15.25

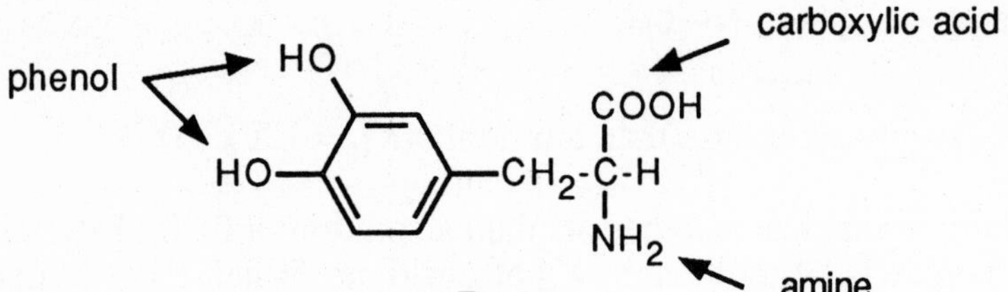

L-Dopa

15.26

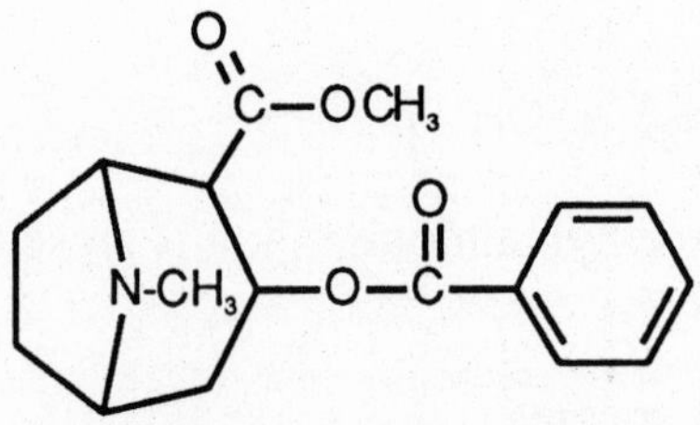

Cocaine is a tertiary amine

15.27

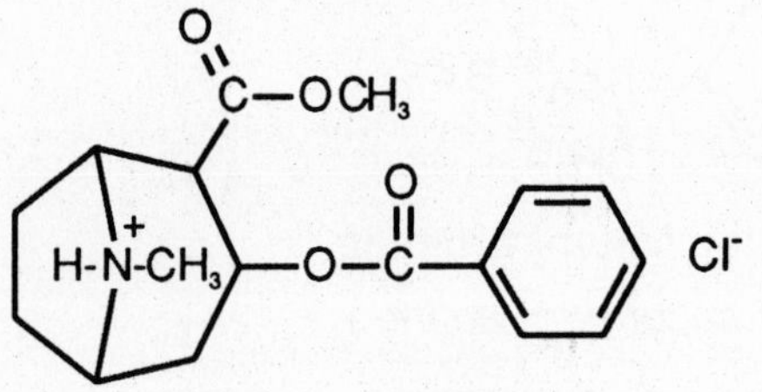

Cocaine hydrochloride

15.28 Neither menthol nor quinine is soluble in water. Upon reaction with HCl, however, quinine is converted into quinine hydrochloride, which is water soluble. Thus, the two compounds could be distinguished by treating samples of each with aqueous HCl and trying to dissolve the resulting product.

15.29 (a)

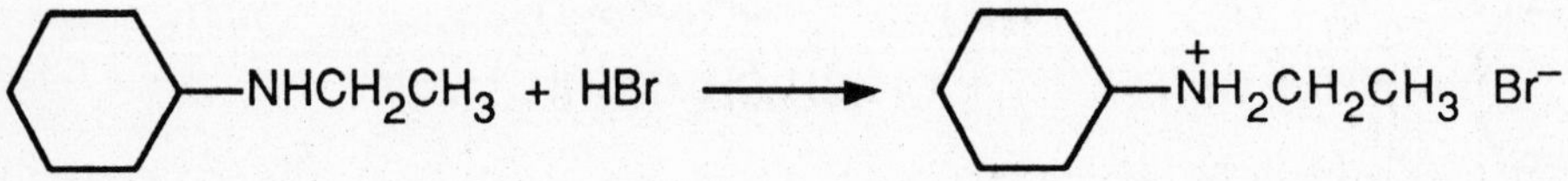

(b)

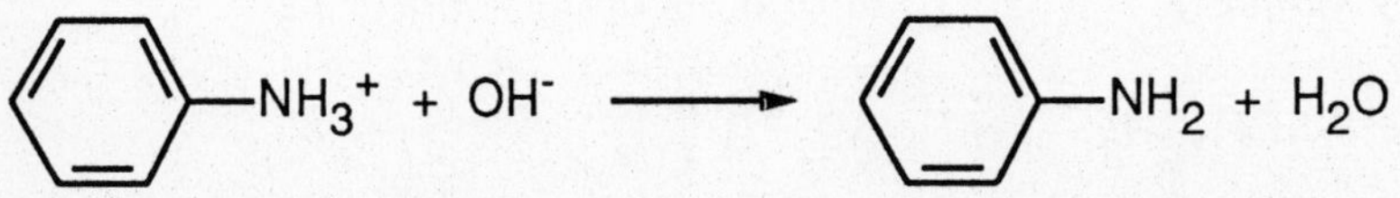

(c)

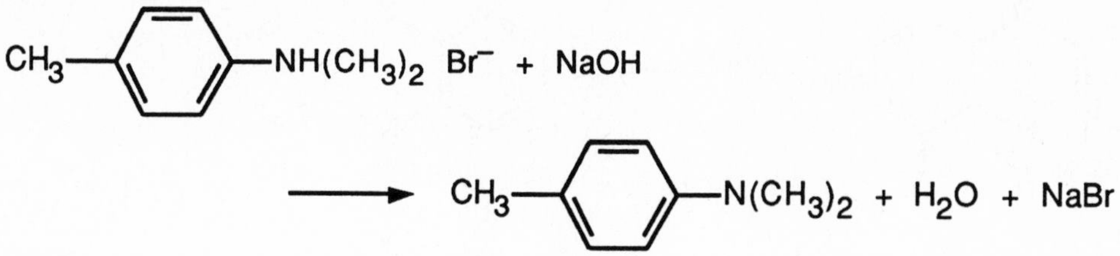

$$CH_3-\underset{}{\langle C_6H_4\rangle}-NH(CH_3)_2\ Br^- + NaOH$$

$$\longrightarrow CH_3-\underset{}{\langle C_6H_4\rangle}-N(CH_3)_2 + H_2O + NaBr$$

(d)

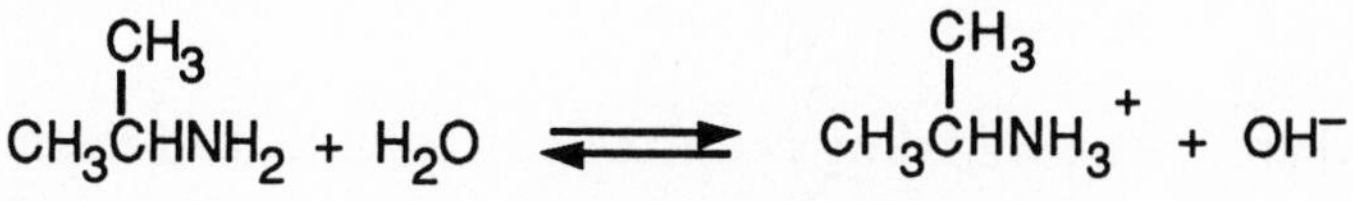

$$\underset{\underset{CH_3}{|}}{CH_3CHNH_2} + H_2O \rightleftharpoons \underset{\underset{CH_3}{|}}{CH_3CHNH_3^+} + OH^-$$

(e)

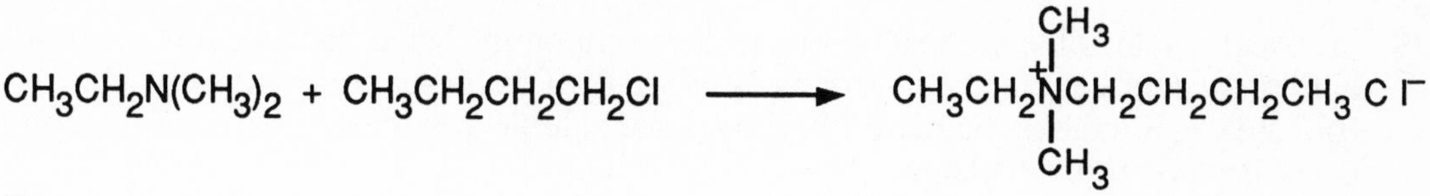

$$CH_3CH_2N(CH_3)_2 + CH_3CH_2CH_2CH_2Cl \longrightarrow \underset{\underset{CH_3}{|}}{\overset{\overset{CH_3}{|}}{CH_3CH_2\overset{+}{N}CH_2CH_2CH_2CH_3}}\ Cl^-$$

(f)

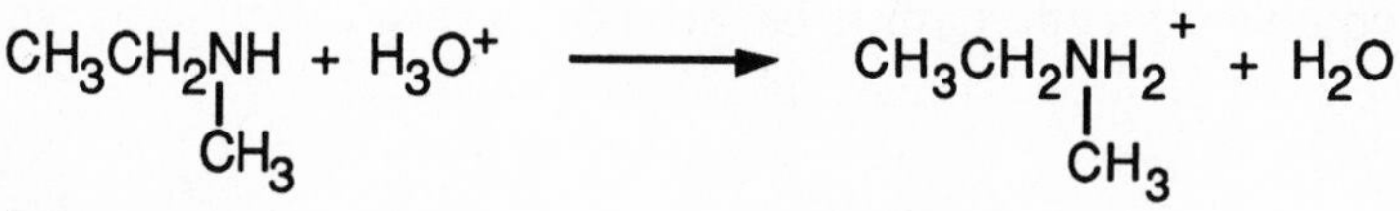

$$\underset{\underset{CH_3}{|}}{CH_3CH_2NH} + H_3O^+ \longrightarrow \underset{\underset{CH_3}{|}}{CH_3CH_2NH_2^+} + H_2O$$

(g)

$$\underset{}{\langle pyridine \rangle N} + HCl \longrightarrow \underset{}{\langle pyridine \rangle \overset{+}{N}{-}H}\ Cl^-$$

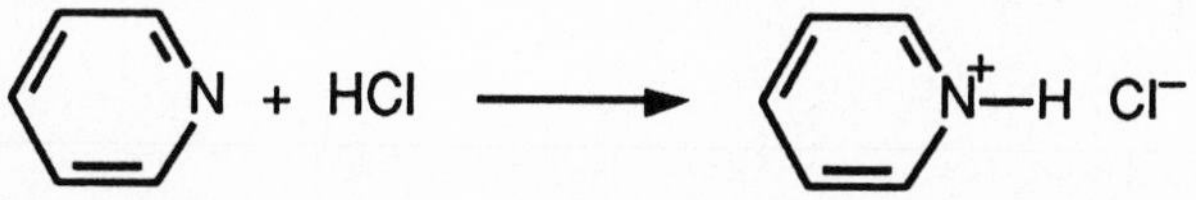

15.30 The ammonium salt pictured does not react with acids or bases because it is neither acidic nor basic.

15.31

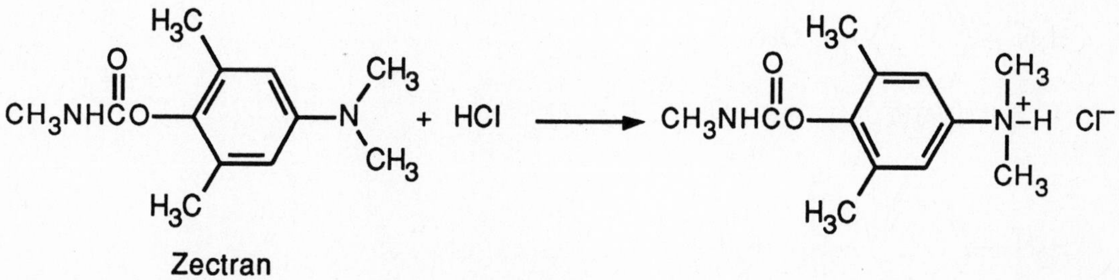

Zectran

15.33 The K_a values of most acidic and basic functional groups that occur in body fluids are such that at pH = 7 they exist in the anionic form.

15.34 The salts of compounds are often more soluble in body fluids than neutral compounds. Also, salts are frequently more readily absorbed than neutral compounds.

15.35 An enteric coating on a drug tablet protects it from being dissolved by stomach acid before it reaches the intestines.

15.36

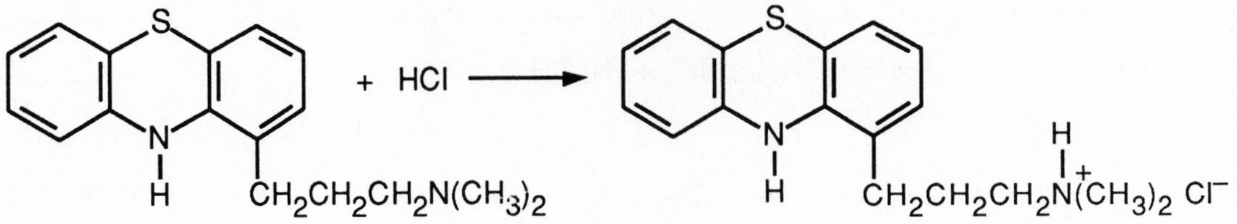

15.37 A prodrug is an inactive compound that is converted to its pharmaceutically active form in the body.

15.38 Prodrugs are used in cases where the needed drug is unstable, insoluble, bad-tasting, or fails to reach the desired site.

15.39 (a) Acetic acid is the highest boiling of the compounds listed because it is more polar and undergoes more extensive hydrogen bonding than the other compounds listed.
(b)(c)(d) *n*-Butane is the lowest boiling, least soluble and least reactive of the compounds listed because it is an alkane.

15.40 Decylamine is much less soluble than ethylamine because of its large alkyl part, which is water-insoluble.

15.41

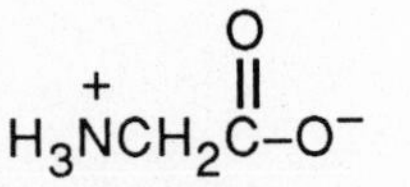

Glycine

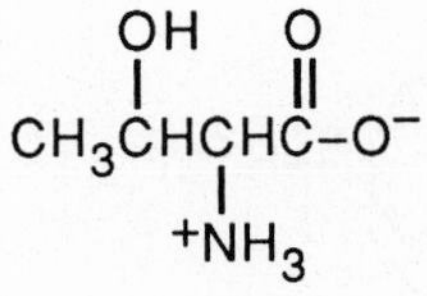

Threonine

15.42

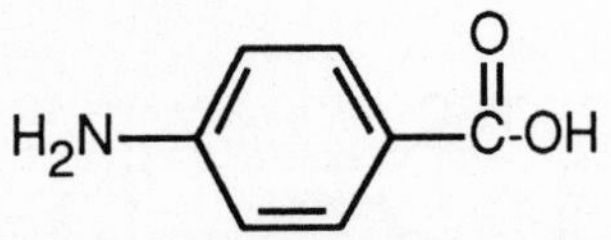

PABA

15.43

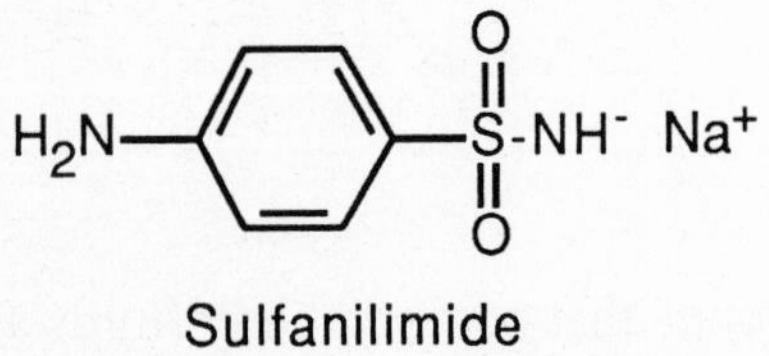

Sulfanilimide

(a) Both PABA and sulfanilimide have *p*-amino-substituted aromatic rings.
(b) The sodium salt form of the drug is used to increase solubility.

15.44

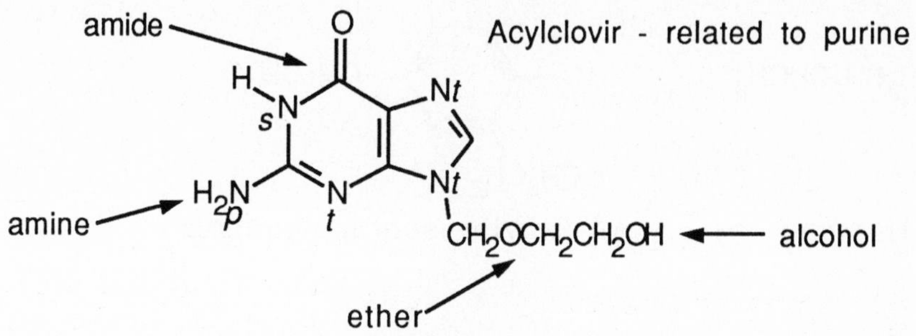

amide → (structure) Acylclovir - related to purine

amine →

ether →

alcohol →

15.45 Trimethylamine, with $K_b = 5.0 \times 10^{-5}$, is a stronger base than pyridine, with $K_b = 1.8 \times 10^{-9}$. Thus the reaction of trimethylamine with pyridine proceeds in the following direction:

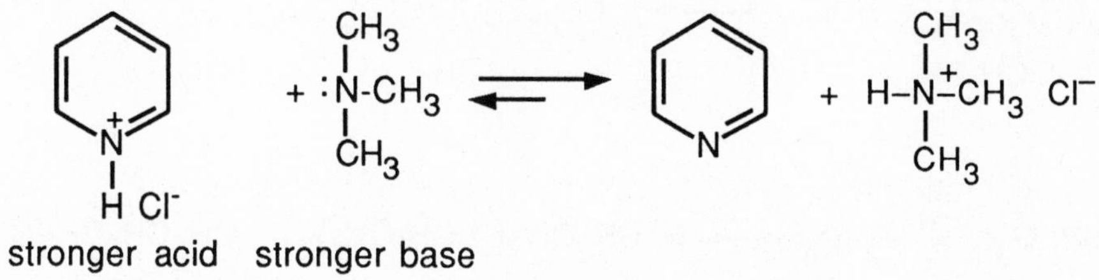

stronger acid   stronger base

15.46

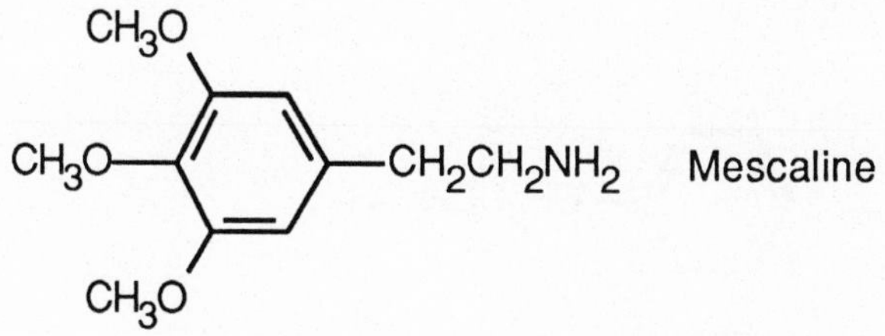

Mescaline

15.47 Sympathomimetic drugs are drugs whose effects mimic those of other drugs.

15.48

Amines	Alcohols
(a) foul smelling	pleasant smelling
(b) somewhat basic	not basic
(c) lower boiling, due to weaker hydrogen bonds, but higher boiling than ethers or alkyl halides	higher boiling, due to strong hydrogen bonds

15.49 Alkaloids are often found to be bitter or poisonous.

15.50 Antihistamines block the sites to which histamines must attach in order to produce their unpleasant effects.

15.51

(a)

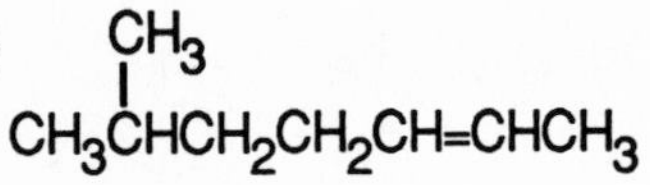

$$CH_3$$
$$CH_3CHCH_2CH_2CH=CHCH_3$$

6-Methyl-2-Heptene

(b)

HO—⟨benzene ring⟩—CH(CH$_3$)$_2$

with CH$_3$CH$_2$ substituent

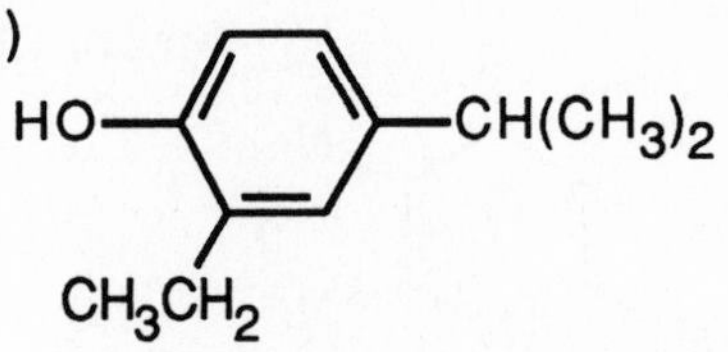

2-Ethyl-4-isopropylphenol

(c)

$(CH_3CH_2CH_2CH_2)_2NH$

Dibutylamine

15.52 (a)

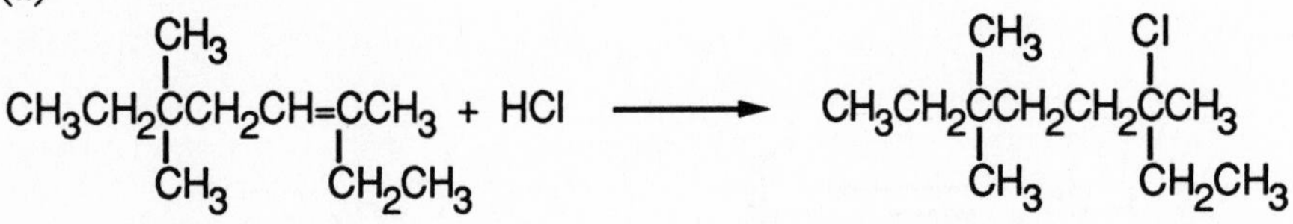

$$CH_3$$
$$CH_3CH_2CCH_2CH=CCH_3 + HCl \longrightarrow$$
$$CH_3 \quad CH_2CH_3$$

$$CH_3 \quad Cl$$
$$CH_3CH_2CCH_2CH_2CCH_3$$
$$CH_3 \quad CH_2CH_3$$

(b)

$$OH$$
$$CH_3CH_2CHCH(CH_3)_2 + H_2SO_4 \longrightarrow CH_3CH=CHCH(CH_3)_2 + CH_3CH_2CH=C(CH_3)_2$$

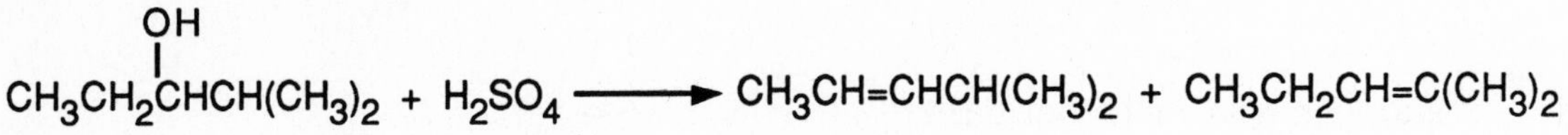

(c)

$$2\ CH_3CH_2SH \xrightarrow{[O]} CH_3CH_2S\text{-}SCH_2CH_3$$

(d)

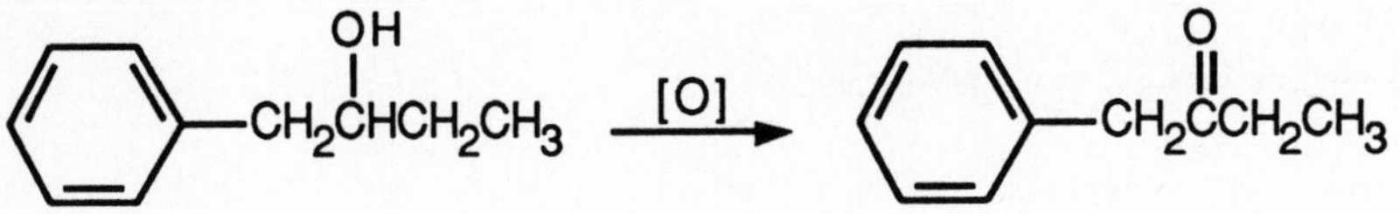

⟨benzene ring⟩—CH$_2$CHCH$_2$CH$_3$ (with OH) $\xrightarrow{[O]}$ ⟨benzene ring⟩—CH$_2$CCH$_2$CH$_3$ (with =O)

(e)

$$CH_3CH_2NH_2 + CH_3CH_2Cl \longrightarrow (CH_3CH_2)_2NH + (CH_3CH_2)_3N$$
$$+ (CH_3CH_2)_4N^+\ Cl^-$$

(f)

$$(CH_3)_3N + H_2O \rightleftharpoons (CH_3)_3NH^+ + OH^-$$

(g)

$$(CH_3)_3N + HCl \longrightarrow (CH_3)_3NH^+\ Cl^-$$

(h)

$$(CH_3)_3NH^+ + OH^- \longrightarrow (CH_3)_3N + H_2O$$

The Chapter in Brief

Amines are compounds that contain one, two, or three organic groups bonded to nitrogen. They can be classified as primary, secondary, or tertiary. Amines are named by citing the organic groups, followed by the suffix *-amine*. Amines are weakly basic and react with acids to form ammonium salts. Many biomolecules have amino groups; among them are nucleotides and neurotransmitters. In plants, amines are called alkaloids.

Self-Test for Chapter 15

Tell whether the following statements are true or false:

1. Of two amines, the one with the larger K_b has the lower pH when dissolved in water.

2. Ammonium salts are water-soluble.

3. Tertiary amines are higher boiling than primary or secondary amines.

4. Morphine and codeine are alkaloids.

5. Quaternary ammonium salts are acidic.

6. Caffeine is a heterocyclic amine.

7. A prodrug is the water-soluble form of a drug.

8. Histamine causes swelling in human tissues.

9. Demerol is a naturally-occurring morphine derivative.

10. The correct name for $CH_3CH_2CH_2CH_2NHCH_3$ is methylbutylamine.

11. The physical properties of low-molecular-weight amines and ammonia are similar.

Complete the following sentences:

1. When the –NH_2 group is a substituent, _____ is used as a prefix.

2. Ephedrine is _____ to dopamine.

3. _____ all contain nitrogen heterocyclic rings derived from either purine or pyrimidine.

4. Epinephrine is an example of a _____.

5. A _____ has a nitrogen atom contained in a ring.

6. The basicity of an amine is measured by _____.

7. Simple amines are water-soluble because of _____ _____.

8. Most amines can be made water-soluble by conversion to _____ salts.

9. An _____ _____ on a drug keeps the drug from being dissolved by acidic gastric juices.

10. A _____ is an inactive compound that is converted to its active form after it is administered.

Match the item in the left column with its partner on the right

1. Trimethylamine   (a) amino acid

2. Atropine   (b) vitamin

3. Pyrrole   (c) primary aromatic amine

4. Tetramethylammonium chloride   (d) tertiary amine

5. Alanine   (e) sympathomimetic drug

6. Dimethylamine   (f) neurotransmitter

7. Pyridoxine   (g) primary amine

8. Doxylamine   (h) heterocycle

9. Dopamine   (i) quaternary ammonium salt

10. Methylamine   (j) secondary amine

11. Amphetamine   (k) antihistamine

12. Aniline   (l) alkaloid

Chapter 16 – Aldehydes and Ketones

16.1

(a)

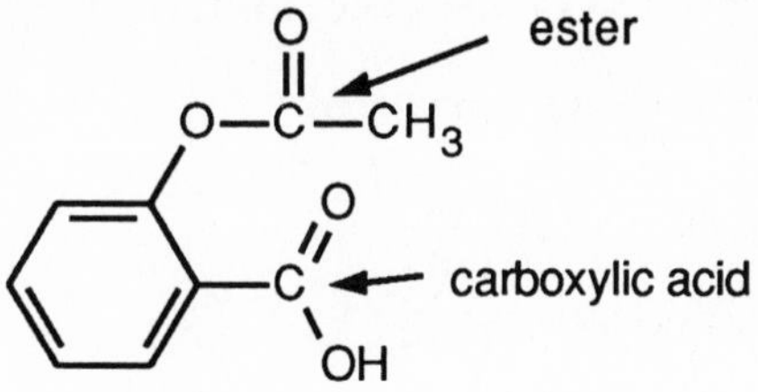

ester

carboxylic acid

Aspirin

(b)

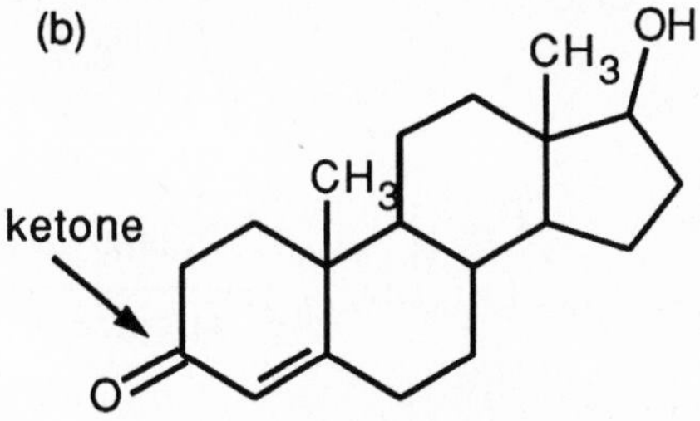

ketone

Testosterone

(c)

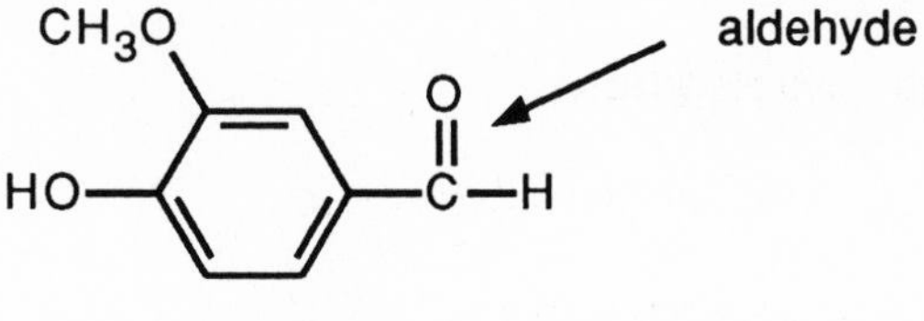

aldehyde

Vanillin

(d)

$C_4H_9\overset{\overset{\displaystyle O}{\|}}{C}CH_3$

Ketone

(e)

$C_4H_9\overset{\overset{\displaystyle O}{\|}}{C}H$

Aldehyde

(f)

$C_4H_9\overset{\overset{\displaystyle O}{\|}}{C}OCH_3$

Ester

16.2

(a)

$CH_3CH_2CH_2CH_2CH_2\text{-}\overset{\overset{\displaystyle O}{\|}}{C}\text{-H}$

Hexanal

(b)

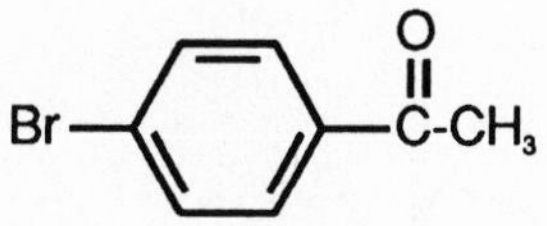

p-Bromoacetophenone

(c)

$CH_3CH_2\overset{\overset{\displaystyle CH_3}{|}}{C}HCH_2\overset{\overset{\displaystyle O}{\|}}{C}CH_3$

4-Methyl-2-hexanone

(d)

$CH_3\overset{\overset{\displaystyle O}{\|}}{C}CH(CH_3)_2$

Methyl isopropyl ketone

16.3

(a)

$CH_3CH_2CH_2CH_2\text{-}\overset{\overset{\displaystyle O}{\|}}{C}\text{-H}$

Pentanal

(b)

$CH_3CH_2\overset{\overset{\displaystyle O}{\|}}{C}CH_2CH_3$

3-Pentanone

(c)

$CH_3CH_2\overset{\overset{\displaystyle CH_3}{|}}{C}HCH_2CH_2\overset{\overset{\displaystyle O}{\|}}{C}\text{-H}$

4-Methylhexanal

16.4

(a)

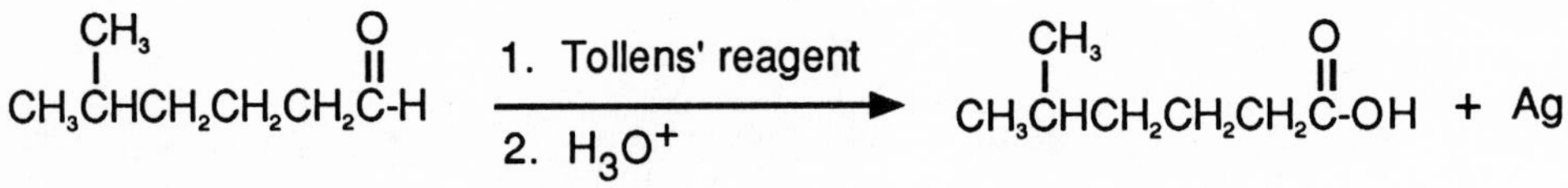

$$CH_3CHCH_2CH_2CH_2\overset{O}{\overset{\|}{C}}-H \quad \xrightarrow[\text{2. } H_3O^+]{\text{1. Tollens' reagent}} \quad CH_3CHCH_2CH_2CH_2\overset{O}{\overset{\|}{C}}-OH \;\; + \;\; Ag$$

with CH_3 substituents on the respective carbons

(b)

$$CH_3CH_2CH_2-\overset{H_3C}{\underset{H_3C}{\overset{\|}{C}}}-\overset{O}{\overset{\|}{C}}-H \quad \xrightarrow[\text{2. } H_3O^+]{\text{1. Tollens' reagent}} \quad CH_3CH_2CH_2-\overset{H_3C}{\underset{H_3C}{C}}-\overset{O}{\overset{\|}{C}}-OH \;\; + \;\; Ag$$

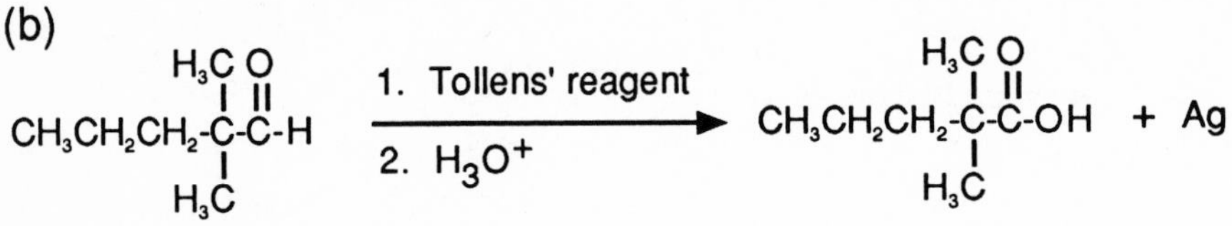

(c)

$$CH_3CH_2\overset{O}{\overset{\|}{C}}CHCH_3 \quad \xrightarrow{\text{Tollens' reagent}} \quad \text{No Reaction}$$

with CH_3 substituent

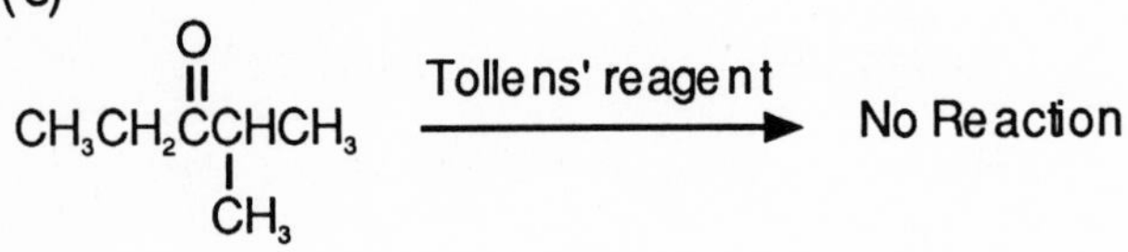

16.5

(a)

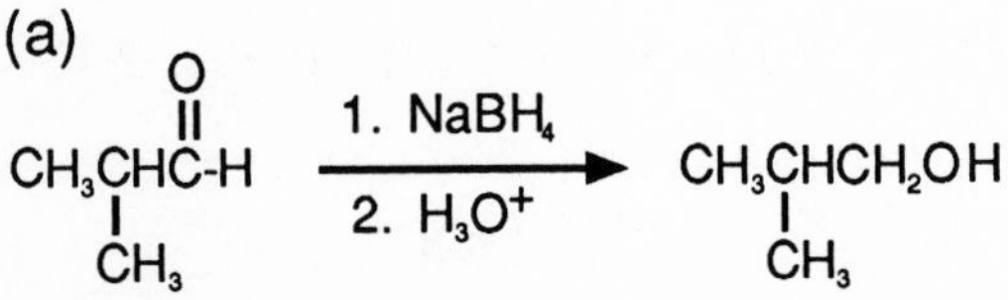

$$CH_3CH\overset{O}{\overset{\|}{C}}-H \quad \xrightarrow[\text{2. } H_3O^+]{\text{1. } NaBH_4} \quad CH_3CHCH_2OH$$

with CH_3 substituents

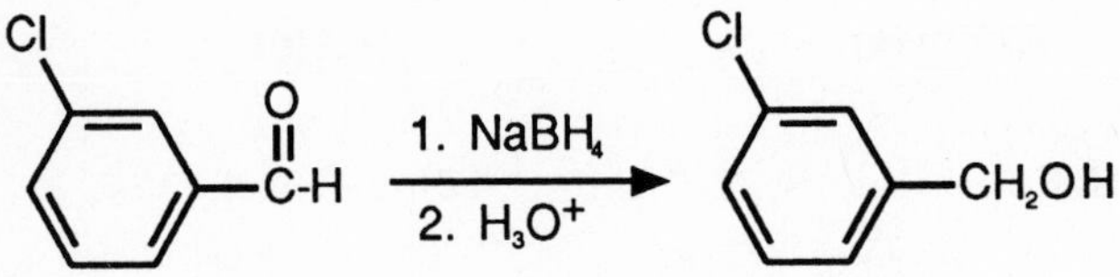

(b)

$$\xrightarrow[\text{2. } H_3O^+]{\text{1. } NaBH_4}$$

(c)

$$\xrightarrow[\text{2. } H_3O^+]{\text{1. } NaBH_4}$$

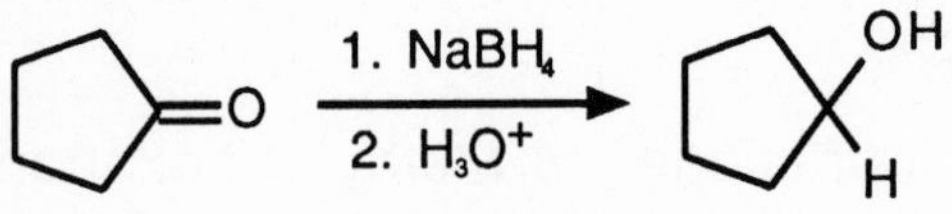

16.6

(a)

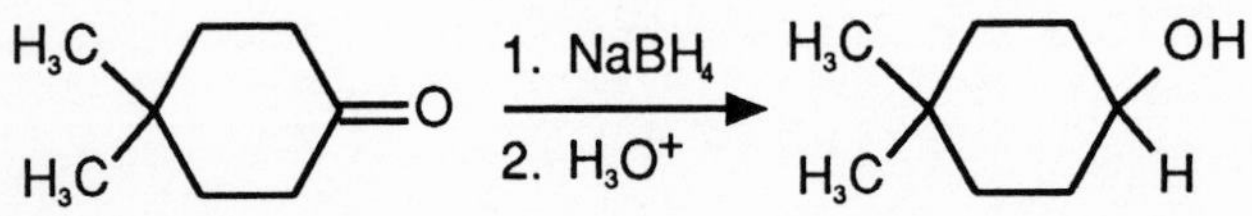

$$\xrightarrow[\text{2. } H_3O^+]{\text{1. } NaBH_4}$$

(b)

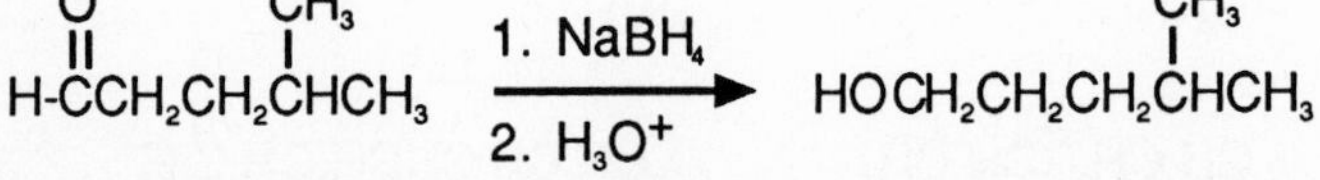

$$H-\overset{O}{\overset{\|}{C}}CH_2CH_2\overset{CH_3}{\overset{|}{CH}}CHCH_3 \quad \xrightarrow[\text{2. } H_3O^+]{\text{1. } NaBH_4} \quad HOCH_2CH_2CH_2\overset{CH_3}{\overset{|}{CH}}CHCH_3$$

(c)

$$CH_3CH_2CH_2CH\overset{O}{\overset{\|}{C}}-H \quad \xrightarrow[\text{2. } H_3O^+]{\text{1. } NaBH_4} \quad CH_3CH_2CH_2CHCH_2OH$$

with CH_3 substituents

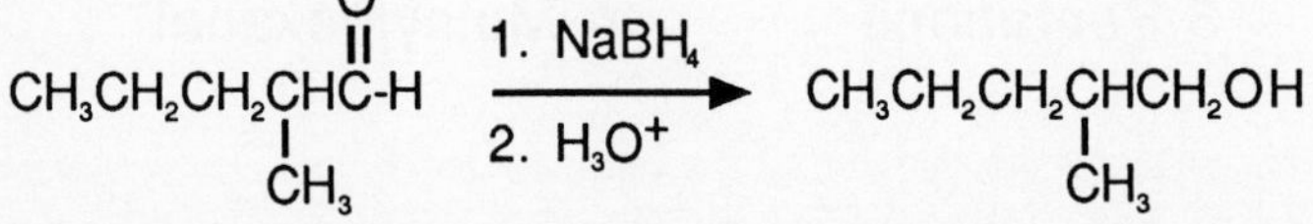

16.7

(a)   CH₃CH₂CH₂CHO Rewrite as:

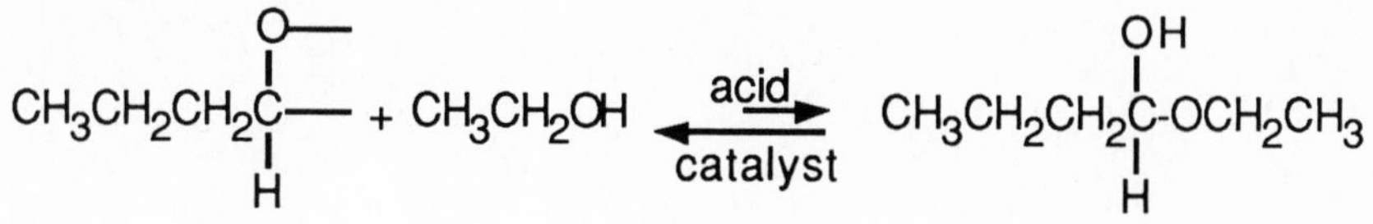

$$CH_3CH_2CH_2\overset{O-}{\underset{H}{C}} \quad + \quad CH_3CH_2OH \quad \underset{\text{catalyst}}{\overset{\text{acid}}{\rightleftharpoons}} \quad CH_3CH_2CH_2\overset{OH}{\underset{H}{C}}\text{-}OCH_2CH_3$$

hemiacetal

(b)

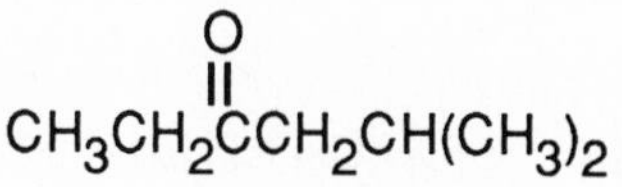

$$CH_3CH_2\overset{O}{\overset{\|}{C}}CH_2CH(CH_3)_2 \text{ Rewrite as:}$$

$$CH_3CH_2\overset{O-}{\underset{CH_2CH(CH_3)_2}{C}} \quad + \quad CH_3OH \quad \underset{\text{catalyst}}{\overset{\text{acid}}{\rightleftharpoons}} \quad CH_3CH_2\overset{OH}{\underset{CH_2CH(CH_3)_2}{C}}\text{-}OCH_3$$

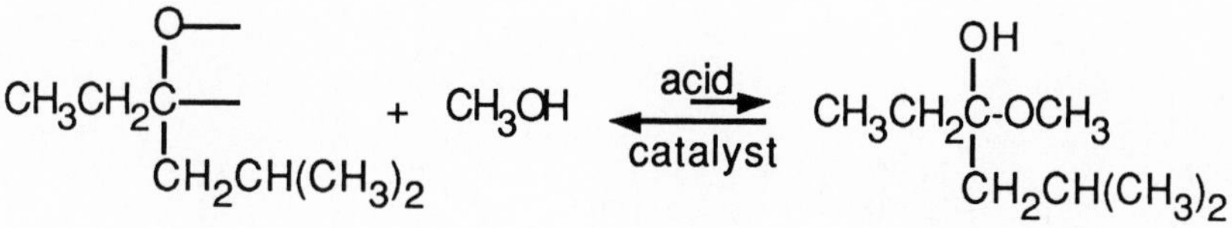

hemiacetal

16.8

(a)

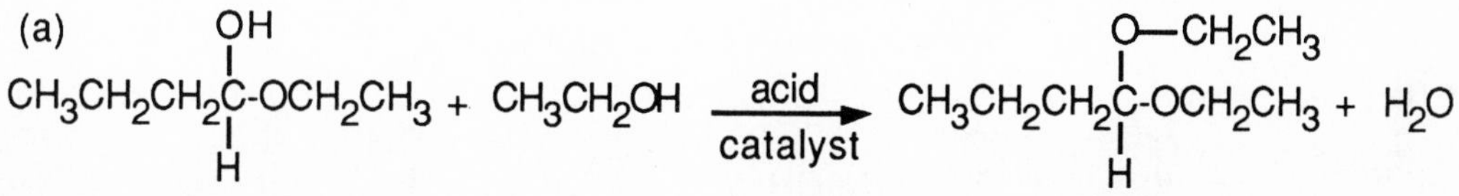

$$CH_3CH_2CH_2\overset{OH}{\underset{H}{C}}\text{-}OCH_2CH_3 + CH_3CH_2OH \underset{\text{catalyst}}{\overset{\text{acid}}{\longrightarrow}} CH_3CH_2CH_2\overset{O-CH_2CH_3}{\underset{H}{C}}\text{-}OCH_2CH_3 + H_2O$$

acetal

(b)

$$CH_3CH_2\overset{OH}{\underset{CH_2CH(CH_3)_2}{C}}\text{-}OCH_3 + CH_3OH \underset{\text{catalyst}}{\overset{\text{acid}}{\longrightarrow}} CH_3CH_2\overset{OCH_3}{\underset{CH_2CH(CH_3)_2}{C}}\text{-}OCH_3 + H_2O$$

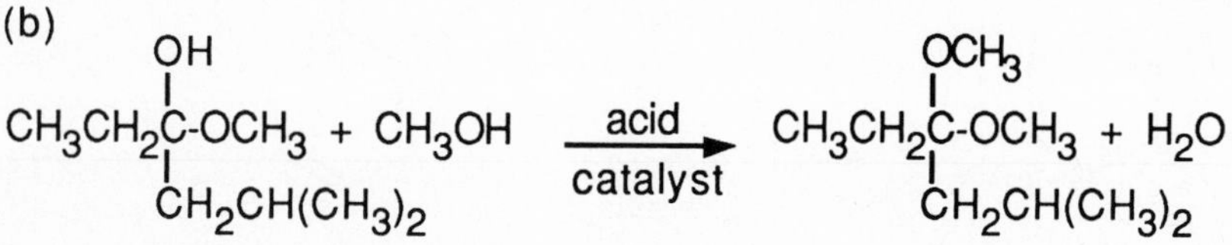

16.9   First, look for a carbon bonded to two different oxygen atoms by single bonds. If one group bonded to the carbon is –OH and the other is –OR (R - alkyl group), the compound is a hemiacetal. If both groups are –OR groups, the compound is an acetal.

(a)

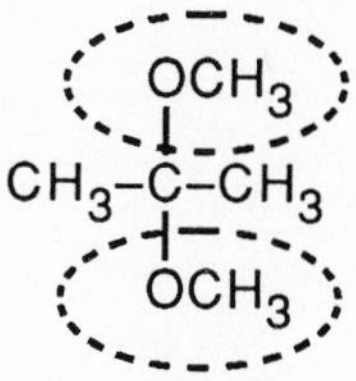

$$CH_3\text{-}\overset{OCH_3}{\underset{OCH_3}{C}}\text{-}CH_3$$

acetal

(b)

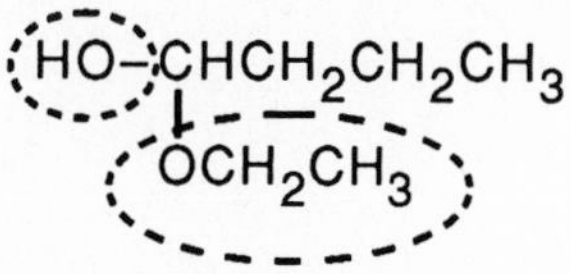

$$HO\text{-}CHCH_2CH_2CH_3$$
$$\overset{|}{OCH_2CH_3}$$

hemiacetal

(c)

$$CH_3\overset{O}{\overset{\|}{C}}CH_2OH$$

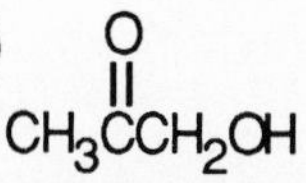

neither acetal
nor hemiacetal

(d)

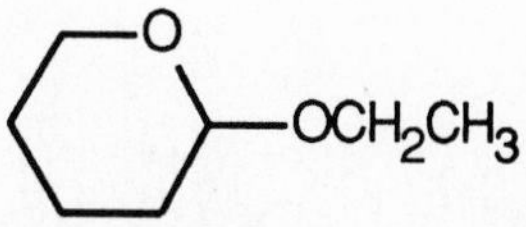

acetal

16.10

(a)

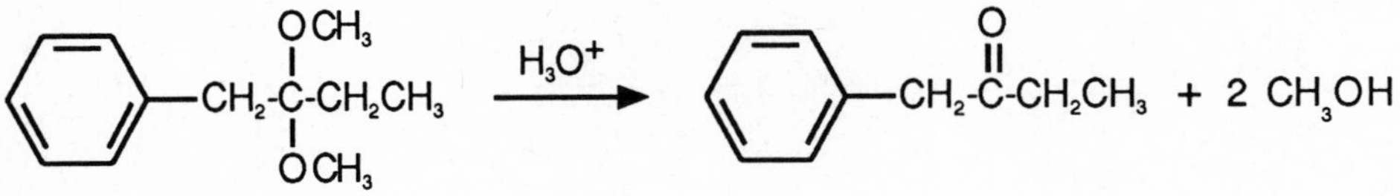

(b)

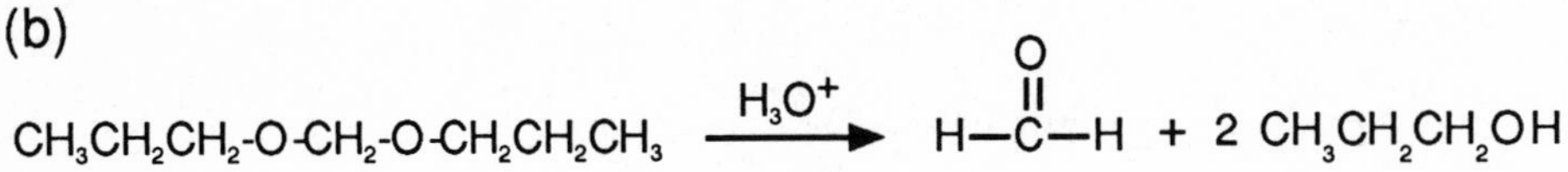

$CH_3CH_2CH_2$-O-CH_2-O-$CH_2CH_2CH_3$ $\xrightarrow{H_3O^+}$ H—C—H + 2 $CH_3CH_2CH_2OH$

16.11

(a)

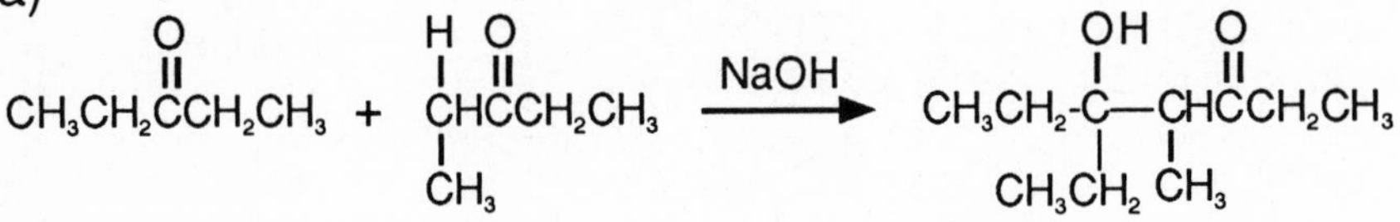

(b)

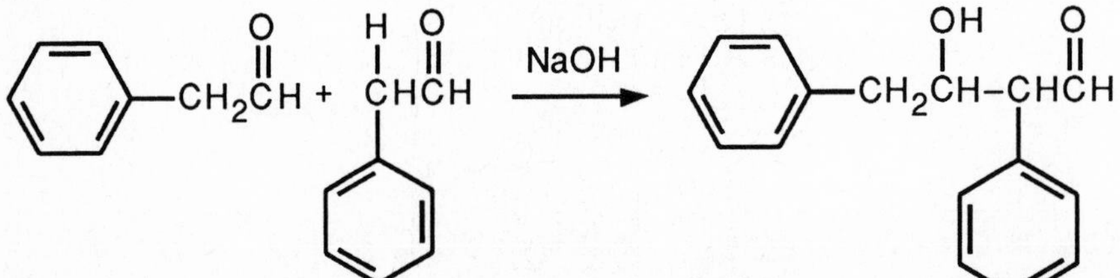

16.12 Compound (a) can't undergo an aldol reaction because it has only one carbon atom (and therefore no hydrogens on a carbon atom next to the carbonyl group).

Compound (b) can't undergo an aldol reaction because it has no hydrogens on the carbon atom next to the carbonyl group.

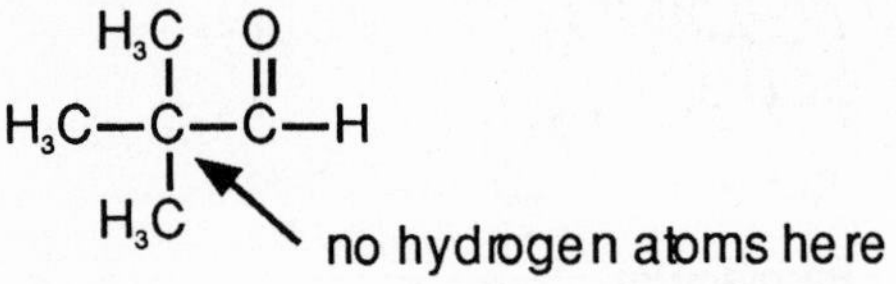

Compound (c) *can* undergo an aldol reaction:

(c)

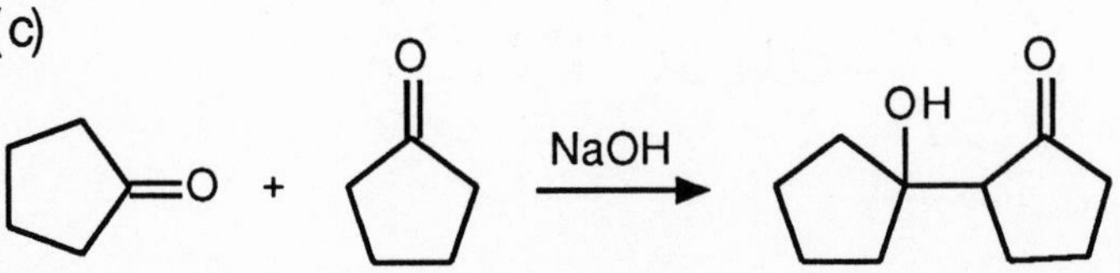

16.13 An aldehyde has a carbon substituent and an -H bonded to the carbonyl carbon; a ketone has two carbon substituents bonded to the carbonyl carbon.

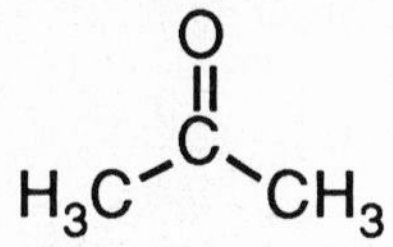

Acetone - a ketone 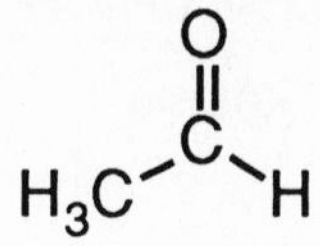   Acetaldehyde - an aldehyde

16.14 The family-name ending -*al* is used for aldehydes; the name ending -*one* is used for ketones.

16.15

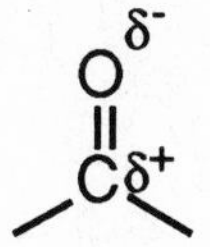

The oxygen is electron-rich, and the carbon is electron-poor.

16.16 There are many possible answers to this question.

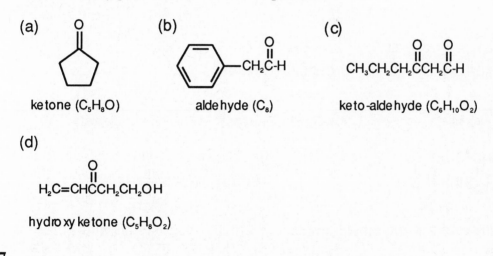

(a)   (b)   (c)

ketone (C₅H₈O)   aldehyde (C₈)   keto-aldehyde (C₆H₁₀O₂)

(d)

H₂C=CHCCH₂CH₂OH

hydroxy ketone (C₅H₈O₂)

16.17

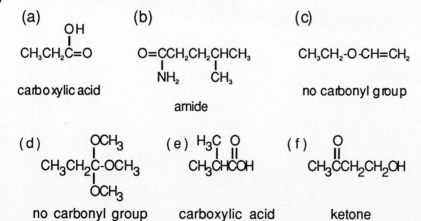

(a)   (b)   (c)

OH
CH₃CH₂C=O   O=CCH₂CH₂CHCH₃   CH₃CH₂-O-CH=CH₂
                    NH₂   CH₃
carboxylic acid   no carbonyl group
                amide

(d)   (e)   (f)

OCH₃   H₃C O   O
CH₃CH₂C-OCH₃   CH₃CHCOH   CH₃CCH₂CH₂OH
OCH₃
no carbonyl group   carboxylic acid   ketone

16.18

(a)

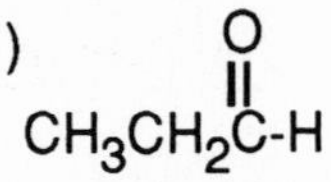

CH₃CH₂C-H
aldehyde

(b)

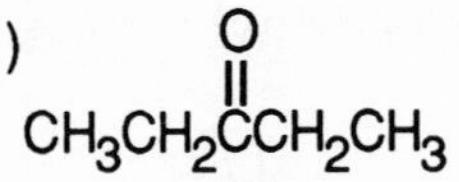

CH₃CH₂CCH₂CH₃
ketone

(c)

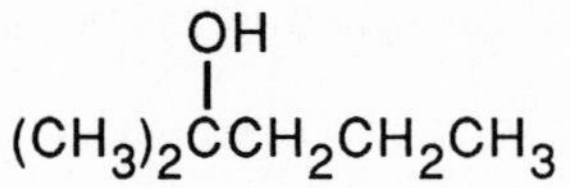

OH
(CH₃)₂CCH₂CH₂CH₃
no carbonyl group (alcohol)

(d)

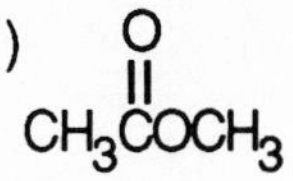

CH₃COCH₃
ester

(e)

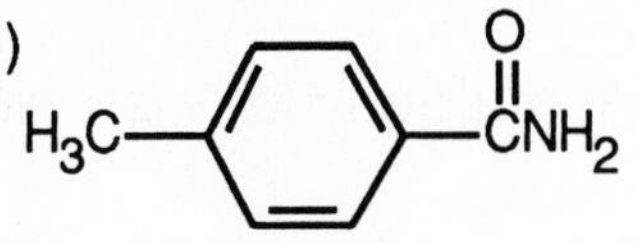

H₃C-〈benzene〉-CNH₂
amide

(f)

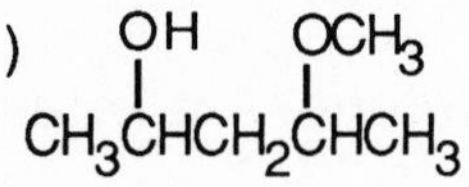

OH   OCH₃
CH₃CHCH₂CHCH₃
no carbonyl group

16.19

(a)

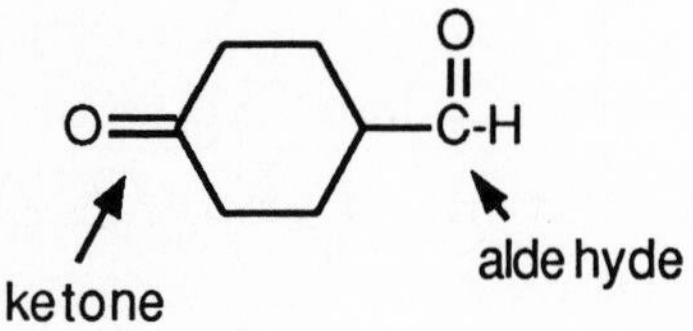

O=〈cyclohexane ring〉-C-H

ketone   aldehyde

(b)

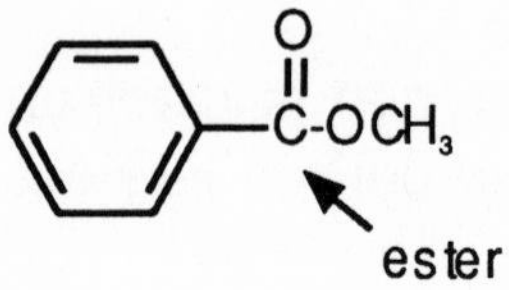

〈benzene〉-C-OCH₃
ester

16.20

(a)

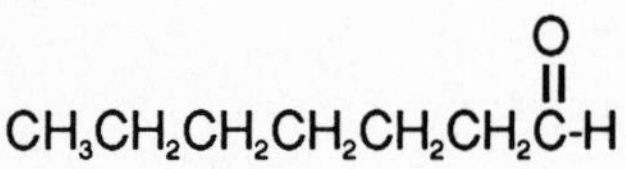

CH₃CH₂CH₂CH₂CH₂CH₂C-H
Heptanal

(b)

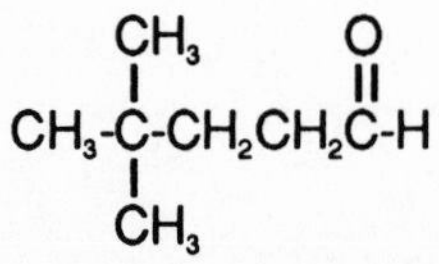

CH₃
CH₃-C-CH₂CH₂C-H
CH₃
4,4-Dimethylpentanal

(c)

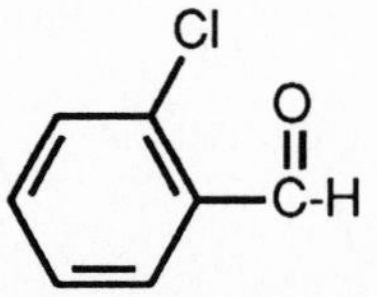

Cl
〈benzene〉-C-H
o-Chlorobenzaldehyde

(d)

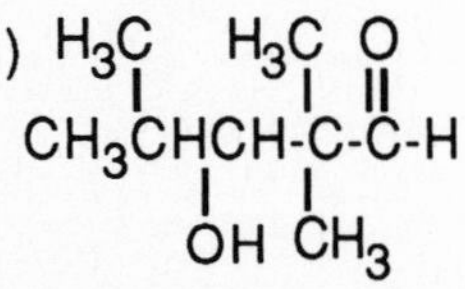

H₃C   H₃C O
CH₃CHCH-C-C-H
OH CH₃
3-Hydroxy-2,2,4-trimethylpentanal

(e)

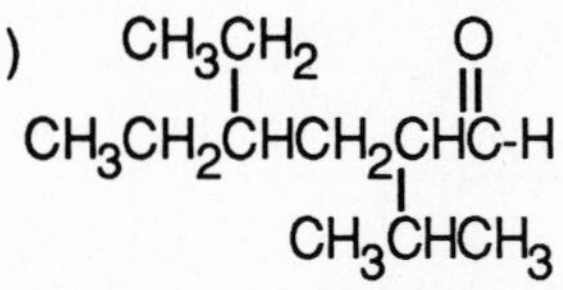

CH₃CH₂   O
CH₃CH₂CHCH₂CHC-H
CH₃CHCH₃
4-Ethyl-2-isopropylhexanol

(f)

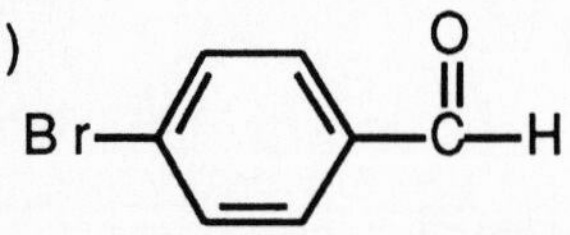

Br-〈benzene〉-C-H
p-Bromobenzaldehyde

16.21

(a)

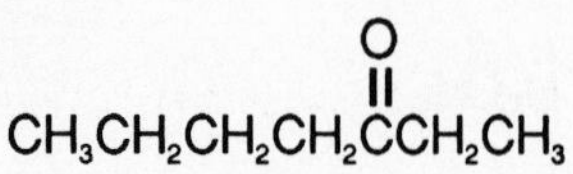

CH₃CH₂CH₂CH₂CCH₂CH₃
3-Heptanone

(b)

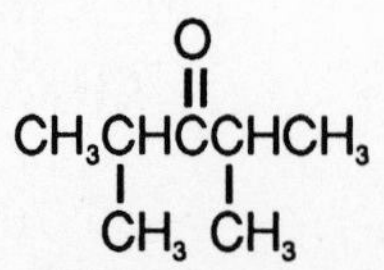

CH₃CHCCHCH₃
CH₃ CH₃
2,4-Dimethyl-3-pentanone

(c)

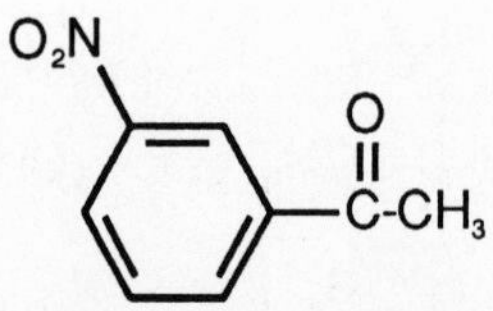

O₂N
〈benzene〉-C-CH₃
m-Nitroacetophenone

(d)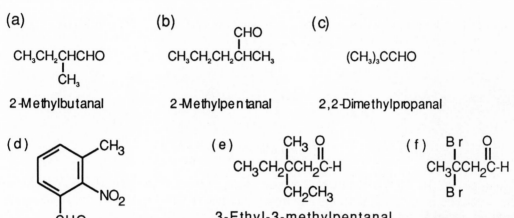

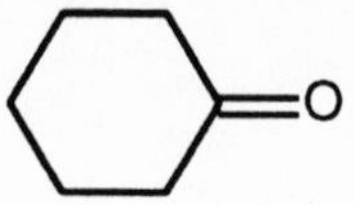

Cyclohexanone

(e)
$$CH_3CH_2\overset{O}{\overset{\|}{C}}CCl_3$$

1,1,1-Trichloro-2-butanone

(f)
$$CH_3CH_2CH_2\overset{O}{\overset{\|}{C}}\underset{\underset{CH_3}{|}}{C}HCH_3$$

2-Methyl-3-hexanone

16.22

(a)
$$CH_3CH_2\underset{\underset{CH_3}{|}}{C}HCHO$$

2-Methylbutanal

(b)
$$CH_3CH_2CH_2\underset{\underset{CHO}{|}}{C}HCH_3$$

2-Methylpentanal

(c)
$$(CH_3)_3CCHO$$

2,2-Dimethylpropanal

(d)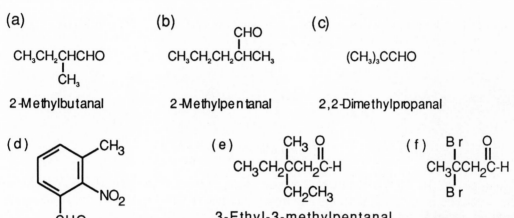

3-Methyl-2-nitrobenzaldehyde

(e)
$$CH_3CH_2\underset{\underset{CH_2CH_3}{|}}{\overset{\overset{CH_3}{|}}{C}}CH_2\overset{O}{\overset{\|}{C}}\text{-H}$$

3-Ethyl-3-methylpentanal

(f)
$$CH_3\underset{\underset{Br}{|}}{\overset{\overset{Br}{|}}{C}}CH_2\overset{O}{\overset{\|}{C}}\text{-H}$$

3,3-Dibromobutanal

16.23

(a)
$$CH_3\overset{O}{\overset{\|}{C}}CH_2CH_3$$

2-Butanone

(b)
$$CH_3\overset{O}{\overset{\|}{C}}CH_2CH_2\underset{\underset{CH_3}{|}}{C}HCH_3$$

5-Methyl-2-hexanone

(c)
$$(CH_3)_3\overset{O}{\overset{\|}{C}}CC(CH_3)_3$$

2,2,4,4-Tetramethyl-3-pentanone

(d)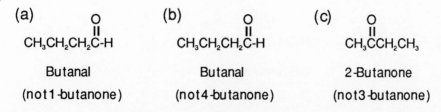

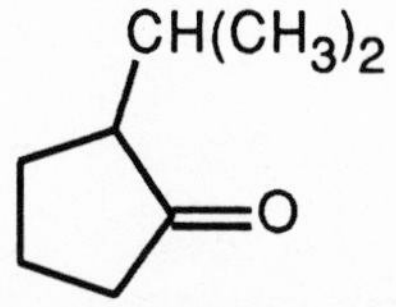

2-Isopropylcyclopentanone

16.24

(a)
$$CH_3CH_2CH_2\overset{O}{\overset{\|}{C}}\text{-H}$$

Butanal

(not 1-butanone)

(b)
$$CH_3CH_2CH_2\overset{O}{\overset{\|}{C}}\text{-H}$$

Butanal

(not 4-butanone)

(c)
$$CH_3\overset{O}{\overset{\|}{C}}CH_2CH_3$$

2-Butanone

(not 3-butanone)

(d) The name cyclohexanal is incorrect because an aldehyde carbon can't be part of a ring.

(e) The name 2-butanal is incorrect because an aldehyde group must be at the end of a chain, not in the middle.

16.25 A *hemiacetal* is produced when an aldehyde molecule reacts with one molecule of an alcohol:

$$\underset{\text{O}}{\overset{\overset{\text{O}}{\|}}{\text{R}-\text{C}-\text{H}}} + \text{R'OH} \rightleftharpoons \text{R}-\underset{\text{OR'}}{\overset{\text{OH}}{\underset{|}{\overset{|}{\text{C}}}}}-\text{H} \qquad \text{A hemiacetal}$$

16.26 An *acetal* is produced when an aldehyde molecule reacts with two molecules of an alcohol in the presence of an acid catalyst:

$$\overset{\overset{\text{O}}{\|}}{\text{R}-\text{C}-\text{H}} + 2\ \text{R'OH} \xrightarrow[\text{catalyst}]{\text{acid}} \text{R}-\underset{\text{OR'}}{\overset{\text{OR'}}{\underset{|}{\overset{|}{\text{C}}}}}-\text{H} + \text{H}_2\text{O}$$

An acetal

16.27 An aldehyde (RCHO) has only one organic group attached to the carbonyl carbon. When the aldehyde is reduced, it yields a primary alcohol (RCH$_2$OH), which also has only one organic group attached to carbon:

$$\overset{\overset{\text{O}}{\|}}{\text{R}-\text{C}-\text{H}} \xrightarrow{\text{NaBH}_4} \text{R}-\underset{\text{H}}{\overset{\text{OH}}{\underset{|}{\overset{|}{\text{C}}}}}-\text{H}$$

A primary alcohol

A ketone (R$_2$C=O) has two organic groups attached to carbon and therefore yields a secondary alcohol (R$_2$CHOH) when it is reduced:

$$\overset{\overset{\text{O}}{\|}}{\text{R}-\text{C}-\text{R'}} \xrightarrow{\text{NaBH}_4} \text{R}-\underset{\text{H}}{\overset{\text{OH}}{\underset{|}{\overset{|}{\text{C}}}}}-\text{R'}$$

A secondary alcohol

16.28

(a)

$$\underset{\text{2-Butanone}}{\overset{\overset{\text{O}}{\|}}{\text{CH}_3\text{CH}_2\text{CCH}_3}} \xrightarrow[\text{2. H}_3\text{O+}]{\text{1. NaBH}_4} \underset{\text{2-Butanol}}{\text{CH}_3\text{CH}_2\overset{\text{OH}}{\underset{|}{\overset{|}{\text{CH}}}}\text{CH}_3}$$

(b)

$$\underset{\text{Butanal}}{\overset{\overset{\text{O}}{\|}}{\text{CH}_3\text{CH}_2\text{CH}_2\text{C-H}}} \xrightarrow[\text{2. H}_3\text{O}^+]{\text{1. Tollens' reagent}} \underset{\text{Butanoic acid}}{\overset{\overset{\text{O}}{\|}}{\text{CH}_3\text{CH}_2\text{CH}_2\text{C-OH}}} + \text{Ag}$$

(c)

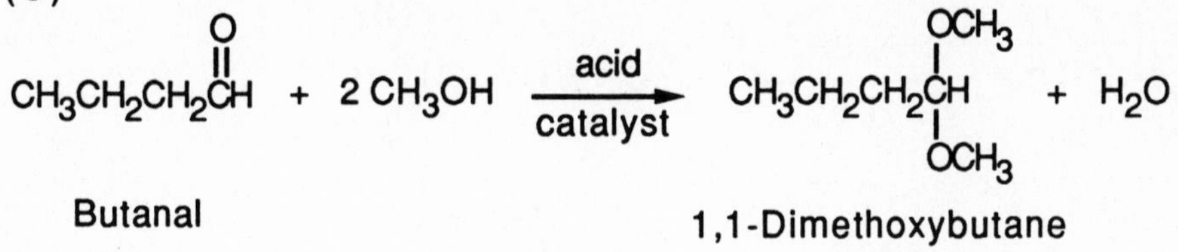

$$CH_3CH_2CH_2\overset{\overset{\displaystyle O}{\|}}{C}H + 2\,CH_3OH \xrightarrow[\text{catalyst}]{\text{acid}} CH_3CH_2CH_2\overset{\overset{\displaystyle OCH_3}{|}}{\underset{\underset{\displaystyle OCH_3}{|}}{C}}H + H_2O$$

Butanal   1,1-Dimethoxybutane

16.29 Remember that only aldehydes react with Tollens' reagent. Ketones are not oxidized.

(a)

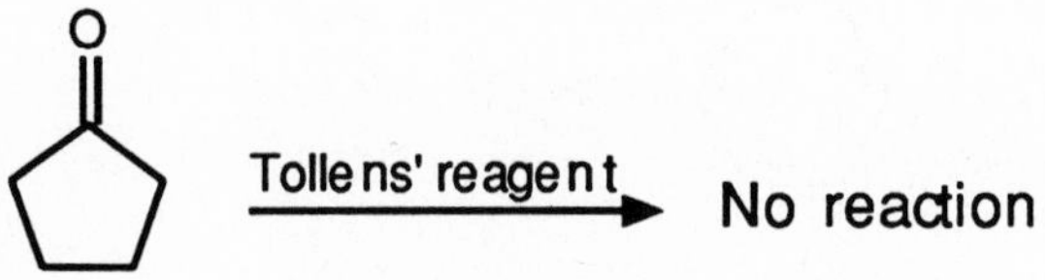

Tollens' reagent → No reaction

(b)

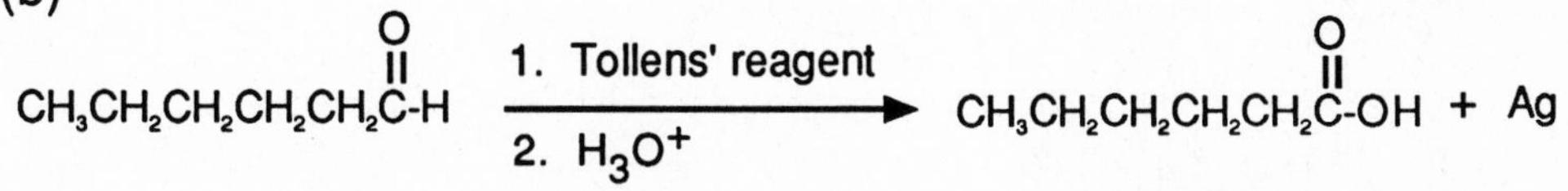

$$CH_3CH_2CH_2CH_2CH_2\overset{\overset{\displaystyle O}{\|}}{C}\text{-}H \xrightarrow[\text{2. }H_3O^+]{\text{1. Tollens' reagent}} CH_3CH_2CH_2CH_2CH_2\overset{\overset{\displaystyle O}{\|}}{C}\text{-}OH + Ag$$

(c)

$$CH_3CH_2CH_2\overset{\overset{\displaystyle CHO}{|}}{C}HCH_2CH_3 \xrightarrow[\text{2. }H_3O^+]{\text{1. Tollens' reagent}} CH_3CH_2CH_2\overset{\overset{\displaystyle COOH}{|}}{C}HCH_2CH_3 + Ag$$

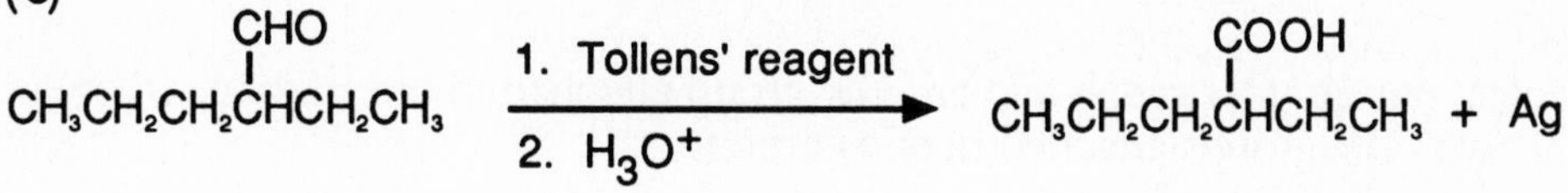

(d)

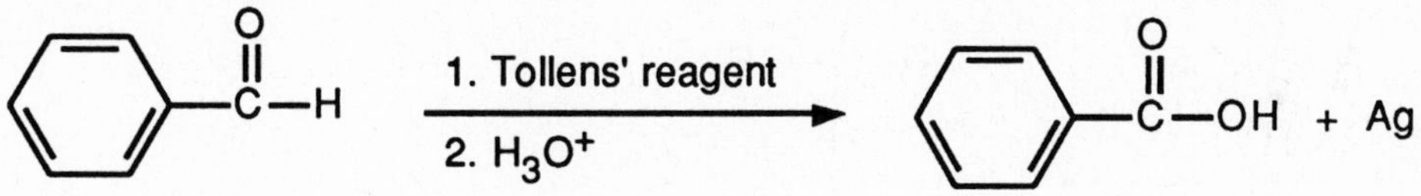

(e)

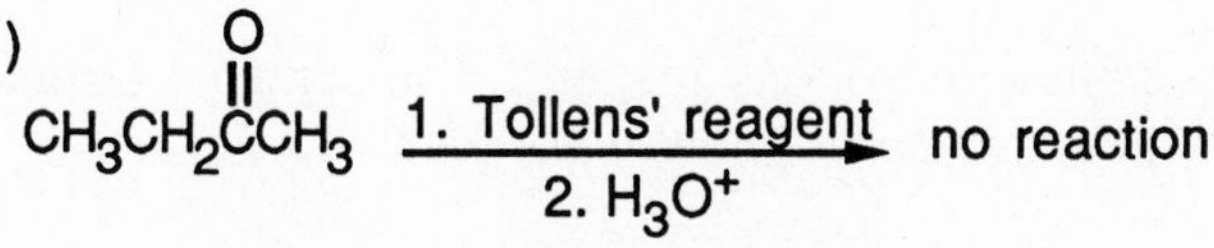

$$CH_3CH_2\overset{\overset{\displaystyle O}{\|}}{C}CH_3 \xrightarrow[\text{2. }H_3O^+]{\text{1. Tollens' reagent}} \text{no reaction}$$

(f)

$$Cl_2CH\overset{\overset{\displaystyle O}{\|}}{C}H \xrightarrow[\text{2. }H_3O^+]{\text{1. Tollens' reagent}} Cl_2CH\overset{\overset{\displaystyle O}{\|}}{C}OH + Ag$$

16.30

(a)

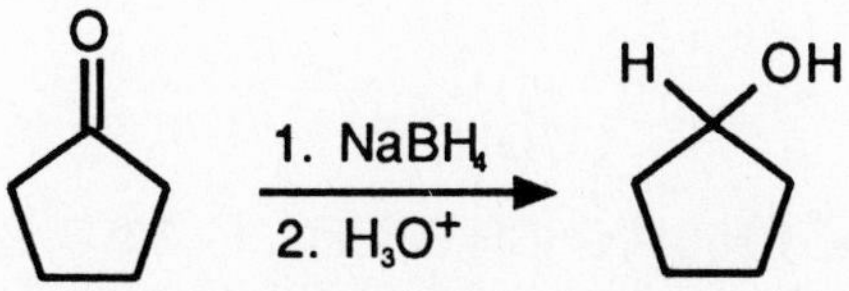

(b)

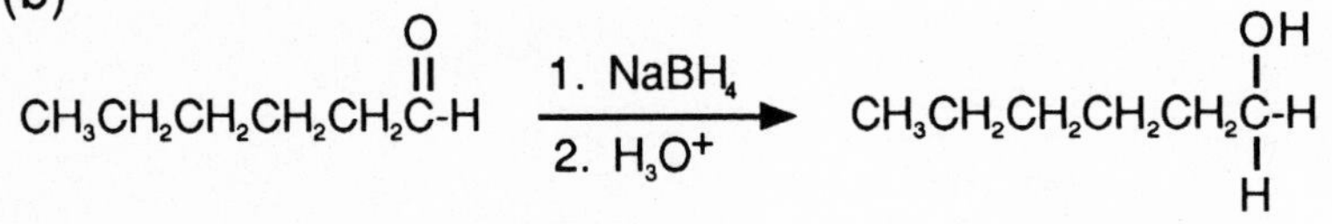

$$CH_3CH_2CH_2CH_2CH_2\overset{\overset{\displaystyle O}{\|}}{C}\text{-H} \quad \xrightarrow[\text{2. } H_3O^+]{\text{1. NaBH}_4} \quad CH_3CH_2CH_2CH_2CH_2\overset{\overset{\displaystyle OH}{|}}{\underset{\underset{\displaystyle H}{|}}{C}}\text{-H}$$

(c)

$$CH_3CH_2CH_2\overset{\overset{\displaystyle CHO}{|}}{C}HCH_2CH_3 \quad \xrightarrow[\text{2. } H_3O^+]{\text{1. NaBH}_4} \quad CH_3CH_2CH_2\overset{\overset{\displaystyle CH_2OH}{|}}{C}HCH_2CH_3$$

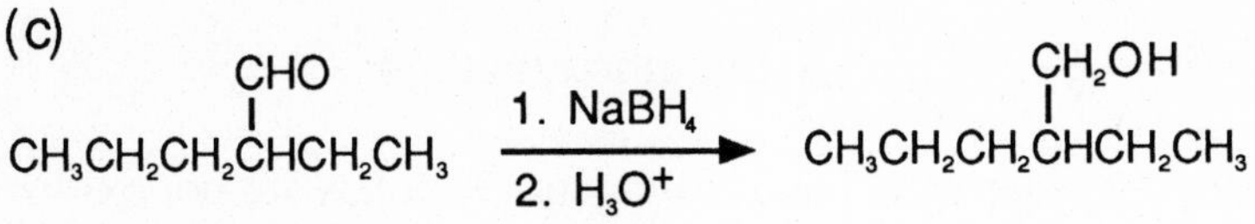

(d)

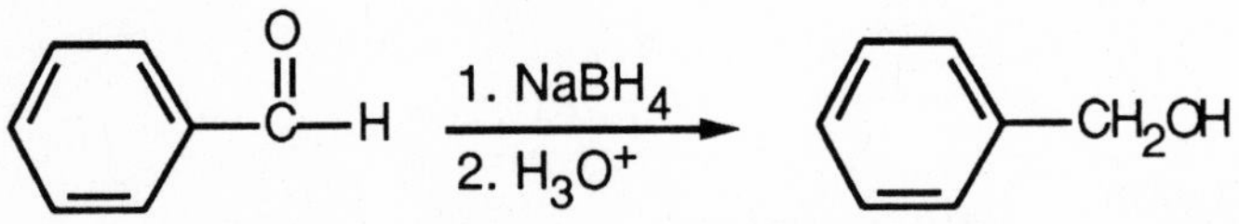

(e)

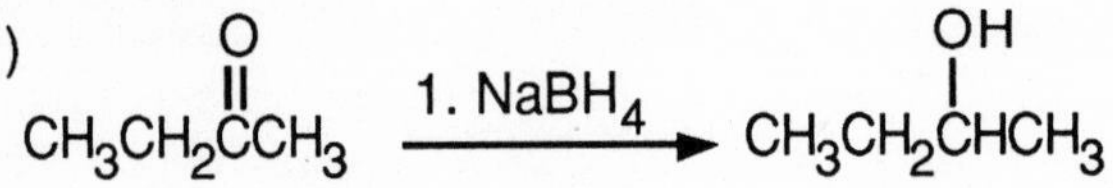

$$CH_3CH_2\overset{\overset{\displaystyle O}{\|}}{C}CH_3 \quad \xrightarrow{\text{1. NaBH}_4} \quad CH_3CH_2\overset{\overset{\displaystyle OH}{|}}{C}HCH_3$$

(f)

$$Cl_2CH\overset{\overset{\displaystyle O}{\|}}{C}\text{-H} \quad \xrightarrow[\text{2. } H_3O^+]{\text{1. NaBH}_4} \quad Cl_2CHCH_2OH$$

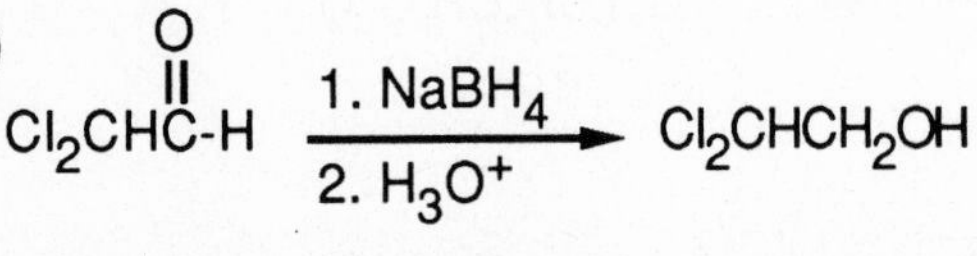

16.31 A hemiacetal has an -OH group and an -OR group attached to one carbon, whereas an acetal has two -OR groups attached to one carbon:

$$\underset{\displaystyle R''}{\overset{\displaystyle OH}{R-C-OR'}} \qquad \underset{\displaystyle R''}{\overset{\displaystyle OR'}{R-C-OR'}}$$

A hemiacetal   An acetal

16.32 Treat a small sample from each bottle with Tollens' reagent. The pentanal sample will react to form a silver mirror, but the 2-pentanone sample will not react.

16.33

(a)

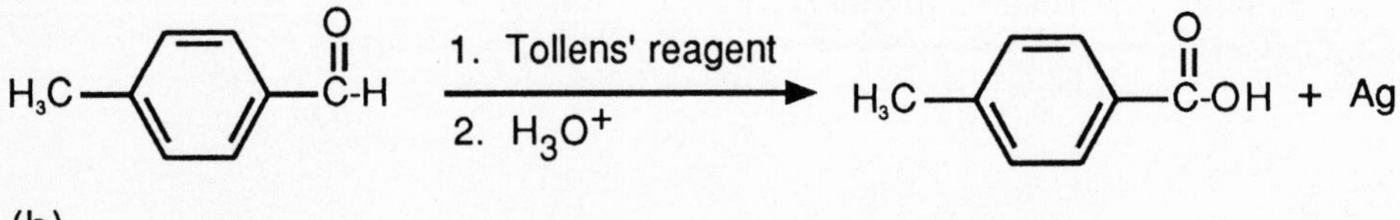

(b)

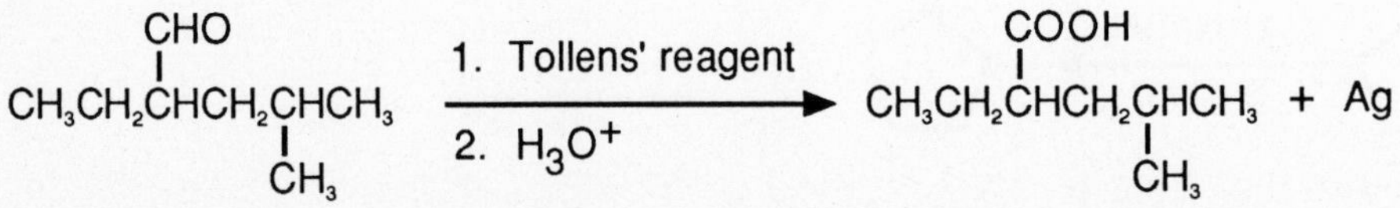

$$CH_3CH_2\overset{\overset{\displaystyle CHO}{|}}{C}HCH_2\overset{\underset{\underset{\displaystyle CH_3}{|}}{}}{C}HCH_3 \quad \xrightarrow[\text{2. } H_3O^+]{\text{1. Tollens' reagent}} \quad CH_3CH_2\overset{\overset{\displaystyle COOH}{|}}{C}HCH_2\overset{\underset{\underset{\displaystyle CH_3}{|}}{}}{C}HCH_3 \quad + \quad Ag$$

(c)

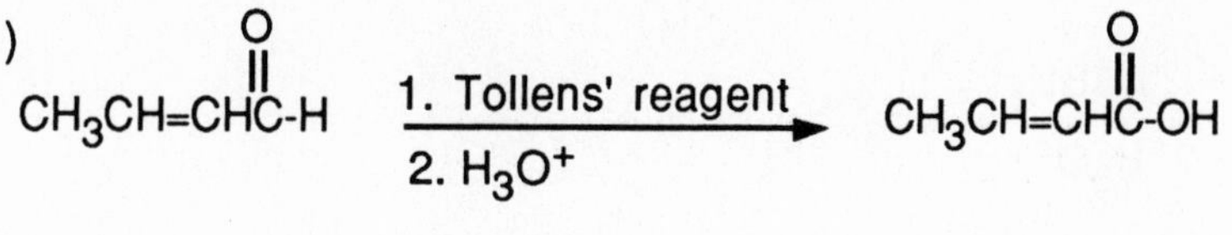

$$CH_3CH=CHC-H \xrightarrow[\text{2. } H_3O^+]{\text{1. Tollens' reagent}} CH_3CH=CHC-OH$$

(d)

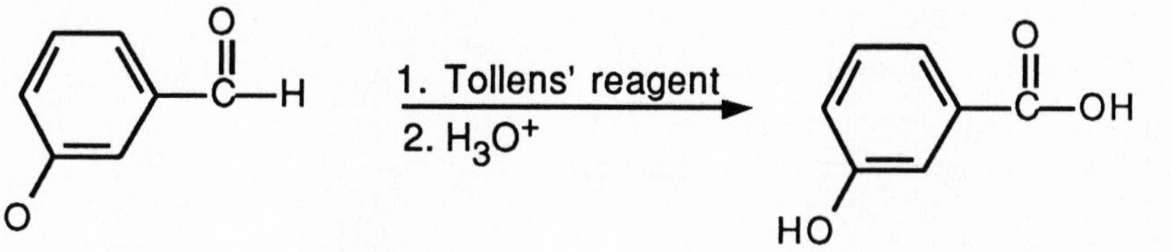

1. Tollens' reagent
2. H_3O^+

16.34

(a)

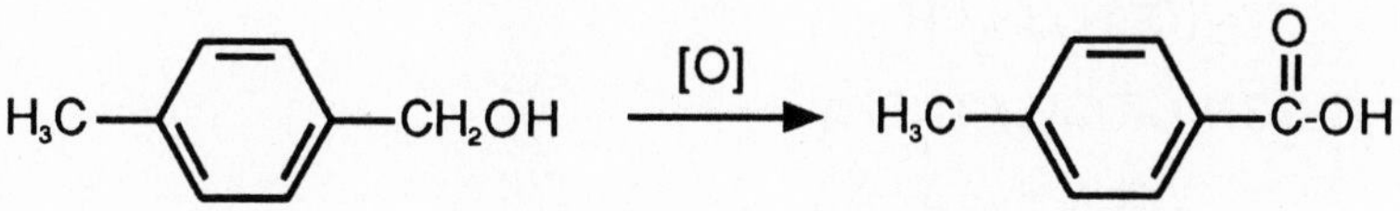

$$H_3C-\overset{}{\underset{}{\bigcirc}}-CH_2OH \xrightarrow{[O]} H_3C-\overset{}{\underset{}{\bigcirc}}-C-OH$$

(b)

$$\underset{\underset{CH_3}{|}}{CH_3CH_2CHCH_2CHCH_3} \overset{CH_2OH}{} \xrightarrow{[O]} \underset{\underset{CH_3}{|}}{CH_3CH_2CHCH_2CHCH_3} \overset{COOH}{}$$

(c)

$$CH_3CH=CHCH_2OH \xrightarrow{[O]} CH_3CH=CHC-OH$$

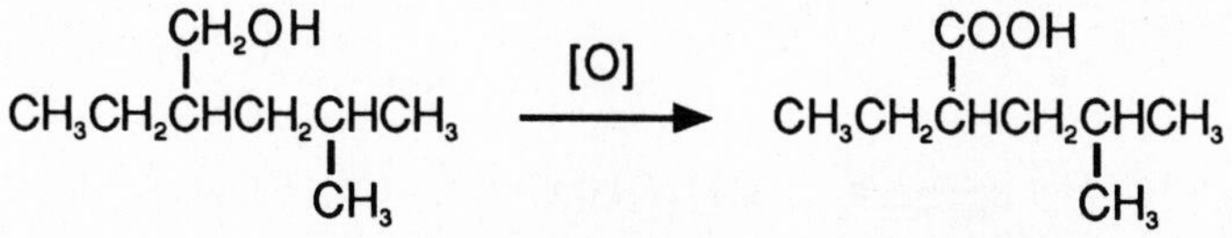

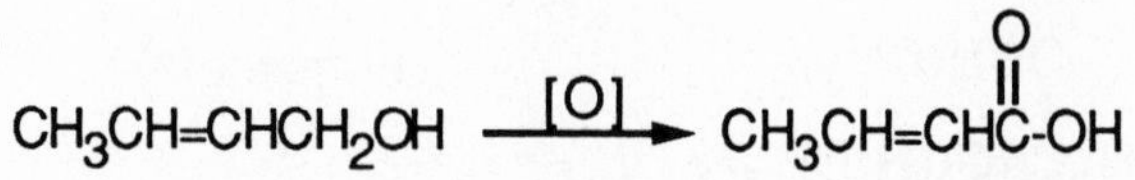

(d)

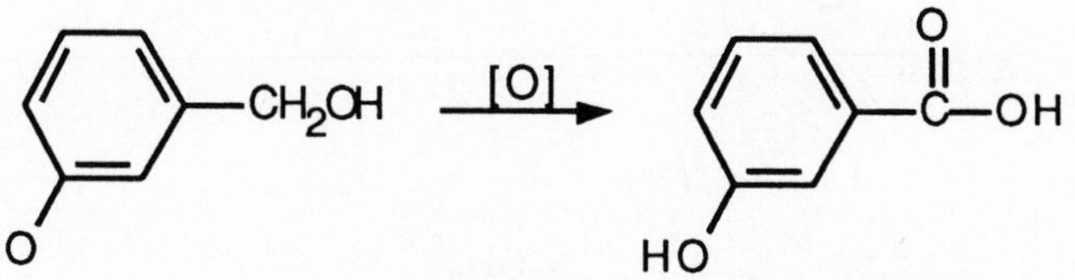

$$-CH_2OH \xrightarrow{[O]}$$

16.35

(a)

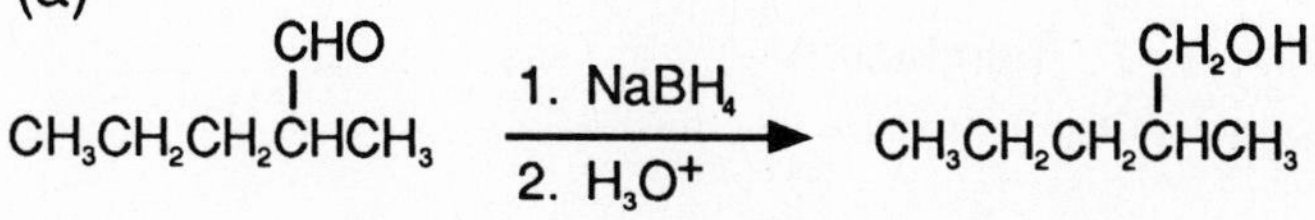

$$CH_3CH_2CH_2CHCH_3 \overset{CHO}{|} \xrightarrow[\text{2. } H_3O^+]{\text{1. NaBH}_4} CH_3CH_2CH_2CHCH_3 \overset{CH_2OH}{|}$$

(b)

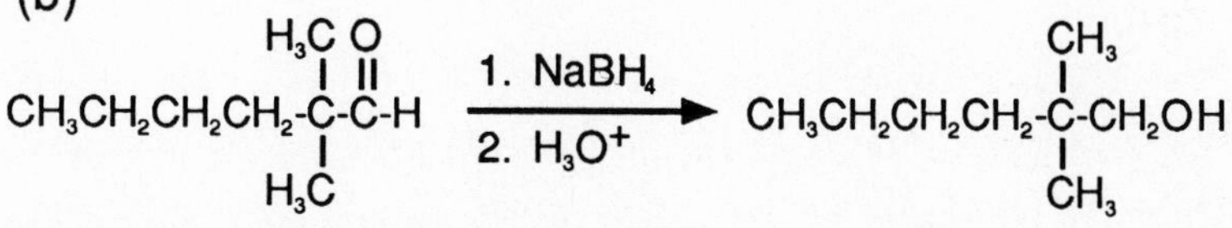

$$CH_3CH_2CH_2CH_2-\underset{\underset{H_3C}{|}}{\overset{\overset{H_3C \ O}{|\ ||}}{C}}-C-H \xrightarrow[\text{2. } H_3O^+]{\text{1. NaBH}_4} CH_3CH_2CH_2CH_2-\underset{\underset{CH_3}{|}}{\overset{\overset{CH_3}{|}}{C}}-CH_2OH$$

(c)

1. NaBH₄
2. H_3O^+

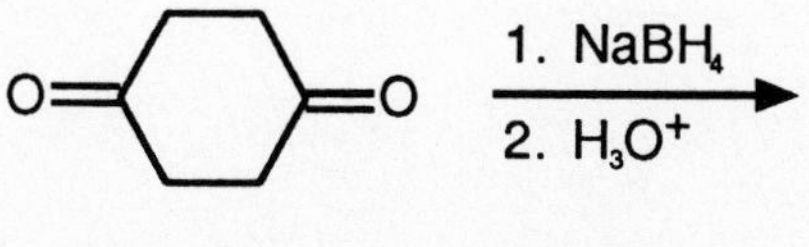

(d)

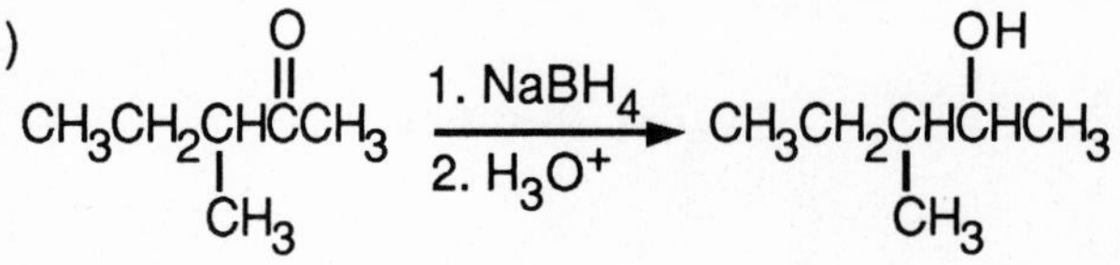
CH3CH2CHCCH3
CH3
1. NaBH4
2. H3O+
OH
CH3CH2CHCHCH3
CH3

16.36

(a)

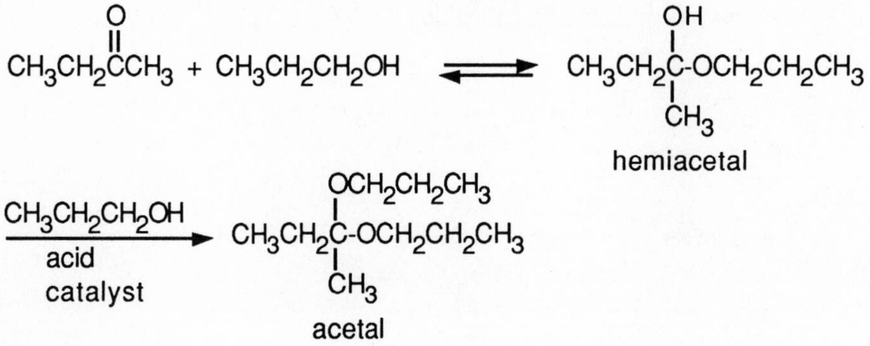
CH3CH2CCH3 + CH3CH2CH2OH
CH3CH2C-OCH2CH2CH3
hemiacetal
CH3CH2CH2OH
acid
catalyst
OCH2CH2CH3
CH3CH2C-OCH2CH2CH3
acetal

(b)

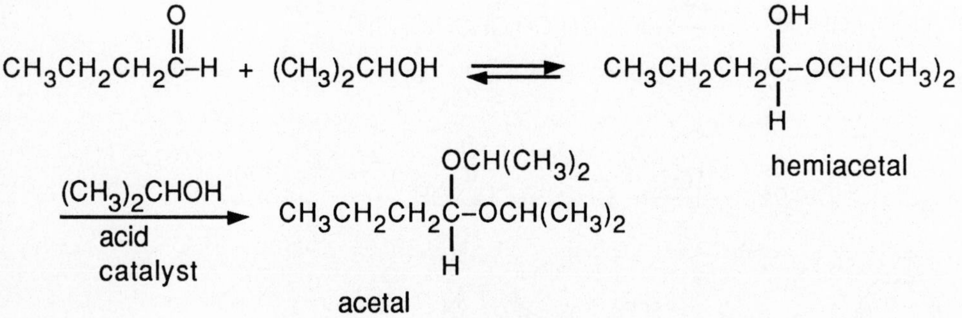
CH3CH2CH2C–H + (CH3)2CHOH
CH3CH2CH2C–OCH(CH3)2
hemiacetal
(CH3)2CHOH
acid
catalyst
OCH(CH3)2
acetal

(c)

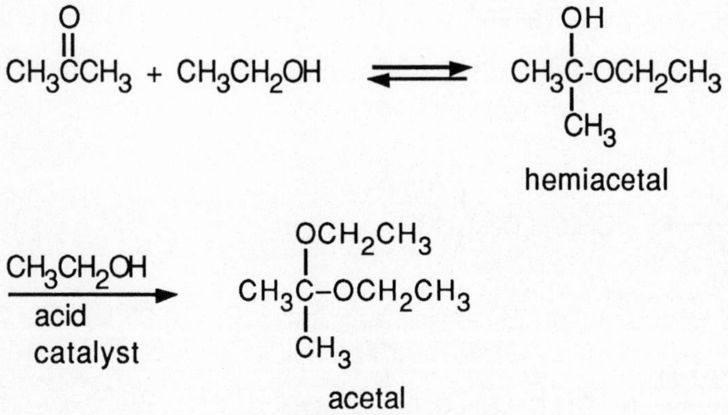
CH3CCH3 + CH3CH2OH
CH3C-OCH2CH3
hemiacetal
CH3CH2OH
acid
catalyst
OCH2CH3
CH3C–OCH2CH3
acetal

(d)

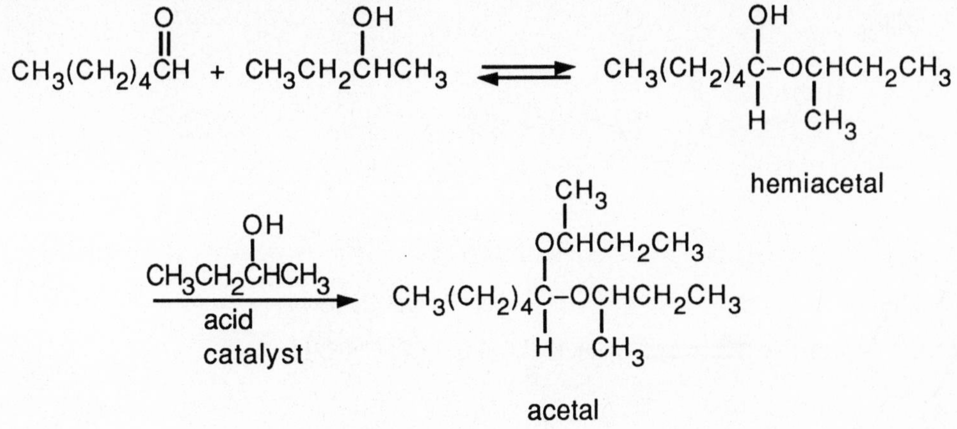

$$CH_3(CH_2)_4\overset{\overset{\textstyle O}{\|}}{CH} + CH_3CH_2\overset{\overset{\textstyle OH}{|}}{CHCH_3} \rightleftharpoons CH_3(CH_2)_4\overset{\overset{\textstyle OH}{|}}{\underset{\underset{\textstyle H}{|}}{C}}-O\overset{}{\underset{\underset{\textstyle CH_3}{|}}{C}HCH_2CH_3}$$

hemiacetal

$$\xrightarrow[\substack{\text{acid} \\ \text{catalyst}}]{CH_3CH_2\overset{\overset{\textstyle OH}{|}}{CHCH_3}} CH_3(CH_2)_4\overset{\overset{\textstyle O\overset{\textstyle CH_3}{|}}{\overset{}{C}HCH_2CH_3}}{\underset{\underset{\textstyle H}{|}}{C}}-O\overset{}{\underset{\underset{\textstyle CH_3}{|}}{C}HCH_2CH_3}$$

acetal

16.37

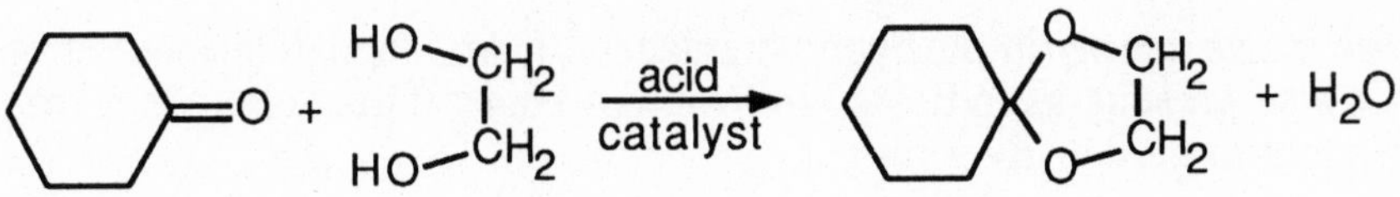

16.38

(a)

$$CH_3CH_2CH_2\overset{\overset{\textstyle OCH_2CH_3}{|}}{CH}-OCH_3 \xrightarrow{H_3O^+} CH_3CH_2CH_2\overset{\overset{\textstyle O}{\|}}{C}-H + CH_3CH_2OH + CH_3OH$$

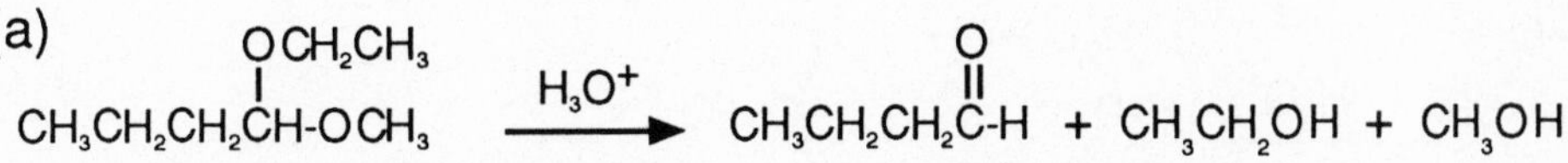

(b)

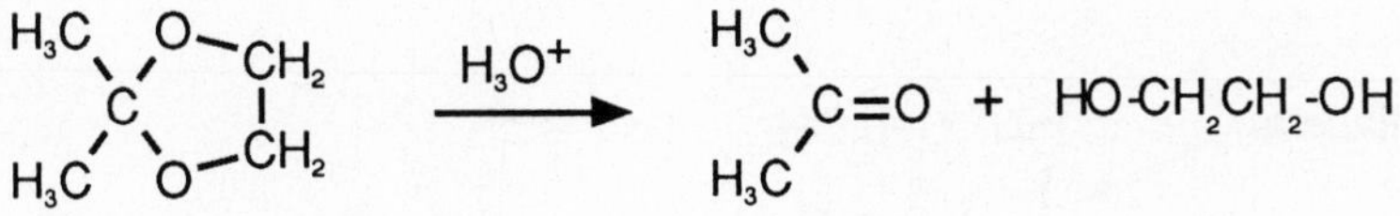

(c)

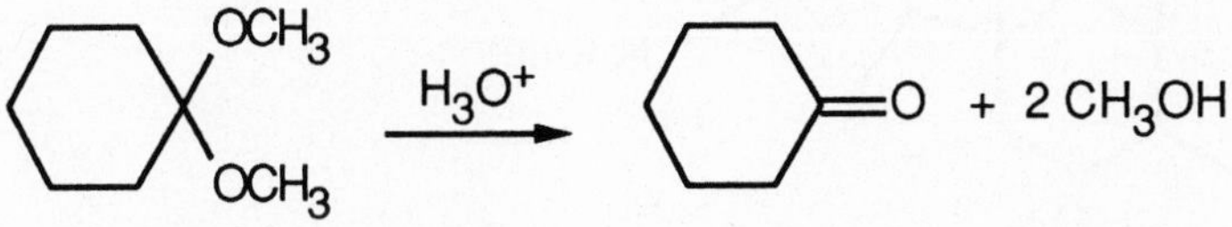

(d)

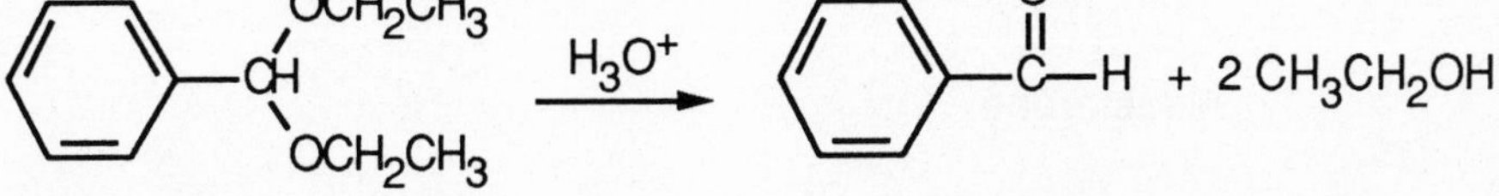

16.39

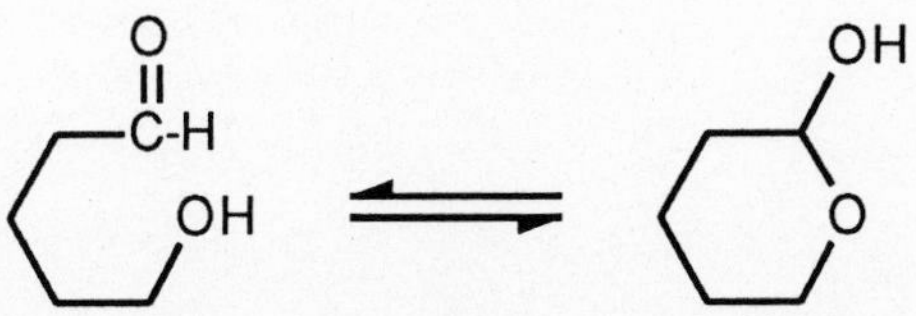

16.40

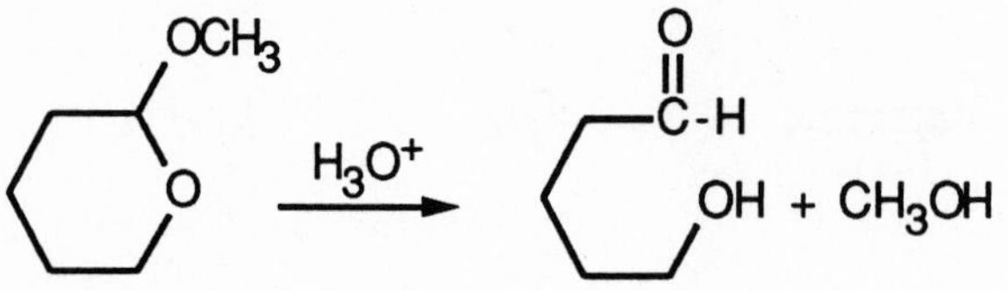

16.41

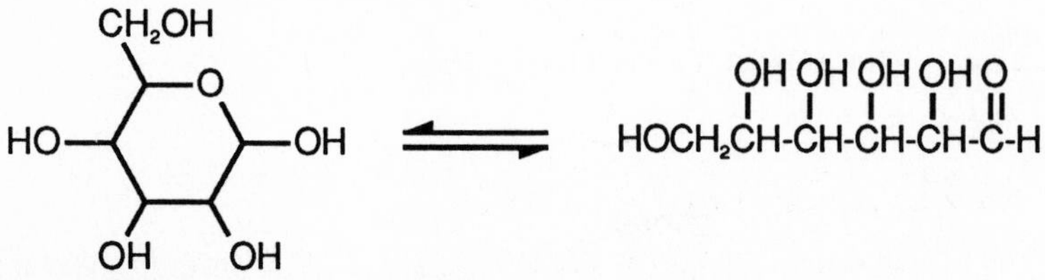

16.42 Although glucose exists mainly in the cyclic hemiacetal form, a small amount of open-chain aldehyde form is also present, as indicated in Problem 16.41. This aldehyde form can react with Tollens' reagent to give a silver mirror.

16.43

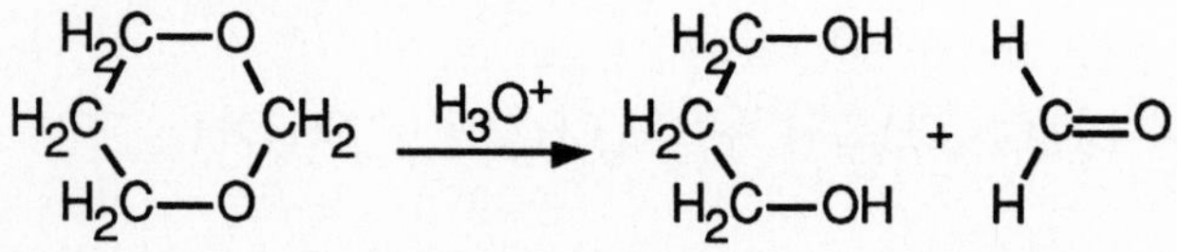

16.44 - 16.45

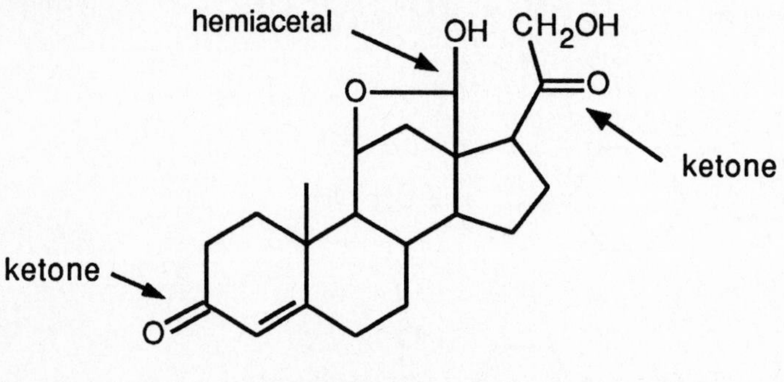

Aldosterone

The hemiacetal group is derived from an aldehyde because the hemiacetal carbon has a hydrogen atom bonded to it.

16.46

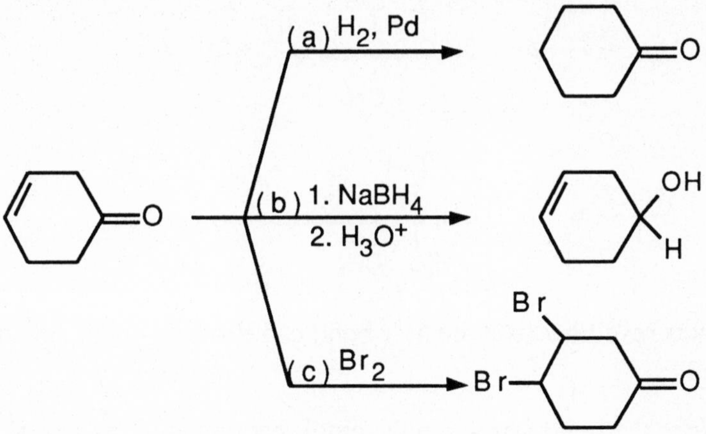

(a) H₂, Pd →

(b) 1. NaBH₄ 2. H₃O⁺ →

(c) Br₂ →

16.47 An aldehyde or ketone must have a hydrogen on the carbon next to the carbonyl group in order to undergo an aldol reaction.

16.48

(a)

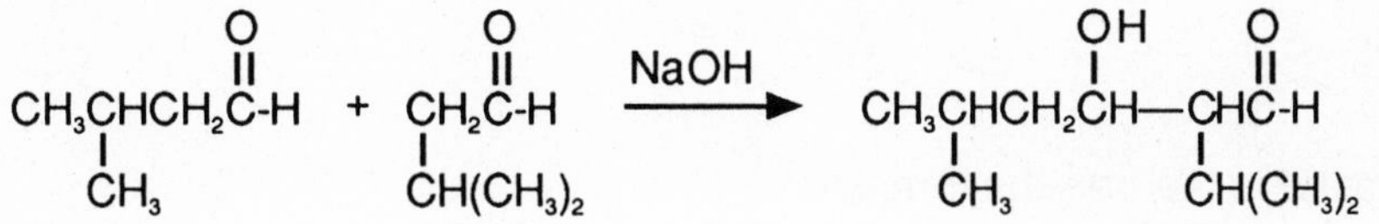

$$CH_3CHCH_2\overset{O}{\overset{\|}{C}}\text{-H} \;+\; CH_2\overset{O}{\overset{\|}{C}}\text{-H} \xrightarrow{\text{NaOH}} CH_3CHCH_2\overset{OH}{CH}\text{—}CH\overset{O}{\overset{\|}{C}}\text{-H}$$

with CH_3 and $CH(CH_3)_2$ substituents

(b)

$$\text{cyclohexanone} + \text{cyclohexanone} \xrightarrow{\text{NaOH}} \text{aldol product}$$

(c)

$$CH_3CH_2\overset{O}{\overset{\|}{C}}CH_2CH_3 \;+\; CH_2\overset{O}{\overset{\|}{C}}CH_2CH_3 \xrightarrow{\text{NaOH}} CH_3CH_2\text{-}\overset{OH}{C}\text{—}CH\overset{O}{\overset{\|}{C}}CH_2CH_3$$

with CH_3, CH_2CH_2, CH_3 substituents

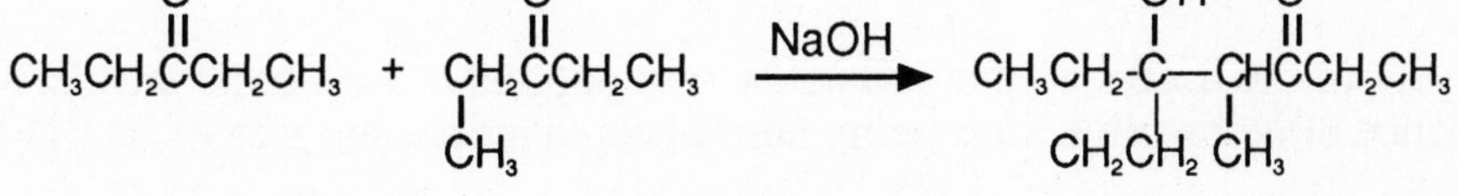

(d)

$$\overset{O}{\underset{}{-CH_2\overset{\|}{C}\text{-H}}} \;+\; CH_2\overset{O}{\overset{\|}{C}}\text{-H} \xrightarrow{\text{NaOH}} -CH_2\overset{OH}{\underset{H}{C}}\text{-}CH\overset{O}{\overset{\|}{C}}H$$

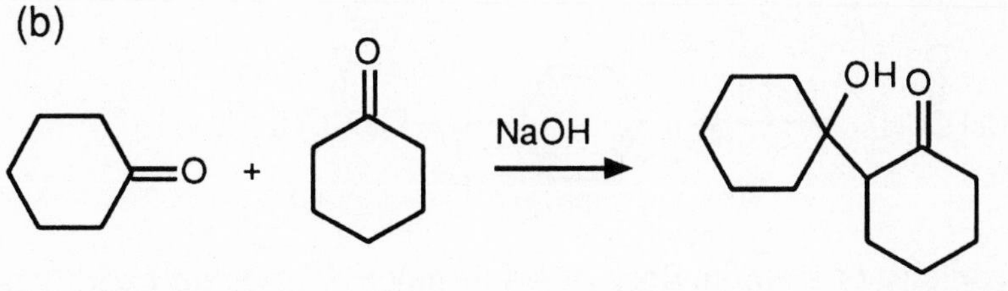

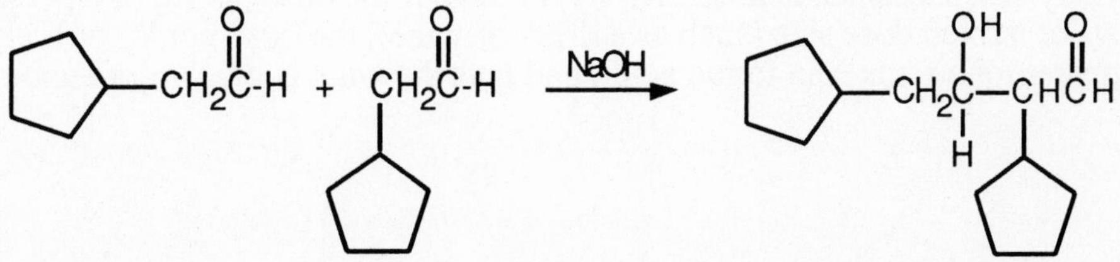

16.49

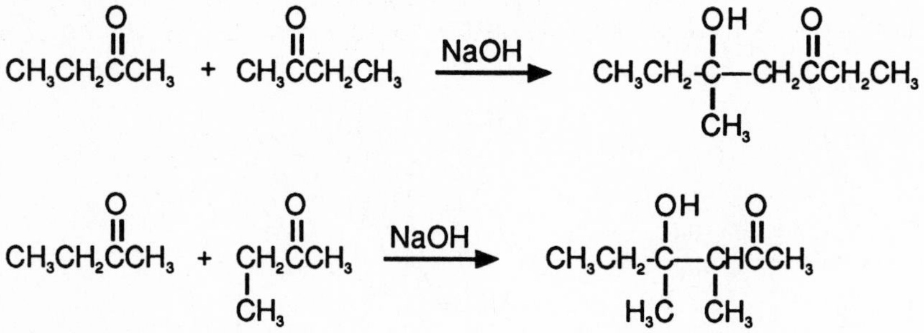

CH₃CH₂C(=O)CH₃ + CH₃C(=O)CH₂CH₃ →(NaOH) CH₃CH₂-C(OH)(CH₃)-CH₂C(=O)CH₂CH₃

CH₃CH₂C(=O)CH₃ + CH₃C(=O)CH₂CH₃(CH₃) →(NaOH) CH₃CH₂-C(OH)(H₃C)-CH(CH₃)C(=O)CH₃

Two different aldol products result because the new bond can form on either side of the ketone.

16.50 To solve this problem, locate the bond formed in the aldol reaction, and then break it. Then, change the hydroxyl group to a carbonyl group, and add a hydrogen to the carbon that was part of the broken bond. This series of steps is the reverse of the series used in Solved Problem 16.4 in the text.

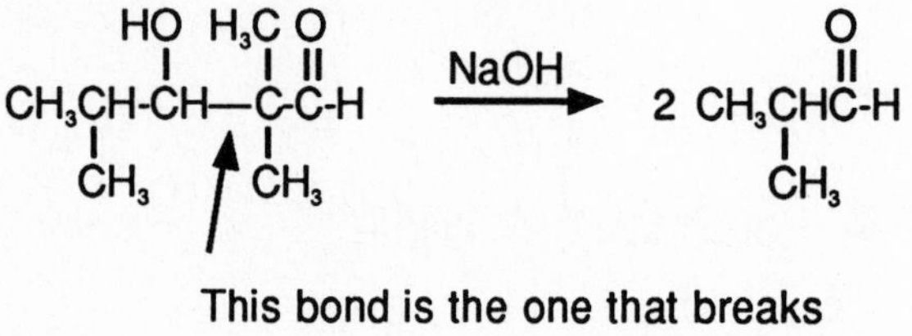

CH₃CH-CH—C-C-H (HO, H₃C, O; CH₃, CH₃) →(NaOH) 2 CH₃CHC-H (O; CH₃)

This bond is the one that breaks

16.51

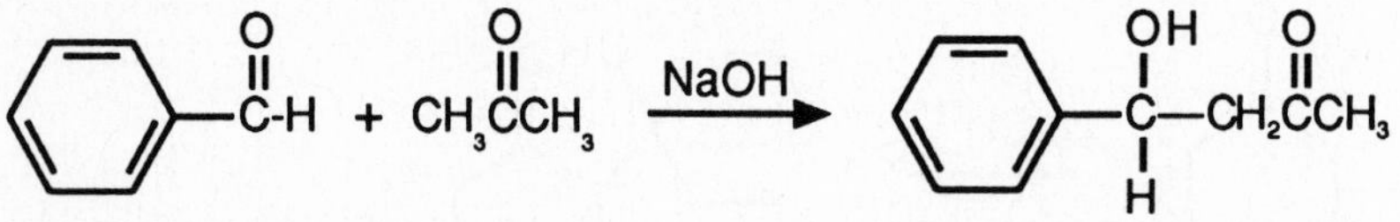

⬡-C(=O)-H + CH₃C(=O)CH₃ →(NaOH) ⬡-C(OH)(H)-CH₂C(=O)CH₃

16.52 *Acute toxicity* is the toxicity of a single dose of a substance. *Subacute toxicity* is the toxicity of a less than lethal dose of a substance over a period of several months. *Chronic toxicity* is the toxicity of a varying dose size over a period of six months to two years.

16.53 LD_{50} is a measure of the dose size that kills 50% of a population. In other words, a person has a 50-50 chance of being alive after being administered a dose the size of its LD_{50} value.

16.54 The toxicity of a substance is measured by the size of the dose per kg of a person's body weight. For a fixed dose size (such as a drink of wine), the dose per kg of body weight is much greater for a fetus than for an adult, and thus the wine is much more toxic for the fetus.

16.55 The oxaloacetic acid ⟶ citric acid reaction resembles an aldol reaction because a bond forms between the carbon next to a carbonyl group and a carbonyl carbon of a second molecule.

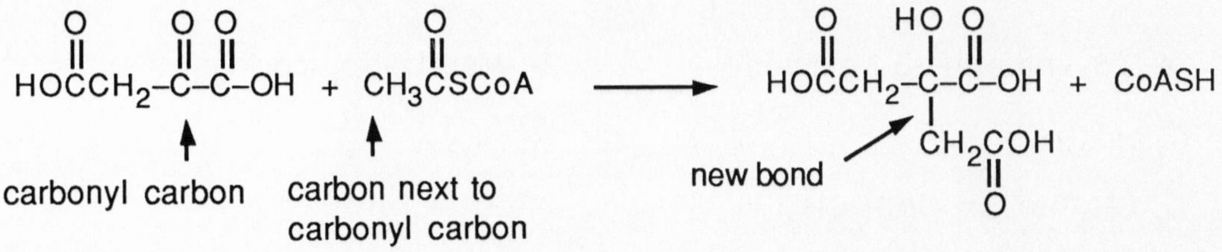

16.56 Benzaldehyde can be identified by its reaction with Tollens' reagent, which forms a silver mirror on the wall of the reaction flask.

16.57 The peach pits contain a cyanogenic glycoside that can release small amounts of HCN after being cleaved by digestive enzymes.

16.58 The cyanohydrin precursor to HCN is non-toxic and is stable inside the millipede's body.

16.59

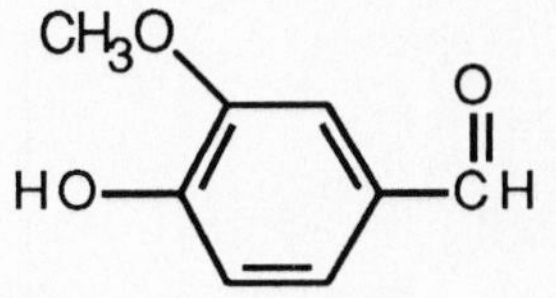

4-Hydroxy-3-methoxybenzaldehyde
(vanillin)

16.60 The alcohol pictured, 2,2-dimethyl-1-propanol, can't be formed from reduction of an aldehyde or ketone because it is a tertiary alcohol. Only primary and secondary alcohols result from reduction of aldehydes and ketones, respectively.

16.61 The portion of the odor due to aldehyde is less stable because aldehydes are easily oxidized to carboxylic acids.

16.62 Formaldehyde in the air can cause bronchial pneumonia and dermatitis. Ingestion of formaldehyde can cause kidney damage, coma and death.

16.63

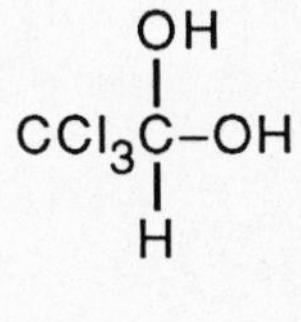

Chloral hydrate

16.64

(a)

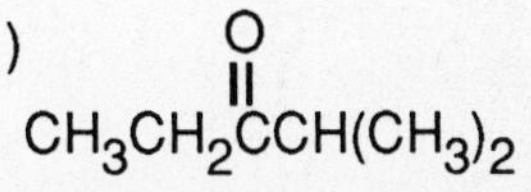

$CH_3CH_2CCH(CH_3)_2$
2-Methyl-3-pentanone

(b)

$CH_2=CHCH_2CH_2CH=CH_2$
1,5-Hexadiene

(c)

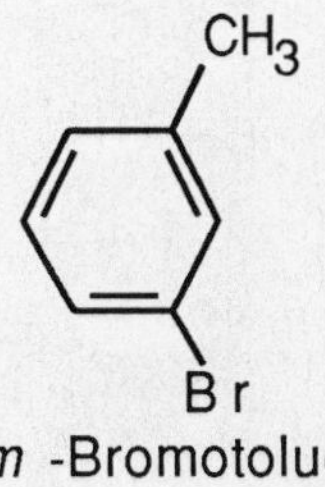

m -Bromotoluene

(d)

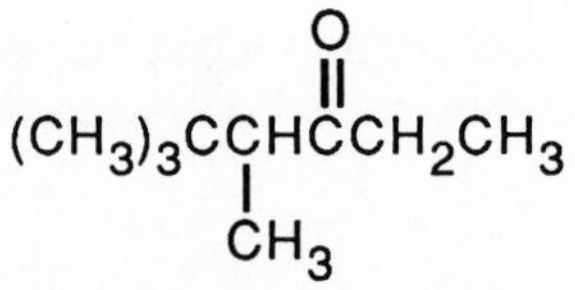

$$(CH_3)_3CCHCCH_2CH_3$$

with O double bond on C, and CH$_3$ below

4.5.5-Trimethyl-3-hexanone

(e)

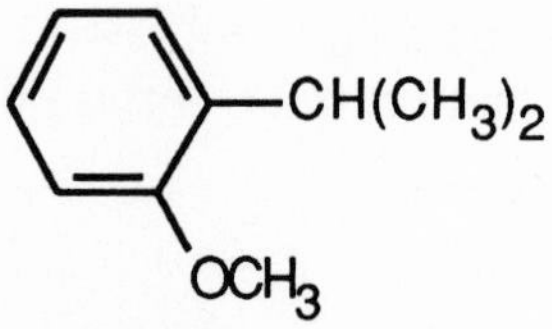

Benzene ring with —CH(CH$_3$)$_2$ and OCH$_3$

o -Methoxyisopropylbenzene

(f)

$$CH_3CH_2C{\equiv}CC(CH_2CH_3)_3$$

5,5-Diethyl-3-heptyne

16.65

(a)

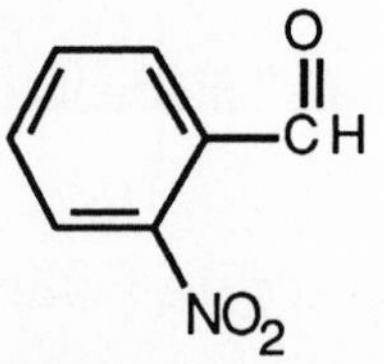

Benzene ring with CHO and NO$_2$

o -Nitrobenzaldehyde

(b)

Cyclopentanone ring with two Cl

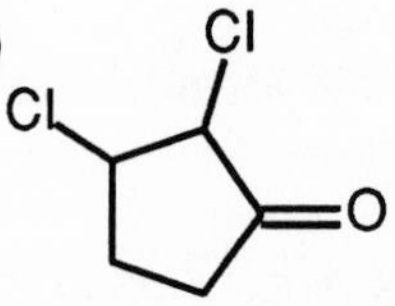

2,3-Dichlorocyclopentanone

(c)

$$CH_3OCH_2CH_2CH_2CH_3$$

Methyl butyl ether

(d) H$_3$C OH CH$_3$

$$CH_3CHCH\text{-}CHCH_3$$

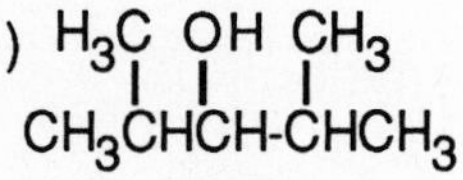

2,4-Dimethyl-3-pentanol

(e)

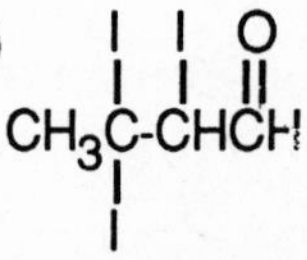

$$CH_3C\text{-}CHCH$$ with I substituents and O

2,3,3-Triiodobutanal

(f)

$$BrCH_2CCHBr_2$$ with O

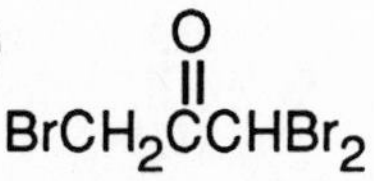

1,1,3-Tribromoacetone

16.66 (a)

$$CH_3CH{=}C(CH_3)_2 + H_2 \xrightarrow{Pd} CH_3CH_2CH(CH_3)_2$$

(b)

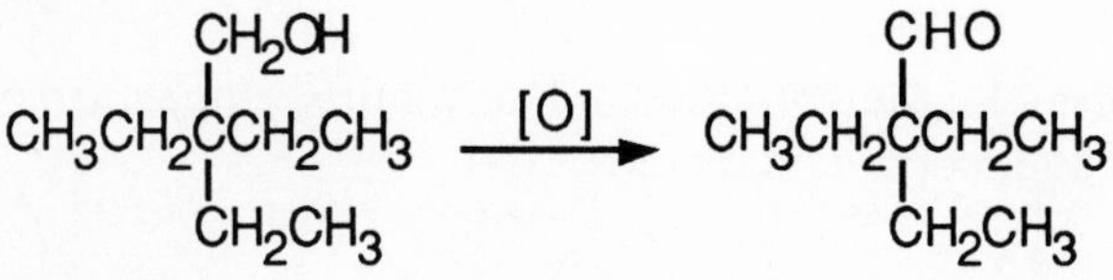

CH$_2$OH

$$CH_3CH_2CCH_2CH_3 \xrightarrow{[O]}$$

CH$_2$CH$_3$

CHO

$$CH_3CH_2CCH_2CH_3$$

CH$_2$CH$_3$

(c)

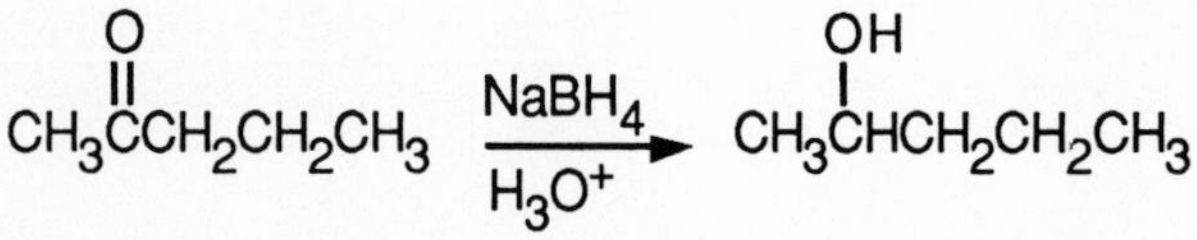

O

$$CH_3CCH_2CH_2CH_3 \xrightarrow[H_3O^+]{NaBH_4}$$

OH

$$CH_3CHCH_2CH_2CH_3$$

(d)

Benzene ring with CH$_2$CH and O + HOCH$_2$CH$_2$CH$_3$ $\xrightarrow[\text{catalyst}]{\text{acid}}$ Benzene ring with CH$_2$C-OCH$_2$CH$_2$CH$_3$, OH and H

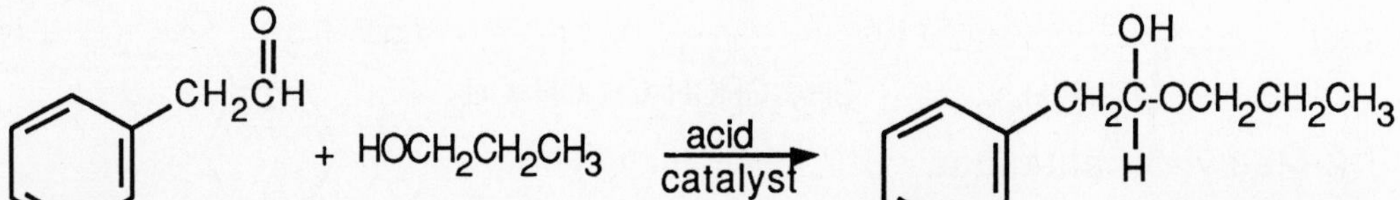

hemiacetal

(e)

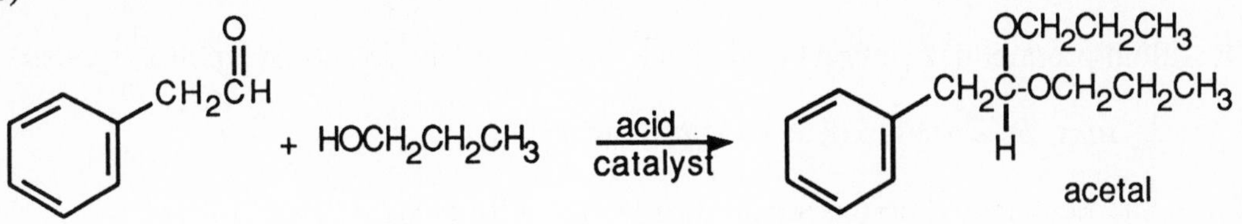

(f)

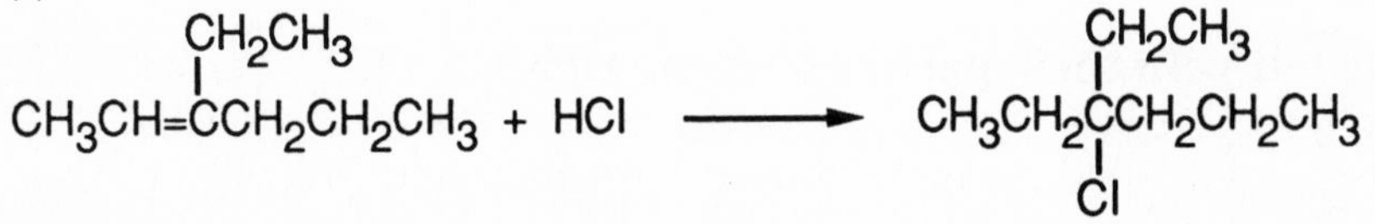

(g)

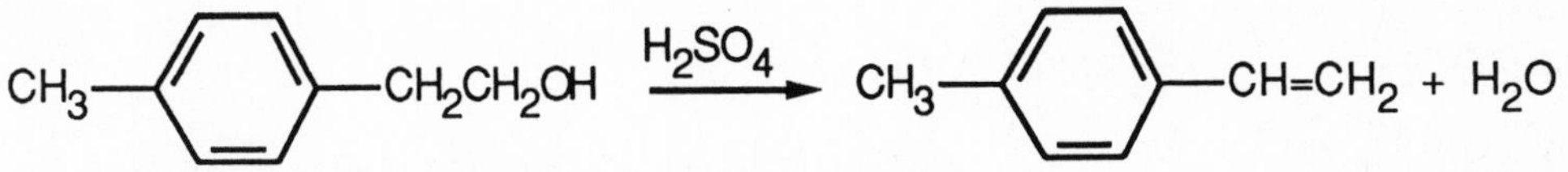

16.67 Treat samples of the two compounds with Tollens' reagent. The aldehyde reacts to yield a silver mirror, but the alcohol doesn't react.

The Chapter in Brief

Aldehydes and Ketones Aldehydes and ketones are compounds that the contain carbonyl groups bonded to either two carbons (ketones) or one carbon and one hydrogen (aldehydes). The family-name ending for an aldehyde is *-al* and that for a ketone is *-one*. Reactions of aldehydes and ketones include oxidation, reduction, acetal formation, and the aldol reaction.

Self-Test for Chapter 16

Complete the following statements:

1. Aldehydes, esters, and ketones are all _____ compounds.

2. The shiny product of oxidation of an aldehyde by Tollens' reagent is _____.

3. _____ is a reaction that converts an acetal to an aldehyde or a ketone.

4. A carbonyl group is polarized, with a partial _____ charge on carbon and a partial _____ charge on oxygen.

5. _____ is a ketone that is widely used as a solvent.

6. Aldol reactions are important because they result in the formation of _____ - _____ bonds.

7. Bonds to the carbonyl carbon of esters and amides are _____ polar than the bonds to the carbonyl carbon on ketones and aldehydes.

8. The conversion of an aldehyde or ketone into an alcohol is said to be a _____ reaction.

9.   Formaldehyde is widely used as a _____.

10.   The initial product of reaction between a ketone or aldehyde and an alcohol is called a _____.

11.   _____ reagent is used to detect sugar in urine.

12._____ can be detected on the breath during starvation.

Match the entries on the left with their partners on the right:

1. $AgNO_3$, NH_3, H_2O (a) Reagent used to form an acetal

2. $CH_3CH_2COCH_3$ (b) Reduces carbonyl groups to alcohols

3. CH_3CH_2COOH (c) An amide

4. CH_3OH, H^+ catalyst   (d) Product of an aldehyde plus Tollens' reagent

5. CH_3CH_2OH (e) Tollens' reagent

6. $CH_3CH_2COOCH_3$ (f) Catalyst for aldol reaction

7. $CH_3CHOHCH_3$ (g) Formaldehyde

8. $NaBH_4$ (h) Product of aldehyde reduction

9. CH_3CHO (i) Yields secondary alcohol when reduced

10. $NaOH$ (j) Ester

11. $HCHO$ (k) Can be oxidized to a ketone

12. CH_3CONH_2 (l) Product of primary alcohol oxidation

Tell whether the following statements are true or false:

1.   Glucose contains an acetal link.

2.   Many sugars are synthesized biochemically by aldol reactions.

3.   Ketones are oxidized by Tollens' reagent to carboxylic acids.

4.   The reduction of aldehydes and ketones is carried out by using NaOH.

5.   An acetal is an alternative name for an ester.

6.   Only aldehydes form acetals.

7.   An aldehyde group always occurs at the end of a carbon chain.

8.   Formaldehyde can't undergo an aldol reaction with itself.

9.   4-Hydroxybutanal can be made by an aldol reaction of acetaldehyde.

10.   Acetaldehyde results from the oxidation of ethanol.

11.   Both aldehydes and ketones can be reduced to alcohols.

12.   Aldehydes and ketones are not capable of forming hydrogen bonds.

Chapter 17 – Carboxylic Acids and Their Derivatives

17.1 CH₃OCH₃   CH₃COOH   CH₃CH₂OH

lowest boiling	highest boiling	high boiling
no hydrogen bonding	forms strongest hydrogen bonds	forms hydrogen bonds

17.2 *N*-unsubstituted amides form the strongest hydrogen bonds because two hydrogens are bonded to nitrogen. Thus, CH₃CONH₂ is the highest boiling and melting amide. CH₃CON(CH₂ CH₃) is the lowest boiling and melting amide because *N*-disubstituted amides don't form hydrogen bonds with each other.

17.3

More soluble	*Less soluble*	*Reason*
(a) CH₃CH₂CONH₂	CH₃COOCH₂CH₃	Amides form hydrogen bonds with water
(b) CH₃CH₂CH₂COOH	C₈H₁₉COOH	The large alkyl part of C₈H₁₉COOH makes it insoluble in water
(c) (CH₃)₂CHCOOH	CH₃CH₂COOCH(CH₃)₂	Carboxylic acids form hydrogen bonds with water

17.4

(a)

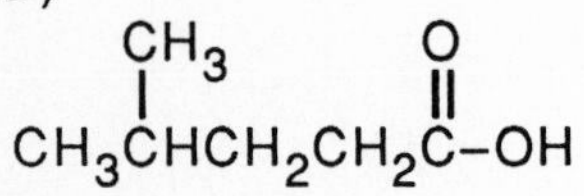

$$\underset{\text{4-Methylpentanoic acid}}{CH_3\overset{\underset{|}{CH_3}}{C}HCH_2CH_2\overset{\overset{O}{\parallel}}{C}-OH}$$

(b)

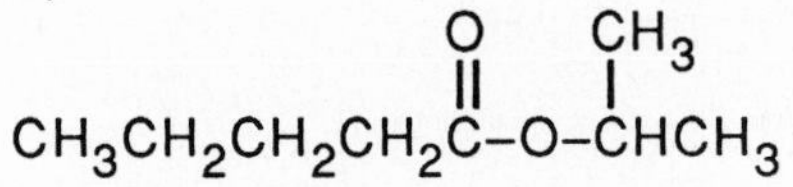

$$\underset{\text{Isopropyl butanoate}}{CH_3CH_2CH_2CH_2\overset{\overset{O}{\parallel}}{C}-O-\overset{\underset{|}{CH_3}}{C}HCH_3}$$

(c)

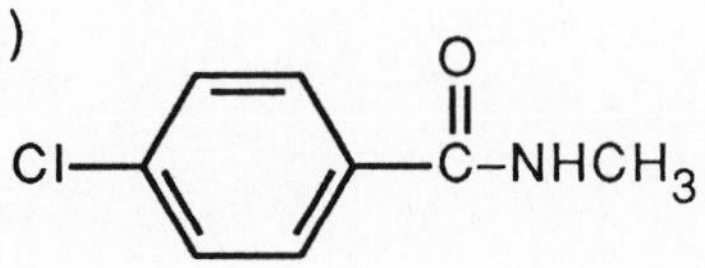

$$\underset{N\text{–Methyl–}p\text{–chlorobenzamide}}{Cl-\langle\text{ring}\rangle-\overset{\overset{O}{\parallel}}{C}-NHCH_3}$$

17.5

(a)

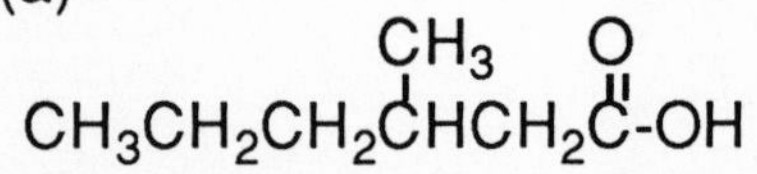

$$\underset{\text{3-Methylhexanoic acid}}{CH_3CH_2CH_2\overset{\underset{|}{CH_3}}{C}HCH_2\overset{\overset{O}{\parallel}}{C}-OH}$$

(b)

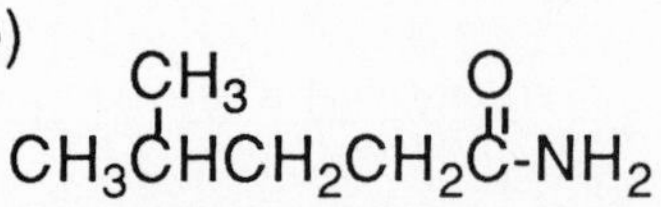

$$\underset{\text{4-Methylpentanamide}}{CH_3\overset{\underset{|}{CH_3}}{C}HCH_2CH_2\overset{\overset{O}{\parallel}}{C}-NH_2}$$

(c)

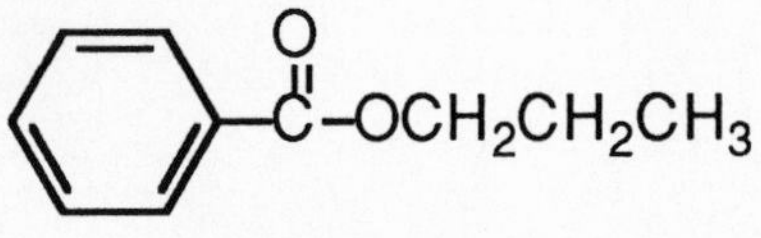

$$\underset{\text{Propyl benzoate}}{\langle\text{ring}\rangle-\overset{\overset{O}{\parallel}}{C}-OCH_2CH_2CH_3}$$

(d)

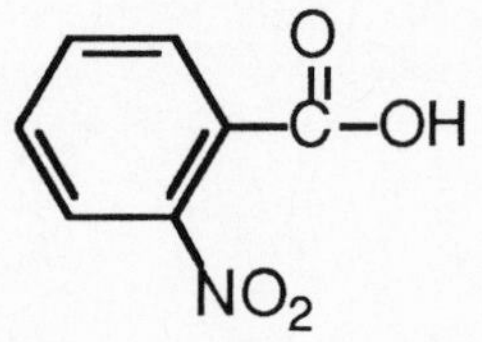

$$\underset{o\text{-Nitrobenzoic acid}}{\langle\text{ring}\rangle\overset{\overset{O}{\parallel}}{C}-OH,\ NO_2}$$

(e)

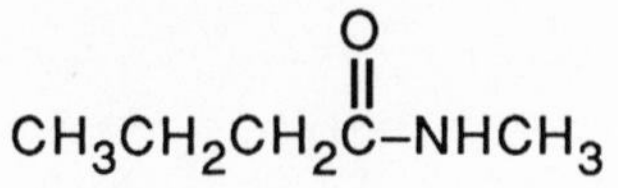

$$CH_3CH_2CH_2\overset{\displaystyle O}{\overset{\displaystyle \|}{C}}-NHCH_3$$

N–Methylbutanamide

(f)

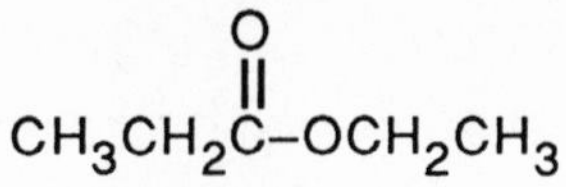

$$CH_3CH_2\overset{\displaystyle O}{\overset{\displaystyle \|}{C}}-OCH_2CH_3$$

Ethyl propanoate

(g)

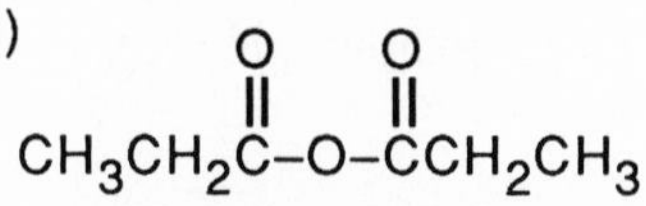

$$CH_3CH_2\overset{\displaystyle O}{\overset{\displaystyle \|}{C}}-O-\overset{\displaystyle O}{\overset{\displaystyle \|}{C}}CH_2CH_3$$

Propanoic anhydride

17.6

(a)

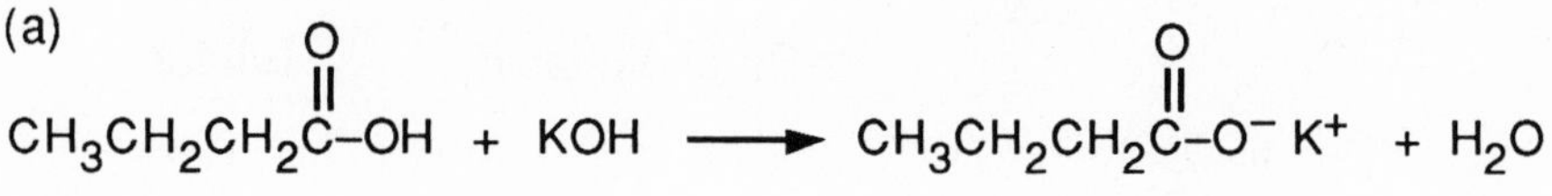

$$CH_3CH_2CH_2\overset{\displaystyle O}{\overset{\displaystyle \|}{C}}-OH \ + \ KOH \longrightarrow CH_3CH_2CH_2\overset{\displaystyle O}{\overset{\displaystyle \|}{C}}-O^- \ K^+ \ + \ H_2O$$

(b)

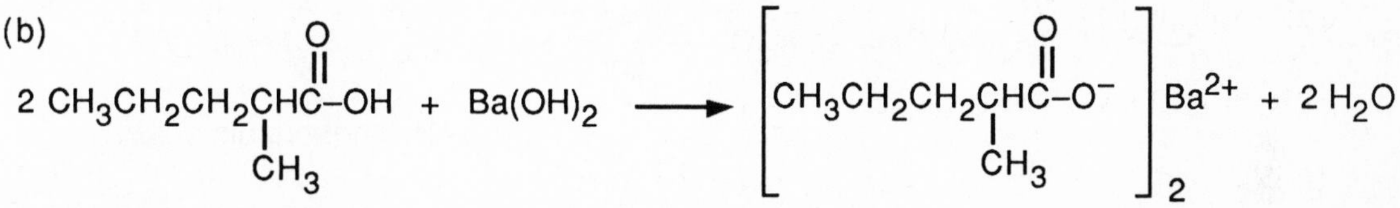

$$2 \ CH_3CH_2CH_2\overset{\displaystyle O}{\underset{\displaystyle CH_3}{\overset{\displaystyle \|}{\underset{|}{CH}}}C-OH \ + \ Ba(OH)_2 \longrightarrow \left[CH_3CH_2CH_2\underset{\displaystyle CH_3}{\overset{\displaystyle O}{\underset{|}{\overset{\|}{CH}}}}C-O^- \right]_2 Ba^{2+} \ + \ 2 \ H_2O$$

17.7

$$\left[H-\overset{\displaystyle O}{\overset{\displaystyle \|}{C}}-O^- \right]_2 Ca^{2+} \qquad H_2C=CH\overset{\displaystyle O}{\overset{\displaystyle \|}{C}}-O^- \ Na^+$$

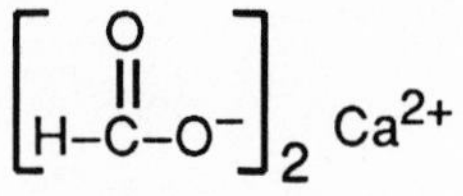

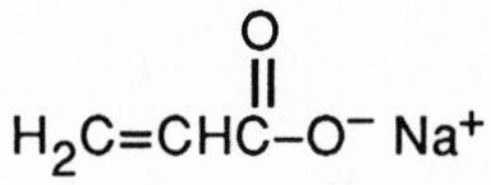

Calcium formate   Sodium acrylate

17.8

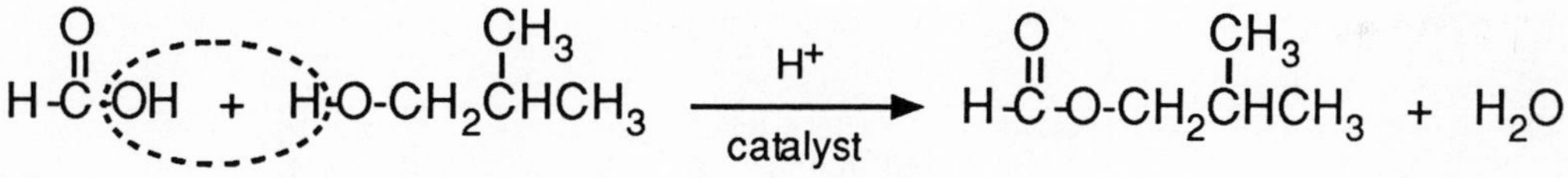

$$H-\overset{\displaystyle O}{\overset{\displaystyle \|}{C}}OH \ + \ HO-CH_2\overset{CH_3}{\underset{|}{CH}}CH_3 \ \xrightarrow[\text{catalyst}]{H^+} \ H-\overset{\displaystyle O}{\overset{\displaystyle \|}{C}}-O-CH_2\overset{CH_3}{\underset{|}{CH}}CH_3 \ + \ H_2O$$

17.9

(a)

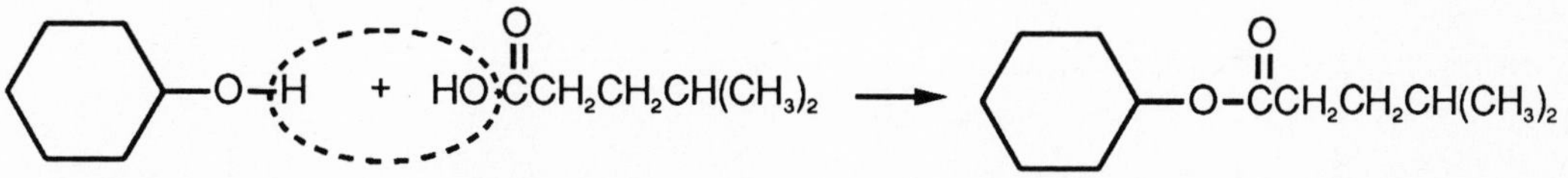

Cyclohexanol   4-Methylpentanoic acid

(b)

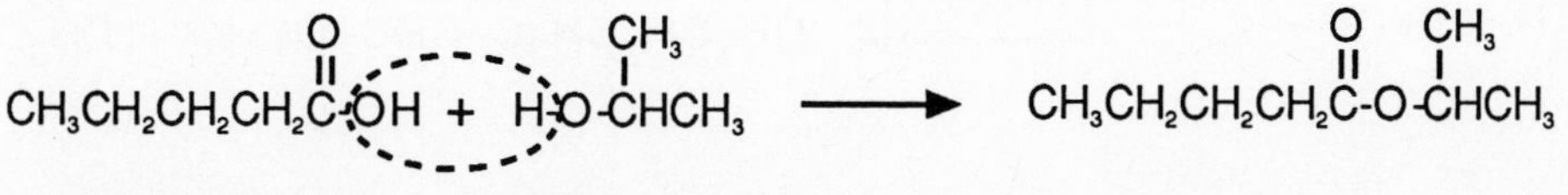

$$CH_3CH_2CH_2CH_2\overset{\displaystyle O}{\overset{\displaystyle \|}{C}}OH \ + \ HO-\overset{CH_3}{\underset{|}{CH}}CH_3 \longrightarrow CH_3CH_2CH_2CH_2\overset{\displaystyle O}{\overset{\displaystyle \|}{C}}-O-\overset{CH_3}{\underset{|}{CH}}CH_3$$

Pentanoic acid   Isopropyl alcohol

17.10

(a)

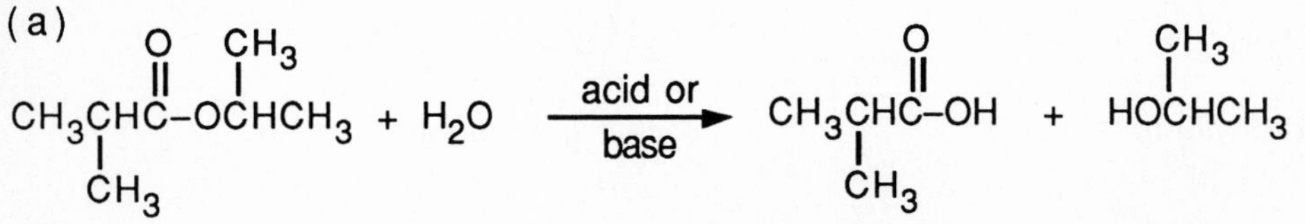

2-Methylpropanoic   Isopropyl alcohol
acid

(b)

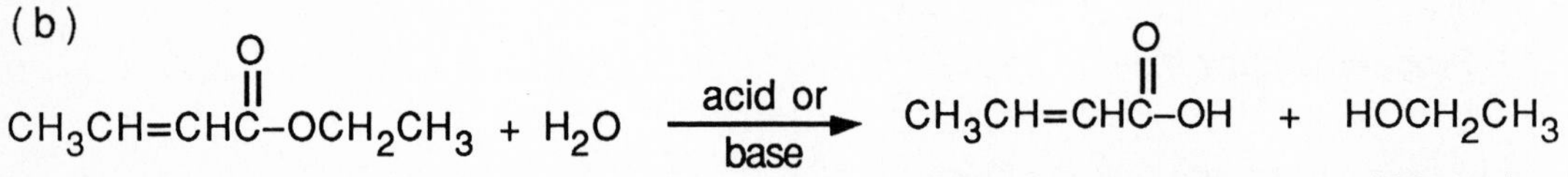

2-Butenoic acid   Ethanol

(c)

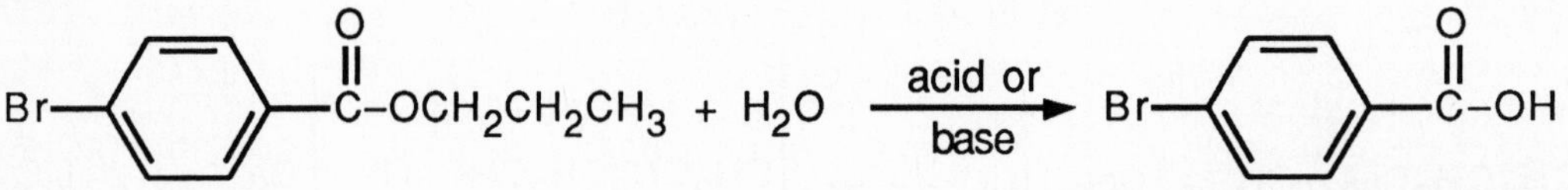

p–Bromobenzoic acid

+ HOCH₂CH₂CH₃

1-Propanol

17.11

(a)

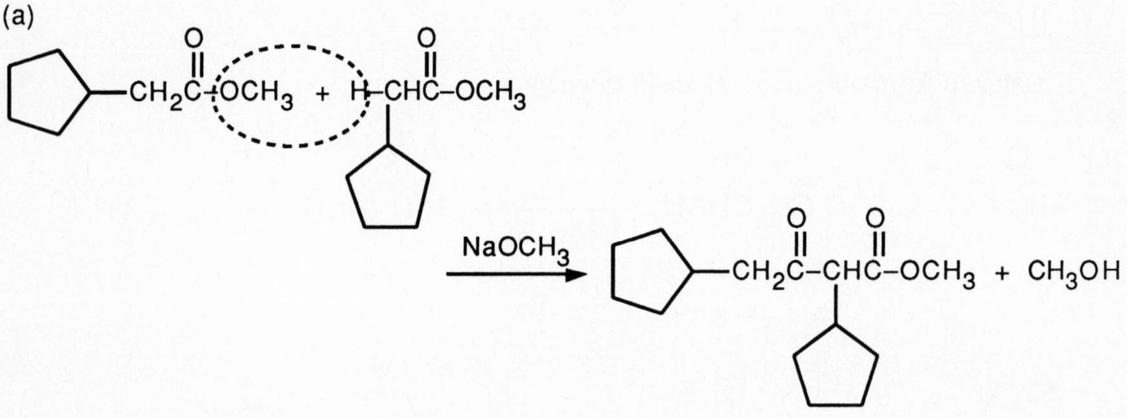

(b)

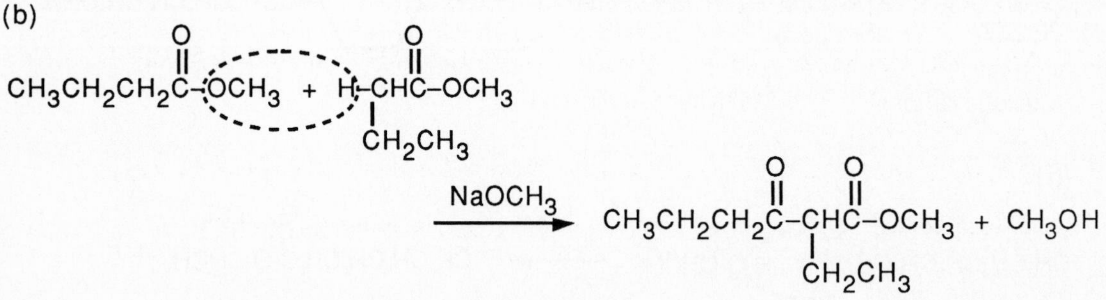

17.12

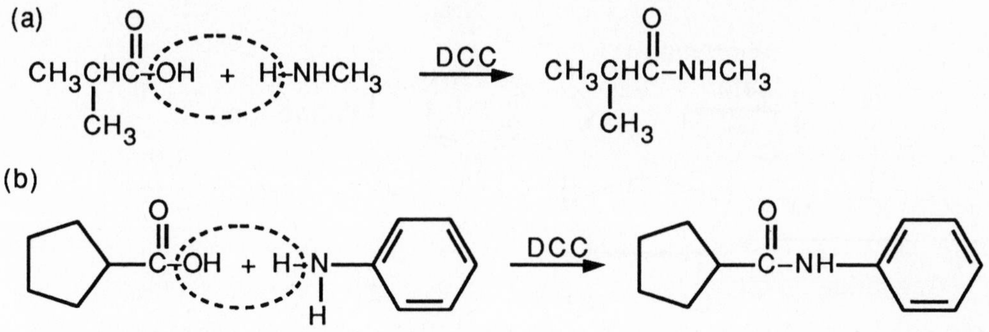

(a)

$$CH_3CHC-OH + H-NHCH_3 \xrightarrow{DCC} CH_3CHC-NHCH_3$$

(b)

$$\text{cyclopentyl-}C-OH + H-N(H)(C_6H_5) \xrightarrow{DCC} \text{cyclopentyl-}C-NH-C_6H_5$$

17.13

$$CH_3CH_2O\text{-}C_6H_4\text{-}NH_2 + HO-CCH_3 \longrightarrow CH_3CH_2O\text{-}C_6H_4\text{-}N(H)-C-CH_3$$

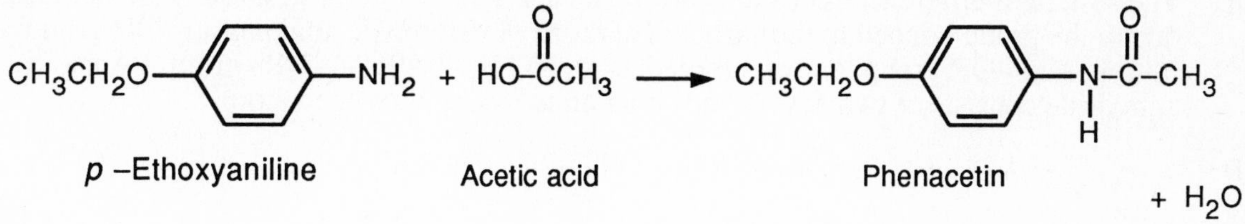

| *p*-Ethoxyaniline | Acetic acid | Phenacetin |

$$+ H_2O$$

17.14

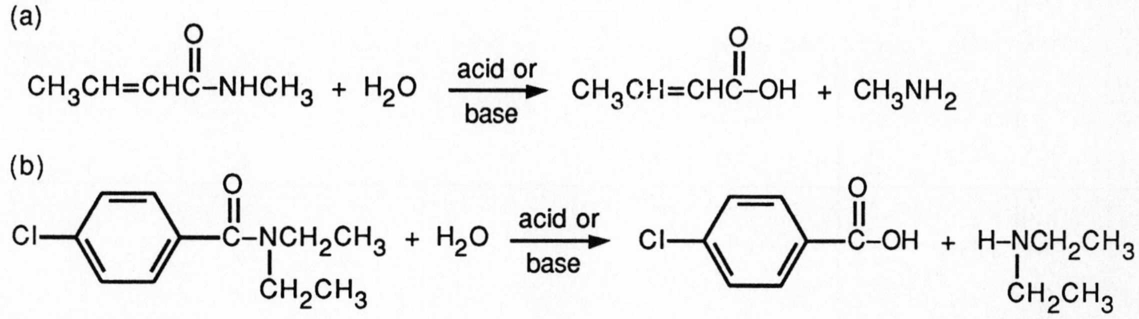

(a)

$$CH_3CH=CHC-NHCH_3 + H_2O \xrightarrow[\text{base}]{\text{acid or}} CH_3CH=CHC-OH + CH_3NH_2$$

(b)

$$Cl\text{-}C_6H_4\text{-}C-N(CH_2CH_3)(CH_2CH_3) + H_2O \xrightarrow[\text{base}]{\text{acid or}} Cl\text{-}C_6H_4\text{-}C-OH + H-N(CH_2CH_3)(CH_2CH_3)$$

17.15

$$CH_3C-NH_2 + H_2O \longrightarrow CH_3C-OH + H_3N$$

| Amide | | Acetic acid | Ammonia |

$$CH_3CH_2OPO_3{}^{2-} + H_2O \longrightarrow CH_3CH_2OH + HOPO_3{}^{2-}$$

| Phosphate monoester | | Ethanol | Hydrogen phosphate anion |

$$CH_3CH_2C-OCH_3 + H_2O \longrightarrow CH_3CH_2C-OH + H-OCH_3$$

| Carboxylic acid ester | | Propanoic acid | Methanol |

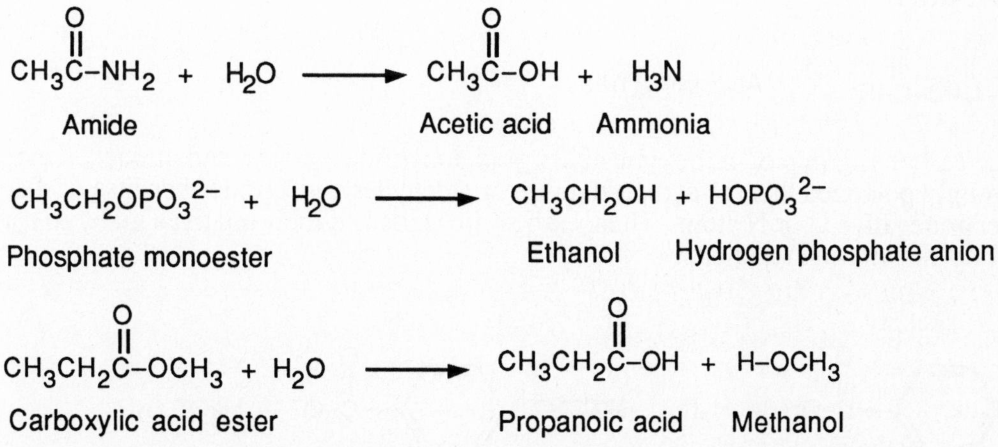

17.16

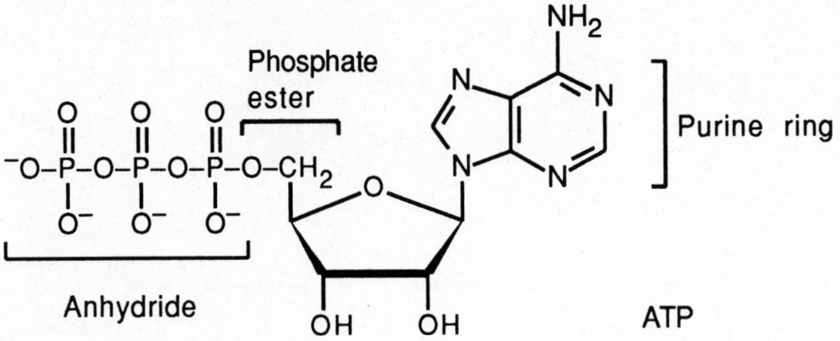

ATP

17.17 The structural differences between carboxylic acids, acid anhydrides, esters and amides are due to the group bonded to the carboxyl carbon. A carboxylic acid has an –OH group, an ester has an –OR group, and an amide has an $-NH_2$, –NHR or $-NR_2$ group. An acid anhydride consists of two acyl groups bonded to a central oxygen atom.

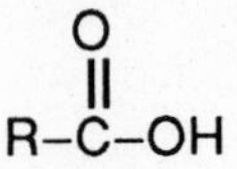

A carboxylic acid

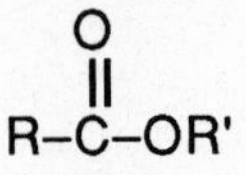

An ester

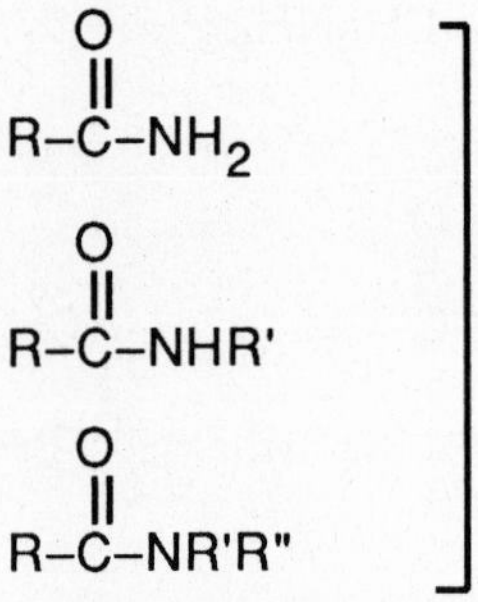

Amides

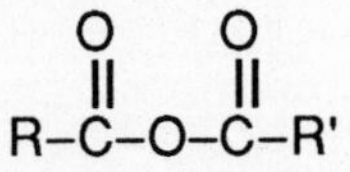

Acid anhydride

17.18 The carbonyl group of carboxylic acids, acid anhydrides, esters, and amides is more strongly polarized that the carbonyl group of aldehydes and ketones because of the electronegative O or N atom. Thus, carboxylic acids and their relatives undergo carbonyl-group substitution reactions.

17.19

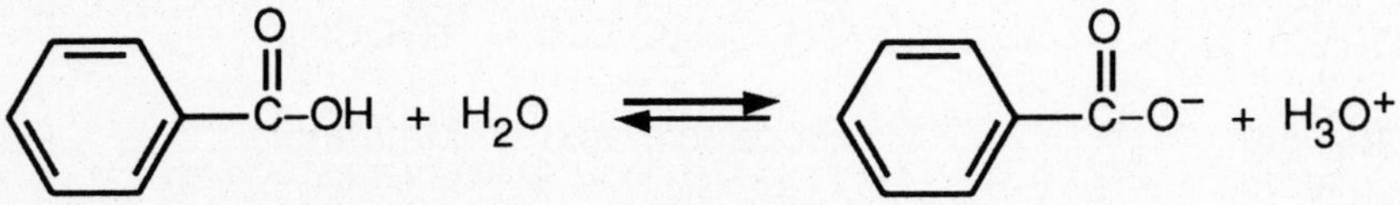

17.20

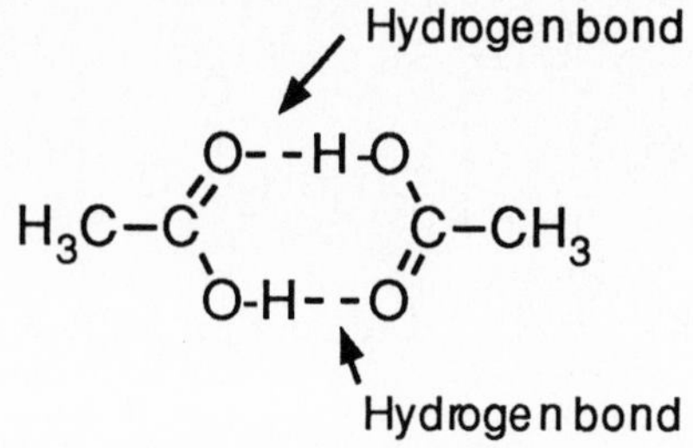

Hydrogen bond

$$H_3C-C \quad C-CH_3$$

Hydrogen bond

17.21

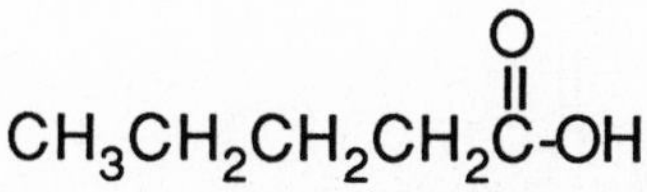

$$CH_3CH_2CH_2CH_2\overset{\overset{\displaystyle O}{\|}}{C}\text{-OH}$$

Pentanoic acid

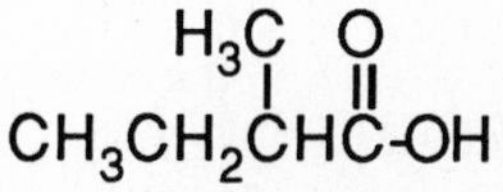

$$CH_3CH_2\overset{\overset{\displaystyle H_3C}{|}}{\underset{}{C}}H\overset{\overset{\displaystyle O}{\|}}{C}\text{-OH}$$

2-Methylbutanoic acid

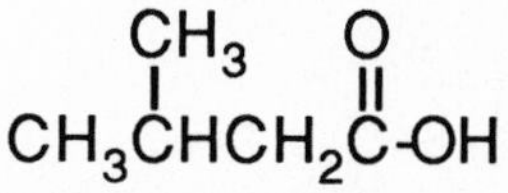

$$CH_3\overset{\overset{\displaystyle CH_3}{|}}{C}HCH_2\overset{\overset{\displaystyle O}{\|}}{C}\text{-OH}$$

3-Methylbutanoic acid

$$CH_3\text{-}\overset{\overset{\displaystyle H_3C}{|}}{\underset{\underset{\displaystyle H_3C}{|}}{C}}\text{-}\overset{\overset{\displaystyle O}{\|}}{C}\text{-OH}$$

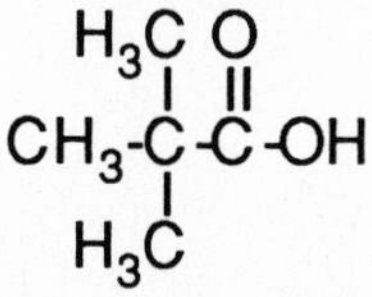

2,2-Dimethylpropanoic acid

17.22

(a)

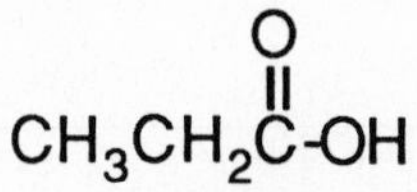

$$CH_3CH_2\overset{\overset{\displaystyle O}{\|}}{C}\text{-OH}$$

In water

(b)

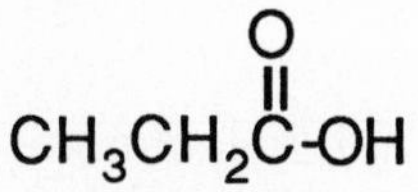

$$CH_3CH_2\overset{\overset{\displaystyle O}{\|}}{C}\text{-OH}$$

at pH = 2

(c)

$$CH_3CH_2\overset{\overset{\displaystyle O}{\|}}{C}\text{-O}^-$$

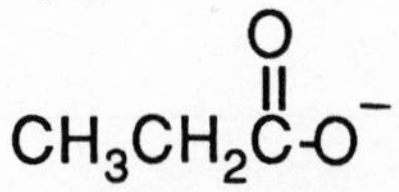

at pH = 12

17.23

(a)

$CH_3CH_2CH_2CH_2CH_2COOH$

Hexanoic acid

(b)

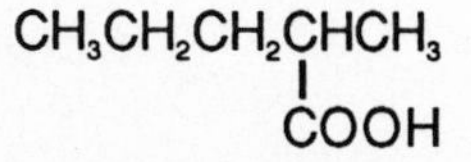

$$CH_3CH_2CH_2\overset{}{C}HCH_3$$
$$\underset{\displaystyle COOH}{|}$$

2-Methylpentanoic acid

(c)

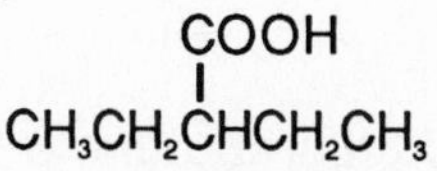

$$\overset{\displaystyle COOH}{\overset{|}{CH_3CH_2CHCH_2CH_3}}$$

2-Ethylbutanoic acid

(d)

▷—CH_2CH_2COOH

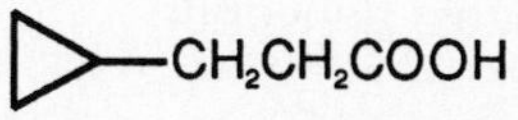

3-Cyclopropylpropanoic acid

(e)

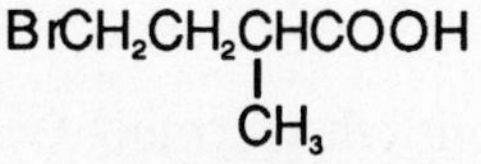

$$BrCH_2CH_2CHCOOH$$
$$\underset{\displaystyle CH_3}{|}$$

4-Bromo-2-methylbutanoic acid

(f)

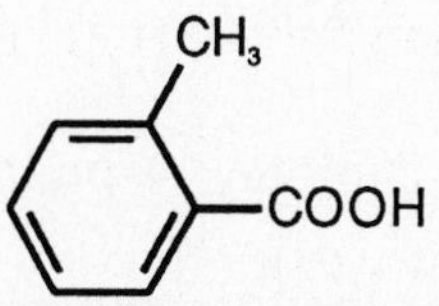

o-Methylbenzoic acid

(g)

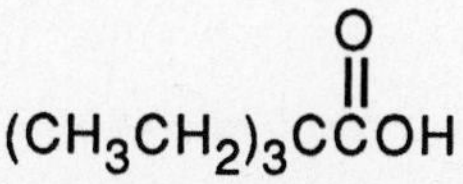

$$(CH_3CH_2)_3C\overset{\overset{\displaystyle O}{\|}}{C}OH$$

2,2-Diethylbutanoic acid

(h)

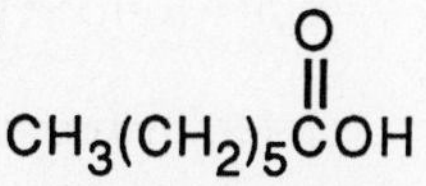

$$CH_3(CH_2)_5\overset{\overset{\displaystyle O}{\|}}{C}OH$$

Heptanoic acid

17.24

(a)

$$CH_3CH_2CHCH_2\overset{\overset{\displaystyle O}{\|}}{C}-O^-\ K^+$$
$$|$$
$$CH_2CH_3$$

Potassium 3-ethylpentanoate

(b)

Ammonium benzoate

(c)

$$\left[CH_3CH_2\overset{\overset{\displaystyle O}{\|}}{C}-O^- \right]_2 Ca^{2+}$$

Calcium propanoate

17.25

(a)

$$\underset{\underset{\displaystyle CH_3}{|}}{\overset{\overset{\displaystyle CH_3}{|}}{CH_3CHCHCH_2}}\overset{\overset{\displaystyle O}{\|}}{C}-OH$$

3,4-Dimethylpentanoic acid

(b)

Triphenylacetic acid

(c) CH₃CH₂

$$\overset{\overset{\displaystyle O}{\|}}{C}-OH$$

m-Ethylbenzoic acid

(d)

$$CH_3CH_2CH_2\overset{\overset{\displaystyle O}{\|}}{C}-O^-\ ^+NH_3CH_3$$

Methylammonium butanoate

(e)

$$CH_3CH_2\underset{\underset{\displaystyle Cl}{|}}{\overset{\overset{\displaystyle Cl}{|}}{C}}\overset{\overset{\displaystyle O}{\|}}{C}-OH$$

2,2-Dichlorobutanoic acid

(f)

$$CH_3CH_2CH_2\overset{\overset{\displaystyle OH}{|}}{CH}CH_2\overset{\overset{\displaystyle O}{\|}}{C}-OH$$

3-hydroxyhexanoic acid

(g)

$$\overset{\overset{\displaystyle CH_3}{|}}{CHC}\underset{\underset{\displaystyle H_3C\ \ CH_3}{|\ \ |}}{}CH_2\overset{\overset{\displaystyle O}{\|}}{C}-OH$$

3,3-Dimethyl-4-phenylpentanoic acid

(h)

Benzoic anhydride

17.26 There are 17 carboxylic acids with the formula $C_7H_{14}O_2$. Any three will do.

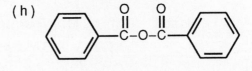

$$CH_3CH_2CH_2CH_2CH_2CH_2\overset{\overset{\displaystyle O}{\|}}{C}-OH$$

Heptanoic acid

$$CH_3CH_2CH_2CH_2\underset{}{\overset{\overset{\displaystyle H_3C}{|}}{CH}}\overset{\overset{\displaystyle O}{\|}}{C}-OH$$

2-Methylhexanoic acid

$$CH_3CH_2CH_2\underset{}{\overset{\overset{\displaystyle CH_3}{|}}{CH}}CH_2\overset{\overset{\displaystyle O}{\|}}{C}-OH$$

3-Methylhexanoic acid

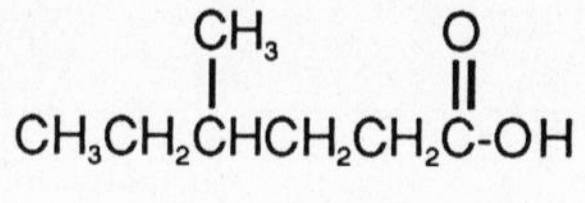

$$CH_3CH_2CHCH_2CH_2\overset{O}{\underset{}{C}}-OH$$

4-Methylhexanoic acid

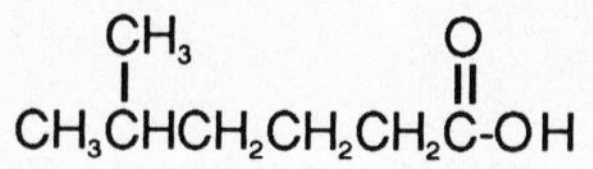

$$CH_3CHCH_2CH_2CH_2\overset{O}{\underset{}{C}}-OH$$

5-Methylhexanoic acid

$$CH_3CH_2CH_2-\overset{H_3C}{\underset{CH_3}{C}}-\overset{O}{\underset{}{C}}-OH$$

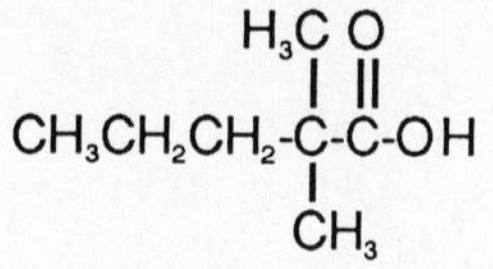

2,2-Dimethylpentanoic acid

$$CH_3CH_2\overset{CH_3}{\underset{}{C}}H\overset{O}{\underset{CH_3}{C}}H\overset{O}{\underset{}{C}}-OH$$

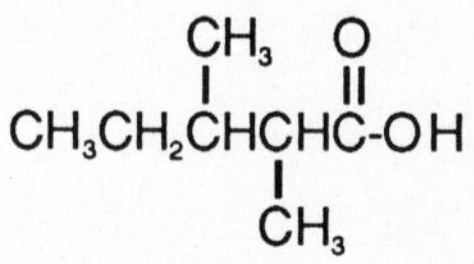

2,3-Dimethylpentanoic acid

$$CH_3\overset{CH_3}{\underset{}{C}}HCH_2\overset{O}{\underset{CH_3}{C}}H\overset{O}{\underset{}{C}}-OH$$

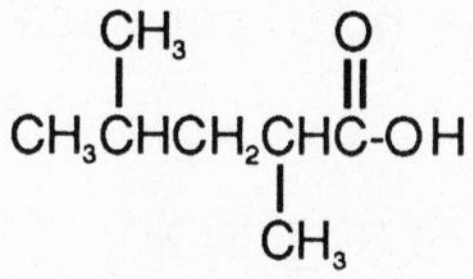

2,4-Dimethylpentanoic acid

$$CH_3CH_2-\overset{CH_3}{\underset{CH_3}{C}}-CH_2\overset{O}{\underset{}{C}}-OH$$

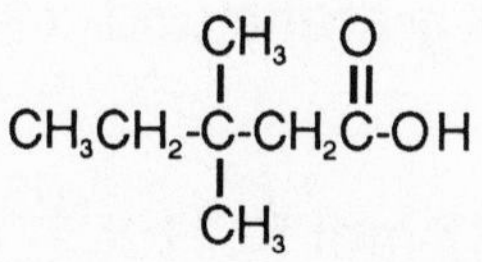

3,3-Dimethylpentanoic acid

$$CH_3\overset{CH_3}{\underset{}{C}}HCHCH_2\overset{O}{\underset{CH_3}{C}}-OH$$

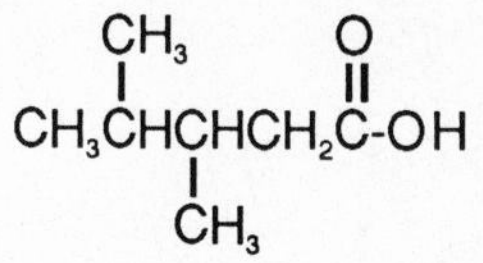

3,4-Dimethylpentanoic acid

$$CH_3-\overset{CH_3}{\underset{CH_3}{C}}-CH_2CH_2\overset{O}{\underset{}{C}}-OH$$

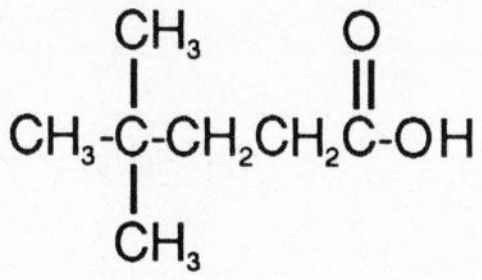

4,4-Dimethylpentanoic acid

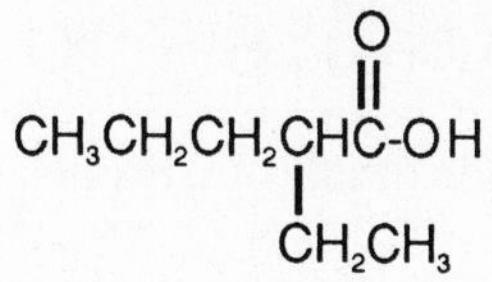

$$CH_3CH_2CH_2\overset{O}{\underset{CH_2CH_3}{C}}HC-OH$$

2-ethylpentanoic acid

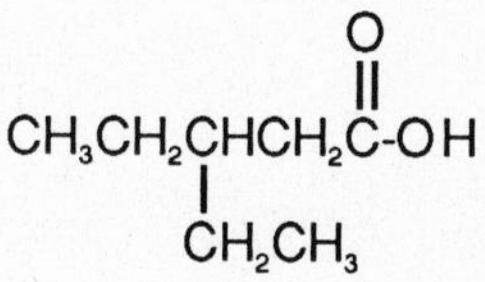

$$CH_3CH_2CHCH_2\overset{O}{\underset{CH_2CH_3}{C}}-OH$$

3-Ethylpentanoic acid

$$CH_3CH-\overset{H_3C}{\underset{H_3C}{C}}-\overset{O}{\underset{CH_3}{C}}-OH$$

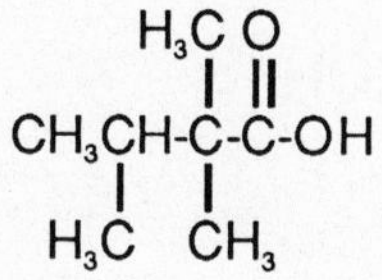

2,2,3-Trimethylbutanoic acid

$$CH_3-\overset{H_3C}{\underset{H_3C}{C}}-\overset{O}{\underset{CH_3}{C}}HC-OH$$

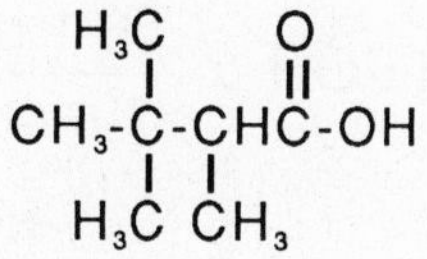

2,3,3-Trimethylbutanoic acid

$$CH_3\overset{H_3C}{\underset{}{C}}HCH\overset{O}{\underset{CH_2CH_3}{C}}-OH$$

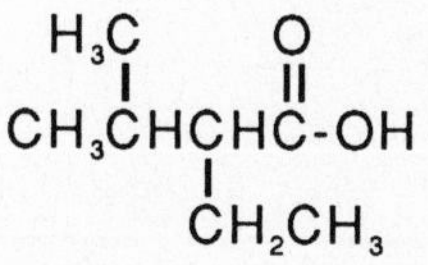

2-Ethyl-3-methylbutanoic acid

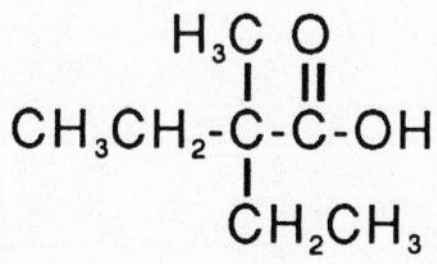

$$CH_3CH_2-\overset{H_3C}{\underset{CH_2CH_3}{C}}-\overset{O}{\underset{}{C}}-OH$$

2-Ethyl-2-methylbutanoic acid

17.27

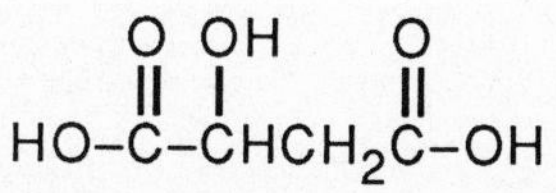

$$HO-\overset{O}{\underset{}{C}}-\overset{OH}{\underset{}{C}}HCH_2\overset{O}{\underset{}{C}}-OH \qquad \text{Malic acid}$$

17.28

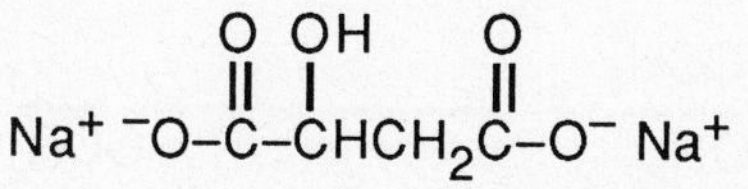

$$Na^+\ {}^-O-\overset{O}{\underset{}{C}}-\overset{OH}{\underset{}{C}}HCH_2\overset{O}{\underset{}{C}}-O^-\ Na^+ \qquad \text{Disodium malate}$$

17.29

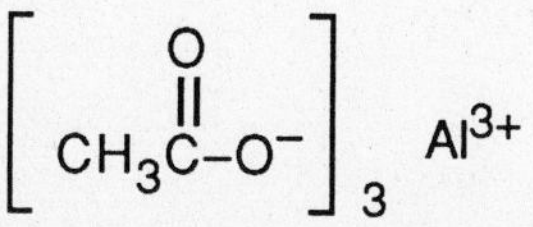

$$\left[CH_3\overset{O}{\underset{}{C}}-O^- \right]_3 Al^{3+} \qquad \text{Aluminum acetate}$$

17.30

(a)

$$CH_3\overset{O}{\underset{||}{C}}\text{-OH} + KOH \longrightarrow CH_3\overset{O}{\underset{||}{C}}\text{-O}^- K^+ + H_2O$$

molar mass of CH_3COOH = 60.0 g; molar mass of KOH = 56.1g

10.0 g acetic acid x $\dfrac{1\,mol}{60\,g}$ = 0.167 mol acetic acid

0.167 mol KOH x $\dfrac{56.1\,g}{1\,mol}$ = 9.37 g KOH

(b)

$$CH_3CH_2\overset{O}{\underset{||}{C}}\text{-OH} + KOH \longrightarrow CH_3CH_2\overset{O}{\underset{||}{C}}\text{-O}^- K^+ + H_2O$$

molar mass of CH_3CH_2COOH = 74.0 g; molar mass of KOH = 56.1g

0.25 L x $\dfrac{2.0\,mol\,propanoic\,acid}{1\,L}$ = 0.50 mol propanoic acid

0.50 mol KOH x $\dfrac{56.1\,g}{1\,mol}$ = 28 g KOH

17.31

$$\begin{array}{c} CH_2COOH \\ | \\ HO\text{-}C\text{-}COOH \\ | \\ CH_2COOH \end{array} + 3NaOH \longrightarrow \begin{array}{c} CH_2COO^- Na^+ \\ | \\ HO\text{-}C\text{-}COO^- Na^+ \\ | \\ CH_2COO^- Na^+ \end{array}$$

0.060 L citric acid x $\dfrac{0.020\,mol\,c.a.}{1\,L}$ x $\dfrac{3\,mol\,NaOH}{1\,mol\,c.a.}$ x $\dfrac{1\,L\,NaOH}{0.040\,mol\,NaOH}$

= 0.090 L NaOH

= 90 mL of 0.040 M NaOH

17.32

$$2CH_3COOH + Ca(OH)_2 \longrightarrow [CH_3COO^-]\,Ca^{2+} + 2H_2O$$

molar mass of $Ca(OH)_2$ = 74.1 g

1.4 g $Ca(OH)_2$ x $\dfrac{1\,mol\,Ca(OH)_2}{74.1\,g\,Ca(OH)_2}$ x $\dfrac{2\,mol\,CH_3COOH}{1\,mol\,Ca(OH)_2}$ x $\dfrac{1\,L}{0.20\,mol\,CH_3COOH}$

= 190 mL acetic acid

17.33

$$HO-\overset{\overset{\textstyle O}{\|}}{C}-\overset{\overset{\textstyle O}{\|}}{C}-OH \ + \ 2 \ NaOH \ \longrightarrow \ Na^+ \ {}^-O-\overset{\overset{\textstyle O}{\|}}{C}-\overset{\overset{\textstyle O}{\|}}{C}-O^- \ Na^+$$

molar mass of NaOH = 40.0 g

(a)

$$0.100 \ g \ NaOH \times \frac{1 \ mol \ NaOH}{40.0 \ g \ NaOH} \times \frac{1 \ mol \ C_2H_2O_4}{2 \ mol \ NaOH} \times \frac{1}{0.0150 \ L} = 0.0833 \ M$$

(b)

$$0.0200 \ L \ NaOH \times \frac{0.300 \ mol \ NaOH}{1 \ L} \times \frac{1 \ mol \ C_2H_2O_4}{2 \ mol \ NaOH} \times \frac{1}{0.0150 \ L} = 0.200 \ M$$

17.34 Chloroacetic acid ($K_a = 1.4 \times 10^{-3}$) is a stronger acid than acetic acid ($K_a = 1.8 \times 10^{-5}$). The larger the K_a, the stronger the acid.

17.35 There are many answers to this question. Here are some possibilities:

(a)

$$CH_3CH_2CH_2CH_2\overset{\overset{\textstyle O}{\|}}{C}-NH_2 \qquad CH_3CH_2\overset{\overset{\textstyle O}{\|}}{C}-NHCH_2CH_3 \qquad H-\overset{\overset{\textstyle O}{\|}}{\underset{\underset{\textstyle CH_2CH_3}{|}}{C}}-NCH_2CH_3$$

Pentanamide   *N*-Ethylpropanamide   *N,N*-Diethylformamide

(b)

$$CH_3CH_2CH_2CH_2\overset{\overset{\textstyle O}{\|}}{C}-OCH_3 \qquad CH_3CH_2\overset{\overset{\textstyle O}{\|}}{C}-OCH_2CH_2CH_3 \qquad H-\overset{\overset{\textstyle O}{\|}}{C}-OCH_2CH_2CH_2CH_2CH_3$$

Methyl pentanoate   Propyl propanoate   Pentyl formate

17.36

(a)

$$CH_3\overset{\overset{\textstyle O}{\|}}{C}-OCH_2CH_2\overset{\overset{\textstyle CH_3}{|}}{C}HCH_3$$

3-Methylbutyl acetate

(b)

$$CH_3\overset{\overset{\textstyle CH_3}{|}}{C}HCH_2CH_2\overset{\overset{\textstyle O}{\|}}{C}-OCH_3$$

Methyl 4-methylpentanoate

(c)

$$CH_3-\overset{\overset{\textstyle H_3C}{|}}{\underset{\underset{\textstyle H_3C}{|}}{C}}-\overset{\overset{\textstyle O}{\|}}{C}-OCH_2CH_3$$

Ethyl 2,2-dimethylpropanoate

(d)

$$\overset{\overset{\textstyle O}{\|}}{C}-OCH_2CH_3$$

Ethyl benzoate

(e)

$$CH_3CH_2\overset{\overset{\textstyle O}{\|}}{C}-O-$$

Cyclopentyl propanoate

17.37 - 17.38

(a)

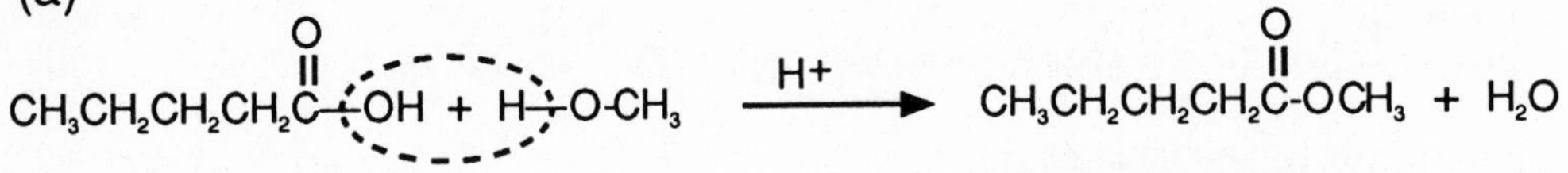

$$CH_3CH_2CH_2CH_2C \underset{\overset{\|}{O}}{\overset{\|}{-}} OH + H-O-CH_3 \xrightarrow{H+} CH_3CH_2CH_2CH_2C-OCH_3 + H_2O$$

Methyl pentanoate

(b)

$$CH_3CH_2CHC-OH + H-O-CHCH_3 \xrightarrow{H+} CH_3CH_2CHC-O-CHCH_3 + H_2O$$

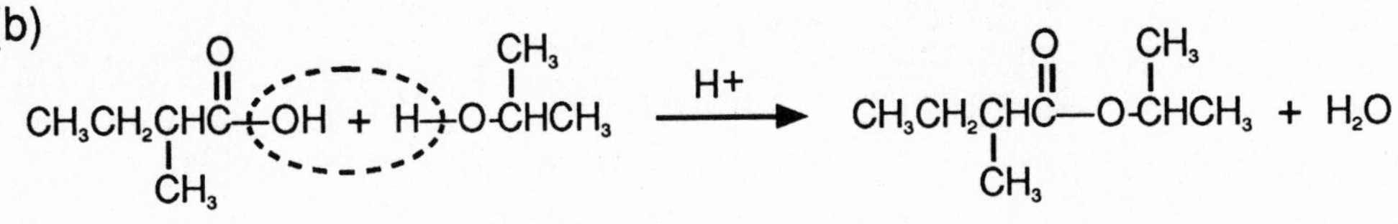

Isopropyl 2-methylbutanoate

(c)

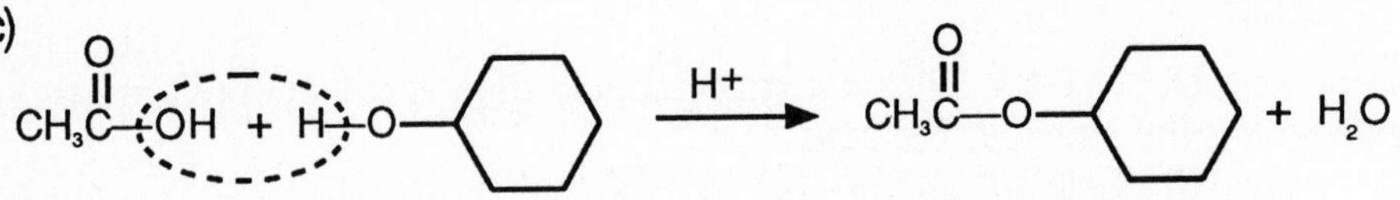

$$CH_3C-OH + H-O-\text{(cyclohexyl)} \xrightarrow{H+} CH_3C-O-\text{(cyclohexyl)} + H_2O$$

Cyclohexyl acetate

(d)

$$\text{(o-hydroxyphenyl)}-C-OH + H-O-\text{(phenyl)} \xrightarrow{H+} \text{(o-hydroxyphenyl)}-C-O-\text{(phenyl)}$$

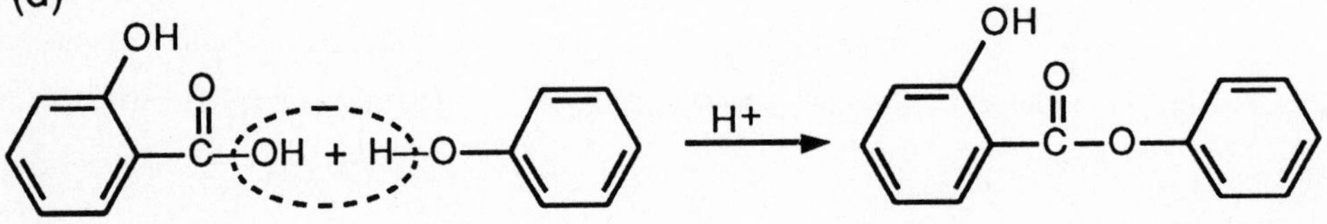

Phenyl o-hydroxybenzoate

17.39 - 17.40

(a)

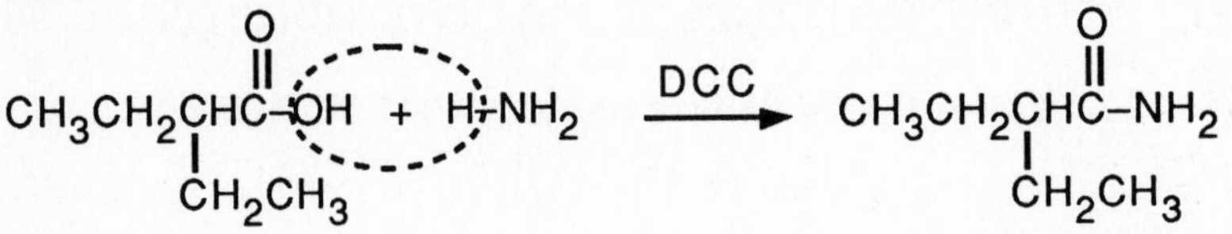

$$CH_3CH_2CHC-OH + H-NH_2 \xrightarrow{DCC} CH_3CH_2CHC-NH_2$$

2-Ethylbutanamide

(b)

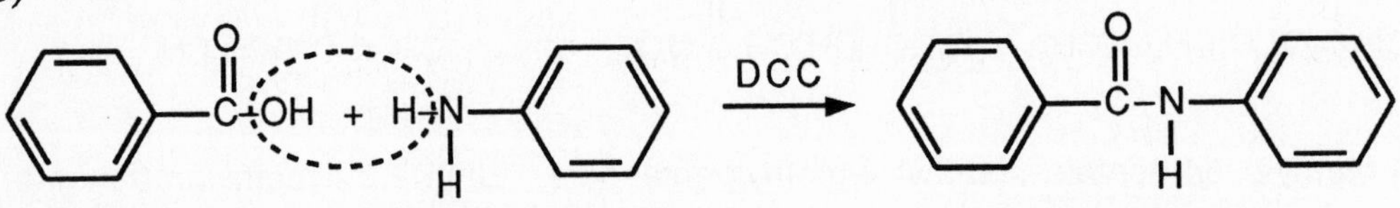

$$\text{(phenyl)}-C-OH + H-N-\text{(phenyl)} \xrightarrow{DCC} \text{(phenyl)}-C-N-\text{(phenyl)}$$

N–Phenylbenzamide

(c)

$$H-C-OH + H-NCH_3 \xrightarrow{DCC} H-C-NCH_3$$

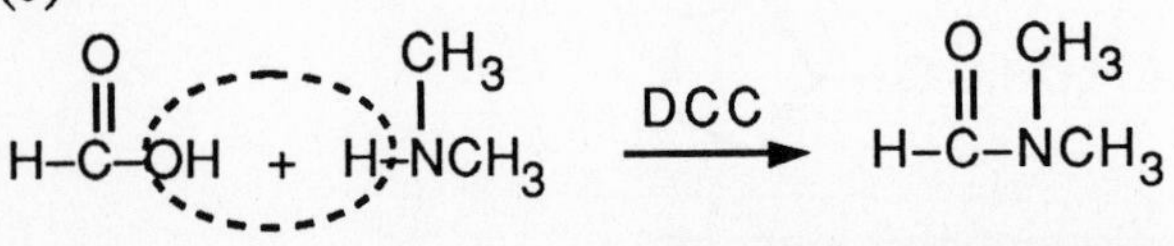

N,N –Dimethylformamide

(d)

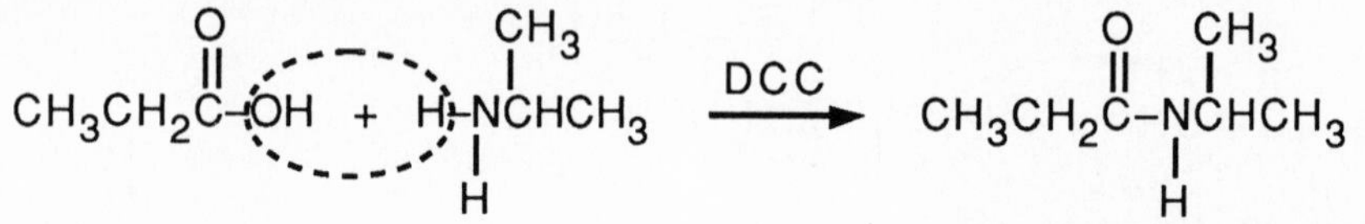

$$CH_3CH_2C-OH \quad + \quad H-NCHCH_3 \xrightarrow{\text{DCC}} CH_3CH_2C-NCHCH_3$$

N–Isopropylpropanamide

17.41 - 17.42

(a)

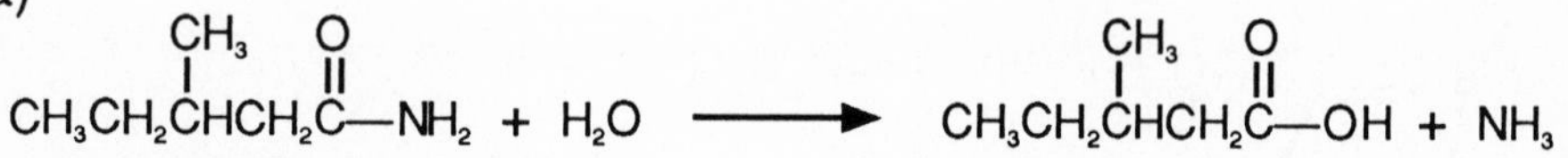

$$CH_3CH_2CHCH_2C-NH_2 + H_2O \longrightarrow CH_3CH_2CHCH_2C-OH + NH_3$$

3-Methylpentanamide

(b)

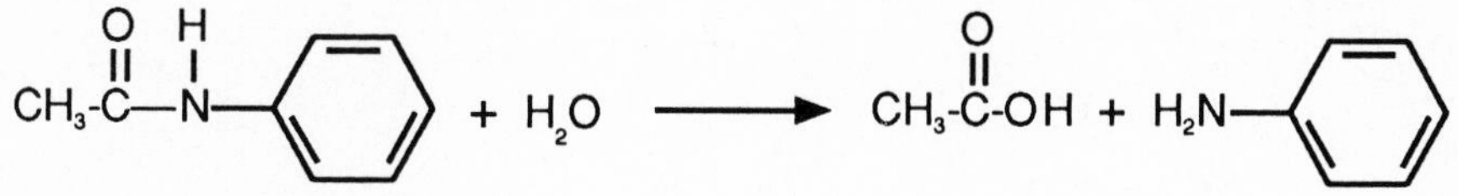

$$CH_3-C-N \text{(phenyl)} + H_2O \longrightarrow CH_3-C-OH + H_2N \text{(phenyl)}$$

N-Phenylacetamide

(c)

$$\text{(phenyl)}C-NCH_2CH_3 + H_2O \longrightarrow \text{(phenyl)}C-OH + H-NCH_2CH_3$$

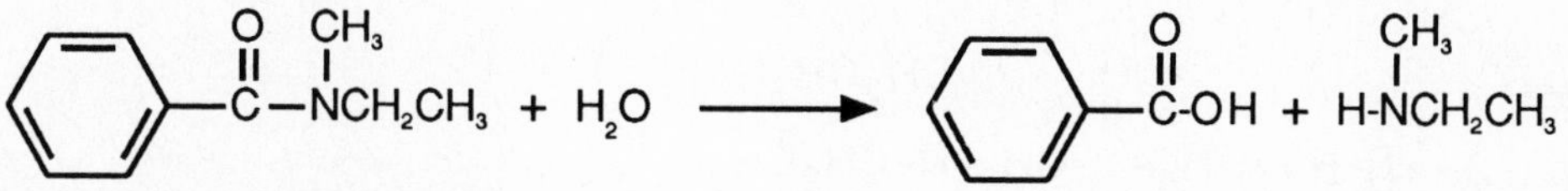

N-Ethyl-*N*-methylbenzamide

(d)

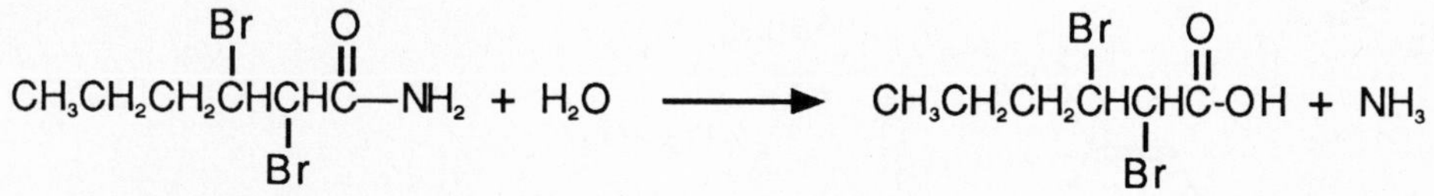

$$CH_3CH_2CH_2CHCHC-NH_2 + H_2O \longrightarrow CH_3CH_2CH_2CHCHC-OH + NH_3$$

2,3,-Dibromohexanamide

17.43 Carboxylic acids, esters, and amides undergo a carbonyl-group substitution reaction:

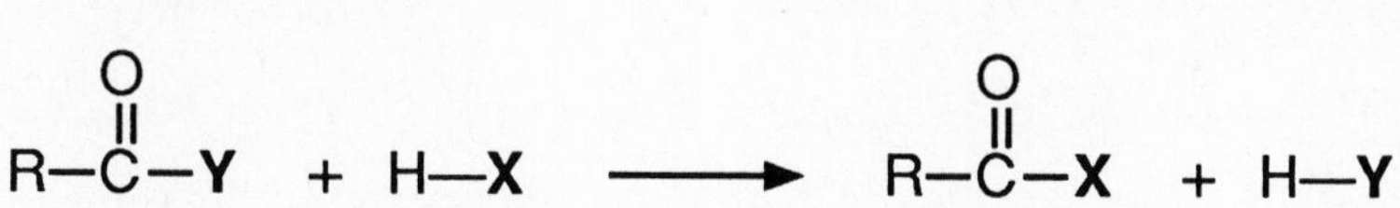

$$R-C-Y \quad + \quad H-X \quad \longrightarrow \quad R-C-X \quad + \quad H-Y$$

17.44

$$\text{(aminophenyl)}C-OH + H-O-CH_3 \longrightarrow \text{(aminophenyl)}C-OCH_3 + H_2O$$

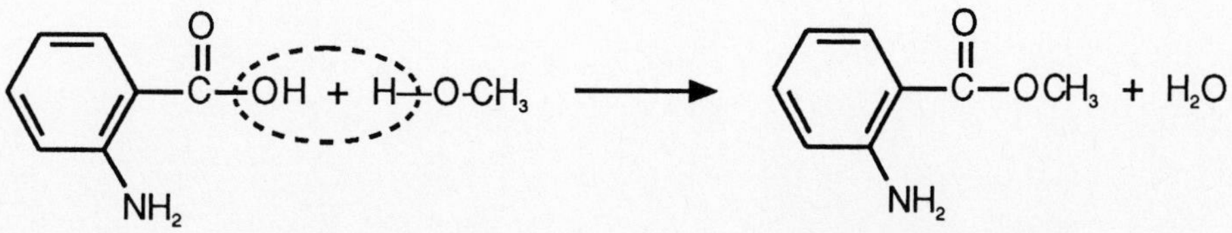

Methyl anthranilate

17.45

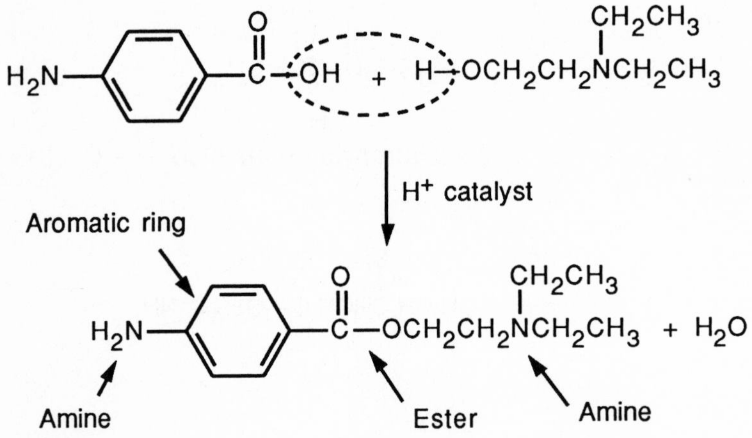

17.46

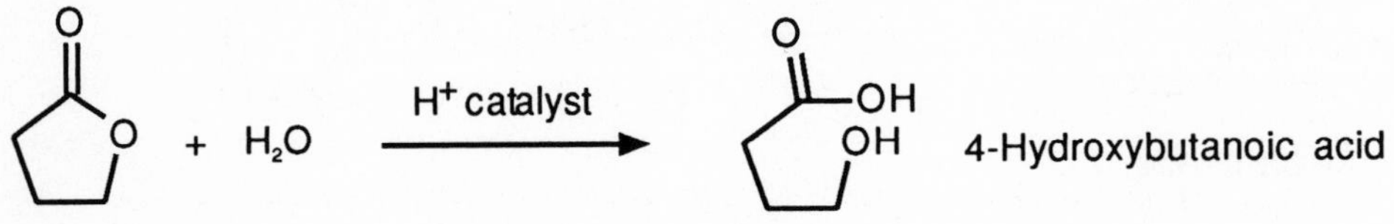

4-Hydroxybutanoic acid

17.47

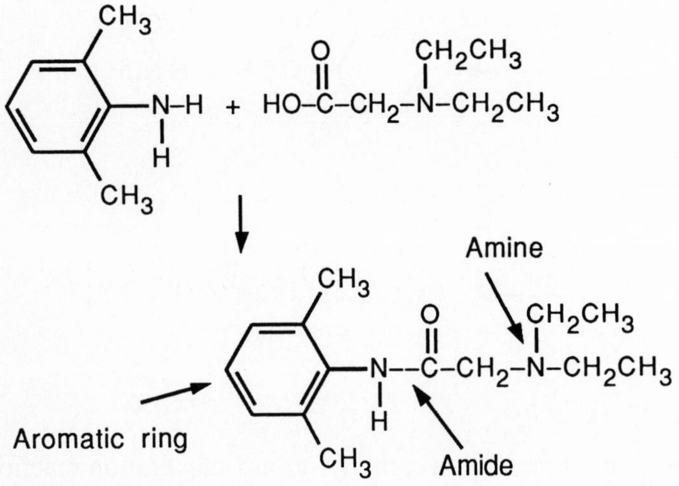

17.48

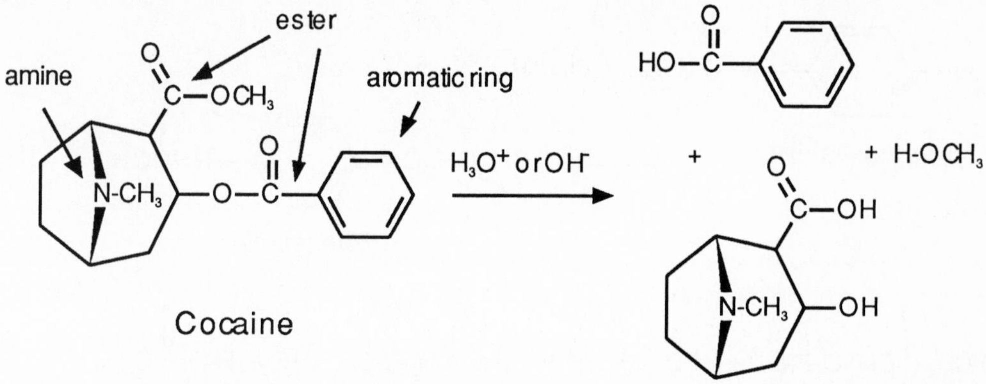

Cocaine

17.49

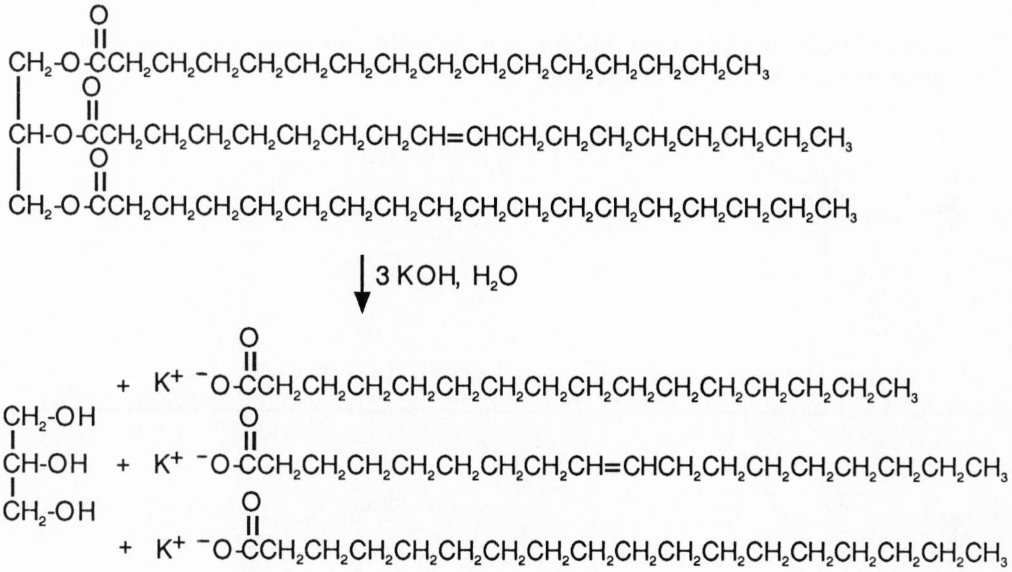

$$\downarrow 3\,KOH,\ H_2O$$

17.50

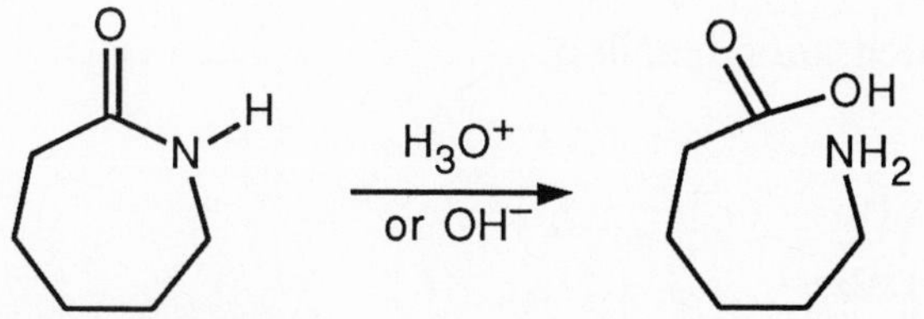

Caprolactam

17.51 There are several ways you might tell samples of pentanoic acid and methyl butanoate apart. One way is to measure their boiling points. Since pentanoic acid forms hydrogen bonds and methyl butanoate doesn't, pentanoic acid has the higher boiling point. Alternatively, you could see which of the two samples dissolves in aqueous $NaHCO_3$. Pentanoic acid dissolves in the base giving bubbles of CO_2 gas, but methyl butanoate does not dissolve.

17.52

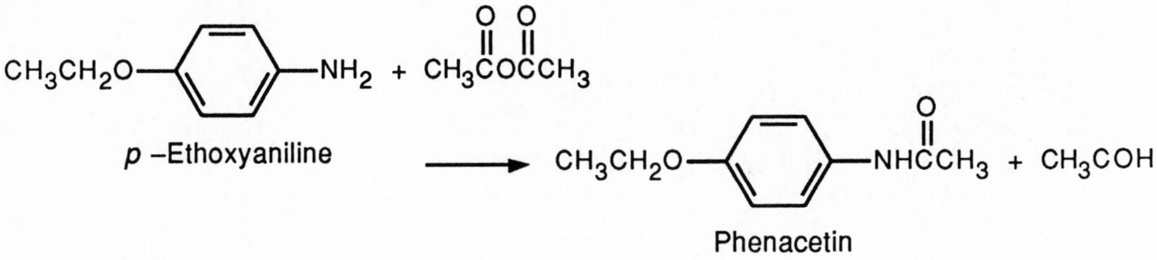

$$CH_3CH_2O-\langle\bigcirc\rangle-NH_2 \ + \ CH_3\overset{O}{\overset{\|}{C}}O\overset{O}{\overset{\|}{C}}CH_3$$

p –Ethoxyaniline

$$\longrightarrow \quad CH_3CH_2O-\langle\bigcirc\rangle-NH\overset{O}{\overset{\|}{C}}CH_3 \ + \ CH_3COH$$

Phenacetin

17.53

$$HO\text{-}CH_2\text{-}\overset{O}{\overset{\|}{C}}\text{-}CH_2\text{-}O\text{-}\overset{O}{\underset{O^-}{\overset{\|}{P}}}\text{-}O^- \ + \ H_2O \ \longrightarrow \ HO\text{-}CH_2\text{-}\overset{O}{\overset{\|}{C}}\text{-}CH_2\text{-}OH \ + \ H\text{-}O\text{-}\overset{O}{\underset{O^-}{\overset{\|}{P}}}\text{-}O^-$$

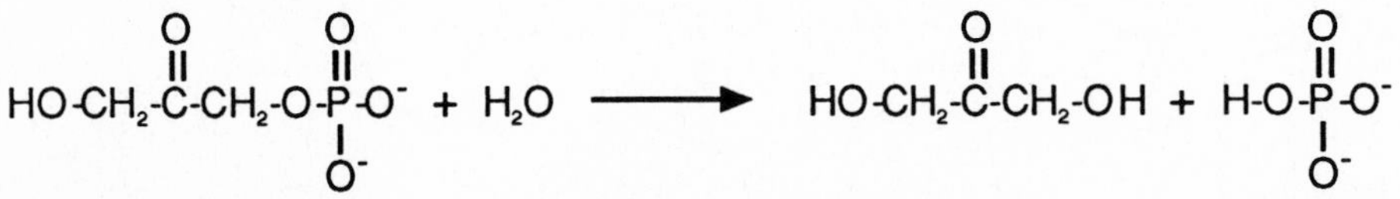

17.54 In order to undergo a Claisen condensation reaction, an ester must have a hydrogen bonded to the carbon atom next to the ester group.

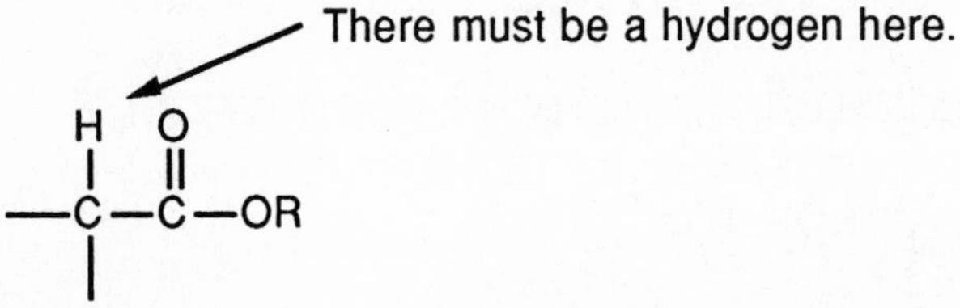

↗ There must be a hydrogen here.

$$-\overset{H}{\underset{|}{\overset{|}{C}}}-\overset{O}{\overset{\|}{C}}-OR$$

17.55 Esters (a) and (b) can't undergo Claisen condensation reactions because they have no hydrogen atoms bonded to the carbon next to the ester group (Problem 17.54).

(a)

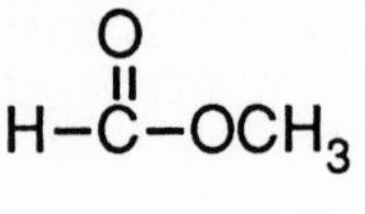

$$H-\overset{O}{\overset{\|}{C}}-OCH_3$$

(b)

$$H_3C-\overset{H_3C}{\underset{H_3C}{\overset{|}{C}}}-\overset{O}{\overset{\|}{C}}-OCH_3$$

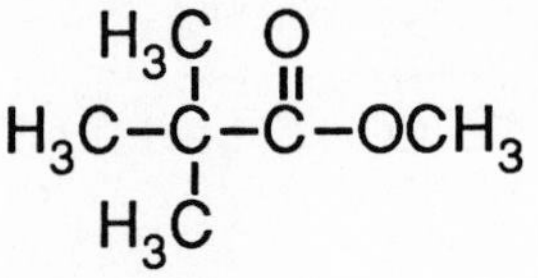

Ester (c) *does* undergo a Claisen condensation reaction:

$$CH_3CH_2\overset{O}{\overset{\|}{C}}\overset{\text{---}}{\overset{\frown}{\underset{\smile}{}}}O\overset{CH_3}{\underset{CH_3}{\overset{|}{C}}}CH_3 \ + \ H\overset{\frown}{\text{---}}CH\overset{O}{\overset{\|}{C}}\text{-}O\overset{CH_3}{\underset{CH_3}{\overset{|}{C}}}CH_3$$

$$\Big\downarrow \ NaOCH_3$$

$$CH_3CH_2\overset{O}{\overset{\|}{C}}-\overset{CH_3}{\underset{CH_3}{\overset{|}{C}}}H\overset{O}{\overset{\|}{C}}\text{-}O\overset{CH_3}{\underset{CH_3}{\overset{|}{C}}}CH_3 \ + \ H\text{-}O\overset{CH_3}{\underset{CH_3}{\overset{|}{C}}}CH_3$$

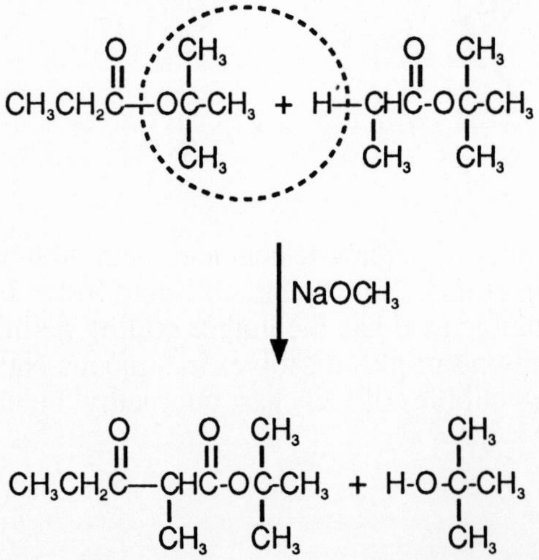

17.56

(a)

$$CH_3CHCH_2\overset{O}{\overset{\|}{C}}\!-\!\widetilde{OCH_3} + \widetilde{H}\!-\!CH\overset{O}{\overset{\|}{C}}\!-\!OCH_3 \xrightarrow{\;NaOCH_3\;} CH_3CHCH_2\overset{O}{\overset{\|}{C}}\!-\!CH\overset{O}{\overset{\|}{C}}\!-\!OCH_3 + CH_3OH$$
$$\underset{CH_3}{|}\qquad\qquad\underset{CH(CH_3)_2}{|}\qquad\qquad\qquad\underset{CH_3}{|}\qquad\underset{CH(CH_3)_2}{|}$$

(b)

$$CH_3\overset{O}{\overset{\|}{C}}\!-\!\widetilde{OCHCH_3} + \widetilde{H}\!-\!CH_2\overset{O}{\overset{\|}{C}}\!-\!OCHCH_3 \xrightarrow{\;NaOCH_3\;} CH_3\overset{O}{\overset{\|}{C}}\!-\!CH_2\overset{O}{\overset{\|}{C}}\!-\!OCHCH_3 + CH_3CHOH$$
$$\qquad\underset{CH_3}{|}\qquad\qquad\qquad\underset{CH_3}{|}\qquad\qquad\qquad\qquad\underset{CH_3}{|}\qquad\underset{CH_3}{|}$$

Isopropyl acetate

17.57 Four products are formed when a mixture of methyl acetate and methyl propanoate are treated with sodium methoxide. Two products result from self-condensation, and two products result from a "crossed" condensation of methyl acetate with methyl propanoate.

$$CH_3\overset{O}{\overset{\|}{C}}\!-\!\widetilde{OCH_3} + \widetilde{H}\!-\!CH_2\overset{O}{\overset{\|}{C}}\!-\!OCH_3 \xrightarrow{\;NaOCH_3\;} CH_3\overset{O}{\overset{\|}{C}}\!-\!CH_2\overset{O}{\overset{\|}{C}}\!-\!OCH_3 + CH_3OH$$

Methyl acetate + methyl acetate

$$CH_3CH_2\overset{O}{\overset{\|}{C}}\!-\!\widetilde{OCH_3} + \widetilde{H}\!-\!CH\overset{O}{\overset{\|}{C}}\!-\!OCH_3 \xrightarrow{\;NaOCH_3\;} CH_3CH_2\overset{O}{\overset{\|}{C}}\!-\!CH\overset{O}{\overset{\|}{C}}\!-\!OCH_3 + CH_3OH$$
$$\qquad\qquad\qquad\underset{CH_3}{|}\qquad\qquad\qquad\qquad\underset{CH_3}{|}$$

Methyl propanoate + methyl propanoate

$$CH_3\overset{O}{\overset{\|}{C}}\!-\!\widetilde{OCH_3} + \widetilde{H}\!-\!CH\overset{O}{\overset{\|}{C}}\!-\!OCH_3 \xrightarrow{\;NaOCH_3\;} CH_3\overset{O}{\overset{\|}{C}}\!-\!CH\overset{O}{\overset{\|}{C}}\!-\!OCH_3 + CH_3OH$$
$$\qquad\qquad\qquad\underset{CH_3}{|}\qquad\qquad\qquad\qquad\underset{CH_3}{|}$$

Methyl acetate + methyl propanoate

$$CH_3CH_2\overset{O}{\overset{\|}{C}}\!-\!\widetilde{OCH_3} + \widetilde{H}\!-\!CH_2\overset{O}{\overset{\|}{C}}\!-\!OCH_3 \xrightarrow{\;NaOCH_3\;} CH_3CH_2\overset{O}{\overset{\|}{C}}\!-\!CH_2\overset{O}{\overset{\|}{C}}\!-\!OCH_3 + CH_3OH$$

Methyl propanoate + methyl acetate

17.58

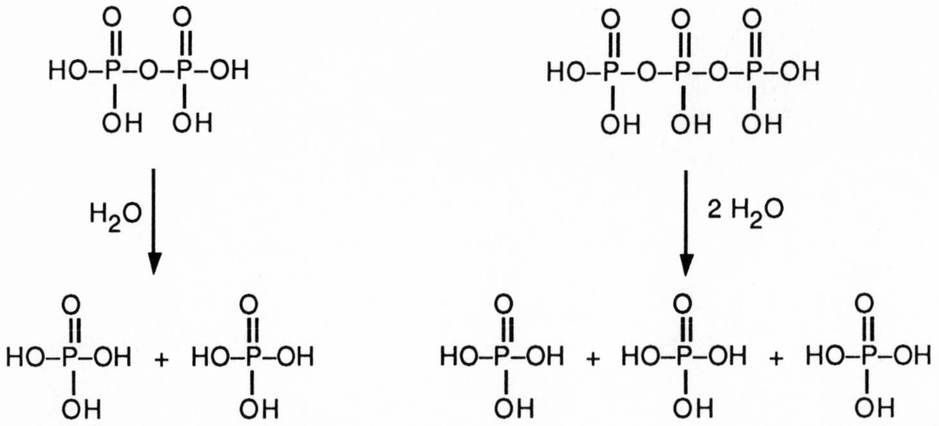

Both pyrophosphoric acid and triphosphoric acid are acid anhydrides because hydrolysis produces two or three acid molecules.

17.59

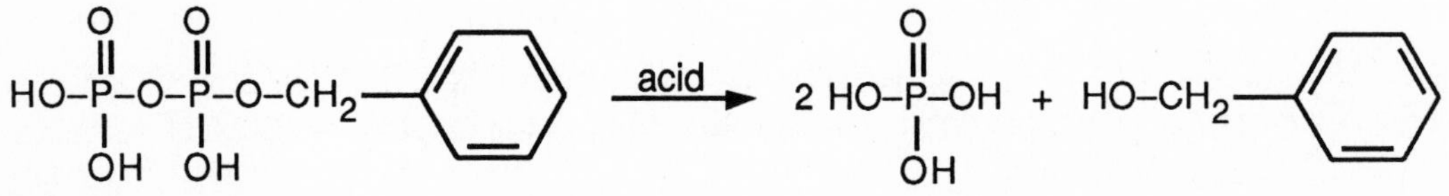

17.60 (a)

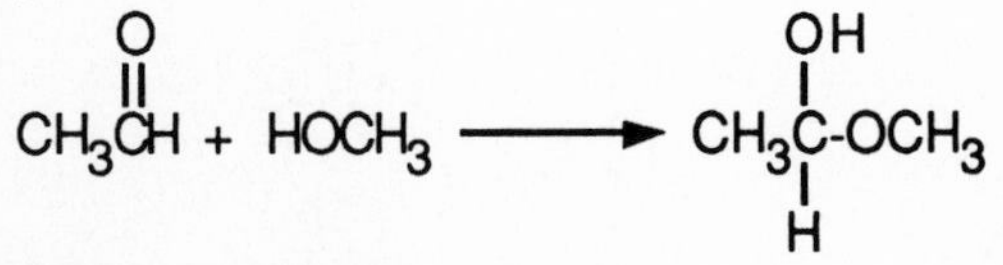

This is an addition reaction.

(b)

$CH_3CH{=}CH_2 + HCl \longrightarrow CH_3CHClCH_3$

This is an addition reaction.

(c)

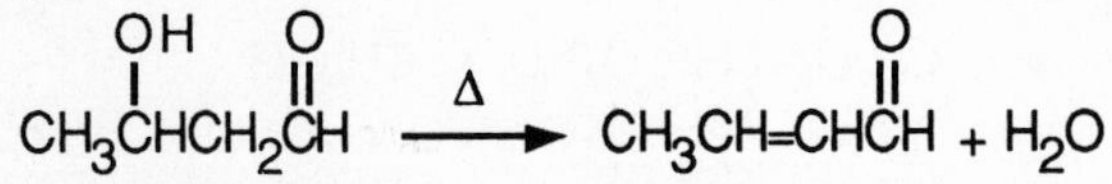

This is an elimination reaction.

17.61

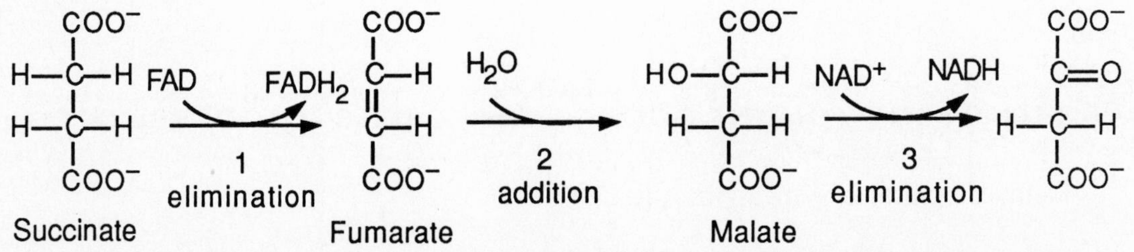

In reaction 1, H_2 is eliminated to produce a double bond. In 2, water is added to the double bond. In 3, an alcohol is oxidized to a ketone.

17.62 Sodium benzoate prevents the growth of microorganisms in acidic food. Potassium sorbate inhibits the growth of molds and fungus.

17.63 A thiol ester has the general formula

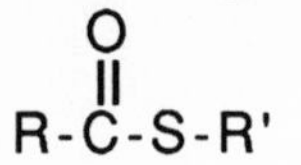

$$\underset{R-C-S-R'}{\overset{\overset{\displaystyle O}{\|}}{}}$$

17.64

17.65

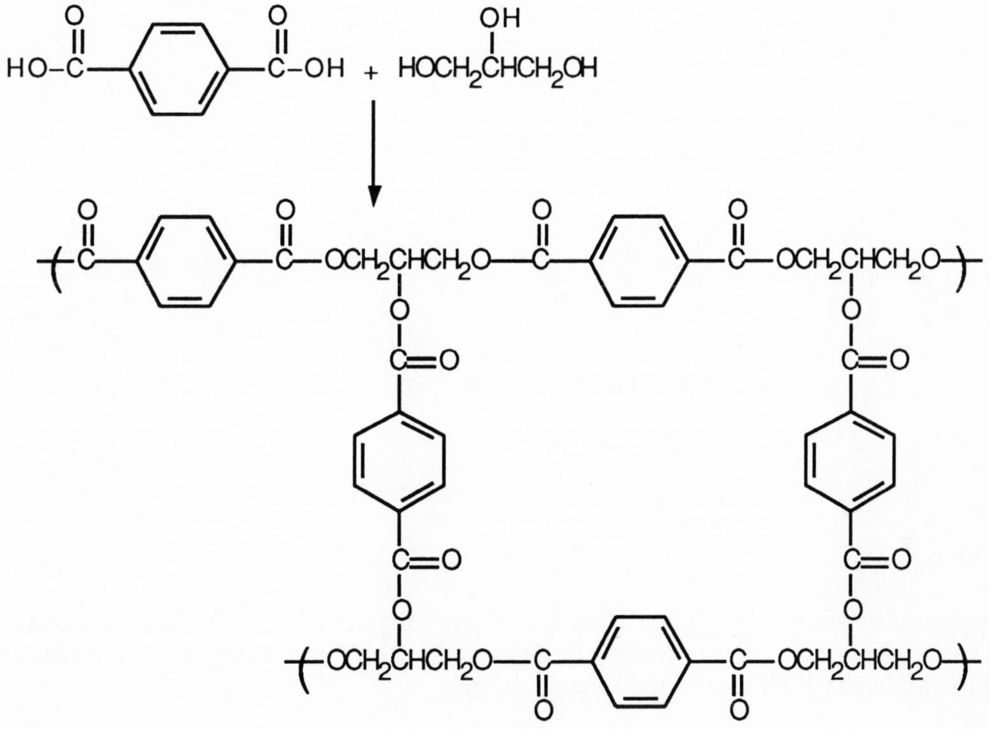

17.66

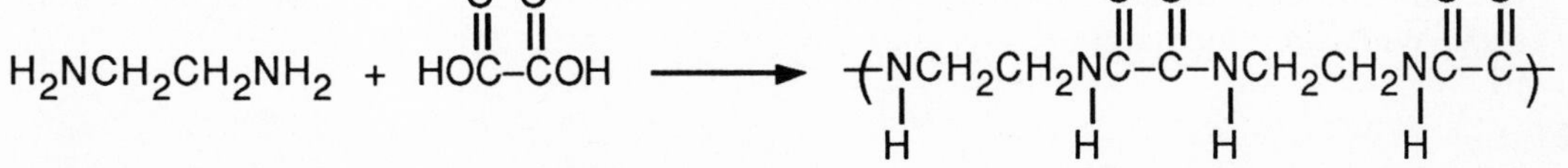

17.67

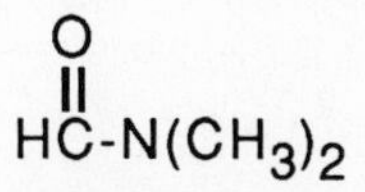

$$\underset{HC-N(CH_3)_2}{\overset{\overset{\displaystyle O}{\|}}{}} \qquad \underset{CH_3C-NHCH_3}{\overset{\overset{\displaystyle O}{\|}}{}} \qquad \underset{CH_3CH_2C-NH_2}{\overset{\overset{\displaystyle O}{\|}}{}}$$

N,N -Dimethylformamide   *N* -Methylacetamide   Propanamide

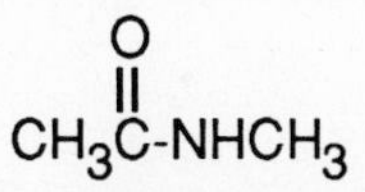

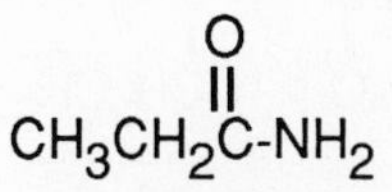

A   B   C

A is the lowest boiling isomer. Since no hydrogens are bonded to nitrogen, no hydrogen bonding between molecules of A can take place. Hydrogen bonding can occur between molecules of B, and thus B is higher boiling than A. C is the highest boiling isomer because two hydrogens are bonded to nitrogen, and thus the most hydrogen bonding occurs between molecules of C.

17.68

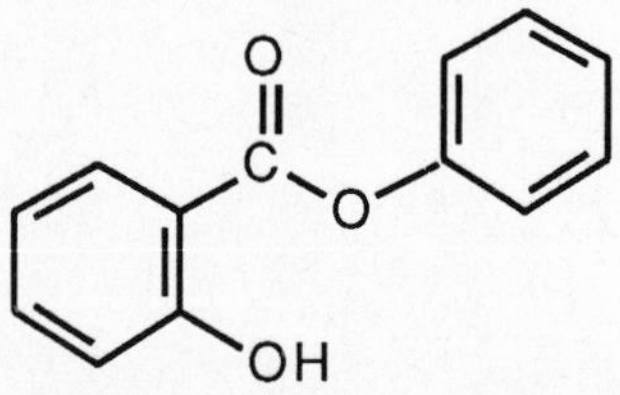

Salol (Phenyl salicylate)

17.69

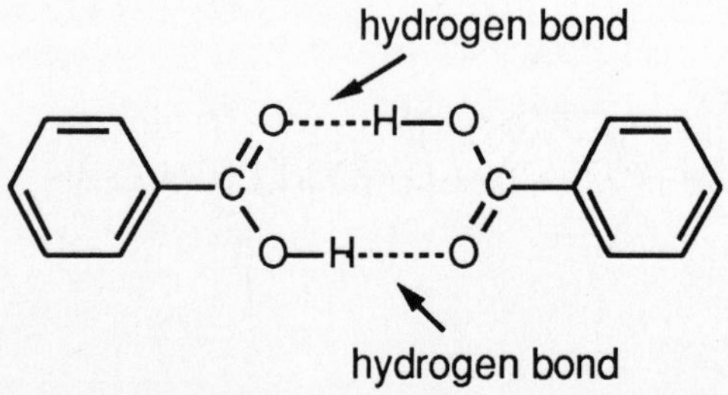

17.70

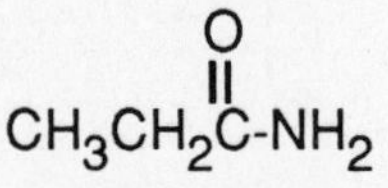

Propanamide

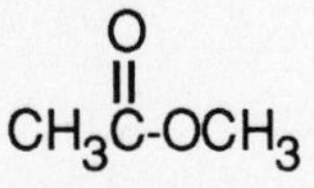

Methyl acetate

Propanamide and methyl acetate are both soluble in water because both are polar molecules and can hydrogen bond with water. Propanamide is higher boiling because molecules of propanamide can hydrogen-bond to each other.

17.71 (1) Benzoic acid has an acidic pH; benzaldehyde is non-acidic.
(2) Benzaldehyde reacts with Tollens' reagent to form a silver mirror; benzoic acid doesn't react with Tollens' reagent.

17.72

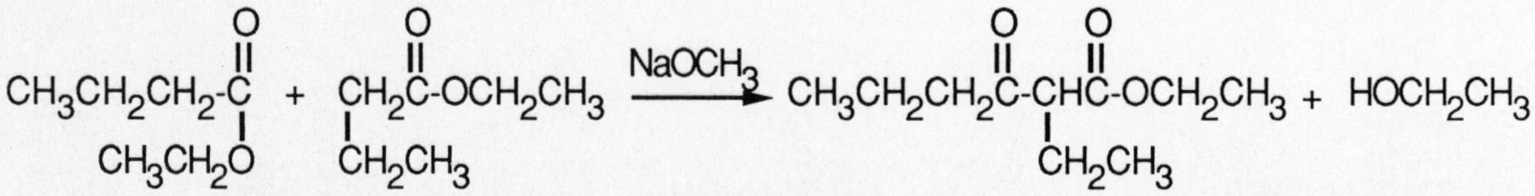

17.73

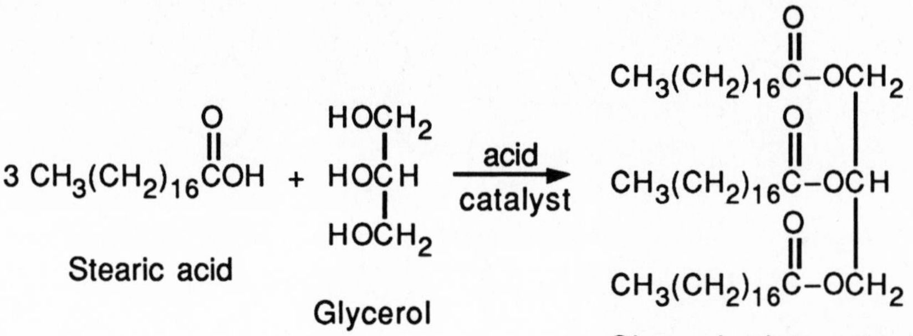

$$3 \ CH_3(CH_2)_{16}\overset{\displaystyle O}{\overset{\|}{C}}OH \ + \ \begin{matrix} HOCH_2 \\ HOCH \\ HOCH_2 \end{matrix} \xrightarrow[\text{catalyst}]{\text{acid}}$$

Stearic acid

Glycerol

$$\begin{matrix} CH_3(CH_2)_{16}\overset{\displaystyle O}{\overset{\|}{C}}-OCH_2 \\ CH_3(CH_2)_{16}\overset{\displaystyle O}{\overset{\|}{C}}-OCH \\ CH_3(CH_2)_{16}\overset{\displaystyle O}{\overset{\|}{C}}-OCH_2 \end{matrix}$$

Glyceryl tristearate

17.74

(a)

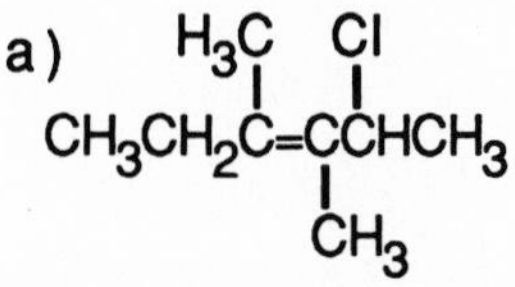

$$CH_3CH_2\overset{\displaystyle H_3C}{\underset{\displaystyle CH_3}{C}}=\overset{\displaystyle Cl}{C}CHCH_3$$

2-Chloro-3,4-dimethyl-3-hexene

(b)

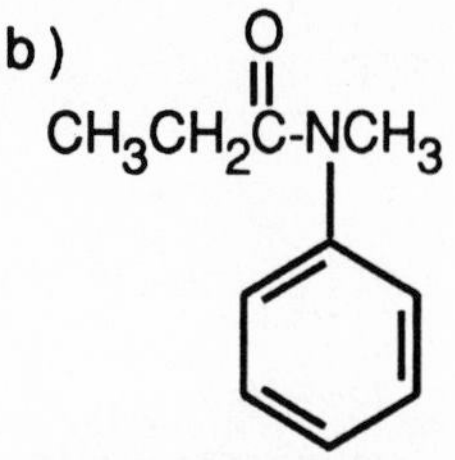

$$CH_3CH_2\overset{\displaystyle O}{\overset{\|}{C}}-NCH_3$$

N -Methyl-N -phenylpropanamide

(c)

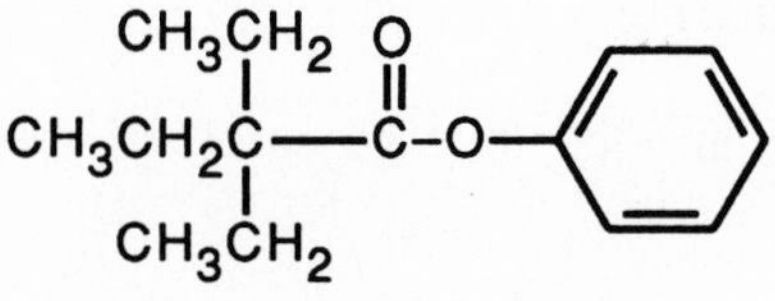

$$CH_3CH_2\overset{\displaystyle CH_3CH_2}{\underset{\displaystyle CH_3CH_2}{C}}-\overset{\displaystyle O}{\overset{\|}{C}}-O-$$

Phenyl 2,2-diethylbutanoate

(d)

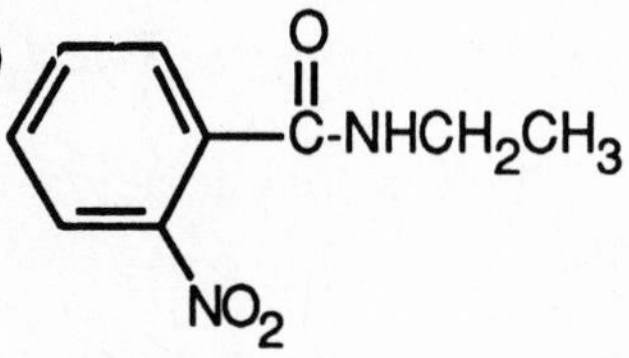

$$\overset{\displaystyle O}{\overset{\|}{C}}-NHCH_2CH_3$$

NO_2

N -Ethyl-o -nitrobenzamide

17.75 (a)

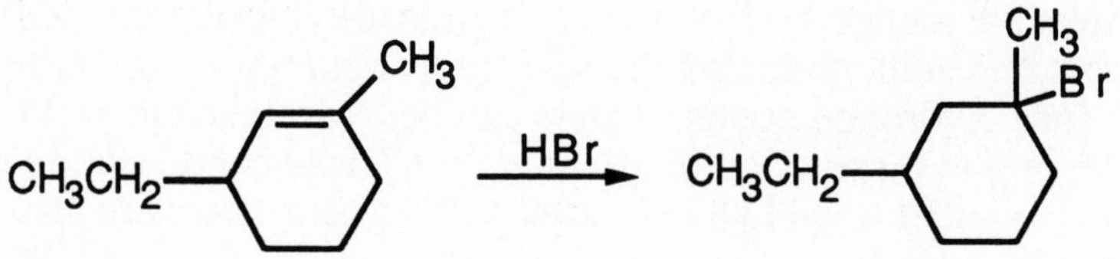

$$CH_3CH_2-\underset{}{\overset{CH_3}{\bigcirc}} \xrightarrow{\text{HBr}} CH_3CH_2-\underset{}{\overset{CH_3}{\underset{Br}{\bigcirc}}}$$

(b)

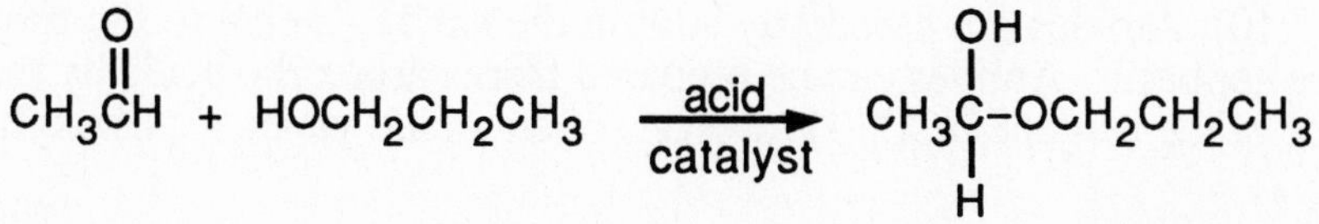

$$CH_3\overset{\displaystyle O}{\overset{\|}{C}}H \ + \ HOCH_2CH_2CH_3 \xrightarrow[\text{catalyst}]{\text{acid}} CH_3\overset{\displaystyle OH}{\underset{\displaystyle H}{C}}-OCH_2CH_2CH_3 \quad \text{(hemiacetal)}$$

(c)

$$CH_3CH_2\overset{\displaystyle O}{\overset{\|}{C}}-O\overset{\displaystyle CH_3}{C}HCH_3 + H_2O \xrightarrow{H_2SO_4} CH_3CH_2\overset{\displaystyle O}{\overset{\|}{C}}OH + HO\overset{\displaystyle CH_3}{C}HCH_3$$

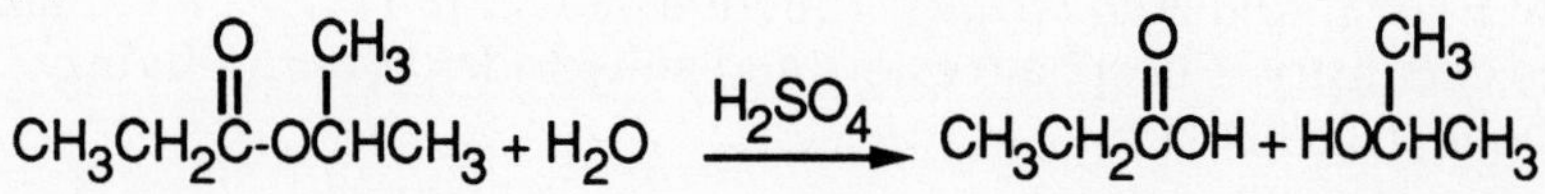

(d)

(e)

$$2 \ CH_3CH_2\overset{\overset{\displaystyle O}{\|}}{C}CH_2CH_3 \ \xrightarrow{NaOH} \ CH_3CH_2\underset{\underset{\displaystyle CH_3CH_2}{|}}{\overset{\overset{\displaystyle OH}{|}}{C}}\!\!-\!\!\underset{\underset{\displaystyle CH_3}{|}}{CH}\overset{\overset{\displaystyle O}{\|}}{C}CH_2CH_3$$

(f)

$$CH_3CH_2CCl_2\overset{\overset{\displaystyle O}{\|}}{C}H \ \xrightarrow{[O]} \ CH_3CH_2CCl_2\overset{\overset{\displaystyle O}{\|}}{C}\!-\!OH$$

(g)

$$CH_3CH_2\overset{\overset{\displaystyle O}{\|}}{C}C(CH_3)_3 \ \xrightarrow[H_3O^+]{NaBH_4} \ CH_3CH_2\overset{\overset{\displaystyle OH}{|}}{C}HC(CH_3)_3$$

The Chapter in Brief

Overview (Section 17.1) Carboxylic acids, esters, and amides undergo carbonyl-group substitution reactions.

Carboxylic Acids (Sections 17.2–17.5) Carboxylic acids are named by adding the suffix *-oic acid* to the root name. Carboxylic acids are high-boiling, and some are soluble in water. The most important reaction of acids is their conversion into esters.

Esters (Sections 17.6–17.8) Esters are named by first specifying the alkyl group bonded to oxygen and then naming the carboxylic acid, replacing the suffix *-oic acid* with *-ate*. Esters are relatively low-boiling, and don't form hydrogen bonds. Esters can be hydrolyzed to yield carboxylic acids and alcohols. An important reaction of esters is the Claisen condensation reaction in which two ester molecules bond together to yield a keto ester. Phosphate esters are also biologically important.

Amides (Sections 17.9, 17.10) Amides are named by adding the suffix *-amide* to the root name. Amides, unlike amines, are nonbasic. Amides can be prepared from carboxylic acids by reaction with amines in the presence of the reagent DCC. Hydrolysis of an amide yields a carboxylic acid and an amine.

Acid Anhydrides, Phosphate Esters, and Anhydrides (Sections 17.111, 17.12) Acid anhydrides are useful reagents in organic chemistry. Phosphate esters and anhydrides occur in living organisms and are key metabolic intermediates.

Organic Reactions (Section 17.13) Addition reactions, elimination reactions, and substitution reactions are three important organic reaction types that occur in living organisms.

Self-Test for Chapter 17

Complete the following sentences:

1. The most common general reaction of carboxylic acids, esters, and amides is called a _____ _____ reaction.

2. Two carboxylic acids can hydrogen bond to each other to form a _____.

3. A carboxylic acid can be dissolved in water by converting it into its _____.

4. The reaction of a carboxylic acid with an alcohol in the presence of an acid catalyst is called an _____ reaction.

5. In carboxylic acids, esters, and amides, the carbonyl-group carbon is bonded to an atom that strongly _____ electrons.

6. Carboxylic acids are named by using the family-name ending _____.

7. $CH_3CH_2COOCH_2CH_2CH_3$ is named _____ _____.

8. Many flavors and fragrances are due to _____.

9. Keto-esters are formed by the _____ _____ reaction.

10. Long-chain carboxylic acids can be found in nature as components of _____.

11. The reaction of an ester with aqueous NaOH to yield a salt and an alcohol is called a _____ reaction.

12. Malonic acid is also known as _____ acid.

Tell whether the following statements are true or false:

1. A carboxylic acid salt is more soluble in water than a carboxylic acid.

2. A *saponification* reaction is the acid-catalyzed hydrolysis of an ester.

3. Amides and amines are both basic.

4. A carboxylic acid is higher boiling than an ester of the same molecular weight.

5. The reagent DCC is used in amide formation.

6. The compound $HCON(CH_3)_2$ is named dimethylformamide.

7. Nitrate esters are important in living systems.

8. Acetic acid is about 1% dissociated in a 1 M aqueous solution.

9. Carboxylic acids are either solids or liquids at room temperature.

10. Esterification can be brought about by treating a carboxylic acid with an alcohol in the presence of NaOH.

11. Pyrophosphoric acid is an phosphate ester.

12. Propanamide is higher boiling than methyl acetate.

Match the entries on the left with their partners on the right:

1. $CH_3COOH + CH_3OH + HCl$ (a) Amide hydrolysis

2. $2 CH_3COOCH_3 + NaOCH_3$ (b) Ester hydrolysis

3. $(CH_3COO^-)Mg^{2+}$ (c) Thioester

4. $CH_3COOCH_3 + NaOH, H_2O$ (d) Used for amide formation

5. $HCOOH$ (e) Phosphate ester

6. DCC   (f) Claisen condensation

7. $CH_3CONH_2 + NaOH, H_2O$ (g) Acid anhydride

8. CH_3OPO_3H (h) Polyester

9. Nitroglycerine   (i) Formic acid

10. Dacron   (j) Ester formation

11. Acetyl SCoA   (k) Acid salt

12. $CH_3COOCOCH_3$ (l) Nitrate ester

Chapter 18 – Amino Acids and Proteins

18.1 Amino acids containing an aromatic ring: phenylalanine, tyrosine, tryptophan

Amino acids containing sulfur: cysteine, methionine

Amino acids that are alcohols: serine, threonine, tyrosine (a phenol)

Amino acids with hydrocarbon side chains: alanine, leucine, isoleucine valine

18.2

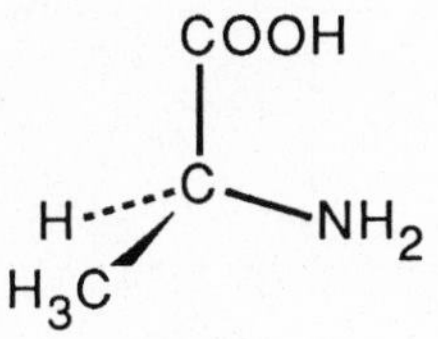

Alanine

18.3

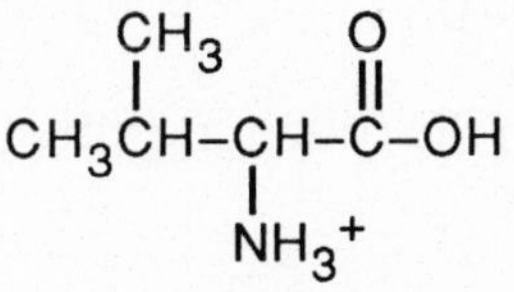

At low pH

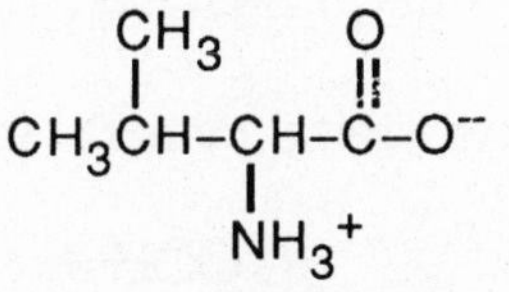

At isoelectric point

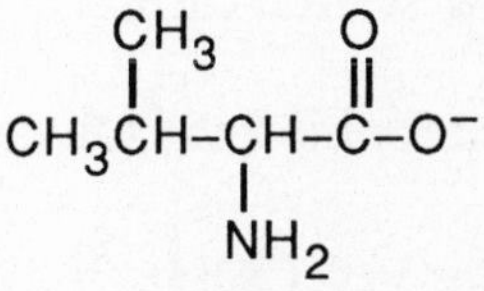

At high pH

18.4

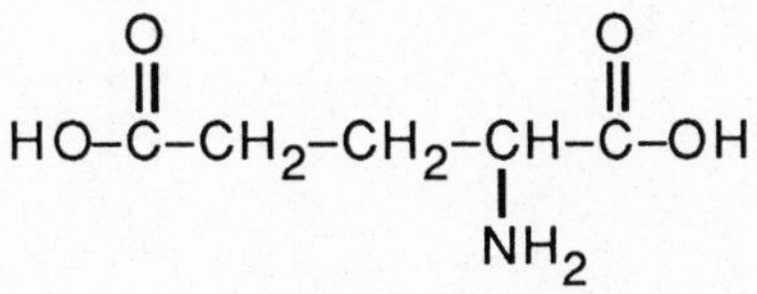

Glutamic acid

Glutamic acid is hydrophilic because its carboxyl group can hydrogen bond with water.

18.5 Handed: (a) glove, (c) screw
Not handed: (b) baseball, (d) nail

18.6 Handed: wrench, beanstalk, bottle cap
Not handed: ruler, pencil, eraser

18.7

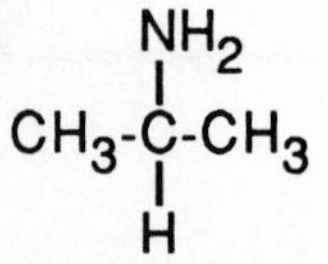

$$\underset{\text{2-Aminopropane}}{\overset{\displaystyle NH_2}{CH_3\text{-}\underset{\displaystyle H}{\overset{\displaystyle |}{\underset{|}{C}}}\text{-}CH_3}} \qquad \underset{\text{2-Aminobutane}}{\overset{\displaystyle NH_2}{CH_3CH_2\text{-}\underset{\displaystyle H}{\overset{\displaystyle *|}{\underset{|}{C}}}\text{-}CH_3}}$$

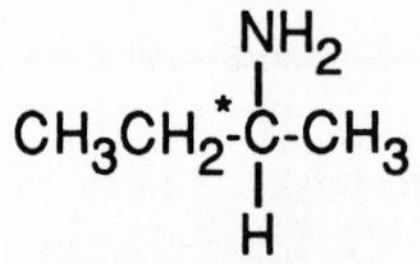

2-Aminopropane is achiral because no carbon has four different groups bonded to it. 2-Butanol is chiral because four different groups are bonded to carbon 2 (–H, –CH$_3$, –NH$_2$ and –CH$_2$CH$_3$).

18.8

(a) 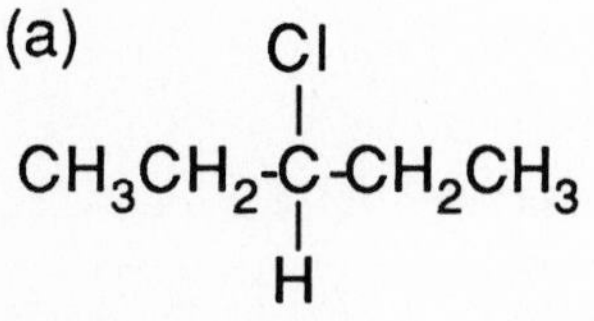
$$\underset{\text{achiral}}{\overset{\displaystyle Cl}{CH_3CH_2\text{-}\underset{\displaystyle H}{\overset{\displaystyle |}{\underset{|}{C}}}\text{-}CH_2CH_3}}$$

(b)
$$\underset{\text{chiral}}{\overset{\displaystyle Cl}{CH_3CH_2CH_2\text{-}\underset{\displaystyle H}{\overset{\displaystyle *|}{\underset{|}{C}}}\text{-}CH_3}}$$

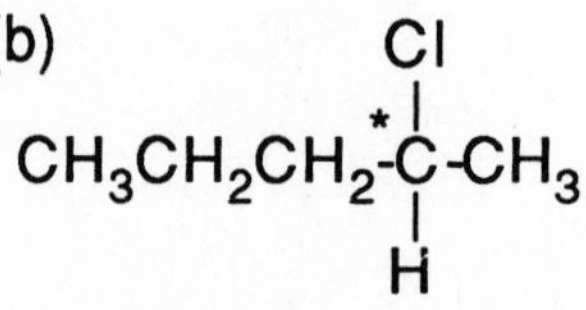

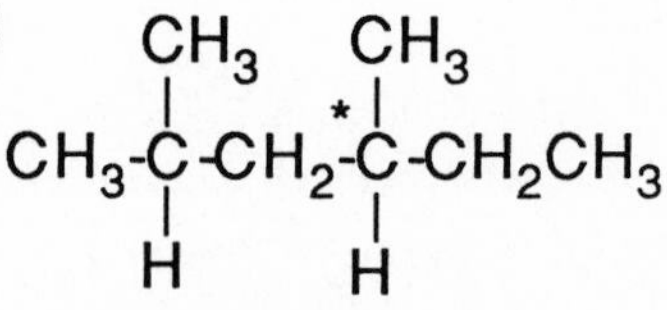

(c)
$$\underset{\text{chiral}}{\overset{\displaystyle CH_3 \quad CH_3}{CH_3\text{-}\underset{\displaystyle H}{\overset{\displaystyle |}{\underset{|}{C}}}\text{-}CH_2\text{-}\underset{\displaystyle H}{\overset{\displaystyle *|}{\underset{|}{C}}}\text{-}CH_2CH_3}}$$

The starred carbon atoms in (b) and (c) each have four different groups bonded to them.

18.9   Threonine and isoleucine have two chiral centers (starred in the following structures).

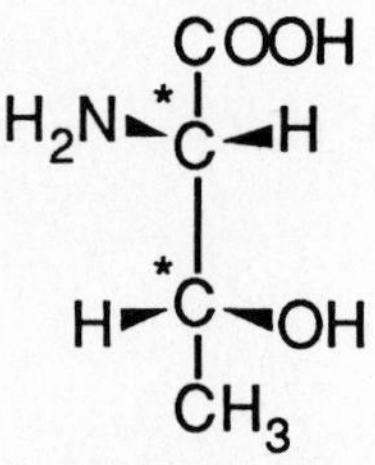

Threonine

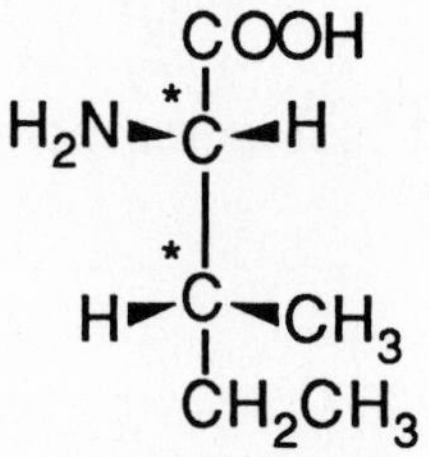

Isoleucine

18.10

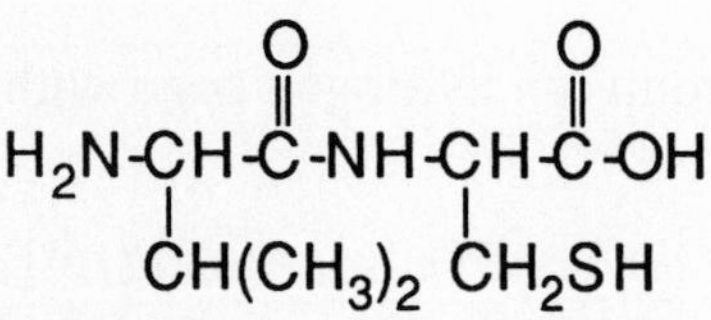

$$\underset{\underset{CH(CH_3)_2 \quad CH_2SH}{}}{H_2N\text{-}CH\text{-}\overset{\displaystyle O}{\overset{\|}{C}}\text{-}NH\text{-}CH\text{-}\overset{\displaystyle O}{\overset{\|}{C}}\text{-}OH}$$

H$_2$N-Val-Cys-COOH

$$\underset{\underset{CH_2SH \quad CH(CH_3)_2}{}}{H_2N\text{-}CH\text{-}\overset{\displaystyle O}{\overset{\|}{C}}\text{-}NH\text{-}CH\text{-}\overset{\displaystyle O}{\overset{\|}{C}}\text{-}OH}$$

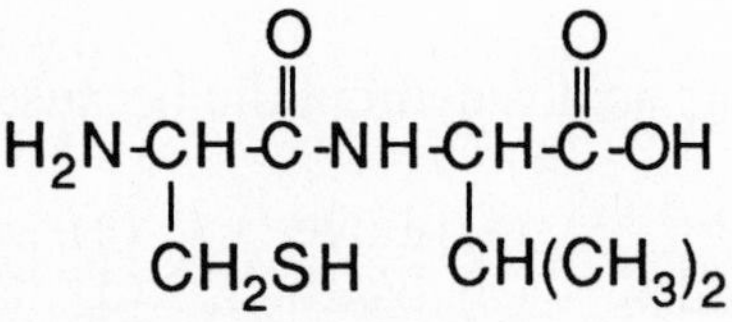

H$_2$N-Cys-Val-COOH

18.11   H$_2$N-Val-Tyr-Gly-COOH   H$_2$N-Tyr-Gly-Val-COOH
H$_2$N-Val-Gly-Tyr-COOH   H$_2$N-Gly-Tyr-Val-COOH
H$_2$N-Tyr-Val-Gly-COOH   H$_2$N-Gly-Val-Tyr-COOH

18.12

(a)

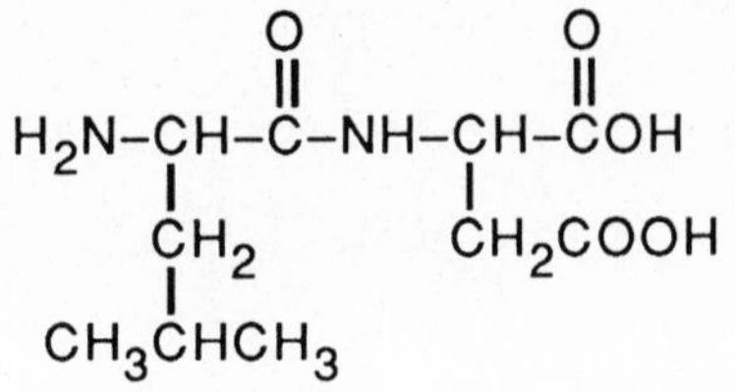

Leucine (Leu) Aspartic acid (Asp)

Leucylaspartic acid

(b)

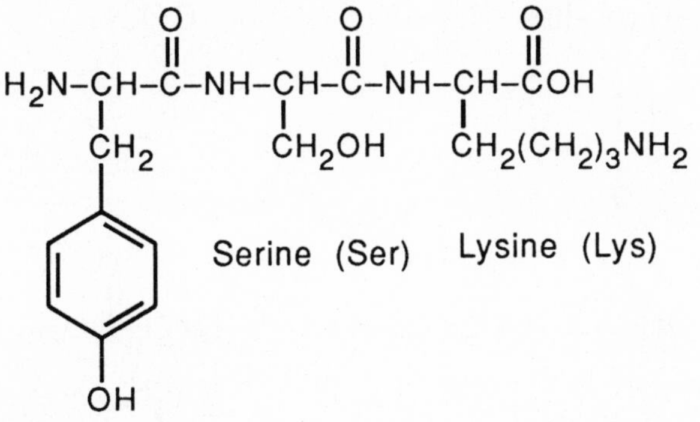

Serine (Ser) Lysine (Lys)

Tyrosine (Tyr)

Tyrosinylseryllysine

18.13

(a)

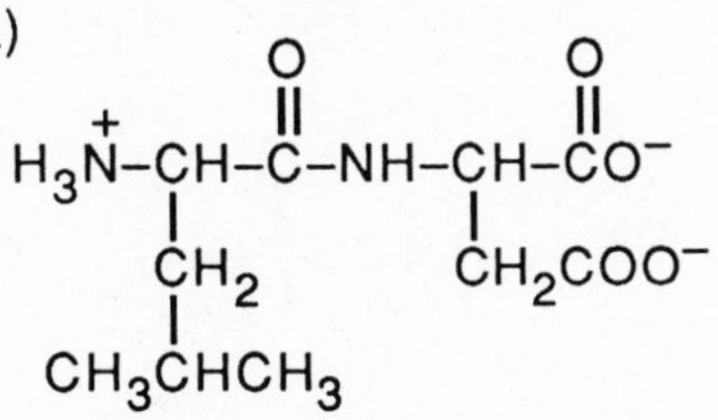

(b)

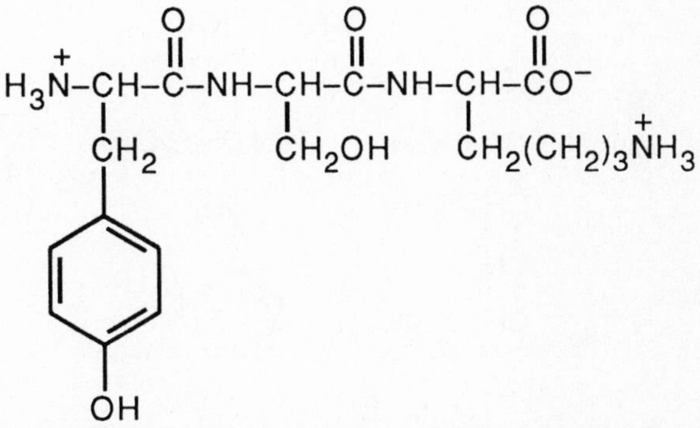

18.14 (a) Glutamine and tyrosine interact through *hydrogen bonds* between the terminal $-NH_2$ group of glutamine and the terminal -OH of tyrosine.

(b) Leucine and proline are pulled together through *hydrophobic interactions* between the alkyl side chain of leucine and the ring portion of proline.

(c) A *salt bridge* occurs between the negatively charged aspartate carboxyl group and the positively charged terminal group of arginine.

(d) The alkyl side chain of isoleucine and the aromatic ring of phenylalanine are held together by *hydrophobic interactions.*

(e) Threonine and glutamine interact through *hydrogen bonding*.

18.15

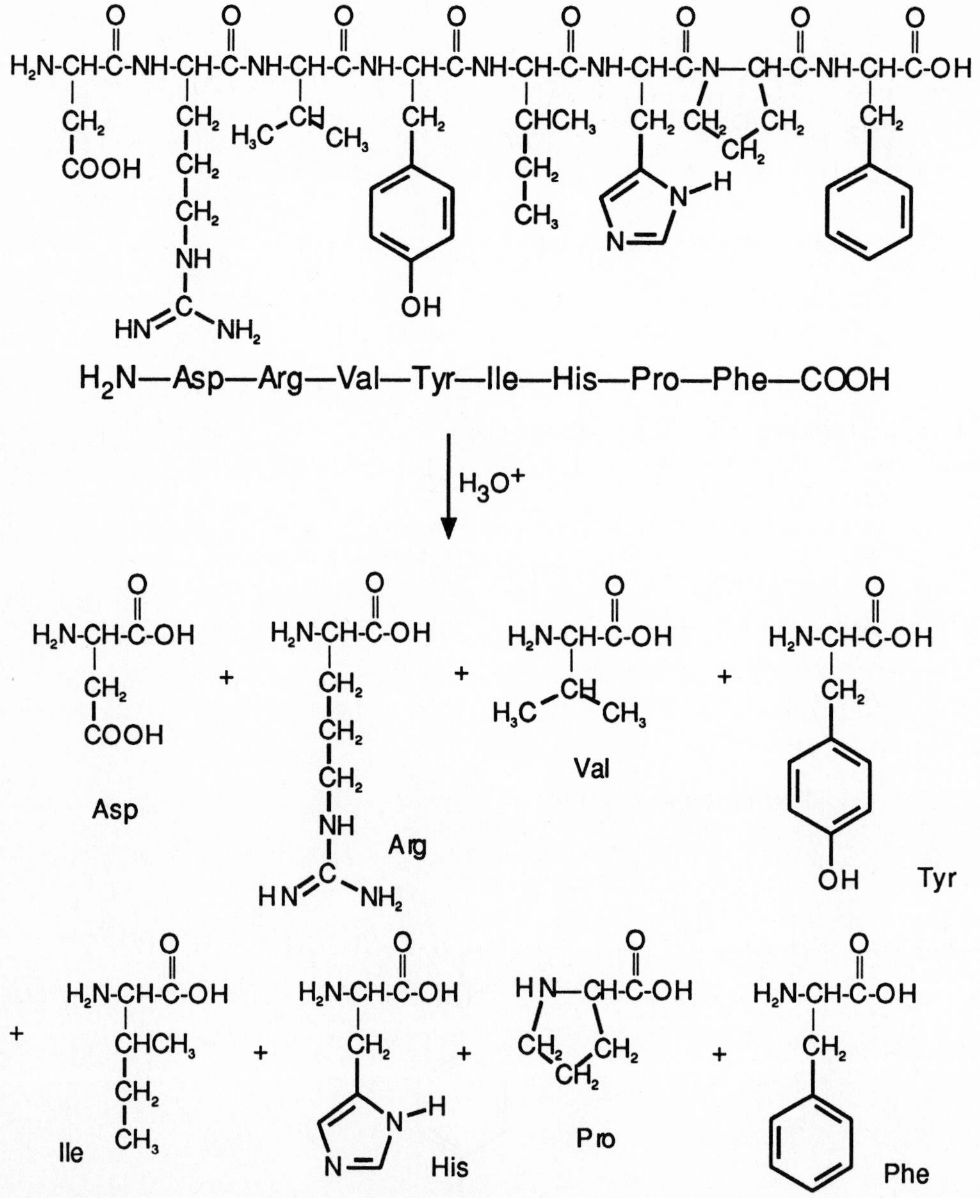

$$H_2N—Asp—Arg—Val—Tyr—Ile—His—Pro—Phe—COOH$$

$$\downarrow H_3O^+$$

Asp   Arg   Val   Tyr

Ile   His   Pro   Phe

18.16 An amino acid is a molecule that contains a carboxyl group and an amino group. Amino acids are the building blocks of proteins.

18.17 When referring to an amino acid, the prefix "α" means that the amino group is bonded to the carbon next to the -COOH carbon. In other words, the -NH₂ and -COOH groups are bonded to the same carbon.

18.18 - 18.19

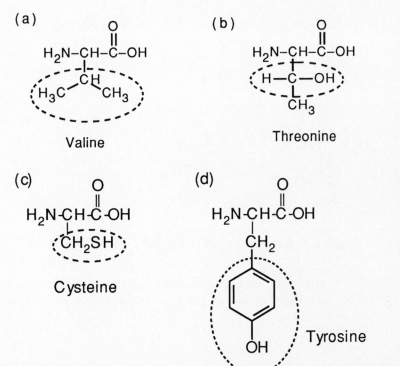

(a)

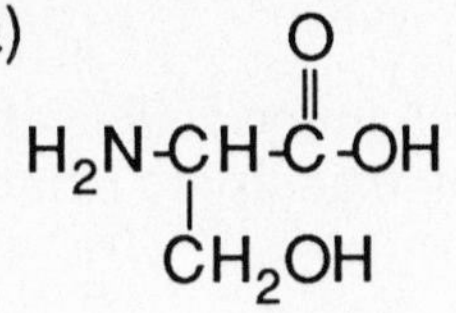

H₂N-CH-C-OH with CH_2OH side chain and C=O

Ser = serine

(b)

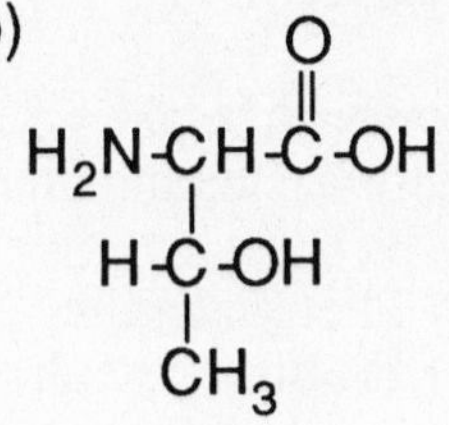

H₂N-CH-C-OH with H-C-OH, CH₃ side chain and C=O

Thr = threonine

(c)

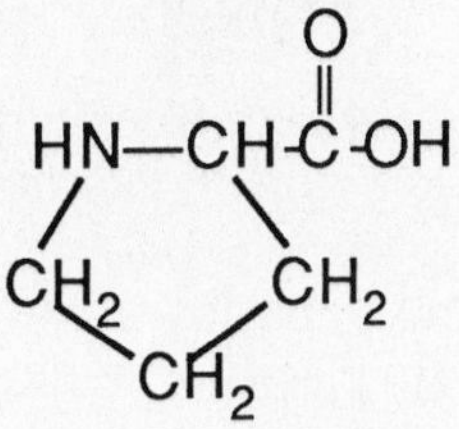

HN—CH-C-OH ring with CH₂, CH₂, CH₂ and C=O

Pro = proline

(d)

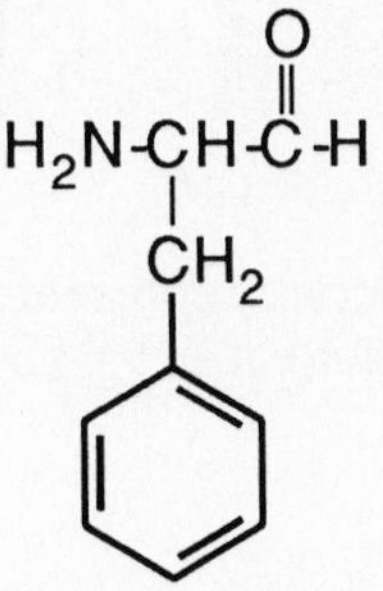

H₂N-CH-C-H with CH₂ connected to benzene ring and C=O

Phe = phenylalanine

(e)

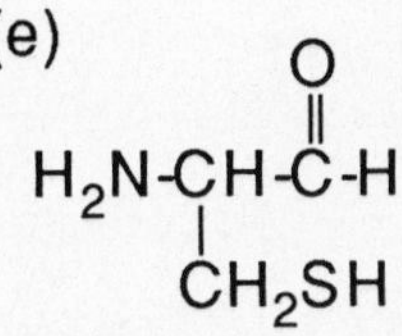

H₂N-CH-C-H with CH_2SH side chain and C=O

Cys = cysteine

18.20

(a)

H₂N-CH-C-OH with CH, H₃C, CH₃ side chain (circled) and C=O

Valine

(b)

H₂N-CH-C-OH with H—C—OH, CH₃ side chain (circled) and C=O

Threonine

(c)

H₂N-CH-C-OH with CH₂SH side chain (circled) and C=O

Cysteine

(d)

H₂N-CH-C-OH with CH₂ connected to benzene ring with OH (circled) and C=O

Tyrosine

18.21 (a) A zwitterion is a dipolar ion. Amino acids exist as zwitterions, having a positively charged $-NH_3^+$ group and a negatively charged $-COO^-$ group.

(b) An essential amino acid is one that the human body can't synthesize. For humans, there are ten essential amino acids, which must be supplied by protein-containing food.

(c) The isoelectric point of an amino acid is the pH at which the amino acid exists predominantly in its neutral dipolar form.

18.22 Amino acids with isoelectric points lower than pH = 5 are acidic; amino acids with isoelectric points higher than pH = 7 are basic; and all other amino acids are neutral.

(a) Lysine - basic   (b) Phenylalanine - neutral
(c) Glutamic acid - acidic   (d) Proline - neutral

18.23

(a)

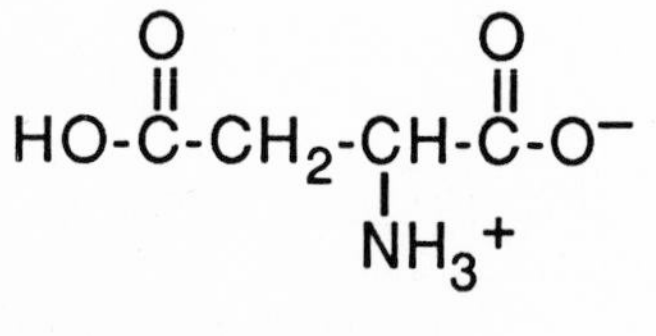

$$HO\text{-}\overset{\displaystyle O}{\overset{\|}{C}}\text{-}CH_2\text{-}\underset{\underset{NH_3^+}{|}}{CH}\text{-}\overset{\displaystyle O}{\overset{\|}{C}}\text{-}O^-$$

This structure represents aspartic acid at pH = 3, its isoelectric point.

(b)

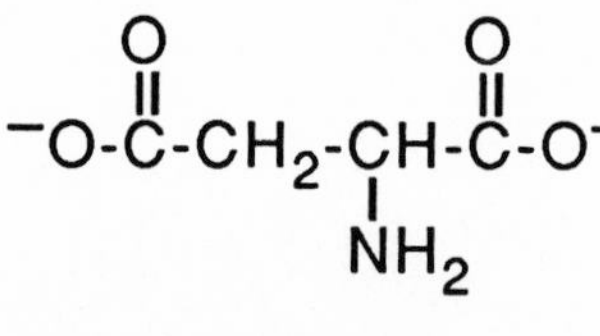

$$^-O\text{-}\overset{\displaystyle O}{\overset{\|}{C}}\text{-}CH_2\text{-}\underset{\underset{NH_2}{|}}{CH}\text{-}\overset{\displaystyle O}{\overset{\|}{C}}\text{-}O^-$$

This structure represents aspartic acid at pH = 13.

18.24 Proline:

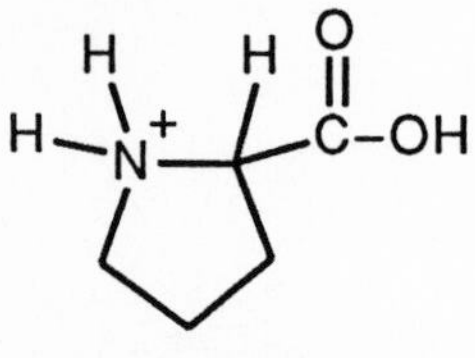

at pH = 1 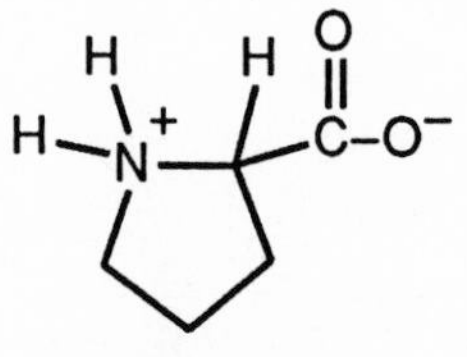   at pH = 6.3 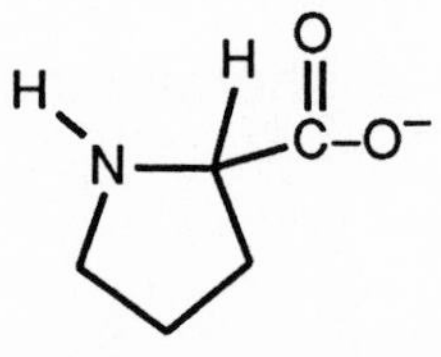   at pH = 9.7

18.25

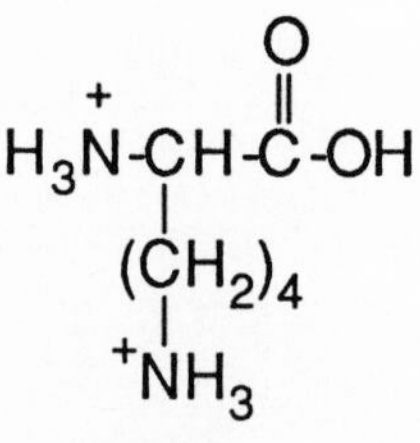

at pH = 1 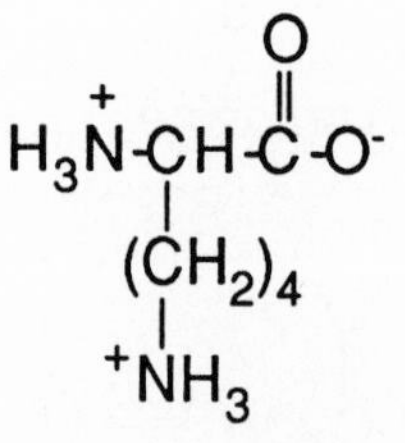   at pH = 6.3 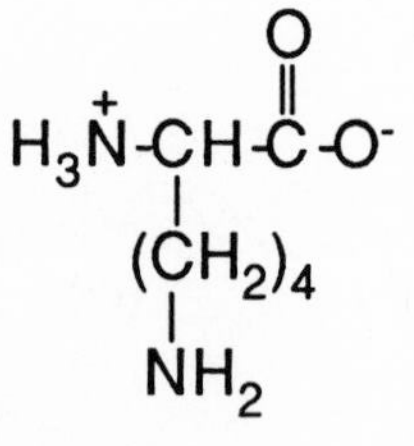   at pH = 9.7

18.26 A chiral object is one that has handedness. An achiral object has no handedness and possesses a plane of symmetry such that one half of the object is an exact mirror image of the other half.

18.27 Chiral: ear, coil
        Achiral: bottle, chair

18.28 Chiral: (a) shoe, (c) light bulb (because of screw threads), (e) house key, (f) pair of scissors
        Achiral: (b) bed, (d) flower pot

18.29 2-Bromo-2-chloropropane has a symmetry plane and is achiral, but 2-bromo-2-chlorobutane does not have a symmetry plane and is chiral.

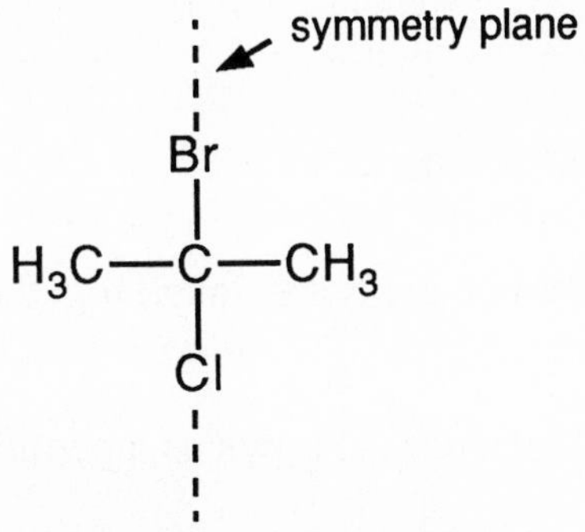

symmetry plane

Br
|
H₃C—C—CH₃
|
Cl

2-Bromo-2-chloropropane

Br
|
H₃C—C—CH₂CH₃
|
Cl

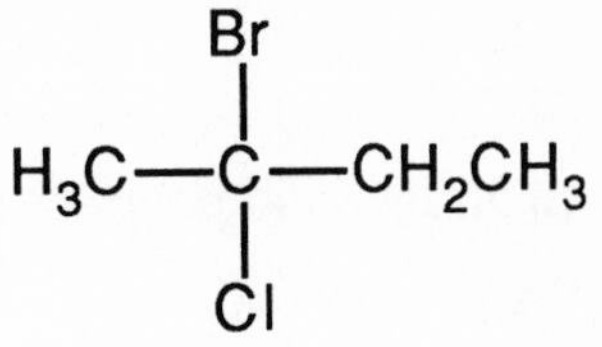

2-Bromo-2-chlorobutane

18.30 First, draw the structure and find the number of different groups bonded to each carbon. A carbon atom bonded to four different groups is chiral.

(a)

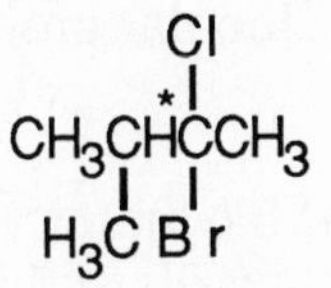

Cl
*|
CH₃CHCCH₃   **2-Bromo-2-chloro-3-methylbutane**
| |
H₃C Br

Carbon 2 is chiral because it is bonded to four different groups: -Cl, -Br, -CH₃ and -CH(CH₃)₂.

(b)

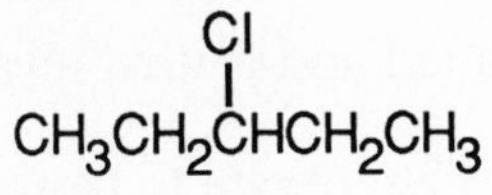

Cl
|
CH₃CH₂CHCH₂CH₃   **3-Chloropentane is achiral**

(c)

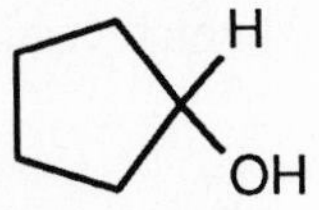

H

OH   **Cyclopentanol is achiral**

(d)

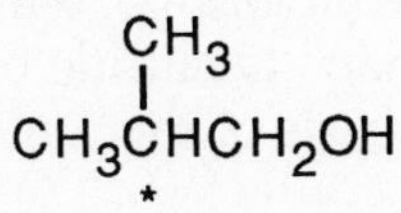

CH₃
|
CH₃CHCH₂OH   **chiral**
*

18.31 Chiral carbons are starred.

(a)   (b)

$$CH_3\overset{*}{C}HCH_2CH_3$$
$$|$$
$$F$$

18.32 A protein is an amino-acid polymer in which the amino acids are linked together by amide bonds.

18.33 A protein containing fewer than fifty amino-acid residues is known as a peptide.

18.34 A simple protein yields only amino acids upon hydrolysis with aqueous acid, whereas a conjugated protein yields other compounds in addition to amino acids on hydrolysis.

18.35 (a) Nucleoproteins contain RNA and protein.
(b) Lipoproteins contain lipids and protein.
(c) Glycoproteins contain carbohydrate and protein.

18.36 Fibrous proteins consist of polypeptide chains arranged side by side. Globular proteins are coiled into nearly spherical shapes.

18.37 Proteins have many functions in the body. Among them are catalysis of biochemical reactions, transport of substances through the body, use as structural materials and as hormones, storage of nutrients, and contraction of muscle fibers.

18.38 (a) *Primary structure* refers to the sequence of connection of amino acids.
(b) *Secondary structure* refers to the orientation of segments of the protein chain into a regular pattern such as an α helix or a β-pleated sheet.
(c) *Tertiary structure* refers to how the entire protein chain is coiled and folded into a three-dimensional shape.
(d) *Quaternary structure* refers to how several protein chains can aggregate to form a larger structure.

18.39 Hydrogen bonding is responsible for stabilizing helical and β–pleated sheet secondary protein structures.

18.40 The disulfide bridges that cysteine forms help to stabilize a protein's tertiary structure.

18.41 Two cysteine residues in a protein can cross-link by forming a disulfide bridge, which occurs when two cysteine thiol groups are oxidized to form a disulfide. Disulfide bridges can connect two different peptide chains or can connect two distant parts of the same chain, introducing a loop in the chain.

18.42 (a) *Hydrophobic interactions* occur between hydrocarbon side chains of amino acids. In a protein, these alkyl side chains cluster in the center of the molecule to exclude water, and are responsible for the nearly spherical tertiary shape of globular proteins.

(b) *Salt bridges* occur between negatively charged and positively charged amino acid side chain groups. They can stabilize the tertiary structure of a protein by connecting two distant parts of a polypeptide chain or by pulling the protein backbone together in the middle of the chain.

(c) Side chains that can form *hydrogen bonds* are located on the outside of a protein, where they can stabilize tertiary structure by forming hydrogen bonds with water. Hydrogen bonds stabilize quaternary protein structure by holding together several protein strands.

18.43 (a) Alanine and isoleucine take part in hydrophobic interactions.
(b) Lysine and aspartate can form salt bridges.
(c) Threonine and glutamine can form hydrogen bonds.

18.44 When a protein is denatured, its three-dimensional structure is disrupted and its ability to catalyze reactions is impaired.

18.45 (a) *Heat* denatures proteins by disrupting side-chain interactions.
(b) *Addition* of a *strong base* interferes with salt bridges.
(c) *Mercury ions* react with -SH groups to precipitate proteins.

18.46 The *N*-terminal amino acid in angiotensin II is aspartic acid, and the *C*-terminal amino acid is phenylalanine.

18.47 Met—Ile—Lys   Ile—Met—Lys   Lys—Met—Ile
Met—Lys—Ile   Ile—Lys—Met   Lys—Ile—Met

18.48

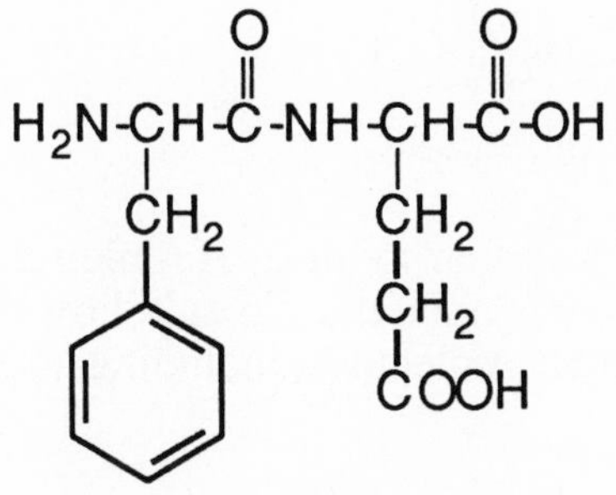

H₂N-Phe—Glu-COOH   H₂N-Glu—Phe-COOH

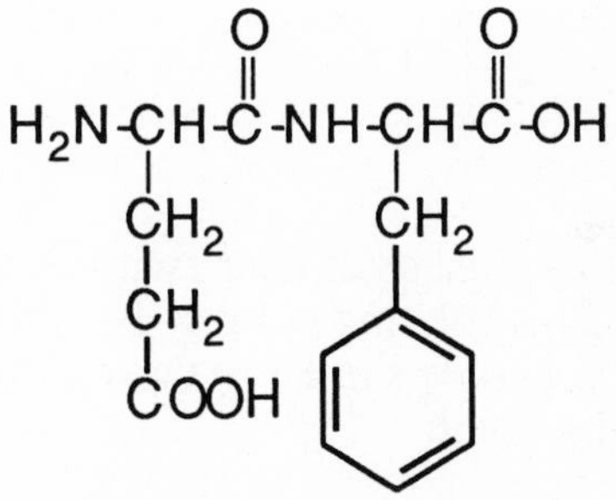

18.49 Amino acids with polar side chains (aspartic acid and asparagine, for example) are likely to be found on the outside of a globular protein, where they can be solvated by water. Amino acids with nonpolar side chains (valine and leucine, for example) are likely to be found on the inside of globular proteins, where they can escape from water.

18.50 If a diabetic took insulin orally, digestive enzymes would hydrolyze it, and the individual amino acids would be absorbed as food.

18.51 - 18.52

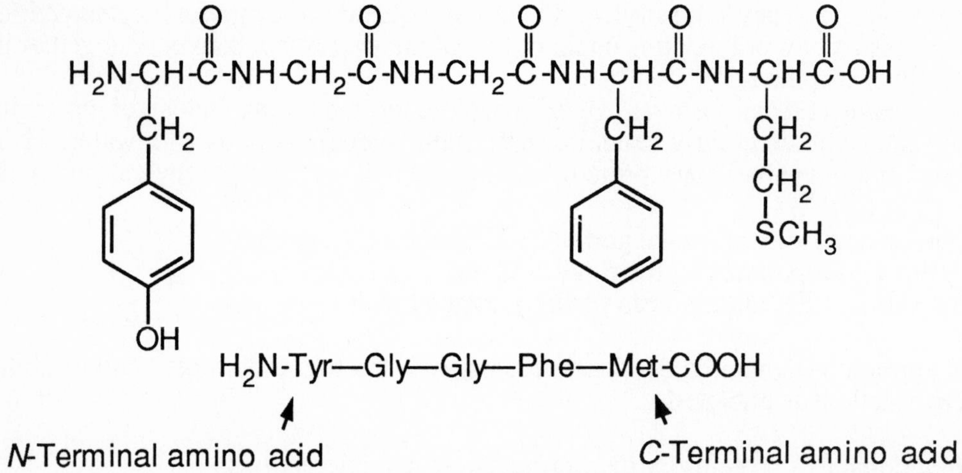

$$H_2N\text{-Tyr}—Gly—Gly—Phe—Met\text{-COOH}$$

N-Terminal amino acid   *C*-Terminal amino acid

18.53

(a)

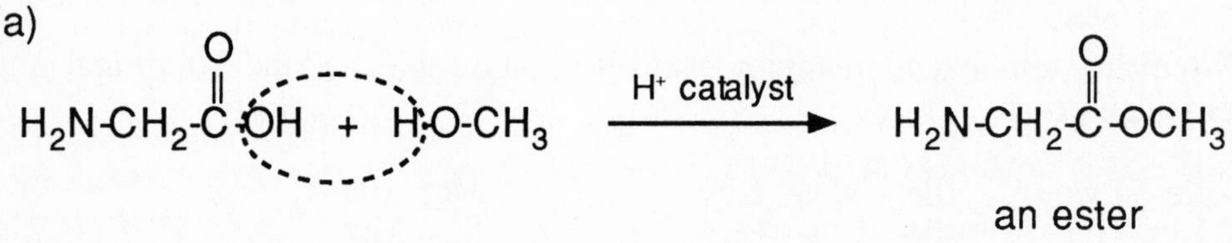

an ester

(b)

an ammonium salt

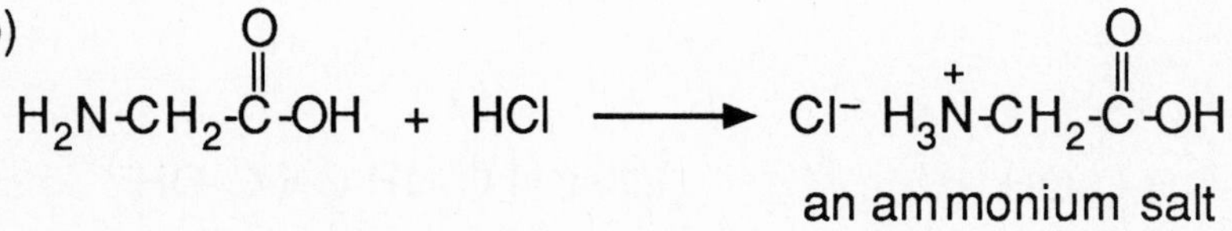

18.54 Amino acids exist as dipolar zwitterions with properties similar to those of ionic salts, including high melting points. The ethyl ester of glycine is not a dipolar salt, however, and thus has properties similar to those of other typical organic molecules, including a relatively low melting point.

18.55 Treatment of glycine with DCC produces not only glycylglycine but also glycylglycylglycine and larger polymers. In addition, reaction of glycine with DCC may yield a *cyclic* dipeptide:

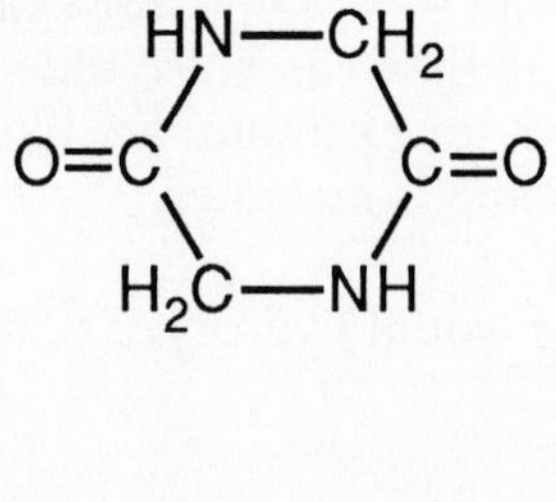

18.56

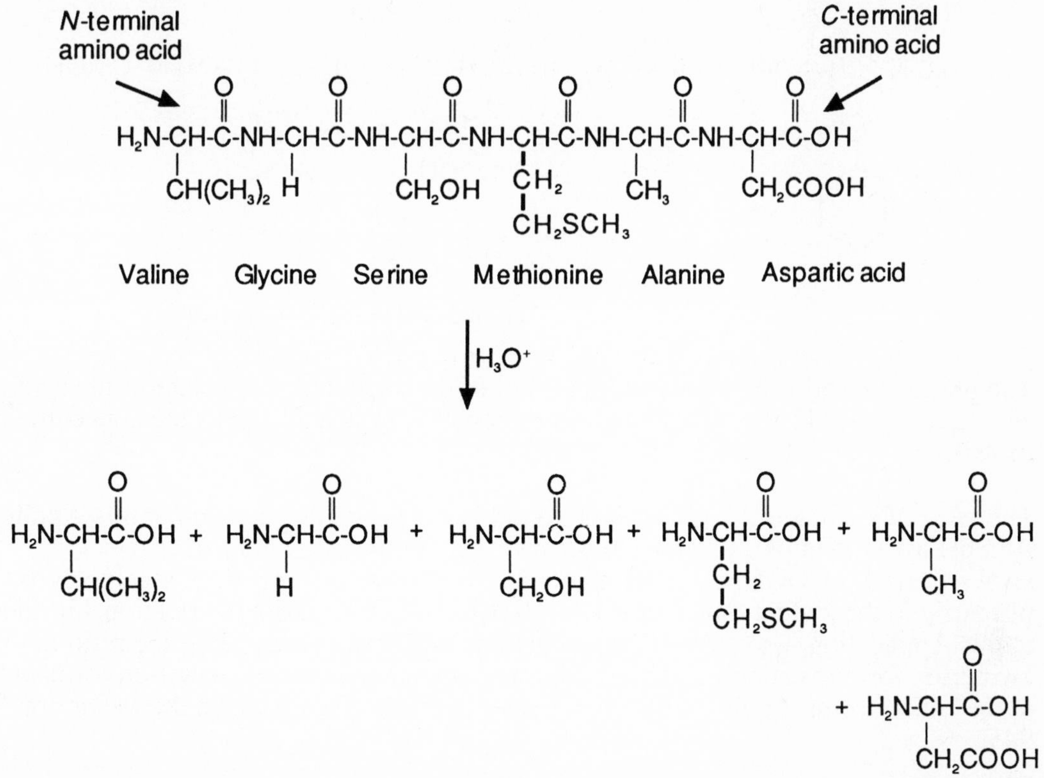

N-terminal amino acid

C-terminal amino acid

$$H_2N-CH-C-NH-CH-C-NH-CH-C-NH-CH-C-NH-CH-C-NH-CH-C-OH$$

$$\overset{|}{CH(CH_3)_2} \quad \overset{|}{H} \quad \overset{|}{CH_2OH} \quad \overset{|}{\underset{CH_2SCH_3}{CH_2}} \quad \overset{|}{CH_3} \quad \overset{|}{CH_2COOH}$$

Valine　　Glycine　　Serine　　Methionine　　Alanine　　Aspartic acid

$$\downarrow H_3O^+$$

$$H_2N-CH-C-OH + H_2N-CH-C-OH + H_2N-CH-C-OH + H_2N-CH-C-OH + H_2N-CH-C-OH$$

$$\overset{|}{CH(CH_3)_2} \quad \overset{|}{H} \quad \overset{|}{CH_2OH} \quad \overset{|}{\underset{CH_2SCH_3}{CH_2}} \quad \overset{|}{CH_3}$$

$$+ H_2N-CH-C-OH$$

$$\overset{|}{CH_2COOH}$$

18.57　A peptide rich in Asp and Lys residues is more soluble in water than a peptide rich in Val and Ala residues. The side chains of Asp and Lys are polar and are better solvated by water than the nonpolar, hydrophobic side chains of Val and Ala.

18.58　At its isoelectric point, a protein has the same number of positive and negative charges and is thus electrically neutral. On either side of the isoelectric point, the protein is charged and is more soluble in a polar solvent like water.

18.59　Since amino acids are both weak acids and weak bases, they can serve as buffers in two different pH regions. Using glycine as an example:

$$H_3N^+-CH_2COOH \overset{K_{a1}}{\rightleftharpoons} H_3N^+-CH_2COO^- + H^+$$

$$H_3N^+-CH_2COO^- \overset{K_{a2}}{\rightleftharpoons} H_2N-CH_2COO^- + H^+$$

The buffering ability of glycine is greatest at pK_{a1} and pK_{a2}. Side chain functional groups of amino acids such as aspartic acid or lysine can also serve as buffers.

18.60

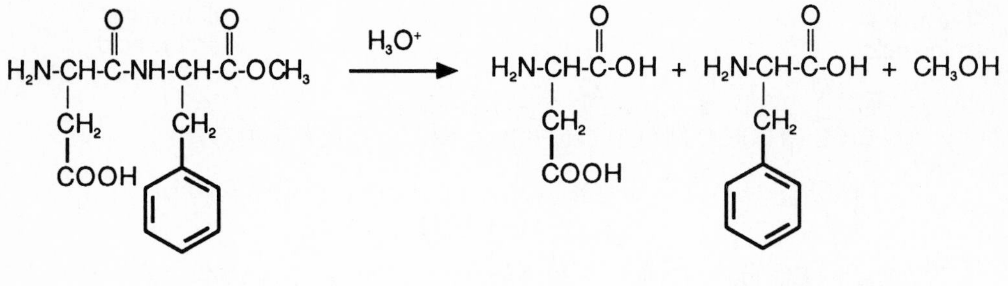

Aspartic acid   Phenylalanine

18.61 The pK_a of an acid is the negative logarithm of the dissociation constant of the acid. It is also equal to the pH at which the concentration of a weak acid equals the concentration of its salt.

18.62 The pK_{a1} of alanine is 2.3 (this can be found in the figure that appears in this Application). At a pH lower than pK_{a1}, alanine exists primarily in the cationic form $H_3N^+–CH(CH_3)COOH$. At a pH above 2.3 (but lower than pH 9.8) alanine exists primarily in the zwitterionic form $H_3N^+–CH(CH_3)COO^-$. From the relationships described in this Application, we can see that at a pH one unit greater than pK_{a1}, the ratio of zwitterion form to cationic form is 10/1; 91% of alanine is in the zwitterion form and 9% is in the cation form. At pH 3.5 an even greater percent of alanine is in the zwitterion form - 94%.

18.63 People need a daily source of protein in the diet because the human body doesn't store protein (the body does store fats and carbohydrates).

18.64 An incomplete protein lacks one or more of the 10 essential amino acids.

18.65 Food from animal sources is more likely to contain complete protein than food from plant sources.

18.66 An amino acid analyzer gives the identity and the quantity of the amino acids in a protein sample.

18.67 Ninhydrin reacts with the protein in fingerprints to give a purple color.

18.68 Pineapple that is canned has been heated to inactivate enzymes. Thus, no enzymatic hydrolysis occurs when canned pineapple is added to gelatin.

18.69 If an aspartic acid residue were substituted for a glutamic acid residue, a health problem might not occur because both amino acids have similar chemical behavior.

18.70 Alpha-keratin has an alpha-helix secondary structure, whereas tropocollagen has a triple-helix secondary structure.

18.71 Bradykinin:

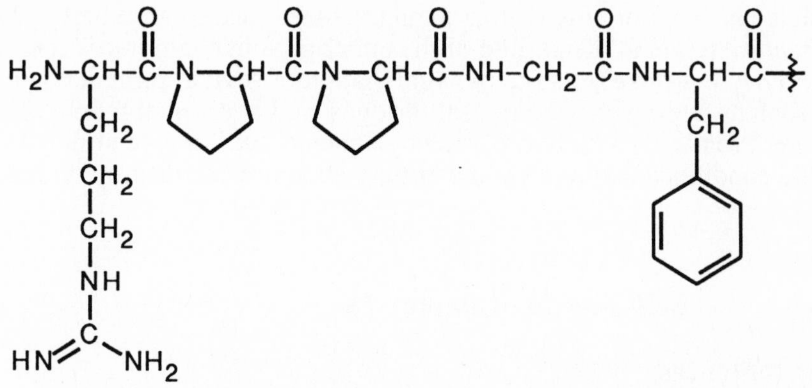

H—Arg——Pro——Pro————Gly——Phe——

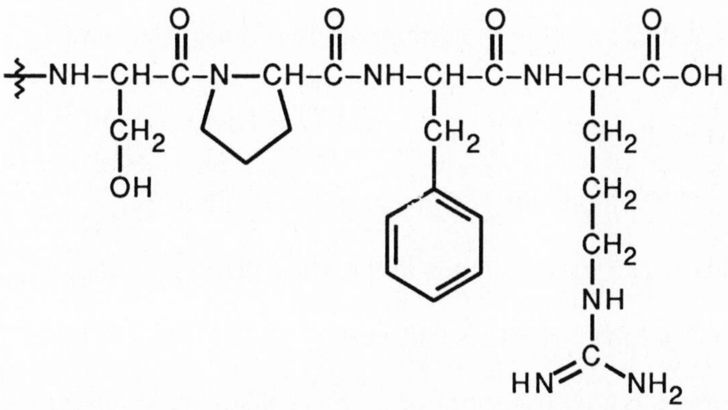

——— Ser—— Pro———— Phe —— Arg ——OH

18.72 The pI of bradykinin is basic because of the two basic arginines.

18.73 Hydrophobic interactions: (b) methionine, (f) phenylalanine, (h) valine.
Hydrogen bonding: (a) glutamic acid, (c) glutamine, (d) threonine, (e) histidine.
Salt bridges: (a) glutamic acid, (e) histidine.
Covalent bonding: (g) cysteine.

The Chapter in Brief

Amino Acids (Sections 18.1–18.5) Amino acids contain an amino group and a carboxylic acid group, and are the "building blocks" of proteins. There are twenty common amino acids; ten must be supplied in the diet, and ten can be synthesized by the human body. Amino acids exist as dipolar ions called *zwitterions*. The pH at which an amino acid exists primarily as its neutral dipolar form is its isoelectric point. Most amino acids do not possess a plane of symmetry and are thus "handed" or chiral.

Peptides and Proteins (Sections 18.6, 18.7, 18.11) Amino acids are linked through peptide (amide) bonds to form peptides and proteins. Peptide chains can also be linked by disulfide bonds between cysteine residues. Proteins can be classified in several ways: by chemical makeup as simple or conjugated, by shape as fibrous or globular, or by biological function.

Structure of Peptides and Proteins (Sections 18.8–18.10, 18.12) The *primary structure* of a protein is the order in which amino acids are connected. *Secondary structure* refers to the way that certain sections of the protein chain are oriented into a regular pattern such as an α helix or a β–pleated sheet. *Tertiary structure* refers to the coiling of the entire protein chain into a specific three-dimensional shape. *Quaternary structure* refers to the aggregation of several protein chains. Noncovalent interactions such as hydrogen bonding, salt bridges, and hydrophobic interactions stabilize a protein's structure. Proteins can be hydrolyzed by aqueous acid to give amino acids, and can be denatured under mild conditions that unravel the tertiary structure and destroy biological activity.

Self-Test for Chapter 18

Complete the following sentences:

1.   The isoelectric point of a neutral amino acid is near pH = _____.

2.   Two molecules that differ only in the arrangement of groups around a chiral carbon atom are called _____.

3.   Amino acids exist as dipolar ions called _____.

4.   The repeating chain of amide linkages in a peptide is called the _____.

5.   A disulfide bond between two cysteines in the same chain produces a _____ in the peptide.

6.   A protein bonded to a carbohydrate is called a _____.

7.   _____ structure refers to how the entire protein is folded and coiled into a specific three-dimensional shape.

8.   In the secondary structure called a _____ _____, polypeptide chains line up in a parallel arrangement held together by hydrogen bonds.

9.   The tripeptide H_2N-Ala-Ile-Leu-COOH contains side chains that are _____.

10.   The amino acids methionine and cysteine are the only two that contain the element _____.

11.   A chain with fewer than 50 amino acids is called a _____.

12.   _____ interactions pull nonpolar side chains together to exclude water.

Tell whether the following statements are true or false:

1.   All amino acids have at least one chiral carbon atom.

2.   Tyrosine and valine can react to form a dipeptide.

3.   Protein denaturation disrupts the primary structure of a protein.

4.   In lysylalanine, lysine is the *N* -terminal residue.

5.   Some amino acids have an isoelectric point near 10.

6.   Simple proteins are more common than conjugated proteins.

7.   β–pleated sheets and α-helixes occur mostly in fibrous proteins.

8.   Amino acids are quite water-soluble.

9.   A peptide is always written with the *N*-terminal residue on the right and the *C*-terminal residue on the left.

10.   Both fibrous and globular proteins are water-soluble.

11.   Proteins may be classified by biological function.

12.   2-Butanol has a chiral carbon atom.

Match the entries on the left with their partners on the right:

1.	Isoleucine	(a) Achiral amino acid
2.	Insulin	(b) Secondary structure
3.	Glycylglycine	(c) Fibrous protein
4.	Glycine	(d) Amino acid that is a secondary amine
5.	β-pleated sheet	(e) Amino acid with hydrocarbon side-chain
6.	Aspartic acid	(f) Globular protein
7.	Collagen	(g) Peptide hormone
8.	Cysteine	(h) Basic amino acid
9.	Albumin	(i) Aromatic amino acid
10.	Arginine	(j) Dipeptide
11.	Proline	(k) Acidic amino acid
12.	Tryptophan	(l) Can form disulfide bridges

Chapter 19 – Enzymes, Vitamins, and Chemical Messengers

19.1 Most vitamin/mineral supplements contain the known essential trace elements, with the exception of cobalt and nickel.

19.2 (a) Fumaric acid hydrase catalyzes the addition of water to fumaric acid.
(b) Squalene oxidase catalyzes the oxidation of squalene.
(c) Glucose kinase catalyzes the transfer of a phosphate group to glucose.
(d) Cellulose hydrolase catalyzes the hydrolysis of cellulose.

19.3 Pyruvate decarboxylase is a lyase.

19.4 Vitamin A is fat-soluble because it has a long hydrocarbon chain. Vitamin C is water-soluble because it has polar hydroxyl groups.

19.5 The family name-ending for an enzyme is -*ase*.

19.6 An enzyme is a large protein molecule that catalyzes biochemical reactions.

19.7 The body needs many thousands of enzymes because each enzyme catalyzes only one particular reaction, and the human body carries out many thousands of biochemical reactions.

19.8 Catalysts speed up reactions by lowering the energy barrier to product formation.

19.9 As opposed to an inorganic catalyst, an enzyme is much larger and more complex. Enzymes also catalyze the reaction of only a single substrate to form a single product, whereas inorganic catalysts usually catalyze the reactions of many substrates.

19.10 (a) Hydrolases catalyze the hydrolysis of substrates.
(b) Isomerases catalyze the isomerization of substrates.
(c) Lyases catalyze the addition of a small molecule, or the elimination of a small molecule.

19.11 A holoenzyme is active as a catalyst and is made up of an apoenzyme (protein part) plus a cofactor (small, nonprotein part).

19.12 A coenzyme is a type of cofactor. A cofactor can be either an inorganic ion or a small organic molecule called a coenzyme.

19.13 An enzyme is a large three-dimensional molecule with a crevice into which its substrate can fit. Enzymes are specific in their action because only one or a few molecules have the appropriate shape to fit into the crevice.

19.14 An enzyme forms an enzyme-substrate complex with the substrate at the enzyme's active site. The substrate is thus in the proper position for functional groups at the active site to carry out a reaction. After the reaction, the enzyme and product separate.

19.15   (a) A *protease* catalyzes this reaction, which is the hydrolysis of an amide.
(b) Either a *dehydrase* or a *decarboxylase* catalyzes this reaction.
(c) A *dehydrogenase* catalyzes the introduction of a double bond into a molecule.

19.16   (a) A *protease* catalyzes the hydrolysis of peptide (amide) bonds in proteins.
(b) A *DNA ligase* catalyzes the formation of a new bond between two small DNA chains.
(c) A *transmethylase* catalyzes the transfer of a methyl group to the substrate.

19.17   A urease is a hydrolase, since it catalyzes the hydrolysis of urea.

19.18   Dimethylurea inhibits urease by competitive inhibition since its structure is similar to that of urea.

19.19   In the lock-and-key model of enzyme action, the crevice of an enzyme has a specific shape (lock) into which only a specific substrate (key) can fit. In the induced-fit model, an enzyme can change its shape slightly to fit the different spatial requirements of a number of substrates.

19.20   A hydrolase (lipase) catalyzes the cleavage of the ester groups of fats.

19.21   A lock-and-key enzyme is more specific than an induced-fit enzyme since it catalyzes the reaction of only one substrate rather than a range of substrates.

19.22

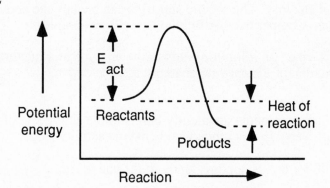

19.23   Since the apoenzyme is the protein part of a holoenzyme, it is more likely to be denatured than the coenzyme.

19.24 Ag^+ acts as a non-competitive inhibitor and binds to the $-SH$ groups of bacterial enzymes, thus killing the bacteria.

19.25   At a high substrate concentration relative to enzyme concentration, the rate of reaction increases as the enzyme concentration increases.

19.26   At a high enzyme concentration relative to substrate concentration, the rate of reaction increases as the substrate concentration increases, up to a point where all enzyme catalytic sites are occupied. The reaction rate then levels off, and adding more substrate doesn't increase the reaction rate.

19.27   At relatively low concentrations, reaction rate increases as either substrate concentration or enzyme concentration increases. When substrate concentration becomes very high, the reaction rate reaches a limit that is determined by the rate of combination of enzyme and substrate, about 10^8 collisions per mole per second.

19.28   (a) Lowering the reaction temperature of an enzyme-catalyzed reaction from 37°C to 27° slows down the reaction.
(b) Raising the pH of an enzyme-catalyzed reaction from 7.5 to 10.5 will probably slow down the reaction, since most enzymes have their optimum rates at close to neutral pH. However, if the enzyme has a rate optimum near 10.5, then the increase in pH from 7.5 to 10.5 will speed up the reaction.
(c) Adding a heavy-metal salt will either stop or slow down an enzyme-catalyzed reaction because heavy metals bind to enzymes, causing noncompetitive inhibition.
(d) Raising the reaction temperature from 37°C to 40°C will probably increase the rate of reaction since most enzymes are not denatured until higher temperatures.

19.29   To function in the very acidic environment of the stomach, an enzyme must operate best at a low pH. To function in the intestine, an enzyme must work at a pH near neutral. An enzyme that is most active at neutral pH will not be active in a strongly acidic environment.

19.30   The three kinds of enzyme inhibitors are competitive inhibitors, non-competitive inhibitors and irreversible inhibitors.

19.31   *Competitive inhibition* occurs when the structure of a second substrate closely resembles that of the normal substrate for an enzyme. The second substrate can occupy the active site and thereby inactivate the enzyme. Competitive inhibition is usually reversible.

Noncompetitive inhibition occurs when an inhibitor binds to the enzyme at a location other than the active site. The conformation of the enzyme changes, and the enzyme is inactivated.

Irreversible inhibition occurs when a molecule covalently bonds to the active site of an enzyme. The active site is thus irreversibly inactivated, and enzyme activity stops.

19.32   In competitive inhibition, the inhibitor bonds noncovalently to the active site.

In noncompetitive inhibition, the inhibitor binds noncovalently with a group away from the active site.

In irreversible inhibition, the inhibitor forms a covalent bond to the active site.

19.33   Irreversible inhibition is the most difficult to treat medically because it occurs at the active site and because of the strength of the bond between the inhibitor and the enzyme.

19.34   Papain is effective as a meat tenderizer because it hydrolyzes peptide bonds and partially digests the proteins in the meat.

19.35   Papain works by hydrolyzing the bee toxin responsible for the swelling reaction.

19.36   Feedback inhibition occurs when the product of a series of reactions is an inhibitor for an earlier reaction. When this product accumulates, it inhibits the enzyme that catalyzes an earlier step in the series. When the amount of product drops, inhibition stops, and product formation is resumed.

19.37 Allosteric enzymes have two types of binding sites; one site is for catalysis of the enzymatic reaction and one site is for regulation of the reaction.

19.38 Positive regulators change the shape of the active site so that the enzymatic reaction proceeds more rapidly. Negative regulators change the shape of the active site so that the reaction rate increases more slowly with increasing substrate concentration.

19.39 A zymogen is an enzyme that is synthesized in a form different from its active form and is later activated. Some enzymes are secreted as zymogens because they would digest or otherwise injure the body if they were secreted in their active form.

19.40 It's less filling and has fewer calories.

19.41 A vitamin is an enzyme cofactor, whereas a hormone regulates enzyme activity.

19.42 A hormone transmits a chemical message from a gland to a target tissue. A neurotransmitter carries an impulse between neighboring nerve cells.

19.43 A vitamin acts as a cofactor for an enzyme and enables an enzyme to catalyze biochemical reactions.

19.44 Vitamins are required in the diet; hormones and enzymes are synthesized in the body.

19.45 The four fat-soluble vitamins are vitamins A, D, E, and K.

19.46 Vitamin C (water-soluble) is excreted in the urine and must be replenished daily, whereas vitamin A (fat-soluble) can be stored in fatty tissue.

19.47 The body's endocrine system manufactures and secretes hormones, which regulate biochemical activities.

19.48 The hypothalamus is primarily responsible for controlling the endocrine system.

19.49 Hormones pass through the bloodstream to their target tissues.

19.50 Endocrine glands include the pituitary, the adrenals, the pancreas, ovary, testis, pineal, thymus, thyroid, and parathyroid glands.

19.51 Hormones travel through the bloodstream and bind to cell receptors, which may be on the outside of a cell, in the cytoplasm, or on the nucleus. The receptors may either release into the cell a substance that activates an enzyme, or may extend into the cell to catalyze sites that are activated when the hormone is attached to the receptor.

19.52 Enzymes are proteins, whereas hormones vary greatly in structure. Some hormones are polypeptides, some are proteins, some are steroids, and some are small organic molecules.

19.53 The same type of lock-and-key specificity exists for both an enzyme/substrate complex and a hormone/receptor complex.

19.54 Cyclic AMP produced by an enzyme on the inner surface of a cell activates enzymes that produce glucose from glycogen.

19.55 Epinephrine raises the blood sugar level by increasing the rate of glycogen breakdown in the liver.

19.56 The human nervous system is made up of the *central nervous system*, which consists of nerves in the brain and spinal cord, and the *peripheral nervous system*, which consists of sensory and motor nerves.

19.57 A synapse is the gap between two nerve cells (neurons). Neurotransmitters released by one neuron cross the synapse to receptors on a second neuron and transmit the nerve impulse.

19.58 *Cholinergic* and *adrenergic* neurotransmitters are two classes.

19.59 The presynaptic end of one neuron releases a neurotransmitter, which crosses the synapse to a receptor site on the postsynaptic end of a second neuron. After reception, the cell transmits an electrical signal down its axon and passes on the impulse. Enzymes deactivate the neurotransmitter so that the neuron can receive the next impulse.

19.60 The autonomic nervous system is responsible for unconscious functions. The somatic nervous system deals with consciously controlled functions like movement.

19.61 Enzyme activity must be monitored under standard conditions because activity is affected by pH, temperature and substrate concentration. The standard is the unit (u) which is the amount of enzyme that converts one micromole of substrate to product at defined standard conditions of pH, temperature and substrate concentration.

19.62 The enzymes creatine phosphokinase (CPK), aspartate transaminase (AST) and lactate dehydrogenase (LDH_1) are increased in the blood after a heart attack because they leak from cells damaged in the heart attack.

19.63 Isoenzymes are enzymes that catalyze the same reaction but differ slightly in structure.

19.64 The body excretes excess water-soluble vitamins, but fat-soluble vitamins accumulate in tissues.

19.66 Penicillin kills bacteria by irreversibly inhibiting an enzyme responsible for the synthesis of bacterial cell walls. Without cell walls, the bacteria die.

19.67 The cells of higher organisms don't have cell walls and are unharmed by penicillin.

19.68

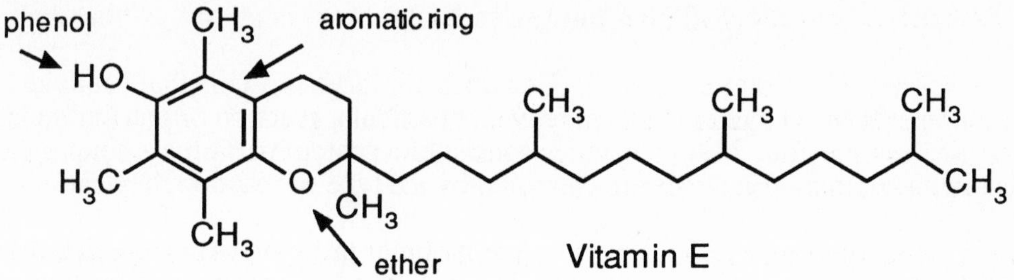

phenol CH$_3$ aromatic ring

HO

H$_3$C

CH$_3$

ether

CH$_3$ CH$_3$ CH$_3$

CH$_3$

CH$_3$ CH$_3$

Vitamin E

19.69

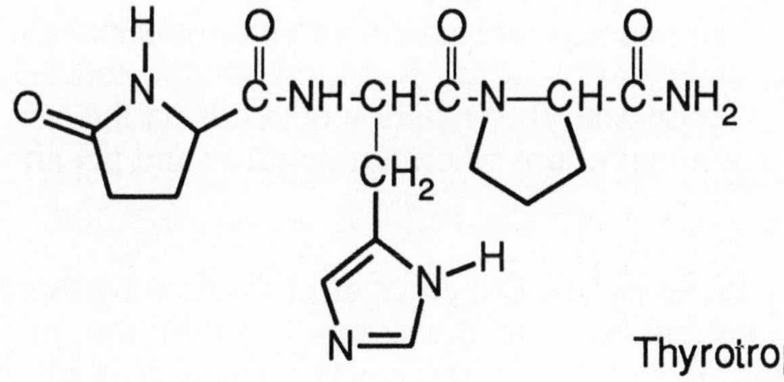

Thyrotropin releasing factor

19.70

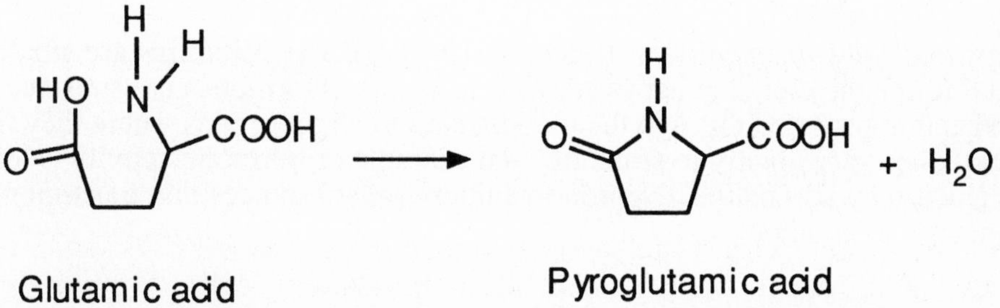

Glutamic acid → Pyroglutamic acid + H$_2$O

Pyroglutamic acid is formed by loss of water from glutamic acid.

19.71

$$1.6 \text{ mg riboflavin} \times \frac{100 \text{ mL wine}}{0.014 \text{ mg riboflavin}} = 11{,}000 \text{ mL} = 11 \text{ L wine}$$

19.72

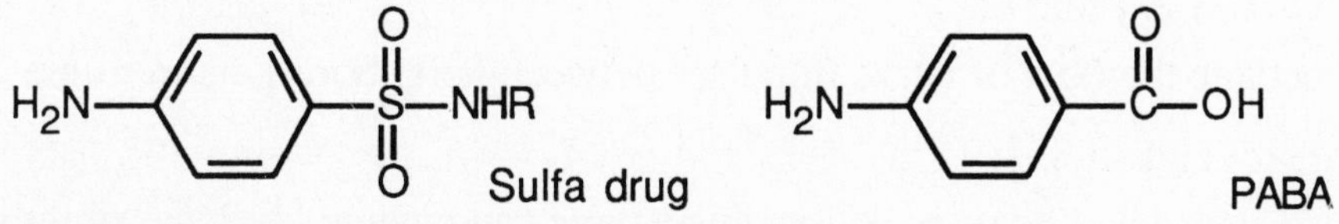

H$_2$N— —S—NHR
Sulfa drug

H$_2$N— —C—OH
PABA

A sulfa drug is structurally very similar to PABA and substitutes for it in folic acid synthesis. The resulting product can't be used for producing the critical enzyme, and the bacteria die.

19.73 The part of an enzyme not involved with catalysis is used to precisely control the shape of the active site and to hold the substrate in place.

The Chapter in Brief

Introduction to Enzymes (Sections 19.1–19.3) Enzymes are large proteins that catalyze biochemical reactions. Many enzymes catalyze only one particular reaction of one particular substrate; others are less specific. Many enzymes consist of a protein part plus a nonprotein cofactor that is often a vitamin. Enzymes are classified by the type of reaction they catalyze.

Enzyme Function (Sections 19.4–19.7) Enzymes are globular proteins with a crevice that contains the active site where reactions take place. The lock-and-key model explains how enzymes are so specific, whereas the induced-fit model explains how some enzymes can accomodate different substrates. An enzyme and a substrate come together to form an enzyme-substrate complex, which is held together by weak noncovalent attractions. Reaction occurs, and the enzyme and product separate. The rate of an enzyme-catalyzed reaction depends on the concentration of enzyme and substratee, and is at a maximum when temperature and pH are optimum.

Enzyme Inhibition and Regulation (Sections 19.8–19.10) Enzymes are inhibited by three types of processes: competitive inhibition, noncompetitive inhibition, and irreversible inhibition. Enzymes are regulated by allosteric control, in which binding a molecule at one site influences binding at other sites. Proenzymes are enzymes that are synthesized in a form different from the active form.

Vitamins, Hormones, and Neurotransmitters (Sections 19.11–19.15) Vitamins are small organic molecules, obtained through the diet, that act as enzyme cofactors. Hormones are substances that are secreted by gland and transported through the bloodstream to target organs where they regulate cellular activity. Hormones vary greatly in structure. An example of hormone activity is the regulation of blood glucose by adrenaline. Neurotransmitters are substances that transmit nerve impulses from one neuron to another.

Self-Test for Chapter 19

Complete the following sentences:

1. An enzyme called a _____ catalyzes the isomerization of a chiral center.

2. _____ are enzymes that have slightly different structures but that catalyze the same reaction.

3. Substances that mediate the flow of nerve impulses between neighboring neurons are called _____.

4. In the _____ - _____ model of enzyme action, an enzyme can change its shape slightly to fit different substrates.

5. In _____ inhibition, an inhibitor changes the shape of an enzyme by binding at a location other than the active site.

6. If the temperature becomes too high, enzymes begin to _____.

7. The catalytic activity of an enzyme is measured by its _____ _____.

8. The _____ secretes releasing factors that pass through the bloodstream to the _____ gland.

9. One neuron is separated from another by a gap called a _____.

10. Cholinergic neurons release the neurotransmitter _____.

11. An _____ enzyme has more than one chain and has binding sites for both substrate and regulator.

12. An enzyme that is synthesized in a form different from its active form is called a _____.

Match the entries on the left with their partners on the right:

1. Papain   (a) Deficiency causes anemia

2. Vitamin D   (b) Deals with consciously controlled functions

3. Hypothalamus   (c) Nonspecific enzyme

4. Autonomic nervous system   (d) Catalyzes hydrolysis of ester groups in lipids

5. Phosphodiesterase   (e) Protein part of enzyme plus cofactor

6. Apoenzyme   (f) Deficiency causes scurvy

7. Somatic nervous system   (g) Deals with unconsciously controlled functions

8. Vitamin B_6 (h) Fat-soluble vitamin

9. Lipase   (i) Gland controlling endocrine system

10. Vitamin C   (j) Protein part of an enzyme

11. Holoenzyme   (k) Catalyzes hydrolysis of cyclic AMP

12. Lyase   (l) Catalyzes loss of small molecule from substrate

Tell whether the following statements are true or false:

1. 98.6°F is the optimum temperature for most enzymes.

2. Hormones travel through the bloodstream to reach target tissues.

3. Adrenaline interacts with enzymes to produces glucose from glycogen.

4. A dehydrogenase catalyzes the loss of H_2O from a substrate.

5. At the active site, the enzyme and substrate are held together by covalent bonds.

6. Vitamins may be small organic molecules or inorganic ions.

7. Hormone releasing factors are small peptides.

8. A neurotransmitter for adrenergic neurons is dopamine.

9.   Copper, cobalt, and selenium are essential enzyme cofactors.

10. Heavy metals cause irreversible inhibition of enzymes.

11. As enzyme concentration is increased, the reaction rate eventually levels off.

12. Hormones, neurotransmitters, and pheromones are all chemical messengers.

Chapter 20 – The Generation of Biochemical Energy

20.1 Use these two facts to solve this problem:
(1) A reaction with a negative ΔG is exergonic; a reaction with a positive ΔG is endergonic.
(2) A reaction with a larger negative ΔG proceeds farther toward products than a reaction with a smaller negative ΔG.
Thus, reactions (a) and (c) are exergonic, and reaction (b) is endergonic. Reaction (a) proceeds furthest toward products, because its ΔG is larger and more negative than the ΔGs of the other reactions.

20.2

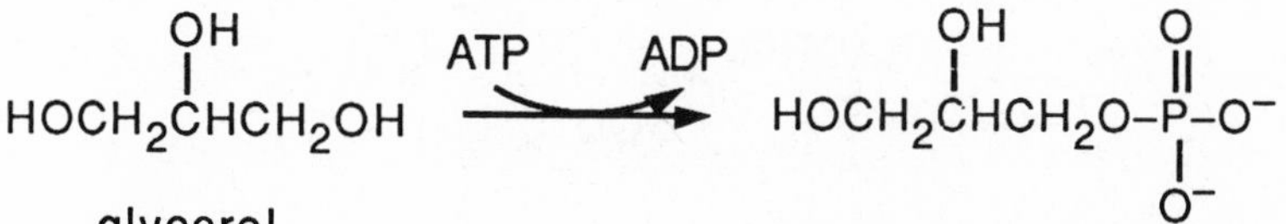

glycerol → glycerol 1-phosphate

20.3 If a metabolic pathway that breaks down a molecule is exergonic (for example), the reverse of that pathway (synthesis) *must* be endergonic. The only way to synthesize the product is to couple the energetically unfavorable reactions with other reactions that are energetically favorable, in a pathway that differs from the reverse of the breakdown pathway.

20.4

Acetyl phosphate	$\longrightarrow$	Acetate + phosphate	$\Delta G = -10.3$ kcal/mol
ADP + phosphate	$\longrightarrow$	ATP	$\Delta G = +7.3$ kcal/mol

Acetyl phosphate + ADP $\longrightarrow$ Acetate + ATP $\Delta G = -3.0$ kcal/mol

The reaction is favorable because ΔG is negative.

20.5 Recall that NAD oxidizes an alcohol to a ketone, and FAD removes two hydrogens from adjacent carbons to yield a double bond.

(a)

HOOC-CH$_2$-CH(OH)-COOH + NAD$^+$ → HOOC-CH$_2$-C(O)-COOH + NADH/H$^+$

(b)

CH$_3$-C(O)-CH$_2$-CH$_2$-COOH + FAD → CH$_3$-C(O)-CH=CH-COOH + FADH$_2$

20.6   The hydrogen atoms removed are circled.

(a)

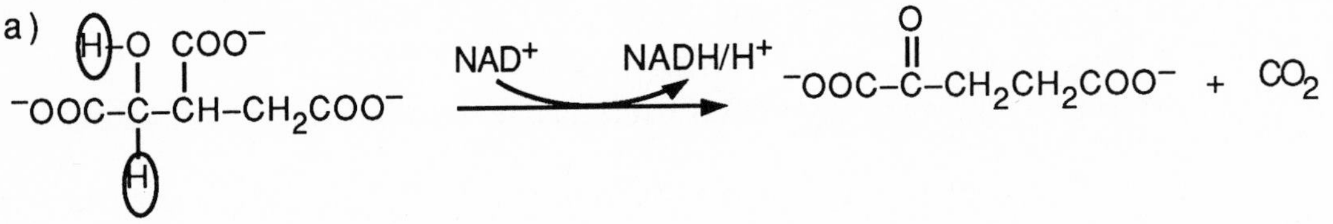

$$^-OOC-C-CH-CH_2COO^- \xrightarrow[NAD^+ \quad NADH/H^+]{} \quad ^-OOC-C-CH_2CH_2COO^- + CO_2$$

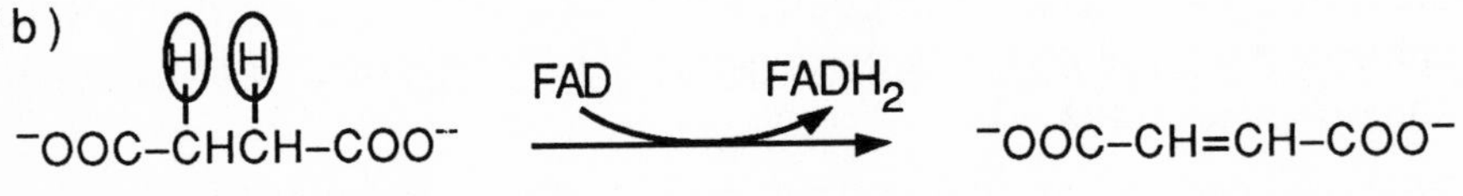

(b)

$$^-OOC-CHCH-COO^- \xrightarrow[FAD \quad FADH_2]{} \quad ^-OOC-CH=CH-COO^-$$

(c)

$$^-OOC-CH_2-C-COO^- \xrightarrow[NAD^+ \quad NADH/H^+]{} \quad ^-OOC-CH_2-C-COO^-$$

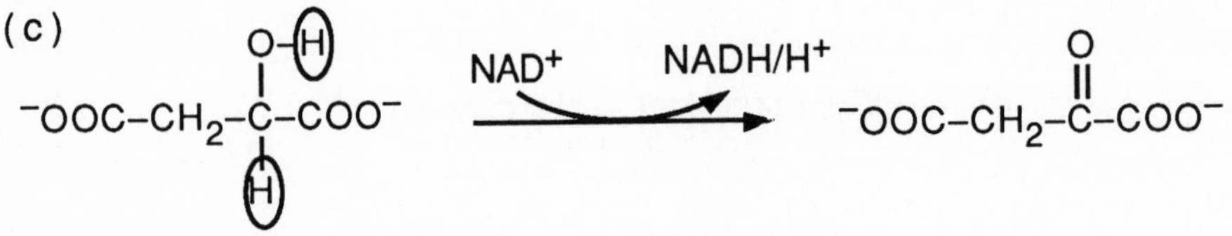

20.7   Citric acid and isocitric acid are tricarboxylic acids.

20.8

$$CH_3C-SCoA + 2 O_2 \longrightarrow 2 CO_2 + HSCoA + H_2O$$

20.9   Production of HSCoA from succinyl CoA is exergonic and provides enough energy to be coupled with phosphorylation of ADP, an endergonic reaction.

20.10

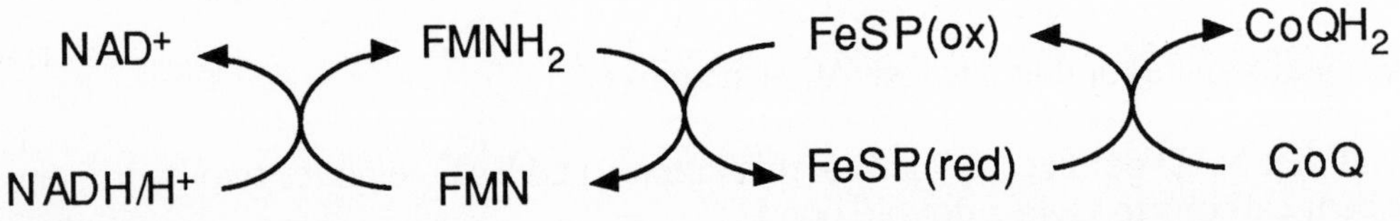

$$NAD^+ \quad FMNH_2 \quad FeSP(ox) \quad CoQH_2$$
$$NADH/H^+ \quad FMN \quad FeSP(red) \quad CoQ$$

20.11   Coenzyme Q is soluble in hydrocarbons because it has a large hydrocarbon portion.

20.12   A reaction that requires energy is endergonic; a reaction that gives off energy is exergonic.

20.13   For a reaction to be spontaneous, it must give off energy and thus have a negative ΔG.

20.14   The sign of ΔG can be used to predict if a reaction is feasible (negative ΔG) or not feasible (positive ΔG).

20.15   Enzymes only increase the rate of reaction and have no effect on either the magnitude or the sign of ΔG.

20.16   Reactions (a) and (c) are exergonic; reaction (b) is endergonic. Reaction (a) proceeds furthest toward products at equilibrium because it has the largest negative value of ΔG.

20.17

Prokaryotic Cells	Eukaryotic Cells
Quite small	Relatively large
No nucleus	Nucleus
Dispersed DNA	DNA in nucleus
No organelles	Organelles

20.18 Prokaryotic cells are found in bacteria and algae; eukaryotic cells are found in higher organisms.

20.19 Organelles are subcellular structures that perform specialized tasks within the cell.

20.20 The *cytoplasm* consists of everything between the cell membrane and the nuclear membrane; the cytosol is the medium that fills the interior of the cell and contains electrolytes, nutrients and enzymes.

20.21 A mitochondrion is egg-shaped and consists of a smooth outer membrane and a folded inner membrane. The inner folds are called *cristae*, and the space between folds is the *matrix*.

20.22 Mitochondria are called the body's "power plant" because 90% of the body's supply of the high energy molecule ATP is synthesized there.

20.23 *Cristae* are the inner folds of a mitochondrion. On the cristae are protuberances where the energy production of the cell takes place.

20.24 Metabolism refers to all reactions that take place inside cells; digestion is a part of metabolism in which food is broken down into small organic molecules.

20.25 Metabolic processes that break down molecules are called *catabolism*. Metabolic processes that assemble larger molecules from smaller molecules are known as *anabolism*.

20.26 The two-carbon molecule acetyl coenzyme A is formed from the catabolism of all three major classes of food.

20.27 *First* ——————————————————————————————————> *Last*

Digestion, citric-acid cycle, respiratory chain, oxidative phosphorylation

20.28 Adenosine triphosphate is the substance formed during catabolism to store chemical energy.

20.29 ATP has a triphosphate group bonded to C5 of ribose, and ADP has a diphosphate group in that position.

20.30 ATP is a high-energy molecule because energy is released when ATP reacts with most other molecules to transfer a phosphate group.

20.31 An ATP molecule transfers a phosphate group to another molecule in anabolic reactions.

20.32

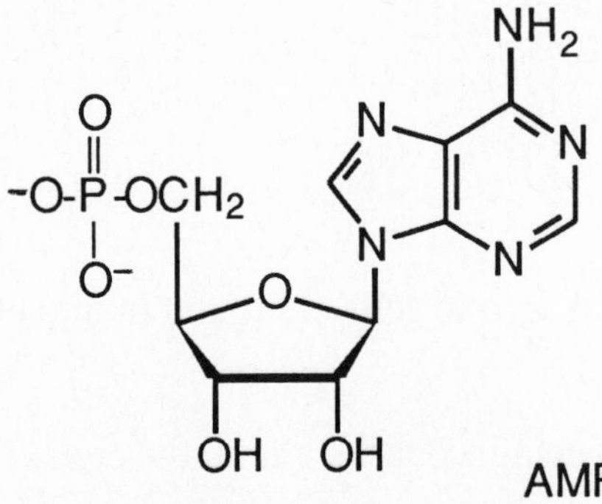

AMP

20.33 A reaction that is energetically unfavorable can be combined with a reaction that is energetically favorable so that the overall reaction is energetically favorable. The two reactions are then said to be coupled.

20.34

1,3 bisphosphoglycerate + H_2O $\longrightarrow$

3-phosphoglycerate + phosphate $\Delta G = -11.8$ kcal/mol

ADP + HPO_4^{2-} $\longrightarrow$ ATP + H_2O $\Delta G = +7.3$ kcal/mol

_____

1,3 bisphosphoglycerate + ADP $\longrightarrow$

3-phosphoglycerate + ATP $\Delta G = -4.5$ kcal/mol

The reaction is favorable because ΔG is negative.

20.35

$$\text{1,3-bisphosphoglycerate} \xrightarrow[\text{ADP}]{\text{ATP}} \text{3-phosphoglycerate}$$

20.36 The hydrolysis of fructose 6-phosphate ($\Delta G = -3.3$ kcal/mol) is not favorable for phosphorylating ADP ($\Delta G = +7.3$ kcal/mol) because the overall ΔG (+4.0 kcal/mol) is positive.

20.37 (a) A dehydrogenated molecule is oxidized.
(b) NAD^+ and FAD are oxidizing agents because they oxidize substrates.
(c) NAD^+ oxidizes secondary alcohols to ketones; FAD oxidizes $-CH_2CH_2-$ to $-CH=CH-$
(d) After dehydrogenation, NAD^+ becomes $NADH/H^+$ and FAD becomes $FADH_2$.

(e)

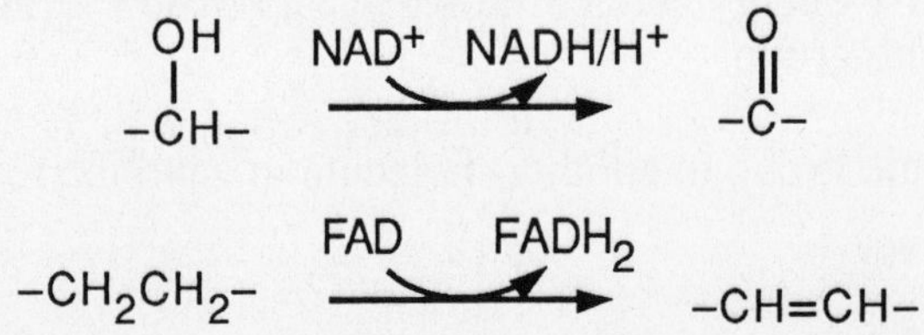

20.38 The citric-acid cycle takes place in cellular mitochondria.

20.39 The citric-acid cycle is also known as the Krebs cycle or the tricarboxylic-acid cycle.

20.40 Oxaloacetic acid acts as the starting point for the citric-acid cycle.

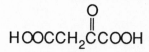

Oxaloacetic acid

20.41 (a) Oxidations occur in the steps in which NAD^+ and FAD are reduced (steps 3, 4, 6, and 8).
(b) Decarboxylations occur in steps 3 and 4.
(c) A hydration occurs in step 7.

20.42 *Substrate-level phosphorylation* occurs when ATP is formed directly, without resulting from reduced coenzymes that enter the respiratory chain. GTP is the high-energy compound that transfers phosphate to ADP to produce ATP.

20.43 One molecule of ATP is directly formed as a result of the citric acid cycle. (Eleven other ATPs are formed from reduced coenzymes from the citric acid cycle that enter the respiratory chain.)

20.44 Three molecules of $NADH/H^+$ and one molecule of $FADH_2$ are produced in the citric acid cycle.

20.45 The two acetyl CoA carbons are oxidized to CO_2 in the citric acid cycle.

20.46 The respiratory chain is also known as the electron-transport system.

20.47 Oxidative phosphorylation refers to formation of ATP from the reactions of reduced coenzymes as they are oxidized in the respiratory chain. *Substrate-level phosphorylation* is the formation of ATP directly as a result of a biochemical reaction.

20.48 In oxidative phosphorylation, reduced coenzymes are oxidized, and ADP is phosphorylated.

20.49 The coenzymes $NADH/H^+$ and FMN initiate the events of the respiratory chain.

20.50 The ultimate products of the respiratory chain are water and energy.

20.51 (a) FAD = flavin adenine dinucleotide
(b) CoQ = coenzyme Q
(c) $NADH/H^+$ = reduced nicotinamide adenine dinucleotide
(d) cyt = cytochrome

20.52 The iron atoms of the cytochromes are oxidized and reduced in the respiratory chain.

20.53 *First* ————————————————————————————————> *Last*

NAD⁺,   iron/sulfur protein,   coenzyme Q,   cytochrome c

20.54

FAD ◄————————► CoQH₂ ————————► 2 Fe⁺³

FADH₂ ————————— CoQ ◄————————► 2 Fe₂⁺²

20.55 Reoxidation of each NADH yields three ATPs; reoxidation of each FADH₂ yields two ATPs.

20.56 If FADH₂ and NADH weren't reoxidized, the body's supply of these coenzymes would be depleted, and the citric acid cycle would stop.

20.57 According to the chemiosmotic theory, a pH differential is caused by the movement of H⁺ ions across the inner mitochondrial membrane. The outside of the membrane is more acidic than the inside.

20.58 A basal metabolic rate is the minimum amount of energy per unit time needed for breathing, maintaining body temperature, circulating blood and keeping all body organs functioning.

20.60 Daily activities such as walking use calories, and thus the body requires a larger caloric intake than that needed to maintain basal metabolism.

20.61 Barbiturates are used in low doses as tranquilizers and at higher doses as sleep inducers.

20.62 Barbiturates are lethal at high doses because they prevent electron transfer in the FMN/FeS/CoQ enzymes and thus keep the respiratory chain from functioning.

20.63 Brown fat, unlike white fat, contains blood vessels, mitochondria and a special protein that uncouples ATP synthesis from electron transport.

20.64 2,4-Dinitrophenol (2,4-DNP) has been used as an uncoupler of ATP synthesis. The uncoupling makes the body burn fat in an attempt to obtain ATP for metabolism. The use of 2,4-DNP was discontinued when it was found that the dose needed to slow ATP synthesis is very close to the dose that stops ATP synthesis, resulting in death.

20.65 The breakdown of molecules for energy must occur in several steps in order to avoid the production of large amounts of heat, to allow for storage of energy, and to control the rate of metabolism. Stepwise breakdown also allows energetically favorable steps to be coupled with other energetically unfavorable reactions.

20.66

$$CoAS\text{-}\overset{\displaystyle O}{\overset{\|}{C}}\text{-}CH_3 \;+\; \begin{array}{c} COO^- \\ | \\ C=O \\ | \\ CH_2 \\ | \\ COO^- \end{array} \xrightarrow[\text{cond.}]{\text{aldol}} CoAS\text{-}\overset{\displaystyle O}{\overset{\|}{C}}\text{-}CH_2\text{-}\begin{array}{c} COO^- \\ | \\ C\text{-}OH \\ | \\ CH_2 \\ | \\ COO^- \end{array}$$

$$\xrightarrow{H_2O} HO\overset{\displaystyle O}{\overset{\|}{C}}\text{-}CH_2\text{-}\begin{array}{c} COO^- \\ | \\ C\text{-}OH \\ | \\ CH_2 \\ | \\ COO^- \end{array} \;+\; CoASH$$

20.67 Evidently the fumaric-acid isomer with a cis double bond cannot act as a substrate for the enzyme that is responsible for the next step in the citric-acid cycle.

20.68 NAD^+ and FAD are oxidoreductases.

20.69

Citric acid cycle step	Process	ATP yield
3	NADH $\xrightarrow[\text{chain}]{\text{respiratory}}$ NAD^+	3
4	NADH $\xrightarrow[\text{chain}]{\text{respiratory}}$ NAD^+	3
5	substrate level phosphorylation	1
6	$FADH_2$ $\xrightarrow[\text{chain}]{\text{respiratory}}$ FAD	2
8	NADH $\xrightarrow[\text{chain}]{\text{respiratory}}$ NAD^+	3
	Net yield per acetyl group =	12

20.70 In the respiratory chain, oxygen is reduced by cytochrome c_3, and it combines with H^+ ions to yield H_2O.

The Chapter in Brief

Energy and Metabolism (Sections 20.1–20.4) All organisms need energy to grow and to carry out their biological functions. Biochemical energy comes from chemical reactions, some of which are exergonic and others of which are endergonic. Most of the energy production in the body occurs in organelles called mitochondria.

Metabolism, the sum of all biochemical reactions that occur in the cell, can be divided into catabolism (the breakdown of molecules) and anabolism (the synthesis of molecules). The overall process of catabolism consists of digestion, the production of acetyl SCoA, the citric-acid cycle, and the respiratory chain.

Adenosine Triphosphate (ATP) and Redox Coenzymes (Sections 20.5–20.7) ATP is the storage molecule for biochemical energy. The exergonic breakdown of ATP can be coupled with an endergonic reaction such that the combination of the two processes is energetically favorable. The coenzymes NAD^+ and FAD are energy carriers that can be reduced and reoxidized, and that enter the respiratory chain.

The Citric-Acid Cycle and the Respiratory Chain (Sections 20.8–20.20) The citric-acid cycle is the body's primary energy producer. The overall function of the cycle is to metabolize acetyl CoA and to produce the coenzymes NADH and $FADH_2$ that enter the respiratory chain. There, a series of reactions produces water, hydrogen ions (H^+), and reduced coenzymes. At sites on the mitochondrial membrane, the hydrogen ions activate the synthesis of ATP. For each acetyl CoA metabolized, 12 molecules of ATP are produced.

Self-Test for Chapter 20

Complete the following sentences:

1.   _____ cells are found in higher organisms.

2.   A → B → C is known as a _____ _____.

3.   ATP is synthesized from _____ and _____.

4.   A reaction that requires energy in order to take place is said to be energetically _____.

5.   The citric-acid cycle is also known as the _____ and as the _____ - _____ cycle.

6.   α-Ketoglutaric acid reacts with acetyl CoA to yield _____ and _____.

7.   Reactions that use the coenzyme _____ remove two hydrogens from an alcohol to yield a ketone.

8.   A complete citric-acid cycle yields _____ molecules of ATP.

9.   _____ is the material that fills the interior of a cell.

10.   _____ are the inner folds of the mitochondria.

11.   The _____ hypothesis states that protons outside of the mitochondrial membrane are unable to migrate back inside spontaneously.

12.   _____ _____ is the minimal amount of energy required to stay alive.

Tell whether the following statements are true or false:

1.   ATP is a higher-energy molecule than ADP.

2.   Both prokaryotic and eukaryotic cells are found in higher organisms.

3.   Anabolism is the breakdown of high-energy molecules.

4. In a reaction that is energetically unfavorable, the energy of the products is less than the energy of the reactants.

5. The third and fourth stages of energy production take place in the mitochondria.

6. A reaction that is energetically unfavorable can use ATP as an energy source.

7. $FADH_2$ donates two electrons to the iron-sulfur protein in the respiratory chain.

8. FAD removes two hydrogens from a carbon chain to yield a double bond.

9. Protons cross the mitochondrial membrane at the cristae.

10. ATP is synthesized only in the respiratory chain.

11. In the synthesis of ATP from ADP, a phosphate ester bond is formed.

12. The reactions of the citric acid cycle may be exergonic or endergonic.

Match the entries on the left with their partners on the right:

1. Mitochondrion

(a) Uses energy

2. Oxidative phosphorylation

(b) Yields one molecule of H_2O

3. Isocitrate

(c) Releases energy

4. Anabolic reaction

(d) Site of energy production in cell

5. Succinyl SCoA $\rightarrow$ succinate

(e) Reduces NAD^+ to $NADH/H^+$

6. Citric-acid cycle

(f) Tricarboxylic acid

7. Malate $\rightarrow$ oxaloacetate

(g) Contains an iron atom

8. Catabolic reaction

(h) Subcellular structure

9. Respiratory chain

(i) Reduces FAD to $FADH_2$

10. Cytochrome

(j) ATP synthesis

11. Succinate $\rightarrow$ fumarate

(k) Yields 2 molecules of CO_2

12. Organelle

(l) Yields acetyl SCoA plus ATP

Chapter 21 – Carbohydrates

21.1

(a)

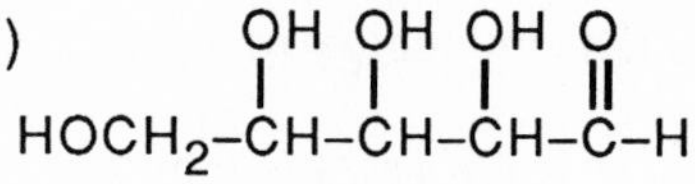

$$\underset{\text{An aldopentose}}{HOCH_2-\overset{\overset{\displaystyle OH}{|}}{CH}-\overset{\overset{\displaystyle OH}{|}}{CH}-\overset{\overset{\displaystyle OH}{|}}{CH}-\overset{\overset{\displaystyle O}{\|}}{C}-H}$$

(b)

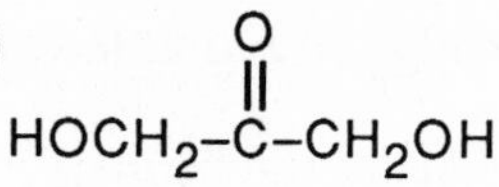

$$\underset{\text{A ketotriose}}{HOCH_2-\overset{\overset{\displaystyle O}{\|}}{C}-CH_2OH}$$

(c)

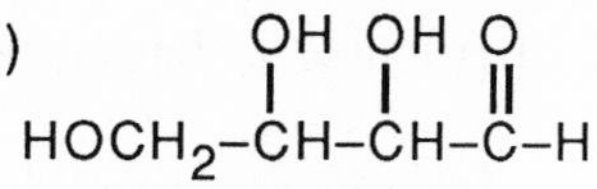

$$\underset{\text{An aldotetrose}}{HOCH_2-\overset{\overset{\displaystyle OH}{|}}{CH}-\overset{\overset{\displaystyle OH}{|}}{CH}-\overset{\overset{\displaystyle O}{\|}}{C}-H}$$

21.2

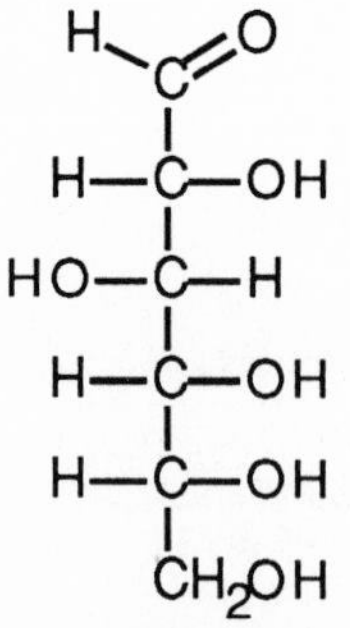

an aldohexose

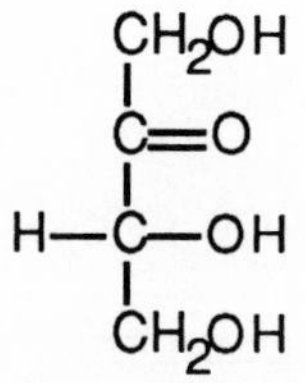

a ketotetrose

21.3

mirror

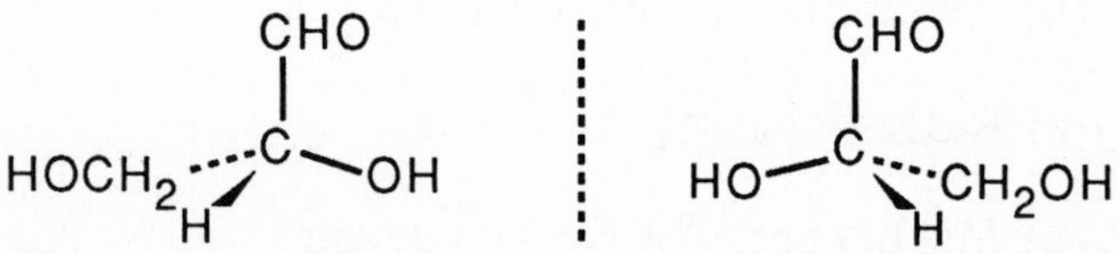

21.4 An aldopentose (see illustration in Sec. 21.1) has three chiral carbon atoms. Using the fact that a molecule with n chiral carbons has 2^n stereoisomers, we calculate that an aldopentose has a maximum of 8 stereoisomers.

21.5

(a)

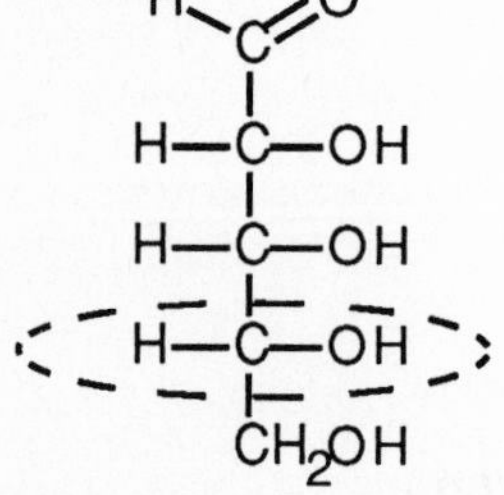

This monosaccharide, which is a pentose, must be ribose. Since the carbon farthest from the carbonyl group (circled) has the -OH group on the right, the monosaccharide is D-ribose.

(b)

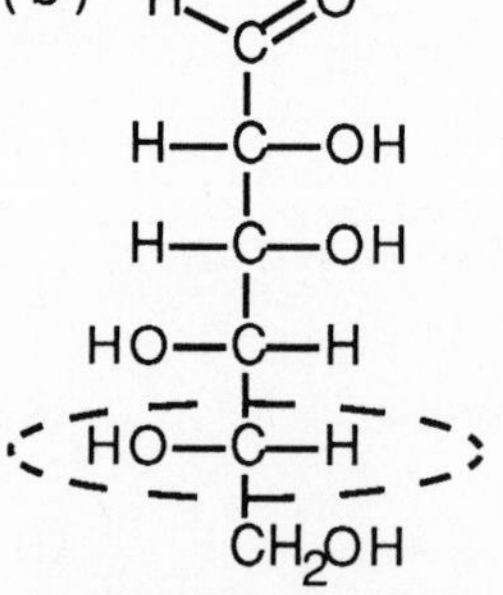

This hexose is an enantiomer of mannose. Since the -OH group of the circled carbon points to the left, the monosaccharide is L-mannose.

21.6

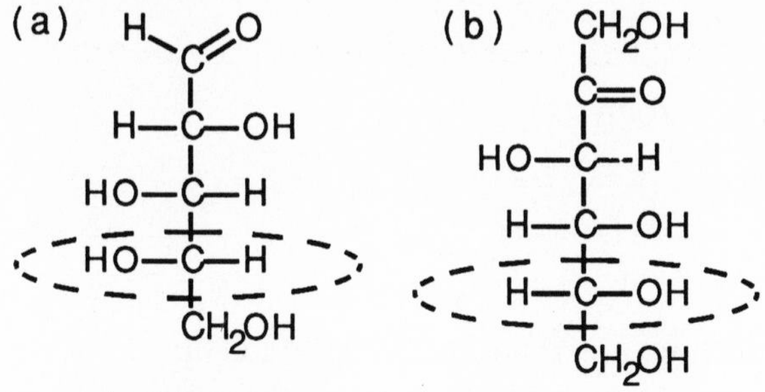

(a)

an L-aldopentose

(b)

a D-ketohexose

21.7

First, coil D-talose into a circular shape:

Next, rotate around the indicated single bond between C4 and C5 so that the -CH$_2$OH group (C6) points up.

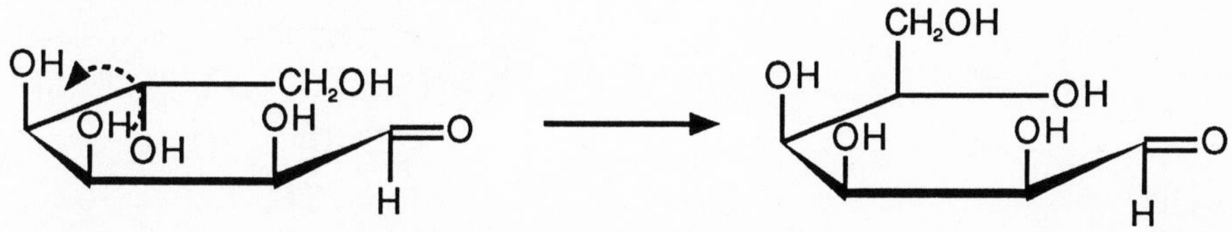

Finally, form a hemiacetal bond between the aldehyde and the -OH group at C5.

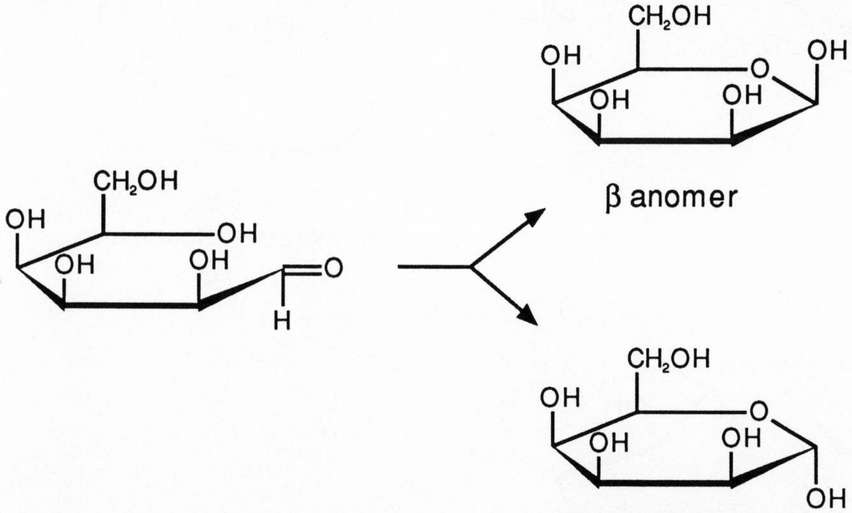

β anomer

α anomer

21.8

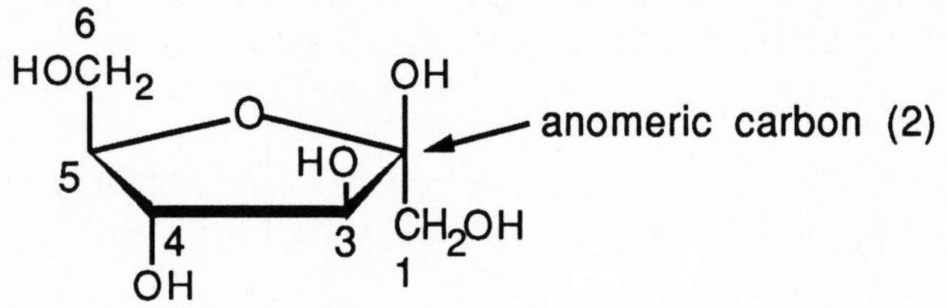
6
HOCH2
OH
anomeric carbon (2)
HO
5
4
3
CH2OH
1
OH

This is the β anomer because the -OH group at the anomeric carbon is up.

21.9 Chiral carbons are starred.

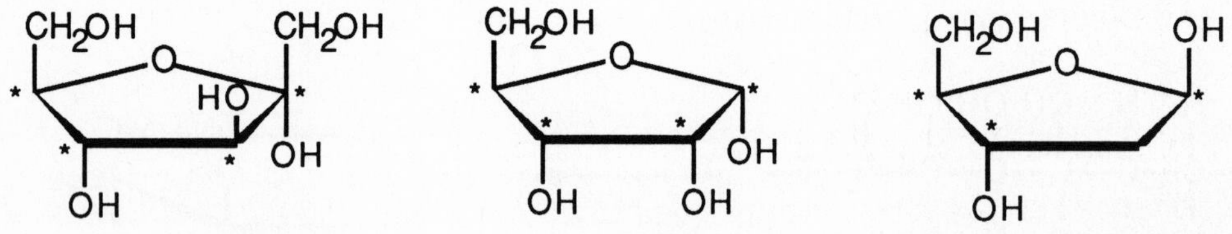
CH2OH
CH2OH
HO
OH
OH
α-D-Fructose
CH2OH
OH
OH
OH
α-D-Ribose
CH2OH
OH
OH
β-D-2-Deoxyribose

21.10

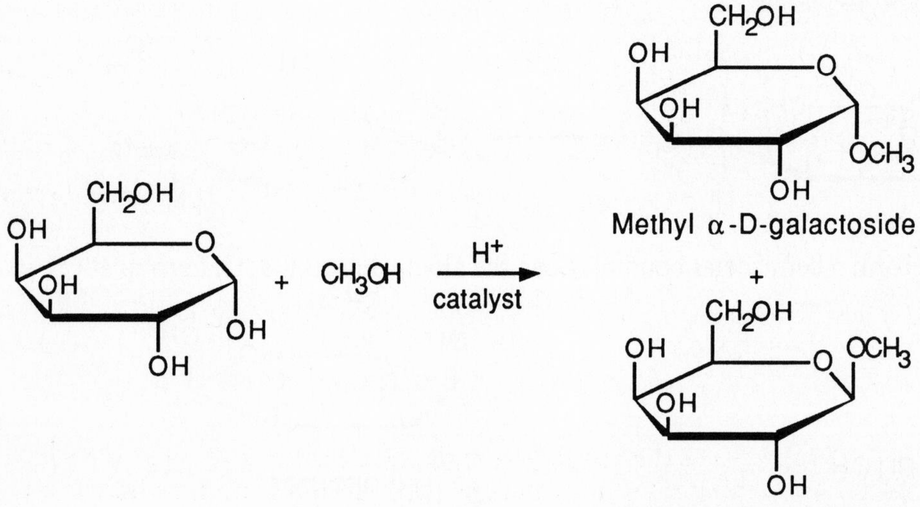
CH2OH
OH
OH
OH
OH
+
CH3OH
H+
catalyst
CH2OH
OH
OH
OCH3
OH
Methyl α-D-galactoside
+
CH2OH
OH
OCH3
OH
OH
Methyl β-D-galactoside

21.11

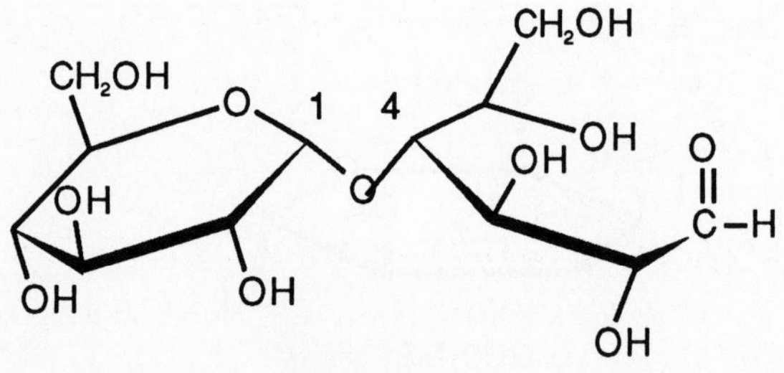
CH2OH
1
4
CH2OH
OH
OH
O
C-H
OH
OH
OH
OH

Maltose

21.12 Cellobiose is a reducing sugar because the hemiacetal linkage in the right-hand ring can exist as an open-chain aldehyde, which reacts with an oxidizing agent.

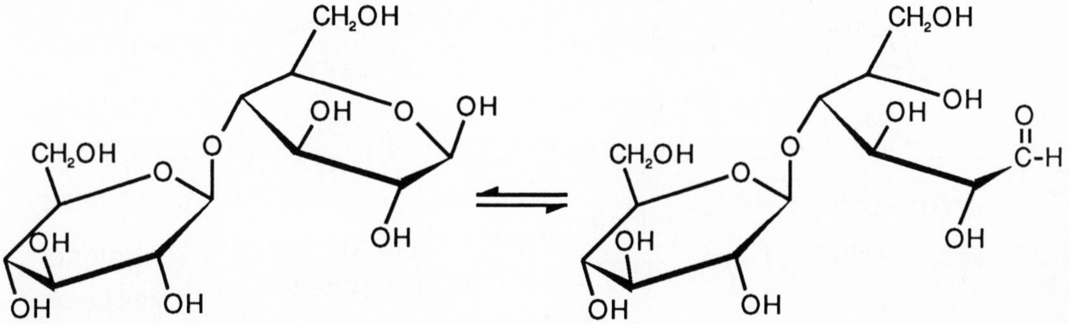

21.13 Cellobiose has a β-1,4 acetal link.

21.14

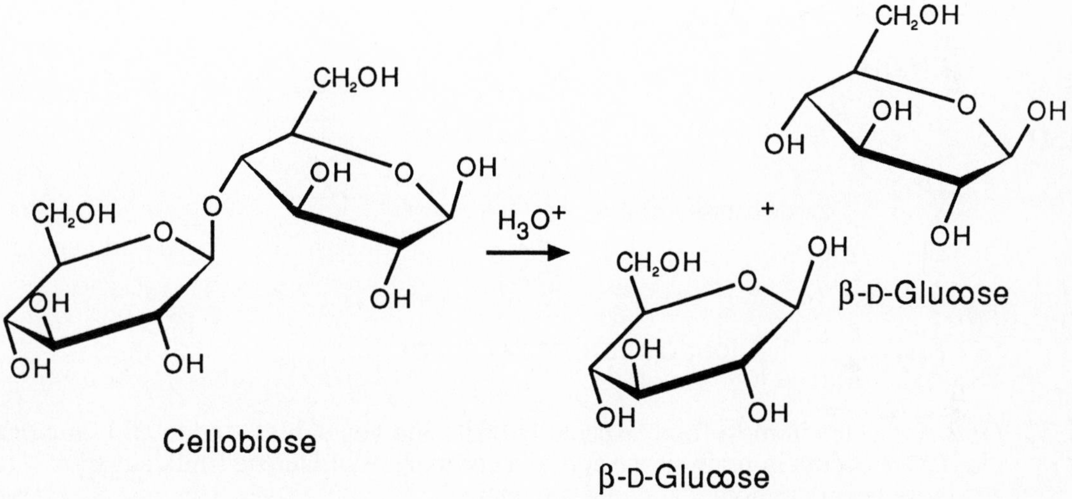

Cellobiose

β-D-Glucose

β-D-Glucose

21.15 Starch has so few hemiacetal units per molecule (only the one at the end of a very long chain) that a positive reducing-sugar reactions with Tollens' reagent or Benedict's reagent is undetectable.

21.16 A carbohydrate is a polyhydroxylated aldehyde or ketone that belongs to one of the biologically most important classes of compounds.

21.17 The family-name ending for a sugar is *-ose*.

21.18 An aldose contains an aldehyde carbonyl group, and a ketose contains a ketone carbonyl group.

21.19

(a)

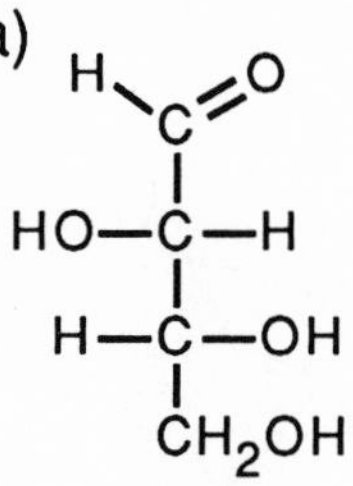

$$
\begin{array}{c}
H-C=O \\
| \\
HO-C-H \\
| \\
H-C-OH \\
| \\
CH_2OH
\end{array}
$$

Threose

An aldotetrose

(b)

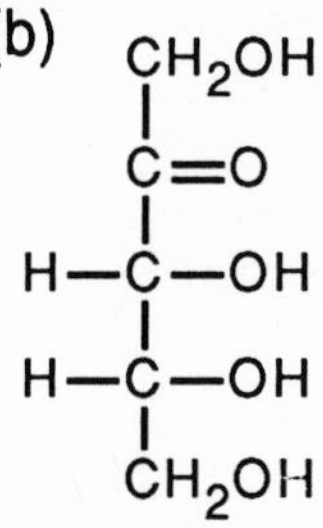

$$
\begin{array}{c}
CH_2OH \\
| \\
C=O \\
| \\
H-C-OH \\
| \\
H-C-OH \\
| \\
CH_2OH
\end{array}
$$

Ribulose

A ketopentose

(c)

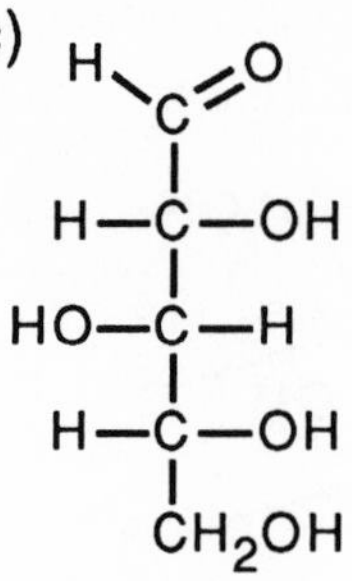

$$
\begin{array}{c}
H-C=O \\
| \\
H-C-OH \\
| \\
HO-C-H \\
| \\
H-C-OH \\
| \\
CH_2OH
\end{array}
$$

Xylose

An aldopentose

(d)

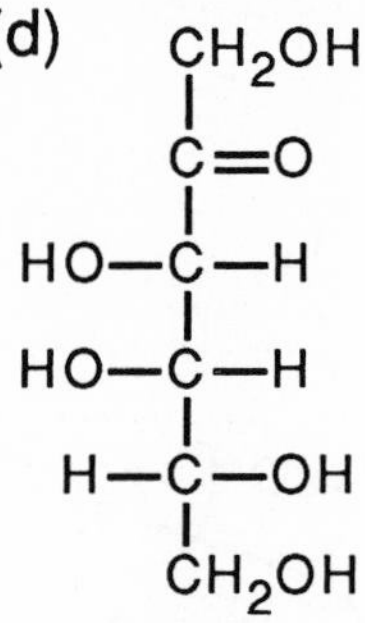

$$
\begin{array}{c}
CH_2OH \\
| \\
C=O \\
| \\
HO-C-H \\
| \\
HO-C-H \\
| \\
H-C-OH \\
| \\
CH_2OH
\end{array}
$$

Tagatose

A ketohexose

21.20

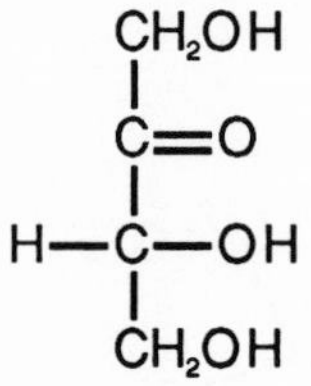

$$
\begin{array}{c}
CH_2OH \\
| \\
C=O \\
| \\
H-C-OH \\
| \\
CH_2OH
\end{array}
$$
A ketotetrose

21.21

$$
\begin{array}{c}
H-C=O \\
| \\
CH_2 \\
| \\
H-C-OH \\
| \\
CH_2OH
\end{array}
$$
← oxygen missing here

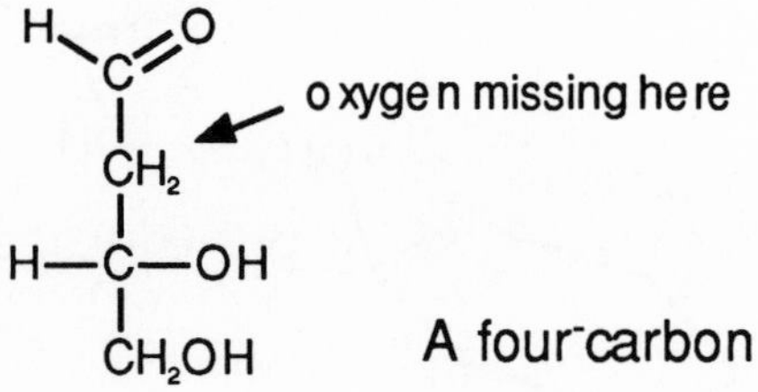

A four carbon deoxy sugar

21.22 *Glucose* occurs in most food, especially fruits and vegetables, and in all living organisms. *Galactose* occurs in brain tissue and as a component of lactose (milk sugar). *Fructose* occurs in honey and in many fruits.

21.23 *Dextrose* is another name for glucose.

21.24 *Enantiomers* are stereoisomers that are mirror images. *Diastereomers* are stereoisomers that aren't mirror images.

21.25 L-Glucose and D-glucose are mirror images.

21.26 L-Glucose is not a good food source because the enzymes in the body are handed and can digest only D-glucose.

21.27

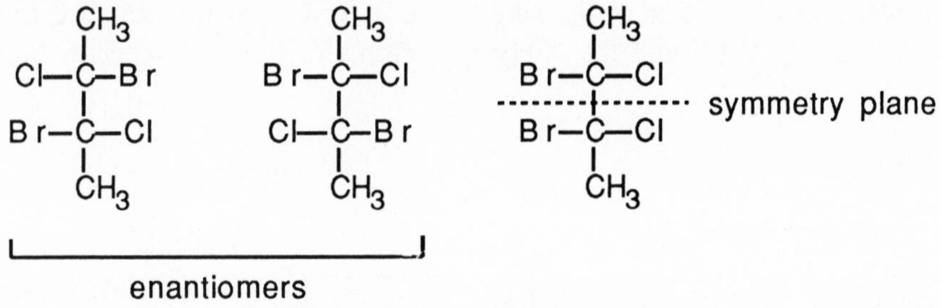

enantiomers

The third stereoisomer doesn't have an enantiomer because it's not chiral.

21.28

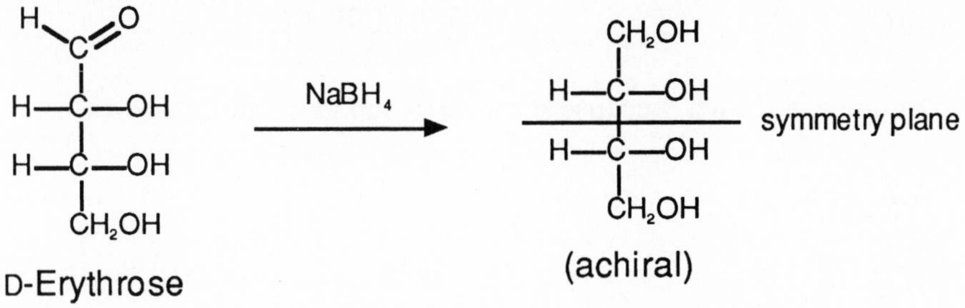

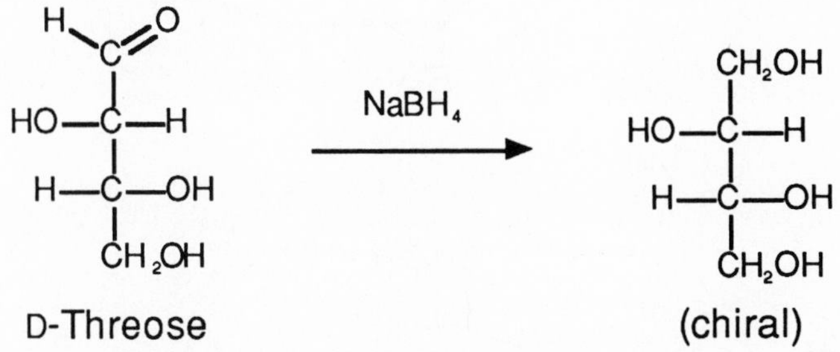

D-Erythrose → (achiral) symmetry plane

D-Threose → (chiral)

The product of reduction of D-erythrose has a symmetry plane and is achiral.

21.29

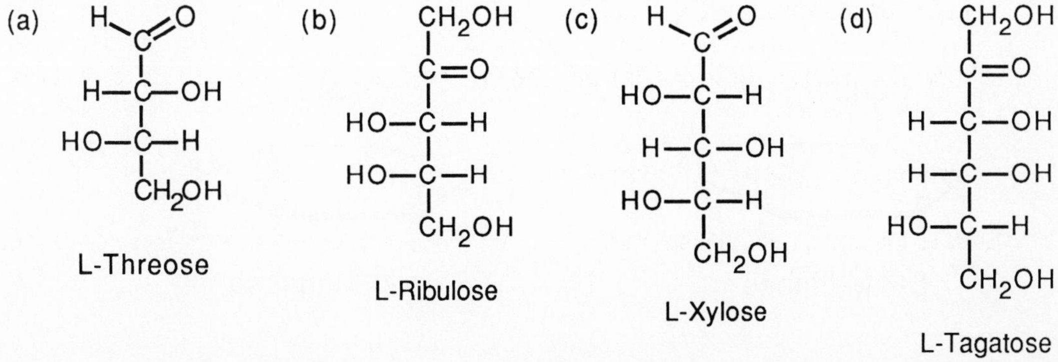

(a) L-Threose (b) L-Ribulose (c) L-Xylose (d) L-Tagatose

21.30 A reducing sugar is one that gives a positive reaction when treated with Tollens' reagent or Benedict's reagent. A sugar must have an aldehyde carbonyl group in order to give this reaction.

21.31 In the β-form of a carbohydrate hemiacetal, the -OH group attached to C1 (the hemiacetal carbon) points toward the same side of the ring as the -CH₂OH group attached to C5. In the α-form, the -OH group at C1 and the -CH₂OH group attached to C5 point toward opposite sides.

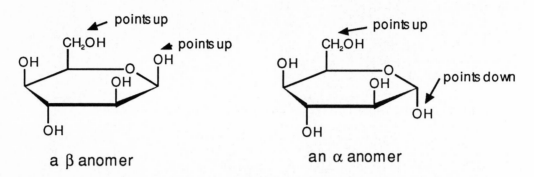

a β anomer   an α anomer

21.32 The α form of D-gulose is shown, because the -OH group at C1 points down.

21.33

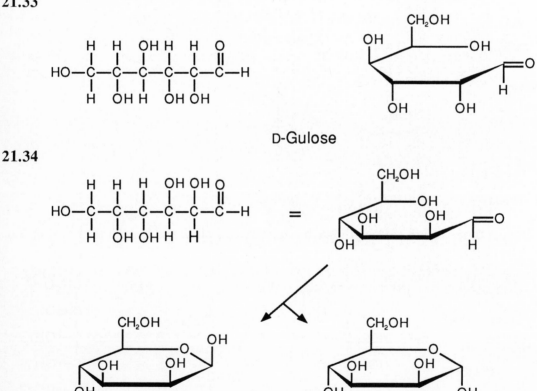

D-Gulose

21.34

β-D-Mannose   α-D-Mannose

21.35

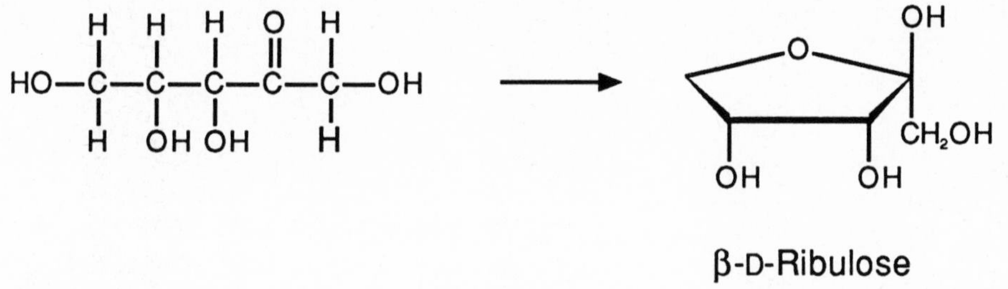

β-D-Ribulose

21.36 - 21.37

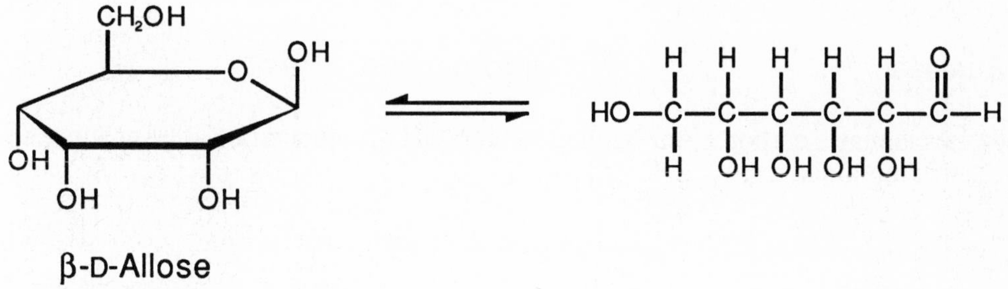

β-D-Allose

21.38

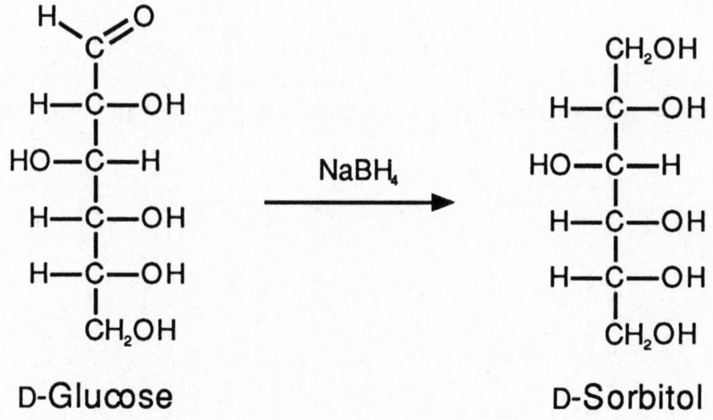

D-Glucose   NaBH₄   D-Sorbitol

21.39

D-Fructose   NaBH₄   D-Sorbitol

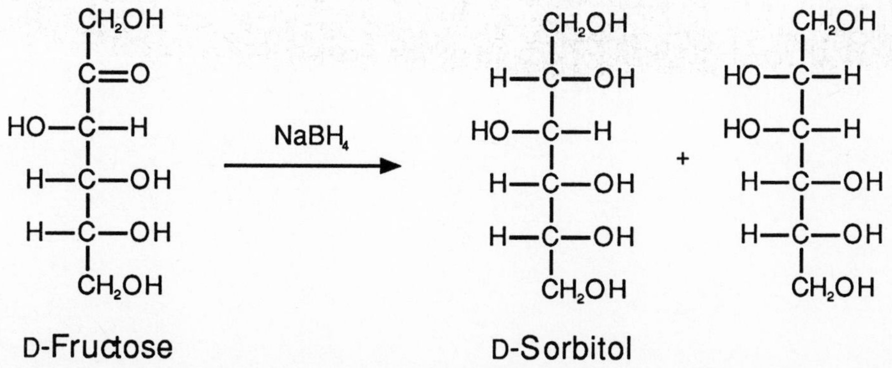

21.40 The reduced carbonyl carbon of glucose has a primary hydroxyl group and is achiral. The reduced carbonyl carbon of fructose is bonded to four different groups and is chiral. Thus, two products, which have different configurations at the reduced carbonyl carbon, are formed from reduction of fructose.

21.41

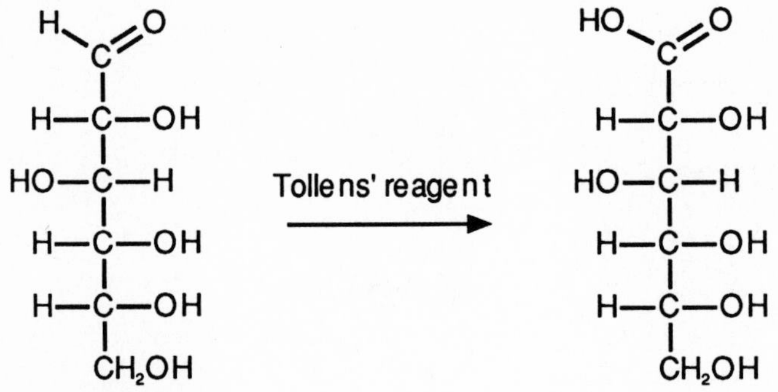

D-Glucose   Gluconic acid

21.42 A hemiacetal has a carbon atom bonded to one -OH group and one -OR group. An acetal has a carbon bonded to two -OR groups.

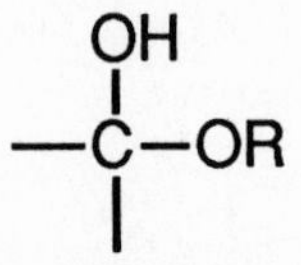

A *hemiacetal* 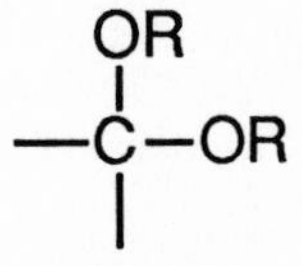   An *acetal*

21.43 A *glycoside* is the acetal product that results from reaction of a carbohydrate with an alcohol.

21.44

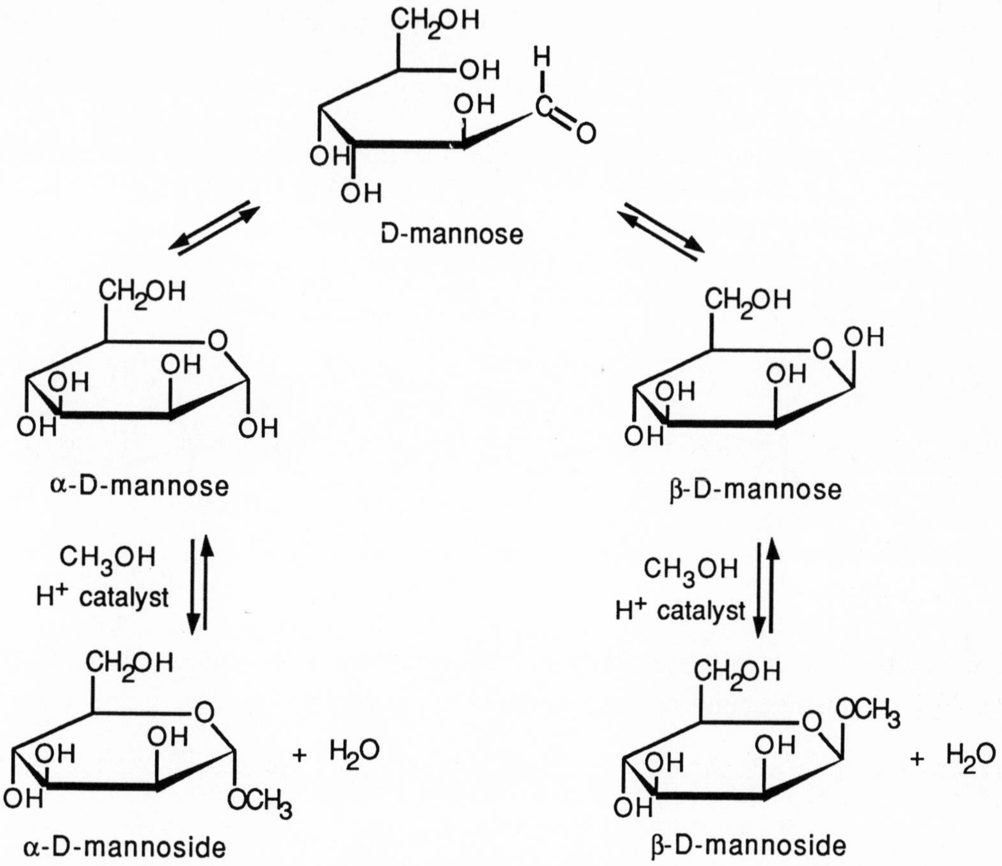

D-mannose

α-D-mannose   β-D-mannose

CH$_3$OH
H$^+$ catalyst

CH$_3$OH
H$^+$ catalyst

+ H$_2$O

+ H$_2$O

α-D-mannoside   β-D-mannoside

21.45

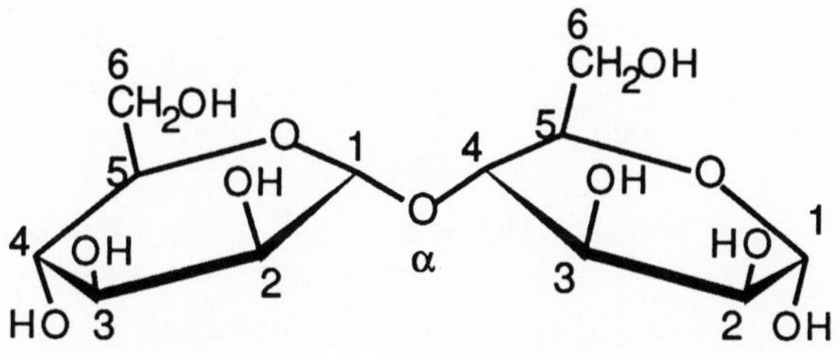

21.46 *Disaccharide*   *occurs in:*   *made from:*

Disaccharide	occurs in:	made from:
maltose	fermenting grains	glucose + glucose
lactose	milk	galactose + glucose
sucrose	many plants	glucose + fructose

21.47 Starch, a major component of the human diet, consists of α-D-glucose units linked together by 1,4-acetal bonds. Cellulose, used by plants as a structural material, consists of β-D-glucose units linked together by 1,4-acetal bonds.

21.48 Amylose and amylopectin are both components of starch and both consist of long polymers of α-D-glucose linked by α-1,4 glycosidic bonds. Amylopectin is much larger and has α-1,6 branches every 25 units along the chain.

21.49 Starch consists of two types of α-D-glucose polymers: *Amylose* is a straight-chain polymer, and *amylopectin* has branches every 25 or so units. Glycogen resembles amylopectin but is larger and contains more branches. Starch is used for food storage in plants, and glycogen is used for food storage in animals.

21.50 Lactose and maltose have hemiacetal linkages that give positive Tollens' test results. Sucrose, however, has no hemiacetal group and is thus unreactive toward Tollens' reagent.

21.51 - 21.52

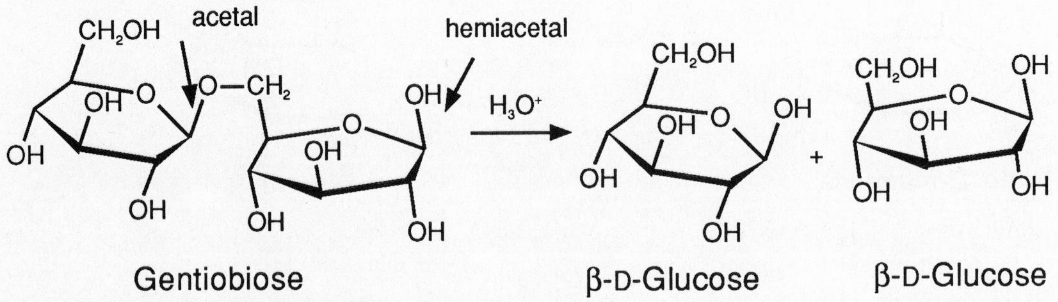

Gentiobiose   β-D-Glucose   β-D-Glucose

Gentiobiose is a reducing sugar because it has a hemiacetal linkage on the right-hand sugar unit. A β-1,6 linkage connects the two monosaccharides.

21.53 - 21.54

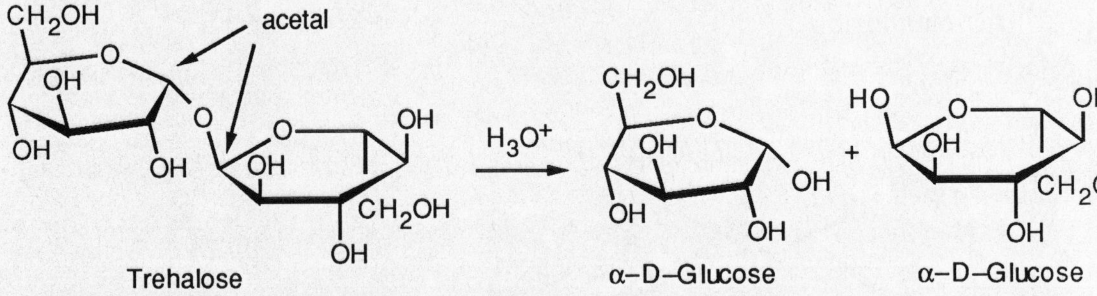

Trehalose   α–D–Glucose   α–D–Glucose

Trehalose is a nonreducing sugar because it contains no hemiacetal linkages.

21.55

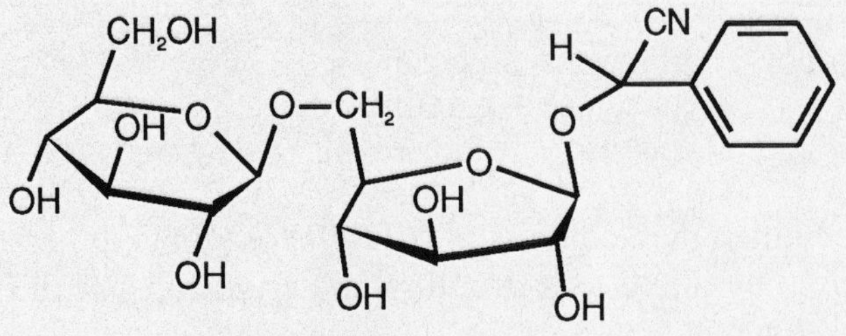

Amygdalin

21.56 An optically active compound is one that rotates the plane of plane-polarized light.

21.57   A polarimeter measures the angle of rotation of a solution of an optically active compound.

21.58   (a) Fructose rotates light to the left to a greater degree than glucose rotates light to the right.
(b) The mixture is called invert sugar because the sign of rotation of the fructose-glucose mixture is inverted from (opposite to) the sign of rotation of sucrose.

21.59   Enantiomers rotate light to the same degree but in opposite directions.

21.60   In a healthy diet, cellulose provides fiber, which aids in the passage of food through the digestive system.

21.61   Pectin and vegetable gum are two kinds of soluble fiber, which can be found in fruits, barley, oats and beans.

21.62   Diabetes is due to a deficiency of insulin, which regulates the movement of glucose from the bloodstream into cells.

21.63   Benedict's test detects all reducing sugars in the bloodstream and is thus not specific for glucose.

21.64   Glucose is oxidized by glucose oxidase to yield gluconic acid and H_2O_2, which reacts with a dye in a peroxidase- catalyzed reaction to yield a colored oxidized dye (and H_2O). The color change, which can be measured, is specific for glucose.

21.65   If incompatible blood types are mixed, the red blood cells clump together, or agglutinate, and death may result. Agglutination occurs when the body's immune system recognizes foreign cells and manufactures antibodies to them.

21.66   An antigenic determinant provokes an immune response that results in the production of antibodies.

21.67   All blood groups have *N*-acetylglucosamine, galactose and fucose as components of their antigenic determinants. Blood group O is the universal donor because it has components common to all blood groups. The other blood groups have additional components of their antigenic determinants that provoke an immune response if blood with incompatible groups is mixed.

21.68   Although artificial sweeteners have caloric value, they are so much sweeter than natural sweeteners that only small amounts need to be used.

21.69

D-ribose and L-ribose are enantiomers that are identical in all properties (melting point, density, solubility and chemical reactivity) except for the direction of rotation of plane-polarized light.

21.70

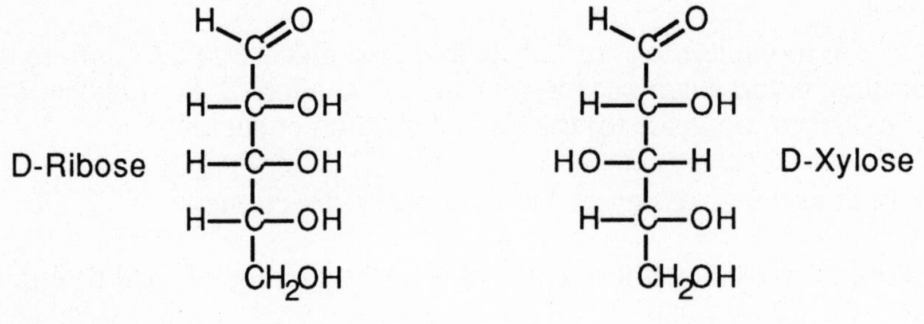

D-Ribose

D-Xylose

D-ribose and D-xylose are diastereomers and differ in all properties listed.

21.71

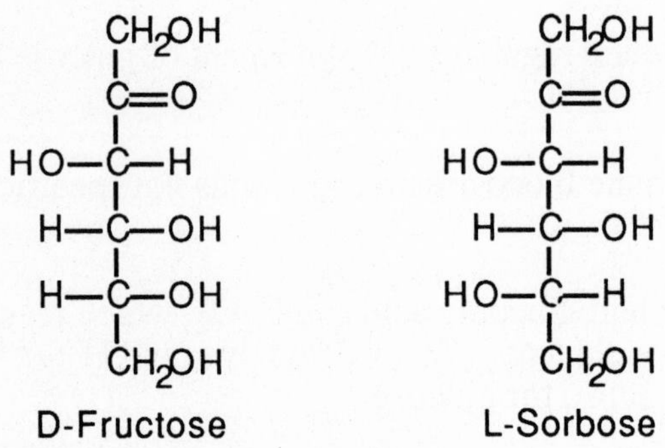

D-Fructose

L-Sorbose

21.72

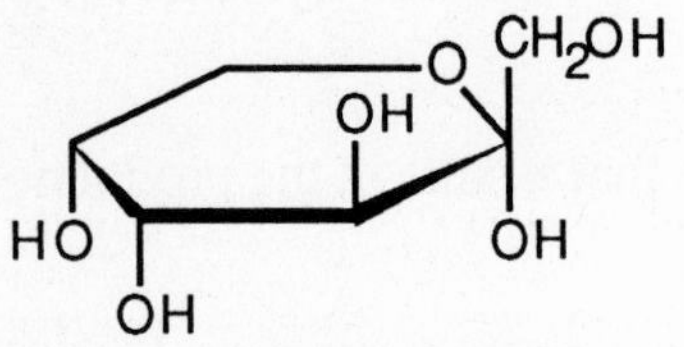

21.73 The α and β hemiacetal forms of monosaccharides are diastereomers because they are not mirror images.

21.74 - 21.75

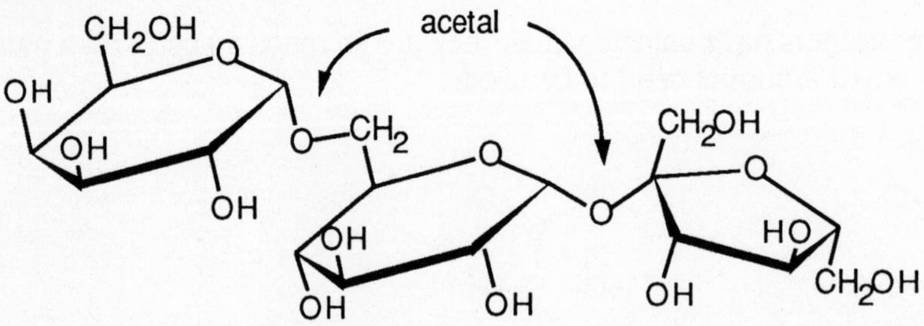

Raffinose is not a reducing sugar because it has no hemiacetal groups.

21.76 The sweet taste of a partially chewed cracker is due to the enzymatic breakdown of starch to glucose.

The Chapter in Brief

Introduction (Sections 21.1–21.3) Carbohydrates are polyhydroxylated aldehydes and ketones. They can be classified either as aldoses or as ketoses, and as monosaccharides, disaccharides, or polysaccharides. Most sugars are chiral and are commonly represented by Fischer projections in which the –OH group of the chiral carbon farthest from the carbonyl group is placed on the right (D form).

Monosaccharides (Sections 21.4–21.6) Glucose is the most widely occurring monosaccharide; it exists mainly as a cyclic hemiacetal. Other important monosaccharides are fructose and galactose. Monosaccharides that react with Tollens' reagent or Benedict's reagent are said to be reducing sugars. Monosaccharides can also react with alcohols to form glycosides, and with other monosaccharides to form disaccharides.

Disaccharides and Polysaccharides (Sections 121.7, 21.8) Maltose, lactose, and sucrose are among the most important disaccharides. Cellulose, starch, and glycogen are important polysaccharides.

Self-Test for Chapter 21

Complete the following sentences:

1. An object that has handedness is said to be _____.

2. Starch molecules are digested by enzymes called _____.

3. The two mirror image forms of a chiral molecule are called _____.

4.   A reaction between an aldehyde carbonyl group and an alcohol hydroxyl group in the same molecule yields a _____ _____.

5. *Levulose* is another name for _____.

6. _____ and _____ are two kinds of starch.

7. The reaction of a monosaccharide with an alcohol yields a _____.

8. _____ is used for food storage in animals.

9. D-Glucose can be classified as a _____.

10. 3-Pentanol is an _____ molecule.

11. A _____ is a stereoisomer that is not an enantiomer.

12. Galactose is an _____ of glucose.

Match the entries on the left with their partners on the right:

1. Maltose   (a) Aldohexose

2. Cellulose   (b) Glucose

3. Methyl glucoside (c) Aldotriose

4. Ribose   (d) Glucose + fructose

5. Fructose   (e) Glucose + glucose

6. Glycogen   (f) Polysaccharide of α-D-glucose

7. Dextrose   (g) Glucose + galactose

8. Glucose   (h) Aldopentose

9. Sucrose   (i) Ketohexose

10. Lactose   (j) Acetal

11. Glyceraldehyde   (k) Animal starch

12. Amylose   (l) Polysaccharide of β-D-glucose

Tell whether the following statements are true or false:

1. All naturally occurring carbohydrates are chiral.

2. Glucose is a reducing sugar.

3. All reducing sugars give a silver mirror with Tollens' reagent.

4. The human body can digest polysaccharides containing β-1,4 acetal links but not α-1,4 acetal links.

5. Achiral objects possess a plane of symmetry.

6. Crystalline glucose is a mixture of α-anomer, β-anomer, and open-chain forms.

7. Sucrose contains both acetal and hemiacetal groups.

8. Amylopectin and glycogen contain 1,4 and 1,6 acetal links.

9. An acetal is an ester.

10. Maltose is a disaccharide composed of glucose and galactose.

11. Two diastereomers rotate plane-polarized light in equal amounts but in opposite directions.

12. All monosaccharides are reducing sugars.

Chapter 22 – Carbohydrate Metabolism

22.1 (a) Lactose + H_2O $\xrightarrow{\text{lactase}}$ glucose + galactose

(b) Sucrose + H_2O $\xrightarrow{\text{sucrase}}$ glucose + fructose

22.2 (a) *Glycogenolysis* is the release of glucose from glycogen.
(b) *Gluconeogenesis* is the synthesis of glucose from lactate.
(c) *Glycogenesis* is the synthesis of glycogen from glucose.

22.3 The following synthetic pathways have glucose as their first reactant:
Glycogenesis: synthesis of glycogen from glucose
Pentose phosphate pathway: synthesis of five-carbon sugars from glucose
Glycolysis: conversion of glucose to pyruvate

22.4 (1) In *Step 6*, 1,3-diphosphoglycerate (high-energy phosphate) is synthesized. In *Step 7*, the energy is harvested in ATP as 3-phosphoglycerate is formed.
(2) In *Step 9*, phosphoenolpyruvate (high-energy phosphate) is synthesized. In *Step 10*, the energy is harvested in ATP as pyruvate is formed.

22.5 The following steps are isomerizations:

Step 2: glucose 6-phosphate ⟶ fructose 6-phosphate

Step 5: dihydroxyacetone phosphate ⟶ glyceraldehyde 3-phosphate

Step 8: 3-phosphoglycerate ⟶ 2-phosphoglycerate

22.6

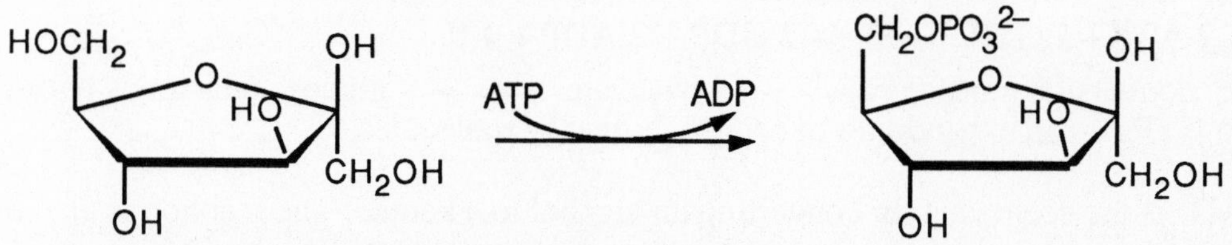

Fructose 6-phosphate enters glycolysis at step 3.

22.7

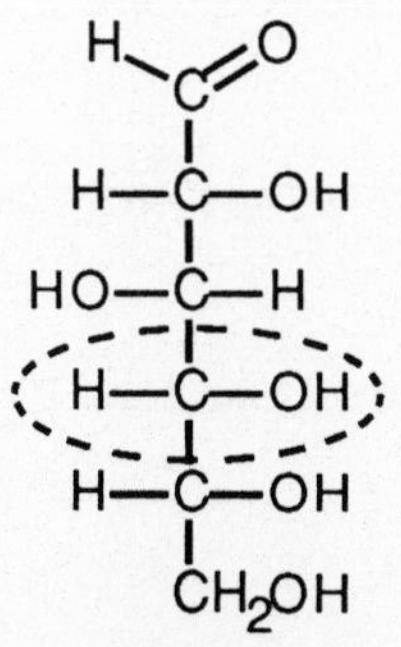

D-Glucose

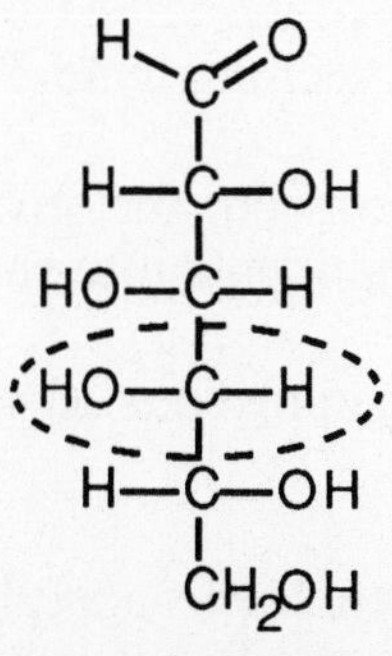

D-Galactose

Glucose and galactose differ in configuration at carbon 4.

22.8 One molecule of CO_2 is formed when pyruvate is converted to acetyl SCoA. Two more molecules of CO_2 are formed in the citric acid cycle; one is formed in the conversion isocitrate —> α-ketoglutarate (Step 3), and the other is formed in the conversion α-ketoglutarate —> succinyl SCoA (Step 4). Since each glucose provides two pyruvates (and thus two acetyl SCoAs), a total of 6 CO_2s are formed.

22.9 Two NADH (yielding 3 ATP each) must be converted to NAD^+ in a process that yields 2 $FADH_2$ (yielding 2 ATP each). Since the two $FADH_2$ molecules yield two fewer ATPs than the two NADH molecules, the catabolism of glucose in this case yields 36 ATPs instead of 38.

22.10 (1) UTP + glucose 1-phosphate ⟶ glucose-UDP + PP_i $\Delta G = +1.1$ kcal/mol

(2) $PP_i + H_2O$ ⟶ 2 P_i $\Delta G = -8.0$ kcal/mol

UTP + glucose 1-phosphate + H_2O ⟶ glucose-UDP + 2 P_i $\Delta G = -6.9$ kcal/mol

The common intermediate for these two reactions is PP_i (pyrophosphate). ΔG for the coupled reactions is -6.9 kcal/mol, indicating an exergonic reaction and a favorable energy change.

22.11 Glycolysis:
glucose + 2 NAD^+ + 2 P_i + 2 ADP —> 2 pyruvate + 2 NADH/H^+ + 2 ATP + 2 H_2O

Gluconeogenesis:
2 pyruvate + 4 ATP + 2 GTP + 2 NADH/H^+ + 2 H_2O

⟶ glucose + 4 ADP + 2 GDP + 6 P_i + 2 NAD^+

2 ATP + 2 GTP ⟶ 2 GDP + 2 ADP + 4 P_i

The conversion glucose ⟶ 2 pyruvate ⟶ glucose consumes two ATPs and two GTPs — an expenditure of four high-energy molecules.

22.12 NAD^+ is the coenzyme for converting an alcohol to a ketone. The reaction is an oxidation.

22.13 Each of the three glucose 6-phosphate molecules yields one CO_2 and one ribulose 5-phosphate molecule. Reactions of the three ribulose 5-phosphate molecules produce two fructose 6-phosphates and one glyceraldehyde 3-phosphate.

22.14 Digestion occurs in the mouth, stomach, and small intestine; it involves the enzyme-catalyzed hydrolysis of food components into small molecules.

22.15 *Aerobic* reactions take place in the presence of oxygen; *anaerobic* reactions take place in the absence of oxygen.

22.16 Under aerobic conditions, pyruvate forms acetyl SCoA.
Under anaerobic conditions, pyruvate forms lactate.
Under fermentation conditions, pyruvate forms ethanol.

22.17 Maltose + H_2O $\xrightarrow{\text{maltase}}$ 2 glucose
This process occurs in the mucous lining of the small intestine.

22.18

Process	*Substrate*	⟶	*Product*
Glycolysis	glucose		pyruvate
Gluconeogenesis	pyruvate & other small molecules		glucose
Glycogenesis	glucose		glycogen
Glycogenolysis	glycogen		glucose

22.19 Glycolysis is also known as the Embden-Meyerhof pathway.

22.20 Pyruvate is the final product of glycolysis.

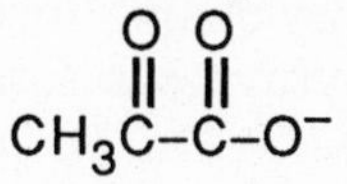

$$CH_3\overset{\overset{O}{\|}}{C}-\overset{\overset{O}{\|}}{C}-O^-$$

22.21 Glycolysis occurs in the cytosol of all cells; the citric acid cycle occurs in mitochondria.

22.22 (a) Phosphorylation:

Step 1: glucose ⟶ glucose 6-phosphate

Step 3: fructose 6-phosphate ⟶ fructose 1,6-diphosphate

Step 6: glyceraldehyde 3-phosphate ⟶ 1,3-diphosphoglyceric acid

(b) Oxidation:

Step 6: glyceraldehyde 3-phosphate ⟶ 1,3-diphosphoglyceric acid

(c) Dehydration:

Step 9: 2-phosphoglyceric acid ⟶ phosphoenolpyruvic acid

22.23

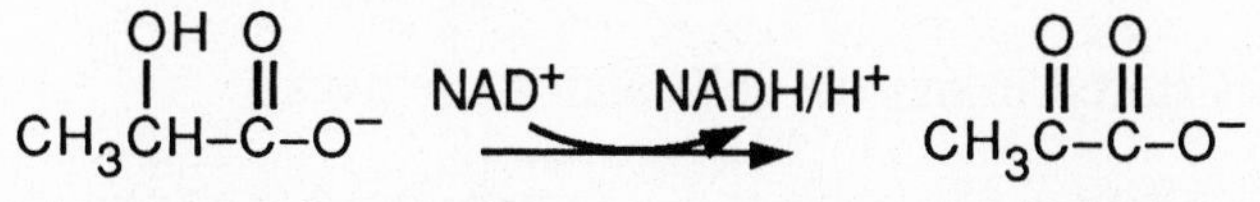

$$CH_3\overset{\overset{OH}{|}}{CH}-\overset{\overset{O}{\|}}{C}-O^- \quad \underset{\xrightarrow{\hspace{1.5cm}}}{NAD^+ \quad NADH/H^+} \quad CH_3\overset{\overset{O}{\|}}{C}-\overset{\overset{O}{\|}}{C}-O^-$$

lactate   pyruvate

22.24 (a) Glycolysis of one mole of glucose produces *6 moles of ATP* (under some circumstances the yield is *8 moles of ATP*).

(b) A mole of pyruvate produces *3 moles of ATP*.

(c) A mole of acetyl SCoA produces *12 moles of ATP*.

22.25

Glycolysis	= 6 ATP
2 x pyruvate ⟶ 2 acetyl SCoA	= 6 ATP
2 x acetyl SCoA (in citric acid cycle)	= 24 ATP
	= 36 ATP

Complete catabolism of one mole of glucose yields 36 moles of ATP.

22.26 If fructose were isomerized to glucose prior to glycolysis, then complete catabolism of one mole of sucrose would yield 72 moles of ATP.

22.27 Catabolism of one mole of sucrose produces four moles of acetyl SCoA.

22.28 The complete catabolism of one mole of sucrose yields 12 moles of CO_2.

22.29 As with sucrose (problem 22.26), catabolism of one mole of maltose yields 72 moles of ATP.

22.30 Under anaerobic conditions NADH can't enter the respiratory chain. Instead, in order to replenish the body's supply of NAD^+, NADH reacts with pyruvate to form lactate and NAD^+.

22.31

Condition	Blood sugar level	Symptoms
hypoglycemia	low	weakness, sweating, rapid heartbeat, confusion, coma, death
hyperglycemia	high	increased urine flow, low blood pressure, coma, death

22.32 Epinephrine causes the immediate conversion of glycogen to glucose 6-phosphate in cells.

22.33 Glucose is initially formed from glycogen during starvation or fasting. When glycogen is used up, glucose is formed from proteins.

22.34 Acetyl SCoA is converted to ketone bodies to prevent buildup in the cells.

22.35 *Juvenile diabetes* is caused by insufficient production of insulin in the pancreas. *Adult onset diabetes* is caused by the failure of insulin to promote the passage of glucose across cell membranes.

22.36 Most of the glycogen in the body is stored in muscle cells and in the liver.

22.37 UTP reacts with glucose to form the high-energy compound UDP-glucose, which carries glucose to the growing glycogen chain.

23.38 Glycogenolysis is not the reverse of glycogenesis; glycogenolysis is energetically favorable, and thus the exact reverse must be energetically unfavorable.

22.39 *Gluconeogenesis* is the anabolic pathway for making glucose.

22.40 Lactate and glycerol are two molecules that can serve as starting materials for glucose synthesis.

22.41 In glucose anabolism, pyruvate is initially converted to oxaloacetate and then to phosphoenolpyruvate.

22.42 The exact reverse of the energetically favorable conversion of glucose to pyruvate is energetically unfavorable and thus doesn't occur in nature.

22.43 The pentose phosphate pathway is used to provide the coenzyme NADPH and to produce ribose 5-phosphate, a sugar used in nucleic acid synthesis.

22.44

If the body needs:	then	*Fate of intermediates in pentose phosphate pathway:*
NADPH		recycled to glucose 6-phosphate for further production of NADPH
ATP		fructose 6-phosphate and glyceraldehyde 3-phosphate enter glycolysis
nucleic acid synthesis		ribose 5-phosphate is major product

22.45 A lack of the enzyme glucose 6-phosphatase gives rise to von Gierke's disease. Symptoms include an enlarged liver and very low blood sugar.

22.46 McArdle's disease is due to a deficiency in the enzyme that catalyzes the breakdown of glycogen to glucose in the muscles. Symptoms include rapid fatigue and muscle cramps on exertion.

22.47 The fasting level of glucose in a diabetic is 140 mg/dL or greater, as compared to a level of 90 mg/dL for a non-diabetic.

22.48 After drinking a glucose solution, both a diabetic and a non-diabetic experience a great increase in blood sugar level in the first hour. After two hours, the glucose level in a non-diabetic returns to near fasting level, while the level in a diabetic remains high.

22.49 Creatine phosphate provides ATP in one step, whereas glucose metabolism takes many steps to provide ATP.

22.50 The distance a person can sprint is limited by creatine phosphate, which is in short supply.

22.51 The NADH formed during glycolysis can't cross the inner mitochondrial membrane. Instead, the hydrogen atoms from NADH/H$^+$ are shuttled across the membrane to form FADH$_2$. FADH$_2$ yields only 2 mol ATP, and thus the energy yield from glycolysis is reduced.

22.52 Galactosemia is caused by the absence of an enzyme that converts galactose to glucose 6-phosphate. Symptoms include cataracts, liver damage and mental retardation.

22.53 Pyruvate can cross the mitochondrial membrane because it is the only molecule in glycolysis that is not a phosphate. (Phosphates can't cross the mitochondrial membrane.)

22.54 Kinase enzymes are usually associated with phosphorylations or their reverse.

22.55 Fructose and glucose have the same net ATP production because fructose can enter glycolysis directly as a glycolysis intermediate.

22.56 Since glucose generated from the hydrolysis of glycogen enters the glycolysis pathway as glucose 6-phosphate, one less ATP is needed (at step 1) and thus one more ATP is produced.

The Chapter in Brief

Overview (Sections 22.1, 22.2) The digestion of carbohydrates begins in the mouth as α-amylase hydrolyzes glycosidic bonds in starches and sugars to yield glucose and other monosaccharides. Glucose can then be used for glycolysis, glycogenesis, and the pentose phosphate pathway, and can be resynthesized by gluconeogenesis or glycogenolysis.

Glycolysis (Sections 22.3–22.9) In the Embden-Meyerhof pathway, glucose is broken down to pyruvate, which is oxidized to acetyl SCoA under aerobic conditions. Acetyl SCoA then enters the citric acid cycle. The total energy output for complete glucose catabolism is 36 ATP per mole of glucose. Other hexoses can also enter the Embden-Meyerhof pathway as glycolysis intermediates. Under anaerobic conditions, pyruvate is reduced to lactate. The pancreatic hormones insulin and glucagon regulate glucose metabolism.

Other Metabolic Pathways for Glucose (Sections 22.10–22.12) In *glycogenesis*, glucose is converted to UDP-glucose and is then transferred to a growing glycogen chain. The reverse process, *glycogenolysis*, releases glucose. In *gluconeogenesis*, glucose can be synthesized from small molecules such as pyruvate or glycerol. In the *pentose phosphate pathway*, glucose is used to synthesize ribose, fructose 6-phosphate, or glyceraldehyde 3-phosphate.

Self-Test for Chapter 22

Complete the following sentences:

1.   The _____ - _____ pathway is another name for glycolysis.

2.   Absorption of food products in the intestine occurs through the _____.

3.   _____ _____ catalyzes the formation of acetyl SCoA from pyruvate.

4.   _____ aids in the passage of blood glucose across cell membranes.

5.   Glycogenolysis may be triggered by the release of _____.

6.   _____ _____ occurs when the enzyme _____ is no longer synthesized in the intestine.

7.   The metabolic response to _____ resembles starvation.

8.   _____ and _____ supply the energy for gluconeogenesis.

9.   When pyruvate is converted to acetyl SCoA, one molecule of _____ is lost.

10. The isomerization of glucose 6-phosphate to fructose 6-phosphate is catalyzed by _____.

11. The hormone _____ stimulates breakdown of glycogen.

12. _____ can lead to mental retardation and death.

Match the entries on the left with their partners on the right:

1.   Glycolysis   (a) Formed by fermentation of pyruvate

2.   Hyperglycemia   (b) Formed from pyruvate under anaerobic conditions

3.   Enolase   (c) Intermediate in glycogen synthesis

4.   Glycogenolysis   (d) Synthesis of glucose from pyruvate

5.   UDP-glucose   (e) Catalyzed the cleavage of fructose 1,6-diphosphate

6.   Ribose 5-phosphate   (f) Low blood sugar

7.   Gluconeogenesis   (g) Synthesis of glycogen from glucose

8.   Ethanol   (h) Product of pentose phosphate pathway

9.   Hypoglycemia   (i) Catalyzes loss of water from 2-phosphoglyceric acid

10. Glycogenesis   (j) Breakdown of glycogen to glucose

11. Lactate   (k) High blood sugar

12. Aldolase   (l) Breakdown of glucose to pyruvate

Tell whether the following statements are true or false:

1.   The pentose phosphate pathway is important because it produces NADH.

2.   Fructose, galactose, and mannose can all enter the glycolysis pathway.

3.   Conversion of glucose 6-phosphate to fructose 6-phosphate requires ATP.

4.   Glycogenesis is the exact reverse of glycogenolysis.

5.   Hyperglycemia is a high level of blood glucose.

6.   The reactions of glycolysis occur in the mitochondria.

7.   36 ATPs are produced for each glucose that passes through the glycolysis pathway.

8.   Glucagon is the storage form of glucose.

9.   All three transformations of pyruvate occur in the human body.

10. Cleavage of fructose 1,6-diphosphate yields two molecules of glyceraldehyde 3-phosphate.

11. Pyruvate is converted to lactate under anaerobic conditions.

12. Each conversion of glyceraldehyde 3-phosphate to pyruvate requires two ADPs.

23.1

$$CH_3(CH_2)_{18}\overset{\overset{\displaystyle O}{\|}}{C}\!-\!OCH_2(CH_2)_{30}CH_3$$

23.2

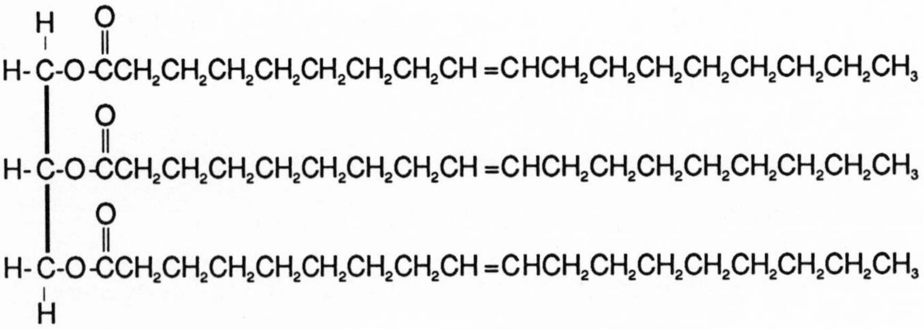

$$H-\overset{\overset{\displaystyle H}{|}}{C}-O-\overset{\overset{\displaystyle O}{\|}}{C}CH_2CH_2CH_2CH_2CH_2CH_2CH_2CH=CHCH_2CH_2CH_2CH_2CH_2CH_2CH_2CH_3$$

$$H-\overset{|}{C}-O-\overset{\overset{\displaystyle O}{\|}}{C}CH_2CH_2CH_2CH_2CH_2CH_2CH_2CH=CHCH_2CH_2CH_2CH_2CH_2CH_2CH_2CH_3$$

$$H-\underset{\underset{\displaystyle H}{|}}{\overset{|}{C}}-O-\overset{\overset{\displaystyle O}{\|}}{C}CH_2CH_2CH_2CH_2CH_2CH_2CH_2CH=CHCH_2CH_2CH_2CH_2CH_2CH_2CH_2CH_3$$

Glyceryl trioleate

23.3

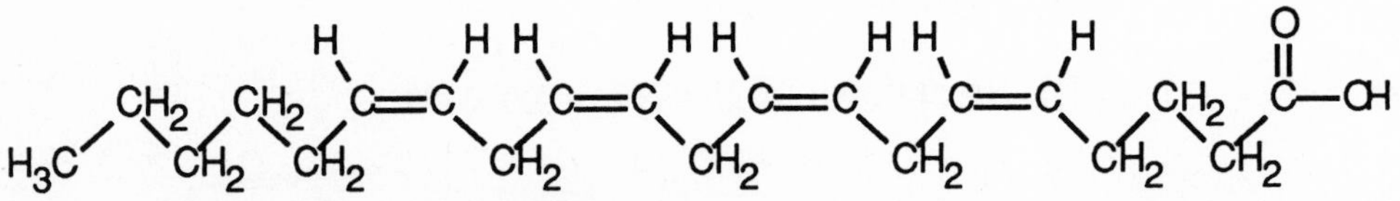

Arachidonic acid

23.4   Glyceryl trioleate (23.2)

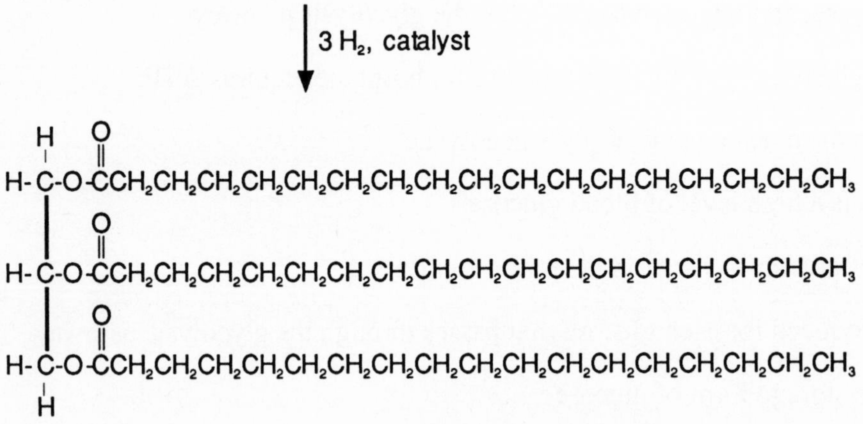

$$\big\downarrow\; 3\,H_2,\ \text{catalyst}$$

$$H-\overset{\overset{\displaystyle H}{|}}{C}-O-\overset{\overset{\displaystyle O}{\|}}{C}CH_2CH_2CH_2CH_2CH_2CH_2CH_2CH_2CH_2CH_2CH_2CH_2CH_2CH_2CH_2CH_2CH_3$$

$$H-\overset{|}{C}-O-\overset{\overset{\displaystyle O}{\|}}{C}CH_2CH_2CH_2CH_2CH_2CH_2CH_2CH_2CH_2CH_2CH_2CH_2CH_2CH_2CH_2CH_2CH_3$$

$$H-\underset{\underset{\displaystyle H}{|}}{\overset{|}{C}}-O-\overset{\overset{\displaystyle O}{\|}}{C}CH_2CH_2CH_2CH_2CH_2CH_2CH_2CH_2CH_2CH_2CH_2CH_2CH_2CH_2CH_2CH_2CH_3$$

Glyceryl tristearate

23.5

$$\left[CH_3(CH_2)_6CH_2CH=CHCH_2(CH_2)_5CH_2\overset{\overset{\displaystyle O}{\|}}{C}-O^-\right]_2 Ca^{+2}\qquad \text{Calcium oleate}$$

23.6

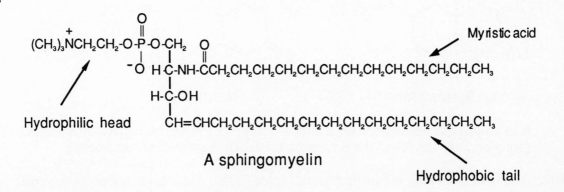

$$
\begin{array}{c}
\quad\ \ \text{H}\quad \text{O} \\
\text{H}-\overset{|}{\underset{|}{\text{C}}}-\text{O}\overset{\parallel}{\text{C}}(\text{CH}_2)_{16}\text{CH}_3 \\
\quad\ \ \quad\ \ \text{O} \\
\text{H}-\overset{|}{\underset{|}{\text{C}}}-\text{O}\overset{\parallel}{\text{C}}(\text{CH}_2)_{16}\text{CH}_3 \\
\quad\ \ \quad\ \ \text{O} \\
\text{H}-\overset{|}{\underset{|}{\text{C}}}-\text{O}\overset{\parallel}{\text{C}}(\text{CH}_2)_7\text{CH}=\text{CH}(\text{CH}_2)_7\text{CH}_3 \\
\quad\ \ \text{H}
\end{array}
\quad\text{or}\quad
\begin{array}{c}
\quad\ \ \text{H}\quad \text{O} \\
\text{H}-\overset{|}{\underset{|}{\text{C}}}-\text{O}\overset{\parallel}{\text{C}}(\text{CH}_2)_{16}\text{CH}_3 \\
\quad\ \ \quad\ \ \text{O} \\
\text{H}-\overset{|}{\underset{|}{\text{C}}}-\text{O}\overset{\parallel}{\text{C}}(\text{CH}_2)_7\text{CH}=\text{CH}(\text{CH}_2)_7\text{CH}_3 \\
\quad\ \ \quad\ \ \text{O} \\
\text{H}-\overset{|}{\underset{|}{\text{C}}}-\text{O}\overset{\parallel}{\text{C}}(\text{CH}_2)_{16}\text{CH}_3 \\
\quad\ \ \text{H}
\end{array}
$$

$$\downarrow \text{ NaOH, H}_2\text{O}$$

$$
\begin{array}{c}
\quad\ \text{H} \\
\text{H}-\overset{|}{\text{C}}-\text{OH} \\
\text{H}-\overset{|}{\text{C}}-\text{OH} \\
\text{H}-\overset{|}{\text{C}}-\text{OH} \\
\quad\ \text{H}
\end{array}
\ +\ 2\ \text{CH}_3(\text{CH}_2)_{16}\overset{\overset{\textstyle O}{\parallel}}{\text{C}}\text{O}^-\ \text{Na}^+\ +\ \text{CH}_3(\text{CH}_2)_7\text{CH}=\text{CH}(\text{CH}_2)_7\overset{\overset{\textstyle O}{\parallel}}{\text{C}}\text{O}^-\ \text{Na}^+
$$

23.7

$$
\begin{array}{l}
\quad\ \ \text{H}\quad \text{O} \\
\text{H}-\overset{|}{\underset{|}{\text{C}}}-\text{O}\overset{\parallel}{\text{C}}\text{CH}_2\text{CH}_2\text{CH}_2\text{CH}_2\text{CH}_2\text{CH}_2\text{CH}_2\text{CH}_2\text{CH}_2\text{CH}_2\text{CH}_2\text{CH}_2\text{CH}_2\text{CH}_2\text{CH}_2\text{CH}_2\text{CH}_3 \quad\longleftarrow \text{Stearic acid} \\
\quad\ \ \quad\ \ \text{O} \\
\text{H}-\overset{|}{\underset{|}{\text{C}}}-\text{O}\overset{\parallel}{\text{C}}\text{CH}_2\text{CH}_2\text{CH}_2\text{CH}_2\text{CH}_2\text{CH}_2\text{CH}_2\text{CH}=\text{CHCH}_2\text{CH}_2\text{CH}_2\text{CH}_2\text{CH}_2\text{CH}_2\text{CH}_2\text{CH}_3 \\
\quad\ \ \quad\ \ \text{O} \qquad\qquad\qquad\qquad\qquad\qquad\qquad\qquad\qquad\qquad\qquad\quad \longleftarrow\ \text{Oleic acid}\\
\text{H}-\overset{|}{\underset{|}{\text{C}}}-\text{O}-\overset{\parallel}{\underset{|}{\text{P}}}-\text{OCH}_2\text{CH}_2\text{NH}_3{}^+\quad\longleftarrow\ \text{Phosphorylethanolamine}\\
\quad\ \ \text{H}\quad \text{O}^-
\end{array}
$$

A glycerophospholipid

23.8

$$
\begin{array}{l}
\qquad\quad\overset{+}{\ } \qquad\qquad \text{O} \\
(\text{CH}_3)_3\text{NCH}_2\text{CH}_2\text{-O-}\overset{\overset{\textstyle\parallel}{}}{\underset{\underset{\textstyle\ }{|}}{\text{P}}}\text{-O-CH}_2\quad \text{O} \\
\qquad\qquad\qquad\quad\ \ {}^-\text{O}\quad \text{H}\,\overset{|}{\underset{|}{\text{C}}}\text{-NH-}\overset{\parallel}{\text{C}}\text{CH}_2\text{CH}_2\text{CH}_2\text{CH}_2\text{CH}_2\text{CH}_2\text{CH}_2\text{CH}_2\text{CH}_2\text{CH}_2\text{CH}_2\text{CH}_3 \quad\nwarrow \text{Myristic acid}\\
\qquad\qquad\qquad\qquad\qquad\quad \text{H-}\overset{|}{\underset{|}{\text{C}}}\text{-OH} \\
\qquad\qquad\qquad\qquad\qquad\quad \text{CH}=\text{CHCH}_2\text{CH}_2\text{CH}_2\text{CH}_2\text{CH}_2\text{CH}_2\text{CH}_2\text{CH}_2\text{CH}_2\text{CH}_2\text{CH}_2\text{CH}_3
\end{array}
$$

Hydrophilic head

A sphingomyelin

Hydrophobic tail

23.9

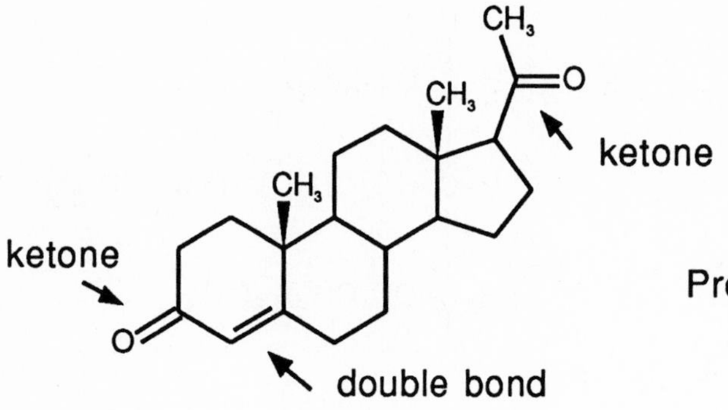

Progesterone

23.10

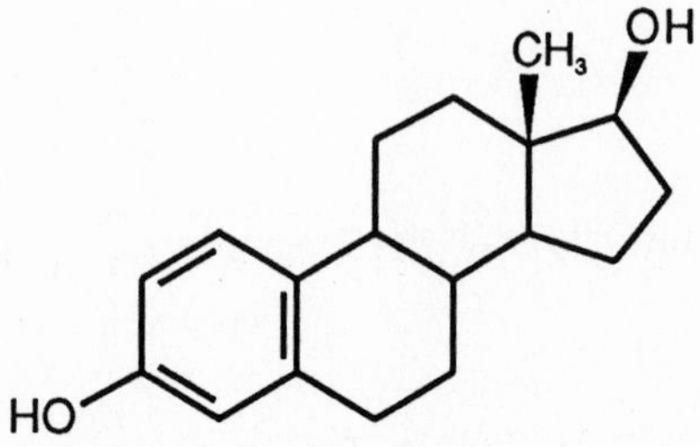

Estradiol 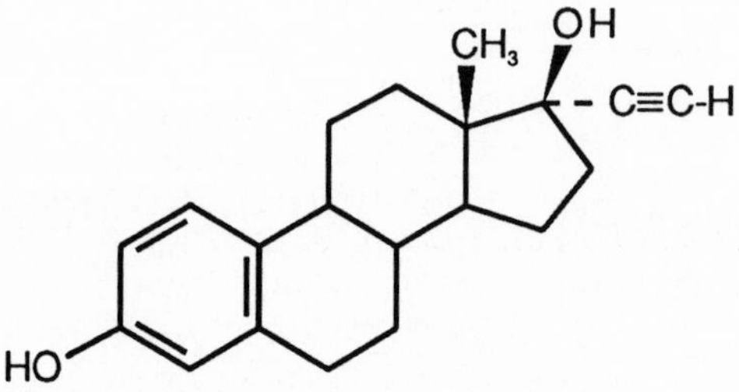   Ethynylestradiol

Ethynylestradiol has a -C≡CH group on the five-membered ring (at C17), whereas estradiol does not. Other than this feature, the two structures are identical. Both are estrogens because they have a steroid structure with an aromatic ring that contains an -OH group.

23.11

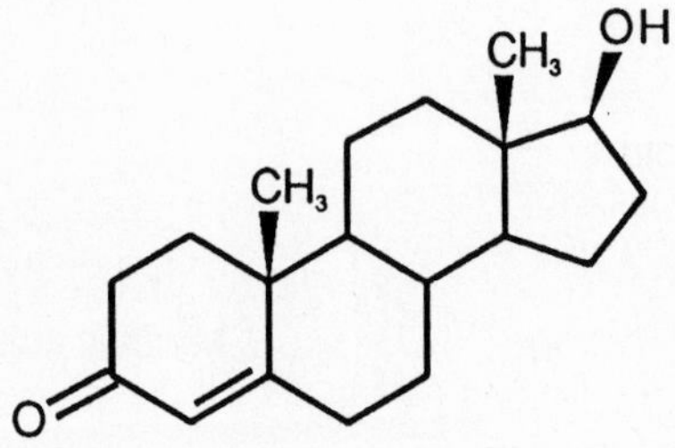

Testosterone 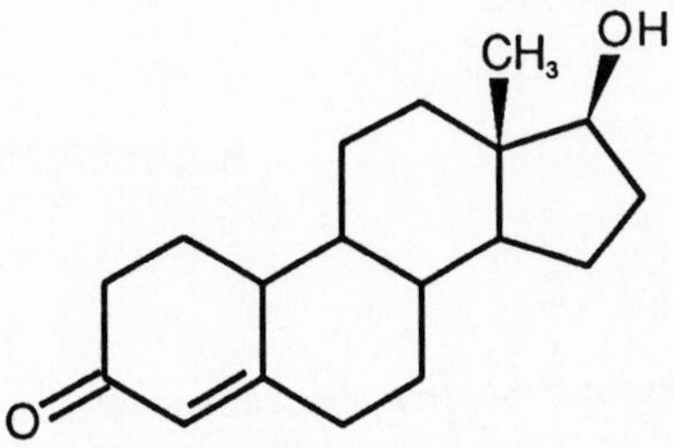   Nandrolone

Nandrolone and testosterone are identical except for the presence in testosterone of a methyl group between the A and the B rings (at C10). Both steroids are androgens.

23.12 A lipid is a naturally occurring organic molecule that dissolves in nonpolar solvents.

23.13 There are many different structural kinds of lipids because many different types of naturally occurring molecules dissolve in nonpolar solvents.

23.14 A fatty acid is a long-chain carboxylic acid having an even number of carbon atoms in the range 12 to 22.

23.15 A fat or oil is a triester of glycerol with three fatty acids - a triacylglycerol.

23.16

$$
\begin{array}{l}
\overset{\text{H}}{\underset{|}{\text{H-C-O-}}}\overset{\text{O}}{\overset{\|}{\text{C}}}\text{CH}_2\text{CH}_2\text{CH}_2\text{CH}_2\text{CH}_2\text{CH}_2\text{CH}_2\text{CH}_2\text{CH}_2\text{CH}_2\text{CH}_3 \\
\\
\text{H-C-O-}\overset{\text{O}}{\overset{\|}{\text{C}}}\text{CH}_2\text{CH}_2\text{CH}_2\text{CH}_2\text{CH}_2\text{CH}_2\text{CH}_2\text{CH}_2\text{CH}_2\text{CH}_2\text{CH}_3 \\
\\
\underset{\overset{|}{\text{H}}}{\text{H-C-O-}}\overset{\text{O}}{\overset{\|}{\text{C}}}\text{CH}_2\text{CH}_2\text{CH}_2\text{CH}_2\text{CH}_2\text{CH}_2\text{CH}_2\text{CH}_2\text{CH}_2\text{CH}_2\text{CH}_3
\end{array}
$$

Glyceryl trilaurate

23.17 The fatty acids in an animal fat are mostly saturated; those in a vegetable oil are mostly unsaturated.

23.18 In animals, fats are used for energy storage, and as components of cell membranes.

23.19 A wax is used as a protective coating for plants and for animal fur and feathers.

23.20

$$\text{CH}_3(\text{CH}_2)_{14}\overset{\text{O}}{\overset{\|}{\text{C}}}\text{-OCH}_2(\text{CH}_2)_{14}\text{CH}_3$$

Cetyl palmitate

23.21 Spermaceti is a wax.

23.22

$$
\begin{array}{l}
\overset{\text{H}}{\underset{|}{\text{H-C-O-}}}\overset{\text{O}}{\overset{\|}{\text{C}}}\text{CH}_2\text{CH}_2\text{CH}_2\text{CH}_2\text{CH}_2\text{CH}_2\text{CH}_2\text{CH}_2\text{CH}_2\text{CH}_2\text{CH}_2\text{CH}_2\text{CH}_2\text{CH}_2\text{CH}_3 \quad\longleftarrow\text{ palmitic acid}\\
\\
\text{A}\quad\text{H-C-O-}\overset{\text{O}}{\overset{\|}{\text{C}}}\text{CH}_2\text{CH}_2\text{CH}_2\text{CH}_2\text{CH}_2\text{CH}_2\text{CH}_2\text{CH}_2\text{CH}_2\text{CH}_2\text{CH}_2\text{CH}_2\text{CH}_2\text{CH}_2\text{CH}_2\text{CH}_3 \quad\longleftarrow\text{ stearic acid}\\
\\
\underset{\overset{|}{\text{H}}}{\text{H-C-O-}}\overset{\text{O}}{\overset{\|}{\text{C}}}\text{CH}_2\text{CH}_2\text{CH}_2\text{CH}_2\text{CH}_2\text{CH}_2\text{CH}_2\text{CH}_2\text{CH}_2\text{CH}_2\text{CH}_2\text{CH}_2\text{CH}_2\text{CH}_2\text{CH}_2\text{CH}_3 \quad\longleftarrow\text{ stearic acid}
\end{array}
$$

H- C-O-CCH₂CH₂CH₂CH₂CH₂CH₂CH₂CH₂CH₂CH₂CH₂CH₂CH₂CH₂CH₂CH₃   ← stearic acid

B H- C-O-CCH₂CH₂CH₂CH₂CH₂CH₂CH₂CH₂CH₂CH₂CH₂CH₂CH₂CH₂ CH₃   ← palmitic acid

H- C-O-CCH₂CH₂CH₂CH₂CH₂CH₂CH₂CH₂CH₂CH₂CH₂CH₂CH₂CH₂CH₂CH₃   ← stearic acid

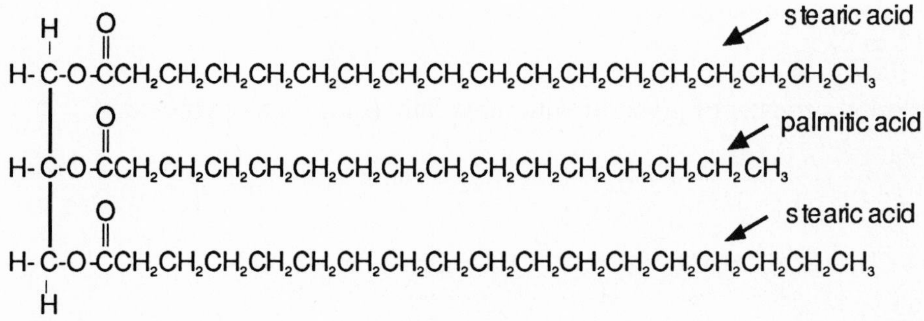

23.23 Molecule A in Problem 14.23 is chiral because four different groups are attached to the central carbon atom of glycerol. Molecule B is achiral because no carbon in the molecule has four different groups attached to it.

23.24

(a)

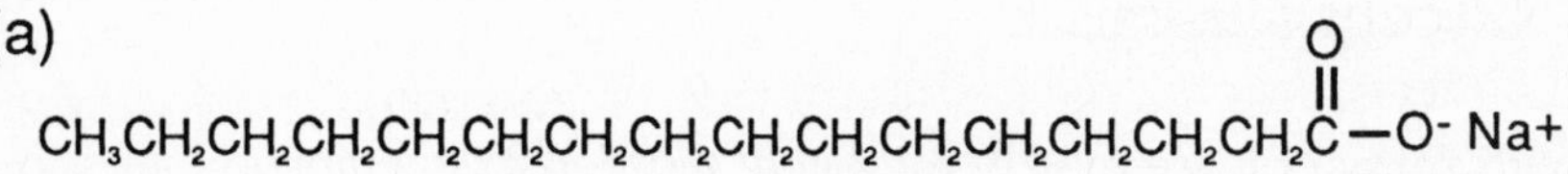

$$CH_3CH_2CH_2CH_2CH_2CH_2CH_2CH_2CH_2CH_2CH_2CH_2CH_2CH_2CH_2\overset{O}{\overset{\|}{C}}-O^- \ Na+$$

Sodium palmitate

(b)

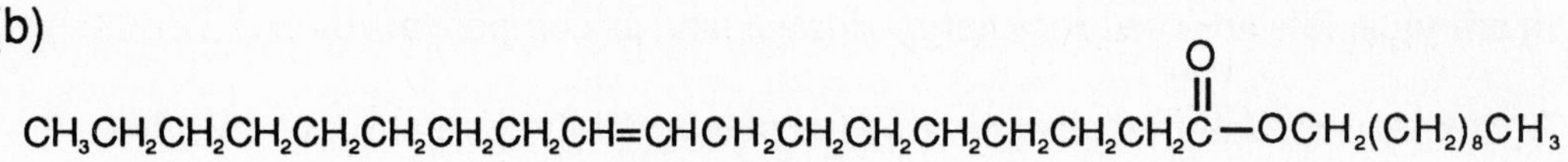

$$CH_3CH_2CH_2CH_2CH_2CH_2CH_2CH_2CH=CHCH_2CH_2CH_2CH_2CH_2CH_2CH_2\overset{O}{\overset{\|}{C}}-OCH_2(CH_2)_8CH_3$$

Decyl oleate

(c)

H- C-O-CCH₂CH₂CH₂CH₂CH₂CH₂CH₂CH=CHCH₂CH₂CH₂CH₂CH₂CH₂CH₂CH₃

H- C-O-CCH₂CH₂CH₂CH₂CH₂CH₂CH₂CH=CHCH₂CH₂CH₂CH₂CH₂CH₂CH₂CH₃

H- C-O-CCH₂CH₂CH₂CH₂CH₂CH₂CH₂CH₂CH₂CH₂CH₂CH₂CH₂CH₂CH₃

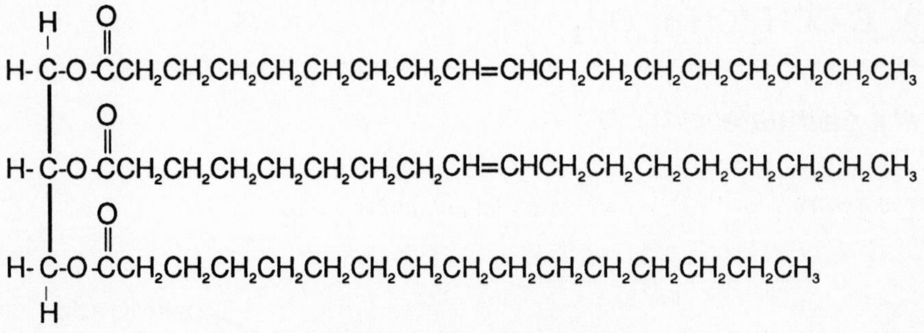

Glyceryl palmitodioleate

23.25 A vegetable oil can be converted into a solid cooking fat by hydrogenating its double bond(s).

23.26

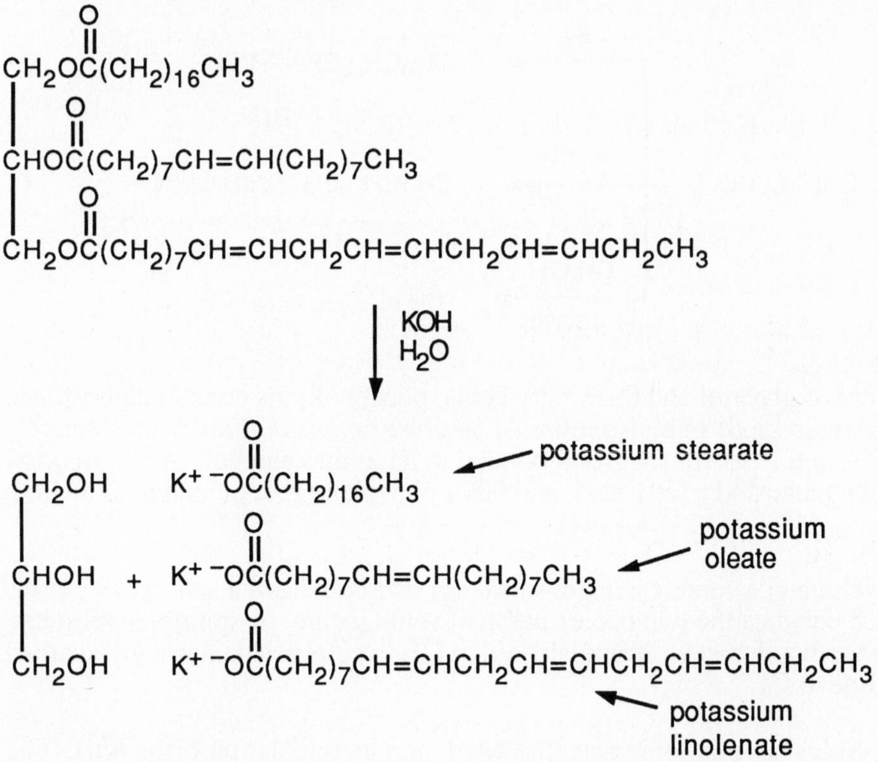

$$\underset{\substack{| \\ CH_2OH}}{\overset{\substack{CH_2OC(CH_2)_{16}CH_3}}{|}}$$

CH$_2$OC(CH$_2$)$_{16}$CH$_3$

CHOC(CH$_2$)$_7$CH=CH(CH$_2$)$_7$CH$_3$

CH$_2$OC(CH$_2$)$_7$CH=CHCH$_2$CH=CHCH$_2$CH=CHCH$_2$CH$_3$

KOH
H$_2$O

CH$_2$OH   K$^+$ $^-$OC(CH$_2$)$_{16}$CH$_3$ ⟵ potassium stearate

CHOH + K$^+$ $^-$OC(CH$_2$)$_7$CH=CH(CH$_2$)$_7$CH$_3$ ⟵ potassium oleate

CH$_2$OH   K$^+$ $^-$OC(CH$_2$)$_7$CH=CHCH$_2$CH=CHCH$_2$CH=CHCH$_2$CH$_3$

⟵ potassium linolenate

23.27

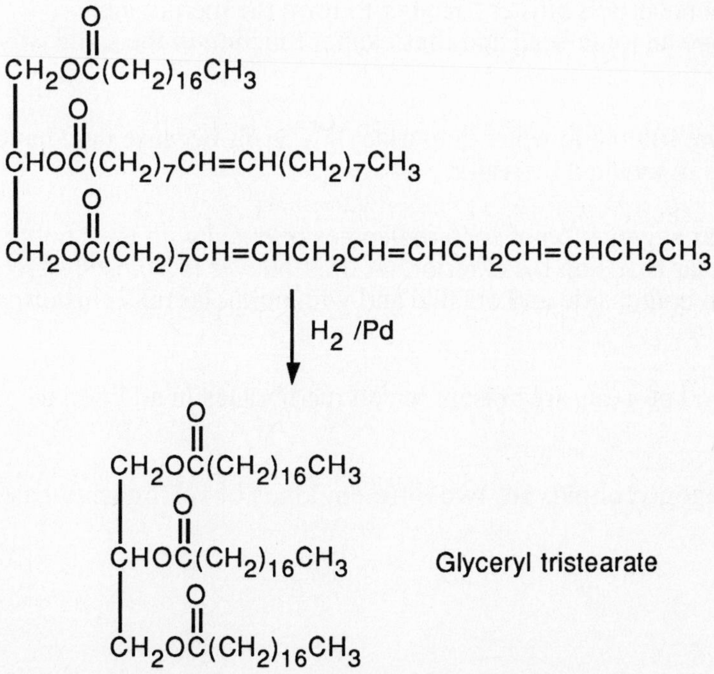

CH$_2$OC(CH$_2$)$_{16}$CH$_3$

CHOC(CH$_2$)$_7$CH=CH(CH$_2$)$_7$CH$_3$

CH$_2$OC(CH$_2$)$_7$CH=CHCH$_2$CH=CHCH$_2$CH=CHCH$_2$CH$_3$

H$_2$ /Pd

CH$_2$OC(CH$_2$)$_{16}$CH$_3$

CHOC(CH$_2$)$_{16}$CH$_3$ Glyceryl tristearate

CH$_2$OC(CH$_2$)$_{16}$CH$_3$

23.28 The product in problem 23.27 is higher melting than the original lipid because the saturated product has fewer bends and can crystallize easier.

23.29

$$CH_3(CH_2)_7CH=CH(CH_2)_7\overset{\overset{\displaystyle O}{\|}}{C}OH$$

$$\xrightarrow{Br_2} \quad CH_3(CH_2)_7\overset{\overset{\displaystyle Br}{|}}{C}H-\overset{\underset{\displaystyle Br}{|}}{C}H(CH_2)_7\overset{\overset{\displaystyle O}{\|}}{C}OH$$

$$\xrightarrow{H_2,\ Pd} \quad CH_3(CH_2)_7\overset{\underset{\displaystyle H}{|}}{C}H-\overset{\underset{\displaystyle H}{|}}{C}H(CH_2)_7\overset{\overset{\displaystyle O}{\|}}{C}OH$$

$$\xrightarrow[H^+\ catalyst]{CH_3OH} \quad CH_3(CH_2)_7CH=CH(CH_2)_7\overset{\overset{\displaystyle O}{\|}}{C}OCH_3$$

23.30 A fat is an ester of glycerol and three fatty acids; phospholipids contain a phosphate group. There are two main kinds of phospholipids: A *glycerophospholipid* is an ester of glycerol, two fatty acids, and a phosphate group bonded to an amino alcohol. A *sphingolipid* is an amide of sphingosine and a fatty acid, and has a phosphate group bonded to an amino alcohol.

23.31 A sphingomyelin and a cerebroside are similar in that both have a sphingosine backbone. The difference between the two occurs at C1 of sphingosine. A sphingomyelin has a phosphate group bonded to an amino alcohol at C1; a cerebroside has a glycosidic link to a monosaccharide at C1.

23.32 Phosphoglycerides have an ionic part (the *head*) and a nonpolar part (the *tail*). The ionic head protrudes outward toward the aqueous environment of the cell and inward toward the cell contents, while the nonpolar tails cluster together to form the membrane. Triacylglycerols do not have an ionic head and thus cannot function in the same way as phosphoglycerides.

23.33 Phosphoglycerides are more soluble in water than triacylglycerols because they have an ionic phosphate group that is solvated by water.

23.34 A soap micelle is a globular aggregation of soap molecules oriented with their nonpolar tails on the interior and their polar heads on the exterior. A lipid bilayer is a closed sheet, with polar groups protruding on both inside and outside and with nonpolar tails clustering in the middle.

23.35 Glycolipids, cholesterol, and proteins are present in cell membranes in addition to phospholipids.

23.36 Sphingomyelins and sphingoglycolipids are two different kinds of sphingosine-based lipids.

23.37

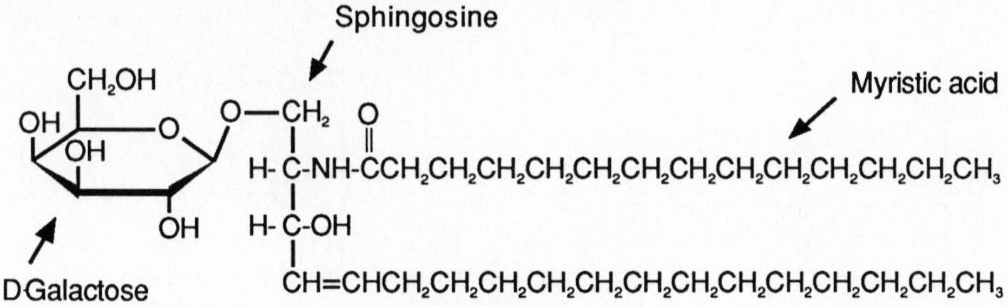

Sphingosine

Myristic acid

CH$_2$OH

OH

OH

OH

D-Galactose

H-C-NH-CCH$_2$CH$_2$CH$_2$CH$_2$CH$_2$CH$_2$CH$_2$CH$_2$CH$_2$CH$_2$CH$_2$CH$_2$CH$_3$

H-C-OH

CH=CHCH$_2$CH$_2$CH$_2$CH$_2$CH$_2$CH$_2$CH$_2$CH$_2$CH$_2$CH$_2$CH$_2$CH$_2$CH$_3$

A cerebroside

23.38

palmitic acid

CH$_2$OC(CH$_2$)$_{14}$CH$_3$

glycerol

CHOC(CH$_2$)$_7$CH=CH(CH$_2$)$_7$CH$_3$

oleic acid

CH$_2$O–P–OCH$_2$CH$_2$CH$_2$NH$_3^+$

phosphate group

propanolamine

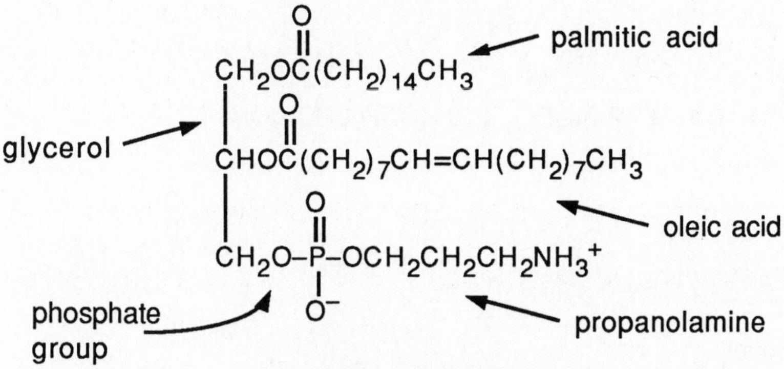

A phosphoglyceride

23.39

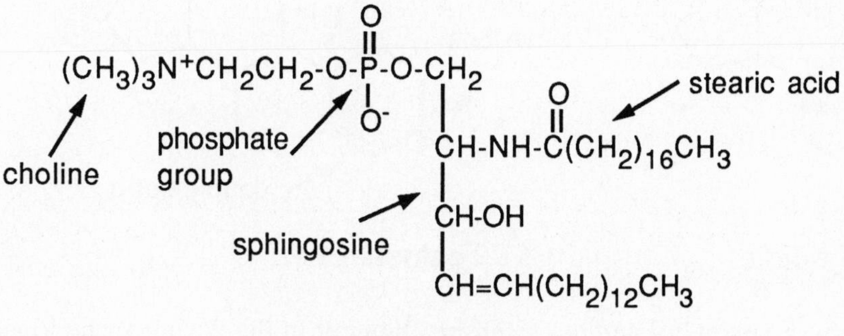

(CH$_3$)$_3$N$^+$CH$_2$CH$_2$-O-P-O-CH$_2$

choline

phosphate group

sphingosine

stearic acid

CH-NH-C(CH$_2$)$_{16}$CH$_3$

CH-OH

CH=CH(CH$_2$)$_{12}$CH$_3$

A sphingomyelin

23.40 Aqueous NaOH cleaves all ester bonds, including phosphate esters.

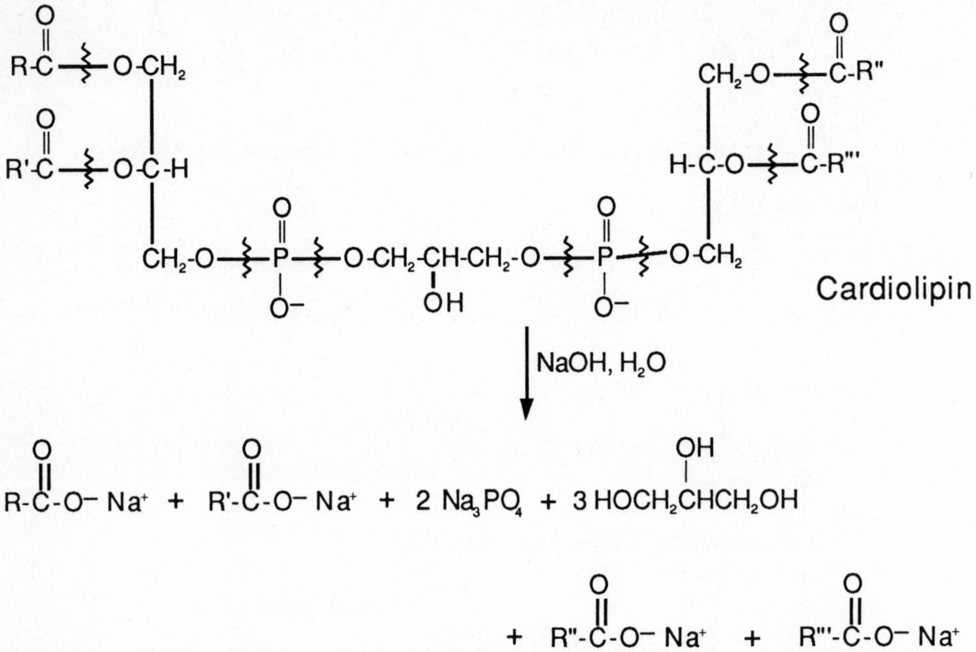

Cardiolipin

NaOH, H₂O

$$R\text{-}\overset{O}{\overset{\|}{C}}\text{-}O^-\ Na^+\ +\ R'\text{-}\overset{O}{\overset{\|}{C}}\text{-}O^-\ Na^+\ +\ 2\ Na_3PO_4\ +\ 3\ HOCH_2CHCH_2OH$$

$$+\ R''\text{-}\overset{O}{\overset{\|}{C}}\text{-}O^-\ Na^+\ +\ R'''\text{-}\overset{O}{\overset{\|}{C}}\text{-}O^-\ Na^+$$

23.41

Estradiol   Testosterone

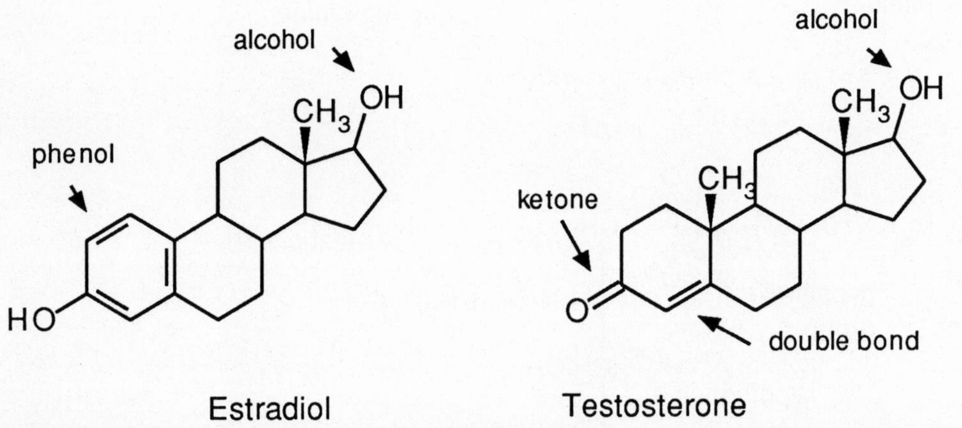

23.42 The differences between estradiol and testosterone all occur in the A ring at the lower left. The A ring of estradiol is aromatic and has a phenol -OH group at C3, whereas a ketone occurs at C3 of testosterone. Additionally, testosterone has a double bond between C4 and C5, and has a methyl group at C10.

23.43

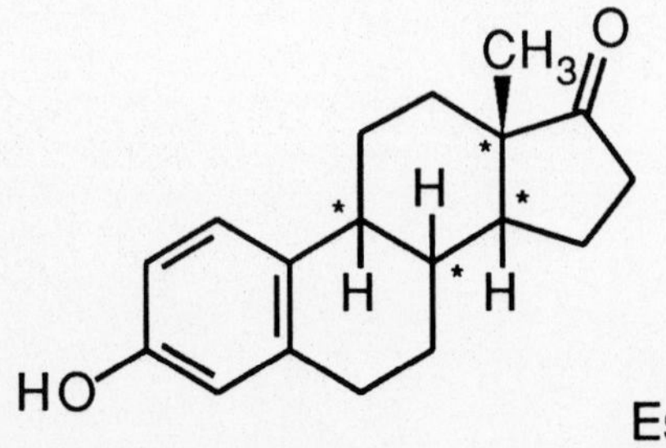

Estrone (chiral centers are starred)

23.44 Cholesterol regulates membrane fluidity and serves as the starting material from which all other steroids are biosynthesized.

23.45

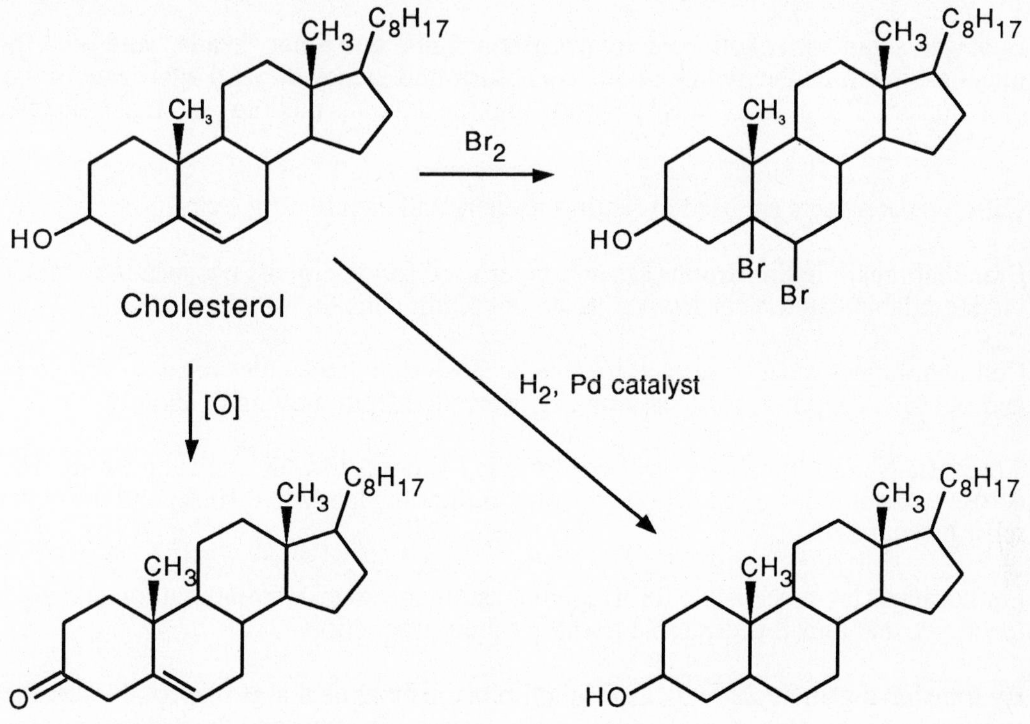

Cholesterol

H₂, Pd catalyst

[O]

23.46

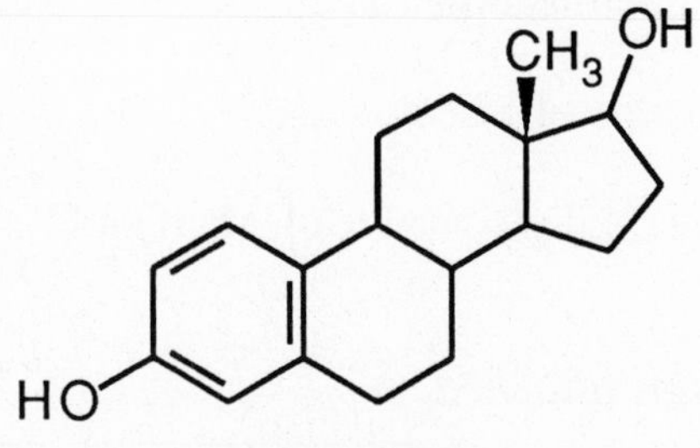

Estradiol

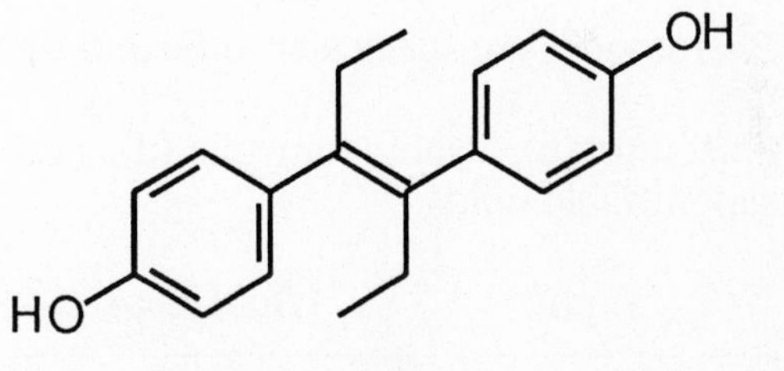

Diethylstilbestrol (DES)

23.47

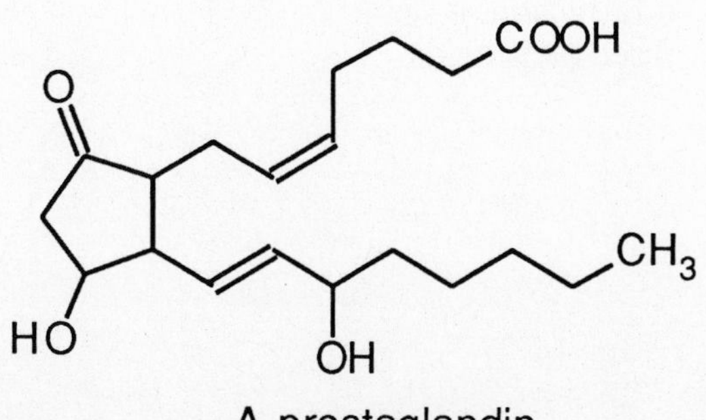

A prostaglandin

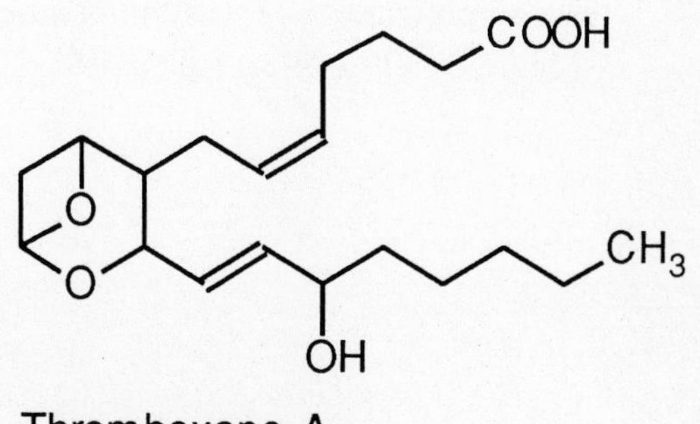

Thromboxane A₂

Thromboxane A₂ is closely related to the prostaglandins.

23.48 Arachidonic acid is the precursor of thromboxane A_2, just as it is the precursor of all other prostaglandins.

23.49 Detergents solubilize greasy dirt in hard water without forming insoluble soap scum.

23.50 Detergents and soaps both have hydrocarbon "tails" and polar "heads," and both form micelles, in which the hydrocarbon "tails" surround greasy dirt and aggregate in the center of a cluster. The polar "heads" protrude into the aqueous medium and make the cluster soluble.

23.51 Cationic detergents are used in fabric softeners and disinfecting soaps.

23.52 Branched-chain hydrocarbons are no longer used for detergents because they aren't biodegradable; bacteria in sewage-treatment plants can't digest them.

23.53 Cell membranes must be semipermeable because some molecules must be able to pass in and out of cells, whereas others must be prevented from moving in and out.

23.54 Active transport requires energy because it is a process in which substances are transported across a membrane in a direction opposite to their tendency to diffuse, and thus energy must be supplied.

23.55 Leukotrienes are responsible for triggering asthmatic attacks, inflammation and allergic reactions, and thus it is desirable to inhibit their production.

23.56 By transferring an acyl group, aspirin inhibits the enzyme that is responsible for the first step in the conversion of arachidonic acid to prostaglandins, and then to leukotrienes.

23.57 A *semiochemical* is used for sending or receiving chemical messages.

23.58 Pheromones are species-specific and trap only one type of insect.

23.59 A lecithin (b), a sphingomyelin (d), a cerebroside (e) and glyceryl trioleate (f) are saponifiable lipids.

23.60

Lipid	*Backbone*	*Groups attached:*
(b) a lecithin	glycerol	a saturated fatty acid, an unsaturated fatty acid, phosphate, choline
(d) a sphingomyelin	sphingosine	a fatty acid, phosphate group, choline
(e) a cerebroside	sphingosine	a fatty acid, a sugar
(f) glyceryl trioleate	glycerol	three oleic acids

23.61

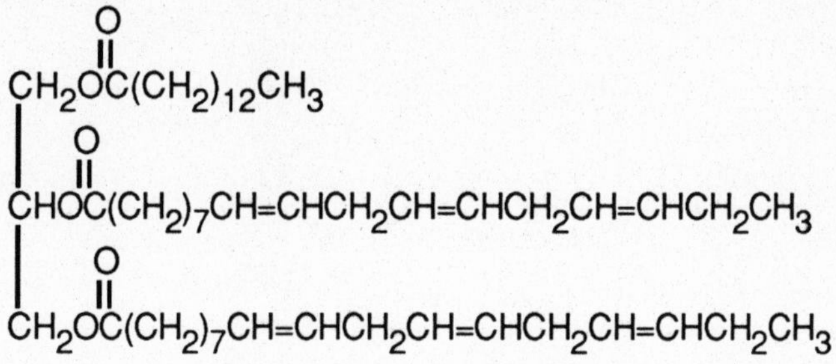

$$CH_2O\overset{\overset{\displaystyle O}{\|}}{C}(CH_2)_{12}CH_3$$

$$CHO\overset{\overset{\displaystyle O}{\|}}{C}(CH_2)_7CH=CHCH_2CH=CHCH_2CH=CHCH_2CH_3$$

$$CH_2O\overset{\overset{\displaystyle O}{\|}}{C}(CH_2)_7CH=CHCH_2CH=CHCH_2CH=CHCH_2CH_3$$

or

$$CH_2O\overset{\overset{\displaystyle O}{\|}}{C}(CH_2)_7CH=CHCH_2CH=CHCH_2CH=CHCH_2CH_3$$

$$CHO\overset{\overset{\displaystyle O}{\|}}{C}(CH_2)_{12}CH_3$$

$$CH_2O\overset{\overset{\displaystyle O}{\|}}{C}(CH_2)_7CH=CHCH_2CH=CHCH_2CH=CHCH_2CH_3$$

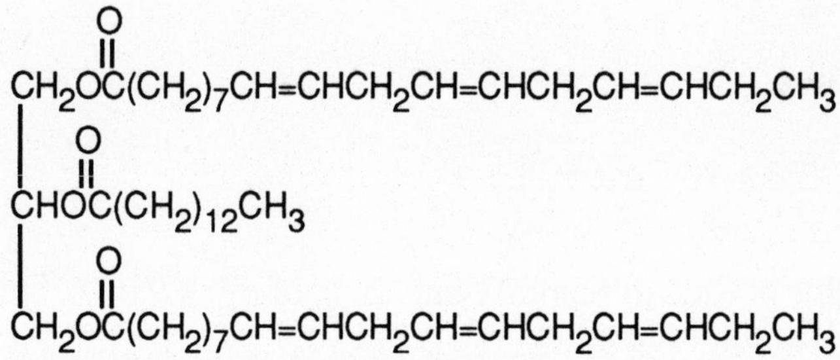

23.62 The fat described in the previous problem would be lower melting than a fat composed of linolenic, myristic and stearic acids, because the former fat is more unsaturated and thus forms crystals with more difficulty.

23.63 Cholesterol is not saponifiable because it contains no ester linkages.

23.64

$$CH_3(CH_2)_{16}\overset{\overset{\displaystyle O}{\|}}{C}\text{-}OCH_2(CH_2)_{20}CH_3 \qquad \text{Jojoba wax}$$

23.65 Sphingomyelins, phosphoglycerides and cerebrosides are abundant in brain tissue.

23.66 Hormones are chemical messengers that mediate biochemical reactions in the body.

23.67 Prostaglandins can lower blood pressure, assist in blood clotting, stimulate uterine contractions, lower gastric secretions and cause some of the pain and swelling associated with inflammation.

23.68 Lecithins emulsify fats in the same way as soaps dissolve grease; the fats are coated by the non-polar part of a lecithin, and the polar part allows them to be suspended in aqueous solution.

23.69

$$\underset{\substack{|\\ \text{CHOCR'}\\|\\ \text{CH}_2\text{OCR''}}}{\overset{\substack{\text{O}\\||\\ \text{CH}_2\text{OCR}\\|\\ \text{O}\\||}}{}} + 3\ \text{NaOH} \xrightarrow{\text{H}_2\text{O}} \underset{\substack{|\\ \text{CHOH}\\|\\ \text{CH}_2\text{OH}}}{\overset{\substack{\text{CH}_2\text{OH}}}{}} + \underset{\substack{\text{O}\\||\\ \text{Na}^+\ ^-\text{OCR''}}}{\overset{\substack{\text{O}\\||\\ \text{Na}^+\ ^-\text{OCR}\\ \text{O}\\||\\ \text{Na}^+\ ^-\text{OCR'}}}{}}$$

Molar mass of fat = 1500 g

Molar mass of NaOH = 40 g

$$5.0\text{ g oil}\ \times\ \frac{1\text{ mol}}{1500\text{ g}}\ =\ 3.3\times10^{-3}\text{ mol oil}$$

Since three mol of NaOH is needed to saponify one mole of oil, 9.9×10^{-3} mol of NaOH is needed to saponify 3.3×10^{-3} mol of oil.

$$9.9\times10^{-3}\text{ mol NaOH}\ \times\ \frac{40\text{ g}}{1\text{ mol}}\ =\ 0.0.39\text{ g NaOH}$$

23.70

$$\frac{200\text{ mg cholesterol}}{1\text{ dL}}\ \times\ \frac{10\text{ dL}}{1\text{ L}}\ \times\ 5.75\text{ L}\ \times\ \frac{1\text{ g}}{1000\text{ mg}}\ =\ 11.5\text{ g cholesterol}$$

An average person has approximately 11-12 grams of cholesterol in their blood.

The Chapter in Brief

Introduction (Sections 23.1) Lipids are a group of biomolecules that are defined by their solubility in nonpolar organic solvents. Lipids are classified as saponifiable or nonsaponifiable depending on whether they contain ester links that can be hydrolyzed by aqueous NaOH.

Waxes, Fats, and Oils (Sections 23.2–23.4) Waxes are esters of long-chain fatty acids with long-chain alcohols; fats and oils are esters of glycerol with three fatty acids. Fats containing unsaturated fatty acids are lower melting than fats containing saturated fatty acids. Unsaturated fats can be hydrogenated to yield saturated fats. When treated with aqueous NaOH, fats and oils yield glycerol and a mixture of fatty acid salts called *soap*. When dispersed in water, soap forms aggregates called micelles, which can solubilize grease.

Membrane Lipids (Sections 23.5–23.8) *Phospholipids* are lipids that contain a phosphate ester group. There are two main classes of phospholipids: *phosphoglycerides* have a glycerol unit, two fatty acids, a phosphate group, and an amino alcohol; *sphingolipids* have a sphingosine unit, two fatty acids, a phosphate group, and an amino alcohol. *Glycolipids* contain sphingosine, one fatty acid, and a sugar unit. Cell membranes are composed of phospholipids arranged in a bilayer.

Other Lipids (Sections 23.9–23.11) *Steroids* are simple lipids based on a four-ring structure; they are used by organisms as emulsifying agents and as hormones. *Prostaglandins* are C_{20} carboxylic acids that contain a five-membered ring with two side-chains; they have a great number of biological effects. Leukotrienes are closely related to the prostaglandins.

Self-Test for Chapter 23

Complete the following sentences:

1. A glycolipid contains an _____ link between sphingosine and a sugar.

2. _____ is a mixture of long-chain fatty acid salts.

3. The carboxylate end of a fatty acid is _____ and the organic chain end is _____.

4. _____ and _____ are two components of cell membranes.

5. The common model of a cell membrane is called the _____ _____ model.

6. Steroid structures are based on a _____ ring system.

7. Prostaglandins are synthesized in the body from a fatty acid called _____ acid.

8. Clusters of soap molecules in water are called _____.

9. _____ are phospholipids that are abundant in brain tissue.

10. Phospholipids aggregate in a closed, sheetlike membrane called a _____ _____.

11. Ethynylestradiol is a _____ steroid.

Tell whether the following statements are true or false:

1. Lipids are defined by their physical properties, not by their structure.

2. Saturated fats are lower melting than unsaturated fats.

3. Sphingolipids contain a carboxylic acid ester group.

4. Cholesterol is synthesized by the human body.

5. Sphingosine is a component of both phospholipids and glycolipids.

6. When soap molecules are dissolved in water, they form a lipid bilayer.

7. Cholesterol is a hormone.

8. The main difference between fats and oil is in their melting points.

9. Cerebrosides are a major constituent of the coating around nerve fibers.

10. Waxes and fats are both carboxylic acid esters.

Match the entries on the left with their partners on the right:

1. Decyl stearate

2. Prostaglandin

3. Choline

4. Stearic acid

5. Progesterone

6. Glyceryl trilaurate

7. Cerebroside

8. Oleic acid

9. Lecithin

10. Linoleic acid

11. Sphingomyelin

12. Cortisone

(a) Female sex hormone

(b) Monounsaturated fatty acid

(c) Adrenocortical hormone

(d) Phosphoglyceride

(e) Amino alcohol

(f) Saturated fatty acid

(g) Polyunsaturated fatty acid

(h) C_{20} acid with a five-membered ring

(i) Sphingolipid

(j) Fat

(k) Glycolipid

(l) Wax

24.1 Dihydroxyacetone enters glycolysis at step 5 and enters gluconeogenesis at the reverse of step 4 in figure 22.5.

24.2

(a)

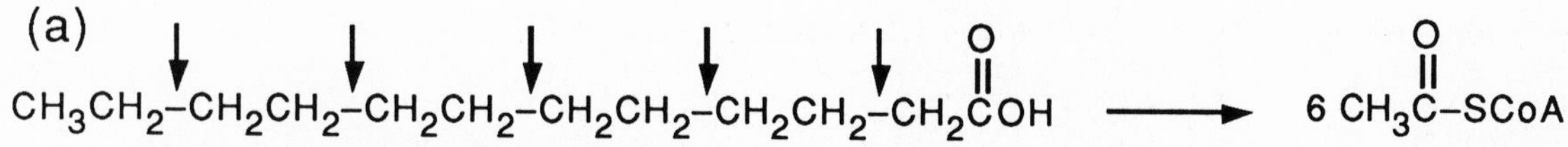

$$CH_3CH_2-CH_2CH_2-CH_2CH_2-CH_2CH_2-CH_2CH_2-CH_2\overset{\overset{\displaystyle O}{\|}}{C}OH \longrightarrow 6\ CH_3\overset{\overset{\displaystyle O}{\|}}{C}-SCoA$$

Five turns of the spiral are needed.

(b)

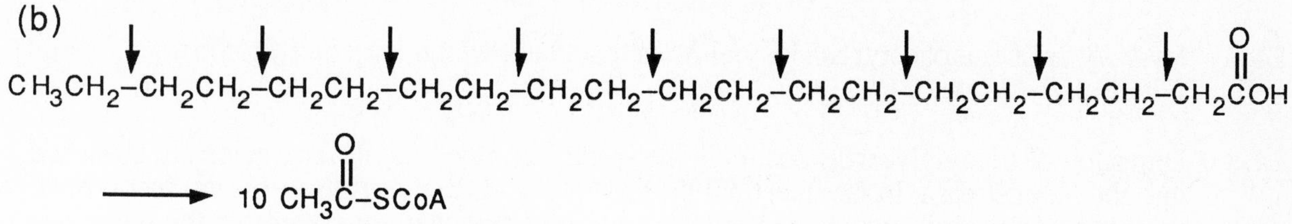

$$CH_3CH_2-CH_2CH_2-CH_2CH_2-CH_2CH_2-CH_2CH_2-CH_2CH_2-CH_2CH_2-CH_2CH_2-CH_2CH_2-CH_2\overset{\overset{\displaystyle O}{\|}}{C}OH$$

$$\longrightarrow 10\ CH_3\overset{\overset{\displaystyle O}{\|}}{C}-SCoA$$

Nine turns of the spiral are needed.

24.3

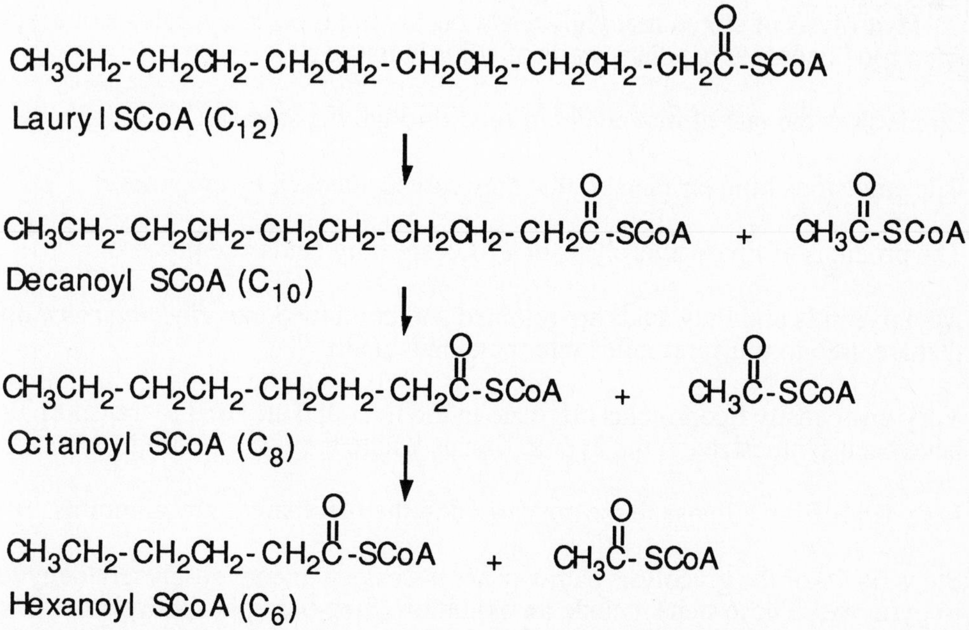

$$CH_3CH_2-CH_2CH_2-CH_2CH_2-CH_2CH_2-CH_2CH_2-CH_2\overset{\overset{\displaystyle O}{\|}}{C}-SCoA$$

Lauryl SCoA (C_{12})

$\downarrow$

$$CH_3CH_2-CH_2CH_2-CH_2CH_2-CH_2CH_2-CH_2\overset{\overset{\displaystyle O}{\|}}{C}-SCoA \quad + \quad CH_3\overset{\overset{\displaystyle O}{\|}}{C}-SCoA$$

Decanoyl SCoA (C_{10})

$\downarrow$

$$CH_3CH_2-CH_2CH_2-CH_2CH_2-CH_2\overset{\overset{\displaystyle O}{\|}}{C}-SCoA \quad + \quad CH_3\overset{\overset{\displaystyle O}{\|}}{C}-SCoA$$

Octanoyl SCoA (C_8)

$\downarrow$

$$CH_3CH_2-CH_2CH_2-CH_2\overset{\overset{\displaystyle O}{\|}}{C}-SCoA \quad + \quad CH_3\overset{\overset{\displaystyle O}{\|}}{C}-SCoA$$

Hexanoyl SCoA (C_6)

24.4 Steps 6,7,and 8 of the citric acid cycle (Fig 20.11) are similar to the first three reactions of the fatty acid spiral.

24.5 Palmitic acid contains 16 carbons and yields 16/2 = 8 acetyl SCoA molecules by going through 8 - 1 = 7 turns of the fatty-acid spiral. The number of moles of ATP per mole of palmitic acid can be calculated in the following way:

Initiation	=	–2 ATP
8 acetyl SCoA x 12 ATP per acetyl SCoA	=	96 ATP
7 turns x 5 ATP per turn	=	35 ATP
Net change	=	129 ATP

24.6

$$1.0 \text{ g palm. acid } \times \frac{1 \text{ mol}}{256 \text{ g}} \times \frac{129 \text{ ATP}}{1 \text{ mol palm. acid}} \times \frac{507 \text{ g}}{1 \text{ mol}} = 260 \text{ g ATP}$$

24.7 *Hydrolysis* of acetoacetyl SCoA yields acetoacetate, which is *reduced* to form 3-hydroxybutyrate.

24.8 Digestion of triacylglycerols occurs in the small intestine. Small fatty acids are absorbed into the bloodstream. In the intestinal lining, fatty acids and acylglycerols are recombined to form triacylglycerols, which are bound in chylomicrons that travel through the lymphatic system to enter the bloodstream.

Hydrolysis of stored triacylglycerols occurs in fat cells; hydrolysis of triacylglycerols from food occurs at capillary walls of adipose tissue.

24.9 Lipids slow the rate of movement of food through the stomach.

24.10 Bile emulsifies lipid droplets so that they can be attacked by enzymes.

24.11 The products of lipase hydrolysis of TAGs are fatty acids and glycerol.

24.12 Acylglycerols and fatty acids are rejoined and combined into *chylomicrons*, lipoproteins that are used to transport lipids into the bloodstream.

24.13 Very low density lipoproteins originate in the liver and are used to transport TAGs that have been synthesized in the liver to tissues where they will be used.

24.14 Fatty acids from adipose tissue are carried in the bloodstream by albumins.

24.15 Steps 6 - 10 of the glycolysis pathway are necessary to convert glyceraldehyde 3-phosphate to pyruvate. These steps include an oxidation (Step 6), a phosphorylation (Step 6), two phosphate transfers to ADP (Steps 7 and 10), an isomerization (Step 8), and a dehydration (Step 9).

24.16 For each molecule of glycerol, 5 molecules of ATP are released in forming pyruvic acid. One ATP results from the conversion of glycerol to glyceraldehyde-3-phosphate, and four more arise from the conversion of glyceraldehyde-3-phosphate to pyruvic acid.

24.17 Eight molecules of ATP are formed in the catabolism of glycerol to yield acetyl SCoA -- the 5 mentioned in Problem 24.16 and an additional 3 in the conversion of pyruvate to acetyl SCoA.

24.18 Twenty molecules of ATP are released in the complete catabolism of glycerol to CO_2 and H_2O -- the 8 molecules mentioned in Problem 24.17 and an additional 12 molecules formed when acetyl SCoA is degraded in the citric-acid cycle.

24.19 Adipocytes are fat cells in which TAGs are stored and mobilized.

24.20 The fatty acid spiral occurs in the mitochondrial matrix.

24.21 The fatty acid spiral is also known as β-oxidation, because the carbon β to the SCoA group (2 carbons away from the SCoA group) is oxidized.

24.22 A fatty acid is converted to its fatty acyl SCoA in order to activate it for catabolism.

24.23 Carnitine is used to transport fatty acyl SCoA's across the inner mitochondrial membrane.

24.24 The sequence is a spiral because the reaction series is repeated on a two-carbon-shortened fatty acid until the original acid is consumed. In a cycle, the product of the final step is a reactant in the first step.

24.25 Each turn of the fatty acid spiral produces 5 molecules of ATP plus one molecule of acetyl SCoA, which enters into the citric acid cycle to yield 12 more molecules of ATP.

24.26 The number of moles of ATP produced per mole of fatty acid is $17n - 7$, where n equals the number of acetyl SCoA's produced. For a 10-carbon acid, $n = 5$; thus, the energy content of $CH_3(CH_2)_8COOH$ (capric acid) is 78 ATP per mole. For a 14-carbon acid, $n = 7$ and the energy content is 112 ATP.

Least energy/mole ⟶ Greatest energy/mole

Molecule	Glucose	Sucrose	$CH_3(CH_2)_8COOH$	$CH_3(CH_2)_{12}COOH$
ATP content/mole	36 ATP	72 ATP	78 ATP	112 ATP

24.27

(a)

$$CH_3CH_2CH_2CH_2CH_2\overset{O}{\overset{\|}{C}}SCoA \xrightarrow[\substack{\text{acetyl SCoA} \\ \text{dehydrogenase}}]{FAD \quad FADH_2} CH_3CH_2CH_2CH=CH\overset{O}{\overset{\|}{C}}SCoA$$

(b)

$$CH_3CH_2CH_2CH=CH\overset{O}{\overset{\|}{C}}SCoA + H_2O \xrightarrow[\text{hydratase}]{\text{enoyl SCoA}} CH_3CH_2CH_2\overset{OH}{\overset{|}{C}}HCH_2\overset{O}{\overset{\|}{C}}SCoA$$

(c)

$$CH_3CH_2CH_2\overset{OH}{\overset{|}{C}}HCH_2\overset{O}{\overset{\|}{C}}SCoA \xrightarrow[\substack{\text{β–hydroxyacetyl SCoA} \\ \text{dehydrogenase}}]{NAD^+ \quad NADH/H^+} CH_3CH_2CH_2\overset{O}{\overset{\|}{C}}CH_2\overset{O}{\overset{\|}{C}}SCoA$$

(d)

$$CH_3CH_2CH_2\overset{O}{\underset{\|}{C}}CH_2\overset{O}{\underset{\|}{C}}SCoA \xrightarrow[\text{transferase}]{\overset{\text{HSCoA}}{\text{acetyl SCoA}}} CH_3CH_2CH_2\overset{O}{\underset{\|}{C}}SCoA + CH_3\overset{O}{\underset{\|}{C}}SCoA$$

24.28

$$CH_3\overset{O}{\underset{\|}{C}}CH_2\overset{O}{\underset{\|}{C}}SCoA \xrightarrow[\text{transferase}]{\overset{\text{HSCoA}}{\text{acetyl SCoA}}} 2\ CH_3\overset{O}{\underset{\|}{C}}SCoA$$

24.29 The number of moles of acetyl SCoA produced from one mole of fatty acid is half the number of carbons in the acid. The number of turns of the fatty-acid spiral is one less than the number of moles of acetyl SCoA produced. (The number of moles of ATP produced equals $17n-7$, where n is the number of moles of acetyl SCoA produced.)

Acid	Acetyl SCoA Produced	Turns of Spiral	Moles of ATP
(a) $CH_3(CH_2)_6COOH$	4	3	61
(b) $CH_3(CH_2)_{12}COOH$	7	6	112

24.30 Three turns of the fatty-acid spiral catabolize caprylic acid, and six turns of the spiral catabolize myristic acid.

24.31 The anabolic pathway for synthesizing fatty acids is called *lipogenesis*.

24.32 Acetyl SCoA is the starting material for fatty-acid synthesis.

24.33 Since the fatty acid spiral is an energetically favorable reaction, its exact reverse is energetically unfavorable and thus doesn't occur.

24.34 Fatty acids have an even number of carbons because they are synthesized from a starting material (acetyl SCoA) that has an even number of carbons.

24.35 Acetyl SCoA is the starting material for the synthesis of all other fatty acids.

24.36 Palmitic acid has 16 carbons and is synthesized from 8 acetyl SCoA units through 7 rounds of the lipogenesis spiral.

24.37 A normal blood cholesterol range is 150-200 mg/dL.

24.38 Atherosclerosis is the formation of cholesterol deposits in the arteries of the brain and heart.

24.39 LDL carries cholesteryl linolenate from the liver to tissues; HDL carries cholesteryl stearate from tissues to the liver, where it is converted to bile and excreted.

24.40 A high HDL/LDL level is better than a low HDL/LDL level because a high HDL/LDL level indicates that more cholesterol is being excreted than is being deposited in arteries.

24.41 Cirrhosis is the development of fibrous tissue in the liver and is due to excessive deposits of triacylglycerols.

24.42 Magnetic resonance imaging primarily monitors the density of hydrogen nuclei in tissues.

24.43 MRI is non-invasive, doesn't require ionizing radiation or contrast medium, and can investigate tissues hidden behind bone.

24.44 An excess of carbohydrates produces an excess of acetyl SCoA. If more acetyl SCoA is produced than is needed in the respiratory chain, it is used to synthesize fatty acids, which are used to produce the triglycerides that are deposited in adipose tissue. Glycogen is also synthesized, but not to the same degree as fatty acids are produced.

24.45 In the fatty acid spiral, the alcohol intermediate is chiral because the hydroxyl carbon is bonded to four different groups.

24.46 Acetone, acetoacetate and 3-hydroxybutyrate are ketone bodies, which are produced when blood sugar is low and the body metabolizes fats. If more acetyl SCoA is produced than can enter the citric acid cycle, it is converted to ketone bodies, in the process known as ketogenesis, to be used as an alternate energy source. Ketone bodies are so named because they either contain the ketone functional group or are directly derived from ketones.

24.47 Ketosis is the condition in which ketone bodies accumulate in the blood faster than they can be metabolized. Since two of the ketone bodies are carboxylic acids, they lower the pH of the blood, producing the condition known as ketoacidosis. Symptoms of prolonged ketoacidosis include dehydration, labored breathing and depression.

24.48

$$\text{Glyceryl trimyristate} \quad \begin{matrix} \text{CH}_2\text{OC}(\text{CH}_2)_{12}\text{CH}_3 \\ | \quad\quad\overset{O}{\overset{||}{}} \\ \text{CHOC}(\text{CH}_2)_{12}\text{CH}_3 \\ | \quad\quad\overset{O}{\overset{||}{}} \\ \text{CH}_2\text{OC}(\text{CH}_2)_{12}\text{CH}_3 \end{matrix} \quad \xrightarrow{\text{hydrolysis}} \quad \begin{matrix} \text{CH}_2\text{OH} \\ | \\ \text{CHOH} \\ | \\ \text{CH}_2\text{OH} \end{matrix} \quad + \quad 3\ ^-\text{OC}(\text{CH}_2)_{12}\text{CH}_3$$

Glycerol is converted to glyceraldehyde 3-phosphate, which enters glycolysis and is converted to pyruvate and yields *one* acetyl SCoA. Each myristate produces 7 acetyl SCoA molecules; three myristates yield *21* acetyl SCoA molecules. A total of *22* acetyl SCoA molecules are formed.

24.49 The complete catabolism of glycerol yields *20* molecules of ATP (Problem 24.18). The complete catabolism of each myristate produces 112 molecules of ATP (Problem 24.26). Catabolism of all three myristates produces *336* molecules of ATP.
The yield from total catabolism of glycerol trimyristate is *356 molecules of ATP*.

24.50 Consider a carbohydrate and a fatty acid with similar molar masses. Glucose (molar mass = 180 g) yields 36 ATP/mole; $CH_3(CH_2)_8COOH$ (molar mass = 180 g) yields 78 ATP/mole (Problem 24.26). Thus, the energy yield per mole from a fat is about twice the yield from a sugar. There are two principal reasons for this difference. (1) A carbohydrate has fewer carbons than a fatty acid of similar molar mass and thus produces fewer moles of acetyl SCoA per mole. (2) Only 2/3 of a carbohydrate's carbons are used to form acetyl SCoA; the other carbons are released as CO_2 in the transformation pyruvate —> acetyl SCoA.

The Chapter in Brief

Breakdown of Triacylglycerols (Sections 24.1–24.3) Dietary triacylglycerols (TAGs) are emulsified by bile in the small intestine. Pancreatic lipase digests some of the TAGs, and the smaller fragments are absorbed. Larger fragments are recombined into triacylglycerols and bound into chylomicrons, which eventually enter the bloodstream. Both dietary and stored lipids are cleaved by lipases to form glycerol and fatty acids. The glycerol enters glycolysis, and the fatty acids enter the fatty-acid spiral. If not needed for catabolism, glycerol and fatty acids can be recombined into TAGs for storage.

Fatty Acid Oxidation (Sections 24.2, 24.5) Fatty acids are activated by reaction with acetyl SCoA and transported to the mitochondrial matrix as carnitine derivatives. The fatty acids then pass through the fatty-acid spiral, in which acetyl SCoA molecules are cleaved from the fatty acid in a four-step process. The process is repeated until the entire fatty acid has been converted to acetyl SCoA. A fatty acid that yields n acetyl SCoA molecules produces $17n-7$ molecules of ATP.

Biosynthesis of Fatty Acids (Sections 24.6, 24.7) Fatty acids can be synthesized from acetyl SCoA in an elongation cycle that uses malonyl SCoA and acyl carrier protein (ACP). At other times, excess acetyl SCoA can be used to form ketone bodies.

Self-Test for Chapter 24

Complete the following sentences:

1.   One _____ _____ is needed for each turn of the fatty acid spiral.

2.   Bile salts solubilize lipids by forming _____.

3.   Triacylglycerols are stored in _____.

4.   TAG synthesis begins with the conversion of glycerol to _____ - _____.

5.   An alternate name for the fatty-acid spiral is ___ - _____.

6.   The first step in the fatty-acid spiral involves introduction of a _____ _____.

7.   _____ is the presence of ketone bodies in the urine.

8.   _____ is a coenzyme for fatty-acid biosynthesis.

9.   _____ is a ketone body containing a hydroxyl group.

10. Chylomicrons are transported in the _____ _____ and in the bloodstream.

11. TAGs that are released from storage are said to be _____.

12. All fatty acids are synthesized from _____.

Match the entry on the left with its partner on the right:

1.	Chylomicron	(a) Lipoprotein rich in lipid
2.	Lipogenesis	(b) Protein that carries fatty acids in the bloodstream
3.	LDL	(c) Solubilizes fats
4.	Carnitine	(d) Hydrolyzes TAGs in adipose tissue
5.	Malonyl SCoA	(e) Lipoprotein that aids in lipid transport
6.	Fatty-acid spiral	(f) Lipoprotein rich in protein
7.	Chyme	(g) Starting material in lipogenesis
8.	Lipoprotein lipase	(h) Ketone body
9.	HDL	(i) Fatty acid biosynthesis
10.	Albumin	(j) Breakdown of fatty acids into acetyl SCoA
11.	Bile	(k) Mixture of partially digested food
12.	Acetoacetate	(l) Carrier of fatty-acid SCoA molecules

Tell whether the following statements are true or false:

1. Bile acids are steroids.

2. TAGs are hydrolyzed by pancreatic lipases to glycerol and fatty acids.

3. Activation of fatty acids for fatty-acid oxidation requires two phosphates to be cleaved.

4. A chylomicron is a type of lipoprotein.

5. Chylomicrons carry fatty-acid SCoA across the mitochondrial membrane.

6. A fatty acid with n carbons requires $n/2 - 1$ turns of the fatty-acid spiral for complete breakdown.

7. TAGs are synthesized starting from glycerol and fatty acid SCoAs.

8. HDL transports cholesterol to tissues, where it can accumulate.

9. A fatty acid with a molecular weight similar to that of glucose yields more ATPs per molecule than glucose.

10. Fatty acid synthesis occurs in mitochondria.

11. The terminal –CH$_3$ group of a fatty acid comes from malonyl SCoA.

12. Most naturally occurring fatty acids have an even number of carbon atoms.

Chapter 25 – Protein and Amino Acid Metabolism

25.1

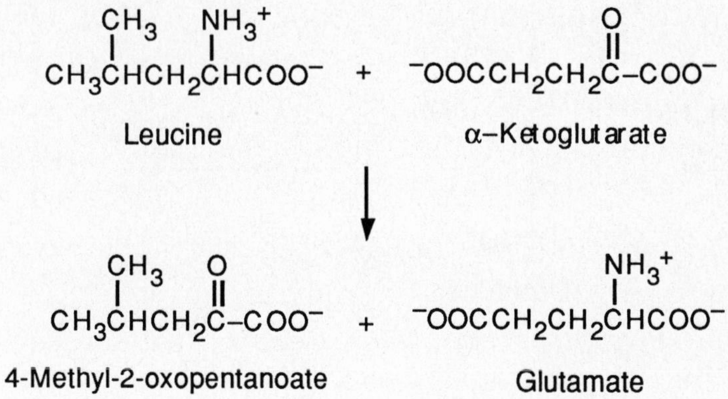

$$\underset{\text{Leucine}}{\overset{\overset{\displaystyle CH_3 \quad NH_3^+}{|\qquad\quad|}}{CH_3CHCH_2CHCOO^-}} + \underset{\alpha-\text{Ketoglutarate}}{\overset{\overset{\displaystyle O}{||}}{^-OOCCH_2CH_2C-COO^-}}$$

$$\downarrow$$

$$\underset{\text{4-Methyl-2-oxopentanoate}}{\overset{\overset{\displaystyle CH_3 \quad O}{|\qquad\;||}}{CH_3CHCH_2C-COO^-}} + \underset{\text{Glutamate}}{\overset{\overset{\displaystyle NH_3^+}{|}}{^-OOCCH_2CH_2CHCOO^-}}$$

25.2

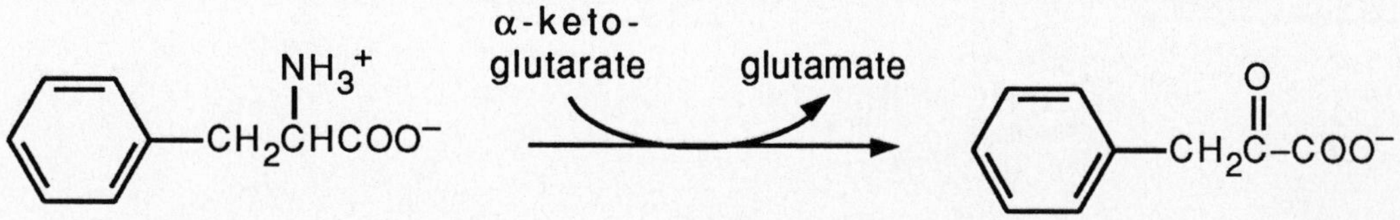

25.3

Fumarate → (addition of water) → Malate → (oxidation of malate) → Oxaloacetate → (reverse transamination) → Aspartate

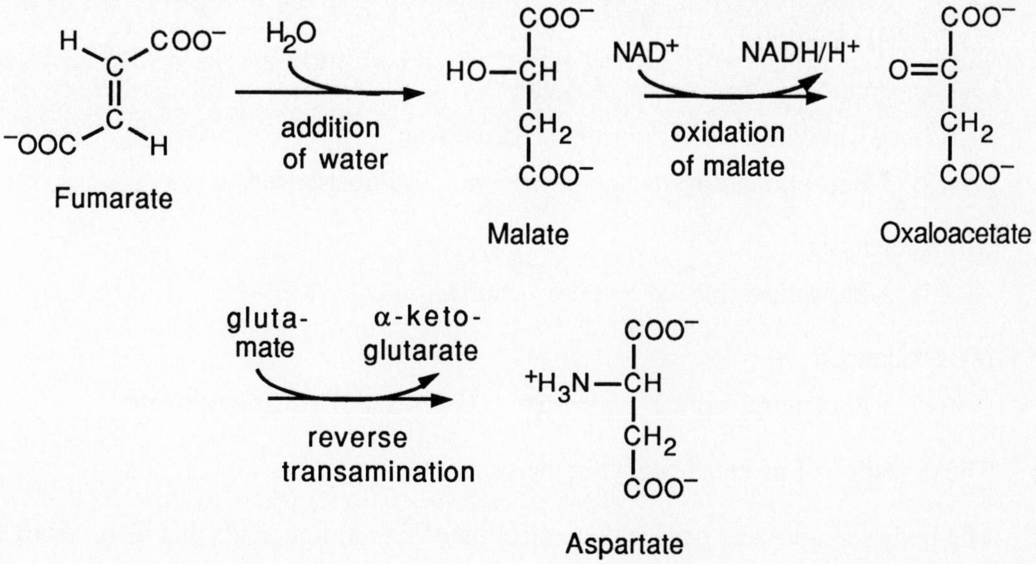

25.4

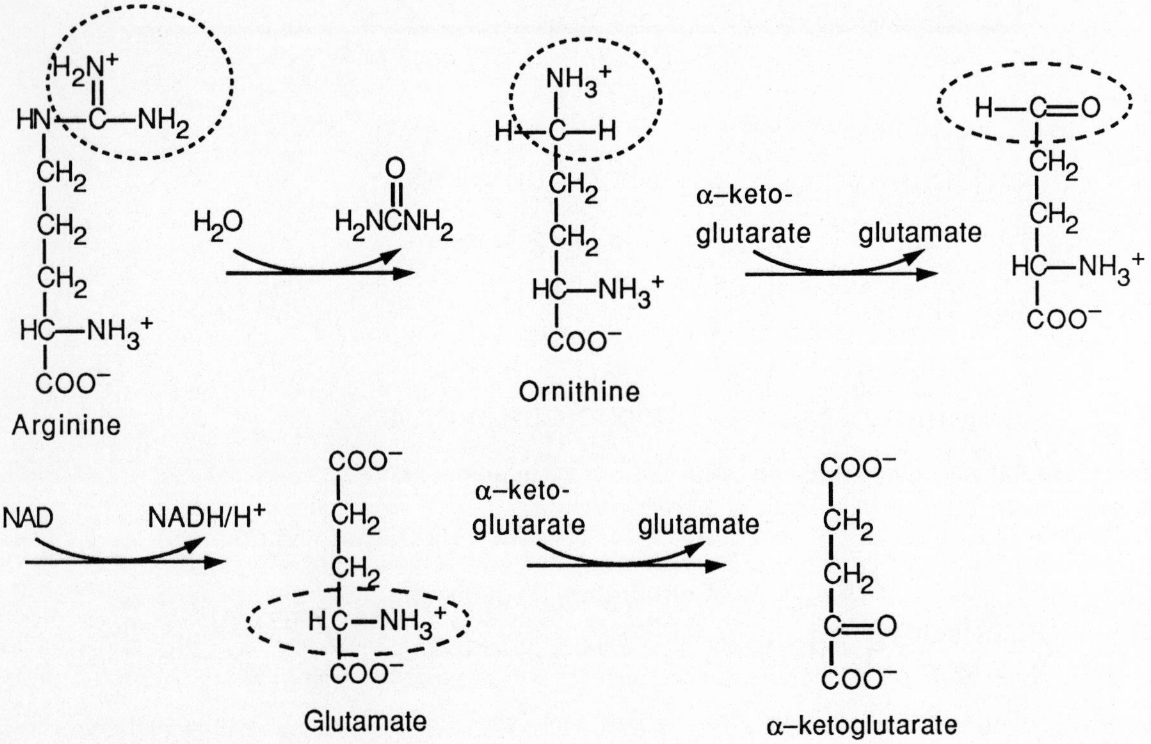

Arginine

Ornithine

Glutamate

α–ketoglutarate

25.5   (a) Transaminations:

(1) Pyruvate ⟶ Alanine

(2) α-Ketoglutarate ⟶ Glutamate

(3) 3-Phosphoenolpyruvate ⟶ 3-Phosphoserine

(b) Hydrolysis:

(3) 3-Phosphoserine ⟶ Serine

(c) Oxidation:

(3) 3-Phosphoglycerate ⟶ 3-Phosphohydroxypyruvate

25.6   The digestion of proteins begins in the stomach.

25.7   The body's amino-acid pool is the collection of free amino acids that result from diet or tissue breakdown.

25.8   Amino acids in the amino acid pool come from the diet, from synthesis from other compounds or from tissue breakdown.

25.9   Amino acids in the amino-acid pool can be used to form tissue proteins or non-protein nitrogen-containing compounds, or they can be catabolized for energy.

25.10   In a transamination reaction, a keto group of an α-keto acid and an amine group of an amino acid change places.

25.11 Pyridoxal phosphate, a relative of vitamin B_6, is a coenzyme that bonds to amino acids and assists in catalyzing transamination reactions.

25.12

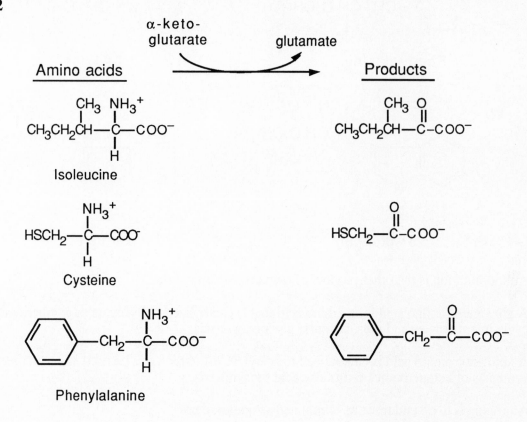

25.14 In an oxidative deamination reaction, an $-NH_2$ group of an amino acid is converted to a keto group, and ammonia is eliminated.

25.15 Either NAD^+ or $NADP^+$ is associated with oxidative deamination.

25.16 Glutamate dehydrogenase is the enzyme associated with oxidative deamination.

25.17

(a)

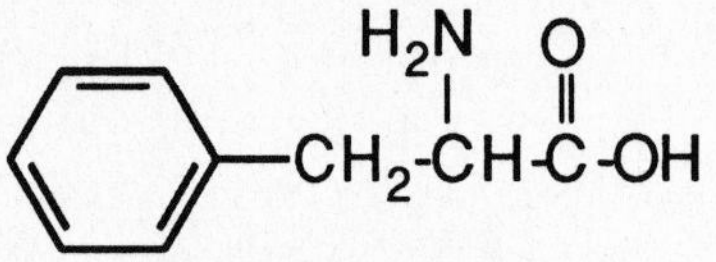

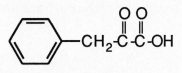

Phenylalanine   α-Keto acid

(b)

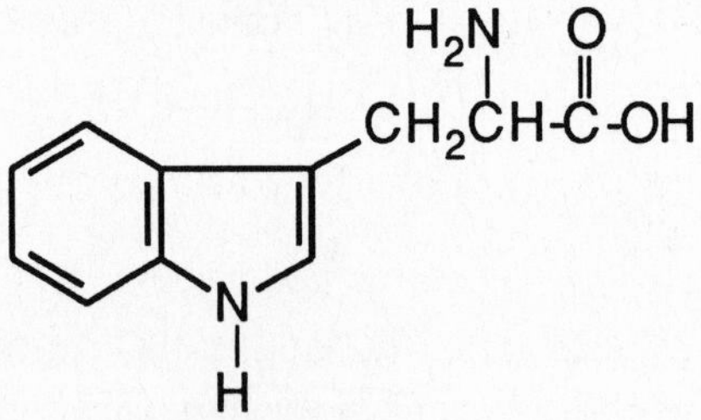

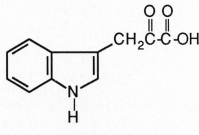

Tryptophan   α-Keto acid

25.18   Ammonium ion is the other product of oxidative deamination.

25.19   A glucogenic amino acid is an amino acid that is catabolized to pyruvate or to citric acid cycle intermediates and thus can enter gluconeogenesis.

25.20   A ketogenic amino acid is catabolized to acetyl SCoA, which can be used either in the synthesis of ketone bodies or in fatty acid biosynthesis.

25.21   Ammonia is toxic and must be eliminated as nontoxic urea.

25.22   The urea cycle might be called the ornithine cycle because ornithine is a key intermediate in the cycle.

25.23   The *urea carbon* comes from carbamoyl phosphate, which is synthesized from bicarbonate produced from CO_2 in the citric acid cycle.
One nitrogen comes from carbamoyl phosphate, which is synthesized from ammonia produced from oxidative deamination.
One nitrogen comes from aspartate.

25.24   Non-essential amino acids can be synthesized in 1-3 steps. Essential amino acids must be provided in the diet.

25.25   α-Ketoglutarate is the starting material for amino acid anabolism.

25.26   Amino acids are made from non-nitrogen metabolites by reductive amination, which is the reverse of oxidative deamination.

25.27   In the body, tyrosine is made from phenylalanine.

25.28 PKU is caused by a genetic inability to convert phenylalanine to tyrosine, leading to the accumulation of phenylalanine and its metabolites in the body. PKU causes mental retardation if not detected early.

25.29 Positive nitrogen balance is the state in which more nitrogen is consumed than is excreted.

25.30 Positive nitrogen balance occurs when new tissue is forming; children, pregnant women and people recovering from starvation or from injuries require positive nitrogen balance.

25.31 Negative nitrogen balance occurs when more nitrogen is excreted from the body than is consumed.

25.32 Negative nitrogen balance results when the diet is inadequate in protein, during starvation, or as a result of illnesses such as cancer and kidney disease.

25.33 *Kwashiorkor* is caused by a diet adequate in calories but inadequate in protein. Symptoms include edema, fatty liver and underdevelopment. *Marasmus* is caused by starvation. Symptoms include muscle wasting and below-normal stature.

25.34 A xenobiotic compound is a compound that is foreign to the body.

25.35 The body responds to a xenobiotic compound in two ways. (1) It reacts with xenophobic compounds to make them less hydrophobic and more water-soluble. (2) Xenophobic compounds are further modified to make them easier to excrete.

25.36 The formation of urea is energy-intensive because two molecules of ATP are consumed during its formation.

25.37 Deaminated amino acids can enter the citric acid cycle, producing ATP to "pay" for the ATP consumed in urea synthesis, (which "disposes" of nitrogen).

25.38

$$CH_3CH(CH_3)CHCOO^-(NH_3^+) \;+\; CH_3C(O)COO^- \;\underset{\text{or ALT}}{\overset{\text{VAT}}{\rightleftharpoons}}\; CH_3CH(CH_3)C(O)COO^- \;+\; CH_3CHCOO^-(NH_3^+)$$

Valine + Pyruvate ⇌ 3-Methyl-2-oxobutanoate + Alanine

The enzyme is either valine aminotransferase or alanine aminotransferase.

25.39 Amino acids can enter the citric acid cycle as the following intermediates: α-ketoglutarate, succinate, fumarate, oxaloacetate and pyruvate.

25.40 Amino acids can be both glycogenic and ketogenic. Amino acids that are catabolized to pyruvate proceed to form acetyl SCoA, which can be used in fatty acid biosynthesis. The pyruvate can also enter gluconeogenesis or enter the citric acid cycle.

25.41 Carbons from some amino acids can be catabolized to acetyl SCoA, which can be used in fatty acid biosynthesis. The fatty acids can enter adipocytes, where fats can be synthesized.

25.42 Tissue is dynamic because its components are constantly being broken down and reformed. Dynamic relationships are common in protein and amino acid metabolism, where proteins are digested and resynthesized, and where amino acids are converted to other amino acids and to carbohydrate intermediates.

The Chapter in Brief

Breakdown of Proteins (Sections 25.1, 25.2) Proteins are denatured in the stomach, hydrolyzed in the stomach and intestine, and the resulting amino acids are absorbed into the bloodstream. The collection of amino acids in the body – the amino acid pool – serves as a source of amino acids for protein synthesis and for conversion into non-nitrogen intermediates that can enter the citric acid cycle, ketogenesis, or lipogenesis.

Reactions of Amino Acids (Sections 25.3–25.5) *Transamination* is a reaction in which the amino group of an amino acid changes place with the α-keto group of α-ketoglutarate. In *oxidative deamination*, the amino group of glutamate is removed and replaced with a carbonyl group to regenerate α-ketoglutarate for transamination. The *urea cycle* provides a route for excreting toxic ammonia as nontoxic urea. Catabolism of glucogenic amino acids yields intermediates in the citric acid cycle; catabolism of ketogenic amino acids yields intermediates that can be used for fatty acid biosynthesis.

Amino Acid Biosynthesis (Section 25.6) Nonessential amino acids can be synthesized from metabolic intermediates via transamination reactions that use glutamate as a source of nitrogen.

Self-Test for Chapter 25

Complete the following sentences:

1. In the transamination reaction of alanine and α-ketoglutarate, _____ and _____ are formed.

2. Infants and children are usually in _____ nitrogen balance.

3. Ketogenic amino acids are catabolized to _____ _____.

4. The first step in the urea cycle is the formation of _____ _____ from ammonia, CO_2, and ATP.

5. A _____ is an enzyme that carries out peptide hydrolysis.

6. The amino acid serine enters the citric acid cycle as _____.

7. _____ _____ is the key reaction in amino acid anabolism.

8. The amino acid _____ is part of the urea cycle.

9. PKU is a metabolic error in converting _____ to _____.

10. In _____, caloric intake is adequate, but protein intake is deficient.

11. Liver damage is associated with a high level of the enzyme _____.

12. The carbon in urea comes from _____.

Match the entries on the left with their partners on the right:

1. Oxidative deamination

2. Ornithine

3. α-Ketoglutarate

4. Serine

5. Trypsin

6. Reductive amination

7. Leucine

8. Phenylketonuria

9. Pepsin

10. Pyridoxal phosphate

11. Transamination

12. Threonine

(a) Hydrolyzes proteins in the small intestine

(b) Process for synthesizing glutamate from α-ketoglutarate + NH_4^+

(c) Ketogenic amino acid

(d) Coenzyme associated with amino acid metabolism

(e) Process that transfers an amino group from an amino acid to α-ketoglutarate

(f) Nonessential amino acid

(g) Intermediate in the urea cycle

(h) Process that regenerates α-ketoglutarate from glutamate

(i) Glucogenic amino acid

(j) Intermediate in both the citric acid cycle and in amino acid metabolism

(k) Hydrolyzes proteins in the stomach

(l) Metabolic disease

Tell whether the following statements are true or false:

1. 3-Phosphoglycerate is a precursor in the synthesis of nonessential amino acids.

2. Protein digestion starts in the mouth.

3. All ketogenic amino acids except lysine and isoleucine are also glucogenic amino acids.

4. Essential amino acids can neither be synthesized nor catabolized in the human body.

5. Some organisms can excrete nitrogen as ammonia without undergoing any harm.

6. Amino acid catabolism occurs in the intestinal lining.

7. Several intermediates in the urea cycle also occur in the citric acid cycle.

8. The urea cycle is an endergonic process.

9. Pyridoxine is a coenzyme associated with transamination.

10. Proline is a nonessential amino acid.

11. Each amino acid is associated with its own transaminase enzyme.

12. Oxidative deamination is the reverse of reductive amination.

Chapter 26 – Nucleic Acids and Protein Synthesis

26.1

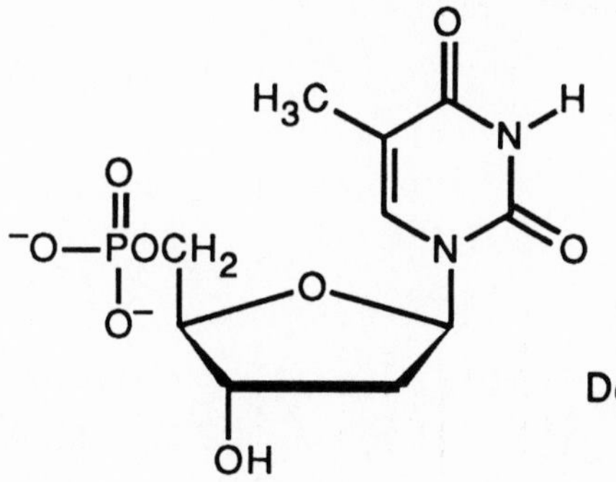

Deoxythymidine 5'-phosphate

26.2

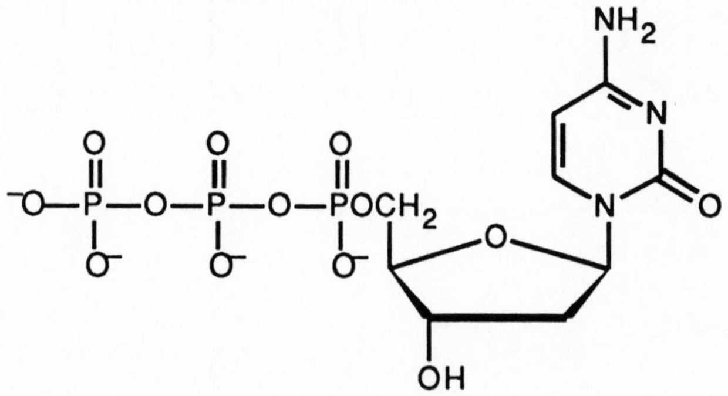

26.3 dTMP - Deoxythymidine 5'-monophosphate
AMP - Adenosine 5'-monophosphate
ADP - Adenosine 5'-diphosphate
ATP - Adenosine 5'-triphosphate

26.4

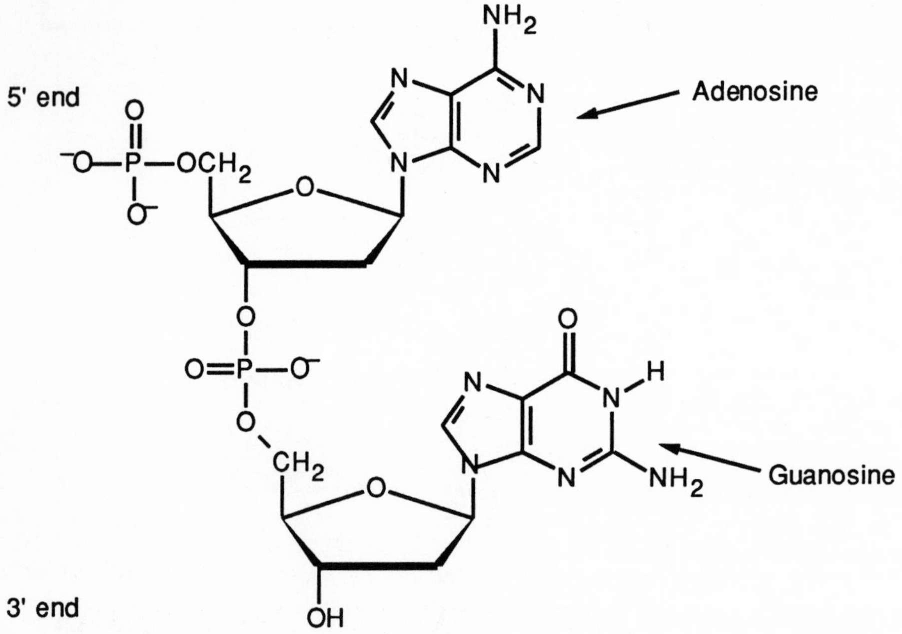

26.5   (a)   Original strand: G-C-C-T-A-G-T

                  Complement: C-G-G-A-T-C-A

         (b)   Original strand: A-A-T-G-G-C-T-C-A

                  Complement: T-T-A-C-C-G-A-G-T

26.6   Adenine has two groups that can hydrogen-bond, but guanine has three. Thus adenin
hydrogen bonds with thymine, which also forms two hydrogen bonds, and guanine
hydrogen bonds with cytosine, which forms three hydrogen bonds. This system of
hydrogen-bonding creates the maximum number of hydrogen bonds possible.

26.7

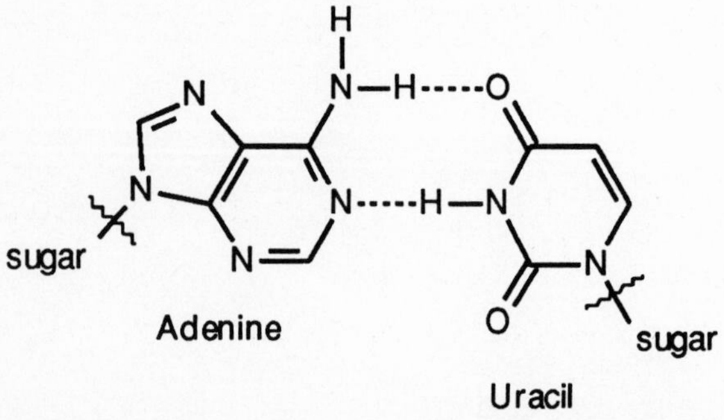

26.8   (a)   Template strand: -G-A-T-T-A-C-C-G-T-A-

                  Complement: -C-U-A-A-U-G-G-C-A-U-

(b) Template strand: -T-A–T-G-G-C-T-A-G-G-C-A-

Complement   -A-U-A-C-C-G-A-U-C-C-G-U-

26.9   *Amino Acid*   *Possible Codons*

(a) Ala	G-C-U,	G-C-C,	G-C-A,	G-C-G		
(b) Phe	U-U-U,	U-U-C				
(c) Leu	U-U-A,	U-U-G,	C-U-U,	C-U-C,	C-U-A,	C-U-G
(d) Val	G-U-U,	G-U-C,	G-U-A,	G-U-G		
(e) Tyr	U-A-U,	U-A-C				

26.10   *Codon*   *Amino Acid*

(a) A-U-U	Ile
(b) G-C-G	Ala
(c) C-G-A	Arg
(d) A-A-C	Asn

26.11 - 26.13

mRNA sequence:	CUU—AUG—GCU—UGG—CCC—UAA
Amino-acid sequence:	Leu——Met——Ala—Trp——Pro—Stop
tRNA anticodon sequence:	GAA—UAC——CGA—ACC—GGG—AUU
DNA sequence:	GAA—TAC——CGA—ACC—GGG—ATT

26.14   The sequence T-G-G on the informational strand of DNA codes for U-G-G on mRNA, and T-G-A codes for U-G-A, which is a stop codon. Instead of adding an amino acid to the peptide chain, chain growth would stop.

26.15   (a)   *Original strand*   *Mutated strand*

DNA	A-T-C	A-T-G
mRNA	U-A-G	U-A-C
Amino acid	Stop	Tyr

(b)   *Original strand*   *Mutated strand*

DNA	C-C-T	C-G-T
mRNA	G-G-A	G-C-A
Amino acid	Gly	Ala

In the first mutation, a protein would add tyrosine instead of stopping. In the second mutation, a protein would add an alanine instead of glycine.

26.16   A nucleotide is a monomer unit of DNA or RNA. It consists of a heterocyclic amine base, an aldopentose, and a phosphoric acid residue.

26.17   Ribose is the sugar in RNA, and deoxyribose is the sugar in DNA. Ribose has an -OH group at carbon 2, pointing down; deoxyribose has no -OH group at carbon 2.

26.18   "Deoxy" means that the oxygen atom attached to carbon 2 of ribose is missing and that there is an -H group on carbon 2 rather than an -OH group.

26.19 Adenine, cytosine, guanine, and thymine are the four heterocyclic bases in DNA.

26.20 Adenine, cytosine, guanine, and uracil are the four heterocyclic bases in RNA.

26.21 Most DNA is found in the nucleus of cells.

26.22 *Messenger RNA (mRNA))* carries the genetic message from DNA to ribosomes.

Ribosomal RNA (rRNA); bonds to protein to constitute the physical makeup of ribosomes, where protein synthesis takes place.

Transfer RNA (tRNA)) transports specific amino acids to the ribosomes, where they are incorporated into proteins.

26.23 *Base pairing* is the hydrogen-bonded pairing of two heterocyclic bases in the double helix of DNA. Adenine pairs with thymine, and guanine pairs with cytosine.
DNA replication is the process by which DNA makes a copy of itself.
Translation is the process by which a genetic message is decoded and used to synthesize proteins.
Transcription is the process by which a genetic message of DNA is transcribed to RNA and is carried to the ribosomes, where protein synthesis occurs.

26.24 A chromosome is an enormous molecule of DNA. A gene is a part of the chromosome that codes for a single piece of information (that is, a single protein) needed by a cell.

26.25 A gene carries the DNA code needed to synthesize a specific protein.

26.26 There are approximately 100,000 genes in the human genome.

26.27 The DNA double helix is held together by hydrogen bonds between base pairs.

26.28 Bases that are complementary always occur in pairs. For example, adenine is always hydrogen bonded to thymine, and guanine is always hydrogen bonded to cytosine.

26.29 DNA is the largest nucleic acid, mRNA is intermediate, and tRNA is the smallest.

26.30 The 5' end of a nucleotide has a phosphate group bonded to carbon 5 of ribose; the 3' end has an –OH group bonded to carbon 3 of ribose.

26.31 - 26.33

Bond between phosphate group and C5 of sugar

Cytosine

Phosphate group

Bond between cytosine and C1 of deoxyribose

Deoxyribose

OH

Deoxycytidine 5'-phosphate

26.34

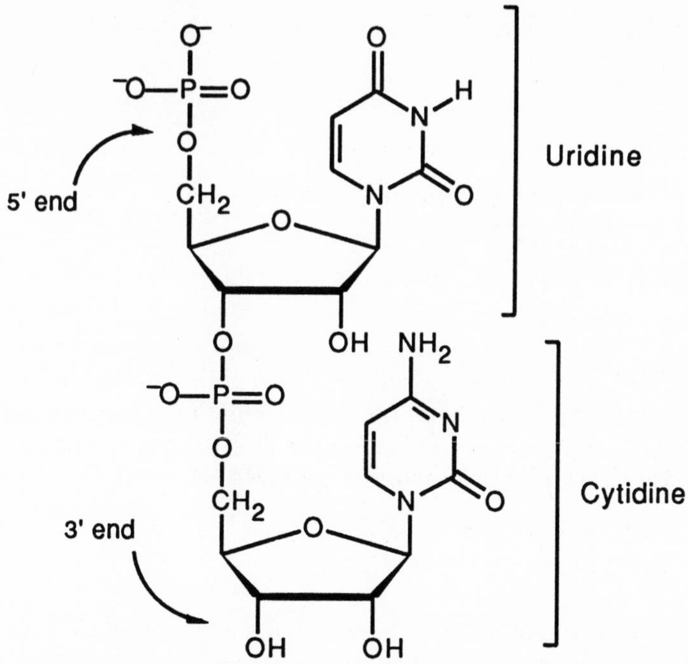

Uridine

Cytidine

26.35 The two DNA strands are named the template strand and the information strand, and they are complementary. The template strand is used for transcription of mRNA and is complementary to mRNA. Thus, mRNA is a copy of the information strand (with U replacing T).

26.36 A codon is a sequence of three nucleotides on mRNA that codes for a specific amino acid in protein synthesis.

26.37 An anticodon is a sequence of three nucleotides that is complementary to the sequence on a codon. The anticodon occurs on tRNA and matches up with the codon on mRNA to orient an amino acid in the correct position for protein synthesis.

26.38 A tRNA molecule is cloverleaf-shaped and contains 70-100 nucleotides. The tRNA anticodon triplet is on one "leaf," and an amino acid bonds covalently to the 3' end.

26.39 Exons and introns are sections of DNA. Exons carry the genetic message, whereas introns do not code for any part of the protein being synthesized. Introns constitute about 90% of DNA and exons 10%.

26.40 Pure   Silver   Taxi
         Pur   Ag   TC

The purines A and G pair with T and C, respectively.

26.41 The percent of A always equals the percent of T, since A and T are complementary. Similarly for G and C. Thus, sea urchin DNA contains about 32% each of A and T, and 18% each of G and C.

26.42

Amino Acid	Codons
(a) Pro	C-C-U, C-C-C, C-C-A, C-C-G
(b) Lys	A-A-A, A-A-G
(c) Met	A-U-G

26.43 - 26.44

Codon	Amino Acid	tRNA Anticodon
(a) A-C-U	Thr	U-G-A
(b) G-G-A	Gly	C-C-U
(c) C-U-U	Leu	G-A-A

26.45 - 26.47
The DNA sequence of the template strand is complementary to the DNA sequence of the informational strand. The mRNA sequence is identical to the DNA sequence on the informational strand, except that U on mRNA replaces T on DNA.

Informational strand:	T-A-C-C-G-A
Template strand:	A-T-G-G-C-T
mRNA:	U-A-C-C-G-A
Dipeptide:	Tyr———Arg

26.48 A mutation is an error in base sequence that occurs during DNA replication. Mutations can occur spontaneously, or they can be caused by chemicals or radiation.

26.49 A mutation in RNA affects only one molecule of RNA; other intact molecules of RNA can still carry out protein synthesis. A mutation in DNA is much more drastic, however, because there is only one molecule of DNA per gene, and any error will be copied into all subsequent DNA molecules during replication.

26.50

	Normal	Mutated
DNA:	A-T-T-G-G-C-C-T-A	A-C-T-G-G-C-C-T-A
mRNA:	A-U-U-G-G-C-C-U-A	A-C-U-G-G-C-C-U-A
Amino acids:	Ile—Gly—Leu	Thr—Gly—Leu

26.51 A mutation must occur in a germ cell (sperm or egg) in order for it to be passed down to future generations.

26.52 If codons were made up of two rather than three nucleotides, only $4^2 = 16$ nucleotide combinations would be possible. Since there are 20 amino acids, it would not be possible to code for all of them with only two nucleotides.

26.53 A hereditary disease is caused by a mutation in the DNA of a germ cell. The mutation affects the amino-acid sequence of an important protein and causes a change in the biological activity of the protein.

26.54 A mutation in DNA may change the biological activity of a protein. When this change leads to uncontrolled cell growth, cancer results.

26.55 Metenkephalin: H_2N—Tyr——Gly—Gly——Phe—Met—COOH
    mRNA: UAU–GGU–GGU–UUU–AUG–UAA
         UAC–GGC–GGC–UUC   UAG
         GGG–GGG
         GGA–GGA

26.56 Using the first set of base pairs above to solve this problem:

  Informational strand: TAT–GGT–GGT–TTT––ATG–TAA
  Template strand: ATA–CCA–CCA–AAA–TAC–ATT

26.57 The presence of introns will make the mapping of the human genome more difficult. When a sequence of bases is mapped, it will be difficult to determine if it codes for a specific protein (as an exon does) or if it is apparent nonsense (as an intron is).

26.58 If you knew your own genetic map, you could learn what diseases might sooner or later be a problem for you, and you might be able to take precautions to postpone your fate. It might be unsettling to know what illness would cause your death, and you would worry about keeping the information confidential.

26.59 Viruses consist of a strand of nucleic acid wrapped in a protein coat and, unlike higher organisms, can't replicate or manufacture protein independent of a host cell.

26.60 In reverse transcription, an RNA virus (*retrovirus*) uses its RNA as a template to synthesize its own DNA, which is then replicated and decoded by the host cell. The host cell also synthesizes viral proteins.

26.61 A vaccine is used to stimulate an organism to produce antibodies against a killed or weakened version of the original virus. It will be difficult to design a vaccine against AIDS because the AIDS virus is constantly mutating.

26.62 The DNA of bacterial cells occurs in plasmids, each of which carries only a few genes. The plasmids are easy to isolate, and several copies of each are present in a bacterial cell.

26.63 A brief outline of recombinant DNA techniques:
  (1) A bacterial plasmid is isolated and treated with a particular restriction endonuclease, which cleaves it at a specific base sequence. The plasmid is left with "sticky ends" - a few unpaired bases at each end.
  (2) The gene to be inserted is excised from its DNA by using the same restriction endonuclease. The gene has sticky ends complementary to the plasmid DNA sticky ends.
  (3) The plasmid DNA and the gene are mixed with DNA ligase, an enzyme that joins the fragments at the sticky ends and which reconstitutes the plasmid.
  (4) The altered plasmid is reinserted into the bacterium. The bacteria replicate rapidly and are soon able to synthesize large amounts of the desired substance.

26.64 Genetically altered bacteria have been used to produce proteins.

26.65 A genetic map might be used to locate a defective gene, all or part of which can be excised with a restriction endonuclease. Using DNA ligase a DNA strand can be inserted to produce a gene capable of coding for the nondefective protein.

26.66 Two possible mRNA sequences for glu are GAA and GAG. Two sequences for val are GUA and GUG, which differ from the glu sequences by one base. Thus, a change in one base can completely alter the structure and function of a protein.

26.67

	Glu	
mRNA sequence:	GAA	GAG
DNA sequence: (template strand)	CTT	CTC

26.68

	A		*B*
original DNA:	TAA	|	TAA
mRNA codon:	AUU	|	AUU
codes for:	Ile	|	Ile
mutated DNA:	TAG	|	GAA
mRNA codon:	AUC	|	CUU
codes for:	Ile	|	Leu

In case A, a DNA mutation from TAA to TAG changes the transcription of mRNA from AUU to AUC. Since both of these codons code for Ile, no change in the synthesized protein occurs.

In case B, a DNA mutation from TAA to GAA changes the transcription of mRNA from AUU to CUU. Since AUU codes for Ile and CUU codes for Leu, the synthesized protein will have an Ile replaced by a Leu. The protein may, however, continue functioning almost normally since the two amino acids are so closely related.

26.69 The chain containing 21 amino acids needs 21 x 3 = 63 bases to code for it. Two three-base codons are needed for the "start" and "stop" codons. Thus, *69* bases are needed to code for the first chain. The chain containing 30 amino acids needs 30 x 3 = 90 bases plus 6 "start" and "stop" bases, for a total of *96* bases.

26.70 Position 9:   Horse amino acid = Gly   Human amino acid = Ser

mRNA codons:	GGU	GGC	GGA	GGG		UCU	UCC	UCA	UCG	AGU	AGC
DNA bases:	<u>CCA</u>	<u>CCG</u>	CCT	CCC		AGA	AGG	ACT	ACC	<u>TCA</u>	<u>TCG</u>

The underlined horse DNA base triplets differ from their human counterparts by only one base.

Position 30:   Horse amino acid = Ala   Human amino acid = Thr

mRNA codons	GCU	GCC	GCA	GCG		ACU	ACC	ACA	ACG
DNA bases:	CGA	CGG	CGT	CGC		TGA	TGG	TGT	TGC

Each group of three DNA bases from horse insulin has a counterpart in human insulin that differs from it by only one base. It is possible that horse insulin DNA differs from human insulin DNA by only two bases out of 165!

26.71 A tRNA bonds covalently to its amino acid by forming an ester bond between the amino acid carboxyl group and the 3' hydroxyl group of the ribose at the 3' end of the tRNA. The tRNA anticodon lines up at the site of protein synthesis by hydrogen bonding to its mRNA codon. Formation of the peptide amide bond occurs at the ribosomes.

26.72 If a protein doesn't have methionine as its first amino acid, the methionine is removed before the protein is activated.

The Chapter In Brief

Structure of Nucleic Acids (Sections 26.1–26.4) The nucleic acids, DNA and RNA, are the chemical carriers of genetic information. DNA is located on chromosomes, which are subdivided into genes. DNA and RNA are polymers made up of nucleotides. A nucleotide consists of a heterocyclic amine base, an aldopentose, and phosphoric acid. The nucleotides are connected by phosphate ester bonds between the phosphoric acid and the aldopentose. DNA exists as a double helix in which two polynucleotide chains are linked by hydrogen bonds between base. The bases pair in a complementary manner, A to T and G to C.

Transmission of Genetic Information (Sections 26.5–26.10) Three fundamental processes take place in the transfer of genetic information. *Replication* is the process by which DNA makes a copy of itself. In *transcription*, the message contained in DNA is transferred to RNA. There are three kinds of RNA - messenger RNA (mRNA), ribosomal RNA (rRNA), and transfer RNA (tRNA). mRNA is synthesized using one strand of DNA as a template. The sequence of RNA nucleotides acts as a code, with groups of three bases as the codons that specify the particular amino acid to be used in protein synthesis. In *translation*, the genetic message is decoded and used to build proteins. Protein synthesis takes place on ribosomes as tRNAs bring the correct amino acids to the site of synthesis. An anticodon sequence on tRNA is complementary to the codon sequence on mRNA.

Gene Mutation (Section 26.11) A mutation is an error in base sequence that occurs during DNA replication. If the mutation occurs in a germ cell, the error is passed on to future generations, and a hereditary disease can result.

Self-Test for Chapter 26

Complete the following sentences:

1.   _____ is the process by which an identical copy of DNA is made.

2.   The two strands of DNA have base sequences that are _____.

3.   When a cell is not actively dividing, its nucleus is occupied by _____.

4.   Mutations may be caused by exposure to _____ rays or to chemicals called _____.

5.   An _____ is a segment of a gene that does not code for protein synthesis.

6.   tRNA binds to an amino acid by an _____ linkage.

7.   A _____ consists of a heterocyclic amine base bonded to an aldopentose.

8. An enzyme called a _____ _____ frees the polypeptide chain from the last tRNA during protein synthesis.

9. An enzyme called a _____ _____ cleaves a DNA molecule at a particular base sequence.

10. The sugar _____ has an -H instead of an -OH at its 2' position.

11. The _____ - _____ model describes DNA as two polynucleotide strands coiled about each other in a double helix.

12. The enzyme _____ _____ catalyzes the bonding of nucleotides to form new strands of DNA.

Match the entries on the left with their partners on the right:

1. 5'end   (a) 3 billion base pairs

2. A-C-G   (b) Cysteine codon

3. U-G-C   (c) Forms three hydrogen bonds

4. Adenine   (d) Coded for by six codons

5. Genome   (e) May cause cancer

6. 3' end   (f) "stop" codon

7. Leu   (g) Purine

8. Cytosine   (h) Occurs only in RNA

9. Somatic-cell mutation   (i) -OH group

10. Uracil   (j) Cysteine anticodon

11. U-G-A   (k) May cause hereditary disease

12. Germ-cell mutation   (l) Phosphate group

Tell whether the following statements are true or false:

1. There are a total of 64 codons for the 20 amino acids.

2. The amount of adenine in an organism's DNA is equal to the amount of guanine.

3. In transcription, mRNA is a copy of the informational strand of DNA.

4. An amino acid codon occurs on tRNA.

5. Peptide bonds are formed at the P binding site of a ribosome.

6. "Pure silver taxi" means that adenine pairs with guanine and thymine pairs with cytosine.

7.   The individual units of RNA and DNA are called nucleotides.

8.   The two strands of the DNA double helix run in the same direction.

9.   Transcription is the process by which the genetic message is decoded and used to make proteins.

10.   Most human DNA contains genetic instructions.

11.   Each amino acid is specified by more than one codon.

12.   The correct name for the RNA nucleotide containing G is guanidine 5'-monophosphate.

Chapter 27 – Body Fluids

27.1 The three principal body fluids are intracellular fluid, extracellular fluid and interstitial fluid.

27.2 Intracellular fluid contains most of the body's water.

27.3 To be soluble in bodily fluids, a substance must be an ion, a gas, a small molecule, or a molecule with many polar or ionic groups on its surface.

27.4 Blood pressure in arterial capillaries is higher than interstitial fluid pressure, and solutes are pushed into interstitial fluid. Blood pressure in venous capillaries is lower than interstitial fluid pressure, and solutes are pushed into venous capillaries.

27.5 The lymphatic system collects excess interstitial fluid, cellular debris, proteins and lipid droplets and ultimately returns them to the bloodstream.

27.6 Antidiuretic hormone, also known as vasopressin, causes a decrease in the water content of the urine.

27.7 Plasma is the non-cellular portion of the blood that contains blood solutes.

27.8 The three main types of blood cells are erythrocytes (red blood cells), platelets and white blood cells.

27.9 *Red blood cells* transport blood gases.
White blood cells destroy invading bacteria.
Platelets assist in blood clotting.

27.10 Lung and intestine contain heparin to combat the formation of life-threatening blood clots.

27.11 Blood serum is the fluid that remains after blood has completely clotted.

27.12 Each hemoglobin can bind with four oxygens.

27.13 Hemoglobin iron must be in the +2 oxidation state in order to bind with oxygen.

27.14 Oxyhemoglobin is bright red; deoxyhemoglobin is dark red-purple.

27.15 When the partial pressure of oxygen drops below 10 mm Hg, hemoglobin is unsaturated. When the partial pressure of oxygen is greater than 100 mm Hg, hemoglobin is completely saturated. Between these pressures, hemoglobin is partially saturated.

27.16 Because of oxygen's allosteric interaction with hemoglobin, uptake of the first oxygen facilitates the uptake of the remaining oxygens. In the reverse direction, release of the first oxygen facilitates the release of the other three oxygens.

27.17 CO_2 can be transported as a dissolved gas, as bicarbonate or bonded to hemoglobin.

27.18 Hemoglobin is 50% saturated with oxygen at 30 mm Hg.

27.19 CO_2 in the blood raises $[H^+]$ in two types of reactions:

(1) Reaction of CO_2 with non-ionized $-NH_2$ groups of hemoglobin amino acids produces H^+.

$$Hb-NH_2 + CO_2 \longrightarrow Hb-NHCOO^- + H^+$$

(2) Carbonic anhydrase catalyzes the reaction of CO_2 with H_2O, producing bicarbonate and H^+.

$$CO_2 + H_2O \xrightarrow[\text{anhydrase}]{\text{carbonic}} HCO_3^- + H^+$$

27.20 (a) Increasing the temperature causes hemoglobin to release more O_2 to tissues.
(b)(c) Production of CO_2 brings about an increase of $[H^+]$, which causes the release of O_2.

27.21 Three types of bodily responses to antigens are inflammation, antibody-directed response and cell-directed response.

27.22 Antihistamines might inhibit the enzyme that produces histamine from histidine.

27.23 Specific immune responses, like enzyme-substrate interaction, involve a fit between a specific antigen and a specific antibody.

27.24 Antibody-directed immune response involves B lymphocytes, a type of white blood cell, which divide into plasma cells that produce identical non-cell-bound antibodies that are specific to the antigen present.

27.25 Memory cells, which are produced from B cells, can quickly produce more plasma cells if the same antigen appears in the future.

27.26 T cells destroy infected cells by releasing a toxic protein that perforates cell membranes.

27.27 A blood clot is a mass of blood cells trapped in a mesh of fibrin fibers.

27.28 Vitamin K and calcium ion are needed for blood clotting.

27.29 Blood clotting can be triggered by either the intrinsic pathway, which occurs when blood is exposed to negatively charged surfaces, or by the extrinsic pathway, which occurs when a substance called tissue factor is released by injured cells.

27.30 Blood clotting enzymes are released as zymogens in order to avoid undesirable clotting in noninjured tissues.

27.31 In addition to filtration, kidneys also recapture water and essential solutes (reabsorption) and excrete excess solutes (secretion).

27.32 $HCO_3^- + H^+ \longrightarrow H_2O + CO_2$

$HPO_4^{2-} + H^+ \longrightarrow H_2PO_4^-$

27.33 Cryopreservation is the freezing of live tissue for storage and reuse.

27.34 Cells rupture as they freeze because the large ice crystals formed rip apart cellular and organelle membranes.

27.35 To avoid formation of large ice crystals, antifreeze chemicals (glycerol, for example) and ice nucleating compounds are used in cryopreservation.

27.36 In order to maintain metabolism, frozen tissues must be able to produce limited amounts of ATP, with no blood supply and no oxygen supply. The metabolites must be nontoxic, and enzymes that accelerate tissue decay must be inhibited more than ATP-producing enzymes.

27.37 Endothelial cells in the brain form tight junctions so that no substances can pass between them.

27.38 In an asymmetric transport system, substances can either be transported into a cell or be transported out of a cell, but not both. For example, there exists a system for transport of glycine out of brain cells, but no system exists for transport of glycine into brain cells.

27.39 Substances that are soluble in membrane lipids can cross the blood-brain barrier. Ethanol crosses this barrier because it's soluble in membrane lipids.

27.40 The substance to be analyzed is combined with a reagent with which it forms a colored product. The quantity of product is determined by using a polarimeter to measure the amount of visible light of a specific wavelength the product absorbs.

27.41 A change in enzyme level in body fluids indicates organ damage.

27.42 Automated analyzers are quick and inexpensive (after their initial cost). They can perform dozens of different tests, and they avoid contamination of the sample by humans and exposure of humans to pathogenic organisms and toxic reagents. They generate few dirty dishes, and they don't take coffee breaks.

27.43 Ethanol is soluble in blood because it is a small, polar molecule.

27.44 A nursing mother's antibodies can be passed to her baby in breast milk.

27.45 When the concentration of sodium in the blood is high, the secretion of antidiuretic hormone (ADH) increases. ADH causes the water content of the urine to decrease, and causes the amount of water retained by the body to increase, causing swelling.

27.46 Active transport is the movement of solutes from regions of low concentration to regions of high concentration, a process that requires energy. Osmosis is the movement of solutes from regions of high concentration to regions of low concentration, a process that requires no energy.

27.47 Active transport is necessary when a cell needs a substance that has a higher concentration inside the cell than outside, or when a cell needs to secrete a substance that has a higher concentration outside the cell than inside.

27.48 In the blood, CO_2 from metabolism reacts to form $HCO_3^- + H^+$. The H^+ is picked up by hemoglobin, which releases O_2, and is carried to the lungs, where it is released and O_2 is picked up.

In the urine, CO_2 reacts to form HCO_3^- and H^+. The HCO_3^- returns to the bloodstream, and the H^+ is neutralized by reaction with HPO_4^{2-} or NH_3.

Whenever excess HCO_3^- accumulates in blood or urine, it can react with H^+ to form $H_2O + CO_3$.

27.49 Three principal functions of blood are *transport*, *regulation* and *defense*. An example of transport is the movement of oxygen-bearing hemoglobin to the tissues. The blood regulates body temperature by redistributing body heat. Blood carries lymphocytes, which help defend the body against foreign invaders.

The Chapter in Brief

Body Water (Sections 27.1, 27.2) Body water consists of intracellular fluid (inside cells), extracellular fluid (mainly blood plasma), and interstitial fluid (between cells). The circulatory system carries blood throughout the body, and the lymphatic system collects excess interstitial fluid. The kidneys regulate the balance between water and electrolytes; antidiuretic hormone controls the water content of the urine.

Blood (Sections 27.3–27.6) Blood is composed of plasma and blood cells, both red and white. The functions of blood include transport, regulation, and defense. Red blood cells transport blood gases (O_2 and CO_2) and regulate pH. Other blood components are responsible for the body's defense against foreign substances. Inflammation and phagocytosis are nonspecific responses to injury. Specific responses to invading substances include antibody-directed immune response and cell-directed immune response. Blood clotting is caused by the protein fibrin plus many clotting factors.

Urine (Sections 27.7, 27.8) The kidney is responsible for filtration, reabsorption of water and solutes, and secretion of solutes. The kidney also assists in regulating the pH of body fluids by acid-base reactions.

Self-Test for Chapter 27

Complete the following sentences:

1. The percentage of heme molecules that carry oxygen is dependent on the _____ _____ of O_2.

2. Antigens can be small molecules known as _____.

3. In the process of blood clotting, _____ are activated to give active clotting factors.

4. Inorganic ions are the major contributors to the _____ of body fluids.

5. Histamine is synthesized from _____.

6. _____ ion and vitamin _____ assist in blood clotting.

7. In _____ _____, substances move from regions of low concentration to regions of high concentration.

8. The three functions of blood are _____, _____, and _____.

9. Bacteria at the site of inflammation are attacked by _____.

10. Arthritis and allergies are known as _____ diseases.

11. _____ is caused by the absence of one or more clotting factors.

12. Fibrin molecules are bound into fibers by cross-links between the side chains of the amino acids _____ and _____.

Match the item on the left with its partner on the right:

1. B cells   (a) Foreign substance

2. Active transport   (b) Enzyme that catalyzes the formation of histamine

3. Fibrin   (c) Movement of solute against a concentration gradient

4. Carbonic anhydrase   (d) White blood cells involved in antibody-directed immune response

5. Erythrocytes   (e) Controls reabsorption of Na^+

6. T cells   (f) Blood protein responsible for clotting

7. Antigen   (g) Enzyme that catalyzes reaction between H_2O and CO_2

8. Histidine decarboxylase   (h) Movement of water in response to a concentration difference

9. Osmosis   (i) White blood cells involved in cell-directed immune response

10. Antidiuretic hormone   (j) Red blood cells

11. Antibody   (k) Protein molecule that identifies a foreign substance

12. Aldosterone   (l) Causes a decrease in the water content of urine

Tell whether the following sentences are true or false:

1. The walls of lymph capillaries are constricted so that lymph can't return to surrounding tissues.

2. Homeostasis is the body's mechanism for halting blood loss.

3. O_2, H^+, and CO_2 all bond to heme.

4. Secreted H^+ is eliminated in the urine as NH_4^+ or $H_2PO_4^-$.

5. When the partial pressure of CO_2 increases, the percent saturation of hemoglobin decreases.

6.   Allergies and asthma are caused by an underproduction of immunoglobulin E.

7.   Blood plasma is the fluid remaining after blood has complete clotted.

8.   Blood clotting begins with the release of tissue factor from injured tissue.

9.   Reabsorption is the movement of solutes and water out of the kidney.

10. The metabolism of food contributes to one's water intake.

11. Lymphocytes surround and destroy bacteria.

12. Caffeine causes increased output of urine.